Fourth Edition

The Ancient World

A Social and Cultural History

D. Brendan Nagle

University of Southern California

Prentice Hall, Upper Saddle River, New Jersey 07458

Library of Congress Cataloging-in-Publication Data

Nagle, D. Brendan
    The ancient world : a social and cultural history / D. Brendan
Nagle. —4th ed.
       p. cm.
    Includes bibliographical references and index.
    ISBN 0-13-080741-9
    1. Civilization, Ancient. I. Title
CB311.N25 1999
930—dc21
                                                   98-18331
                                                   CIP

Editorial/production supervision
       and interior design: *Harriet Tellem*
Acquisitions editor: *Todd R. Armstrong*
Manufacturing buyer: *Lynn Pearlman*
Editorial assistant: *Holly Jo Brown*
Cover design: *Bruce Kenselaar*

This book was set in 10/12 Baskerville by The Composing Room of Michigan, Inc. and was
printed and bound by RR Donnelley and Sons. The cover was printed by
Phoenix Color Corp.

 © 1999, 1996, 1989, 1979 by Prentice-Hall, Inc.
Simon & Schuster/A Viacom Company
Upper Saddle River, New Jersey 07459

Printed in the United States of America
10 9 8 7 6 5 4 3 2

ISBN 0-13-080741-9

Prentice-Hall International (UK) Limited, *London*
Prentice-Hall of Australia Pty. Limited, *Sydney*
Prentice-Hall Canada, Inc., *Toronto*
Prentice-Hall Hispanoamericana, S.A., *Mexico*
Prentice-Hall of India Private Limited., *New Delhi*
Prentice-Hall of Japan, Inc., *Tokyo*
Simon & Schuster Asia Pte. Ltd., *Singapore*
Editora Prentice-Hall do Brasil, Ltda., *Rio de Janeiro*

For Pat, Garrett, and Eliza

Contents

PART THREE: THE ROMAN WORLD

Maps

Preface

Modern authors of social and cultural history can generally assume that their readers will share a number of fundamental presuppositions about the nature of present-day society. For example, they can take for granted that there will be no argument with the proposition that society is very different from or even opposed to the state and its institutions. Similarly, they do not have to establish that the modern state is a complex mosaic of classes and cultures that interact with a large number of public, semipublic, and private bodies such as churches, corporations, educational institutions, labor unions, branches of government, cultural organizations, and the like.

Unfortunately, a similar set of shared presuppositions does not exist for the ancient world. In a majority of cases none of the institutions mentioned here existed in antiquity, and those that did functioned at such a rudimentary level that they counted for little. Even the ancient world's class system operated on a set of principles quite different from that of the modern state. Particularly in their classical formulations, ancient societies were tightly knit communities in which political, cultural, and religious life closely intermingled. Society was not something set apart from the state but was, instead, closely identified with it. As a result, it is possible to write of ancient society as an independent sphere of human activity in the modern sense only in a very limited way, but what this book seeks to do is to pursue the distinctive forms society took in the ancient world and especially the unusual relationship between society and the state that characterized the social order of antiquity. Detailed descriptions of the highly integrated world of the classical period are given, placing special emphasis on its culture, social structures, moral values, and political processes. The inner workings of the Athenian democracy and the Roman Republic are discussed at length, and art, literature, and religion—especially how they functioned, vis-à-vis society—receive prominent attention. At the same time, recognizing that the closely unified societies of the classical period changed radically over the course of time, special consideration is given to the much-altered world of the Hellenistic period (third to second centuries B.C.) and the Roman Empire (first to fifth centuries A.D.). The last chapter describes the new society that began to make its appearance toward the end of antiquity, laying the foundations for the modern world.

In the years since the first edition of this textbook appeared, a great deal has been written on the social history of antiquity. Despite this outpouring, the social history of the ancient world remains at an early stage of its development. For example, any attempt to write a comprehensive survey of the family or gender relations from Sumerian to Byzantine times will quickly demonstrate the sketchiness of our sources and the lack of scholarly investigation into particular periods or areas. However, enormous strides have been made, and this new edition makes a special point of adding to and updating the social material in the text. Where appropriate, emphasis has been placed on the interconnections that permeate the history of the Near East, Greece, and Rome.

I owe special thanks to the following people, who at one stage or another in this book's publishing history made helpful critical suggestions: Thomas A. Anderson, Jr.; Richard Beal; John A. Brinkman; Stanley M. Burstein; T. F. Carney; Stefan Chrissanthos; Walter Donlan; H. A. Drake; Katherine F. Drew; Rory Egan; John K. Evans; Arther Ferrill; Gerald E. Kadish; Richard W. Kaeuper; Barbara Kellum; John A. Koumoulides; Eric Leichty; Michael Maas; W. J. McCoy; Richard E. Mitchell; Jasonne G. O'Brien; Kate Porteus; Chris Rasmussen; Lee Reams; Brigette Russell; and Joanne Scurlock.

Chapter 1

The Early Civilization of Mesopotamia and Egypt

WHY MESOPOTAMIA?

As far as we can tell, the great leap from peasant village to true city occurred around 3000 B.C. in the land of Sumer, in the southern part of Mesopotamia. Here, for the first time, human energies were channeled into the creation of great temple complexes and large-scale irrigation and flood-control projects. Directing these operations was a talented elite that drew on the then revolutionary information storage recovery technique of writing to control the collection, storage, and redistribution of the agricultural surpluses on which this new mode of human organization depended.

Paradoxically, this spectacular development took place in what is, from many viewpoints, a hostile environment. The climate of central and southern Mesopotamia is dry and subtropical, with temperatures reaching 120°F in the summer and with an average annual rainfall of less than 10 inches. Unlike the Nile, which floods at a time suitable for the cereal crop cycle, the Tigris and Euphrates flood between April and June, too late for the summer planting and too early for the winter. As a result, agriculture is possible only by means of artificial irrigation and careful crop management. To bring moisture to the fields at the low water levels of the planting seasons, deep canals must be dug and maintained. Silting is a perennial problem that can be resolved only by unending labor and a high degree of community cooperation.

Salinization is another challenge, especially in the south, where the low water table encourages salt to collect and rise to the surface when the fields are not properly

1

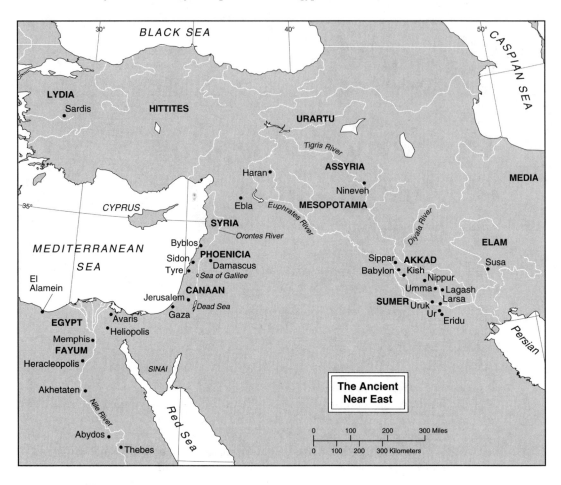

The Ancient Near East

leached by fresh inundations. Without adequate drainage, the soil quickly becomes sterile, making it difficult if not impossible to restore to productivity. The rivers, with their unpredictable and often violent floods, are yet another threat to the cities and villages precariously located along their banks. Without human intervention, southern Mesopotamia hovers between swamp and desert. Yet it offers immense advantages over the surrounding regions. When properly irrigated, the land is immensely fertile, and in antiquity it was one of the richest food-producing areas in the world. The rivers themselves are excellent means of transportation, and their regular burden of mud, though not as rich as that of the Nile, is the basis for the natural fertility of the region. It was these factors and, most important, the organizational abilities of the Mesopotamians themselves that sustained the brilliant civilization that flourished there for thousands of years, one that has never ceased to influence our own culture.

THE AGRICULTURAL REVOLUTION

The story of the growth of Mesopotamian civilization begins in the fringes of the region, in the foothills of the Zagros Mountains to the north, and in the hills of Palestine and Lebanon to the west. There, between 8000 and 6000 B.C., occurred an extraordinary event that changed forever the history of the region: the Agricultural, or Neolithic, Revolution.

That it was a revolution there can be no dispute. It transformed the way human beings lived and shattered a tradition over 2 million years old. However, why the Agricultural Revolution occurred at this precise time is still largely a matter of conjecture. Why, for instance, did it not occur during one of the earlier interglacial periods when, presumably, the same conditions prevailed? It is difficult to find any uniformly satisfying answers. We know that agriculture developed more or less simultaneously in many different parts of the globe, so it is unlikely that it resulted from any single cause such as climatic change or population growth, although both have been offered as explanations. We also know that the move to agriculture was not always permanently successful. In some places it was tried for a while and then abandoned. It is even possible that certain plants and animals were domesticated more than once and by different peoples.

Most modern explanations of the origins of agriculture tend to emphasize the role of microenvironments and longstanding human-plant and human-animal relationships. Such factors as changing climatic conditions, the presence of animals and plants that offered good potential for domestication, and the cultural and technological levels of achievement of the human populations present undoubtedly played important roles in the development of agriculture.

The Technology of Agriculture

The key to understanding agriculture is the process known as domestication. Domestication was the essential technological breakthrough that allowed human beings to escape the age-old system of hunting and gathering and to control the production of food rather than being at the mercy of what sustenance the terrain might offer at any given moment.

Domestication can be defined as a primitive form of genetic engineering in which certain plants and animals are brought under human control, their objectionable characteristics eliminated, their favorable ones enhanced and in the case of animals, can be induced to reproduce in captivity. If wild animals cannot be induced to breed in captivity they cannot be domesticated. Modern domesticated cattle, sheep, and pigs, for instance, look only remotely like their lean, mean, and fast-moving ancestors. Domestication is best viewed as the creation of an artificial environment in which the chosen plants or animals come to exist exclusively. Left alone, domesticated species either die or revert to their original wild forms. Because herds, farms, orchards, and gardens are permanent, static entities, once they came into being the old hunting-gathering forms of social organization had to be replaced.

Hunters and gatherers place a low value on possessions and a high value on mobility. Always on the move, they carry only a few tools and weapons with them. Agriculture reverses this way of life. It cannot be practiced without a commitment to permanence and the accumulation of large amounts of material goods. Homes, villages, and storage facilities must be constructed; fields cleared, divided, and fenced; herds built up and maintained; and tools fabricated. Constant effort is required to maintain all of these. Once settled, farmers may not move again for generations. Pastoralists are equally committed to their flocks and herds.

For practical purposes, hunting-gathering bands always remained small, in the range of 30 to 50 people. Larger groups would have been difficult for most environments to sustain; smaller ones could not reproduce themselves. Agriculture, by contrast, knew no limits as far as population growth was concerned. Thus, where hunting-gathering bands restricted their numbers, agricultural communities tended to expand them. Children could be put to work in the fields or gardens at an early age, and at harvest time it was essential to maximize the number of people who could be mobilized. Overpopulation was solved by emigrating and opening up new land for cultivation. By about 6000 B.C., villages with populations in the thousands were common throughout the Near East.

Counting the Cost for Society: The Impact on Gender Roles

The growth of population and the accumulation of material goods changed the way human beings lived. Under hunting-gathering conditions a rough egalitarianism prevailed; no one had (or needed) more than anyone else. What was the point of accumulating things that could not be carried from place to place during long nomadic treks? In the settled conditions of agriculture, however, this was not the case. Now there was a reason to expand one's possessions, whether farm or flock. Wealth was its own self-evident justification. Material goods could be accumulated, enjoyed during one's lifetime, and then passed on to the next generation. With the Agricultural Revolution inequality became, for the first time, an aspect of the human condition, because not everyone could be equally successful in the quest for material possessions.

The new way of life had a powerful impact on gender relations. With the introduction of agriculture, the role and status of women changed. It is estimated, for instance, that in some present-day hunting-gathering groups, women contribute over 70 percent of the daily food supply and as a result have a higher status than their counterparts in agrarian societies. In hunting-gathering bands children are usually spaced at three- to four-year intervals (by means of late weaning), whereas in agricultural societies women have frequent pregnancies and spend more time caring for small children. Finally, men dominate agriculture wherever it involves the use of the plow and herding. As their roles changed and as they lost the ability to contribute directly to the economic well-being of the community, the status of women declined.

Another factor contributing to this decline was the emergence of a form of public life. In hunting-gathering bands hierarchy was minimized and authority rested in the hands of the most trusted and able members of the community as well as the elders. Everyone knew everyone else and the older members of the community mediated disputes. This changed with the development of large villages, where more formal and less personal methods of administering justice and maintaining order became necessary. Men easily assumed the new roles of judges, which complemented their responsibility for defending villages from outside marauders and policing the more unruly members of the village community; the power of coercion and patriarchal control went hand in hand. The realm of justice, administration, and warfare was defined as an arena of public concern under male control in opposition to, and superior to, the private realm of the family and the household to which women, children, servants, and, for the first time, slaves were assigned. This distinction between public and private realms is a key to understanding ancient society.

The results of the Agricultural Revolution were thoroughly mixed. It is usually regarded as a great leap forward for humankind, as indeed it is if we focus only on its ability to provide large food surpluses and to create new and more varied jobs for men. In other respects, though, it posed challenges in terms of cooperation and the ownership of goods that have never been adequately solved.

Apart from its lowering of the status of women, the agricultural way of life created new stresses for everyone. Herds and farms had to be maintained. There were new sources of friction over boundary lines, possessions, and the equitable distribution of goods and responsibilities. Relations between men and women and between children and their parents changed. New relations between haves and have-nots, masters and servants, owners and nonowners, freemen and slaves, came into being. Warfare was a much more serious business than in the past. There was now something worth fighting over beyond mere disputes about hunting territory. There was valuable booty in the form of movable goods and people who could be put to work for their new masters. Herds and farms could be appropriated, and their previous owners enslaved.

It is undoubtedly true that plain superiority in force allowed agriculturalists to overwhelm hunting-gathering peoples everywhere in the world. It was not a peaceful process. Even when not in direct confrontation, agriculturalists always encroached aggressively on the territories of hunters and gatherers. The problems that arose from rapid population growth were solved as surplus population moved on, into the territories of hunters and gatherers. In all of the sustained confrontations between agriculturalists and hunters and gatherers, the latter have always lost. Today, what was once the only way of life for the human race is practiced by a tiny and ever-shrinking percentage of people in the most inaccessible parts of the globe. In the great sweep of human history the only two other events that can be compared to the Agricultural Revolution in terms of their effects on human relations are the State and Urban Revolution (to be considered next) and the Industrial Age Revolution—the age in which we live.

THE STATE AND URBAN REVOLUTION

About the middle of the sixth millennium (ca. 5500 B.C.), groups of settlers driven by a mixture of enterprise and growing population pressure made their way down into the plains of the Tigris and Euphrates rivers and took up residence in the more promising riverbank environments. In the marshy south, fish and wild fowl contributed to the diet of the settlers, and in the central steppe area, sheep, cattle, and goats were raised. Having brought with them the grains they had cultivated in the northern hills and valleys, the settlers quickly found that barley could tolerate the somewhat more salty farmlands of the south, and wheat did better in the north. There was a catch, however: both crops required drainage and irrigation.

Initial irrigation efforts occurred on a small scale, but it was soon learned that the volume of grain from the irrigated patches of farmland was disproportionate to the amount of land irrigated and a lot more than had been produced by means of dry-farming techniques in the surrounding hill country. The settlers also found that date palms flourished along the irrigation ditches and riverbanks and provided a high-calorie source of food that was easily stored. Through the transfer and adaptation of techniques and crops that had proved successful in one area to a potentially richer area, the foundation for a truly self-sustained agricultural economy was established in southern Mesopotamia between 5000 and 3000 B.C.

The archaeological sources demonstrate that during the fourth millennium (4000–3000 B.C.) there were many widespread, uniformly distributed agricultural settlements in southern Mesopotamia that practiced small-scale irrigation and mixed food production with food gathering. There were also a number of religious centers, such as the one at Uruk, which by 3500 B.C. was a substantial ceremonial hub surrounded by a large number of towns and villages. Around 3000 B.C. Uruk suddenly expanded and, drawing population from the surrounding communities, became a true city with a population of approximately 50,000 people. This pattern of rural incorporation was repeated again and again throughout southern Mesopotamia, and then spread west toward Syria and north into Elam.

Urbanization was not brought about solely by the need for concentrating resources for irrigation, although the advantages of large-scale organization for such purposes must have been clear by this time. The growth of population, the resulting need for greater productivity, ecological factors, and the need for defense against competing communities nearby would all have contributed, though it is hard to identify any one of them as the primary cause. An important, if not essential, role was played by the centers of common worship scattered throughout Mesopotamia. These focal points of community life, with their temples and priesthoods, must have been attractive places for craftsmen and traders to settle, and their presence in turn attracted the local landowners and farmers. Thus the temples became centers of economic as well as religious activities. The need for a place of refuge might have been a final factor that drew the population from the scattered towns and villages to the city center. Thick walls, adequate supplies of food, and a large population would have been effective in deterring potential aggressors, whereas small or poorly defended villages or towns would have been tempting targets.

The Social Consequences of Urbanization

Coming soon after the Agricultural Revolution, the State and Urban Revolution introduced yet another set of social relations and released new floods of human energy. Because the form of the state that first emerged in Mesopotamia was the independent, self-sufficient city with its attached rural territory, the term *city-state* was coined to describe the phenomenon. However, it was also possible for the state to evolve with little or no urbanization. Early Egypt is a good example of this latter kind of development.

In the city-state (or state), kin and tribal loyalties are, by definition, subordinated and replaced by political ties. The new organization is something much more than just a large town. Political ties are human relations of an entirely new kind; indeed, it is their existence that makes possible all of civilization. Population size is not the only factor. An agricultural town might have a huge population and still not qualify as a city-state. What makes a city-state different from an agricultural town is the synergy created by its people interacting with each other on the basis of political relationships rather than traditional blood ties.

The concentration, diversity, and complexity of population and organization characterize states and city-states. These features encourage the specialization of craft and the stimulation of new ideas, arts, and technologies. Thus even a small Mesopotamian city-state had the capacity to outperform entire groups of villages or towns whose collective population was much larger. Consider just one common example: warfare. Because it had significant numbers of specialized craftspeople, a city-state was able to produce and store huge quantities of weapons of all kinds. Its bureaucrats could keep track of supplies of metal and other materials needed in warfare. These officials could also find, draft, and equip large numbers of soldiers, and then supply them even at great distances from home. When new technologies such as chariots were introduced, it was again the cities that had the wealth and resources to obtain them in large numbers. Kings and their officers provided specialized leadership. In addition, the city itself, together with its temples, gods, religious festivals, and homes, provided an identity and a sense of belonging for its inhabitants. The city-state had become something worth fighting for, and propaganda and ideology emerged simultaneously with its appearance.

The price paid for the new way of life came in the form of weakened family and kin relations and the unequal stratification of society into privileged and less-privileged classes. Justice was administered on the basis of impersonal law, and the state assumed a monopoly of power to wage war, punish criminals, and execute any other policy it established. Family and clan heads lost their special power to rule their own kin. Private wars and vendettas between individuals or groups of individuals were outlawed. Religious rituals that previously had been exclusively clan affairs were now to be shared by everyone, clan members or not. In gender relations, the state reinforced the changes that the introduction of agriculture had brought about between males and females. The public realm of politics, administration, management, religion, warfare, and economics was enormously expanded, and men were the principal beneficiaries. This was especially true in societies such as those of Mesopotamia, where warfare was a regular part of life. New areas of human endeavor, such as art and monumental architecture, came into being. The invention of writing opened the possibility of careers in a dozen new fields, which were almost exclusively restricted to males. Women benefited from generally rising standards of living, better food supplies, and the more stimulating life of the city. Trade brought luxury goods and contact with the outside world. Religion, as always, offered its own special sphere of activities that were solely female. In general, however, women's exclusion from the most significant parts of the public realm meant their restriction to the less-privileged private world.

EARLY MESOPOTAMIAN HISTORY: THE SUMERIAN PERIOD (3100–2000 B.C.)

Around 3100 B.C., at the same time that the city-state emerged, Mesopotamia passed another threshold: it went from prehistory to history. For the first time we learn the names of some of the men and women involved in these revolutionary changes and of the places where they lived. All of the earliest names of people, such as the Sumerian Uanna-Adapa (better known in its Hebrew form, Adam), are legendary, the inventions of later writers, but the earliest cities mentioned, such as Eridu, Sippar, and Shuruppak, are places familiar in later times.

EVENTS OF EARLY MESOPOTAMIAN HISTORY

Agricultural Revolution	8000–6000 B.C.
Development of agriculture in Mesopotamia	ca. 5500 B.C.
State and Urban Revolution: emergence of the world's first cities and states in Sumer	ca. 3100 B.C.
Sargon of Akkad unifies Mesopotamia: world's first empire	ca. 2240 B.C.
Decline of Sumer; sack of Ur	ca. 2000 B.C.

A little is known about the principal linguistic and ethnic groups of Mesopotamia at the time of the State and Urban Revolution. The northern and middle Euphrates region was inhabited by people who spoke a Semitic language called Akkadian (better known as its dialects, Babylonian and Assyrian); in the south the language groups were Sumerian and Elamite. Neither of the latter is related to any known language group, although it is generally assumed that they were probably at one time more widespread than the present records indicate. We do not know where any of these people originated. All of them emerge into the sudden light of history with their languages and cultures wholly formed. It is possible that the Sumerians, the creators of urban society, were not native to the region. Despite the difference in language among the three major ethnic groups, Sumerians, Elamites, and Semites, they soon became culturally indistinguishable from one another. All of them adopted some form of the Sumerian city-state and adapted the Sumerian technique of writing to their own languages. They fought among themselves with about equal ferocity, their capacity to do so having been immensely enhanced by their successful urbanization.

From the beginning, Mesopotamia fluctuated between times of unification, when one or another city succeeded in dominating some or all of the others, and times of fragmentation, when the individual city-states went their own anarchic ways. At an early date the city of Kish gave some kind of unity to the states of Sumer, and the title *King of Kish* became synonymous with *King of Sumer.* Another city, Nippur, provided the religious sanction for Sumerian overlordship, and in times of extraordinary danger the leaders of the cities assembled there to elect one of their number to the kingship. Eventually, the endorsement of the priesthood of Nippur became an essential part of the legitimation process and was eagerly sought by would-be contenders for the overlordship of Sumer.

Although the unity of the cities under the leadership of one of their number represents one aspect of Mesopotamian political life, another, more common characteristic was the struggle of the cities among themselves over boundaries and irrigation water. We know, for example, of the quarrels around 2500 B.C. between Lagash and its neighbor Umma over a stretch of territory that lay between them. We learn first that

> the *ensi* [governor] of Umma, at the command of his god, raided and devoured the Guedin, the irrigated land, the field beloved of Ningirsu [the god of Lagash].[1]

The phalanx of Lagash, however, led by its *ensi* Eannatum, attacked the invaders and "heaped up piles of bodies on the plain."[2] A century or so later the tables were reversed when Lugalzaggesi of Umma sacked Lagash, and an unknown author wrote the following lament over the ruined city:

---

[1]Georges Roux, *Ancient Iraq* (Harmondsworth, UK: Penguin, 1966), p. 131. By permission of George Allen and Unwin Ltd.

[2]Ibid.

Eannatum leads the army of Lagash into battle (left) assisted by the god Ningirsu (right), who holds a net symbolically containing the enemies of his city.

> The men of Umma have set fire to the temple Antasurra [in Lagash], they have carried away the silver and the precious stones. . . . They have shed blood in the temple of E-engur of the goddess Nanshe.[3]

Despite this setback, Lagash recovered, and two centuries later its leader, Gudea, was dedicating huge temples, extending the city's irrigation network, and fostering long-distance trade. Yet 200 years after that, Lagash was embroiled with Larsa, another Sumerian city, and temporarily came under its control.

This kind of endless warfare exhausted Sumerian energies and periodically gave outsiders an opportunity to meddle in Sumerian affairs. Around 2350 B.C. Sargon, the powerful Akkadian ruler of Agade in the middle Euphrates region, seized his opportunity and conquered Sumer, declaring himself "King of Kish, Uruk, and Ur." He went on to build an empire—the world's first—that stretched from Syria to the Persian Gulf. For a brief time, the fiercely independent city-states of Mesopotamia were forced to stop their quarreling and accept the overlordship of Sargon, his family, and his appointees.

Sargon's empire lasted through the long and vigorous reign of his grandson, Naram-Sin, but then sank slowly into anarchy, aptly described by the words of the Sumerian List of Kings: "Who was king? Who was not king!" Various enemies, among them the Amorites of the Syrian desert fringes, the peoples of the Zagros Mountains, and the seething cities of Sumer, had a hand in its downfall. After its collapse, Ebla in Syria, the "Akkad of the North," which had been sacked by Naram-Sin, recovered and held sway over northern Mesopotamia, while in the south the individual city-states once more became independent.

[3]From Samuel Noah Kramer, *The Sumerians: Their History, Culture, and Character* (Chicago: University of Chicago Press, 1963), pp. 322–323. © 1963 by the University of Chicago Press.

ENHEDUANNA: THE WORLD'S FIRST AUTHOR

When Sargon conquered Sumer he was faced with a major problem in reconciling Sumerian-speaking southerners and their Akkadian-speaking conquerers. His approach was to try to fuse the two cultures by identifying Akkadian and Sumerian gods with each other and by appointing members of his own family to religious positions in Sumerian temples.

One of these appointees was his daughter, Enheduanna, whom he made high priestess of both An, the god of heaven, at Uruk, and of Nanna, the moon god, at Ur. Her portrait, as well as two long, well-crafted cycles of hymns that she wrote, survives, thus making her the world's first known literary figure. In the hymns the Sumerian goddess Inanna is syncretized (identified) with her Akkadian counterpart, the goddess Ishtar. So successful was Enheduanna in smoothing over the differences between north and south that long after Sargon's dynasty disappeared, the king of Sumer continued to appoint his daughter to the position of high priestess of Ur and Uruk. Sometimes these priestesses outlived even their own dynasties and became the legitimating link between one dynasty and the next.

THE SACK OF UR

O Father Nanna [the chief god of Ur], that city into ruins was made . . .
Its walls were breached; the people groan;
In its lofty gates, where they were wont to promenade, dead bodies were lying
　　about;
In its boulevards, where the feasts were celebrated, scattered they lay . . .
In its places, where the festivities of the land took place, the people lay in heaps
　　. . .
Ur—its weak and its strong—perished through hunger . . .
O Nanna, Ur has been destroyed, its people have been dispersed.

Source: From "A Sumerian Lamentation," trans. S. N. Kramer in James B. Pritchard, ed., *Ancient Near Eastern Texts: Relating to the Old Testament*, 3rd ed. with Supplement. Copyright © 1950, 1955, 1969, 1978 by Princeton University Press. Excerpt, pp. 459–460. Reprinted by permission of Princeton University Press.

Between the fall of Sargon's empire and the rise of Babylon under Hammurapi 400 or so years later, Sumer had a brief revival, the so-called renaissance of Ur III (ca. 2100–2000 B.C.). Under the vigorous leadership of Ur-Nammu, temples were rebuilt, and Ur's ziggurat, a pyramidal mud-brick tower, was erected. Overseas trade developed, and irrigation was extended. One of Ur-Nammu's greatest achievements was the publication of a code of laws intended to systematize and make public the customary rules by which cases were decided. This late flourishing of Sumer under Ur's leadership was the last major effort of the Sumerians as an independent people. Continuing pressure from the Amorites and from Elam gradually weakened Ur, and the city was finally captured and sacked, probably by the Elamites.

World Views: Ancient and Modern

In dealing with any of the societies of the ancient world, but especially those in their early phases, it is important to recognize that we are dealing with peoples whose viewpoints are radically different from our own. This is not simply because they lived long ago and did not possess industrial and scientific know-how, but also because they started out with different assumptions about the world and the place of human beings in it.

Most modern Western societies are made up of conglomerations of competing (and sometimes cooperating) public, semipublic, and private bodies such as business corporations, unions, churches, government agencies, schools, clubs, and private societies of all kinds. The term *civil society* is given to this kind of society. Private life is highly developed, and most citizens, except those who choose a life in politics or government, have little to do with the public realm. Life in modern industrialized countries revolves around jobs, families, social acquaintances, and private organizations to which people belong. Self-expressive individualism is at least officially encouraged. In fact, one of the highest compliments we can bestow on people is to say that they think for themselves.

To understand most ancient societies, however, we must reverse many of these assumptions. Outside the family there was little or no difference or separation between public and private realms. Society and the state practically coincided. All of the institutions of society—family, government, religion, and economic and cultural spheres—were integrated with one another. The community, not the individual, was supreme. People were supposed to fit in, not "find themselves." There were no private codes of morality or independent lifestyles. However, individualism could express itself in one area: the choice of one's personal gods. Because the religions of Mesopotamia and Egypt were polytheistic, a great variety of cults were available for every need, every occasion, and every taste. There was no single set of religious doctrines and related moral rules to which a person had to adhere, as in monotheistic religions.

Religion and Society

In the Mesopotamian world view, the cities and their inhabitants, together with their domestic animals and even the land itself, belonged to the gods; specifically, they belonged to the god or goddess of each particular city. Reversing modern assumptions, individual men and women were thought to exist for the sake of the gods, not for their own self-fulfillment.

According to the Mesopotamian creation myth, the gods had become tired of working for a living and thus had created human beings to take their place. But in this way, although they had solved the problem of work, the gods came to depend on humans to supply them with their food, drink, clothing, and shelter. The inhabitants of Mesopotamian cities were not merely engaged in the secular, humdrum tasks of making a living or raising a family. As servants of the gods, they participated in a much larger drama in which the gods themselves were the principal actors: the job of making the universe work.

For Mesopotamians, the universe—the cosmos—was seen as an orderly whole. However, it had not started out that way, and there was no guarantee that it would remain orderly. There was always the possibility that it would slip back into its original form, and then both gods and humans would disappear into the watery, inert chaos of the world's origins.

According to the Akkadian creation myth, the *Enuma Elish* ("When on High"), at the beginning the universe consisted of an undifferentiated, watery mass. There were two basic elements: the fresh waters (the male principle), known as Apsu, and the salt waters (the female principle), known as Tiamat. From these two original deities all the other gods were born. The gods were so rowdy that their parents decided to destroy them. When the gods got wind of this plan, they were horrified, but they took heart when one of their number, the god of intelligence and wisdom, Ea, succeeded in putting their father, Apsu, into a trance and then killing him. Ea next constructed his dwelling on top of the monstrous remains of Apsu, which thus became the earth. Understandably, Tiamat was disturbed by her spouse's destruction and rounded up the forces of chaos to continue the war with her upstart children. The gods were again dismayed, but this time they found a champion in the storm god Marduk. After a titanic struggle, Marduk defeated Tiamat and used part of her body to form the sky, and then went on to create the rest of the universe, including the human race.

Despite the gods' apparent victory, there was no guarantee that the forces of chaos might not recover their strength and overturn the orderly creation of the gods. Gods and humans alike were involved in the perpetual struggle to restrain the powers of chaos, and they each had their own role to play in this dramatic battle. The responsibility of the dwellers of Mesopotamian cities was to provide the gods with everything they needed to run the world. Without this support, the gods could not perform their proper function; it was an awesome responsibility for the people of Mesopotamia. At least in early times, it had the effect of inspiring them to superhuman tasks.

The role of the city and its inhabitants in the maintenance of the cosmos was brought home with great force at the time of the major festivals. Most of these were associated in some way with the agricultural cycle of the year. They were enacted to keep the natural world functioning properly. Mesopotamians did not view the world as a natural system functioning on its own, independent of human agency, but as something that had to be activated by their personal intervention. The fertility cycle, for instance, could be made to function only by means of a religious ritual in which a marriage between the *ensi,* or king of the city, and the priestess of Inanna took place. Similarly, each year when the flooding Tigris and Euphrates threatened to bring back the primeval watery chaos, the victorious battle of the gods was reenacted in ritual form, and the triumph of gods and humans over chaos was ensured for another year. Given these attitudes, the importance of the temple in Mesopotamian life can easily be appreciated.

Temples   The temples where the gods lived varied in size, shape, and function. The main god or goddess of the city had the largest temples and lived there with his or her family and relatives. Scattered throughout the various regions of the city were neighborhood chapels consisting of a small, open courtyard and a pedestal for a statue of the god or goddess.

Some temples were built on top of high mud-brick towers called ziggurats. At Ur, for instance, the ziggurat of Ur-Nammu's time was over 70 feet tall and had a base of 150 by 200 feet. It was composed of three separate stories connected by ramps of stairs. It was sealed by an 8-foot-thick layer of baked bricks set in bitumen. To give its huge bulk a sense of lightness, its lines were slightly curved, a technique also used by the Greeks in the building of the Parthenon, the famous temple of Athena at Athens. Ziggurats were regarded by Mesopotamians as staircases between heaven and earth, the connecting link between gods and humans. The people of Israel, who knew these structures well, took a different view and mocked them in the story of the Tower of Babel as symbols of human arrogance.

Other types of temples were built on level ground, usually surrounded by a number of spacious courtyards, each one opening into the other. These courtyards were lined with rooms that served as lodgings for the priests and temple workers, schools, libraries, workshops, and storehouses. All day long the courtyards were full of people coming and going, men and women bringing their offerings to the gods, merchants supplying the worshipers, drovers with their animals, idlers gossiping in the shade, temple attendants coming and going. Some of the temples were huge. At Uruk the building dubbed the Limestone Temple by its excavators measured over 350 by 100 feet and was built on a base of limestone brought from a quarry 40 miles away. The temple at Adab dedicated to the mother goddess Nin-tu had seven magnificent entrances with impressive names such as *Lofty Gate* and *Door of Refreshing Shade.*

The temple buildings themselves were divided into three rooms by partitions or curtains, one behind the other. These rooms had doors of precious wood and ceilings and walls paneled with sweet-smelling cedar. Lions, bulls, and griffins guarded the entrances. In the innermost room was the statue of the god or goddess surrounded by votive offerings, pots of flowers, and incense burners. In the room immediately preceding the god's was an altar or table for offerings and meals, along with a large basin for the sacred washings. Daily, to the sound of music, hymns, and prayers, the god was washed, clothed, perfumed, fed, and entertained by minstrels and dancers. In clouds of incense, meals of bread, cakes, fruit, and honey were set before the deity, along with offerings of beer, wine, and water. Animals were slaughtered, and portions of the sacrificial meat burned in his honor. On feast days the statues of the deities were taken in solemn procession through the courtyard or the streets of the city accompanied by singing and dancing.

Large numbers of priests were involved in the daily worship of the god or goddess. Some of them had highly specialized jobs, such as those who recited incantations, interpreted dreams, or anointed the statues of the deities. Others were singers or musicians. Women had important roles to play. As we have seen in the case of Enheduanna, the daughter of Sargon of Akkad, the high priestess was often of royal blood. There were other priestesses called *naditu* (the term meant "barren" or "fallow") who could marry but were not allowed to have children while they remained attached to the temple. The oddity of not being allowed to bear children while being married was handled by allowing the *naditu* to obtain a second wife for her husband. This second wife acted as childbearer for him and as a servant for the first wife. Surrogate motherhood has a long history!

Palaces   The other essential institution of the Mesopotamian city-state was the palace. As population and prosperity increased, the cities became less vulnerable to the old threats of natural disaster and starvation but more exposed to destruction at human hands. Their accumulated wealth could be looted, their population enslaved, and their canal system destroyed or taken over. The cities, accordingly, sought for more and more effective defensive (and offensive) measures. The principal of these was the kingship. From about 2600 B.C. onward the kings became central to the organization of the cities, not just ad hoc war leaders chosen for a particular campaign. The maintenance of the army and of the city fortifications was institutionalized and put under the control of the king.

The king's administration was modeled on that of the temple and imitated its protocol. Like the god, the king was surrounded by his servants. Often located in the same area and surrounded by the same thick protecting walls, palace and temple together came to form a kind of sacred city within the city proper.

Many of the palaces were beautifully laid out and handsomely decorated. The palace at Mari in northern Mesopotamia is considered one of the gems of Near Eastern architecture. It covered 7 acres and had over 300 well-planned rooms and sunny courtyards paved with gypsum. The walls were decorated with paintings. The audience room where the king received ambassadors and the throne room where he held court formed the heart of the palace. Other parts of the building were used for lodging the garrison, guests, scribes, and other attendants of the king. There were also chapels for the king's private devotions and schoolrooms for training palace personnel. Other sections of the palace were given over to workshops, armories, archives, kitchens, and storerooms. Bathrooms had floors sealed with bitumen. Efficient clay pipes provided excellent drainage, and when the palace was excavated, 3,500 years after its destruction, they were found to be still working.

Among the most important functionaries of the temples and palaces were the scribes, whose exclusive understanding of the complicated cuneiform (wedge-shaped) script made them key figures in the administration of the city. Incoming taxes and tribute were recorded along with the yields of the temple's and palace's possessions. The amount of inventory and the disbursement of goods from storage were recorded, for it was as distribution and regulatory agencies that these two key institutions performed their most important functions.

Thousands of contracts, payrolls, vouchers, labels, wills, marriages, deeds of property, and lists of inventories have survived. Some of the correspondence of the kings with fellow monarchs, provincial governors, and army chiefs has also come down to us. The letters between them admonish, order, request information, threaten, and boast. Canals are ordered dug or cleared, troops are mobilized, goods (usually arms or food) or the return of an escaped prisoner is requested, crimes are reported, and strange events that might reveal the will of the gods are noted, along with the details of pragmatic marriage and property arrangements.

THE IDEALS OF MESOPOTAMIAN LAW

In peace the kings of Mesopotamia were supposed to be the upholders of justice and the protectors of the weak and poor against the rich and powerful. This ideal is expressed in the epilogue of the law code of Hammurapi, king of Babylon (ca. 1792–1750 B.C.), part of which appears in this box. Hammurapi's code, although more systematic than any known prior collection, was by no means the first publication of laws for Mesopotamia, although it probably was the first regionwide promulgation. The existence of such an accessible source of law undercut the influence of local authorities, for by providing individuals with knowledge of the law, Hammurapi empowered them to seek justice on their own behalf.

That the strong might not oppress the weak, and that they should give justice to the orphan and the widow I have inscribed my words upon my monument and established them in the presence of my statue, "King of Justice," in Babylon. . . .

These are the just laws which Hammurabi, the wise king established and by which he gave the land stable support and good government. . . . Let any oppressed man, who has a case, come before my image, "King of Justice." Let him read the inscription on my monument! Let him give heed to my weighty words! And may my monument enlighten him as to his case and may he understand his case! May he set his heart at ease! And let him exclaim: "Hammurabi indeed is a ruler who is like a real father to his people." . . .

In the days that are yet to come, for all future time, may the king who is in the land observe the words of justice which I have written upon my monument! May he not alter the judgments of the land which I have pronounced, or the decisions of the country which I have rendered. May he not efface my statutes! If that man have wisdom, if he wish to give his land government, let him give attention to the words which I have written upon my monument! And may this monument enlighten him as to procedure and administration, the judgments which I have pronounced, and the decisions which I have rendered for the land! Let him justly rule the Black-Head people [the traditional name for the Sumerians]. Let him pronounce judgments for them and render for them decisions! Let him root out the wicked and the evildoer from the land! Let him promote the welfare of his people!

Source: Based on *The Code of Hammurabi,* trans. Robert F. Harper (Chicago: University of Chicago Press, 1904), pp. 99–103.

Mesopotamian Society

Although Mesopotamians believed that the city and its inhabitants belonged to the gods, this was not meant to be taken in the literal sense that the god, through the temple, owned all of the land of the state. In early times especially, the temples were undoubtedly among the largest landholders, but even then the nobility as well as ordinary free citizens owned large amounts of land.

In Sumerian times (ca. 3000–2000 B.C.) it is estimated that about half the population was made up of commoners or free citizens. Below the free citizenry were the dependents or clients of the nobility and the temples. These people did not own land and worked, often as tenants, for the nobles and priests. At the bottom of the social pyramid were the slaves. Throughout Mesopotamian history, they never seem to have been very numerous.

The Mesopotamian system was not based on caste, but it is safe to assume that most people born into a particular status or occupation remained in it for the rest of their lives. However, catastrophe or, less likely, extraordinary good luck could change a person's status overnight. Because warfare was constant, there was always the possibility of enslavement for noble and commoner alike. Economic hard times could have the same result because it was legal for a father to sell his wife and children into slavery for up to three years; he could even sell himself. Conversely, the status of a slave was not immutable. A slave could work to escape from bondage by setting aside income earned while a slave, and there was always the possibility of being freed as a gesture of generosity or kindness by one's owner. Slaves also had a number of rights. They could own property, engage in business activities, and even give evidence in court—more than women could do in most Western societies until recent times. If a freeman took a slave as his mistress and had children by her, she could not be sold, and on his death she and her children were automatically free. If a freewoman married a slave, her children were born free. Hence the gulf between slave and free was not as great as it was to be in other societies, especially because the stigma of race was not present to perpetuate the memory of people having once belonged to a servile class.

Women had important legal rights. They could own property and slaves, engage in business, and appear in court as witnesses. Marriage was monogamous, although in practice a man could have a concubine, especially if his wife was not able to bear children. Parents or elders of the clan usually arranged marriages. Betrothal was recognized when the groom presented his father-in-law with a gift of money, which was lost if he broke off the engagement. Upon marriage the bride assumed possession of these gifts and of the dowry given to her by her own family. The dowry was regarded as inalienable; that is, it could not be sold or given away by her, and on her death it went to her children. If there were no children, the dowry reverted to her father's family. In case of divorce, which was easy for a man to obtain but difficult for a woman, the dowry went with the wife. In a husband's absence, the wife could administer his estate; if he died, she inherited the same share in his estate as her children. She could marry again at will and still keep her original dowry.

Daily Life   The excavated houses of Ur give a good idea of how ordinary Mesopotamians lived. Made of mud brick, the houses often shared common walls. Their doors opened onto narrow, winding streets. Yet the blank exterior walls, with their single small doorways and uninteresting appearance, gave little idea of the comfort, quiet, and privacy that existed within. The thick mud-brick walls gave insulation from the heat of the summer, the cold of the winter, and the noise of the city. Rooms were arranged around a bright, open courtyard where most of the cooking and family living took place. Sometimes there was a second story or a small attached garden, but generally space in the city was at a premium. Walls were usually painted white, and floors were covered with a layer of hard gypsum.

Mesopotamian food was plain but plentiful. Barley was the staple of the south, wheat of the north. Vegetables, cheese, and fish were always available, and most meals would have been accompanied by milk or beer; Mesopotamians were especially fond of the latter. Because a good deal of land was devoted to herding, Mesopotamians probably ate more meat than many other ancient peoples. For dessert there were figs and dates or a thick sweet treacle made from dates or grapes.

Children were under the complete control of their parents and could be disinherited or, as we have seen, even sold into slavery for a period of time. In normal situations, however, children were cherished and loved as they are in all societies. Their education was largely informal. They learned from being members of a family and observing its older members at work. Most of all, they learned from belonging to the vibrant communities that were the cities of Mesopotamia. Crowded, narrow streets, marketplaces covered with awnings, and busy, sun-filled plazas around the great temples were all within walking distance of everyone's house. Traders from distant lands brought their wares to the city, and visitors and travels were at hand at all times. The cities themselves were constantly abuzz with activities of one kind or another. Perhaps a major trial or some other public business was under way; the assemblies of citizens were consulted on major issues throughout a good portion of the history of Mesopotamia. There were great festivals to the gods on a regular basis. War and preparations for war were common, and building activities were always going on. If the inhabitants tired of the city, there was always the local countryside with its interesting and intricate network of canals and ditches to be explored.

Besides the informal education that took place in the streets of the cities, there were schools that prepared promising students (or at least those whose parents could afford the fees) for a career in the temple or palace bureaucracy or one of the many professions. Many years were spent memorizing the thousands of tiny wedge-shaped signs of cuneiform and becoming familiar with the methods of administration used in the temples and palaces. For specific professions such as medicine, engineering, business, and accounting, specialized vocabularies had to be learned. Because so much of Mesopotamian life revolved around irrigation and farming, specialists were needed who could do the surveying required to establish claims of ownership and help keep disputes out of court. There was even an opportunity for genuine research, because the schools served as libraries and the depositories for records, technical manuals, and literary works of all kinds.

Moral Values and the Afterlife   In early Mesopotamian society, primary emphasis was placed on the virtue of obedience to the gods and subservience to the needs of the community. An orderly world was not possible without firm authority. The ideal society was described as follows:

> Days when one man is not insolent to another, when a son reveres his father,
> Days when respect is shown in the land, when the lowly honor the great.[4]

Although survival in a hostile environment dominated the concerns of these early years, in time Mesopotamians began to look beyond the restrictive ties of their communities, and at the beginning of the second millennium (ca. 2000 B.C.) the needs of the individual—fears, guilt, and sufferings—began to be heard for the first time. Complaints and petitions were not directed to the gods on high but to the individual's own personal god, who might, if sufficiently pressed, do something to help.

One such complaint from the period has survived in literary form, by an author sometimes known as the Sumerian Job. In this tale a just, wealthy, and benevolent man is struck down suddenly with sickness and misfortunes of all kinds. Even so, he says he will continue to praise his god and will keep lamenting until he is heard:

> My god, the day shines bright over the land, for me the day is black . . .
> Tears, lament, anguish, and depression are lodged within me,
> Suffering overwhelms me like one chosen for nothing but tears,
> Malignant sickness bathes my body.
> How long will you neglect me, leave me unprotected?[5]

The afflicted man goes on to say that though he realizes that the blame for his misfortunes rests on him, he asks that his hidden faults may be revealed in order that he may seek forgiveness for them.

For Mesopotamians the afterworld was a dreary and cheerless place, ruled by a fearsome hierarchy of demons. At most it was a dismal reflection of life on earth. No one was exempt from it, not even the heroes who struggled to avoid being dragged down into it. Of these the best known was Gilgamesh, one of the early rulers of Uruk, about whom there developed a cycle of tales that ultimately came to make up the *Epic of Gilgamesh,* probably the finest product of Near Eastern literature outside the Hebrew scriptures.

In one of the early versions of this epic, the hero, Gilgamesh, is saddened by the thought of death brought home to him by the sight of "dead bodies floating in the river's waters," and he determines to make a name for himself before his own death:

> I peered over the wall,
> Saw the dead bodies floating in the river's waters,
> As for me, I too will be served thus, verily it is so!
> Man, the tallest, cannot reach to heaven,
> Man, the widest, cannot cover the earth. . . .
> I would enter the "land," would set up my name,
> In its places where the names have been raised up, I would raise up my name,
> In its places where the names have not been raised up, I would raise up the names of
> the gods.[6]

---

[4]H. Frankfort et al., *Before Philosophy* (Harmondsworth, UK: Penguin, 1949), pp. 212–213. Originally published as *The Intellectual Adventure of Ancient Man* (Chicago: University of Chicago Press, 1946). By permission of the University of Chicago Press.

[5]Kramer, *The Sumerians: Their History, Culture, and Character,* p. 128.

[6]Ibid., p. 193.

In a later version Gilgamesh next sets off in quest of adventure with his companion Enkidu and a number of volunteers, and after crossing high mountains they vanquish a great monster. However, Enkidu is slain by the gods for an act of impiety, and in broken-hearted grief Gilgamesh leaves the city and the kingship, and wanders in the steppe clothed in animal skins:

> "My friend, my younger brother—who with me in the foothills hunted wild ass, and
>   panther in the plains;
> Enkidu my friend . . . who with me could do all . . .
> Now—what sleep is this that seized you?
> You have grown dark and cannot hear me."
> He did not raise his eyes.
> [Gilgamesh] touched his heart; it was not beating.
> Then he covered his friend, as if he were a bride. . . .
> His voice roared out—a lion. . . .
> Again and again he turned towards his friend, tearing his hair and scattering the tufts,
>   stripping and flinging down the finery off his body.[7]

In the hope of avoiding a fate similar to that of Enkidu, he sets off to visit the immortal Utnapishtim. On the way he is given this piece of advice:

> Gilgamesh, whither are you wandering?
> Life, which you look for, you will never find.
> For when the gods created man, they let death be his share, and life withheld in their
>   own hands.
> Gilgamesh, fill your belly—day and night make merry, let days be full of joy, dance
>   and make music day and night.[8]

Finally, Utnapishtim reconciles him to his mortality, though there are other adventures before Gilgamesh returns home. This magnificent poem, which deals with such eternal human problems as sickness, old age, death, fame, and the craving for the unattainable, can be considered a metaphor for Mesopotamia's own heroic struggle to resist decay and leave a name for itself among the peoples of the Earth.

THE EGYPTIAN ALTERNATIVE: THE OLD AND MIDDLE KINGDOMS

Egypt had considerably more potential for unification than its great northern neighbor, Mesopotamia. Early in its history unity was achieved and maintained—though not without occasional relapses into anarchy—under the rule of a god-king, the pharaoh.

---

[7]Frankfort et al., *Before Philosophy*, p. 225.
[8]Ibid., p. 226.

Ecology and Unity

The Nile was an important factor in this early achievement of national unity, for it provided a first-class means of transportation up- and downstream. A steady northern wind propelled ships sailing against the current, and traffic moving in the opposite direction had the assistance of the flow of the river itself. Outside the delta the habitable land of Egypt does not extend more than 15 miles on either side of the Nile, and often much less, so military control of the river could be easily translated into control of Egypt itself.

Beyond the advantages of good communication, Egypt was lucky to have defensible frontiers. To the east and west, fearsome deserts offered protection and reduced potential invasion routes to two easily defended passageways, the Gaza Strip to the northeast and the route from Libya through El Alamein in the west. Although Egypt's southern border with Nubia (the Sudan) was sometimes troublesome, there was no threat from equatorial Africa thanks to a vast, impenetrable marsh known as the Sudd, in the southern part of the Sudan.

Egypt was also blessed in other respects. The natural environment of the Nile valley made the practice of agriculture much less demanding than it was in Mesopotamia. Annually, the Nile flooded the river valley from desert wall to desert wall to a depth of 3 to 4 feet, leaving behind a fertile layer of mud as it receded. The flooding began in early June, and by October the river had returned to its normal channel, just in time for the winter planting of cereal crops—the reverse of the situation in Mesopotamia. Because the water table remained high, no irrigation was necessary. Salinization was not a threat, as the flood waters were sufficient to leach out any salts left by the rapid evaporation of surface water.

Another piece of good fortune for Egypt was the existence of naturally occurring flood basins. Periodically over the centuries, the Nile had changed its course, leaving behind banks of mud roughly paralleling the river. These natural levees could be turned into reservoirs by damming their ends and trapping the water of the flood between them after it had reached its maximum extent. These flood basins, as they are called, could then be tapped for water for second crops or drained later in the year and planted.

This environment of naturally occurring flood basins was found in both Upper and Lower Egypt. Little technical expertise was required to exploit it. Only at critical moments was there any need for concerted community efforts. By contrast, in Mesopotamia, maintenance of the much more sophisticated radial irrigation system called for much higher standards of technical and managerial competence and greater community involvement. When the population of Egypt expanded, however, and more land was needed to support it, the manipulation of the flood basins could be critical to survival. Simply by guaranteeing stable public order, a regional elite could build considerable political power.

A combination of technical expertise in managing large-scale irrigation of this kind along with control of trade goods seems to have led to the emergence of the state in Egypt. At first the communities of Upper Egypt competed among themselves

---

EVENTS OF EARLY EGYPTIAN HISTORY

Egypt unified under the pharaohs	ca. 3100 B.C.
The Old Kingdom	ca. 2700–2200 B.C.
Great pyramids built	ca. 2600–2200 B.C.
Collapse of central government (Intermediate Period)	ca. 2180–2040 B.C.
Revival of Egypt: the Middle Kingdom	ca. 2040–1780 B.C.

---

for dominance, a great struggle perhaps reflected in the myth of the battle between the brothers Osiris and Seth. The region around Abydos finally emerged supreme and brought all of Upper Egypt under its control. Next came the conquest of the north by a combination of diplomacy, war, and dynastic marriages. By around 3100 B.C. all of Egypt had been securely and, as it turned out, permanently unified. The final architect of Egyptian unity was the pharaoh Narmer, or Menes, as he is known traditionally.

The new kings built their capital at the strategic site of Memphis, just south of the delta, and over the next several centuries consolidated their rule. Probably no other dynasty in history has been so successful in creating an effective yet apparently timeless form of government. For thousands of years Egyptian pharaohs were able to convey to their subjects a sense of permanence and eternity while constantly adjusting the system to meet new needs. Yet the unifiers of Egypt and the kings of the first dynasties are shadowy figures known only by their names and fine, rectangular mastabas (tombs). It was only during the period known as the Old Kingdom (ca. 2680–2180 B.C.) that the full glory of Egyptian unity and the techniques by which it had been achieved were revealed.

The Pharaoh's Power: The Mythological Viewpoint

The challenge to the early pharaohs was how they were to maintain their rule over the vast land of Egypt. Pharaonic Egypt was over 750 miles long, and in its early years it contained a wide diversity of peoples and cultures. Its natural inclination was toward fragmentation, not unity. A continuing subtheme of Egyptian history was the struggle between the central power of the kings and that of the local authorities in the provinces. Favorable factors such as defensibility and good communication have already been mentioned, but Egyptian unity and stability were not an accident of environment. They were instead created by the Egyptian people themselves, in particular of their gifted ruling class. In many ways the Egyptian social and political system is even more alien to us in the West than the Mesopotamian. It is the opposite of what we have come to regard as a desirable form of government. What worked for Egypt in ancient times was a benign, theocratic totalitarianism: a dictatorship of a god-king.

The competent, serene faces of the Egyptian ruling classes. Spanning a period of over 2,000 years of continuous history are Methethy (left), the manager of a large estate (ca. 2340 B.C.); Sennuwy, wife of an Egyptian governor of the Sudan (ca. 1950 B.C.) (top right); and a high official of the Ptolemaic administration (ca. 80 B.C.) (right).

In Egyptian belief, the sun rose daily and traveled across the sky to the western horizon, where it entered the underworld. From there, after fighting off the forces of chaos and disorder, it emerged the following morning with renewed strength and repeated its daily passage through the sky. Similarly, the Nile was thought to pass through a cycle of birth and death. For months it lay as a muddy stream between fields burned brown by the hot sun. Then, miraculously, it gathered force and swelled until it overflowed its banks and spread a great mantle of water over the dry countryside. Gradually shrinking, it left a rich deposit of silt from which the new crops sprang.

The Egyptians believed that this orderly world had been brought into existence by the gods and fixed by them for all time in the first moment of its creation. There was no evolution, no development, just repetition. The interworking of its parts and the balance of its elements were described by the term *ma'at,* which can be translated as "order," "justice," or "truth." The course of the stars, the sequence of day and night, and the passage of all things from life to death were part of this universal, unchanging *ma'at.* The cosmos did not advance or retreat or develop; it repeated itself in an "eternal now." What lay outside this was exceptional, an aberration that had to be endured until the gods restored order.

Although the universe was created in this fashion, it was not an infallible mechanism in which the activity of the gods or humans was irrelevant. As in Mesopotamia, the gods were always victorious in the struggle to maintain order, but the struggle always had to be renewed. When it came to maintaining the *ma'at* of Egypt, the gods delegated one of their number, Horus, the son of Osiris, to be the guarantor of its balance and harmony. His function was to ensure the continuing existence and activity of the gods on earth by means of religious acts and to maintain the natural order such as the flow of the Nile and the fertility of the soil. His authority was neither political, social, nor economic, but cosmic. He did not rule by the consent of the governed but by a decision of the gods.

The archetypal myth of Egypt was the succession of Osiris by his son Horus. According to this myth, the reigning king, Osiris, was killed by his brother Seth and his body dismembered. Ultimately it was put together again by Osiris's faithful wife, Isis, and he became the Lord of the Dead, while his son Horus succeeded him as Lord of the Living. Pharaoh did not succeed pharaoh in linear, human succession as one king might succeed another. Instead, every living pharaoh was Horus and every dead one was Osiris. Alternatively—because for Egyptians one religious viewpoint did not replace but complemented another—the king at death either went up to heaven to be united with Re (the Sun God), his father, or he was the Nile dying and coming to life. In order to ensure his successful passage to the next world, whether as Re or Osiris, it was necessary to guarantee the preservation of his physical remains and supply him with all the essentials for the transition.

Although the authority of the pharaoh was unchallengeable, it was not, theoretically at least, dictatorial. The pharaoh was charged by the gods with the care of Egypt, not as his private possession for his own personal enjoyment but in accordance with the original act of creation. In the words of one of the pharaohs, Merikare, he was the "shepherd of his people . . . who spends the day caring for them." One of the earliest of the kings' insignia was the shepherd's crook. The other was the threshing flail, a symbol of the king's mastery of cereal agriculture.

Ideally, the pharaoh was accessible to everyone, for Egyptian justice aimed not for a kind of Mesopotamian system of law administered according to known, universal codes of behavior but for a more flexible, personal system. The king alone was the source of all law and could adjust it according to the particular circumstances of the case before him. Naturally, the pharaoh did not administer justice personally to the millions of Egyptians, but his delegates did so in his name, and as far as we can tell the ideology was taken seriously.

Pharaonic Power: The Historian's View

The optimistic, mythological view of the world fabricated by the pharaohs of the first two dynasties and perfected in the Old Kingdom had a very realistic foundation. From the beginning of Egyptian history the pharaohs avoided the most anarchic aspect of Mesopotamia: the multiplication of independent city-states. Cities of this type, protected by powerful walls, full of independent-minded citizens, ruling themselves and trading with each other and with the outside world were not allowed to develop once pharaonic power was established over a united Egypt. Egyptian cities were unwalled, administrative centers, serving the will of the pharaoh. Interestingly, one of the very earliest depictions of a pharaoh shows one of them tearing down the walls of a city. Unlike Sargon or Hammurapi, the Egyptian pharaoh did not have to deal with dozens of city-states, each with its own established traditions, bureaucracy, and government system that could frustrate the decision making of the central authority. The pharaoh stood at the head of a powerful national bureaucracy that owed its allegiance in theory, and generally in practice, to him alone, and extended its influence to every corner of Egypt.

The economic and commercial roles of the pharaohs also contributed to their tight control of the land. As the population of Egypt grew, so did its dependence on the system of irrigation. From a technical viewpoint, this did not involve any major problems. As long as political disorder could be avoided, the system usually worked effectively. The pharaohs made this connection clear in their propaganda and emphasized their roles in opening new canals and expanding land under cultivation. Another tool in the hands of the pharaohs was their control of long-distance trade. Given Egypt's peculiar geography, that was something well within their grasp.

In the ancient world, the possession of prestige goods—precious metals, brightly colored clothes, feathers, jewelry, and weapons—was a crucial element of status. The owners of these goods were seen as people of importance, who had the power to do good or evil to their underlings. The pharaohs carefully guarded their monopoly of prestige goods and equally carefully doled them out as signs of royal favor. Conveniently, Egyptian burial customs, which dictated that the dead be buried with rich grave goods, meant that there was always a need for new treasures to take their place. Thus the position of the pharaoh as the key distributor of prestige goods remained intact from generation to generation. As pyramid builders they were also, as we shall shortly see, the largest employers in the land.

The pharaohs' manipulation of their own mortuary or burial system showed their genius in creating a national government to its fullest extent. Long before the people of the south became the rulers of Egypt, they had buried their dead kings in fine tombs filled with rich funeral offerings. During the Old Kingdom this practice was enlarged, and the tombs of the pharaohs grew more and more magnificent. In form they took the shape of large, rectangular brick buildings erected over central burial chambers. In the reign of King Djoser (ca. 2670 B.C.), however, Imhotep, the pharaoh's master builder, came up with a new and extraordinary burial monument: the step pyramid complex. This consisted of six of the old-style tombs squared and superimposed on each other to a height of over 200 feet, surrounded by a huge, walled courtyard containing a number of temples. All of the buildings, including the pyramid, were of stone. Succeeding pharaohs continued to build step pyramids, and eventually the true pyramid with smooth sides evolved.

The pyramids were not just burial places where the king's body was deposited and then forgotten. Worship of the king continued actively at all of the pyramid complexes. Priests attended the temples, and whole villages of workmen existed to maintain the pyramid and its accompanying buildings in good repair. Estates throughout Egypt were assigned to each pyramid complex to supply its financial and material needs.

In the context of the Egyptian view of the universe, the pyramids—of which some 80 are known—served as visible symbols of the pharaoh's divine rule of Egypt, unifying the land in a common, official religion that transcended all local religions. Just as in the Mesopotamian myth all Mesopotamians were engaged in some way in the cosmic drama of the gods, so too Egyptians believed they were involved with the pharaoh and the gods in the maintenance of their land. The burial of the king, as well as his passage from this world to the next, was not simply a private affair of importance only to the royal family and its retinue but an event of national significance. The ritual cycle by which the living pharaoh, the god Horus, became Osiris, Lord of the Underworld, guaranteed the survival of Egypt itself. By expressing this act in architectural form in the building of the pyramids, the kings of the Old Kingdom stumbled on—or perhaps cunningly devised—a method of unifying all Egyptians in a single religion of ancestor worship in which the pyramids served as giant reliquaries. Even if the religious symbolism were to lose its force, the effect of the great looming mass of the pyramids along the skyline for 100 miles west of Memphis could not be missed. Their existence guaranteed the legitimacy of the rule of the kings and offered convincing proof of their power. The message could be read by peasant and nobleman alike: the pharaohs had supreme power and no one else in the land possessed anything like it. They were indeed gods.

Although pillaged and stripped of its original covering of limestone, the Great Pyramid still suggests something of the power and resources of its creator, the pharaoh Cheops (ca. 2600 B.C.).

Temples, Rituals, and the Afterlife

Although the cult of the pharaoh occupied the most prominent place in the national religion, Egyptians also worshiped thousands of gods, goddesses, spirits, and sacred objects. Tolerant and conservative, they were reluctant to part with old rituals and deities. Although the country's size and cultural complexity contributed to the perpetuation of local gods, there was a constant interchange among them as the individual cults expanded, contracted, and blended with each other—or disappeared.

Animal gods abounded. Seth, the rival and murderer of Osiris, was depicted with a doglike body, long neck, upright tail, and squared ears. Horus appeared as a falcon and also as a falcon-headed man. The vulture goddess Nekhbet was the tutelary goddess of Upper Egypt, while her opposite in Lower Egypt was the cobra goddess Wadjet. Hathor had a human head but a cow's ears, horns, and body. Other gods, such as Min, Ptah, Atum, and Amen, by contrast, never appeared as animals and were always depicted in human form. There was a great mingling of divine personalities and traits as the political fortunes or popularity of individual gods rose or fell. When Narmer, the unifier of Egypt, moved from Hierakonpolis to Memphis, the god of the latter city, Ptah, came into prominence, and at a later date Re of Heliopolis, not far from Memphis, rose to a position of dominance. The pharaoh, originally identified only with Horus, soon came to be identified also as the son of Re.

The cult of the gods was of such central importance to Egyptian life that it is understandable why the temples rose to such prominence. Built of stone, these monuments were created to last forever, and like the tombs of the pharaohs, they became part of the eternal landscape of Egypt.

Egyptian temples were laid out axially, with one room or courtyard leading to another, each one progressively removed from the outside world. Darkness increased room by room until finally the chapel of the cult image was reached. Here only specially designated priests could perform the daily round of liturgical acts that guaranteed the presence of the god in the cult image. These rituals, performed in accordance with the movement of the sun across the heavens, maintained the temple in harmony with the rhythm of the cosmos and were essential to the continued presence of the gods. The rites began each morning with the opening of the sanctuary doors as the sun was rising. The cult statue was anointed, clothed, and fed, and at that moment it was believed that the god took possession of it. Twice more, at midday and in the evening, the god was fed and entertained. As the sun set, he departed to join the sun in his nightly passage through the underworld.

The priests who performed these tasks were laymen who spent part of the year in the service of the temple and the remainder in their normal secular occupations. They were not the guardians of a divine revelation or a caste set aside to perform rituals or preach salvation to the unconverted. They had no ethical role to play, and no one would have thought to consult them on matters of morality. Their principal function was assisting the pharaoh in his most important function: the maintenance of the divine order of creation (*ma'at*). The priests' job was simply to see that the temple operated properly. It was a technical role requiring ritual cleanliness, not inner purity.

In Egyptian belief, existence after death without some connection with the body was unthinkable. When a man died, his vital self, his *ka,* continued to exist in the tomb and was sustained by its contents. "Going to one's *ka*" was used as an expression for dying. Contracts were made and corporations formed to see that the dead were supplied with all the essentials they needed in the hereafter. Another aspect of the dead person also survived death. This was his *ba,* his individualized self or interior consciousness. Personified as a bird, the *ba* could escape the confines of the tomb but required the corpse in order to retain its identity. A final aspect of the deceased was the *akh,* or Transfigured Spirit, whose abode was heaven. The *akh* was the deceased in transcendent form, without earthly ties, but unlike the *ba* the *akh* did not retain a connection to the body. It is the most spiritualized of the various concepts the Egyptians had of death.

It is odd that although we know a great deal about the concern of the Egyptians for the afterlife and the meticulous care they gave to preparing for it, we are not completely clear about what they thought that life was like. For some it was simply a repetition in its most earthly form of their existence in this world, whereas for others it was a form of reintegration in the cosmic processes. In this latter belief, the souls of the dead became transfigured beings and joined the sun in its daily passage through the sky, or they became stars in the heavens: "Spirit to the sky, corpse into the earth!"[9] For others, death was an escape from the troubles of life:

Death is before me today
Like a sick man's recovery,
Like going outdoors after confinement.

Death is before me today
Like a well-trodden way,
Like a man's coming home from warfare.

Death is before me today
Like the clearing of the sky,
As when a man discovers what he ignored.

Death is before me today
Like a man's longing to see his home
When he has spent many years in captivity.[10]

Art, Literature, and Society

Egyptian art was primarily sacred rather than secular. Tomb paintings and inscriptions served primarily religious and magical purposes, and played an essential part in supplying the dead with all the essentials of life in the hereafter. They were neither decorative nor artistic in our sense of these words. Second, the state and its needs, especially in the early period, overwhelmed the personal and private side of Egyptian life.

All the great monuments—the pyramids of the Old Kingdom and the temples of the empire period—reflected the power and majesty of the pharaoh and the gods, not of the individual. Egyptian art was intended to emphasize the unchangeable and the eternal, not the fleeting moment of the present. In their reliefs the pharaohs appear disproportionately large, dominating the figures of their enemies and their own officials. Great emphasis is placed on the ideal of the pharaonic order by the careful disposition of the king and his followers in clear, well-organized registers, whereas his enemies appear in front of him as stunned, chaotic masses. In unruffled calm the pharaoh triumphantly drives the rabble from the battlefield or stands before prostrate bodies and discarded weapons. The message is simple: Egypt is a land cared for by a divine being whose word preserves the order of the land. Evil, by contrast, is a challenge from the demonic outside world that will, in due course, be checked by the might of the king.

Literature, especially in the early period, was mainly a matter of public rather than private expression. It had a practical purpose, serving primarily the needs of the state, religion, and the bureaucracy. Thus the tombs of the pharaohs were inscribed

[9]H. Frankfort, *Ancient Egyptian Religion* (New York: Harper & Row, 1961), p. 100.

[10]Miriam Lichtheim, trans., *Ancient Egyptian Literature: A Book of Readings* (Berkeley: University of California Press, 1976), p. 168. Reprinted by permission of the University of California Press.

with spells and incantations, the so-called pyramid texts, to ensure the triumphant immortality of the god-kings. These magical charms, hymns, and prayers aimed to advance the king past obstacles he might encounter and protect him from danger. Later these texts were appropriated by the nobles and commoners who could afford to have them inscribed on their coffins in a kind of democratization of the hereafter.

The Egyptian scribal or bureaucratic system led to the development of a "how to get along in the organization" kind of literature known as wisdom literature. Typically it made suggestions on how to handle one's superiors and inferiors and how to prevent one's private life from getting in the way of one's career. One of the most famous wisdom writers, Ptah-hotep, urges the use of initiative and constant effort to get ahead. Eloquence is a useful accomplishment. "It is," he says, "a real craftsman who can speak in counsel, for speaking is more difficult than any other labor." A scribe should speak the truth, but not exceed it; he should not answer more than he is asked. A successful bureaucrat is always a good listener:

> If you are the one to whom a petition is made, be calm as you listen. . . . Do not rebuff the petitioner before he has swept out his body or before he has said that for which he came. The petitioner likes attention to his words better than the fulfilling [of them]. . . . It is not necessary that everything about which he has petitioned should come to pass, but a good hearing is soothing to the heart.[11]

The scribe should look after his friends and dependents because "one never knows what may happen tomorrow." Greed is dangerous, an incurable disease that makes friends bitter, alienates one's superiors, creates bad relations with parents, and leads to divorce. A man should look after his wife: "Feed her belly, clothe her back." Some advice went beyond the pragmatic and emphasized moral values:

> Do not jeer at a blind man nor tease a dwarf,
>   Neither interfere with the condition of a cripple;
> Do not taunt a man who is in the hand of God [an epileptic]
>   Nor scowl at him if he errs.
> Man is clay and straw,
>   and God is his potter;
> He overthrows and he builds daily.[12]

With the exception of love poetry, the hymns and poetry of Egypt concentrated on the celebration and proclamation of the greatness of the pharaohs and the gods. In endlessly repeated refrains, their mighty acts were reviewed without any attempt at developing a narrative account:

> How great is the lord of his city:
>   he is a canal that restrains the river's flood water!

[11]John A. Wilson, *The Culture of Ancient Egypt* (Chicago: University of Chicago Press, 1965), p. 93.

[12]W. K. Simpson, ed. *The Literature of Ancient Egypt* (New Haven, CT: Yale University Press, 1973), p. 262 © 1973 by Yale University Press.

> How great is the lord of his city:
>   he is a cool room that lets a man sleep until dawn!
> How great is the lord of his city:
>   he is a walled rampart of copper of Sinai!
> How great is the lord of his city:
>   he is an overflowing shade, cool in summertime!
> How great is the lord of his city:
>   he is a warm corner, dry in wintertime![13]

The reason for this approach was not lack of inspiration but rather the intention of the ancient Egyptian poet, whose object was to evoke rather than analyze or narrate. His aim was to instill in his audience a sense of the fidelity, magnificence, or power of the god or pharaoh, and the endless repetition of the writing had the effect of arousing awe or confidence or mystery, whichever was desired. Unlike the modern poet, who composes almost always for a reading public, his ancient counterpart wrote for public events such as rituals honoring the pharaoh, court liturgies and dramas, burials, processions, and victory celebrations. Dull facts were elevated into religious acts and became part of the ongoing cosmic liturgy, the very opposite of modern poetry, which dwells on subjective moods and feelings or individuals' reactions to the outside world.

Egypt to the End of the Middle Kingdom

For almost 1,000 years the pharaohs were able to keep tight control of Egypt. The administration was highly centralized, and provincial officials and elites had little independence. By the reign of Pepy II (2275–2185 B.C.), however, there were signs that the influence of the pharaoh was declining and that some of his delegates and representatives were beginning to act like kings themselves.

Part of this loss of power by the central administration was caused by the need to maintain the numerous and economically unproductive pyramid complexes with their huge staffs and large endowments. Over the years, rewards to faithful and successful officials constituted another drain on the pharaohs' resources, and inner power struggles, about which we know little, took their toll also. Another factor that seems to have contributed to the decline was a succession of unusually low flood years that led to crop failure, famine, and public disorder. If anything was calculated to strip away the myth of pharaonic absolutism, it was the failure to guarantee public order and an adequate food supply. By the end of the sixth dynasty (ca. 2180 B.C.), the centralized authority of Egypt had virtually evaporated, and all the land was in turmoil. Pyramids and tombs were looted, and the endowments for their support were swept away. Memphis ceased to function as the administrative center of the country, and the individual regions of Egypt were left to fend for themselves. At this point Egypt entered what is known as the first Intermediate Period (ca. 2180–2040 B.C.).

[13]Lichtheim, *Ancient Egyptian Literature,* pp. 199–200.

Some districts fared better than others during this time of chaos. In the north, the provincial rulers of Herakleopolis succeeded in maintaining order in their district and eventually even regained control of the rich delta area. Under the kings of Herakleopolis, Egyptian literature flourished, and for a brief moment a form of individualism emerged. Old standards, values, and even religious beliefs were challenged.

In the *Story of the Eloquent Peasant,* which dates from this time, a farmer demands justice for himself from the king. The tale begins with the peasant going off to the market to sell his produce, but on the way he is seized and beaten by a royal official for no apparent reason. The peasant complains to the official's superior, who is so impressed with the peasant's eloquent plea for justice that he informs the king and has the peasant's speech written down. In the end the peasant wins his case and is awarded compensation.

One of the kings of the First Intermediate period, Khety II (ca. 2100 B.C.), is credited with the composition of a book of instructions for his son, Merikare. Some of the book offers practical advice on subjects such as the protection of the frontiers and the suppression of revolts, but most of it talks about proper conduct and just dealing with one's fellow men. Merikare is advised by his father that he should protect the oppressed and the weak and that the gods prefer "the character of one just of heart than the sacrificial ox of one who does mischief."

During this period access to immortality was democratized as well. In the Old Kingdom immortality had been restricted to the pharaoh, his closest family members, and officials, but it was now assumed that it was available to anyone who could afford the appropriate burial ritual and magic spells. There was even the suggestion that immortality might depend on proper behavior in life and not just on properly performed rituals. The deceased was sometimes depicted in judgment before the sun god Re in a judicial process known as the counting of character, in which Re measures the individual's virtues against his faults.

While the kings of Herakleopolis were supporting this unusual liberalization of thought, another powerful dynasty was establishing itself in the obscure town of Thebes in the south. The Thebans eventually felt strong enough to challenge the Herakleopolitan kings and, after some skirmishing, defeated them and reunited all of Egypt. With the emergence of this new dynasty (the eleventh dynasty), Egypt entered a new period of its history, the Middle Kingdom (ca. 2040–1780 B.C.).

Although natives of Thebes, the new monarchs moved their capital north to a more strategically located place, It-tawy, just south of Memphis. Large sections of the Fayum area were brought under cultivation, and power was once more concentrated in the hands of the central administration. Nubia in the south, an important source of gold, was reconquered, and the copper and turquoise mines of Sinai were opened once more. Egyptian influence was felt in Palestine and Lebanon.

For administrative convenience Egypt was divided into three large geographical regions and the territories of the individual provinces, the nomes of Egypt, were carefully surveyed and demarcated. The god Amen, "The Hidden," came into prominence, and, grafted onto the sun god Re, he became "Amen-Re, King of the Gods."

The understanding of kingship itself changed. The remote, inaccessible god-king of the Old Kingdom evolved to become the Good Shepherd or Herdsman of his people.

The Middle Kingdom did not have the fabulous good fortune of the Old Kingdom, however. The eleventh dynasty was succeeded in due course by the powerful kings of the twelfth, but after two centuries, for unknown reasons, the succession failed. The next dynasty was a weak one. It found itself unable to stop a serious economic decline, and the kingship changed hands rapidly. As the power of the pharaohs again faded, the officials of the palace and bureaucracy came to the fore. Among them were a surprising number of immigrants from western Asia bearing the names of a Semitic-speaking people, the Amorites. For the first time in history, the outside world was about to intrude on Egypt's blissful isolation.

Chapter 2

An Age of Empires: The Near East, 2000–1000 B.C.

A TIME OF TURMOIL: NEW PEOPLES EAST AND WEST

Around 2000 B.C. the Near East went through a period of rapid transformation. Peoples came and went with bewildering speed. Some have familiar names; others are complete strangers to us. The Sumerians were eclipsed by newcomers, the Amorites, from the Syrian desert fringes. Babylon appeared for the first time, as did Assur, the principal city of the Assyrians. The Israelites now entered history along with their mentors and enemies, the Canaanites. In the west, two Indo-European–speaking peoples, the Hittites and the Mycenaean Greeks, emerged. Mesopotamia alternated between fragmentation and brief periods of unity. Egypt, as usual, had the reverse experience: occasional lapses from unity followed by the restoration of the traditional pharaonic order for long periods. The lands between these old centers of power were a mosaic of kingdoms, tribal groups, and independent city-states, a battleground of peoples, cultures, and empires.

MESOPOTAMIA IN THE AGE OF HAMMURAPI

Of the newcomers, the Amorites had the most immediate visible impact. Their presence had been felt as early as 2300 B.C., when the Sumerians described them in unflattering terms as people who "knew nothing of farming or civilized life." It would be a mistake, however, to take these disdainful words at face value. The world of western Asia was forever being shaped and reshaped by the interaction of the settled in-

---

KEY EVENTS IN THE AGE OF HAMMURAPI

Amorite expansion in western Asia	ca. 2100–1900 B.C.
Age of the Hebrew patriarchs: Abraham, Isaac, Jacob	ca. 1800–1600 B.C.
Reign of Hammurapi of Babylon	ca. 1792–1750 B.C.
Emergence of Canaanite, Hittite, and Hurrian peoples	ca. 1800 B.C.
Hittite sack of Babylon	ca. 1600 B.C.
Kassite rule of Mesopotamia	ca. 1600–1200 B.C.

---

habitants of the region and their seminomadic pastoralist neighbors. Herders lived on the fringes of cities and agricultural villages in a symbiotic relationship. Families or individuals detached themselves and went to work in the towns or settled down as farmers. Sometimes the movement was in the opposite direction, from city to desert fringe. Culturally and ethnically, there was little difference between the two communities. They usually spoke the same or closely related languages and worshiped the same gods.

Toward the end of the third millennium, when the Semitic-speaking Amorites began to infiltrate into Mesopotamia, no great dislocation of culture occurred. The newcomers rapidly assimilated the Sumerian-Akkadian culture and adopted Akkadian as their official language. Sumerian gods were worshiped under Semitic names, and the old Sumerian epics and myths were translated and passed on with only minor alterations. In other respects, however, the arrival of the Amorites had a lasting influence. The division of Mesopotamia into states ruled by Amorite kings broke down the old system of city-states, and under powerful Amorite dynasties great kingdoms came to dominate Mesopotamia. Babylon rose to prominence under the leadership of Hammurapi (ca. 1792–1750 B.C.), whose ancestors had settled in the middle Euphrates region some centuries before, while a little farther to the north, on the Tigris, the Amorite dynasty of Shamsi-Adadi installed itself at Assur.

A good general, a wily diplomat, and a superb administrator, Hammurapi was at first limited in influence to the area around Babylon, but as time went on he succeeded in consolidating all of southern Mesopotamia under his rule. He avoided antagonizing the rulers of Assyria while gaining control of the south. Later, when Shamsi-Adadi died, he turned his attention northward and incorporated Assyria in his empire.

Symbolic of Hammurapi's unification of Mesopotamia was his great law code, which was promulgated throughout Babylonia as a universal model that the various communities were to imitate in their practice of law. It was not a constitutional law code requiring obedience to specific statutes or regulations. Nor was it the first code of laws by any means, because it had been customary for Sumerian kings to correct abuses by issuing edicts and making collections of laws for their own cities. Hammurapi's, however, was the first code intended to provide an example for an entire region composed of many different peoples, each with its own code of laws.

In some respects Hammurapi's code was harsher than the preceding Sumerian codes, substituting death or mutilation for crimes that had previously been punished by compensation in kind or money. Nevertheless, in many ways it was remarkably progressive. In the area of family law it offered protection to women and children from arbitrary treatment, poverty, and neglect. Although a man might divorce his wife for misbehavior, if he divorced her for not producing sons, he had to give her money "to the amount of her marriage price" (§138) and had to make good to her "the dowry which she brought from her father's house" (§138). The code even protected a woman from her own children: "If a man gives to his wife a field, garden, house, or goods and delivers to her a sealed deed, after [the death of] her husband her children cannot enter a claim against her" (§150). The code concludes with the benevolent wish that the readers would regard Hammurapi as a "ruler who is like a real father to his people . . . he has established prosperity for the people for all time and given good government to the land."[1]

In the end, even the genius of Hammurapi could not overcome the sheer diversity of the peoples in Mesopotamia, coupled with the longstanding traditions of independence of its cities. After his death, his empire evaporated, although his dynasty maintained itself in Babylon for another 150 years until the city was sacked by an invading Hittite army.

In the centuries following the collapse of Babylon, Sumer and Akkad came under the control of the Kassites, a people from the Zagros Mountain region. Perhaps challenged by this intrusion from the outside, the scribes and priests of the temples began to reexamine the great literary and religious traditions of the past. Canonical (i.e., approved) versions of ancient stories and legends were established as well as the proper forms for the singing of incantations and omens. Epics, hymns, prayers, and rituals of all kinds were standardized, among them the *Epic of Gilgamesh*.

Despite this conservative tendency, there was considerable change in other aspects of religious belief. A more personalized religion emerged, and the gods were called on to pay more attention to the plight of the individual. Along with the rise of this kind of individualized religion came a corresponding weakening of the old social order and of people's faith in the dependability of the gods. There was a feeling that it was no longer sufficient to view disasters as mere accidents over which even heaven had no control. People began to protest the injustices of the gods, who seemed to permit the evil to prosper and the good to suffer. These attitudes were to crop up again and again in Mesopotamian history and indeed throughout world history.

Abraham, the Patriarchs, and the Origins of Israel

Besides decisively influencing Mesopotamia, the Amorites had a major impact on the lands to the north and west. They settled in large numbers in Syria and merged with the already well-established urban culture they found there. To the south of Syria, in the land later called Canaan (and later still Palestine), the arrival of the Amorites was marked by widespread destruction. This was followed by a quick re-

---

[1]Robert F. Harper, trans., *The Code of Hammurabi* (Chicago: University of Chicago Press, 1904).

THE PROBLEM OF SUFFERING AND EVIL: A BABYLONIAN VIEW

In the literary work known as the *Ludlul bel Nemeqi* ("I will praise the Lord of Wisdom"), the writer, a kind of Babylonian Job, protests that he has been abandoned by his personal gods and inflicted with all kinds of undeserved suffering:

> My god has forsaken me and disappeared,
> My goddess has failed me and keeps a distance,
> The benevolent angel who [walked] beside me has departed.
> My protecting spirit has taken to flight, and is seeking someone else
> My strength is gone; my appearance has become gloomy. (1:43–47)

> My flesh is flaccid, and my blood has ebbed away.
> My bones have come apart, and are covered [only] with my skin.
> My tissues are inflamed. (2:92–96)

These afflictions have come upon him despite close attention to religious observances:

> For myself, I gave attention to supplication and prayer:
> To me prayer was discretion, sacrifice my rule.
> The day for reverencing the god was a joy to my heart;
> The day of the goddess's procession was profit and gain to me.
> The king's prayer—that was my joy,
> And the accompanying music became a delight for me. (2:23–28)

Why the gods acted in this mysterious fashion is beyond the sufferer's understanding. His solution to the problem is akin to one of those offered by Job: believing that man is too insignificant and too limited to know the will of the gods:

> I wish I knew that these things [his religious observances] were pleasing to one's
>   god!
> What is proper [pleasing] to oneself is an offense to one's god,
> What in one's own heart seems despicable is proper to one's god.
> Who knows the will of the gods in heaven?
> Who understands the plans of the underworld gods?
> Where have mortals learnt the way of a god? (2:34–38)

Source: W. G. Lambert, trans., *Babylonian Wisdom Literature* (© Oxford University Press, 1960), by permission of Oxford University Press.

covery and the restoration of urban life. From Canaan groups of Amorites and other Semitic-speaking peoples penetrated into Egypt, and, as the Hyksos, set themselves up as an independent power in the delta. It is against the background of these unsettled conditions that the wanderings of Abraham and his descendants, the patriarchs of Israel, are best set.

The stories about Abraham and his wife, Sarah, are described in colorful detail in the first book of the Bible, the Book of Genesis. The tales begin with the emigration of Abraham's father, Terah, and his large extended family from Ur in southern

Mesopotamia to Haran in Syria. There Abraham is told by his god: "Leave your relatives, and your father's home, for the land I will show you; and I will make of you a great nation. . . . Through you shall all the families of the earth invoke blessings on one another" (Gen. 12:1–3). Abraham responds to the call and, leaving Syria, makes his way to Canaan. Later in life, and contrary to all expectations, because his wife Sarah is old and childless, he becomes the father of a son, Isaac. In Canaan, Abraham enters into a covenant, or contract, with his god, and once more the promises made earlier are repeated, together with the promise that the land of Canaan will belong to his descendants. The rest of the Book of Genesis tells of the experiences of Abraham's descendants: his son, Isaac, his grandson Jacob, or Israel, and Jacob's twelve sons, the ancestors of the twelve tribes of Israel. During a famine in Canaan, Jacob and his sons emigrate to Egypt, where one of them, Joseph, was already in a prominent position in the pharaonic administration.

There are complicated problems involved in trying to identify the precise time and place of the activities of the Hebrew patriarchs, and even in trying to decide whether they are to be taken as individuals or personifications standing for whole tribes. The Genesis stories are based on ancient oral traditions that had a long and complex history of transmission before they were first written down, perhaps sometime in the tenth century B.C. at the time of David or Solomon, centuries after they were supposed to have taken place. Most scholars believe that there is a basic core of truth to the stories, but there is no agreement as to exactly when the wanderings of the patriarchs took place. Special attention must be given to the role that theological interpretation has played in the handing down of these stories and to the shape they finally took in the last editing of the Book of Genesis, sometime during or after the Babylonian captivity (587–538 B.C.).

Whatever position is taken regarding the historicity of the stories about Abraham, there can be no doubt that for the biblical authors of both the Hebrew scriptures and the New Testament, Abraham was a key figure in the history of salvation, the first beneficiary of the mighty "saving acts" of God. The god who spoke to him in Haran and who made a covenant with him in Canaan was identified as the same god, Yahweh, who later spoke to Moses and the prophets, and who was eventually recognized as the God of all peoples, the creator of the world, the Lord of History. Theologically, Abraham is recognized as the preeminent model of the man of faith, one who responds obediently to God's gracious invitation of salvation. In a broader sense, Abraham is often seen as the type of man who is willing to trust his own inner vision and, against all odds, is prepared to follow it wherever it leads. In one way or another, either in its religious or its secular interpretation, the model of Abraham is firmly lodged in the culture of the West.

The Wanderings of the Indo-Europeans

Besides the Amorites, other peoples were on the move in the period around 2000 B.C. Among these were the Hurrians, a non–Semitic-speaking people who moved from the region of present-day Armenia southward. They eventually occupied a great half-circle of territory stretching from northern Mesopotamia across Syria into Anatolia. In this strategic location they became the transmitters of the cultural traditions of Mesopotamia to peoples farther to the west, including the Hittites, an Indo-European–speaking people emerging in Anatolia.

Today Indo-European languages are more widespread and spoken by more people than any other languages in the world. These languages are spoken from India to the westernmost part of Europe and throughout the Americas. Indo-European–speaking peoples seem to have originated in the steppes of Eurasia, near the northern coasts of the Aral, Caspian, and Black seas. The recent domestication of the horse in the Eurasian steppe and the development of chariot warfare gave them a technological edge in battle over their more civilized opponents.

The exact date of the dispersal of the Indo-Europeans is furiously disputed. At some point, perhaps after 2000 B.C., emigrants from the Eurasian steppe left their homelands and headed west and south. Some of the western emigrants settled in Greece, where, after mingling with the original inhabitants, they emerged about 1600 B.C. as the proto-Greek people known as the Mycenaeans. Others continued farther west and eventually settled in every part of Europe. Some of the southern emigrants passed through Iran and headed east through Afghanistan, making their way slowly toward India. Yet others settled among the peoples of the Zagros Mountains in southwestern Iran, and, as the dominant elite among the Kassites, took control of the ancient centers of civilization, Sumer and Akkad. They were a conservative people with a gift for ruling. They stayed out of the power politics of the region and gave southern Mesopotamia its longest period of peace in its history—over four centuries—from around 1600 to 1200 B.C.

The Hurrians of northern Mesopotamia accepted an Indo-European ruling aristocracy, and together the two peoples built up a powerful kingdom that dominated all of that region for several centuries. Known as the Kingdom of Mitanni, it was far more active in the affairs of western Asia than the more circumspect Kassite kingdom to the south. At its zenith, Mitanni dealt with Egypt as an equal, and the daughters of its rulers married into the Egyptian royal family. The majority of the gods of Mitanni were of Hurrian origin, such as the storm god, Teshub, his consort, Hepat, and the grain god, Kumarbi. Several bear familiar Indic names, including Varuna, the sky god, and Indra, the god of war.

THE HITTITE EMPIRE

The immigrants who had the greatest long-term impact on western Asia were the Indo-European speakers who settled as a kind of warrior caste in Anatolia. For centuries the region had traded its metals and timber with the resource-poor peoples of Syria and Mesopotamia. By about 1700 B.C. these Indo-European infiltrators had assimilated most of the high culture of Anatolia, and one of their leaders decided to set himself up as regional king. He seized the abandoned fortress of Hattusas and ruled from there, extending his power first to surrounding areas of Anatolia and then into Syria. From the name of his capital he is known as Hattusilis I ("the man of Hattusas"). His successor, Mursilis I, sent a raiding party down the Euphrates. Babylon was sacked, and the dynasty of Hammurapi brought to an end (1595 B.C.). Thereafter, due to overextension and infighting in the royal family, the Hittites barely managed to hold on to their Anatolian homeland.

Hittite resurgence in Anatolia and Syria began around 1450 B.C. During the early part of the fifteenth century B.C. Hittite expansion was blocked by the power of the Kingdom of Mitanni. Gradually, the Hittites built up their strength, and under the able king Suppiluliumas, they decisively defeated Mitanni in Syria. Under pressure on their eastern border from their former tributary state, Assyria, the Kingdom of Mitanni crumbled. The Hittites now found themselves in direct contact in Canaan with the Egyptians, who had recently ejected the Hyksos and were pressing northward in quest of defensible borders. When Suppiluliumas died in about 1335 B.C., the Hittite empire was at its height.

For administrative purposes, the Hittites borrowed Mesopotamian cuneiform writing techniques for their inscriptions and records, and communicated in Akkadian with neighboring states. Thousands of inscribed tablets have been found in the royal archives of Hattusas. They give a good picture of Hittite foreign relations during the zenith of the empire and also, to a lesser extent, of Hittite culture. Although they borrowed heavily from the cosmopolitan high culture of western Asia, the Hittites also made their own unique contributions.

Much of Hittite mythology was derived from that of their Hurrian neighbors, who in turn had borrowed from Mesopotamian sources. The myth of the struggle for overlordship among the gods is one such example. According to this story, the supreme sky god, Anu, was castrated by his chief subordinate, Kumarbi. In turn Kumarbi's son, Teshub, the storm god, rebelled, and after a tremendous battle succeeded in usurping his father's position. The same story in modified form was repeated centuries later by the Greek poet Hesiod, and there is a possibility that the myth had reached the Greeks by way of the Hittites. According to native Hittite belief, their monarchs were the representatives on earth of the god Tarhuntas, and every spring they celebrated their god's victory over the dragon of chaos in a local version of the Babylonian story of the triumph of Marduk over Tiamat. In Hittite mythology the gods needed the help of mortals, who, through magic rituals, could aid their deities.

Despite such borrowings, the Hittites explored other cultural avenues independently. Although the Greeks are usually credited with being the inventors of secular literature, the Hittites spoke frankly of their own history in nonmythological fashion. The success of the early Hittite kingdom was ascribed, for instance, to the harmony of the ruling family, whereas later disasters were recognized as the result of lack of cooperation at the highest levels.

Like their Mesopotamian counterparts, the Hittite kings promulgated codes of laws, but they were original in the development of international law. Wars were to be undertaken only after proper legal procedures had been followed and a declaration of war proclaimed. Treaties with equal powers, such as Egypt, were carefully drawn

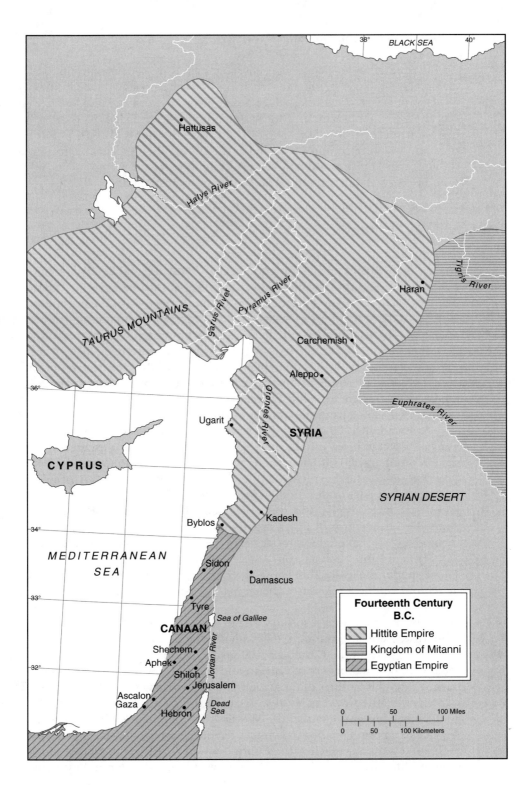

Fourteenth Century B.C.

Hittite Empire

Kingdom of Mitanni

Egyptian Empire

41

up and phrased in legal language, covering such issues as the extradition of fugitives and support for the legitimate succession in their respective royal houses. A different kind of treaty was developed for lesser, or vassal, powers. Here, greater emphasis was given to the obligation of the vassal, and imperative clauses, such as "You shall not covet any territory of the land of Hatti" (which sounds like one of the Ten Commandments), were commonly used. For these and other reasons, some scholars have thought that Hittite vassal treaties served as a model for the covenant or treaty between Israel and Yahweh—the Old Covenant or Testament.

THE EGYPTIAN EMPIRE

During the Old and Middle Kingdoms (ca. 2700–2200 and 2040–1780 B.C., respectively), the geographic isolation and cultural superiority of Egypt had allowed its inhabitants to maintain an attitude of smug superiority toward the outside world. The peoples of the north were characterized as "miserable," inhabiting lands cursed by quarrelsome and unsettled populations, "short of water, bare of wood, and painful because of mountains," whereas Egyptians lived in serenity, ruled by a god-king. There was some truth to the Egyptian stereotype of their northern neighbors, but the emergence of powerful Amorite coalitions in Syria and Canaan and contemporaneous weakness in the ruling Egyptian dynasty meant that Egypt was no longer able to keep its distance from the outside world.

From about 1700 B.C. onward, waves of emigrants and invaders from Syria and Canaan began to move into Egypt. They settled in the delta area, and eventually one of their numbers had sufficient power to set up an independent kingdom there. They were known to the Egyptians as the detested Hyksos ("foreign princes"). Their strength lay in part in their military technology. The horse-drawn chariot, recently introduced into western Asia, was a complete novelty to the Egyptians.

The humiliation of Egypt lasted about a century and a half. Finally rousing themselves, the Egyptians came to terms with the new political and military realities. From around 1560 B.C. on, a series of wars of liberation were launched from Thebes under the leadership of the brothers Kamose and Ahmose. The Hyksos were driven out, and a new dynasty, the eighteenth, uniting all of Egypt, was established by Ahmose.

The new pharaohs resolved never to submit to foreign domination again. It was a fateful decision and committed Egyptians to a fundamental rearrangement of their way of life. Beyond the Gaza Strip, defensible frontiers were to be found only far to the north, on the borders of Canaan and Syria. If Egypt was to be secure, it would have to extend its control of these regions and be willing to pay the price of extended contacts with the world of western Asia. To the south, Egypt's principal source of gold, Nubia, lost at the end of the Middle Kingdom, had to be recovered.

Over a period of about a century, Egyptian armies campaigned in Canaan and Syria and eventually reached the Euphrates, where they collided first with the Kingdom of Mitanni. Then, after the Hittites overwhelmed Mitanni, Egyptians and Hit-

---

THE EGYPTIAN EMPIRE: THE NEW KINGDOM

Hyksos invasion of Egypt	ca. 1750–1550 B.C.
New Kingdom, or Empire Period	ca. 1550–1100 B.C.
Revolution of Akhenaten	1363–1347 B.C.
Tutankhamen	1347–1338 B.C.
Invasions of the Sea Peoples and the decline of Egypt	ca. 1200 B.C.

---

tites found themselves locked in combat for control of Syria and northern Canaan. At one point a great battle was fought at Kadesh, with each side claiming victory, but the situation eventually stabilized as Egyptians and Hittites, the latter threatened by the rising power of Assyria on their eastern flank, recognized their limitations. A treaty of "good peace and brotherhood" was arranged around 1280 B.C., and thereafter the two powers cooperated effectively. Control of Nubia was restored, and deep in the Sudan, over 1,200 miles from the northern capital at Memphis, the pharaohs erected vast temples to overawe the local people and to facilitate the exploitation of the rich resources, primarily gold, of the south.

Complications of Imperial Rule

The maintenance of an empire that saw Egyptian fighting forces deep in the Sudan and as far north as Syria brought into existence new classes of imperial bureaucrats and army officers. The empire could not be maintained without reorganizing the Egyptian administrative and economic system. Egyptian society and culture were also affected by the acquisition of an empire. Opportunities for advancement and the necessity of having a standing army in distant places meant that Egyptians were placed in lasting contact with foreigners and that large numbers of outsiders found their way into Egypt. With them came new cultural influences and pressure to break away from the old system. To the new administrators, army officers, and merchants, who now came to exercise more and more power, many Egyptian customs must have seemed peculiar.

As commander of the army and a bureaucracy dominated by new men, the pharaoh was particularly susceptible to alien influences. As early as the reign of Thutmosis III (1490–1436 B.C.), one of Egypt's great empire builders, there were indications of a break with tradition. In art, simplicity and economy were replaced by overdecoration and monumentality, and traditional rigidity in portraiture began to give way to a new fluidity of movement. In religious thought there was a tendency toward identifying Egyptian gods with foreign gods. Because most of the principal divinities of Egypt were natural forces anyway, this could be accomplished with relative ease. Re, the sun god, came to be identified with his Akkadian counterpart, Shamash, and Seth with the Canaanite Baal. Although innocuous on the surface, these tendencies spelled danger for the highly integrated religious system of Egypt, where the position of the pharaoh and his brother-gods was unique and could not tolerate identification with the deities of other lands without suffering a loss of power.

There were other threats to the old order. The material success of the empire meant rewards and enrichment for the agencies that claimed to be responsible for Egypt's victories abroad. The temple and priesthood of Amen-Re at Thebes accumulated enormous wealth and prestige from the god's support of the original wars of liberation from the Hyksos and the subsequent expansion of Egyptian military might outside Egypt. The new army became one of the main supports of the pharaoh, but it, along with the administrative apparatus that supported it, also constituted an independent source of power within the palace. These were new forces that in times past had not existed within the framework of the Egyptian state.

The real challenge lay in the interpretation of the pharaoh's position in the sacred nation of Egypt. Was he a god-king who ruled the state by his word directly, the representative of the gods on Earth, or merely the channel through which the divine guidance came? It was an important distinction, not a theological quibble. The first theory represented the old, absolutistic approach, which, with some modifications, had sustained Egyptian society over the millennia. The pharaoh was the state; he sustained it and made it function, not just in theory but in actuality. The other ideology, reflecting the realities of the changes in Egypt since the Hyksos, viewed the pharaoh as central to the state, but only as an instrument of the gods, who, with the priests and bureaucrats at his side to help him, ruled the kingdom. Still, Egyptians had always lived with contradictions in their system; it was not part of their psychology to try to resolve contradictions or be bothered by inconsistencies, which they preferred to live with rather than try to resolve. For once, however, the contradictions were brought out into the open and became an issue of public debate (Egyptian style, of course). This came about through the emergence of one of the most remarkable religious visionaries in history, the pharaoh Akhenaten.

Akhenaten succeeded to the throne as Amenhotep IV, but in the sixth year of his reign he dropped this name, which honored the god Amen, in favor of a new name, Akhenaten: "He who serves Aten willingly." Aten was the sun disk, the purest manifestation of the sun god Re, who had been worshiped from the earliest times in Egypt. He was thought of as the loving creator of all things and the sustainer of life on Earth.

Although this change in name represented a significant challenge to the entrenched priesthood of Amen at Thebes, it did not much affect the traditional religious life of Egypt. The next step that Akhenaten took, however, did have revolutionary significance: the worship of the other gods, particularly of Amen, was suppressed. The temples were closed, and even the worship of Osiris came to a standstill. Everywhere the pharaoh's workmen blotted out the name of Amen wherever they found it, along with the names of other gods, in the belief that the elimination of a god's name led to his annihilation, at least as far as humans were concerned—out of sight, out of mind. The public festivals of the gods ceased. A new capital called Akhetaten ("horizon of Aten") was constructed midway between Thebes and Memphis to emphasize the break with the old ruling regime. There Aten was worshiped in open, sun-filled courts, unlike the dark recesses of the traditional temples where

THE HERESY OF AKHENATEN

Egypt was a land of many gods, with a place and a role for all of them. In traditional Egyptian belief, the sun god made his circuit of the sky in the company of other gods and at night passed through the underworld, where he struggled with the forces of chaos. In Akhenaten's theology, however, Aten was the sole god; in his manifestation as the sun disk, he made his journey across the sky alone, in solitary splendor. He was the creator god, who, without the help of any other deity, cared for his creatures:

> How many are your deeds,
> Though hidden from sight,
> O Sole God beside whom there is none!
> You made the earth as you wished, you alone,
> All peoples, herds, and flocks;
> All upon earth that walk on legs,
> All on high that fly on wings. . . .

> Your rays nurse all fields,
> When you shine they live, they grow for you;
> You made the seasons to foster all that you made,
> Winter to cool them, heat that they taste you.
> You made the far sky to shine therein,
> To behold all that you made;
> You alone, shining in your form of living Aten,
> Risen, radiant, distant, near.

Source: Miriam Lichtheim, trans., *Ancient Egyptian Literature: A Book of Readings* (Berkeley: University of California Press, 1976), pp. 98–99. Reprinted by permission of the University of California Press.

the gods had previously dwelt. Surrounded by his family, courtiers, bureaucrats, and army officers, Akhenaten spent the remainder of his 17-year reign pursuing his religious vision of a purified and reformed temple-state.

If Akhenaten had been able to replace what he had taken away with something just as attractive, the revolution might have had some permanent effect, but the heretical pharaoh seems to have been content, as far as Egypt at large was concerned, with curtailing the worship of the traditional gods and not much more. His position was clear: As god-king of Egypt, he was to be worshiped, while in turn he worshiped Aten. Thus identified with Aten, he was to be worshiped by all Egyptians. By emphasizing his position as the god-king of Egypt and claiming the exclusive right to worship Aten, Akhenaten reasserted in the strongest terms the old ideology of absolutism and arrogated to himself all the old powers of the pharaoh—and then some. There was great logic and simplicity in his action. By eliminating the complicated, confusing system of the gods of Egypt, Akhenaten was able to undercut the competing powers of the priesthoods and temples that sustained them and regain the absolutism of the pharaohs of old, who had ruled without challenge from any institution. It was an attempt to restore the old *ma'at*, the true order of things.

Yet despite these clearly defined tendencies, there were contradictions in Akhenaten's reforms. His new religion was extremely personal, limited to him and those immediately connected with him. If the major gods of Egypt had always been somewhat distant and unapproachable, Aten was no exception. Akhenaten's emphasis on *ma'at* led to another contradictory development: his humanization in art. In place of the traditional, stiff, eternally young pharaoh, Akhenaten was portrayed realistically with sloping shoulders, protruding stomach, and elongated head. Others in his retinue were similarly depicted, and unusual prominence was given to relaxed family scenes and to the women and children of the pharaoh's household. Instead of an austere, triumphant king, the pharaoh now appeared as an affectionate father playing with his children or conversing with his wife. Language and literature were encouraged to reflect the spoken tongue, and foreign words and everyday colloquialisms were permitted to enter the official, secular documents, although the classical language of Egypt remained dominant in religious communication.

It seems almost miraculous that Akhenaten was able to get away with his revolution without provoking a revolt. The old priesthoods and the old elites were outraged, but the army remained loyal to him, and there is no indication of civil unrest. Perhaps the whole reform movement sailed right over the heads of the vast majority of ordinary Egyptians, whose folk religion was unaffected by changes in the official religion that seemed so important to the elites. An attack on Akhenaten and his immediate successors did not occur for another 50 years, and then only when a new dynasty assumed power. At that time his mummy was destroyed and his memory denigrated, and efforts were made to eliminate all references to him. As in the case of other embarrassing episodes in their history, Egyptians, like other peoples, tried to forget about Akhenaten and his unwanted reforms.

There is evidence that Akhenaten made some kind of a compromise toward the end of his reign. Certainly his successors were forced to accept the failure of his revolution. After his death, his son-in-law, Tutankhaten, was forced to make a full surrender by changing his name to Tutankhamen and thus dropping the reference to Aten, abandoning Akhetaten, and returning to Thebes and the full control of the old oligarchies of priests and bureaucrats. The attempt to go back to an earlier age failed, and the pharaohs were forced to accept the realities of the present age and their diminished position in it. The empire, which had been neglected by Akhenaten, was once more given the full attention of the Egyptian government, but the power of the pharaoh continued to decline and with it the power of Egypt. As one author puts it, "The foundation stone of ancient Egypt had been cracked."[2]

Egyptian Society in the New Kingdom

From earliest times Egyptians had a very different view of life from that of their counterparts in Mesopotamia. Social life in Mesopotamia began and ended with the city. A Mesopotamian was first and foremost a citizen of his hometown—Larsa, Babylon,

[2]John A. Wilson, *The Culture of Ancient Egypt* (Chicago: University of Chicago Press, 1965), p. 234.

Unidentified royal couple from Amarna, possibly Akhenaten's son-in-law Semenkhara and his daughter Meritaten.

Ur, or some other—and only in a cultural sense a Sumerian or Akkadian. There was no such thing as a Sumerian or Akkadian nation. There were empires from time to time when one city ruled another, but never a period when the people of Mesopotamia regarded themselves as citizens of a single state or nation.

Although Egypt had plenty of diversity, it was much more a nation than Mesopotamia. Egyptians had a clear idea of themselves as Egyptians, and everyone else was regarded as simply non-Egyptian, often as not even human. After centuries of pharaonic rule, Egyptians shared a common language and a homogeneous culture. In many other respects, however, ordinary Egyptians probably differed little from men and women in Mesopotamia. Each individual Egyptian was embedded in his own local society, its customs, its religious practices, and its temples, and had little interest in what happened around the next bend of the Nile. Each worked his own small plot of land, but owed much of his time and labor to the great landowners or temples.

In the New Kingdom, the temples of Egypt became enormously wealthy. According to one famous document known as the Harris Papyrus, temples owned, among other property, 169 towns; 500 gardens, vineyards, and orchards; 88 ships; and half a million cattle. On the basis of this document and other sources of information, it has been estimated that up to one-fifth of the people and one-third of the arable land came under the control of the temples. Still, being under the control of the temples did not mean enslavement, any more than did service in the administration of the pharaohs. The people who worked for the temples—the priests, scribes, herdsmen, cultivators, and artisans—were assigned small farms for their subsistence. Within the limited scope of career options in the ancient world, theirs was not such a bad situation. They had a certain amount of independence, while also participating in a much larger institution with important local responsibilities and contacts with the outside world.

Because Egyptian society as a whole was less subject to the stresses of city life and the endless wars between city-states and outside invaders that characterized much of Mesopotamia, we can guess that the Egyptian peasant led a more placid, less demanding life. He and his wife had an eternal place in the scheme of things, as their parents had had before them and their children would have after them. Their personal fortunes were not likely to rise or sink, except as the fortunes of the whole community might rise or sink. Here and there an ambitious or disgruntled son might decide to escape into the army. A more prosperous peasant might manage to get an able son into a scribal school, but there was no impulse toward self-improvement, no itch to change things. Egyptians were content with their simple pleasures: their families, their homes, their beer, and the occasional festival that broke the monotony of daily life. If they were of the reflective type, they might occasionally think of their place in the great cosmic scheme of things, which the gods had designed and which gave them a secure and orderly—if dull—existence. However, they were not much agitated by the thought of any other viable alternative.

Daily Life   Life in Egypt was not particularly demanding, certainly not by modern standards, and for long periods of the year there was little or nothing to do. The rhythms of life were dictated by the seasons, not machinery or the clock—or the need to keep up with the neighbors. Irrigation was not nearly as complex or labor-intensive as it was in Mesopotamia, where canals and ditches constantly had to be dug or cleared of accumulated silt. Egyptian farmers merely had to wait for the annual inundation of the Nile to subside in order to plant their crops; if they wanted to raise a second crop, they had to be prepared to manipulate the flood basins that paralleled the river in both Upper and Lower Egypt. Here some real work and perhaps some coordination with others at the village level were necessary.

It was true, of course, that unusually large floods or, more likely, too low floods could cause catastrophe, and successive poor inundations could bring about famine and the collapse of the social order. Still, if the pharaohs were able to bail out their starving Hittite allies in Syria, as they did on one occasion, they should usually have been able to ship grain up- or downstream within Egypt itself as long as the problem was localized and they were fully in command of the administration. If they were not, as was the case at the end of the Old Kingdom, then Egypt could fall apart.

Wheat and barley bread were the staple foods of Egypt, but, in the north especially, beef was common. Some kinds of fish were taboo, but this must not have deterred many in times of real need. There were enormous quantities of vegetables. Fruits included primarily figs and dates, but grapes, apples, and pomegranates were also available during the New Kingdom. Honey and treacle made from dates were used as sweeteners. Milk, butter, and cheese were common. Pigeons, ducks, and geese were kept both for their eggs and for their flesh. The favorite drink was beer, though wine, often sweet and spicy, was also available.

As in Mesopotamia, the houses of all classes were made of mud brick and timber, and ranged in size and style from the magnificent palaces of the pharaohs and the villas of the nobles to the simple houses of the peasants and workers. Although mud sounds like an unpromising material, anyone familiar with the adobe house of the American Southwest will recognize what practical, cheap, and attractive homes can be built with it. Floors, ceilings, and walls were often painted in brilliant colors. Favorite motifs included animals, trees, plants, and people in the various activities of daily life. Egyptians loved flowers and water, and the villas of the nobles always had enclosed gardens full of plants, fruit trees, and pools of water.

The Family and the Status of Women   The Egyptian family, like the family elsewhere in the ancient world, was not a simple nuclear family of husband and wife and perhaps children but a large corporation made up of the living and the dead. Egyptians maintained a lively interest in their relationship to their ancestors, and genealogies were maintained in the family archives. There was a practical aspect to this custom, as there was to every facet of Egyptian life. A stable family life depended on a secure economic foundation, and this in turn demanded that the family property be preserved and handed down intact from one generation to the next. Good records and titles to land were an essential aspect of the transmission of the family heritage and property.

Fathers had great power over their children, even over the property of their grown sons. Mothers seem to have been particularly venerated. A standard claim to virtue in tomb inscriptions was the claim that the deceased was "beloved by his mother." Children were expected to care for their parents in their old age; daughters, at least, were obligated by law to do so. If art is any guide, husbands and wives had warm and loving relationships. They are often shown seated side by side, the husband's arm resting on his wife's shoulders, while her hand lies on his forearm. Daughters are represented in art with the same tenderness as sons.

Throughout Egyptian history women enjoyed a high degree of freedom and were often able to function on much the same level as men. Why this was so is not immediately apparent, and no Egyptians have left any records of their investigation of a subject that has only recently become a topic of interest to Western historians. Perhaps the reason lies in part in the fact that neither men nor women enjoyed political freedom, and Egyptian interest in or respect for the military was never very high. As a result, some of the clubby, exclusive institutions that males in other societies dominated to the exclusion of women did not exist in Egypt. Property, politics, and military responsibilities did not intermingle as they often did in other ancient lands. Women could own property, retain it throughout their marriage, and dispose of it as they wished. Contracts between men and women were arranged as between equals.

In the Old Kingdom the sage Ptah-hotep advised a husband regarding his wife: "Fill her belly and clothe her back. . . . Make her heart glad as long as you live, [but] you should not contend with her at law," the implication presumably being (on at least one reading of the text) that a husband could not assume that the law or the sympathy of the judge would automatically be on his side. Divorce was a matter of one party repudiating the other, although in practice social pressures must have made it much less easy than it seems. Marriage contracts were often drawn up with financial conditions that would have made the dissolution of a marriage hardly worth the effort unless there was some very pressing reason. Another reason why divorce was probably not common is that although Egyptian marriages were monogamous, concubinage was often tolerated. If a wife did not produce children, there was no need to divorce her; children could be raised through a concubine. Even where a concubine was admitted to the family, the first wife had precedence and, if divorced, had to be well compensated. It was once believed that brother-sister marriages were widely practiced among Egyptians. It is true that such marriages occurred at times in the royal family, but they do not seem to have been tolerated among ordinary people, although marriages between half-brothers and half-sisters did occur. The belief in the frequent occurrence of brother-sister marriages perhaps derives from a misunderstanding of Egyptian love poetry. In this form of poetry, lovers refer to each other as "brother" and "sister"; by New Kingdom times, the term *sister* had also come to mean "wife."

The myth of Isis, the warm and courageous wife of Osiris, held a central place in Egyptian mythology, and undoubtedly underlay and sustained the prominent position of women in Egyptian society. Isis was an important role model and symbol for all women, but Egyptians were also aware that women were influential in palace politics and sometimes had very visible roles in the government of Egypt. One of the figures in the founding of the Old Kingdom, Queen Mer-Neith of the first dynasty, was, according to one opinion, a ruling pharaoh in her own right. She was probably the daughter of Djer, the third pharaoh after the founder, Narmer; the wife of the next king, Djet; and the mother of the next two, Den and Anedjib. The tombs of the queens in the first dynasty were as large as their husbands', suggesting the importance of their roles as unifiers of the land, if, as is suspected, some of them were princesses from Lower Egypt. Coming from the recently conquered north, they would have been in a position to reconcile that region to its absorption by the south. Ahhotep, the mother of Kamose and Ahmose, who liberated Egypt from the hated Hyksos conquerors during the second Intermediate Period, was praised on a great stele (pillar) at Karnak for having rallied the army of Egypt and put a stop to a rebellion. In unusual times the queens even won the position of pharaoh for themselves and ruled as kings in their own right. At the end of the Old Kingdom, Nitocris became pharaoh, as did Sebeknofru at the end of the Middle Kingdom. The best-known female pharaoh was the powerful Queen Hatshepsut, who ruled as king for 21 years and whose magnificent mortuary temple in western Thebes is considered an architectural masterpiece.

EGYPT IN DECLINE

Toward the end of the New Kingdom, the pharaonic system of government was beginning to show signs of wear. Royal religious authority declined along with the pharaoh's military and political power. For centuries there had been a slow decay at work in the government and in the ideology of pharaonic rule. Since the unification of Egypt over 2,000 years before, Egyptian society had been sustained by a comprehensive, mythological world view, an effective belief system that successfully prevented society from fragmenting into warring factions of temples, bureaucratic elites, and regional groupings. A god-king, unquestionably accepted by his subjects not out of fear but out of a shared belief in the way the cosmos worked, had been the key to Egypt's success in the past. The great pyramids, the huge temples that were built in the empire period, the efficient bureaucracy, and innumerable other highly visible symbols sustained this view and reassured ordinary Egyptians that they were uniquely blessed by the gods. Less highly visible, but of complementary importance, was the predictable and stable succession of the pharaohs and their ability to maintain internal order while defending Egypt against outsiders.

However, following the death of Merenptah (1224–1204 B.C.) of the nineteenth dynasty, there were problems in the succession, and the remaining pharaohs of the dynasty reigned for an average of only six years each, ending in the military usurpation of Sethnakht, who founded the twentieth dynasty. Succession problems also plagued this dynasty. After the 31-year reign of Rameses III (who may well have been assassinated), the next five pharaohs (Rameses IV–VIII) ruled for an average of only five years each. The upheavals of the Middle East ca. 1200 B.C., which led to the loss of Egypt's territories in Canaan and direct attacks on Egypt itself, also contributed to the weakening of the monarchy. Other factors were at work, such as inflation, the depletion of the Nubian gold mines, lack of access to the copper mines of Sinai, and, as always, regionalism. Toward the end of the New Kingdom (ca. 1100 B.C.) there was an unprecedented concentration of power in the hands of individuals other than the pharaoh, such as the Egyptian commander in Nubia, the high priest of Amen, and the commander of the army. There was increasing bureaucratic corruption at the local level. The central administration was weakened as powerful families were able to convert some key administrative departments into private, hereditary fiefdoms. The Merybast family, for instance, held major offices under all the pharaohs from Rameses III through Rameses XI, including vizierships, high priesthoods, army commands, royal stewardships, and the mayoralty of Thebes. The king's own family came into greater prominence, with royal princes carrying out major rituals formerly reserved to the king; sometimes even royal butlers were designated, in the absence of the pharaoh, to perform these tasks. In the reign of the last king of the New Kingdom, Rameses XI, the real power lay in the hands of a military man, Heri-Hor, who simultaneously held the positions of vizier, high priest of Amen, and commander-in-chief of the armed forces.

After Rameses' death in 1085 B.C., Egypt divided once again (the third Intermediate Period, ca. 1085–664 B.C.). For about a century the south remained in the hands of the descendants of Heri-Hor. Then came the rule of an Egyptianized Libyan dynasty (ca. 940–730 B.C.), followed by a brief Nubian dynasty (ca. 760–656 B.C.). The Nubians, ruling from Thebes through a royal priestess known as the "God's wife of Amen," attempted to justify their claim to the throne by reviving traditions of the great past such as building pyramids and using the names of pharaohs of the Old Kingdom. The Nubians were soon hustled out of Egypt by a new Mesopotamian

---

EGYPT IN DECLINE

Invasions of the Sea Peoples	ca. 1200 B.C.
Libyan dynasties	ca. 940–730 B.C.
Nubian dynasties	ca. 760–656 B.C.
Nubians and Assyrians struggle for control of Egypt	671–663 B.C.
Egyptian recovery: the Saite pharaohs	664–525 B.C.
Persian conquest of Egypt	525 B.C.
Egypt conquered by Alexander the Great	332 B.C.

---

power, the Assyrian Empire. Memphis and Thebes were both sacked, and statues of the pharaoh were taken to Assyria to decorate the king's palace at Nineveh. There was a brief period of national unity under a native dynasty (the Saite dynasty) before another great power, Persia, intervened to make Egypt a province in a gigantic empire reaching from the Mediterranean to India.

During these years of turmoil and instability, pharaohs could appeal to the authority of the past, but the reality of Egypt's position in world politics belied any such claims. Egypt itself had changed considerably during these centuries. For millennia, Upper Egypt had dominated the north. Now this position was reversed as the delta region grew by internal colonization, and for the first time in Egypt true cities emerged. Greater numbers of people found shelter behind their walls, and the kings of the north grew rich on their ability to exploit Egypt's resources in the developing markets of the eastern Mediterranean. Egyptian religion lost its vitality and turned inward to magic, witchcraft, and demonology. If tomb paintings are any indication of a change in viewpoint, the Egyptians of the late period seem to have abandoned their exuberant enjoyment of life, and instead sought security in rigid organization and conformity. By the time of the Greeks, Egyptian society was tightly organized, with priests and warriors enjoying special positions of prominence. Preoccupied with ritual, they were, in the eyes of Greek historian Herodotus, who visited Egypt in the fifth century B.C., the most god-fearing people. At the same time the incredible accomplishments of the past, the evidence of Egypt's great antiquity, the pyramids and temples, and the land's great wealth and population were an inspiration to such new peoples as the Greeks, who had nothing in their homeland to compare to the monuments of Egypt and whose memories went back centuries, as compared to millennia. If much had been taken, much remained. The Greeks borrowed heavily from the Egyptians, especially the belief that human beings could accomplish great things. This was not exactly what the pharaohs had in mind when they had erected their famous monuments, but for the people of the next age, such a misinterpretation was irrelevant.

Chapter 3

The Near East
to the Persian Empire

THE NEW PEOPLES OF THE NEAR EAST

Around 1200 B.C. the Aegean, Anatolia, and the Near East were convulsed by one of the greatest ethnic upheavals of their long history. Old empires crumbled and were swept away, several so completely that their existence was not even suspected until resurrected by archaeologists and linguists in recent times. Many new peoples, among them the Iranians, Israelites, Philistines, and Phoenicians, made their appearance for the first time.

As in the past, the new peoples came from the north and the desert fringes of Syria. The northern peoples came in two unconnected movements. One of these originated in the Aegean and Anatolian area. Its component peoples were called the Sea Peoples by the Egyptians, although the innocent-sounding name belies the disasters they brought to the eastern Mediterranean. The other northern people, the Iranians, arrived with less fanfare, or to be more accurate, the people they overcame left no written records of what the conquest was like. From the desert fringes of the Near East itself came the Aramaeans.

The Sea Peoples and the Philistines

The Sea Peoples were not entirely strangers to Egypt and the eastern Mediterranean. On and off between 1300 and 1200 B.C. the pharaohs had recruited mercenaries from the Aegean and Anatolian areas for their armies. Troops from these regions served in the personal bodyguard of Rameses II and saved the day at the battle of

NEW PEOPLES IN THE NEAR EAST

Invasions of the Sea Peoples	ca. 1200 B.C.
Arrival of the Philistines	ca. 1200–1100 B.C.
Aramaean expansion in Syria and Mesopotamia	ca. 1100–900 B.C.
Emergence of the Phoenicians	ca. 1100–900 B.C.
Exodus from Egypt	?1250 B.C.
Israelite conquest of Canaan	ca. 1200–1000 B.C.
David and Solomon	ca. 1000–922 B.C.

Kadesh when the Egyptian army was on the verge of being annihilated by the Hittites. They were not always so accommodating, however. Sometimes they found it more profitable to make common cause with the Libyans of North Africa and raid the delta area of Egypt whenever a good opportunity presented itself.

At some point around 1250 B.C. the peoples of the Aegean and Anatolia themselves came under pressure. Some of the problems seem to have been caused by their own warlike tendencies, but others were caused by disturbances from elsewhere. In any case, around 1200 B.C. the two old and stable powers of the west, the Mycenaean and Hittite kingdoms, along with some lesser states in the region, collapsed, and streams of refugees, migrants, and freebooters were let loose on the eastern Mediterranean. Cities all along the coast, including such legendary places as Troy and Sidon, were overwhelmed. Some of the migrants settled down in the newly conquered territories, and others moved on. The Egyptians were bundled out of Canaan, but when the Sea Peoples tried to force their way into Egypt itself, they were stopped by Rameses III. Some of the prisoners taken in battle were settled in Egypt and served as mercenaries for the pharaohs. Other survivors turned back up the coast and took over the Canaanite cities of the district between Gaza and Mount Carmel. Identified by the Egyptians as the Peleset, they gave the name Palestine to the region. They are also known, and perhaps better known to us, as the Philistines of the Hebrew Scriptures.

The Philistines brought from the Aegean and Anatolia their own distinctive artistic, political, and military traditions. They were genuine intruders in a region that had long been dominated by Semitic-speaking peoples with a strong indigenous culture. Although they were a minority, the Philistines managed to maintain themselves for several centuries as an independent people by means of their superior fighting and organizational abilities and their monopoly of an important new technology, the production of iron. Although iron is not intrinsically superior to bronze, it is cheaper to produce on a large scale, and its basic ores are more common. In the new Age of Iron a government could put more soldiers in the field for the same cost as it could by using the old technology of bronze production. Outside the realm of warfare, the introduction of iron made metal a common material in the household and on the farm for the first time. This could mean increased food production as iron-tipped agricultural implements made agriculture more efficient and brought difficult soils, such as clays, into cultivation.

> ### IRON VERSUS BRONZE
>
> The key to the usefulness of iron is carburization, the process by which carbon molecules are made to combine with molecules of iron to form carbon steel.
>
> In terms of tensile strength, unforged iron is not much stronger than copper (32,000 psi, or pounds per square inch) and well below cold-hammered bronze (120,000 psi). By contrast, even a low-carbon steel has a tensile strength of 140,000 psi, and when cold-hammered the strength reaches 245,000 psi.
>
> The impulse to move from the use of copper and bronze to iron and steel apparently resulted from the chaotic conditions created by the activities of the Sea Peoples. The normal trade routes were disrupted, and it became difficult to find tin, the principal component of bronze. In response, the smiths of Anatolia, a region rich in iron, improvised a solution. They discovered that by means of repeated heatings in a hot charcoal furnace, iron could be made into an exceedingly hard metal. Without knowing the chemistry involved, they had discovered the art of steel manufacturing. From this time onward (around 1000 B.C.), carburized iron came into common use for tools, cooking and farm implements, and, above all, weapons. Mass production of pure steel (as opposed to partially steeled or carburized iron) was not achieved until the mid-1860s A.D., when Bessemer and Siemens perfected their techniques of production and made the Age of Steel possible.

Some aspects of Philistine life are strongly reminiscent of the kind of society found in the Homeric epics, the *Iliad* and the *Odyssey*. Philistine cities were ruled by warrior aristocracies under weak kings, and the people at large seem to have had some say in the decision-making process. The kings acted in concert, and individuals among them could be overruled by their fellow kings in council. Some of the most vivid stories in the Books of Samuel in the Bible tell of the conflicts between the Philistines and their mortal enemies, the Israelites. Among the best known of these is the tale of Goliath, the Philistine hero who challenged the Israelites to single combat in Homeric fashion, expecting to fight a fully armed warrior of his own age, status, and experience. Instead, he died ignominiously at the hands of an unarmed, untried youth, David. Needless to say, we sympathize with David, as the author of Samuel intended, but from the Philistine viewpoint the encounter would have been regarded as a dishonorable accident that only proved the underhanded tactics of their opponents. Other well-told stories are the death in battle with the Philistines of the first king of Israel, Saul, and his son, Jonathan, the beloved friend of David. The Book of Judges recounts the story, much appreciated by Hollywood, of the love of the Israelite Samson for the Philistine Delilah and her betrayal of him to her kinsmen. The Philistines, like so many lesser-known peoples in history, owe their fame less to their own achievements than to the fact that they were the enemies and foils of peoples who later rose to prominence.

The Phoenicians

To the north of the Philistines, the old Canaanite cities of the coast slowly recovered from the effects of the migrations of the Sea Peoples. The inhabitants of these cities are known to us as the Phoenicians, from the name later given them by the Greeks, but culturally they were indistinguishable from the other inhabitants of the land between Syria and Egypt. They never formed a single nation. Like the Philistines, the Phoenicians are known, for the most part, only through the unflattering accounts of their enemies.

The access of the Phoenicians to the sea and their mastery of it gave them an independence their inland neighbors and kinsmen sorely lacked. Located on headlands or islands off the coast, their cities were difficult, if not impossible, to capture. Around 950 B.C. the Phoenicians began conducting trading voyages as far west as Spain, and in the following centuries they established commercial networks all over the Mediterranean. Sidonians founded Cadiz in Spain, and around 800 B.C. citizens of Tyre, the leading city in Phoenicia, founded Carthage, destined to become the rival of Rome for control of the Mediterranean centuries later. For centuries Greek and Phoenician colonists fought each other inconclusively for control of Sicily. Enterprising Phoenician traders voyaged as far afield as the tin mines of Britain and down the coast of West Africa as far as modern Sierra Leone.

In their strategic location between Mesopotamia and Egypt, the Phoenicians were in a position to borrow at will from both of these old centers of high civilization. As Canaanites, they were themselves the inheritors of a rich, local cultural tradition. However, besides the abundant cedar forests of Lebanon and a small snail from which they derived a marvelous red or purple dye, their natural resources were insignificant. Nevertheless, with these they did wonders. They imported cloth from abroad, dyed it, and reexported it throughout the Mediterranean. Ivory and ebony from India, Africa, and Syria and gold, silver, and precious stones from Yemen and Anatolia were worked into ornaments, furniture, and exquisite pieces of jewelry. The Phoenicians' own hinterland produced respectable wine and olive oil, which were also exported. In due course, glass and silk were added to their trade goods. Light in weight and extremely valuable, these exports were welcome everywhere. The Phoenicians prospered, and their opulence and self-assured cosmopolitanism provided the prophets of Israel with ready-made symbols of indulgent materialism. "O Tyre," said the prophet Ezekiel,

> You say . . . "I am perfect in beauty." Your wealth, merchandise and wares . . . will sink into the heart of the sea on the day of your shipwreck. . . . By your great skill in trading you have increased your wealth, and because of your wealth your heart has grown proud . . . you think you are wise, as wise as a god.
>
> —*Ezekiel 27:3, 28:5–6*

Besides being traders in material goods, the Phoenicians were also the bearers of the ancient high cultures of the Near East to the lands to the west. The old world had much to offer to the new. Just one example will suffice. Some centuries before the development of their trading empire, a phonetic alphabet of a mere 22 letters had evolved in Canaan. This brilliant invention neatly solved the difficulties involved in learning the unwieldy cuneiform and hieroglyphic systems of writing in use in the

Near East for millennia. Now the basics of written communication could be mastered in a matter of months instead of years. The rapid acceptance of the new alphabet by such peoples as the Greeks is one of the world's earliest and most successful examples of technology transfer. There can be no doubt that the sudden flowering of a literary culture among the Israelites and a literary, philosophic, and scientific culture among the Greeks was connected with their successful and complete acceptance of this new technology. In the case of the Greeks, the mastery and adaptation of the Phoenician alphabet represent an early example of a peripheral culture borrowing from a more advanced one and then leapfrogging ahead of it.

Aramaeans and Israelites

While the Sea Peoples were wreaking havoc along the coast between Anatolia and Egypt, the inland districts of the Near East were experiencing serious disturbances of their own. Possibly encouraged by the collapse of Hittite power in Syria and the activities of the Sea Peoples on the coast, vast confederations of seminomadic peoples on the fringes of the Syrian desert began to migrate toward the more developed regions of the Near East. This movement was widespread and powerful. The most prominent among the migrants were the Aramaeans. They settled throughout Syria, then crossed the Euphrates, and began to infiltrate southward into Mesopotamia.

The movement of the Aramaeans roughly paralleled that of the Amorites almost 1,000 years before and had equally important results. The language of the newcomers, Aramaic, slowly came to replace the older languages of the region such as Akkadian (Babylonian and Assyrian), Canaanite, and Hebrew, and eventually Aramaic became the general language of business and diplomacy in the entire Near East. Like the Phoenicians, the Aramaeans also adopted the alphabet developed by the Canaanites and spread it wherever they went. It was from the Aramaeans that the Persians and later the Arabs derived their scripts. The result was the eventual disappearance of the ancient cuneiform style of writing throughout the Near East.

Everywhere they settled, the Aramaeans established kingdoms. Some were small, others quite large and powerful. One of the most important of these was the kingdom of Damascus in Syria. The ancient state of Assyria was almost overwhelmed, but in the end, by dint of constant fighting, it managed to survive intact. In the south the Aramaeans gradually adapted themselves to urban lifestyles, and centuries later, under the Aramaean dynasty of the Chaldaeans, Babylon experienced the most glorious phase in its long history.

At some point in the waning years of the Egyptian Empire, the second major event in the history of the Israelites occurred: the Exodus from Egypt. Along with the covenant of Abraham, this event became the central historic and religious experience of the people of Israel.

Although the biblical description of the Exodus seems to support a massive departure of Abraham's descendants from Egypt, a close study of the texts and of nonbiblical evidence produces a much more complex picture. It seems that at least some of the Israelites (those who later identified themselves as the descendants of Abraham's grandson Jacob, or Israel) went down to Egypt with the Hyksos in the seventeenth and sixteenth centuries B.C., and were expelled with them. The majority, along with the other inhabitants of Palestine, became subjects of Egypt during the Empire period. Many must have been brought into Egypt as forced laborers, and others may have gone there voluntarily. Some enjoyed a brief triumph over Egypt at the time of Akhenaten, when, as members of the Habiru, or landless people, they invaded and settled in central Palestine, only to be resubjected when the Egyptian Empire revived under Rameses II. Perhaps at this time some were brought into Egypt to work on the great building projects that were initiated in the delta region by the pharaohs of the nineteenth dynasty. One of these groups somehow escaped, possibly during the rule of Rameses II, and fled into the desert of Sinai under the leadership of the Egyptianized Moses. There they met other tribes with whom they amalgamated and, inspired by the visionary genius of Moses, adopted the worship of Yahweh, perhaps a local god of the Sinai Peninsula.

There is no hope at this point of disentangling the exact nature of Moses' belief from its later development at the hands of other, equally gifted people, but it is clear that the Exodus and the making of the covenant (the so-called Old Testament) at Mount Sinai were fundamental to the development of Israel's religion. It was in the desert that the Israelites became a people and achieved self-conscious identity. The Exodus itself became lodged in the nation's consciousness as a central symbol of liberation by the power of Yahweh. Just as centuries earlier Yahweh had intervened in history to call Abraham out of Mesopotamia, now he acted to free Abraham's descendants from the hand of the most powerful king on earth, the pharaoh. This belief in the intervention of God in history became one of the most characteristic tenets of Israel's religion. It survived transplantation to a new land and countless subsequent challenges from changing cultural, economic, and social conditions.

The Conquest of Canaan and the Kingdom of David

The Canaan out of which Israel was to emerge had already been fought over many times. By the time of the arrival of the group led by Moses at some date in the thirteenth century B.C., the early Amorite invaders had long since mingled with the original inhabitants to such an extent that the two were indistinguishable. Together they constituted a people who shared a common culture that reached from Egypt to southern Syria. The Canaanites were in contact not only with the civilizations of Mesopotamia and Egypt but also with the Minoan and Mycenaean cultures of the Aegean area, whose pottery exports have been found widely throughout Palestine and Syria. Whereas the coastal and river valley regions were thickly settled, the mountainous areas were only sparsely occupied. An agricultural people, the Canaanites worshiped the fertility gods Baal and Astarte, and the myths and ritual practices associated with them were to be assimilated, in part, by the invading Israelites.

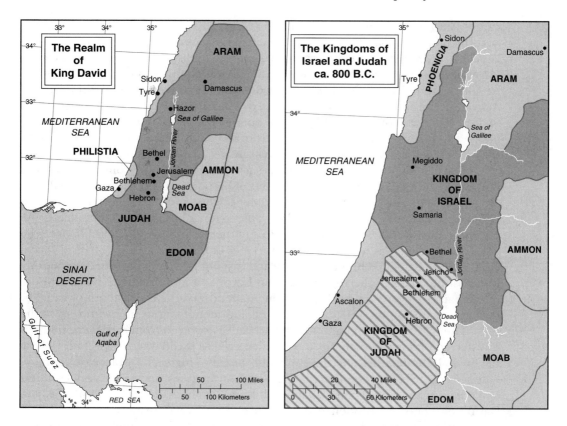

The conquest of Canaan was a slow process that took several centuries to complete. Initial toeholds were achieved in the mountainous areas and only gradually in the more settled regions. The newcomers brought a religion whose appeal extended to the Israelites who had not gone down to Egypt or who had settled in central Palestine as Habiru, as well as to others not completely assimilated by the Canaanites. At the same time, non-Israelite groups such as the Kenites entered Palestine and were absorbed by one or another of the tribes who claimed descent from Abraham. By the eleventh century B.C. a loose confederation of tribes sharing a common sanctuary at Shiloh had come to consider themselves members of a single kinship group, worshiping the same god and descended from the same ancestor. By a process involving in part conquest and in part assimilation, the people of Israel had come into existence.

There was as yet nothing that could strictly be called a state. The individual tribes were ruled by councils of elders, and in times of great stress charismatic leaders, the so-called judges of the Scriptures, rose to lead individual tribes or groups of tribes in military ventures. Among them were such well-known figures as Deborah, Gideon, and Samson, whose successful exploits opened up new areas for settlement or repelled enemy assaults. However, the judges proved unable to defend these hard-won gains against new enemies. From the east the Ammonites, the descendants of earlier Amorite invaders, pressed in, assisted by the Aramaeans of Syria. From the west the powerful coalition of Philistine city-states threatened the very existence of Israel. Armed with iron weapons and chariots, the Philistines were able, in the early stages of the conflict, to confine the Israelites to the mountainous areas of Palestine. At Aphek around 1050 B.C. they soundly defeated the forces of Israel, captured the Ark of the Covenant, and went on to destroy the Israelites' main tribal sanctuary at Shiloh. Under the pressures of Philistine encroachment as well as internal developments, the Israelites reluctantly turned from the charismatic leaders of the past to the more efficient institution of the monarchy.

The first king was Saul, whose early successes gave respite from the Philistines but who in time succumbed to the pressures of his position and became mentally deranged. His successor, David, had gained experience as a guerrilla leader and as a mercenary under the Philistines, and was able to unite both his own immediate supporters in the southern tribes and the tribes of the north in a successful alliance. The Philistine menace was overcome, and the cities of the seacoast submitted to David. Gradually, he extended his power north and east until the Israelite kingdom became the most powerful in the region between Egypt and Mesopotamia. But David did more than create an empire. He fundamentally altered the constitution of Israel by formally espousing the religion of Yahweh and identifying its cult with that of the state. The Ark of the Covenant, which had been recovered from the Philistines, was transferred with great solemnity to Jerusalem, where David intended to build a temple for it. Jerusalem became the capital of the new kingdom. In place of the loose federation of tribes, a central monarchy with court, scribes, and professional soldiers and administrators was created. Although Jerusalem had been a Canaanite city and David's own personal residence, it now became a national shrine.

David's son Solomon (ca. 961–922 B.C.) extended these lines of development even further. Closely allied to the Phoenician king of Tyre, Solomon set about consolidating his father's religious innovations by building a great temple at Jerusalem with the assistance of Phoenician craftsmen and artists. Friendly relations were also maintained with Egypt and other powers. The army was expanded and strengthened, and the frontier cities fortified. A merchant fleet was created in the Red Sea, and Solomon attempted to exploit the commercial possibilities of his kingdom's strategic location on the trade routes between Phoenicia, Syria, and Arabia. Cultural activities were also significant, and the great deeds of the times of Saul and David along with the traditions of Israel's early history were collected and given literary form.

Solomon's vision far outdistanced the resources of Israel, and not long after his death the empire disintegrated. The northern tribes reasserted their independence and established their capital at Samaria. Although Judah in the south remained faithful to the Davidic kings and the principle of dynastic succession, the northern state reverted to a version of the old system of charismatic leadership. For the next two centuries the two states lived side by side, alternately at peace or at war, both rendered progressively impotent by the growing power of Assyria, the first cosmopolitan empire of the ancient Middle East.

THE GLORY OF ASSYRIA AND BABYLON

By the end of the ninth century B.C., Mesopotamia and Palestine had fully recovered from the effects of the great disturbances that had occurred at the end of the second millennium, and had begun to reach new heights of economic prosperity. Assyria survived the period of unrest by dint of constant fighting, its hardy peasantry forming the nucleus of its powerful army. The founder of the empire was Adadnirari II (911–891 B.C.), but it was his grandson Ashurnasirpal II (883–859 B.C.) who, with his campaigns in Syria and Phoenicia and his construction of a magnificent palace at Kalhu, signaled the emergence of a new Assyria. Although checked briefly in 853 B.C. by the combined forces of Syria, Phoenicia, and Israel and by internal problems of succession, Assyrian power revived under the tireless organizer and conqueror Tiglathpileser III (744–727 B.C.). Damascus fell, and Assyrian armies reached the Mediterranean seacoast. To the north the powerful state of Urartu, occupying much of what was later Armenia, was humbled. Babylon was brought under strict control. In 722–721 B.C. Samaria, the capital of Israel, fell, and thousands of its citizens—the Lost Ten Tribes—were deported to Mesopotamia and vanished from history. Foreigners were introduced in their place, and with the remnants of the Israelite population came to form the Samaritan people of later times. Judah in the south survived precariously as a vassal kingdom of Assyria. When Babylon revolted in 689 B.C., Sennacherib (704–681 B.C.) destroyed it, although his son and successor, Esarhaddon (680–669 B.C.), thought it wise to have it rebuilt. In 671 B.C. Egypt was subdued, but quickly rebelled and had to be beaten down again eight years later.

On the death of Ashurbanipal in 627 B.C., a dynastic struggle racked the Assyrian state. Babylon again revolted, and under the Aramaean (or Chaldaean) Nabopolassar (625–605 B.C.) made common cause with the Medes of Iran and bands of Scythian nomads from Eurasia, who had been active in the Middle East for the preceding half-century. In 614 B.C. Assur fell, and two years later Nineveh was captured. By 609 B.C. the remnants of the Assyrian army were being stamped out in northern Mesopotamia.

The Assyrian Empire consisted of an extraordinarily assorted collection of peoples and states that the Assyrians held together by means of a powerful army, meticulous organization, and occasional calculated acts of brutality. The army was an integrated fighting force of infantry, cavalry, and special forces such as slingers and archers. It was the first army to combine systematically engineering and fighting techniques. Its engineers developed siege engines, built bridges, dug tunnels, and perfected supply and communication systems. Its widespread use of iron weaponry enabled it to put large numbers of soldiers into the field.

Always confronted with the sheer diversity of their empire, the Assyrians worked on effective techniques of control. Cities that revolted were sometimes laid waste as examples to others. To break up local loyalties, whole populations were moved elsewhere, where they were given land and urged to intermarry with the resident population. The concern of the Assyrians for their new subjects can be seen in

The hard realities of Near Eastern politics: King Jehu of Israel does obeisance to Shalmaneser III of Assyria.

their administrative correspondence and contrasts sharply with the frightful image they emphasized in their propaganda. Trade and industry flourished as never before. Roads were constructed, cities grew, and the arts developed. Fine, realistic friezes of hunting and battle scenes were created to decorate the great palaces of the kings, and collections of all sorts of materials (literary, scientific, and other) were compiled. The last of the major kings, Ashurbanipal, was a polymath who received a scholarly education:

> The art of the Master Adapa I acquired: the hidden treasure of all scribal knowledge, the signs of the heaven and the earth. . . . I have solved the laborious problems of division and multiplication. . . . I have read the artistic script of Sumer and the obscure Akkadian.[1]

His great library, of which 20,000 tablets have come down to us, include the Akkadian version of the *Epic of Gilgamesh.*

[1]D. D. Luckenbill, *Ancient Records of Assyria and Babylonia* (Chicago: University of Chicago Press, 1926–1927), vol. 2, p. 379. Permission given by Nellie Luckenbill Scheel.

A SECOND AGE OF EMPIRES

Rise of the Assyrian Empire	ca. 750 B.C.
Assyrian conquest of Israel (the Northern Kingdom)	721 B.C.
Fall of the Assyrian Empire: destruction of Nineveh	612 B.C.
Babylonian or Chaldaean Empire	612–539 B.C.
Fall of Judah (the Southern Kingdom) and destruction of Jerusalem	587 B.C.
Babylonian Captivity	587–538 B.C.
Cyrus of Persia captures Babylon	539 B.C.
Alexander of Macedon overthrows the Persian Empire	334–330 B.C.

With the collapse of Assyria, the Near East temporarily reverted to its older, fragmented form. Most of the efforts of the Babylonians were directed toward the development of their own immediate holdings in Mesopotamia and to the subjection of Syria and Palestine, not to the maintenance of a vast empire on the Assyrian model. Under its Chaldaean leaders, Babylon became one of the most splendid cities in the world. Temples were rebuilt, the priesthoods enriched, and religious customs revived. The great ziggurat Etemenanki—the Temple of the Foundation of Heaven and Earth—almost 200 feet tall, dominated the city, which was surrounded by a circuit of great walls 10 miles in length. The famous Hanging Gardens were constructed by Nebuchadrezzar for the pleasure of his Median queen, who missed her mountainous homeland.

The Fall of Judah and the Babylonian Captivity

While the Medes extended their power westward into Asia Minor and came into conflict with the kingdom of Lydia, the Babylonians advanced into Syria and Palestine. There they were opposed by the Egyptians, who had belatedly come to the aid of the Assyrians, but these forces were soon swept aside and driven back within the confines of Egypt. Judah quickly submitted to Nebuchadrezzar (604–562 B.C.), but when the Babylonians withdrew, it rebelled again, despite the warnings of the prophet Jeremiah. In 598 B.C. the Babylonians were back, and early in the following year Jerusalem surrendered. The king and the leaders of the community were deported to Babylon, and the city itself was thoroughly plundered. Unrest continued under the Babylonians as it had under the Assyrians, as the different parts of the empire tried to gain independence, often supported by Egyptian assurances of help. In 589 B.C. a scattered revolt, which included Judah and the city of Tyre, began. As the Hebrew prophet Jeremiah had predicted, the Babylonians struck swiftly, and Jerusalem was soon under siege. In the summer of 587 B.C. it was captured and burned, and its walls razed. More of the population was deported, and the remainder, mostly the rural peasants, were left leaderless. With the elimination of the ruling house of David and the destruction of Solomon's temple, the history of Israel seemed ended forever.

Nebuchadrezzar was soon succeeded by the eccentric Nabonidus (555–539 B.C.), reflections of whom appear in the scriptural Book of Daniel, which was composed in the Hellenistic period. Nabonidus quickly quarreled with the priesthood of Marduk at Babylon and began interfering in the religious life of the city. An antiquarian visionary, he tried to revive ancient religious rituals and at Haran in northern Mesopotamia built a temple to the moon god, to whom he was particularly devoted. Disgusted by the continuing opposition of the Babylonian clergy to his religious schemes, he withdrew to a desert oasis, leaving his son Belshazzar to serve as regent.

THE PERSIANS

While the power of the Chaldaean dynasty declined, a new people in the north were carving out a realm for themselves. In 553 B.C. one of the minor Indo-European tribes of Iran, the Persians, successfully challenged the overlordship of the Medes, and Cyrus the Achaemenian established a new ruling dynasty. The Medes acquiesced in the new arrangement, and Cyrus led both peoples successfully westward, where they overthrew the kingdom of Lydia and conquered the Greek cities of the Asia Minor coastline. Next the Persians turned their attention to Mesopotamia and, conspiring with the disaffected priests of Babylon, obtained control of the city peacefully in 539 B.C. The next year Cyrus issued an edict ordering the reestablishment of the temple at Jerusalem. Subsequently, a number of the exiles in Babylon returned to Jerusalem and despite enormous obstacles rebuilt the temple. The project was completed in 515 B.C., but to the disappointment of those who remembered the glories of the old temple, did not compare to the original. Jerusalem had become an unimportant town in a small province of the huge Persian Empire.

The Persian Empire, which by 525 B.C. included Egypt, was the largest that had yet been created in the ancient Near East. Organized into provinces under independent governors called *satraps,* the empire united all the land from Greece to Afghanistan and from the Caucasus to the Sudan. It offered peaceful conditions, stable coinage, excellent communications, and a good deal of tolerance to its subjects. It continued the cosmopolitan tendencies of the Assyrian Empire. Culturally backward, the Persians used Aramaic as the standard language of administration and diplomacy, and adapted the arts of Mesopotamia to their own needs. The Persian religion, which consisted of the worship of a large pantheon of gods and spirits, was presided over by a priestly caste called the *magi.* At some date in the sixth century B.C. the prophet Zoroaster (Zarathustra) reformed the primitive magian religion, condemning blood sacrifice, magic, and the pantheon of gods. He proposed instead an impressive theology that pitted the supreme god of light and truth, Ahura-Mazda, against the forces of evil, Ahriman, in a battle into which all humans were drawn on one side or the other. According to Zoroaster, humans are morally responsible for their actions, and in the end there will be a general judgment that will see the good and evil separated and appropriately rewarded or punished. Although Zoroaster met a violent end, his reforms became an enduring part of the Persian religion as well as many others in the Greco-Roman period.

RELIGION AND CULTURE IN ISRAEL

The earliest stages of Hebrew religious history are set against a background of tribal organization and seminomadic life. Whereas the Egyptians and Mesopotamians looked back to heroic kings and divine founders, the Israelites celebrated their humble origins in the cultic refrain, "A wandering Aramaean was my father," and regarded their experiences in the desert of Sinai as a golden age of youth and innocence: "When Israel was a child," declared the prophet Hosea, "I came to love him and from Egypt I called him" (Hos. 11:1). Nomadic ideals of brotherhood, hospitality, and asylum as well as the system of the vendetta profoundly influenced the development of religion, law, and culture in Israel, preventing it from evolving along the same lines as its highly organized neighbors. Yahweh, the god the Israelites had encountered in the desert, had no need of the apparatus of a state to fulfill his promises to his people or to communicate with them.

The first great challenge that the newly arrived Israelites experienced was how to ensure the survival of the religion of Moses in the seductive atmosphere of Canaan. The god of Israel was a desert god, austere and uncomplicated in his demands of loyalty, intolerant of rivals, and well suited to the needs of a nomadic people. The gods of Canaan, by contrast, were the sensuous fertility deities of an agricultural people. But much of Israel's nomadic experience was irrelevant to the new environment, and thus a new lifestyle had to be learned. The Israelites were now as permanently settled on the land as the Canaanite farmers among whom they lived. In a situation in which it was hard to tell what was most effective—magic or ritual or just good farming practices—it was easier to take over the whole apparatus of cultivation of the soil from the Canaanites, religious and secular alike. To some extent this is what happened. By a gradual process the Canaanite agricultural festivals were adapted to the needs of the Israelites and given a place in the traditional history of Yahweh. The tug of the old Canaanite gods and goddesses remained strong, however, and it was not until after the Babylonian Captivity (587–538 B.C.) that Yahwism finally triumphed.

The second great challenge faced by the Israelites came when the community of Yahweh was radically transformed by the work of its early kings. From a loosely organized coalition of tribes participating in a cultic league, Israel emerged by the middle of the tenth century B.C. as one of the most powerful states in the Middle East, with borders reaching from Egypt's frontier to Syria. Imitating its neighbors, Israel employed professional soldiers and administrators. In place of the independent clans and tribes making their own decisions, the court at Jerusalem now imposed taxes, declared wars, and made treaties. Yet no divine sanction accompanied the selection of Jerusalem as the capital of the state. It was "David's city," an old Canaanite stronghold that he had seized by his own efforts. From exclusive dependence on

Yahweh, who had raised up leaders at moments of national peril, Israel had come to depend on the chariots and soldiers of the kings. The first task facing the new kingdom was therefore to bring the new institutions of the monarchy into accord with the old, and the form that this adaptation took led to the development of an enduring, if controversial, tradition in Hebrew religious thought. Yahweh, who in times past had made a covenant at Sinai with Moses and the Israelites, now entered into a similar relationship with David and his descendants. David was to become Yahweh's adopted son, whose task it was to shepherd and rule Yahweh's people and to wage his wars. By bringing the Ark of the Covenant to Jerusalem and constructing a temple there, the task was complete: the city had become a national sanctuary, a holy place, its foundation celebrated by an annual festival recording the arrival of the Ark in the city.

The Beginnings of the Hebrew Bible

Although the monarchy of David entered into the national tradition of Israel, it always remained in tension with the Israelites' earlier beliefs that had emphasized unconditional dependence on Yahweh. David's military census and his professional soldiers together with Solomon's aggrandizement of the state at the expense of the tribes brought about a fierce reaction that found expression in the rise of the prophets, whose origins can be traced to the charismatic leaders of the period of the conquest of Canaan. Of equal importance, however, was the rise of a powerful cultural movement that demanded that a literary form be given to the experience of the Israelites. Sometime between 950 and 800 B.C. a number of writers, some of whom were members of the palace hierarchy at Jerusalem and some of whom were associated with other great shrines, decided that the nation needed a story of its origins. Possessing an astonishingly wide vision, they tried to make sense of the chaotic mass of legends, songs, cultic practices, prayers, sayings, rituals, proverbs, and laws that constituted the traditions of the different tribes. Some of these elements had already been given literary form, but there was as yet no comprehensive narrative of the history of Yahweh's great deeds and of the experiences of the people of Yahweh from the time of Abraham (and indeed earlier). It was to this task that the group of writers under David and Solomon turned, producing the bulk of the material found in Genesis, Exodus, Numbers, Judges, and Samuel.

After the kingdom divided following the death of Solomon, the Northern Kingdom (Israel) developed its own version of the national tradition. The theme of these writers was a great one: to trace how Yahweh had acted on behalf of Israel in the past, and how individuals and the nation as a whole had responded to these acts. With artistry and psychological insight they described the faith and the doubt of Abraham; the indulgence of Jacob by his father, Isaac; the jealousy of Joseph's brothers; the character of the mordant and depressed Saul; and the greatness and the weakness of David. In some instances they used a variety of advanced literary techniques, such as the placing of speeches in the mouths of the protagonists, whereas at other times the simplicity of the original account was allowed to stand unadorned. To this day, some of the stories in Genesis and the tale known as the Succession Document (2 Sam. 9–20; 1 Kings 1–2), which tells of David's troubles with his family and the revolt of his son Absalom, stand as masterpieces of historical narration.

The Prophets

Although the narrative writers tackled the problems of their times from the viewpoint of a sophisticated intellectual class interested in connecting the past with the present, the prophets took a more direct approach and assaulted the evils of the day by means of sermons and symbolic actions. Unlike the priests and kings, whose offices were hereditary and whose tasks were prescribed by rules and precedents, the prophets claimed to convey messages directly from God. Some wrote or at least had their followers record their comments, whereas others, such as Elijah and Elisha, did not write, although some of their sayings and pronouncements have survived.

Amos, the first of the great writing prophets, made his appearance in the Northern Kingdom in the eighth century B.C., some time before its destruction by the Assyrians. Amos spoke at a time when Israel had just defeated Damascus, but for the prophet the victory was no assurance of continued peaceful occupation of the land but rather a prelude to disaster. The people had been unfaithful to the demands of the covenant on which the possession of the land depended and had neglected the weak and the poor, while thronging to worship God by sacrifices and gifts at the various shrines throughout the kingdom:

> I hate, I despise your religious feasts; I cannot stand your assemblies. . . .
> Away with the noise of your songs! I will not listen to the music of your harps.
> But let justice roll on like a river, righteousness like a never failing stream!

> Hear this, you who trample the needy and do away with the poor of the land . . .
> skimping the measure, boosting the price and cheating with dishonest scales,
> buying the poor with silver and the needy for a pair of sandals, selling even the
>   sweepings with the wheat.

—Amos 5:21–24, 8:4–6

Hosea also preached in the Northern Kingdom, but somewhat closer to the time of its destruction than did Amos. His message was essentially the same as that of his predecessor, although he did not stress social negligence so much as the cult of idols and the political errors that this had led Israel to commit. His uniqueness consists of his contribution of a new terminology to describe Israel's failure. He spoke of his nation's sin as that of a wife who is unfaithful to her true husband (God) and runs instead after lovers (idols). Hosea describes the relationship that was established between God and Israel during the days of the Exodus as being like a marriage contract, but Israel had become unfaithful. Nevertheless, Yahweh so loves Israel that he will take her back again:

> How can I give you up, Ephraim? How can I hand you over, Israel?
> How can I treat you like Admah?
> My heart is changed within me; all my compassion is aroused.
> I will not carry out my fierce anger, nor will I turn and devastate Ephraim.
> For I am God, and not man—the Holy One among you.
> I will not come in wrath.
>
> *—Hosea 11:8–9*

In typical prophetic fashion, Hosea made his point by way of symbolic action: he actually took a prostitute as a wife and loved her despite her infidelities.

The greatest prophet of the eighth century B.C. was Isaiah (Isa. 1–40). Like Hosea, Isaiah regarded the basic problem facing Israel as the lack of loving closeness to God among the people. Self-satisfied and smug, they instead were pursuing their own ways without paying attention to the terms of the covenant. Isaiah saw Assyria as the instrument of God's judgment on Israel, but one that would itself be disciplined after fulfilling God's purposes. However dark a picture he painted, however, Isaiah offered hope for the future and predicted a glorious kingdom ruled by a king who would sway the hearts of people by love rather than by force or fear.

The Deuteronomist Historian

Although the eighth century B.C. closed with the destruction of the Northern Kingdom and the deportation of many of its inhabitants, the bulk of its theological traditions and its literature passed into the possession of Judah, the Southern Kingdom. Among these were the traditions regarding the ancient covenant renewal ceremony held at the sanctuary at Shechem. Here a particular viewpoint of the history of Israel had been given special preeminence and eventually found its way into written form that today is the core of the Book of Deuteronomy. This book in turn came to form the preface or introduction to a panoramic history of Israel from the occupation of the land to the fall of Jerusalem in 587 B.C., composed by an anonymous writer of the sixth century B.C., usually called the Deuteronomist Historian (D).

This interpretation of Israelite history is the most thoroughgoing in the Bible and one of the most impressive intellectual feats of the ancient world. It attempts to account for the fall of both the Northern and Southern Kingdoms in terms of the Sinai covenant, which both of them failed to observe. Out of all the nations, God had chosen Israel to be his special possession, not because of any merit on its part but solely because he loved it:

> The Lord did not set his affection on you and choose you because you were more numerous than other peoples, for you were the fewest of all peoples. But it was because the Lord loved you and kept the oath he swore to your forefathers that he brought you out with a mighty hand and redeemed you from the land of slavery, from the power of Pharaoh king of Egypt. Know therefore that the Lord your God is God; he is the faithful God, keeping his covenant of love to a thousand generations of those who love him and keep his commands.
>
> *—Deuteronomy 7:7–9*

However, God could not be served with divided loyalty:

> Hear, O Israel: The Lord our God, the Lord is one. Love the Lord your God with all
> your heart and with all your soul and with all your strength.
>
> *—Deuteronomy 6:4–5*

The promise of the land was a conditioned promise to be fulfilled only if Israel was faithful to the covenant. For the Deuteronomist Historian, the entire period between the occupation of the land and the fall of the kingdoms was an endless cycle of infidelity. With each failure to live up to the terms of the covenant came a dissolution of the tribes or a failure of the monarchy. Worship of idols is viewed as inherently divisive and destructive. King after king "did evil in the sight of the Lord," with the result that the purpose for which the land was given was annulled. Because kings and people were unfaithful to him, God used the events of international history to punish his people. It was not God who had failed but the people and especially the kings, who were expected to live up to the high standards of an idealized Davidic kingship. Both the covenant at Sinai that Yahweh had made with Israel as a whole and the covenant he had made with the dynasty of David had been repeatedly broken. As a result, God had allowed both the Northern and Southern Kingdoms to fall prey to their enemies.

The Babylonian Exile and Monotheism: The Priestly History

The capture of Jerusalem and the dissolution of the Davidic state had a profound effect on the development of the next round of literary compositions that found their way into the Old Testament—Deutro, or Second Isaiah (Isa. 40–66)—and the anonymous compilation known as the Pentateuch (the first five books of the Bible). Second Isaiah has some of the most beautiful language of the Old Testament. This anonymous prophet addressed himself to the question of the restoration of Israel and what form it was to take. Although the Deuteronomist Historian hinted at a solution in the form of a renewed monarchy under a king after the likeness of David, Second Isaiah rejected this, saying that God has no need of temples or kingdoms but is more concerned with the human spirit:

> This is what the Lord says:
> "Heaven is my throne and the earth is my footstool.
> Where is the house you will build for me? Where will my resting place be?
> Has not my hand made all these things, and so they came into being?" declares the
>   Lord.
> "This is the one I esteem: he who is humble and contrite in spirit, and trembles at my
>   word."
>
> *—Isaiah 66:1–2*

What counted was not God's material presence but his spiritual presence within his people. God is fettered by neither temple nor people; his power rules the world and the course of history. With Second Isaiah true monotheism finally makes its appearance. Yahweh is no longer just the god of the nation of Israel, but the supreme God of all people, beside whom the deities of the nations are nonexistent.

Among those deported to Babylon at the time of the destruction of Jerusalem were the priests who had attended to the temple and conducted its rituals. This group in particular must have felt the impact of the end of the regular cult practices, and it responded characteristically. Faced with the problem of ensuring that the generation now growing up in Babylon would not lose contact with the viewpoint, laws, and customs of the nation and be swallowed up like the deportees of the Northern Kingdom, the Jerusalem priests made an effort to bring all the ancient traditions together into a comprehensive whole. Their work of compiling and editing can be traced in the first four books of the Old Testament—Genesis, Exodus, Leviticus, and Numbers—and is called *P,* or the Priestly History.

Convinced that the destructions of 721 and 587 B.C. came as a result of the failure of the people to know and obey the law, the priests resolved that this would never happen again. Taking the accounts of the older writers, they inserted new materials concerning cult practices and rituals and added a fresh editorial viewpoint: the belief that the God who in the beginning had called Abraham from the midst of the sinful people of Mesopotamia and snatched his descendants from Egypt would once more repeat the miracle for them. It was these writers who composed or appended the story of creation to Genesis (1:1–2:3) and organized the material of the early history of men from the time of Adam to Abraham, demonstrating artistically the care of God for Israel's ancestors and in particular his power, as contrasted with the nonexistent power of the deities of other nations. Their aim was to prove through history that despite appearances to the contrary, God had always cared for his people. Thus, although Jerusalem had been destroyed by the Babylonians, their gods were still nothing compared to Yahweh. Unlike the cosmological myths of the nations where the gods struggled against the forces of chaos, Yahweh was depicted as above and beyond these battles. He stood outside the forces of nature, and was neither one of them nor their sum total. For the composers of the Priestly History, the work of creation was an orderly process in which God systematically and calmly brought into being the whole universe. There was no danger of the creating deity or of the world itself falling victim to the forces of chaos, as in the pagan myths. Furthermore, it was this same God who continued to care for his people even in their apparently desperate circumstances, surrounded and about to be engulfed by the materially and culturally powerful peoples of Mesopotamia.

The Evolution of Judaism

Postexilic Israel was radically different from the Israel that preceded it. Gone was the structure of the state, the kings, their administrators, their staffs, and their armies. Politically speaking, Israel was reduced to the role of an insignificant temple-state in the huge empires of the Persians and of the Macedonians who succeeded them. The glorious restoration promised by the prophets had not come to pass. The Day of the

Lord, when a reckoning of history was to be made, had been postponed. Nor were the inhabitants of this new, shrunken state the only people who claimed descent from Abraham. There were large communities of Jews, as they now began to be called, in Egypt, Mesopotamia, and elsewhere, and the needs of this new people of Yahweh were altogether different from those of the Israel of the past. More and more it was the observance of the Mosaic law that determined who belonged to the community of Israel and who did not. The formation of the Jewish religion was under way. It should be understood, however, that the term *Judaism* was (and is) a very loose term covering many different interpretations of Israelite theology and law.

The essential problem faced by the restored community in Judah was how it was to live until the promises of restoration made by the prophets were fulfilled. There was complete agreement that the tragic destruction of Jerusalem and the Babylonian exile had occurred because of the infidelity of Israel to Yahweh and his covenant, and the new community was determined that such a tragedy would not repeat itself. The difficulty lay in determining exactly what constituted loyalty to the covenant. What were Yahweh's expectations? What, precisely, were the terms of the covenant?

In the past the covenant had been somewhat loosely defined in terms of a personal relationship between God and his people. Now a more precise definition of this relationship was sought so that henceforth there would be no misunderstanding of what Yahweh expected of the individual and the community. The laws of the past regarding moral behavior, ritual, and worship now began to be interpreted as constitutional mandates regulating behavior, whereas previously they had been regarded, as they were in all the ancient Mesopotamian law codes, as simply descriptions of legal practice. Henceforth the key to proper behavior was whether a particular action was or was not in conformity with the law of Israel. To live in conformity with the terms of the covenant meant that knowledge of the law as embodying Yahweh's wishes was essential. The new era was inaugurated sometime around 400 B.C., when the scribe Ezra read the Mosaic law to the assembled community and explained it to them. The Feast of the Tabernacles was then held, and after it the people solemnly committed themselves to observe the law in all its requirements.

The new approach had the advantage of exactitude. Those who knew and obeyed the law could be assured that they were, minimally, not violating the covenant. The question of what constituted the Law of God rose to foremost importance, and it became the task of a whole class of professional interpreters to determine the answer. Prophets were not as needed so much as skilled editors, theologians, scholars, and lawyers. In addition, the presence of large communities of Jews outside Judah called for different kinds of institutions to meet their needs, and in time the synagogue, a place of prayer and instruction, took its place beside the family as a major focus of Jewish life.

Society in Israel: The Family and the Status of Women

Social and economic conditions in Israel's early centuries were very different from those in Egypt or the city-states of Mesopotamia. Farming depended on available rainfall, not on irrigation. There were no huge, intrusive bureaucracies governing everyday life. Even the ideology of land ownership was different. In Israel, Yahweh was the sole lord of the land, but he had no earthly representative to claim the land on his behalf. Religious practices put limitations on the use of land: the poor were allowed to glean the leftovers from the harvest, and passers-by could satisfy their hunger by helping themselves to crops along the wayside. Even the land itself got a rest: every seventh year it was to be left fallow.

In another and more fundamental sense, the social underpinnings of life in Israel and in its powerful neighbors were different. The Israelites believed that the desert had been their birthplace; there they had become a people, and from there they had emerged to occupy Canaan. They looked back with nostalgia to the idealized visions of desert simplicity and equality. This belief was at the root of the prophets' opposition to amassing great wealth, to "joining field to field," to taking interest on loans, and to the whole cycle of agricultural and commercial life. In early times pastures and watering holes had been held in common, and boundaries had been left poorly defined. Even the occupation of the land of Canaan had been worked into this idyllic picture of communal brotherhood. It was believed that at the time of the invasion, equal lots had been cast to decide which tribe was to get which portion of the land. The belief went even deeper. The ideal Israelite was the faithful man who had Yahweh himself for his lot or portion:

> The Lord is my portion, my share, and my cup;
> Thou holdest my lot.
>
> —*Psalms 16:5*

There was deep attachment to the family's ancestral land, and many devices were available for keeping it within the family. Daughters who received land were expected to marry within the clan, and if a landowner died childless, the inheritance reverted to his brothers or uncles. A man was bound to marry his widowed, childless sister-in-law.

From early times Israelite families were patriarchal. One of the common words used to describe the family in Hebrew is *beth ab,* "the house of one's father." In the early period the family consisted of a man's wife (or wives), his sons and their wives, his servants, and the resident aliens, widows, and orphans who lived under his protection. A husband had practically despotic power over his family in these early years. Children could be sold into slavery by their father or even put to death by him as clan head. Wives, like children, came under the direct and immediate control of their husbands. Along with servants and cattle, they were listed among a man's possessions.

As was the custom throughout most of the ancient world and is still common in many countries, marriage was regarded primarily as an alliance among families and as a way of cementing clan relations and excluding outsiders. In marriage an Israelite woman left her parents and was joined to her husband's clan, adopting his ancestors and religious customs. A husband had wide grounds on which to divorce his wife, but she could not divorce him. When repudiated, however, she took with her all her personal property as well as whatever goods she had received from her parents.

With the growth of the monarchy and the development of urban living, many of these practices died away or were mitigated. Living conditions in towns set a limit on the number of families that could be housed under one roof. It began to be expected that sons would leave their father's house upon marriage and set up their own homes. The state took into its hands such traditionally familial prerogatives as blood vengeance and the more severe forms of family discipline. Clan solidarity was deliberately weakened by the state, and in time the idea of individual responsibility emerged. The prophet Jeremiah argued against the old proverb "The fathers have eaten sour grapes, and the children's teeth are set on edge," saying that the individual, not his parents or ancestors, is responsible for his own sins (Jer. 31:29).

Before the Babylonian Exile women participated in public assemblies as singers, dancers, and priestesses, and shared fully in the annual cycle of agricultural festivals. The cult of the Canaanite goddess of fertility, Astarte, gave a prominent place to women in its mythology and cult practices. Despite the protests of the prophets, women served in shrines and sanctuaries as sacred prostitutes, following traditional Mesopotamian practices. However, after the Exile and the complete victory of Yahweh over the competing gods of Canaan, the public role of women in religion was drastically curtailed. Now only a single male deity, Yahweh, was to be worshiped; all others, male and female alike, were banned. Worship was centralized in Jerusalem, and all the local, rural shrines were destroyed. Temple rituals were the sole responsibility of an organized, hereditary, male priesthood. Women, along with children, foreigners, slaves, and imbeciles, were excluded from the inner precincts of the temple, where the main activities and sacrifices took place. When the synagogue evolved, women were allowed to participate in its services but they were not required to attend. Because the law did not allow mothers to carry their infants outside the home on the sabbath, this meant that at certain times in their lives many mothers would have been unable to attend the synagogue or, if they lived in Judah, the Temple at Jerusalem.

The increasing prominence of the law after the Exile also had an important impact on the status of women. A large portion of the Mosaic law was devoted to ethical prescriptions deriving from the primary law of the covenant, the Ten Commandments, but the law was also dedicated to prescriptions regarding ritual purity. As greater and greater emphasis was given to monotheism, the concept of Yahweh's holiness grew in importance. If he were to be approached, it had to be by people whose hands as well as hearts were clean. Holiness and uncleanness were incompatible. Anything having to do with the worship of Yahweh, whether it was the sacred vessels used in the sacrifices, the temple itself, or the priests, had to be without blemish. If Yahweh was holy, then his people, too, had to be holy: "You shall be holy, for I, the Lord your God, am holy" (Lev. 19:2). To fulfill its destiny as a sacred nation, Israel had to exclude every form of impurity, moral or ritual.

Among the many items deemed ritually impure in the holiness code of the law were discharges of the body such as blood and semen. The emission of semen in sexual intercourse produced uncleanness in both man and woman, but it was of short duration. By contrast, menstrual blood and the blood of childbirth made a woman impure for much longer periods. If a woman gave birth to a male child, she was unclean for 7 days, and a 33-day period had to elapse before she could enter the sanctuary; the amount of time was doubled if the child born was female. The practical result of this was that, for a large portion of their lives, women were regarded as unclean, and could not enter the temple or participate in cultic activity.

Another change that had far-reaching consequences for the status of women in postexilic Israel was the strengthening of the family as a social unit. Concubinage disappeared, and married children were urged to set up their own households. This had the effect of firmly consigning women to the private realm of the family and to their roles as mothers, wives, and homemakers. The influence of this division of gender responsibilities was to be enormously expanded in later centuries with the emergence of Christianity as the majority religion of the Mediterranean world. This ancient gender division has had incalculable effects on the status of women to the present day.

Apocalyptism and Eschatology

Despite the growth in the importance of the law in the development of Judaism, the old way of regarding the covenant did not disappear entirely. Yahweh was still viewed as the Lord of History, but more attention now began to be paid to his future ordering of history than to his actions in the past. As early as the sixth century B.C., the intervention of Yahweh, now seen as the God of all peoples and of all human history, began to be interpreted in new ways. It took the form of apocalyptism, the revelation of the hidden plan of God in history; its content was a focus on the final events (in Greek, the *eschata*) or eschatology, of world history.

In the apocalyptic view of things, the present world is meaningless, evil, and destined for destruction. In due course God will intervene to bring it to a fitting end and inaugurate his kingdom. In the meantime, the faithful must patiently await this final intervention of God in history.

Apocalyptic writers fleshed out this vision by borrowing Persian imagery and interpreting history as a great cosmic struggle between the forces of good and evil. They surveyed all of history up to their own time in symbolic language and then looked to the future, where they saw a titanic conflict throughout the world: Israel is attacked by the devil using the empires of this world as his instruments. There is much suffering, but in the end God intervenes. Satan and his forces are overthrown, the old order is swept away, and God creates in its place a new heaven and a new Earth. The chosen are then called into his kingdom to enjoy everlasting bliss.

Apocalyptic viewpoints were shared by many Middle Eastern peoples besides the Jews, though we tend to know more about Jewish and Christian apocalyptic ideas because of the survival of such books as Daniel and Revelations. Daniel is the earliest biblical work in the fully apocalyptic style. Although purporting to have been written in the sixth century B.C., it was actually composed in the second. Its intent was to console the Jews of Palestine who were suffering violent persecution at the hands of their Macedonian overlords. The author of the book attempted to answer the question of when the world would end and predicted that after a succession of four world empires—the Chaldaean Empire of the Babylonians, a Median Empire, and the Persian and Macedonian empires—a Messianic "Son of Man" would establish a kingdom over which he would rule forever. It was in a context where apocalyptic viewpoints such as these circulated—and dominated—that the most influential religions of the West germinated.

Chapter 4

The Emergence of Greek Civilization

GEOGRAPHY AND HISTORY

Greece is a difficult country to classify geographically. From one viewpoint it looks like a typical Mediterranean country. Most of its contacts are with the Near East or other Mediterranean lands. It enjoys a mild Mediterranean climate with cool, wet winters and dry, hot summers. The grape and the olive grow well there. Yet from another perspective Greece must be regarded as part of Europe, and in particular of the Balkans, of which it is a peninsula extending into the Mediterranean. Through the Black Sea it has contacts with the steppe lands of Eurasia. Aristotle was right to say that "the Hellenic people occupy an intermediate geographical position."

Yet another perspective on the subject comes from the poetically minded Plato, who said of his fellow Greeks: "We sit like frogs around a pond." By the "pond," he meant the Aegean Sea, the common meeting place and battleground of the Greek states surrounding it. Plato's description is, in fact, quite accurate. No part of mainland Greece is more than 35 miles from the sea. At least before industrialization brought smog, a traveler sailing across the Aegean never lost sight of land; some mountaintop, such as Mount Ida on Crete, Mount Athos or Mount Olympus on the mainland, or some island or headland, was always visible on the horizon.

Perhaps this is the best way to think of Greece: a country with a lake at its center. In contrast to the well-defined states of Mesopotamia and Egypt, with their great rivers and flat, alluvial plains, Greece is a land of diversity. Sharply defined regions made up of bays, gulfs, scattered islands, headlands, mountain valleys, and coastal plains set a pattern of fragmentation that is in turn reflected in Greek politics and history.

Precisely because of this diversity there has never been a Greece—or Hellas, as the Greeks called it—the way there has been, say, an Egypt. Greeks have been united to the extent that they have shared a common language and some common cultural practices. But Greece never became a unified state. No city rose the way Rome did in Italy to unify the land and give it a national identity and citizenship. Greeks always remained citizens of particular cities. There were Corinthian citizens, Athenian citizens, and Theban citizens, but never Greek citizens.

THE ORIGINS OF GREEK CULTURE

The earliest periods of Greek history—the Mycenaean Age and the following Dark Ages—are a blend of European warrior traditions and of influences reaching Greece from western Asia and Egypt.

The middle centuries of the second millennium were a period of comparatively great wealth in Europe. By about 1500 B.C. a uniform material culture emphasizing military display extended over much of the continent. Goods were accumulated to impress others and provide proof of status. Yet there were no cities, no great temples or palaces along Mesopotamian or Egyptian lines. No complex political hierarchies and no massive bureaucracies attempted to regulate life. European preferences ran to looser forms of social and political organization such as the chiefdom, a type of society where the person in authority maintained himself by his ability to acquire and redistribute prestige goods to his followers. The possession of gleaming weapons and armor, exotic clothes, beautiful women, large retinues of followers and servants, and herds of cattle, sheep, and horses were both a proof and a guarantee of the chief's authority. Chiefs doled out gifts as marks of esteem to their followers and as ways of building their own power. Surrounded by their companion warriors and the elders of the community, these chiefs presided over small territorial kingdoms. They spent much of their time in hunting and athletics, and still more time in idleness and feasting. "There is nothing more perfect than a banquet," says Odysseus, Homer's hero, in anticipation of one of the many feasts he attended. Swaggering, brawling, heavy-drinking, and touchy, the chiefs fought each other in endless rounds of warfare. The more famous ones were buried under large earthen mounds, surrounded by their weapons, hunting dogs, chariots, horses, and, on occasion, their favorite retainers. Huge stone and earth burial mounds, fortifications, and religious assembly areas demonstrate that these chiefdoms were at times capable of truly large-scale undertakings.

It is from the perspective of this age-old culture of Europe as much as from the viewpoint of the influences of the Middle East that we need to approach the study of Greek history. In Greece there was never any simple, one-time-only transference of technology or culture from East to West—conquest by Egypt, for instance—but rather a long period of picking and choosing by the Greeks themselves. Greece was preeminently a borderland region, and, like so many borderland areas, it benefited from being on the fringes of two worlds. Although far enough away from the major powers of the Near East to escape political domination (and too poor to be considered worth conquering), Greece was close enough for a rich cultural and commercial interchange to take place. The Greeks themselves dictated the terms of the exchange.

THE MINOAN AND MYCENAEAN AGES

In the 1870s A.D., great interest in early Greek history was stimulated by the spectacular finds of amateur archaeologist Heinrich Schliemann at the sites of ancient Troy and Mycenae. This interest was maintained by the discovery in A.D. 1900 of a massive palace complex of Knossos on Crete by Sir Arthur Evans. Hundreds of sites have since been excavated in the Aegean and the adjacent Balkan areas, and archaeologists and historians have continuously struggled to place the different finds in some kind of cultural and chronological order. The result has been the slow unfolding of one of the most brilliant of the world's once-forgotten cultures.

Minoan Crete

We have no idea what the people of early Crete called themselves. Evans dubbed them "Minoans" after their legendary King Minos, famous in Greek myth for his palace with its maze (the labyrinth) and its inmate the Minotaur, the half-man, half-bull offspring of his adulterous wife.

It was perhaps by way of Anatolia (in modern Turkey) that civilization first made its way to Crete around 2500 B.C. Five hundred years later the people of Crete were organizing their lives around complex structures called "palaces" by Evans. There were at least four major palaces—at Knossos, Phaistos, Mallia, and Zakros—but smaller complexes have also been found elsewhere on the island.

The palaces were complicated structures consisting of a honeycomb of residential and storage rooms designed around a large courtyard. The palaces varied considerably in size; Knossos, for example, covered over 185 acres, with a population of about 12,000. They were well constructed. The lower courses of the walls consisted of stone and the upper generally of mud brick with timber reinforcements to help resist earthquake shocks, which were common in Crete. Illumination for the inner rooms was provided through light wells, and drainage and water supplies were good. Oil, wine, and grain were stored in huge jars, and goods such as clothes were kept in lead-lined stone chests. Many of the rooms and passageways were decorated with colorful frescoes depicting various aspects of Cretan life. The men appear beardless, wearing codpieces or kilts, and the women have elaborate hair designs and dresses with flounced sleeves and pinched waists. Exquisite garden scenes portray flourishing plant and animal life. Minoan artists excelled at jewelry; they produced marvels of delicate carvings in ivory, faience, gold and silver, and precious and semiprecious stones. They were also masters at vase painting, especially on marine themes.

The Minoan-Mycenaean World

Most of our understanding of Cretan society depends on our interpretation of the functions of the palaces. Presumably kings presided over them, as they did in Mesopotamia, receiving their legitimacy from their religious and military roles. Unlike Mesopotamia, however, there were no large temple complexes on Crete. Worship was conducted in mountain caves and at mountaintop sanctuaries. The palaces themselves may have been religious centers, a belief sustained by the alignment of the palace at Knossos with Mt. Iouchtas and that at Phaistos with the Kamaros cave sanctuary. It is unclear what kinds of political relations existed among the palaces of Crete. They probably maintained themselves as independent, self-ruling states, with Knossos, perhaps, exercising some kind of honorary overlordship.

Writing was present on Crete in pictographic form from the third millennium B.C., but at some time after 1700 B.C. a syllabic script called Linear A by the archaeologists was introduced. It has not been deciphered, but its successor, Linear B, dating from the time of the arrival of the Mycenaean mainlanders (ca. 1450 B.C.), has been identified as Greek. Both were used for recording palace transactions and keeping inventories of food, clothes, weapons, and the like. Most of the writing perished long ago because it was done on clay tablets, skin, and bark. Only the accidental burning of an archive, which baked the tablets hard, has preserved any of them. It is from these rather limited sources that we have to make our inferences about life in the palaces. In general, it is safe to infer that the palaces functioned as regulators of the various commercial, agricultural, and industrial activities that took place in the regions surrounding them. Trained scribes and administrators kept track of and controlled local life, but how closely they did so is hard to tell. The size and wealth of the palaces indicate something more than merely local exploitation of agricultural riches, and there appears to have been a substantial volume of overseas trade. Minoan exports consisted of such things as wool, oil, and timber as well as finished goods, including pottery; raw materials and luxury items were the principal imports. Located on the fringes of both the barbarian and civilized worlds, Crete was in an ideal position to act as a trade intermediary. Its merchant and naval fleets must have been significant, and efficient-looking warships make their appearance in the frescoes from the nearby island of Thera.

If the temple-states of the Near East are to be taken as models for Crete, we should probably expect to find a close intermingling of religious and civic life. Female deities were common. Predominant among them was the Great Mother Goddess, who is depicted in many forms, including that of a goddess grasping two snakes—the symbols of her divinity—and that of a huntress, the so-called Lady of the Beasts. Trees and pillars were worshiped (in a way reminiscent of Canaanite practice), and the sanctuaries located on the mountaintops suggest the "high places" that the Hebrew prophets attacked so often.

THE EMERGENCE OF THE GREEKS

European Bronze Age	ca. 2500–1200 B.C.
Minoan Age	ca. 2200–1400 B.C.
Indo-European incursions	ca. 2300–2000 B.C.
Mycenaean Age	ca. 1600–1100 B.C.
Dark Ages	ca. 1100–800 B.C.
Evolution of the *polis* and settlement of Greeks overseas (the colonial movement)	ca. 750–500 B.C.
Evolution of the hoplite (heavy infantry or phalanx) style of fighting	ca. 700 B.C.
Archaic Age	ca. 800–500 B.C.
Arrival of the Persians in the Aegean	545 B.C.
Classical Age	ca. 500–300 B.C.

What shows up in the archaeological record is almost exclusively the remains of elite life. Women (at least of the upper classes) were prominent in Minoan religious and social life. They appear in processions and at athletic events, and they even participated in the mysterious bull-leaping ceremony. The majority of ordinary people who actually did the work of building the palaces and maintaining the economy are, as is often the case, archaeologically invisible.

Minoans and Mycenaeans

Sometime around 1450 B.C. Mycenaeans from mainland Greece came to power in Crete. How this came about is unclear, but most historians believe the island was conquered by force. A number of sites show signs of destruction at this time, but the destruction was not massive. A Mycenaean elite simply replaced a Minoan elite in the palaces. Probably little changed in the countryside among the rural population. Recordkeeping was in Greek, as evidenced by the introduction of a new script, Linear B. There is good reason to believe that Knossos dominated most of central and western Crete until about 1200 B.C., when it was burned and looted, a victim of the unrest that also brought down mainland Mycenaean palaces.

THE MYCENAEAN AGE

The Mycenaean Age of Greece lasted over twice as long as the Classical Age of Greek history (ca. 500–300 B.C.), yet we know more about some years, months, and even days of the latter than we do of the four and a half centuries of the Mycenaean, despite the existence of more than 5,000 tablets dealing with the period in a language we can translate. Unfortunately, most of them concern a single year in the life of only one mainland palace toward the end of the thirteenth century B.C., and the rest relate to Mycenaean Knossos of over two centuries earlier. None refers to what we could call traditional historical events—battles, treaties, invasions, laws, internal struggles for power, and the like—and what passes for Mycenaean history is principally a reconstruction of its beginning and end, and an attempt to evoke from the archaeological evidence some idea of the kind of life associated with the different phases of Mycenaean development.

The first phase of Mycenaean civilization is the Shaft Grave era, which lasted from roughly 1600 to 1500 B.C. It is known principally from the contents of the 5 shaft graves uncovered by Schliemann in A.D. 1876 (one more was discovered later in the same grave circle) and the 24 found by Greek archaeologists in A.D. 1951 and 1952. The former were the richer and yielded an incredible trove of golden crowns, diadems, masks, and jewelry as well as hundreds of swords, daggers, spearheads, knives, axes, arrowheads, and shields. There were also gold and silver goblets, alabaster and faience vases, rings, combs, disks, silver boxes, pieces of amber, and fragments of linen armor. The graves represent about a century of use and were periodically opened for new burials.

Except for the graves themselves, which indicate continuous occupation of the site for a long time, there is no evidence of the palaces or dwellings that went with them. They may be buried under later buildings or have been of such a temporary nature that they rapidly disappeared and were eventually replaced by more permanent structures. The contents of the graves suggest a warlike society engaged in raiding and fighting but also open to foreign contact and especially susceptible to Cretan influences. Although much of the art is specifically Mycenaean, with its peculiar interest in violent, narrative scenes and bizarre monsters and animals, the influence of Minoan artists and craftsmen is everywhere apparent. We thus should see early Mycenaean society as being fairly typical of the warrior culture that extended over much of Bronze Age Europe, but differing from it because of the close contact between the Mycenaean aristocrats and the high civilization of Crete.

By the mid-fifteenth century B.C. the Mycenaeans were still burying their dead in communal fashion, although they were now placed in great beehivelike *tholos* (vaulted) tombs under mounds of earth. We know of more than 80 of these tombs, scattered from Thessaly to the Peloponnese, but few have been found intact, although those that have survived probably provide a fair indication of what all of them contained. Three tombs, Vaphio, Myrsinochorion, and Dendra, supply the bulk of the remains. These include the usual arsenal of weapons, with the addition of something that had not been found before: a bronze cuirass with greaves and a boar-tusk helmet with metal cheek pieces. The Vaphio tomb also contained a hoard of beautiful gems and gold drinking cups.

The tombs themselves are indicative of the growing power and technical ability of the Mycenaeans. One of them, the Treasury of Atreus, dates from around the end of the *tholos*-tomb period and represents the culmination of Mycenaean architectural ability. Having survived intact for over 3,000 years, it is one of the architectural wonders of the world. Its vault, over 40 feet high inside, was the largest in the world until Hadrian built the Pantheon in Rome in the second century A.D. Closely fitting blocks of stone form a marvelous corbeled vault, and the huge entryway is roofed by blocks weighing over 100 tons. Although the Treasury of Atreus is contemporary with the palace phase of Mycenaean culture, there is again no evidence of palaces and towns during the main period of the *tholos* tombs.

Mycenaean Palaces   Sometime in the fifteenth century B.C. the Mycenaean assimilation of Cretan civilization was complete, and around 1400 B.C. the Mycenaean world entered its third and most developed phase: the period of the palaces. Simultaneously, in foreign trade Minoans gave way to mainlanders as the middlemen in the commerce between Europe and the east, and Mycenaean wares began to appear in Egypt, Syria, Phoenicia, and Sicily and southern Italy in the west. The militaristic Mycenaean chiefdoms of the past now became more like the palaces of Crete: administrative centers attempting, on Minoan lines, to control the commercial, industrial, and agricultural activities of the regions they ruled. One of the main concerns of the palaces was the maintenance of the force of chariots on which their defense rested.

We know of major palaces at Mycenae, Tiryns, Athens, Orchomenus, Thebes, and Pylos. There may be others among the hundreds of known but unexplored sites. None of the main palaces is as large or as elaborate as their Cretan counterparts. Mycenae, for instance, was only 74 acres, compared to 185 for Knossos. Unlike the Cretan palaces, the typical Mycenaean palace had as its center a great hall, or *megaron,* whose focus was a central hearth. It was entered through a wide, columned portico from a courtyard. The techniques of construction used in Crete were also used on the mainland, although the Mycenaean palaces tended to be a lot darker than those on Crete. They were well drained and had good water supplies. The *megaron* served as a central meeting place where the king could hold court, receive reports, give banquets, and generally conduct public business. Outside the great hall were the residential quarters and storage facilities for wine, oil, grain, textiles, metals, and war materiel. There were workshops for the smiths, masons, potters, chariot builders, wheelwrights, tailors, and textile workers, who were essential to the palace's functioning. All were closely supervised by a corps of administrators who were able to write; handwriting experts have determined that these were not professional scribes but palace administrators who had other functions to perform.

As economic centers, the palaces were by no means negligible. One of them, Pylos, controlled the production of 400 smiths in groups of up to 26; at Mycenaean Knossos there were almost 600 textile workers. The smiths at Pylos received exact amounts of metal intended for the manufacture of specific items so that control over production remained exclusively in the hands of the central administrators. This corps of closely supervised specialists provided for the needs of the individual kingdoms as well as for the export market. Thousands of stored pots ready for use or distribution have been found at Pylos and Thebes, and the tablets clearly indicate that there was large-scale production of wool on Crete and flax on the mainland, as well as of more common products such as oil, wine, fruits, spices, honey, and livestock. A network of roads, some of which can still be traced, together with their bridges and culverts, also played an important role in the Mycenaean economy.

Mycenaean society had at its head a king, or *wanax* as he is called in the Linear B tablets, assisted by a number of officials, the "Followers" or "Companions," who acted as the king's delegates and enforced his will throughout the kingdom. They also acted as his military commanders. At Pylos, for example there were 11 regiments, each commanded by a "Follower." Although they owned rural estates, the Followers actually lived in the capital. In the countryside lived yet another group of aristocratic landholders. The approximately 200 villages and towns found at Pylos were administered by officials with the title *pasireu* or *basileus,* the same title given centuries later by Homer to the Greek chiefs at Troy. Some estates were held by women with religious titles, evidently priestesses who presided over the cults of female deities. Tenants and subtenants cultivated the land on behalf of the landowners, but in addition to the nobility and tenants there was a class of small landholders who leased and worked public land. Collectively the landowners were known as the *damos*

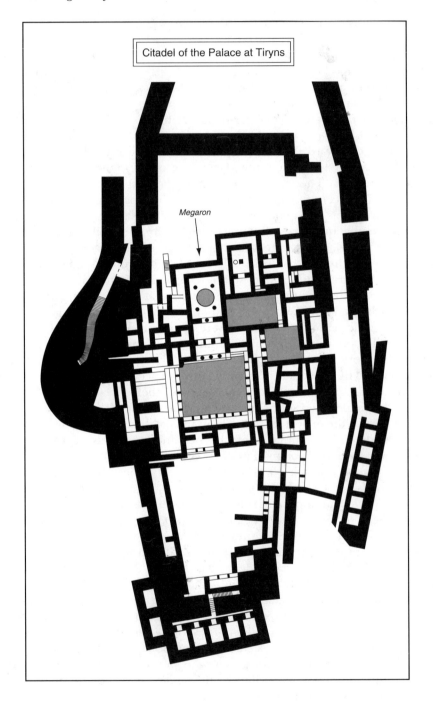

Citadel of the Palace at Tiryns

Megaron

(in later Greek, *demos,* or "people"). All citizens were expected to serve in the armed forces and had their own arms. There is evidence of slaves at the bottom of society, and they seemed to have played a major role in the industrial activities of the palaces. It is unlikely that a free merchant class existed because it was at least the intention of the palaces to exercise complete control over all commercial activities.

Religion had an integral role in the organization of palace activities, and the gods were served by a variety of priests and priestesses. Altars were located by the hearths of the great halls, which suggests a traditional association of throne, hearth, and altar. Although the Great Mother Goddess was a major deity all over Greece, as she was on Crete, the male deities Zeus, Poseidon, Hermes, Apollo, and Dionysus are represented strongly in the Linear B tablets. Athena, Hera, Artemis, and Ares also appear in the tablets.

The End of Mycenaean Civilization

About a century or a century and a half after their founding, all the Mycenaean palaces, with the exception of Athens, were attacked and burned. In some instances the surrounding areas were so disastrously affected that major social and economic changes resulted. When the palace at Pylos was destroyed, the site was never reoccupied, and the population of the region dropped to perhaps 10 percent of what it had been. In Boeotia the number of occupied sites dropped from 27 to 3, and in Laconia from 30 to 7. The surviving inhabitants withdrew to more defensible places or fled to other parts of Greece, such as Achaea or Attica, or even overseas. Mycenae and Attica recovered, but a second round of disturbances around 1150 B.C. finished off the former. By the end of the century Greece had entered a period of economic, social, and technological backwardness. All the arts of high civilization—writing, fresco painting, seal engraving, faience making, ivory carving, even the shaping of stone for building purposes— were lost. The trade network that had united the Aegean area with the Near East collapsed, and Greece slipped into a period of isolation broken by only the most limited contacts with the outside world.

The identity of the destroyers of Mycenaean civilization is one of the great mysteries of ancient history. The Greeks of later ages did indeed know something of the calamities of the late thirteenth and twelfth centuries B.C., but not their magnitude. They believed that the sack of Troy was the beginning of a period of troubles for all of Greece and that when the returning heroes reached their homelands, they found them unsettled by intrigues, political unrest, and pressures from outside invasion. Of the wholesale decline from high civilization into barbarism, however, the Greeks knew nothing.

Modern explanations range from many differently identified groups of invaders to hypotheses of catastrophic climatic change resulting in prolonged droughts and social unrest. In all the explanations at least one factor remains constant: the latter half of the thirteenth century B.C. and the whole of the twelfth were periods of widespread disturbances and destruction, not just in Greece proper but all over the Aegean world and the eastern Mediterranean. About 1220 B.C. Egypt was invaded by a coalition of Libyans and northern peoples, and in the list of the

Despite its massive defensive walls, a section of which is shown here, Mycenae was violently assaulted and sacked in the twelfth century B.C.

invaders' names is the suggestive title *Akaiwasha* or *Achaean,* the principal title given by Homer to the Mycenaean Greeks at Troy. Thereafter Egypt was constantly on the defensive against outsiders. Around 1200 B.C. the empire of the Hittites in Asia Minor was overwhelmed and its capital at Boghazkoi destroyed. Along the coasts of Asia Minor, Syria, and Phoenicia, a whole string of sites including Troy (level VIIa), Tarsus, Mersin, Ugarit, and Sidon went up in flames. We even have a record of the communications between the last king of Ugarit and the king of Cyprus in which there are complaints about threatening fleets of pirate ships.

In about 1190 B.C. Egypt was again invaded by northerners (the Sea Peoples), among whom are named the Peleset (the Philistines) and the Denyen (Danaans), one of the titles given by Homer to the Mycenaeans. At some point in the midst of these confusing movements of peoples the Mycenaean centers of power came under attack and collapsed. We do not know the exact chronology of the fall of the individual palaces, which quite easily could have been the handiwork of different groups of invaders arriving from varying places at different times or even the result of internal squabbles among the Mycenaeans themselves. There is no evidence of massive migrations of peoples; rather, there are suggestions of continuing unrest and small groups of raiding parties who at times combined to take on major projects such as the invasion of Egypt (or even the destruction of Troy as described by Homer, a joint effort of a number of states). In such a world the highly structured palace organization of the Mycenaeans, which depended on trade and widespread contacts with the east and north, would have had difficulty maintaining itself. Its essential imports and exports would have had little chance of getting through to their destinations, and the complicated social and organizational arrangements of the palaces would have had difficulty operating under the strained and unsettled conditions of the times.

THE DARK AGES

The darkness of the period following the collapse of Mycenaean society was brightened by a number of technological and cultural developments. In the eleventh century B.C. Athens, which had survived the upheavals and become host to numerous refugees, began to produce a fine new pottery called protogeometric. Iron, which had been known before the invasions, came into more general use for both weapons and agricultural implements. Masses of Greeks fleeing from the collapsing world of the Mycenaeans emigrated to Asia Minor and the offshore islands, where they laid the foundations for the rich culture that was to develop and flourish there for a millennium. Perhaps most importantly, memories of the great past survived in the songs of wandering bards or minstrels, and these eventually culminated in the epics of Homer composed at the end of the Dark Ages (750–725 B.C.).

Heroic poetry is common in many cultures. Such epics as the *Song of Roland* (French) and the *Cattle Raid of Cooley* (Gaelic) recount the deeds of the superhuman heroes of previous times. In a similar way, the bards of the Greek Dark Ages kept alive the exploits of long-dead warriors by borrowing from different eras of the past, whether from Mycenaean times, the period of the collapse of the palaces, or the subsequent Dark Ages. Over the centuries the traditions developed, and certain plots, such as the deeds of the Seven Against Thebes, the siege of Troy, and the Heracles legends, became standardized and were elaborated in great detail. The art of the poet was demonstrated by his ability to take a well-known tale and reweave it in such a way that, while remaining true to the basic story, he captivated his audience and made it sympathetic to his interpretation of the event. Thus Odysseus wept when he heard the tale of Troy sung, and congratulated (as well he could) the bard with the words,

> Demodocus, I praise you as the most outstanding of men. Either the Muse, Zeus' child taught you, or Apollo himself. You sing exceedingly well of the achievements of the Achaeans, their sufferings, and their labors. You might say you had been there yourself or heard the tale from someone who was.[1]

Although deriving from the bardic tradition, the poems of Homer have a complexity and sophistication not found in any other heroic poetry. They contrast noticeably with the savagery of the Celtic epics, for example. The Homeric tales are

---

[1]Homer, *The Odyssey*, 8.487–491.

bloody enough, but they are never bizarre. They are filled with a deep sense of humanity—its greatness, its sufferings, and its limitations.

Homeric Society

There is a debate over the identification of the society described by Homer. How much of his material derives from Mycenaean times? The poet talks knowledgeably of boar-tusk helmets and certain types of shields that he himself could not possibly have seen because he lived in later times, although they are indeed Mycenaean. Yet he knows nothing of the bureaucratic activities of the palaces that the decipherment of Linear B has revealed. Could Homeric society belong to the period of the fall of Mycenaean society, and is the story of the destruction of Troy a memory of that time? Or perhaps we should look at the period of the migrations to Asia Minor. Or, as seems most likely, is Homeric society to be assigned to a time in the Dark Ages themselves?

Although due allowance must be made for Homer's ability to transform the material that came down to him from many different periods, it is still possible to trace in broad outline the type of society whose moral values his poems enshrine. It was a world of small, practically autonomous units, each one economically self-sustaining and inward-looking. Their rulers were chieftains (*basileis,* sing. *basileus*) whose principal function was the preservation of the community in the face of constant outside aggression. They maintained themselves by forming a circle of companions, warriors like themselves, drawn from their own families, the community at large, and even footloose wanderers who had proven fighting ability. This social system was inherently unstable, however. The ruling chief had to maintain his position by providing lavish feasts for his friends and followers, giving gifts, and above all, showing successful leadership in battle. Strategic marriage alliances and success in the hunt and in athletic competitions were also important. Any one of his rival chiefs, especially the more charismatic types, might supplant him if he began to show weakness in any one of the required areas of competence.

It was this lifestyle that the bards of the Dark Ages celebrated in their songs. Homer's Greeks at Troy are portrayed as a loosely knit band of roughly equal chieftains supporting their paramount leader, Agamemnon, in a quest for honor, booty, and excitement (not necessarily in that order). The *Odyssey* is in good measure the story of what happens to a chiefdom when its ruler is gone for a long time and his relatives (his son in this instance) and retainers are unable to maintain the family's position. Immediately, other local chieftains begin to infringe on the paramount chief's household. When Odysseus returns he must reassert his authority with overabundant bloodshed.

The upper-class women of the Homeric sagas are very different from both their respectable but almost invisible counterparts of later times and the not-so-respectable courtesans (*hetairai*) who provided female companionship for those who could afford it. The women of the epics are clearly valued members of society. When

Long after Homer, the tradition of reciting selections from his poems became a permanent feature of one of Athens's great festivals, the Panathenaea. Here one of the competing rhapsodes recites his verses.

Odysseus goes off to Troy he has no reservations about leaving his household in the hands of his wife, Penelope, who in fact lives up to his expectations. She is presented as a clever and resourceful woman who for years outwits a houseful of suitors. Throughout the *Odyssey,* the goddess Athena acts as his adviser, and on occasion is needed to prod him into vigorous or even bloody action. Nausicaa, the princess of Phaeacia, counsels the shipwrecked Odysseus on how to get a favorable hearing in her father's palace: he is to throw himself at her mother's feet and ask her for help. Nevertheless, the role of women is clearly circumscribed by the conditions of heroic society itself. In an environment of intense competition women are used as pawns in marriage alliances and prizes in war. A sexual double standard prevailed. At Troy almost all the warriors had their mistresses, and Odysseus spent many years in a dalliance (admittedly divinely coerced) with the beautiful nymph Calypso. Yet the infidelity of Helen or Clytemnestra was seen as a threat to the very existence of the social

---

THE HOMERIC SYSTEM

In this episode from the *Iliad*, the heroes Sarpedon and Glaucus, allies of the Trojans, discuss their reasons for fighting. First, they have a contract with their own people, the Lycians; second, because death will come to all, they have a duty to themselves to die fighting bravely and winning glory.

> Sarpedon said to Glaucus, son of Hippolochus: "Glaucus, why do we receive special honors in Lycia in terms of food and drink? Why are the choicest portions of meat served to us and our cups of wine kept brimming over, and why do men look up to us as though we were gods? Moreover, we were given a large estate by the banks of the river Zanthus, fair with orchard lawns and vineyards and wheat-growing land. Therefore it is our duty to take our stand at the head of the Lycians and bear the brunt of the fight so that one Lycian may say to another: 'Our princes in Lycia eat the fat of the land and drink the best wine, but they are fine fellows; they fight well and are always at the front of the battle.' My good friend, if we could avoid this fight and live on forever, ageless and immortal, I would neither press forward myself in battle nor bid you to do so, but death in ten thousand shapes now hangs over our heads, and no man can escape him. Therefore, let us go forward and either win glory for ourselves or yield it to another."

—Homer, *The Iliad* (trans. Samuel Butler), 12.309–328

---

order itself. These gender roles and patterns of behavior were to have a long history in Greek social relations.

OUT OF THE DARKNESS: THE ARCHAIC AGE

The Greek Recovery, 850–700 B.C.

In the ninth century B.C. the Greek world, along with the rest of the eastern Mediterranean, began to emerge from the political chaos and economic depressions of the previous centuries. Western Asia, under the leadership of Assyria, revived first, and Greece soon followed.

Many factors were involved in the recovery. One of these was the simple fact that the Aegean world was close to the rich East, which could be easily reached by sea. Phoenician merchants were soon displaying their attractive manufactured goods to interested Greek buyers. On the Greek side the driving force was the desire of the aristocracy for luxury goods of all sorts to enhance their political and social standing. Good internal lines of communication provided by the Aegean, and the accessibility of central Europe and the Black Sea region, with their rich resources of grain, lumber, metals, and slaves, were also important reasons for the revival.

The Greeks were not content to remain on one end of a trade route controlled by middlemen. By 800 B.C. a permanent Greek trading post was established at Al-Mina in Syria. It played an important role not only in trade but also in the exchange of ideas and technology for the next 200 years. Shortly afterward, Greek traders appeared in the Bay of Naples, where the attraction was the excellent iron that could be obtained from the Etruscans of Italy. By 650 B.C. the Greeks had become so indispensable even in Egypt that the pharaohs allowed them to build a trading enclave at Naucratis, only 10 miles from the royal capital.

Migrations   As Greece recovered, its population quickly increased. It is estimated that between 800 and 750 B.C. the population of Athens quadrupled, and that in the next 50 years it doubled again. In response to the threat of famine from overpopulation, the confinements of life at home, and the opportunity for a better lifestyle, Greeks left their homes in the eighth century B.C. in a wave of overseas migration. Although some of the migrations were individual affairs, most were the organized activities of overcrowded communities. The emigrants were sent out by their states explicitly to establish new foundations (misleadingly called colonies) abroad. Between 750 and 500 B.C. hundreds of sites on the Black Sea coast, Sicily, southern Italy, and the western Mediterranean were occupied by land-hungry Greeks. With deliberate self-consciousness they set out to create new homes, maintain their culture, and resist assimilation. The leaders of these expeditions were aristocrats who were given special responsibility for choosing the site, dividing the land, and drawing up the laws for the new foundations.

A somewhat similar movement was occurring across the southern rim of the Mediterranean. Here Phoenician merchants established trading posts along the coast of Africa as far as the Atlantic and maintained links with their home states in Lebanon and Syria. By 600 B.C. the Mediterranean was unified as it had never before been, even in Mycenaean times.

Hoplite Warfare   One of the key factors that ensured the success of the Greek colonial movement was military superiority. Around 700 B.C. there evolved a new style of infantry fighting using heavily armed bands of soldiers in massed units called phalanxes. The individual infantryman (or *hoplite,* in Greek) wore a metal breastplate, helmet, and greaves, and carried a large round shield that he supported by means of a hand grip and a strap over his forearm. He was armed with a sword and thrusting spear.[2]

The success of a phalanx was proportional to its weight, speed, and, above all, solidarity. Eight men deep and as wide as the available troops permitted, it was irresistible as long as it stayed together. The increasing wealth of ordinary individuals and a plentiful supply of metal began to make this style of fighting a possibility throughout the Greek world. It made obsolete any less organized form of fighting. This new military strength enabled the Greeks to establish themselves and then

---

[2]The armor of the hoplite was lightened and in some cases eliminated over the next several centuries.

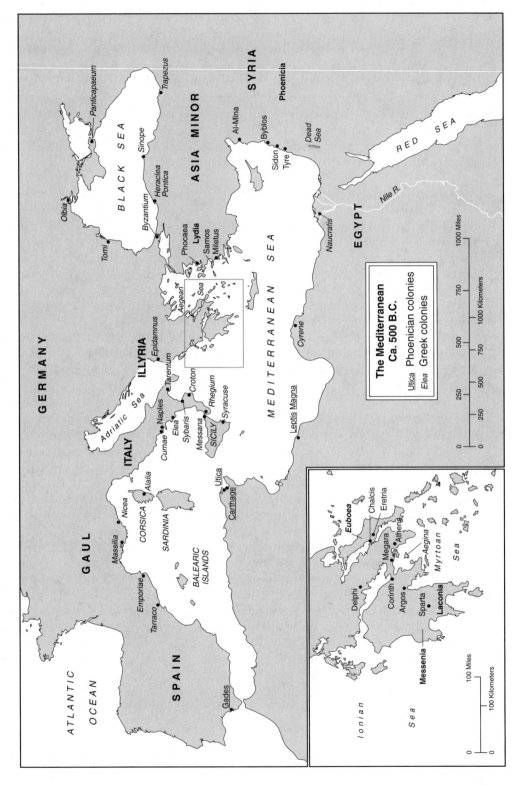

The Mediterranean
Ca. 500 B.C.

Utica Phoenician colonies
Elea Greek colonies

GERMANY

ATLANTIC
OCEAN

GAUL

Massilia
Nicea
Emporiae
Tarraco

SPAIN

Gades

CORSICA
Alalia

SARDINIA

**BALEARIC
ISLANDS**

Utica
Carthage

ITALY

ILLYRIA
Epidamnus

Adriatic Sea

Tarentum

Cumae
Naples
Elea
Sybaris
Croton
Messana
Rhegium
SICILY
Syracuse

Leptis Magna

Cyrene

MEDITERRANEAN SEA

Aegean
Sea

Phocaea
Lydia
Samos
Miletus

Tomi

Olbia

Byzantium

Heraclea
Pontica

Sinope

BLACK SEA

Panticapaeum

Trapezus

ASIA MINOR

SYRIA

Al-Mina
Byblos
Sidon
Tyre

Phoenicia

Dead
Sea

RED SEA

Nile R.

EGYPT

Naucratis

1000 Miles

750

500

250

0

1000 Kilometers

750

500

250

0

Euboea
Chalcis
Eretria

Megara
Athens
Aegina

Myrtoan
Sea

Delphi

Corinth
Argos
Sparta
Laconia

Messenia

Ionian
Sea

100 Miles

100 Kilometers

0

0

92

maintain their superiority over the less organized native inhabitants of the regions in which they settled as colonists. There were some exceptions to this generalization. Several Italian peoples, principally the Etruscans and Latins, assimilated the new techniques and successfully resisted Greek encroachment on their coastlands: for example, no Greek cities were founded north of Naples. To the south the Phoenicians held off the Greeks and, outside of one foundation in Libya, prevented their expansion in Africa. Needless to say, the new style of fighting also offered plenty of opportunities for Greeks to fight among themselves, earning the title of "war-mad Greece" for their land.

The Crisis of the Old Order   The impact of population growth, economic prosperity, overseas emigration, and the development of phalanx-style hoplite warfare shattered the old order of Greece. People engaged in trade and manufacturing often gained huge fortunes and promptly sought to make even more. As one of them, poet-reformer Solon of Athens, stated, "There is no end to wealth; for those of us who have the most possessions rush to double them." Some of those who profited were aristocrats, but many were not. Inevitably, others were left behind. Worse, aristocrats sometimes found themselves outstripped by their more enterprising nonaristocratic neighbors. Many of the new overseas foundations thrived and overshadowed the home states, demonstrating what might be accomplished in the freedom of the new communities.

Ready for battle, a formidably armed hoplite takes leave of an old man, possibly his father. Heavily equipped infantrymen such as this one constituted the principal strength of both Greek and Roman armies.

Along with wealth came the experience of travels in foreign lands and sometimes radically new ideas about the distribution of power and the privileges that went with it. The old Homeric world of the aristocracy, with its fixed realities, crumbled. Even the gods were affected. Homer's gods cared nothing for justice. Like the aristocrats whose values they reflected, they were interested mostly in honor and feasting. However, they were now found wanting in a world where injustice and excess were the norm. People began to expect more from their gods.

Under these circumstances it would have been understandable if the Greeks had settled for the accumulation and enjoyment of wealth, as did their Phoenician rivals to the south. It was even more likely that unending strife between rich and poor would have stifled any further growth, and that the newly founded Greek cities throughout the Mediterranean would have been swallowed up in short order by the native peoples who surrounded and outnumbered them. Yet none of these things happened, and the Greeks went on to found a civilization that was to flourish for the next thousand years. Few peoples in history addressed the problems of justice, political order, human freedom, and the demands of society as thoroughly and frankly as did the Greeks during the Archaic Age (800–500 B.C.). The principal response of the Greeks to the crisis of the old order was to create the city-state, or *polis* (pl. *poleis*).

Response to the Crisis: The *Polis*

As the economic recovery got under way in Greece, villages, especially those with religious shrines or defensible high points, became centers where merchants could set up shop and exchange their imported pots, metal goods, and cloth for local products. It was always expensive to import goods over long distances, and as the population increased it made more sense for the producers of the goods that were exported in exchange—the potters, metal and textile workers, armorers, and smiths—to relocate wherever the local population was large enough to support them. Soon the old centers became economic and cultural focal points as well as places of worship and refuge. The local aristocracy and their retainers made their homes there. The term *polis,* previously reserved for just the citadel, now began to be applied to the entire center as well as the surrounding countryside. A *polis* might eventually evolve into a true urban center with a marketplace (*agora*), temples, public buildings, walls, aqueducts, and so on, as happened at Athens, or it might remain just as a collection of villages, as the Spartans preferred.

What made the *polis* unique was not so much its physical reality as the state of mind that went with it. Authority was viewed in a new light in the *poleis*. It was clear to their inhabitants that they were not like the Egyptians or the Mesopotamians, people who lived in large kingdoms under the control of kings. At the same time, the old Greek arrangements of the past were insufficient. Kinship was still important but inadequate. The people were not subjects or merely kinsmen, though. What were they? The answer that eventually emerged was that they were citizens.

Authority, *polis*-dwellers decided, rested not on divine kings, priests, bureaucrats, or military leaders but on the people as a whole. The community was sovereign. It could make its own laws and constitutions. Neither its magistrates nor institutions such as families, religious associations, social classes, or economic categories of people were above or beyond the law. An entirely new kind of relationship between members of the community developed that depended not on kinship relations or obedience to others but on a commonly agreed-upon body of law and a shared way of life. This development did not happen all at once. It took centuries for these ideas to evolve, and even longer for their various social and economic implications to be worked out. As we shall see in the case of Sparta and Athens, the Greeks could approach the problem of *polis*-building from very different viewpoints.

Origins of the Polis

How did the Greeks stumble on these ideas? The reasons are complex, and for the most part the precise answers are lost in the remoteness of time. One important element, certainly, was the fact that the Greeks had long enjoyed traditions and institutions of a quasidemocratic character. The kings that had existed were not all-powerful, but more like firsts among equals. The aristocracy was not feudal; that is, other social classes did not owe it inherited obligations in return for land. Although different in its lifestyle from the rest of the community, the aristocracy was not separated from the ordinary people by complex social customs, language, and attitude, as was the case of European aristocracies in recent times. No European princess, for instance, is likely to have done her own and her brothers' laundry with such willingness as did Nausicaa, the daughter of the king of Phaeacia in Homer's *Odyssey.* The Greek upper classes moved from being a warrior aristocracy wielding power through armed might to being a political and cultural aristocracy with ease.

Pressure from the development of hoplite warfare also contributed to the evolution of the *polis.* In Homer we read of assemblies of the people being called upon to voice their opinion on a number of subjects. In the eighth and seventh centuries B.C. the people, with perhaps up to a third armed in hoplite fashion and having learned to fight together, was a formidable element. As the primary defender of the *polis* it could not be denied a share in political power should it choose to demand it, which in time, and in different ways, it did. It is interesting that the practice of burying warriors with their arms ceases at the same time that hoplite warfare develops. Valuable arms, instead of being buried in the ground to honor the dead, were passed on, more practically, to the living. Apparently community needs triumphed over aristocratic display. The aristocracy remained key players in the new *poleis,* but they were no longer the sole players.

Other factors contributing to the formation of the *polis* were the absence of any major rival military power that could have swallowed up the entire Greek world, the impressive example of the new overseas foundations, and the traditional ability of the Greeks to articulate their problems in attractive, convincing discourse. In one respect the Greeks were just lucky. The Assyrians never pushed as far west as the Aegean, and when the Persians made their appearance, at least the mainland Greek *poleis* were strong enough to repel them. The other two elements, however, occurred not by luck but by design. Greek high culture was a powerful and original development, unique in that unlike most high cultures elsewhere it was not confined to an elite. This important aspect of early Greek history will be treated later in this chapter (see "Culture and Society in the Archaic Age").

Social Transformation   One of the many consequences of the rise of the *polis* was a decline in the visibility of upper-class women. Another was the rise in the self-consciousness and exclusivity of *polis* citizens.

In Homer's time one of the strategies aristocrats used to maintain their power was to seek marriage alliances with other aristocratic families. Women were seen as possessing social importance in their own right, for they were the connecting links between important families. As such they enjoyed considerable freedom, at least compared to well-to-do Greek women in later periods. (We know little of the poor of Homer's day, and there was no middle class.) They traveled and were present at banquets when guests and ambassadors from other states were received, and they participated in conversations at which important decisions were made.

With the development of the *polis,* however, the main decision-making site shifted from the houses of the aristocracy to the public places of the city. Although the assembly had long been called upon to approve important issues presented to it, it now began to assume more general control over the decision-making process. By definition the assembly consisted of the armed men of the community—the property owners who made up the bulk of the phalanx. Accordingly, as the aristocracy's dominance of policy making was restricted, the influence of the women of their households also receded or at least became less visible. In the end they could only indirectly influence affairs of the state through their husbands, sons, or other kinsmen.

Another consequence of the development of the *polis* was the widening of the base of the military class in both numbers and ideology. Anyone who could afford hoplite armor and weapons could claim a place in the phalanx, and the ideology of aristocratic combat, in a slightly modified form, was appropriated by the citizens at large. Paradoxically, militarism grew rather than retreated with the decline of the glory-seeking aristocracy, as more men participated actively in military affairs and shared the military culture than ever before. War went from the activity of a small group of professionals to the business of an entire community. Correspondingly, a new ideology of warfare evolved. War was now justified as a community act, a service of the people for the people, rather than an activity that brought glory and wealth to an individual or a small class of specialists in the art of war. This "democratization" of war had immense consequences for the future; whereas it helps explain how, in the name of freedom, a handful of insignificant cities could heroically defy empires, it also accounts for the endless, bitter rounds of wars the Greeks fought among themselves.

Another consequence of the rise of the *polis* was the narrowing of the definition of who belonged to the community and who did not. It gave a powerful impetus to the development of a sense of "us" and "them," those inside and those outside the *polis*. Gradually there developed a feeling of privilege and an awareness of what might be lost by letting outsiders share in the benefits of *polis* membership. Aristocrats, generally, had a broader sense of self-interest and sought to create alliances through marriage with outside communities, but with the growth of the *polis* ordinary citizens came to view such practices with suspicion. Democratic Athens passed a law in the fifth century B.C. making it a requirement for citizenship that both parents be Athenian. Aristotle remarks of this process: "When a state begins to have a large enough population it gradually [restricts its population] first by dropping sons of a slave father or mother, then those whose mothers only were citizens, and finally citizenship is confined to the children of citizens on both sides." The ultimate extreme of this development was reached at Sparta, where foreigners were rigorously excluded and suspicion of the outside world became a fixed feature of the culture. From this perspective, citizenship, the greatest invention of the Archaic Age, became a new if broader form of aristocracy.

THE EXAMPLE OF TWO CITIES: SPARTA AND ATHENS

Although the typical *polis* had the basic structure of assembly, magistrates, and council, and shared common assumptions about what constituted citizenship, there was a wide variety of local forms. For instance, there was no agreement on how widely the franchise should be extended. Oligarchic forms of the *polis* tended to restrict the active participation of citizens in political affairs to property owners, whereas democratic states were more liberal in this regard. Whether oligarchic or democratic, the citizens voted directly, not through representatives. A decision to wage war, for instance, was taken by those who would do the fighting themselves, not by professional politicians who would stay safely at home. This was a sobering aspect of Greek politics that made issues such as war a serious business, not to be undertaken lightly. Even in a strictly oligarchic state, though, a citizen could still voice his opinion in the assembly, participate in religious affairs, and own property.

There was no chronological uniformity of development of the *polis*. Some areas of Greece, especially those near the Aegean, rapidly evolved *polis* forms of society, whereas others in more remote areas of the country followed suit only centuries later (if at all). Two of the classical states of Greece, Sparta and Athens, illustrate these tendencies but were by no means the only forms of the *polis* to evolve. In fact, in many ways they are atypical, for we know more about Athens than about any other *polis*, and both Sparta and Athens were larger and more powerful than the average *polis*.

Sparta

Sparta's *polis* constitution was the earliest and most radical to appear. Like Thessaly and a few other regions of Greece, Sparta had a large subject population, probably the descendants of the original inhabitants who had been conquered centuries earlier but had not been assimilated. These were called *helots* and had the status of state slave. They belonged to the state, and could not be bought or sold by individual Spartans. In the eighth century B.C., when other Greek states were seeking new land overseas,

Sparta solved its population problem by conquering neighboring Messenia and reducing its inhabitants to *helot* status. As a consequence, the total subject population greatly outnumbered the native Spartans and thus presented a constant threat. After the outbreak of a major revolt of the *helots* in the seventh century B.C. Sparta had to assume a permanent wartime position in order to subordinate completely the community to the demands of the most effective method of fighting then known, hoplite warfare. Only by this means could the minority Spartans hope to maintain superiority over the unarmed, unorganized *helots* and beat back interference by hostile outsiders. If the hoplite phalanx demanded totally dependable, fearless, physically strong individuals with great powers of endurance and a willingness to lose their individuality in the group, then society would have to be redesigned to produce such individuals.

The process began by relieving Spartan citizens of the necessity of work. This was achieved by assigning to every eligible male enough property and a sufficient number of *helots* to work it. Barracks life became the norm for male citizens, making it possible for the Spartan army to be called up at a moment's notice.

The Spartan System   The Spartan's daily life was an endless round of military and athletic exercises. By any standard Spartan life was different. Normal family life was nonexistent. Children from age 7 were raised by the state, and males and females given roughly equal education. For a good portion of their lives men did not eat or live at home but with their fellows in mess halls. Unlike Greek women elsewhere, Spartan women could own property and marry whomever they chose. The use of gold and silver money was banned, and individual Spartans were forbidden to engage in crafts or business, for neither family ties, individual ambition, nor the desire for riches could be allowed to interfere with the state's demand for total commitment from its citizens. Or, at least, such was the ideal. Foreigners were kept out of Sparta, and Spartans were forbidden to travel without special permission. Male citizens could vote in the assembly and elect annual magistrates. Two hereditary kings provided military leadership, and together with 28 elected men (who had to be over the age of 60), they constituted a permanent council, the *Gerousia*. The assembly voted on key issues such as war and peace, and had some judicial competence; it elected the members of the *Gerousia* and other magistrates. The *Gerousia*, in turn, prepared the agenda for the assembly and had important judicial functions. Five annually elected magistrates called *ephors* acted as executive officers of the state and had wide supervisory powers.

From a military viewpoint the results of the Spartan system were spectacular. The Spartan phalanx was virtually unbeatable; for three centuries the *helot* population was kept under firm control, and outsiders were deterred from even contemplating an invasion of Sparta. Spartan women had more freedom than any women in antiquity or possibly than any women before modern times. In the end it was only the deterioration of the system itself that left Sparta vulnerable to the outside world.

The Weaknesses of Sparta   From nonmilitary viewpoints, however, the Spartan experiment was less than successful. Ironically, as the world's first effort in communism it was dependent on the enserfment of the vast majority of the inhabitants of Sparta. Furthermore, high culture was slowly suffocated by the barracks-style life. The importance of achieving equality and uniformity wore down traditional norms of aristocratic excellence in art and poetry because these, it was presumed, promoted the individual rather than the group and, even worse, might encourage independent thought and criticism. By 550 B.C. Spartan pottery and metalwork, which had been of excellent quality, were in sharp decline. In the key areas of constitution building and military practice, however, the Spartans were trailblazers, and they gloried in the term they gave themselves as citizens: the Equals (*Homoioi*). It was a beguiling ideal, and one that has attracted the admiration of a certain segment of Western intelligentsia from Plato to Karl Marx.

Sparta's constitution went a long way toward showing other Greeks what could be accomplished by way of social engineering, should they have the stomach for it. The Spartans had done a lot more than merely harmonizing the elements of the state in order to achieve justice: they had eliminated most of the obstacles to social harmony, such as glaring economic inequalities, individual ambition and greed, and even family ties. It was a model that other Greeks either could not or did not need to follow.

Athens

In Athens the process of constitution building took a very different path. To begin with, Athens had no subject population of the kind that Sparta had created. Hence Athenian society did not need to reflect so wholly the needs of security and hoplite warfare. The problems that were more typically faced and solved in Athens were the sharing of political power between the established aristocracy and the emerging hoplites and other classes, and the adjustment of aristocratic lifestyles to the lifestyles of the new *polis*. It was the harmonious blending of all of these elements that was to produce the classical culture of Athens.

The Athenian System   Entering the *polis* age, Athens had the traditional institutions of other Greek protodemocratic states: an assembly of adult males, an aristocratic council, and annually elected magistrates. Within this traditional framework the Athenians, between 600 and 450 B.C., evolved what Greeks regarded as a fully fledged democratic constitution, though with a more limited franchise than is seen in modern times.

SOLON   The first steps toward change were taken by Solon in 594 B.C., when he broke the aristocracy's stranglehold on elected offices by establishing wealth rather than birth as the basis of office holding, abolishing the economic obligations of ordinary Athenians to the aristocracy, and making the assembly a court of appeal in certain cases. The strength of the Athenian aristocracy was further weakened during the rest of the century by the rise of a type of government known as a tyranny, which is a form of interim rule by a popular strong man, not the ruthless dictator that the term suggests to us. The Peisistratids, as the succession of tyrants were called (after the founder of the dynasty, Peisistratos), strengthened Athenian central administration at the expense of the aristocracy by sending out judges on circuit, producing Athens's first national coinage, and embellishing and adding festivals that tended to focus attention on Athens rather than on the various local villages of the surrounding region. By the end of the century, the time was ripe for more change. The tyrants were driven out, and in 508 B.C. a new reformer, Cleisthenes, gave final form to the developments already under way.

Cleisthenes   Cleisthenes' principal contribution to the creation of the democracy at Athens was to complete the long process of weakening family and clan structures, especially among the aristocrats, and to set in their place purely local corporations called *demes,* which became the point of entry for all civic and most religious life in Athens. Out of the *demes* were created 10 artificial tribes of roughly equal population. From the *demes,* by either election or selection, came 500 members of a new Council, 6,000 jurors for the courts, 10 generals, and hundreds of commissioners. The Assembly was sovereign in all matters, but in practice delegated its power to subordinate bodies such as the Council, which prepared the agenda for the meetings of the Assembly, and the courts, which took care of most judicial matters. Various committees acted as an executive branch, implementing policies of the Assembly and supervising, for instance, the food and water supplies and public buildings. This widescale participation by the citizenry in the government, although it varied in degree, distinguished the democratic form of the Athenian *polis* from other, less liberal forms.

The effect of Cleisthenes' reforms was to establish the superiority of the Athenian community as a whole over local institutions without destroying them. National politics rather than local or *deme* politics became the focal point. At the same time, entry into national politics began at the deme level and gave local loyalty a new focus: Athens itself. Over the next two centuries the implications of Cleisthenes' reforms were exploited to the full.

During the fifth century B.C. the Council of 500 was extremely influential in shaping policy, but in the next century it was the mature assembly that took on more and more decision-making responsibility. By any measure other than that of the aristocrats, who had been upstaged by the supposedly inferior "people," the Athenian democracy was a stunning success. Never before, or since, have so many people been involved in the serious business of self-governance. It was precisely this opportunity to participate in public life that provided a stimulus for the rapid and brilliant unfolding of classical Greek culture. The seeds for this unfolding were thus sown in the Archaic Age.

POLIS SOCIETY

Modern societies make a very clear distinction between society and the state. We generally assume that if the two are not opposed, there is at least a good deal of tension between the them. Bureaucracies, police forces, armies, and other elements of the public realm are clearly set off against the private sphere, which is characterized by voluntary associations of all kinds. There is no danger that we will confuse the legislative, judicial, or executive branches of government with society itself.

The Greek *polis,* on the other hand, had none of the semipublic bodies such as business corporations, unions, churches, universities, professional societies, and newspapers (now called civil society) that have such an important role in modern societies. The *polis* was a highly integrated type of community in which society and state were so closely linked that it was difficult—and mostly unnecessary—to make a distinction between them. In fact, the two generally coincided. The state was the citizenry and the citizenry was the state. Power was not delegated to permanent institutions such as legislatures, courts, or professional classes of soldiers, lawyers, administrators, or politicians. There was no separate government apart from the citizenry. *Polis* citizens could not say "The government can do nothing right" because they would be talking about themselves. Power was not scattered, as it is in the modern state. It rested fully in the hands of the people, however narrowly that term was defined. Understandably, it was over conditions of entry into this happy decision-making group that most of the internal battles in Greek cities raged. *Polis* citizenship was worth having and worth protecting; hence its exclusivity.

Because the city-state was a kind of hereditary or family-held corporation that required for membership the possession of a certain amount of "stock" (at a minimum, citizen parentage), it was understandably difficult to obtain admission to its ranks. Foreigners might reside for generations in a particular city without being granted the franchise. Part of the reason for this was economic. Unlike the modern state, which tends to regard the individual's right to accumulate money as something privileged, the *polis* looked on wealth with a communitarian eye. The rich were expected to perform expensive public services or liturgies, which could range from giving banquets to erecting public buildings and maintaining war ships. Money coming into the state from any source, whether as booty, tribute, or tax, was regarded as the property of the community. Citizens could thus hope to benefit by the corporate profits of the state and hence were unwilling to admit outsiders whose numbers would dilute the "take" of citizens by birth. At a deeper level, Greeks had trouble with the idea of allowing aliens access to land, the economic basis of *polis* life. Possession of land implied a right and a duty to participate in community affairs. Besides, in any given *polis* the amount of land available was fixed and could be increased only by conquest. Naturally, in times of emergency or revolution these rules were bent for the moment, but there was always a tendency to return to exclusivity.

Citizens, Slaves, and the Economy

The citizens of a *polis* constituted only a portion, sometimes only a small portion, of the total population. The remainder consisted of a variety of people with different statuses. Some were foreigners and they in turn could be permanent residents (*metics*) or just visitors. There were slaves and freed slaves who did not possess citizenship. Freed slaves had the status of metics. And among citizens themselves there were gradations. A great deal of diversity existed among individual city-states, and there is no way of telling what percentages of these groups might have been found in any particular *polis* at any given time.

Slavery itself varied greatly from region to region and it also varied whether it was urban or rural, domestic or industrial. In Sparta, for instance, land was worked by *helots* owned by the state. In other parts of the Greek world such as Thessaly and Sicily, large holdings were worked by a variety of tenants, serfs, and slaves. In most of Greece, however, small holdings were the rule. If the farmer owned a slave the two worked side by side on the land. In cities and towns, slaves, if not used for domestic purposes, were often rented out by their owners. They were allowed to keep a portion of their earnings and might, if lucky, eventually save up enough to buy their freedom (which did not usually include citizenship). There were no slave-specific tasks, as in New World forms of slavery, and Greece, of course, had no equivalent to the modern factory system in which workers endlessly perform the same repetitive tasks. Instead, skilled craftsmen, whether free or slave, worked in shops, independently or in small groups, usually responsible for performing all the tasks to produce a particular item, such as shoes, furniture, or wheels for carts. The mines were the worst places for slaves to work, and it is here, perhaps, that we find the closest parallels to New World–type slave systems or the slavery currently found in some of the developing countries of the world.

Although slaves and freemen often worked side by side, there was an essential difference between the two. Free laborers, independent craftsmen, small farmers, and traders almost never worked full-time for someone else for wages. It was hard for Greeks to distinguish full-time employment for wages from slavery. Working for someone else meant that hours were fixed. Workers could not choose to come or go as they desired, or produce what they wanted or in the way they wanted. They had no control over the circumstances of their work. They could be let go at will, without an explanation. Most demeaning of all, they had to compete with others just to have one of these jobs. Better to have a small farm and independence than be subjected to the whims of an employer. Naturally, this attitude depended on long-established cultural practices, a willingness to accept a low standard of living, and, for the most part, the simple absence of any other alternative.

Society and the Family

Anyone observing another culture, either past or present, does so as an outsider. Inevitably we see it, at least at first, through the lens of our own cultural values. Even after we think we know it well, natives will tell us we are still not getting it. This is especially true in the matter of gender and the family, where our own values and assumptions are hard to dismiss. In the case of ancient Greece this is especially taxing because, even apart from its remoteness in time, almost all information we have comes to us through male interpreters and tends to concern the better-off segments of society. Perhaps one way to break into the mentality of Greeks of the *polis* age regarding gender and the family is to look at some of our own presuppositions about these subjects and then try to make comparisons with Greek ways of thought.

The Economy, Education, and Personal Identity
In modern times we assume that as we enter adult life we have available a wide variety of career choices and lifestyles. Connected with this assumption is the belief that the primary role of parents is to raise and educate their children so that they can function well in a world of business, industry, and the professions. We assume that the accumulation of money is largely for the purpose of consumption for an improved personal lifestyle. We think of work, usually for others, as the normal full-time occupation for men and women alike, and that it is almost always done outside the home. We admire and praise hard work and are suspicious of those noted for their laid-back attitudes, lack of punctuality, and other kinds of "undependability."

In Greece, on the other hand, there were few or no job choices or careers. Some Greeks had their own businesses, but most people, perhaps 90 percent, worked for themselves at agriculture. This type of employment was demanding at certain times of the year, but left much free time in off seasons. In Greece, as in most premodern societies, the majority of people did not work full-time. Thus, there was generally time for politics and military campaigning. Except for the landless and the truly poor, one's labor was not a commodity to be sold on a labor market. Working for someone else was a confession of poverty and an inability to maintain a real, independent household. Lifestyles were generally simple and undemanding: there was no fancy cooking, no fast-changing styles in either housing, furniture, transportation, or clothing. Greek culture was not a consumer culture characterized by disposability. Clothes were often passed on from one generation to the next. Dwellings and land passed from parent to child and formed the main basis of the survival of the next generation. Houses, even those of the rich, were plain and functional, not ostentatious. This is not to say that the wealthy who could afford to display their wealth did not do so. Rather, they did it publicly through liturgies, or acts of public service such as sponsoring choruses or gymnastic displays at festivals or paying for war ships and contributing special war taxes, rather than through grand houses and other types of conspicuous consumption.

Formal education, we assume today, occurs outside the home in schools and universities. We take for granted the inadequacy of families to fully educate their children and therefore expect that well-developed educational systems will exist independently of the family, sustained by the state. Modern children will attend school from a very early age to young adulthood, in the case of students attending college. By contrast, most education in ancient Greece was informal: it was acquired as part of the normal process of growing up in the community. Only later in Greek history did an educational system independent of the family and the city come into existence, and then only for a small percentage of the population. Much of a *polis* male's identity was formed in the public realm: hanging around the agora, palaestra, or gymnasium; attending public functions such as the courts, the assemblies, and festivals; and service with the army, either on campaign or preparing for campaigns. The private realm of work and the household, by contrast, did not have the kind of over-whelming importance or prestige it does in modern societies. Women's education was also informal, focusing on the home, the farm, the homes of relatives and friends, daily trips to the fountain, and especially the religious cycle of festivals.

Marriage   Marriage for modern people is the product of mutual affection and compatibility; spouses generally do not differ significantly from each other in age, education, or income. We have free choice in whom we select for a mate. The ideal family is one where warm, loving relationships predominate. We accept that most children born to parents are likely to grow to maturity. Children are cherished for their own worth, not because they represent some kind of investment in the future, a kind of old-age insurance policy. On the contrary, we feel that parents are responsible for providing for their old age. That parents and their adult children may be separated by vast distances and see each other only rarely is a given. No one feels uncomfortable with the idea of men and women living singly in their own separate households, leading their own independent, unsupervised, strictly private lives. We regard divorce as a necessary evil—often an extremely difficult, wrenching experience. In recent times women have obtained the right to vote, control and dispose of property, serve on juries, run for public office, and generally have independent careers on a par, at least *de jure,* with men. With some restrictions, women have the same legal public standing as men. Above all, men and women both assume a great deal of freedom, and especially privacy, in how they choose to live. Our identity is formed largely by our activity in private, not the public sector.

For ancient Greeks marriages were usually arranged affairs. It was taken for granted that if there was to be real affection between the spouses, it would develop after the marriage. Formal betrothals before marriage were common and could occur at a very young age. The sister of Demosthenes, the famous Athenian orator, was 5 when she was betrothed, although this may be an exception because she was an orphan. Marriages were usually between males aged about 30 and girls between 14 and 18. High infant mortality rates meant that husbands and wives had to harden themselves to the loss of many children, especially in the critical ages of 1 to 5. The strange story circulated that it was the custom for Persian men not to meet their children until they were 5 so that they should not suffer the pain of loss, but this tale was clearly a parable reflecting the emotional experience of the Greeks in dealing with the loss of beloved children.

Children were an economic necessity, not a choice: in old age parents expected their children to care for them, and in Athens they could legally compel them to provide support. However, there were limitations on how many children a family could support. In particular, there were reasons for not raising all female offspring. Girls without dowries did not have much chance of making a good marriage or even getting married at all, so fathers who knew they could not provide dowries for their daughters felt pressure to abandon them at birth before they became, technically speaking, members of the family. Because they had not received names or been ritually inducted into the family, these infants had no real existence in the eyes of the community; exposing them, as abandonment was called, was regarded as a morally neutral act. Many of these infants were exposed in clay pots or jars intended to serve as their coffins. Some exposed infants, possibly most, were raised by people who made a job of saving abandoned children and bringing them up for sale as slaves. Sometimes the fathers of dowryless girls set them up as concubines. Prostitution was state regulated in some cities, and at Athens a percentage of the profits from brothels went to the building of a temple to Aphrodite. Conversely, it might make sense in some situations to raise a daughter rather than a son. Where a family already had a son, an additional son or sons would lead to depletion of the property. Greeks did not practice primogeniture, the transmission of the family property intact to the firstborn son, but instead divided the property among the children. In a situation like this a daughter could be married off less expensively, with the additional benefit of creating a new family alliance.

The Household   There was no equivalent in Greek for the world *family* in English, in the sense of a husband, wife, and children. Instead Greeks had households, or *oikoi*. These were associations of husband, wife, children and possibly slaves, and property. A Greek household (or *oikos*) was the principal means of subsistence of almost all Greeks. Without property there could be no household. There was no economy separate from privately owned farms and small businesses, which provided jobs in our sense of the word. The *oikos* generally derived its income from two sources: the property that the husband owned and the income from the dowry that the wife brought with her. A wife was not a slave in her own household, firmly under the thumb of her despotic, patriarchal husband, who arranged everything without her knowledge or consent. On the contrary, wives ran the household and were well informed on domestic finances and participated fully in family decision making. It is perhaps best to think of a *polis*-style household as a kind of corporation, jointly managed by the partners—husband and wife—for a common goal.

A wife's domestic power rested on a number of bases. First was her position as one of the matrons of the *polis*. She thus possessed membership in a powerful group vested by the community with the moral authority and duty of upholding its standards; there was and always has been an important distinction between the status and importance of grandmothers and mothers, on one hand, and unmarried female members of the household on the other. Men may have made the rules, but it was the mothers of the community who saw that they were obeyed. Second, a wife's power derived from the fact that she belonged to two households: her natal household and the one formed by the partnership with her husband. If she did not like the way her husband was handling domestic affairs, either as it concerned her personally or in regard to economic matters, she could bring pressure to bear on him: "improve, or my dowry and I depart." Because in many instances the husband's lifestyle depended on the income of the dowry, this was a powerful incentive to conform to a wife's wishes. Naturally, when the wife's dowry was unimpressive, her power was proportionately less. Nevertheless, should wife and dowry leave, the husband was still responsible for the support of the children who remained in his keeping. Divorce could be initiated by either husband or wife and no stigma seems to have attached to the breakup of a marriage. Divorce did not, as it so often does in our society, imply isolation and descent into poverty for former wife and children; the wife simply returned to her parental household to await the next arranged marriage. Another source of influence for the wife lay in the fact that most marriages were political or economic alliances between families. Hence, the mistreatment of wives or the mismanagement of household affairs was of concern outside the immediate family. Great pressure came from the in-laws, who maintained a keen interest in their married female family members.

Gender Roles and the Politics of Reputation   *Polis* life was like life in a large village. Everyone knew everyone else and everything about everyone: what each family was worth, who was married to whom, when and for how long. All scandals, past and present, were common knowledge. In this environment of face-to-face existence, honor and shame, the "politics of reputation," were all important. A household's reputation depended on how well it was managed. Everyone knew whether the husband was a good farmer and how well his wife ran the household. Everyone knew whether the husband treated his wife well and was a good father, a dependable comrade in the battle-line, a wise councillor, a fair judge, a regular attendee of the meetings of the assembly—in short, whether he fulfilled his communal obligations, public as well as private, and how far he fell short in doing so. The sexual purity of his household was an essential component of a man's honor. Violation of it by adultery or the sexual activity of unmarried children, male or female, could destroy a man's reputation and with it the ability of the household to function. So serious was this danger that at Athens a thief taken in a household—not to mention an adulterer caught in the act—could be killed with impunity.

In general, only men could function in the public realm, whereas a woman's power sphere was the private world of the household and of other women. For obvious functional reasons (not to mention ancient custom), women did not serve in the army or the navy. Juries, assemblies, the gymnasium, and the agora (the public meeting place of the community) also belonged in the male realm. The bulk of discussion in the assemblies, or at least the most important issues, involved war or things related to war, the quintessential sphere of males. Judicial procedures were often rowdy affairs. Because there was no police force and no public prosecutor's office, the appearance of witnesses in court and the enforcement of judgments afterward depended on the ability of plaintiffs to round up their friends and coerce the compliance of their opponents. Conversely, men were not supposed to intrude in the domestic affairs proper to women. But women, except perhaps the richest of the rich, for whom seclusion was a proof of status, did not spend their time confined to their houses. They had a vigorous social life of their own, visiting their neighbors, going on errands, making trips to the fountain, going on pilgrimages to religious shrines, and participating in local and city festivals. If the family was a small corporation, then the male was its designated representative in public. Nevertheless, his public behavior was always subject to critique at home and measurement against standards of family honor. The householder, the *kurios,* did not act as a solitary individual in public but as the representative of his household and its honor.

Life Choices Whether the separation of male and female realms is to be seen in positive or negative terms is a subjective affair and can be argued indefinitely. It betrays bias to assume that glory lay only in one area and repression in the other. In reality, neither men nor women had much choice in life. The *polis* decided most of the important issues of life for everyone. Men were forced to serve in the army or navy for almost their entire lives, or at least until they were too old to be any use. Public service on juries and commissions and in assemblies was obligatory, morally if not always legally; not pulling one's weight in a *polis* could lead to social ostracism. Heads of households were responsible for the recreation or perpetuation of their families, the worship of the ancestors, and the maintenance of the family's economic worth. The state insisted on this; it was not a matter of choice. From the viewpoint of the *polis* the family was not a private unit so much as an essential, functional part of the larger community. Loss of traditional families, or their failure to function properly, was a loss to the state itself. Dysfunctional families were a public liability. Society insisted that families adequately dower their marriageable female members; not to do so was shameful. Squandering a patrimonial inheritance also brought shame. Parents could not disinherit their children, or at least not without grave difficulty. Property did not exist for the satisfaction of personal needs or wants. In fact, for both men and women property was something held in what amounted to trust for the next generation; if lost by neglect or extravagance, it was almost impossible to replace. It was not a matter of just going out and getting a job: there were no jobs. One had one's inherited land or property and lived off that; dependence on casual, part-time labor was precarious. Because privacy was almost nonexistent in the small, face-to-face society of the *polis,* there was little hope that these social obligations could be avoided. At Athens, even an outsider could interfere in family affairs on the grounds that its improper management was negatively affecting him as a member of the community.

A *polis* was a partnership of partnerships, an alliance of families that was supposed to work together to make the whole system work. Roles of male and female, young and old, married and unmarried were clearly subordinated to this goal and so were clearly defined. There was little angst about identity. Except among the very rich, individual expression of lifestyle was not encouraged, and even the very rich had to worry about public opinion. There was a certain logical wholeness to the public and private realm of *polis* life: along with ownership of land and property went the duty of defending it when threatened from within or without. Within the community, defense of one's property meant having a wide network of friends to help in court cases and other emergencies; against outside enemies there was the phalanx consisting of groups of like-minded, self-interested property owners. Drills, maneuvers, exercise in the gymnasium, and discussion of war and peace in the assembly were logical, correlative aspects of self-defense. Civilian and military spheres complemented each other precisely: Citizenship depended on ownership of land and ownership of land in turn enabled the citizen to participate in the defense of the *polis.* It is significant that as soon as the *polis* lost its ability to exercise its independent military power in the age after Alexander, gender roles also were affected.

CULTURE AND SOCIETY IN THE ARCHAIC AGE

Between 800 and 500 B.C. the Greeks critically reexamined their entire cultural heritage in light of their experiences of emigration, *polis* building, and contact with non-Greeks. It was a time of heady liberation from old ways of doing and thinking, a period of discovery, exploration, and invention. New standards and tastes were formulated that were to become normative for the next thousand years, not to be replaced until the rise of Christianity in the late Roman Empire. Perhaps the most important aspect of these cultural developments was that they were not confined to a segregated, self-satisfied elite but spread throughout the fabric of Greek *polis* society.

No central institution or group of people directed this process of discovery and revision. Greeks in dozens of cities in the Black Sea, Mediterranean, and Aegean regions found themselves engaged in the same task of exploring a wide array of ideas, technologies, institutions, and art forms. Festivals that blended mythology and ritual with competitions in music, dancing, poetry, and athletics were introduced everywhere. Temples were built to house the cult statues of the gods, and created a whole new industry for artists, craftsmen, builders, and architects. Poetry, the mass medium of the age, was deeply rooted in Greek cultural life. Huge audiences enjoyed poetry along with dancing and music as a normal part of their lives. It was not the special preserve of an educated elite, but the traditional means by which moral values and information were passed on from generation to generation.

Literacy spread widely among not only the elite but also other strata in Greek society. Eventually one of the distinguishing characteristics of Greek *polis* life was the presence of inscriptions put up around the city to inform its inhabitants of such matters as their laws, magistrates, treaties, obligations to the gods, and ancestors. For the first time in history ordinary people had direct access to written sources of information. In the past only the power brokers of society had this privilege. Mythology and legend became the subject of an extensive and varied literature that was in turn critically evaluated by the first secular philosophers and scientists. Systematic empirical investigation of the natural world was initiated along with the first attempts to apply mathematics to scientific problems. Philosophy and the social sciences got their start. The canons of Greek art and architecture were laid down.

Greek Ethnicity

Among the many discoveries of the period was the Greeks' realization that they shared a common language, religious institutions and customs, and even supposed descent from the same ancestor. According to Athenian historian Thucydides, the

Greeks did not even have a name for themselves until after Homer. It was only in the eighth century B.C., during the period of recovery, that the terms *Hellas* for Greece and *Hellenes* for Greeks came into common usage. By the sixth century B.C. the unity of Greek culture was an established fact. When two of the most prominent intellectuals of the sixth century, Xenophanes and Pythagoras, were forced to flee their home states in Asia Minor, they were able to find refuge in distant Sicily and southern Italy. There, surprisingly, they found a congenial cultural atmosphere that allowed their genius to flourish. This cultural unity of the Greek world should not be taken for granted. If anything, Greeks, scattered among a dozen peoples and regions, should have quickly lost their identity and been absorbed or simply have disappeared. Like all other aspects of human culture, good as well as bad, the unity of Greek culture was a product of human endeavor, a human artifact, not a given. It did not just "happen."

Hesiod and the Justice of the Gods

It was the genius of Homer and the bardic tradition that first gave unity and order to Greek culture and religion. A short time after Homer, probably around 700 B.C., another great poet, Hesiod, rounded out Homer's picture of the Greek gods by explaining how they had come into being in the first place. He did this in the *Theogony* by adding an adaptation of the Hurrian/Hittite story of the origin of the gods to Homer's ordering of the Olympian family of gods into the Olympian Twelve. In another poem, *The Works and Days,* Hesiod attempted to bring similar order to the human world by describing evolution in terms of five ages: the Golden Age, the Silver Age, the Bronze Age, the Heroic Age, and finally Hesiod's own age, the Iron Age. The origin of these myths was Eastern, but Hesiod gave his tale of the origin of the gods and humans a peculiarly Greek twist. He did not claim to speak on the authority of the state or of a powerful priesthood but only of the Muses, who inspired all poets and artists. It was left to the individual reader (or listener, more likely) to decide about the credibility of his account.

Hesiod's contribution to the evolution of Greek culture was equally fundamental in his invention of terms to describe what the Greeks were experiencing in their transition from the heroic age of Homer to the more structured, less exuberant world of the *polis*. Hesiod was the first Greek to devise a moral and political vocabulary suitable for life in the new state. He went beyond the purely personal relationship of humans and gods that had characterized the Dark Ages to a more abstract, general series of relationships. Hesiod's terms are still poetic: Zeus is responsible for the order of the universe. One of his wives is Custom; his daughter Justice watches the behavior of humans and reports back to Zeus, who then punishes individuals and communities for their transgressions. Other daughters of Zeus are Social Order and Peace. This may not seem like much of an advance, but it is important in that it represents a major shift from Homer's casual assumption of the primacy of honor over every other value to the primacy of justice and order. It is Hesiod who begins the process of transforming Zeus from a god of strength and force to a divinity responsible for a rational and just world, the Zeus of the *polis* religions.

The Impact of Homer and Hesiod   The poems of Homer and Hesiod circulated widely. Each poet offered a way of looking at the world of gods and humans that was universal. Their poetry rose above the narrowness of local cultures. It was as valid for mainland Greece as for the scattered outposts of Hellenism throughout the Mediterranean and Black Sea regions. Their mythology was not bound up with the ritual of any single city or shrine, but encompassed all of the Greek—and even non-Greek—world. In a time and place where ritual and religion were very much local affairs, Homer and Hesiod provided a universal framework for all of Greek religion.

The myths of Homer and Hesiod also contributed to the unity of Greek culture by providing a quasihistory that bound all Greeks together as sharers in a common past. Homer established the siege of Troy as a pivotal point in Greek history, and other legends filled in the void on either side. Limited though it was, his picture of early times was sufficient to give the scattered Greeks of the Archaic Age a sense of where they fit into history and how, chronologically and historically, they were linked with each other.

Religion and the *Polis*

The religion of the *polis* was first and foremost a collection of cults and rituals specific to each *polis*. The modern term for this is *civil religion,* to distinguish it from the great, modern cosmopolitan religions of the world. Each Greek state had its own calendar of festivals, and its own gods and goddesses, spirits, and mythology. In addition there were the cults and legends of its heroes and of the ancestors of its families. Their worship, the maintenance of their temples and shrines, and the performance of rites in their honor were at the heart of Greek religious practice.

The object of *polis* religion was practical. Its most important function was to guarantee the good will of the gods and thereby the survival of the city. There were also rituals of a more personal type, such as those that aimed at helping individuals through the great events of life—birth, adolescence, marriage, and death—and easing young men and women into the realities of military and domestic life. There was no formal system of doctrine or morality, as is found in contemporary religions. Greek priests and priestesses were responsible for the proper performance of rituals; they were not the mediators of revelation, preachers of the divine word, forgivers of sin, or interpreters of a divine scripture or tradition. They were not gurus or saints who, in their own lives, had exhibited the qualities of a particular religion. Mythology served as a commentary explaining, connecting, and rationalizing the conflicting aspects of the civil religion.

All citizens were expected to worship the gods in appropriately prescribed ways. Ritual, private as well as public, was pervasive. It involved every aspect of life. At

THE LIBERATED INDIVIDUAL

The upheavals of the Archaic Age provoked different responses in different people. Many were shaken badly by the disintegration of the traditional patterns of life. Some sought to control what looked like disorder by means of laws and constitutions. Hence, the Archaic Age was a time of great lawgivers, such as Lycurgus at Sparta and Solon at Athens. Quite another response came from those who turned in upon themselves in an effort to make sense of their emotions and the life of the spirit. In these writers we catch the first glimpse of the self-aware individual whose attempts to come to grips with his or her emotions look quite modern.

Liberated from aristocratic concerns with self-image, the high-born Archilochus of Paros felt free to criticize indiscriminately rich and poor, aristocrat and commoner. He had no qualms about adjusting the aristocratic code to his own personal needs and could make clear-cut judgments about his own wants:

I have no desire for the gold of Gyges,
Nor does envy have power over me;
I am not jealous of what the gods have,
Nor do I desire to rule.

—Archilochus

Sappho of Lesbos could similarly assert her own judgment against the prevailing assumptions of society:

A company of horsemen or of infantry
Or a fleet of ships, some say,
Is the black earth's finest sight,
But to me it is what you love.

—Guy Davenport, trans., *Sappho: Poems and Fragments* (Ann Arbor: University of Michigan Press, 1965), no. 25. Copyright © by the University of Michigan Press, 1965.

We should not read too much into these words. Neither poet's individualism is wholly modern. Both Archilochus and Sappho regarded emotions as imposed from the outside, much as Homer did, rather than as coming from within themselves. Still, they went beyond Homer in seeing the passions as participating in the laws and movements of the universe and as being worth examining in their own right. In the next century the spirit of individualism was pushed even farther by critical intellectuals and independent-minded professional soldiers, craftsmen, and even athletes.

Athens at the height of its power, festivals occurred on about half of the days of the year (but only a portion involved the whole community), and this number does not take into account the innumerable local rural festivals. The gods, like humans, were assumed to love beauty and a good show. They enjoyed dancing, singing, and athletics as well as feasting in their honor. At Athens, plays to honor the gods became permanent features in many state festivals. Needless to say, showing disbelief in the gods by not participating in their worship was regarded as dangerous to the well-being of the state.

Temples   Among the first public buildings the *polis* needed were suitable dwelling places for their gods. Many if not most *poleis* were founded on sites that had long-standing religious associations, so it is understandable that the first major buildings erected by Greeks in the Archaic Age were temples. Thus the needs of the civil religion drove Greece's long experimentation in the interrelated fields of architecture and sculpture and created the connection, never completely broken, between art and the people. *Polis* art was a public affair, aimed primarily at honoring the gods. It involved all the people, not just an elite who treated it (along with the artists they patronized) as their private affair. *Polis* art was a living functional art, not a museum art. The patrons of the arts at this stage of Greek history were the people themselves.

The primary function of the temple was to house the statue of the god (or goddess) and provide a suitable setting for sacrifice, the principal act of worship, which took place in front of the temple. Therefore, it was important that the temple have the correct appearance. To give it special dignity, the place where the cult statue was housed (the cella) was provided with a surrounding colonnade of pillars and an extended roof. Greeks went to great lengths to achieve the right proportions between the various parts of the temple: the size of the cella compared to the rest of the temple, the width and height of the columns, the size of the roof and the entablature, and so on. The basic form was simple and orderly, but the possibilities for subtle shifts in proportion were enormous. Many ratios were tried. One temple on the island of Samos, for instance, shows that the architect used measurements based on the square root of 2 (approximately 12:17); others found the square roots of 3 and 5 intriguing. In any case, the general theory evolved that a well-designed building should conform to certain mathematical ratios.

Once built, the temple provided an opportunity for sculpture and painting to make the divinity's house even more beautiful. Apart from the cult statue itself, which was often a major work of art, the gable ends (the pediments) and the spaces in the entablature above the columns (the frieze and metopes) provided dramatic locations for carvings. Hence, through its building program the *polis* created an entire industry that employed architects, masons, craftsmen, sculptors, and painters and laborers, whose livelihoods were then tied to the life of the *polis*. Because all buildings once erected immediately begin to deteriorate, a permanent, skilled staff was required to maintain what was a major part of the infrastructure of the city.

Apart from their obvious religious functions and their centrality in *polis* life, temples had other roles. Citizens took pride in their public buildings. In time the grandeur and beauty of the temples became important assets as cities competed for honor and power. Certainly, one of the principal sources of Athenian self-esteem was the city's beautiful buildings. Even in antiquity they were tourist attractions. That is not to say that Greek temples didn't also serve mundane purposes. Money and precious goods were deposited there for safekeeping. They were the sites of dedications of grateful (or just hopeful) petitioners. Eventually, temples and their surrounding areas became filled with statues and dedications of all kinds, particularly war booty. A visitor to Delphi joked that one couldn't turn around without bumping into some god or hero.

RELIGION: DOMESTIC AND PUBLIC

Most major *polis* religious ceremonies involved the sacrifice of animals, followed by a banquet or the distribution of meat. Individuals also performed sacrifices in fulfillment of domestic religious duties. The following is part of a deposition by the grandsons of a man called Kiron, who are trying to prove the genuineness of their citizenship:

> As is to be expected with his grandchildren, he never performed a sacrifice unless we were present. In fact, as was appropriate, we were present and took part in all sacrifices, whether the ritual was great or small. We were invited not only to domestic rites but also to the Rural Dionysia (a country festival). We sat with him at public entertainments and went to his house for all the festivals. He thought the festival of Zeus of the Store Chamber particularly important. He performed all of it himself and admitted to it neither slaves nor free-born men who were not members of the family. Nevertheless, *we* shared in the ceremony, laying our hands on the victims, making our offerings along with his, and participating fully in the rituals. Meanwhile he prayed for our health and wealth just as you would expect a grandfather to pray. Yet if he did not assume that we were his daughter's children . . . he would not have done any of these things and would instead have involved the person who now claims to be his nephew.

—Isaeus, *On the Estate of Kiron*, 15–17

Although the Archaic Age was in one sense a time of excitement and liberation, it was also one of great moral and psychological uncertainty. It was impossible that such huge social, cultural, and political upheavals would not have been accompanied by similar disturbances at the psychological and spiritual level. The civic religion of the *polis*, though effective in its public functions, did not answer all the private needs of individuals. How were people to cope with all the problems of daily life in an age of change? Who knew what was right and what was wrong during this revolutionary time?

Traditional explanations accounted for personal disasters in old-fashioned ways: they were the consequences of one's own sins or mistakes (conscious or unconscious), or the sins or mistakes of one's parents or even of earlier generations. Motive, it seemed, counted for little. What mattered was not to make mistakes, thus avoiding the negative consequences—pollution or defilement in Greek eyes—that came with them. The problem was how to know what acts were unjust or sinful and what ritual acts of atonement should be offered to remove them. Limitations set by divine providence were easily overstepped, and Greek legends were full of tales of hubris, the arrogant but often unknowing violation of the proper order. The legend of Oedipus, the savior of Thebes who killed his father and married his mother, is a prime example. Divine wrath (*nemesis*) always followed on the heels of hubris, whether intentionally or not.

In this kind of world, knowledge of the will of heaven was vital, but the Greeks had no sacred texts or authorized representatives of the gods to provide the necessary information. However, they did have seers and prophets who would answer questions for a fee by examining the flight of birds or the entrails of sacrificed animals. Every city had such oracles and seers, but in sufficiently important cases or if one had the resources, the petitioner could go to one of the famous sources of oracles, such as Delphi, where Apollo himself could be questioned. Answers sometimes were found in dreams. Sleeping in temples to await a message from the god or goddess in a dream was one popular though not foolproof method. The historian Herodotus tells of the tyrant Hippias, who had been expelled from Athens but was returning with Persian help, hoping to regain control of the city. He interpreted a dream that he had slept with his mother to mean that he would recover Athens and die in old age in his homeland. Unfortunately for Hippias, the Persians were beaten at the battle of Marathon, and Hippias never returned to Athens.

The Mysteries   Although the *polis* had some great attractions as a place to live and offered many possibilities for the development of the human spirit, it could also be mean, ugly, and limiting. It was always intrusive and demanding. Tensions in a small Greek *polis* were often unbearable. People lived too close together, were too closely related, and knew too much about each other for any real privacy. Antagonisms among and between families were handed down from generation to generation. Then as now, an occasional escape from the suffocating aspects of daily life was essential to mental health. One of these escape valves was the mystery cult.

The mystery cults were ancient pre-*polis* religions accessible only through a process of individual initiation. Some belonged to particular clans and families, but others were open to anyone desiring the experience of closeness to a particular deity. The most famous were those of Dionysus and Orpheus. Another was the cult of Demeter at Eleusis near Athens. All three were open to men and women alike, and were not limited to the citizens of any particular city. Most of the mystery religions promised the initiate freedom from the terrors of death and entrance into a blessed life in the next world (and sometimes even in the present). Almost all were associated with some myth as well as aspects of agricultural magic. Erotic activity and intoxication also played roles.

The Bacchic rituals of Dionysus offered an opportunity for an immediate, tangible encounter with the divine and an escape from the limiting round of daily life. Wild, collective frenzies or orgies helped the individual lose him- or herself in the group and enter into communion with Dionysus, "the Liberator," through an induced state of madness. Typically, the rituals were held at night in places far from the scenes of daily life. There was nothing official or organized about the Bacchic rituals. They were the spontaneous responses of individuals to the inspiration of the god. The main stimulants were sex and alcohol, but the frenzy itself was very much a mass phenomenon, and as such was regarded as both divine and wholesome. In contrast to Apollo, Dionysus brought a message that was democratic and liberating. Whereas Apollo told people to achieve security by learning their place in society, Dionysus told his followers to forget their differences and lose their individuality in the common personality of the group. In modern times much has been made of the Apollonian and Dionysian aspects of culture, the first supposedly representing the preeminence of the intellect and the other of the emotions, but in the Archaic Age at least, both gods served a similar, essentially nonrational role in the lives of the Greeks.

Compared to the Bacchic mysteries, those at Eleusis seem models of proper behavior. The ceremonies were performed publicly in buildings specially constructed for these purposes under the guidance of an authorized priesthood. The initiation hall at Eleusis, whose foundations can still be seen, could hold several thousand, and it is likely that a majority of Athenians belonged to the cult, although anyone, including slaves and foreigners, could be admitted.

The secrets of initiation at Eleusis were well guarded. The rituals in some way concerned the myth in which Pluto, the god of the underworld, carries Persephone away to Hades as her mother, Demeter, goddess of cereal grains, mourns. The myth concludes with the return of Persephone from Hades for part of the year and the subsequent restoration of fertility to the fields by her mother. Initiates seem to have sought to share in the joy of the reunion of mother and daughter and in the banishment of hunger and poverty.

The mystery religions represented significant divergence from key aspects of traditional Greek religion in their belief in the afterlife, which was at odds with the gloomy Hades of Homeric religion where the dead had only the barest of existence, and their emphasis on individuality, which contrasted with the collective approach of the *polis* religions. Greeks took these contradictions in stride. These beliefs would have immense influence on Socrates and his disciple Plato and through them on the subsequent evolution on Western philosophic and mystical thought.

Athletics

Since Homeric times athletics had been the preserve of the aristocrats, for they alone had the leisure time to keep fit and to practice the different events. However, athletics were not just an upper-class recreation; they were also a serious part of the way aristocrats prepared for war.

Funeral games held at the burials of prominent people traditionally offered opportunities for the demonstration of athletic prowess. In the seventh and sixth centuries B.C., however, athletic contests were added to other ceremonies honoring the gods. For example, games were performed in honor of Zeus at Olympia, Poseidon at Corinth, Athena at Athens, and Apollo at Delphi. As many as 50,000 people are known to have attended the Olympic Games, and because the other pan-Hellenic games were held on similar two- or four-year cycles, it was possible for the religiously or athletically minded to attend a festival every year. Initially amateur in the sense that aristocrats were the main participants, the games soon became the preserve of professionals, and winners achieved international status.

The practical value of athletics as a way of preparing for war was recognized by the citizens of the developing *polis*. Over time the gymnasium and the palaestra (wrestling ground) became essential features of all Greek towns. There men gathered to learn and maintain their athletic skills. Gymnasiums were also the centers of important cultural activities. Plato, for instance, established his school at the site of one of Athens's gymnasiums, the Academy, and Aristotle founded his at another, the Lyceum.

As always, the Greeks found a voice to record their feelings about the victors in the games and to proclaim that there was more to athletic victories than the herb crowns that were given as awards. Pindar, one of the greatest Greek poets, made a living composing choral songs in honor of athletic victors. For Pindar, athletics brought together a number of important elements in human life: youth, strength, grace, and the will to win. It was in the moment of victory that the human being as athlete came closest to the gods and to immortality. Pindar also took into account the connection between athletes and their communities. An athlete's victories, Pindar noted, honored not just the athlete and his family but the whole *polis*.

The Symposium

The adaptability of the aristocracy was one of the keys to the relatively peaceful evolution of the *polis*. Yet despite the assimilation of many of its traditions and institutions into society in general, as in the case of athletics, some aristocratic practices were kept intact and remained a focal point of the aristocratic lifestyle.

In the Dark Ages the warrior feast of the aristocracy had been a practical social institution used by chiefs to strengthen their position in the community. By means of regular feasting, the local aristocrat could show off his wealth, boast of his exploits, and distribute gifts to key individuals. He could deepen friendships while intimidating potential rivals. In the Archaic Age, when the aristocracy had lost its exclusive control of military and political power, the warrior feast became their symposium, a feast consisting of elaborate drinking rituals, songs, dancing, poetic contests, games, and musical performances. Erotic activity, both hetero- and homosexual, was an accepted, although not necessary, aspect of the symposium.

The Symposium and Art

The importance of athletics to the aristocracy, together with the habit of performing naked for most events, had a significant influence on the development of Greek art. By watching athletes practice, artists had the opportunity to work out the difficult problems of depicting human anatomy correctly. There was also a direct connection between art and athletics through the equipment needed for the symposium.

Greek wine did not come in bottles but in large ceramic containers called amphorae. Because Greeks believed that drinking undiluted wine was both barbaric and bad for their health, they always mixed it with water. (A side benefit of this custom was to make the wine last longer and to allow someone to drink for long periods without becoming severely intoxicated.) Getting the right mix of wine and water became, in the context of the symposium, a kind of ritual. Special vessels and containers—large mixing bowls, jugs, ladles, and cups—were necessary.

Understandably, well-off hosts wanted to serve their guests from the best-quality ceramics. A demand thus arose for pottery decorated with subjects that interested participants in a symposium: feasting and the activities of the symposium itself, mythology, erotic acts, athletics, and warfare. The scenes were expected to be recognizable and appealing. In response, Greek artists developed unexcelled skills in the difficult task of depicting human figures on the curved surfaces of vessels of all sizes and shapes. Pleasure in the naturalistic portrayal of the human figure was a characteristic of Greek art from this time forward. Painted pottery of this type found a much wider market than the symposium and was popular with Greeks in general. In this way, yet another aristocratic institution was appropriated by the ordinary citizens of the *polis*.

The *Polis,* Temples, and Science

The development of the *polis* during the Archaic Age stimulated all aspects of Greek culture. Sometimes, as in the case of architecture, sculpture, and painting, the influence of the *polis* was direct and obvious; in other areas, such as literature, philosophy, and science, it was more indirect.

Science and Philosophy   Some architects and builders, as we have seen, were interested in the mathematical aspects of architecture, including the theory that a well-designed building should conform to certain ratios. It was only a step from such thinking to infer that the beauties and harmonies of nature itself and even of society and politics might also depend on ratios inherent in the natural order of things. Oddly, the poets Homer and Hesiod had also pointed toward a scientific way of viewing the world. Hesiod, in particular, by giving a coherent structure to Greek religion and creating such abstractions as Strife and Chaos, moved his readers in the direction of coherent, orderly thought about religion and how the world of gods and humans had come into being.

The decisive move toward a wholly nonmythological view of the universe was made by a number of original thinkers who lived in Ionia in Asia Minor in the sixth century B.C.: Thales, Anaximander, and Anaximenes. They went beyond Hesiod's abstractions and mythological personifications. Instead of picturing the universe as ultimately dependent on the activity of the gods for its order and harmony, they explained it in secular and material terms. Mythological language was eliminated; nature was to be approached in a detached, objective way by means of reason alone. Out of this rational investigation (which they called *historia*) was to come a comprehensive explanation of nature (*theoria*). They speculated about the makeup of the universe: What was its original substance? How had it come into being? How did things change physically? How had an orderly universe arisen out of chaos? Their answers were given in material terms, as when Thales said the original substance of the universe was water. The explanation may seem naïve, but what was important was that new kinds of questions were being asked. The old explanation of the origins of the universe as the primordial struggle of the gods to bring order out of chaos was laid aside in favor of an explanation rooted in the makeup of nature itself.

Science and the Polis   Some of the Ionian scientists' organizing ideas may well have been inspired by the *polis* itself. They saw how laws and constitutions could bring order to the world of human society and speculated that something similar to law ruled the material world. For Anaximander the basic law of the universe was reciprocity or exchange; justice, so to speak, was built into the nature of the universe itself. Such opposites as hot and cold and wet and dry formed orderly systems of natural exchange. Winter succeeds summer, just as cold and wet succeeds hot and dry; birth and death and strength and weakness are similarly balanced opposites, held together by natural tension. Pursuing this idea, he envisioned the universe as consisting of a motionless Earth in the center of a perfectly spherical universe. The Earth, being equidistant from all points of the sphere surrounding it, needed no support. Again, the relevance of Anaximander's thought is not so much its specific form as the way he went about his analysis. The key in this instance is the dominance of geometric thinking. Anaximander thought of the universe in terms of geometric space. In this understanding, the Earth and the heavenly bodies have their appropriate locations. Distances between them could, at least theoretically, be measured geometrically. This was a major shift from a qualitative vision of the universe that thought of qualitatively superior heavens, for instance, dominating a qualitatively inferior Earth. Anaximander's model had the potential to sweep away the whole idea of a hierarchically arranged universe and replace it with a material structure in which no part was intrinsically superior to any other.

Pythagoras   Another thinker of this period, the mystical philosopher Pythagoras, reflected on the nature of music. How was it that music differed from noise or just sound in general? He concluded that the explanation was that music consisted of certain proportions, rhythms, and measures. In studying the subject more closely, he and his followers discovered something more significant: there was a relationship between musical harmonies and numerical ratios. They found that the intervals of the scales could be expressed in terms of mathematical ratios: the octave, for example, is 1:2; the fourth, 4:3; and the fifth, 3:2. The realization that music was not just a haphazard series of sounds that pleased the ear but depended on underlying mathematical relationships was an intoxicating insight that sent Pythagoreans looking for numerical relationships in everything. A statue, for instance, might be beautiful because of certain proportions; the health of the body could depend on a balance of contending elements; the social order on the harmony of different classes; and so on. They were often carried away by absurd, mystical numerologies, but they had stumbled on a powerful investigative tool: the assumption that nature could be un-

---

THE GODS ANALYZED

The critic Xenophanes of Colophon (lived ca. 550 B.C.) aimed his barbs at athletes ("It isn't boxers or pentathlon experts or wrestlers or track stars who pay the bills of the *polis*") as well as Homer and Hesiod ("Homer and Hesiod attribute to the gods all that in reality is shameful and disgraceful: theft, adultery and lying to one another"), but he reserved his most penetrating comments for the way Greeks thought about the gods themselves:

> If oxen, horses and lions had hands and could sketch or make works of art the way men do, horses would depict gods like horses and the gods of oxen would look like oxen. . . . [*Not surprisingly*] Ethiopians have gods with snub noses and curly hair, while Thracians have gods with grey eyes and red hair!

—Xenophanes, *fragments 11, 15, 16*

---

derstood mathematically and that mathematical measurements underlying the physical realm could be discovered.

This insight was particularly valuable for astronomy, the subject in which the Greeks, outside mathematics itself, made the most progress. Pythagorean assumptions about the importance of mathematics profoundly influenced Plato, as we shall see, but Aristotle, the other great figure of classical philosophy and science, remained truer to the Ionian traditions of empirical, hands-on research. Unfortunately, the kind of mathematization of science that the Greeks launched (and that has been characteristic of Western science ever since) could also be a dead end. By inventing idealized relationships between bodies—for example, by insisting that circular motion was more perfect than other forms of motion—Greek investigators let themselves become entranced with purely mathematical explanations and the elegance of geometric proofs. They neglected to put as much effort into applying mathematics to the observation and measurement of natural phenomena. For most Greeks, especially the followers of Plato, nature was always the realm of the approximate, of opinions; the material world was too gross and inferior to participate, except very distantly, in the provable world of mathematics.

What might have happened had the Greeks not been so hampered by some of their nonscientific assumptions and had instead initiated the scientific and industrial revolution in the fifth or fourth centuries B.C.? Why this did not happen has been the subject of a good deal of speculation. It must be significant that Hephaistos, the god of fire and technology, was something of a buffoon and always had an inferior position among the Olympians. Unlike Athena, patron of potters and weavers, he was never fully integrated into the Greek *polis*. Perhaps what this says is that the explanation for the failure of the science and technology of the ancient world is to be sought in social and cultural values rather than in the work of the scientists, engineers, and technicians.

Chapter 5

The Wars of the Greeks

PERSIANS AND GREEKS

During the Archaic Age the peoples of Greece and the Near East exchanged goods and ideas, but the Aegean world was well outside the reach of Near Eastern power rivalries and empire building. This all changed, however, when the Persians conquered Asia Minor (modern Turkey) in 547 B.C. Suddenly the Aegean world became part of Near Eastern politics; the Aegean was no longer an isolated lake.

The first phase of the integration of Greece into Near Eastern political and military affairs began as the Persians attempted to establish their western frontier. In 547 B.C. it was not clear how far Persia could or would go. Even for an expanding, conquering people there were limits to their capacities. Strategically their empire suffered geographic weakness in two regions. The first was in the northeast, between the Caspian Sea and the Hindu Kush mountains, where Persia was open to invasion from the nomads of the Eurasian steppe. The second was in the northwest, where Greeks and Macedonians, and beyond them the nomadic Scythians around the Black Sea, posed potential threats.

Whether the Persians needed to extend their frontier farther west and north was left undecided after their initial conquest of Asia Minor; one reason was that they were busy elsewhere. In 539 B.C. they expanded into Mesopotamia, taking over the Babylonian Empire, and in 525 B.C. they added Egypt and Libya to their dominions. Then in 499 B.C. some of the Ionian Greek states of Asia Minor led by Miletus rebelled. They received a little assistance from Athens and Eretria on the mainland, but Sparta and the other states of Greece prudently refused to become involved. For three years the war carried on indecisively, with the Persians slowly gaining the upper hand. Eventually they succeeded in bringing Miletus under siege, and a great sea battle was fought off the nearby island of Lade in 494 B.C. Almost as soon as the two fleets became engaged, the Samian and Lesbian contingents deserted the Greeks, and the remaining rebels were overwhelmed. Miletus, until then the cultural center of the Greek world, was taken and razed by the Persians, and its population deported or sold into slavery.

Marathon: The Campaign of 490 B.C.

The Persians still had accounts to settle with Athens and Eretria, the two mainland cities that had been involved in the revolt. Under the command of Datis and Artaphernes, the Persian fleet sailed directly from Samos to Euboea, where Eretria, after a brief siege, was betrayed from within and sacked. Embarking from Eretria, the Persians next crossed the narrow Euboean channel and landed on the plain of Marathon, thereby provoking an anxious and crucial debate in the Athenian Assembly as to whether to go out to meet the Persians or to wait until they arrived before the city itself. When the decision was made to advance to Marathon, a runner was dispatched to Sparta, and the 9,000 hoplites of Athens marched out to meet their enemies. At Marathon they were joined by 1,000 Plataeans, and together the citizens of the two cities confronted the Persians.

Several days passed as the Athenian generals debated whether to attack immediately or to wait for the Spartans to arrive. The most powerful personality among the generals and the most experienced in the ways of the Persians was Miltiades, who had been involved with the Persian king Darius in an expedition across the Danube. After much debate he succeeded in persuading his fellow generals not to wait any longer and to follow his proposal for handling the superior numbers of the enemy. When the two forces engaged, the Persians extended their line of battle to envelop the smaller Greek army. Anticipating this action, Miltiades had weakened the center and strengthened the wings so that when the two lines met, the Athenian center gradually gave way but the wings routed their opponents and closed in from behind on the Persian center. Outmaneuvered, the Persians fled to their ships—losing, according to Herodotus, 6,400 men to the Athenian and Plataean losses of 192. Delayed by the celebration of a religious festival, the Spartans arrived too late for the battle but examined the battlefield and made note of the light weapons of the Persian infantry and the tactics of Miltiades.

The resounding defeat of the Persians in a set battle after the disasters of the Ionian revolt was a surprise to both Persians and Greeks but most of all to the Athenians, who saw their victory as a vindication of their decision to adopt the democratic constitution of Cleisthenes in 508 B.C. They could reflect that it was the Assembly, not the Areopagus Council (ruling council of Athens), that had made the crucial decisions of the war, first to aid the Ionians and then to fight at Marathon. Nevertheless, the significance of the battle should not be exaggerated, either as a vindication

THE GREEK WARS WITH PERSIA

Persian conquest of Asia Minor	546 B.C.
Ionian Rebellion	499–494 B.C.
Battle of Lade and destruction of Miletus	494 B.C.
Battle of Marathon	490 B.C.
Invasion of Xerxes	480 B.C.
Battles of Thermopylae, Artemisium, and Salamis	480 B.C.
Battles of Plataea and Mycale	479 B.C.
Delian League founded	478–477 B.C.

of the worth of the Athenian democracy or as a victory over the Persians. The latter had no intention of destroying Athens as they had Eretria, but merely wished it to take back the exiled tyrant Hippias and acknowledge the general overlordship of Persia.

In the decade following the Persian invasion, the democracy of Athens advanced to new levels of citizen participation. In the past the nine archons (magistrate) had been elected from the first two census classes, which guaranteed that the well-to-do would dominate the Areopagus and hold all the important magistracies. In 487 B.C., however, a modification was introduced whereby archons were no longer directly elected but instead were selected by lot from a group of candidates who were directly nominated by the *demes* (local divisions of Attica). Once the connection between the voting public and the magistracies was broken, the archonship lost its power, and the generalship, which remained directly elective, took its place in terms of political importance.

These years were also a time of intense political rivalry and fundamental decision making. The two most prominent figures in Athens were Aristides and Themistocles, who struggled with each other over issues of naval policy and political power. When a rich vein of silver was struck at the mines of Laurium, Themistocles persuaded the people to devote the income to ship construction, and by 480 B.C. Athens had a fleet of some 200 triremes (oared war ships). Ostracism, the process by which an individual could be exiled for 10 years by a majority vote, was used for the first time in 488 B.C.; its purpose was to guard against the overly ambitious or to make a clear-cut decision on conflicting policies advocated by different individuals. By exiling one person the people could endorse the policy of his opponent and ensure themselves clearly defined goals; they also removed an obstacle to attaining those goals. Initially, persons connected with the Peisistratids were ostracized, but in 482 B.C. Aristides, Themistocles' rival, was exiled. By this act the people aligned themselves solidly behind Themistocles' policy of naval expansion and in effect chose him as their commander-in-chief for the anticipated second Persian invasion.

The Second Persian Invasion

Persian preparations for a major invasion of Greece had been under way since the repulse at Marathon, but a revolt in Egypt in 487 B.C. and the death in the following year of Darius, the Persian king, gave the Greeks a long respite. It was not until 480 B.C. that the Persians, under the leadership of Darius' weak son Xerxes, were ready to march.

On this occasion Persian aims called for a major invasion and the permanent addition of Greece to their empire. The Greeks, for their part, had to be prepared to cope with an assault by land and sea, though their most serious problems were to be found within their own ranks. Argos, the traditional enemy of Sparta, stood aloof, and north of the isthmus of Corinth only Athens could be depended on. Thessaly agreed to participate, but on the condition that the allies protect it from invasion. When this proved impracticable, the Thessalians promptly went over to the enemy.

The line of defense finally chosen was based on Thermopylae on the landward side and Artemisium at the northern tip of Euboea on the seaward. The object of this strategy was to compel Xerxes to choose between forcing his way through the 50-foot-wide pass of Thermopylae, where Persian cavalry and superiority in numbers would be useless, or marching inland and reaching central Greece by a land route and thus losing contact with the fleet. The Greek strategy meant that it was essential for them to hold both land and sea positions because the loss of either one would lead to a flanking movement. Once the decision was made, the Greeks under the Spartans Leonidas and Eurybiades took up their positions. Leonidas had about 7,000 men with him and Eurybiades 280 ships, of which 147 were Athenian, commanded by Themistocles. Opposing them was an army of enormous proportions and a naval force of over 1,200 Phoenician, Greek, Egyptian, and Carian war ships. Fortunately for the Greeks, a storm destroyed 400 of these ships before the first engagement, and an additional 200 were sunk by another storm after an attempt to round Euboea and trap the Greeks at Artemisium.

Both the land and sea engagements at Thermopylae and Artemisium lasted a period of days. The Persian land forces could make no headway against the strongly positioned Greeks, and at sea the Greeks held their own despite heavy losses. It was finally the land position that was turned, when on the third day the Persians, with the help of a Greek traitor, succeeded in getting behind Leonidas' army, forcing him to dismiss the bulk of his forces. Only 400 Thebans, 700 Thespians, and 300 Spartans remained with him to make a final stand. As the battle progressed, the Thebans surrendered, leaving the Spartans and Thespians to fight on alone to the end. With the land position lost, the fleet had no choice but to retreat, and all of central Greece was abandoned.

Despite the heroism displayed at Thermopylae and Artemisium, the Greeks were now in the familiar position of seeing the overwhelming resources of the Persians prevail over their own. There was no hope of defending Attica, so the Athenians

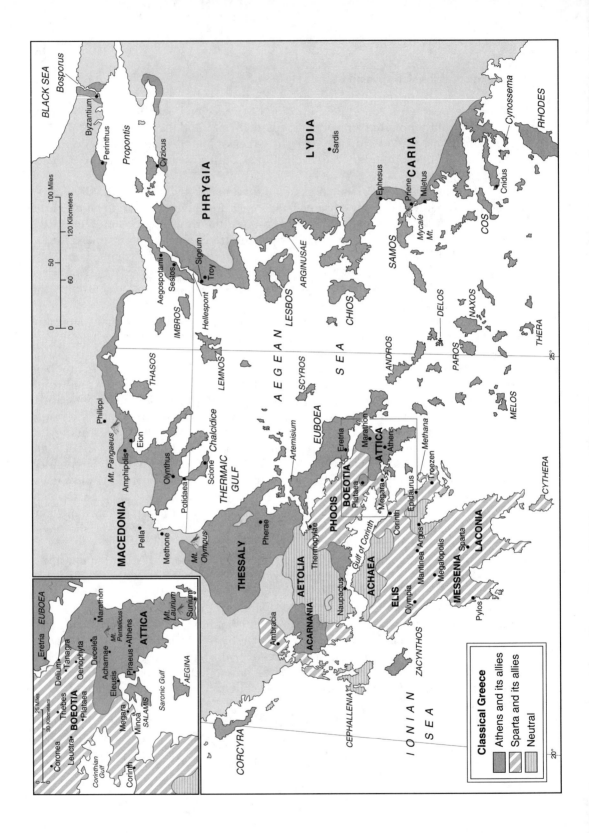

Classical Greece

- Athens and its allies
- Sparta and its allies
- Neutral

GREEK DISUNITY

Using the example of Phocis and Thessaly, the Greek historian Herodotus candidly gives one of the main reasons why the Greek states chose one side or the other during the second Persian invasion:

> The Phocians were the only people in this area who had not joined the Persian side, and in my opinion the motive which swayed them was simply and solely their hatred of the Thessalians: for had the Thessalians declared in favor of the Greeks, I believe the men of Phocis would have lined up with the Persians.

> —Herodotus, *The History of the Persian Wars* 8.30

---

evacuated their population to Salamis, Aegina, and Troezen, although a small contingent remained on the Acropolis, hoping to hold it against the Persians.

Salamis and Plataea   The decision the Greeks now faced was whether to fight at Salamis or withdraw to the isthmus of Corinth. Themistocles urged the first course and persuaded the Spartan commander to hold firm. For three weeks, hoping that the Persians would attack them in the narrow waters of the bay, the outnumbered Greeks waited, with discontent rising steadily in their ranks. Finally, recognizing that withdrawal was inevitable, Themistocles sent a trusted slave to the Persians with the message that the Greek fleet was preparing to depart and that he was ready to support Xerxes henceforth. The Persians, who were planning to attack anyway, were delighted and believed the news. They immediately sent a blocking force around Salamis to prevent escape and placed troops on an island at the mouth of the bay. There was now no alternative to fighting, but the Greeks, thanks to Themistocles, were able to dictate the terms under which the battle would be fought.

At dawn the Persian ships began to move into the narrows, the Ionian Greeks on the left and the Phoenicians on the right. As they advanced, the huge armada began to crowd into the confined waters of the bay, and the Greeks were able to maneuver against them and ram at will. By nightfall the bulk of the Persian fleet had been put out of action, and the hopes of a Persian victory in 480 B.C. were over. It was now late in September, and Xerxes, having lost control of the sea and the means of supplying his huge land forces, withdrew to Asia, leaving a substantial contingent behind in Thessaly to continue the war.

Between September and August of the next year (479 B.C.), the Greeks managed to preserve their fragile unity. After attempting to seduce Athens from the league, the Persian commander, Mardonius, ordered the razing of the city and then withdrew to Boeotia, where he awaited the arrival of the allies on ground of his own choosing. The main Greek effort was now to be on land. To oppose an estimated 300,000 Persians, the Greeks by a supreme effort had assembled about a third of that number, mostly hoplites and light infantry. The commander-in-chief was the Spartan regent Pausanias, and Aristides, who had fought with Themistocles at Marathon, commanded the Athenian contingent.

The problem faced by Pausanias was the same as that of the Athenians at Marathon: how to engage the enemy infantry without first being cut to pieces by the superior Persian cavalry. For several weeks the Greeks waited in the foothills, hoping the Persians would be tempted to attack, all the while suffering incessant cavalry raids and difficulties with supplies. When their main source of water was blocked by a Persian attack, Pausanias decided to withdraw farther up in the hills toward the city of Plataea. The movement was to be executed at night, but it proved to be impossible to coordinate the actions of 100,000 men. When daybreak arrived, the Athenians and Spartans were lagging behind. To all appearances the Greek army was breaking up, and Mardonius ordered an immediate assault. The Persians advanced under a cloud of arrows, but the Spartans, having learned from the Athenian experience at Marathon, waited until the appropriate moment and then charged, with devastating effect. When Mardonius fell, the Persians broke and fled to their camp in the plain. While this battle was going on, the Athenians fought a separate engagement with the Boeotians and drove them from the field. Athenians and Spartans then assaulted the camp and annihilated their disorganized enemies. The battle of Plataea was as much a Spartan victory as Salamis had been an Athenian one, and it was the discipline and valor of the Spartan hoplite phalanx in an extremely difficult situation that turned what looked like certain disaster into victory.

Probably not more than a few days later another major battle, fought at Mycale in Asia Minor, resulted in the destruction of Persian naval power in Ionia. Although Salamis and Plataea had saved mainland Greece from conquest, Ionia, with its exposed hinterland—even after Mycale—was another problem. The best the Spartans could recommend to the Ionians was that they should abandon Asia altogether, but the Athenians, who had longstanding connections with this part of the world, raised objections. When the Spartans sailed home, the Athenian flotilla under Xanthippus remained behind and with the support of the Asiatic Greeks went on to clear the Persians out of Sestos, a strategic base controlling the Hellespont, Athens's lifeline to the grain-producing Black Sea region. Thus, as early as 479 B.C. the divergent aims, military resources, and social structures of Sparta and Athens were revealed, and the fragile unity of the Greeks began to disintegrate.

THE MILITARY SITUATION AFTER THE PERSIAN WARS

From the Persian perspective the expedition of Xerxes had been an embarrassment, but the integrity of the empire was not threatened. The war had been lost as a result of errors, not lack of resources. If anything of importance was settled by the war, it was that henceforth the Persian border with Greece was Asia Minor, and preferably included the seacoast. The Greek mainland was not worth conquering.

From the Greek point of view, the consequences of victory in the Persian wars were more complicated. The old inter-Greek arrangements of the Archaic Age were forever altered. In the past the freewheeling independence of the various *poleis* did not threaten the freedom of Greece as a whole. But now, with the Persian threat at hand, this old system no longer worked. In fact, Greek fecklessness had almost lost them the war. Some Greeks, such as the historian Thucydides, recognized that the only thing that had saved Hellas was the fact that the Persians made more mistakes than the Greeks did. And there was no assurance that the next time the Greeks would be so lucky. Persia was not going to go away. It remained an active threat, always meddling, always probing. The Greek states therefore needed to decide how to cope with this situation. But were they sufficiently flexible to adjust? Was the freedom of Greece as a whole compatible with the freedom of each individual city? In the end it was the tragedy of the Greeks of the *polis* age that they were unable to preserve both sets of freedoms.

The prestige Sparta enjoyed after the battle of Plataea suggested that it should remain the head of the Greek alliance, but neither the logic of the military situation nor Sparta's own constitution would permit this. There was the further problem that, after the battles of Marathon and Salamis, Sparta now had a potential rival in Greece: Athens.

Sparta was a hothouse society, so tightly organized that its citizens could not survive long as Spartans outside its immediate environment. This fact was brought home immediately after the war when Leotychidas, the commander of Mycale, was accused of corruption and fled into exile. More important than the inability of individual Spartans to survive outside Sparta was the inability of the Spartan army to operate for long periods away from home. Alone among the Greek states, Sparta depended on the enserfment of the *helots,* masses of fellow Greeks of a homogeneous background who could be kept under control only by perpetual military surveillance. As a result, the army could never be absent from Laconia for long without inviting rebellion by the *helots.* In addition, although Sparta's system of government was ideally designed to satisfy the needs of a nation of soldiers and serfs, it was in every other respect slow and cumbersome, quite incapable of providing the kind of leadership needed by the volatile and anarchic Greek states of the Aegean.

However, the military problems transcended Spartan limitations as a state. Even if its power had been based on some other, less explosive social arrangement than the serfdom of the *helots,* Sparta still would not have been able to cope with the situation faced by the Greeks of Asia. After Plataea, defense against the Persians did not call for massive land armies but rather for both large and small fleet operations against widely scattered targets. Persian garrisons continued to maintain footholds in Europe for 15 years or more after Plataea, and major naval offensives were a possibility until Athens made peace with Persia in 448 B.C. However, the Greeks had to be prepared to handle both massive fleet concentrations of 300 or more ships, as happened at the battle of the Eurymedon River (ca. 468 B.C.), as well as the endless probing of Persian satraps looking for weak spots in the Greek defensive screen up and down the coast. Out-factions in the Greek cities were always ready to call in the Persians when bested by their enemies. The Persians were still able to control large segments of Greek Asia through cooperative tyrants and oligarchies. What the Greeks needed was a well-informed central organization that could coordinate strategy and concentrate their scattered forces to counter the enemy's great strength—in short, centralized command and control over military resources.

Other factors also made it difficult for a state such as Sparta to provide leadership to the Greeks after the repulse of the Persians. First, the theater of war was now the eastern and northern Aegean, not mainland Greece, where Sparta had traditionally operated. Then, whereas almost any city could field a hoplite phalanx, the same was not true of a fleet of triremes. Sparta was least endowed with the resources necessary to sustain a navy. Ships were extremely expensive. Large crews were needed to operate them, and large sums of money were required merely to keep the fleet in existence. Even when not in use, hulls had to be maintained, equipment stored, and crews trained. A fleet with its dockyards, arsenals, harbors, and trained personnel such as ship architects and skilled workmen constituted a huge capital investment. The financing of crews was a major burden. The trireme had a complement of 200 men; a good-sized fleet of about 200 ships required at least 40,000 rowers, marines, and officers (and obviously a much larger population from which to draw their numbers). Unlike hoplites, who were largely self-sustaining and who paid taxes in time of war, many of the rowers would have been propertyless. The state that aspired to naval power had to have either a large population, a lot of money, or both. Naval warfare tended to favor (as it still does) the development of large fleets by the few states that possessed the necessary resources. It is not surprising that by midcentury only Athens, Lesbos, Chios, and Samos were making significant contributions in ships to the anti-Persian alliance, with Athens predominating.

The Athenian Alliance (Delian League)

Although the Greek league headed by Sparta remained intact, Athens—with the enthusiastic support of the Greeks in the east—created another alliance, the Delian League, in the winter of 478–477 B.C. Its purpose was both offensive and defensive. It aimed to preserve Greek freedom and to conduct active reprisals against the Persian Empire to obtain plunder to offset the expenses of the league. We are not certain of the organizational structure of the alliance. Whatever the arrangement, Athens controlled the decision-making process. Although autonomy was guaranteed to each member, Athens supplied the commanders for all military operations, appointed the league treasurers, and took half of all the loot taken. The amount of contributions was determined by Aristides, who was popular among the allies and whose reputation for honesty had earned him the title "the Just." The meeting places of the League and the treasury were at the temple of Apollo and Artemis at Delos.

The league's first actions were to drive the Persians out of Eion, their most important stronghold in northern Greece, and to coerce Naxos back into the league after an attempted secession. When a large fleet of 350 ships supported by an army was assembled in Asia about 468 B.C. by the Persians, Cimon, the son of Miltiades, led the league's forces against it and obtained a complete victory by land and sea at

The trireme, of which this is probably a representation, was the principal war ship of Greek fleets in the fifth and fourth centuries B.C. Propelled by oars, it was used to ram enemy ships. Because of the lack of adequate illustrations of the vessel, it is still uncertain how the rowers were seated.

the battle of the Eurymedon. He then went on to the Hellespont, where he cleared out more Persian garrisons.

In the meantime, Themistocles, despite the objections of the Spartans, supervised the rebuilding of the walls of Athens and the fortifications of Piraeus, the port of Athens. It was his genius as well as his downfall to have an extraordinary ability to anticipate the future and then devote all his efforts to bringing others around to his views. He had been able to carry the Athenians with him in the years before the second Persian invasion, and now he espoused an anti-Spartan policy, which at the time was not acceptable to the Athenians. Cimon was solidly pro-Spartan, and in the public debate between the two, Themistocles lost and was ostracized, probably in 472 B.C. When he continued his anti-Spartan activities at Argos, Sparta protested. Pursued by both Athenian and Spartan agents, he fled first to Epirus and then to the Persians, who welcomed him and appointed him governor of the district of Magnesia in Asia Minor, where he died. As it turned out, Themistocles' assessment of the situation in the Greek world after Plataea was right; he had correctly interpreted Sparta's resentment at being ousted from the position of leader of the Greeks as well as its growing fear of Athens. Within 10 years his policies were taken up and given definitive form by Ephialtes, Pericles, and the radical democrats.

THE GREAT WAR BETWEEN ATHENS AND SPARTA

The "First" Peloponnesian War (460–446 B.C.)

In the late 460s and 450s some radical alterations were made in the Athenian constitution. These changes were spearheaded by aristocrats Ephialtes and Pericles, but the underlying cause was the way in which the Athenian democracy was developing. Unlike hoplite warfare, which was the preserve of the middle classes, naval warfare called for masses of rowers who had nothing more to offer than their muscle power and their willingness to sit for small wages in cramped spaces for long periods. As

Athens's power shifted more and more toward naval operations, the political influence of the rowers of the fleet grew proportionately and was exercised in the Assembly with the assistance of such leaders as Pericles.

In the mid-460s the democrats began whittling away at the still-significant power of the Areopagus. In 462 and 461 B.C. they were finally able to pass a series of laws that eliminated the last vestiges of the old aristocratic constitution and inaugurated the full democracy. The jurisdiction of the Areopagus, which had originally included the right to try magistrates and supervise the administration of the laws, was now transferred to the popular courts and the Council. Only cases of religious significance (these included homicide) were left to that venerable body. At the same time, pay was introduced for the jurors. Shortly afterward (458–457 B.C.) the archonship was opened to the third class, the *zeugitae,* and arrangements were made for the selection by lot of the councillors from all of the citizens, without prior election.

Cimon and Pericles   At the time that these reforms were taking place, Cimon, still the most powerful individual in Athens, was in Laconia helping the Spartans put down the revolt of the *helots* that had broken out after the disastrous earthquake in 464 B.C. Unfortunately for Cimon, the Spartans, fearing that the "adventurous and revolutionary spirit of the Athenians" (the words are Thucydides') would affect their own citizens and subjects, sent him and his troops back to Athens ignominiously. The Athenians were enraged, and with the encouragement of Ephialtes and Pericles, Cimon's opponents, formed an alliance with Sparta's enemies Argos and Thessaly. In the following year (461 B.C.) Cimon was ostracized, and the Athenians under new leadership committed themselves to an anti-Spartan policy. Soon after the ostracism of Cimon, Ephialtes was murdered, and his assassins were never identified, although an oligarchic plot was suspected. This left Pericles as the principal spokesman for the new policy and for the democracy at large, a position he held until his death 30 years later.

Pericles was the son of Xanthippus, the commander of the Athenian detachment at the battle of Mycale; his mother, Agariste, was the daughter of the famous Cleisthenes, the founder of the Athenian democracy. Despite his aristocratic background, Pericles was a dedicated democrat who was single-minded in his devotion to Athens. Although not a brilliantly original thinker, he was a first-class orator and a capable general. His judgment was sound, and under his guidance Athens flourished.

External events accelerated the development of a thoroughgoing anti-Spartan policy in Athens. In 459 B.C., after years of meddling by its aggressive neighbor, Corinth, Megara left the Spartan alliance and sought help from Athens. This was a major coup, as possession of Megara meant control of access to Attica from the Peloponnese, a strategic factor of incalculable importance because the only serious threat to Athens could come from a land invasion by the Spartans and their supporters. With Athens now involved against Corinth, Aegina joined in the fray but was defeated by Athens and in the following year incorporated in the Athenian alliance

(457 B.C.). The same year a Spartan army operating in Boeotia had difficulty returning home, as the Athenians occupied the exits through the mountains as well as the coastal route. Some Athenians persuaded the Spartan commander to attack Athens and try to overthrow the democracy before the final stages of the city's fortifications, the Long Walls connecting it with Piraeus, were completed. Although the Spartans were victorious at the bloody battle of Tanagra, they suffered such severe losses that they were forced to withdraw. A few months later another Athenian army marched into Boeotia and after a victory at Oenophyta took control of that region. The year 457 B.C. thus marked the high point of Athenian success in Greece.

Mainland Greece was not the only theater of war in these years. An inscription recording the names of 177 men from a single Athenian tribe who were killed in action in Cyprus, Egypt, Phoenicia, the Peloponnese, Aegina, and Megara in one year gives an idea of the widespread nature of Athens's military operations. The eastern involvement came about as part of Athens's ongoing policy of protecting the Greeks by weakening Persia whenever possible. Thus, in 460 B.C., when a fleet of ships of the Athenian alliance operating in Cyprus was invited to help the rebel king of Egypt, Inaros, in his fight against the Persians, they accepted quickly. At first all went well. The Phoenician naval forces were defeated, and Memphis was occupied. Then the Persians began to recover, and in 455 B.C. both the Egyptians and Greeks were badly defeated. The latter managed to hold out until the following year but finally surrendered. The defeat in Egypt was a major setback for the Athenian alliance, the first it had suffered since it had been formed 20 years earlier.

With the annihilation of the Egyptian expedition, the Athenians transferred the treasury of the Delian League to Athens for safety (454–453 B.C.) and recalled

A mourning Athena reads a list of names of fallen soldiers.

Cimon. Two years later Athens entered into a five-year treaty with Sparta, but by 450 B.C. had recovered sufficiently to send Cimon with 200 ships to Cyprus, where the Persians were defeated by land and sea. The following year, however, Cimon died. With his death the impulse to continue the war against Persia evaporated.

From Alliance to Empire

With the removal of the Delian League's treasury to Athens, the allies ceased to meet, and henceforth actions were taken unilaterally by Athens. Yet there had been indications that the alliance would or could turn into an empire from the very beginning. The treasurers of the league as well as the commanders of its joint forces had always been Athenian, and the policy of Athens dominated its decision making. Secession was ruled out as an option of league members at an early date, when first Naxos and then Thasos (465 B.C.) were coerced into remaining. The tribute of the alliance was used legitimately to subsidize the Athenian fleet, but the application of funds to rebuild the Athenian temples destroyed by the Persians raised a storm of protest, both inside and outside Athens. Probably in the early 440s Athenian weights, measures, and coinage were made obligatory throughout the alliance. By 446 B.C. Athens was claiming that all cases involving the death penalty, exile, or loss of civil rights should be subject to appeal to its courts. By mid-century the alliance of Athens and its allies had become an empire.

If the Athenian Empire is to be judged solely by the standards of autonomy and freedom as defined by the Greeks, there is no way it can be justified. Some writers have argued that the empire benefited the lower classes, wherever they existed, because it protected them from their own rapacious oligarchies. There may have been no great enthusiasm for Athens among the lower classes of the various cities, but it was the lesser of evils to be subject to the Athenian people than to their own wealthy classes.[1] To this extent the Athenian Empire may be considered to have been popular among its subjects. Others support the opinion of a contemporary of Thucydides, who said that the allies did not want to be subject to either an oligarchy or a democracy but simply "to be free with whatever kind of government they could get."[2]

During its five-year truce with Sparta, the advantageous arrangements Athens had built up in Greece began to disintegrate. Argos renounced its treaty with Athens in 451 B.C. and made a 30-year pact with Sparta instead. Then Pericles' proposal for a Panhellenic congress at Athens to discuss the restoration of the temples destroyed by the Persians came to nothing. In 446 Athens lost Boeotia at the battle of Coronea, and later in the year Euboea and Megara revolted. The former was recovered by the swift action of Pericles, but Megara was lost for good. Athens was once more exposed to a land attack by Sparta. In midwinter of that year Athens negotiated a new peace treaty with Sparta that was supposed to last for 30 years.

[1]G. E. M. de Ste. Croix, *The Origins of the Peloponnesian War* (Ithaca, NY: Cornell University Press, 1972), p. 4.

[2]Cited by D. W. Bradeen, "The Popularity of the Athenian Empire," *Historia 9* (1960):268.

The Peloponnesian War (431–404 B.C.)

Corcyra and Corinth   In 435 B.C. Corinth and its colony Corcyra came to blows over a colony established by the latter. The Corcyreans won the battle, but instead of accepting defeat, Corinth began building a new fleet. Corcyra, which had traditionally avoided alliances, found itself isolated in the face of a major effort by Corinth and its allies. In desperation Corcyra turned to Athens to seek an alliance. A delegation was sent to present the thorny matter to the Athenian Assembly in 433 B.C. At issue was whether Athens should make an offensive alliance with Corcyra and break the 30-year treaty with Sparta, make only a defensive alliance with Corcyra and provoke the ire of Corinth, or make no alliance at all and probably see Corcyra's considerable navy fall into the hands of Corinth and the Peloponnesian League. The Athenians settled for the defensive alliance, sending only 10 ships to keep an eye on the situation. However, a major battle was fought between the two contestants, and when the Corcyreans were on the verge of defeat, the Athenians intervened. The Corinthians, deprived of their victory, withdrew in a rage. The battle was a major triumph for Athens. Both Corinth and Corcyra had suffered heavily, whereas Athens's fleet came through unscathed, and the 30-year treaty remained intact.

The clash with Corinth made Athens reflect on one of its tributary allies in northern Greece, Potidaea, which was also a colony of Corinth and annually received magistrates from Corinth, the mother city. In an attempt to anticipate Corinthian retaliation in this area, Athens ordered the Potidaeans to get rid of their system of Corinthian magistrates, pull down a section of their wall, and give up hostages. Potidaea refused and obtained the support of Macedonia and Sparta, who promised to invade Attica if the city was attacked. A general revolt in the area began in 432 B.C. Corinthian and other Peloponnesian "volunteers" arrived to help Potidaea, but by the end of the summer all these forces had been beaten, and the city was under siege by the Athenians.

The final spark that set off the war was the Megarian decree. Athens accused its neighbor Megara of cultivating and thereby violating the sacred land of Demeter and Persephone at Eleusis. As punishment, Athens excluded the Megarians from entering the Athenian agora and the harbors of the empire, an action that would have devastated the economy of Megara. Technically the 30-year treaty had not been infringed, but considerable damage had been done to a member of the Peloponnesian League.

These three events—the Corcyrean-Athenian treaty, the siege of Potidaea, and the Megarian decree—provoked a major debate at Sparta. Athens was given an ultimatum to withdraw the Megarian decree and end the siege of Potidaea or face war. To make sure the proposal was rejected, Sparta added the demand that Athens restore the autonomy of Aegina. Understandably, Athens refused to accept these terms. The war came about because Sparta was ready to challenge Athens to prevent any further growth of its power. "The war was made inevitable," said Thucydides in his summary of the causes of the war, "by the growth of Athenian power and the fear this inspired among the Spartans."

WARS FOR THE HEGEMONY OF GREECE

Peloponnesian War	431–404 B.C.
Sicilian Expedition	415–413 B.C.
Battle of Arginusae	406 B.C.
Battle of Aegospotami	405 B.C.
Surrender of Athens	404 B.C.
Thirty Tyrants at Athens; restoration of the democracy	404–403 B.C.
Persia dictates peace in Greece	387 B.C.
Spartan seizure of Theban acropolis	382 B.C.
Battle of Leuctra ends Spartan hegemony	371 B.C.
War with Phocis ends Theban hegemony	355–346 B.C.

The Outbreak of War   The strategy Pericles proposed for the conduct of the war was to emphasize Athens's naval strength while husbanding its limited hoplite reserves. Athens had already learned the cost of holding its land approaches through Megara and Boeotia, and Pericles argued that Athens could survive a war with the Peloponnesians only by avoiding major infantry battles and by instead sending naval expeditions to weaken and disrupt the Spartan alliance. According to this strategy, Athens had to be prepared to sacrifice rural Attica to the invaders. Athens would have to behave as an island, relying on its navy to guarantee its food supplies. Accordingly, when the Peloponnesian army appeared in Attica in 431 B.C., the people and their flocks had withdrawn to Euboea or within the Long Walls. Because the Spartans were not prepared for a lengthy siege, they could only ravage the countryside and withdraw. The invasion of Attica was to become an annual occurrence during the long war.

The following year a plague broke out in Athens. By the time it ceased in 426 B.C., perhaps one-third of the population had been wiped out. Among those who died was Pericles. Nevertheless, his strategy was still generally followed. Athens set out to harry the enemy by creating a ring of bases on islands and headlands around the Peloponnese and using these to foment rebellion among the *helots* and the allies of the Spartans. From the island of Minoa, Athens was able to blockade Megara; from Cythera, Athens could intercept ships sailing to Sparta from Africa. There were major bases at Zacynthos, Cephallenia, Corcyra, Naupactus, and Acarnania, and the forts on the promontories of Pylos and Methana allowed Athens to conduct direct attacks on Messenia and the territories of Epidaurus and Troezen. It was at Pylos that one of the major Athenian successes of the war came in 425 B.C., when a detachment of Spartans was cut off and forced to surrender by the generals Cleon and Demosthenes. Sparta, already hard pressed, sued for peace. Hoping for larger gains and egged on by Cleon, the Athenians refused to come to terms. However, operations thereafter were not so successful. A large force of Athenians was badly defeated at Delium in Boeotia, and in the north the brilliant Spartan general Brasidas successfully provoked Athenian allies to revolt. His success in winning over the important city of Amphipolis led to the banishment of the historian Thucydides, who had the misfortune to be the commander of some Athenian forces in the area at the time. However, Brasidas was killed shortly thereafter in an Athenian attempt to recover Amphipolis. In the same encounter Cleon also died (422 B.C.).

By this time both sides were ready to negotiate, and in 421 B.C., under the terms of the peace of Nicias (negotiated by the Athenian general of that name), most of the bases captured by Athens around the Peloponnese were to be given up. Sparta in turn was to relinquish claim to the northern cities that had revolted. However, neither side lived up to the terms of the treaty. In addition, Megara, Corinth, and Boeotia refused to sign the agreement; technically they were still at war with Athens. Scione, one of the states that had revolted, was not included in the terms of the treaty, and when it was taken by the Athenians, all the male citizens were executed and the rest of the population sold into slavery. A similar fate befell Melos.

The Sicilian Disaster   In the first round of the war, Athens fared better than Sparta. The Athenian alliance was practically intact, but Sparta's had been shaken. Sparta needed time to reassemble its forces, and this it managed to do despite the efforts of Alcibiades, a gifted but mercurial relative of Pericles who had risen to power in Athens, to exploit the opposition of Argos to Sparta and use Argos as a means of undermining the Peloponnesian League.

When an opportunity arose for Athens to exploit its alliances in Sicily, Alcibiades persuaded the assembly to send an expedition, despite Nicias' objections that Athens's true interests lay in the Aegean. From the beginning the expedition was a disaster. Its commanders were an ill-fated trio: the unwilling Nicias, his opponent Alcibiades, and another general by the name of Lamachus. Shortly after they arrived in Sicily, Alcibiades was recalled to face charges of having profaned the Mysteries of Eleusis. Although there was no proof, his freewheeling way of life made him a natural suspect. Rather than face trial, he fled to Sparta. There he advised the Spartans to set up a fortified base at Decelea in Attica and support the Syracusans. Mismanaged from the beginning, the expedition finally succumbed to the poor generalship of Nicias and the unexpected strength of the Syracusans. In all, 200 ships and 40,000 men were lost by the end of the two-year campaign (415–413 B.C.). Worse, the war with Sparta was resumed in 414 B.C., and in the following year Decelea was fortified. From a position of prestige and strength two years earlier, Athens was suddenly fighting for its life.

The Fall of Athens   Cut off by Decelea from Euboea's food supply and confronting the revolt of its major allies Lesbos and Chios, Athens seemed at the end of its resources. More alarming, Sparta was now ready to accept financial help from Persia. From 412 B.C. onward the satraps of Asia Minor regularly supplied money for the maintenance of Sparta's fleet. In return, the Spartans turned over the Greeks of Asia to their enemies. Alcibiades, having lost favor at Sparta, transferred his counsels to the Persians and pretended to be in a position to sway the satraps for or against whomever he recommended. Encouraged by this belief, the Athenians entered into negotiations with the Persians and were informed by Alcibiades that if they abandoned their democratic constitution and set up an oligarchy, they would draw Persian support away from the Spartans. Plans were laid accordingly for the introduction of an oligarchy. One group, led by Antiphon and Peisander, favored a narrow oligarchy, but another, led by Theramenes, favored a more liberal arrangement. In 411 B.C., in its temporarily demoralized condition, the Assembly was persuaded to accept an oligarchy in which ostensibly 400 were involved, but in fact it was controlled by a handful of conspirators. It immediately began negotiations with the Spartans and abolished pay for public services. A plan to introduce a similar oligarchy in Samos, where the bulk of the Athenian fleet was located, failed, and the democracy maintained itself under the leadership of Thrasybulus and Thrasyllus. One of the fleet's first acts was to invite Alcibiades to return, and he was promptly elected to the generalship. A proposition to sail to Athens to restore the democracy was turned down, but it was decided that the 400 oligarchs had to go. Impressed by the strength of the democracy on Samos, Theramenes turned on the extreme oligarchs.

While all this was going on at Athens, the fleet won two important victories at Cynossema and Cyzicus. Athens regained control of the vital grain route through the Hellespont, which it had briefly lost. Encouraged by these successes, Athens restored the full democratic constitution and prepared to carry on the war as before.

The initiative now passed to the Peloponnesians and the Persians. Sparta had a piece of good fortune when the Persian king sent his able son, Cyrus, to Asia to coordinate efforts against the Athenians and at the same time stumbled upon an able commander in the person of the general Lysander. Athens tried desperately to match the efforts of its enemies, and raised money by melting down precious objects of gold and silver and pressing its allies for further contributions. Some successes were achieved, and at Arginusae in 406 B.C. the Spartan fleet under Callicratidas was defeated, though the victory was overshadowed by the aftermath. Because of a storm the generals were able neither to recover the bodies of the dead nor to rescue survivors in the wrecked ships, and a hysterical assembly condemned the generals to death.

The end of the war came swiftly. Lysander, well bankrolled by Cyrus, assembled yet another fleet and surprised the Athenians, who had beached their ships at Aegospotami in the Hellespont. A total of 171 Athenian ships, along with their crews and marine contingents, were taken. Only 8 ships under the general Conon escaped. Following the now well-established practice of executing prisoners, Lysander killed the 3,000 Athenians he found among the captured crews and released the rest. By the end of the year (405 B.C.) Athens was blockaded by land and sea, and negotiations for peace had begun. Corinth and Thebes proposed that all the Athenian males be massacred and the rest of the population sold into slavery, but Sparta settled for the destruction of the Long Walls, the fortifications of Piraeus, and the abandonment of the empire. The fleet was to be given up, except for 12 triremes, and Athens was compelled to become an ally of Sparta. The terms were accepted, and in 404 B.C. the great war between Sparta and Athens came to an end.

THE ARROGANCE OF POWER

The Athenians could see no future for themselves except to suffer what they had made other people suffer. There was the example of the citizens of small states whom they had injured [such as Scione and Melos, whose populations they had massacred or sold into slavery], not because these states had done something to the Athenians, but because they had acted out of the arrogance of power.

—Xenophon, *Hellenica 2.2.10*

THE HEGEMONY OF SPARTA AND THEBES

After its victory over Athens, Sparta was no more capable of coping with being the leader of the Greeks than it had been after the battle of Plataea 75 years earlier. Yet by 404 B.C. Sparta had arrived at the conclusion that only by maintaining an empire could its security be ensured. The internal and external obstacles were enormous, however, and the burden of empire destroyed Sparta even more effectively than it did Athens.

Sparta's own losses in the Peloponnesian War had been significant. Only about 3,000 Spartiates (full citizens) remained, and the numbers continued to decline as a result of constant war and social change. In the past Sparta had been able to conserve its peculiar society by rigorously isolating itself from the rest of the world. Now that Sparta had made the decision to take Athens's position as peacemaker in the Aegean, it was forced to expose its society to the unsettling influences of normal Greek life. Tribute from the empire and loot from wars poured into Sparta in violation of its traditional norms, and the wealth began to concentrate in private hands. More and more of the first-class citizens (the Equals) lost their share of land and dropped out of the ranks of the first class. With so much power and influence at stake, the ephors, kings, and council struggled among themselves, and public policy oscillated between violent extremes. Spartan governors abroad ruled through narrow oligarchies and were almost universally hated.

The experience of Athens was probably typical. There a group of oligarchs known as the Thirty Tyrants, led by the extremist Critias, crushed the moderate opposition of Theramenes. They executed 1,500 of the democratic leaders and forced 5,000 others into exile. Estates were indiscriminately confiscated. It was not long before the exiles, led by Thrasybulus, the democrat who had organized the fleet against the oligarchs in 411 B.C., attempted to return. In 403 B.C. they seized Piraeus. After Critias was killed in fighting, negotiations ensued, and by the end of the year the democracy had been restored. By an act of fine statesmanship, further internal strife was avoided, and amnesty was extended to all but the Thirty Tyrants.

Sparta's most basic problem was its lack of resources for maintaining an empire. It possessed neither the financial superiority nor the manpower needed to control the anarchic world it had inherited from Athens. After the Peloponnesian War, other states recovered with astonishing rapidity. Trade resumed, populations expanded, and soon Sparta found itself only one of many cities with aspirations to empire. Its reputation as a champion of Greek liberties, which to some extent might have compensated for its internal weakness, was tarnished by its blatant betrayal of the Asian Greeks to the Persians during the later years of the Peloponnesian War. More important, the same problems inherent in maintaining naval power that had forced Athens to create an empire—the need for capital for ships and crews—now plagued Sparta. An adequate navy could be maintained only through significant imperial revenues or Persian subsidies, neither of which was seen as an acceptable alternative by Greek public opinion.

The Military Revolution

Perhaps the most important problem facing Sparta after the Peloponnesian War was the fact that a military revolution had begun that affected not just Sparta but all states that had built their power on heavy infantry alone. This revolution was to spell their doom.

After years of war, Greece was full of men ready to serve whomever was willing or able to pay their wages. The normal citizen levy of hoplites might suddenly find itself confronted with an experienced body of mercenaries hired by its opponents. While wearing down their enemy's citizen soldiers with their mercenaries, the other side could husband its own citizen manpower resources. Professionalism spread throughout the Greek military world at every level, from the ordinary soldiers to the generals. The century after the Peloponnesian War was a time of mercenaries, rootless soldiers who had no loyalty to any city, only to their profession of arms. Like the men in the ranks, generals and their staffs were for hire.

Besides professionalism there was another reason for the military revolution: the limitations and weaknesses of hoplite warfare had been demonstrated conclusively during the Peloponnesian War. Long contact with Persia in the east and with Sicily in the west, as well as the experience of the war itself, encouraged innovation. Light infantry (*peltasts*) came to play a progressively larger role in battle. Armed with only shield, dagger, and javelin, these soldiers were trained to run close to the hoplite phalanxes, hurl their javelins, retreat, and then attack again. At Lechaeum in 390 B.C. *peltasts* under the able leadership of the Athenian general Iphicrates cut to pieces a detachment of regular Spartan hoplites. Other specialized units such as slingers and archers also came into play, and cavalry could not be ignored.

These new forms of warfare along with increasing professionalism among all ranks went against traditional Greek practice. Formerly, the ownership of land, service in the military, and citizenship went hand in hand. This meant that property owners were the primary defenders of the state. On the other hand, *peltasts* came from the poorer classes or from outside of Greece altogether. They were cheaper to arm than hoplites, but still needed much training. Hence they tended to be professionals, unattached to their cities or places of origin, unstable elements in an already unstable world. Archery was practiced only in Crete; slingers came from Rhodes; the best light cavalry was Middle Eastern or North African. The army of the future that combined all of these elements would be unbeatable, but it would also be revolutionary not just in a military but also in a social, political, and economic sense. Significantly, the advanced states of Greece failed or were incapable of making the transition. Instead it was backward, despised Macedonia that took the decisive step.

The Rise of Thebes

In 401 B.C., with Spartan connivance, Cyrus, the Persian viceroy in Asia, raised a large force of Greek mercenaries and attempted to unseat his brother Artaxerxes II, the ruling king of Persia. He failed, and the Greek cities of Asia that had supported Cyrus called in terror upon the Spartans to defend them against Persian reprisals. The Spartans, sensing an opportunity for plunder, sent an army under the king Agesilaus. Although the Spartans were generally successful on land, Spartan naval power was destroyed by the Persian fleet at the battle of Cnidus in 394 B.C. By a strange quirk, the commander of the Persian fleet was Conon, the Athenian general who had escaped from the disaster of Aegospotami in 405 B.C. and had fled to the Persians with a handful of ships. With this battle the victory of Sparta over Athens was undone, and Conon was able to go on to help in the rebuilding of the Long Walls at Athens. Meanwhile, Sparta's heavy-handedness, Persian subversion, and the natural tendency of the Greek states to combine against the most powerful had brought about the unlikely coalition of Athens, Corinth, Thebes, Argos, and Euboea against Sparta. Persia aided with lavish subsidies. As a result, Sparta was forced to withdraw its army from Asia and once more abandoned the Greek cities there to the Persians. By 388–387 B.C. Sparta had had enough and sent the envoy Antalcidas to the Persian king to seek a negotiated settlement. Despite the efforts of the allies, represented by Conon, the king favored Sparta and in 387 B.C. dictated a peace whose terms were left to Sparta to be enforced: the peace of Antalcidas, or the King's Peace. Given this breathing space, Sparta devoted its energies to eliminating the most dangerous of the alliances formed against it. Of these, the special understanding between the Boeotian and Chalcidian leagues and the recent union of Corinth and Argos seemed the most dangerous. Sparta succeeded in all of its efforts, but its garrisoning of the acropolis of Thebes in 382 B.C. in support of a narrow, pro-Spartan oligarchy led to disaster. Two years later a group of Thebans, led by Pelopidas and Epaminondas and supported by Athenian "volunteers" (because Athens was technically still at peace with Sparta), liberated Thebes. Gradually the Spartan hold on Boeotia was broken. Athens, making common cause with Thebes, reorganized its maritime empire in 377 B.C. Guaranteeing autonomy of its members, the Second Empire, as it was known, was initially very popular. Under the generalship of Callistratos, Chabrias, and Iphicrates, Spartan seapower was easily contained. Meanwhile, Theban supremacy in central Greece began to worry Athens, and in 374 B.C. Athens sought peace with Sparta. It was of short duration, but alienation from Thebes was growing, and in 371 B.C. a more permanent peace, the peace of Callias, was negotiated. Freed from the danger of Athenian intervention, Sparta immediately attacked Thebes, and to the astonishment of Greece, the Thebans, led by Pelopidas and Epaminondas, swept their enemies from the field with great slaughter at the battle of Leuctra (371 B.C.). Sparta was reduced to 800 full citizens, and its power was at an end. In the winter of 370–369 B.C. and again in 368 B.C., the Thebans and their allies entered the Peloponnese and restored the independence of Messenia, thereby destroying the economic base of Spartan power. Megalopolis, the newly founded capital of the Arcadian League, hemmed in Sparta from the north and barred access to Messenia should Sparta ever contemplate reconquering that region.

Thebes had thus become the predominant power in Greece and for a brief time maintained its hegemony. Its strength was derived from its federal constitution, which embraced practically all of Boeotia. In an unusual development, the league created an assembly open to all its members, which decided common issues of policy. The individual districts elected the generals, judges, and financial officers. The democratic basis of the league enabled the Thebans to draw upon a much larger reserve of manpower than either Athens or Sparta or almost any other single city possessed, but Thebes frittered it away after its two great leaders died in battle—Pelopidas in Thessaly in 364 B.C. and Epaminondas at the battle of Mantinea two years later. The immediate cause of Thebes's decline was a war with the minor state of Phocis (Third Sacred War, 355–346 B.C.). By drawing on the resources of the temple of Delphi, which they had seized, the Phocians were able to hire great numbers of mercenaries. With these they wore down the citizen levies of Thebes. At almost the same time, Athens lost the power it had slowly built up in the new alliance by succumbing to the old temptation of attempting to convert the league into an empire. The Social War (357–355 B.C.) deprived Athens of practically all its allies. Along with Sparta and Thebes, Athens joined the list of states that had exhausted themselves in trying to build empires on bases that were too narrow.

Chapter 6

Classical Athens

THE EARLY CLASSICAL PERIOD (ca. 490–450 B.C.)

To an uninvolved observer, the descent of the Persians on mainland Greece in 490 B.C. might have looked like the preliminary step to the inevitable absorption of an unimportant fringe area into a world empire. There would have been no way to tell that in a little over a century and a half the Greeks would be on the verge of reversing this position and that their former consciousness of inferiority and weakness would have given way to a sense of invincibility, not just on the battlefield but in cultural matters also.

In this reversal of fortune Athens had a major role, first in the military sphere by leading the fight against the Persians and then in the field of culture, for it was in Athens in this period that the culture of Greece reached full maturity in a great many areas: sculpture, painting, architecture, philosophy, drama, oratory, history, and, above all, political sophistication. Whole new disciplines were created and reached levels that in some instances have never been excelled; others were launched to achieve full growth later.

Classical Culture: What Made the Difference?

The close relationship between society and the state, common in all *polis*-type societies, reached its highest level of development in Athens. The Athenian people were collectively legislators, judges, and administrators; quite literally they controlled their own destinies. How this tightly knit society stimulated and provided the essential environment for the cultural growth that occurred in Athens in the classical period is a complex question. It cannot be treated fully here except to comment on the close connection that existed in these years between the intellectual and artistic community and society at large. The great dramatists presented their plays as part of an essential civic function to all Athenians, not just to the knowledgeable or those who could afford the price of theater tickets. Socrates and other philosophers taught and debated in the marketplace, the agora. Even the more strictly organized philosophical schools of Plato and Aristotle, the Academy and the Lyceum, respectively, were located in the public gymnasiums, also important community gathering places. The great rhetoricians did not address professional politicians and jurists but the masses of the Athenian people in the courts, in the assemblies, and at festivals. Art was intended for public use and entertainment, not the private adornment of the palaces of kings or the residences of the rich. The themes of the plays were not trivial; the playwrights debated different understandings of theological issues, ranging in scope from the deep religiosity of Aeschylus to the apparent blasphemy of Euripides. Although a split ultimately developed between the people and a segment of the intellectual community, segregation of society by culture was practically unknown. There was also a tendency to give the greater achievements of the classical period a permanent, or at least repetitive, character, which meant that they continued to mold subsequent generations long after the disappearance of the society that had brought them into being. A good example is the art of the period, which was enshrined in the great public buildings and statuary of Athens. The achievements of the great tragedians were also given quasipermanence by means of revivals of their plays at public festivals. The educational system, formalized in this period in the important schools of Isocrates, Plato, and Aristotle, guaranteed that a lasting form would also be given to the ideas and philosophies developed at this time.

Discipline and Order: The Vision of Aeschylus

One of the most important consequences of the Athenian efforts to order the state by means of constitutions and laws was the development of a sense of individual freedom and responsibility. The constitution of Cleisthenes had replaced tyrannic and aristocratic whim with predictable, man-made laws. In the past a man's primary relationship had been to his family, clan, and brotherhood members, but now it was directed immediately to his fellow citizens from all over Attica. The citizen now came face to face with the state—in fact, he *was* the state. At the same time, the decline in the importance of kinship ties led to a weakening of the old group-style morality, and in its place arose an ethical system based on personal responsibility and giving special emphasis to the duties of citizens to one another.

The worth of constitutions and law and of the new idea of individual responsibility was dramatically boosted by the Greek victories in the Persian wars. These successes seemed to vindicate completely the concepts of discipline, order, and individual freedom against the world of the barbarians, which now began to be viewed as the epitome of the tyrannical and the unrestrained. It was the barbarians who, by attempting to step beyond their allotted place in the cosmic order, had brought down on themselves divine retribution. It was also very clear that the innocent suffered along with the guilty. It was to this contradictory working of cosmic justice, which at once put down the mighty but also made the innocent suffer, that people turned their attention.

The lifetime of Aeschylus (ca. 525–456 B.C.) spans almost the entire first period of the Classical Age. He fought at Marathon and possibly at Salamis, and he lived until after the establishment of the full Athenian democracy. His earliest surviving play, *The Persians* (472 B.C.), is not a triumphal proclamation of the superiority of the Greeks but rather a thoughtful analysis of the Persian loss. The barbarians were defeated not because of the higher quality of the Greeks but because due order had been violated. They had arrogantly stepped beyond the bounds assigned to them by providence, and Zeus, the guarantor of cosmic order, had humbled them at Salamis. Other plays by Aeschylus reflect similar themes. Oedipus, who killed his father and married his mother, violated order, with disastrous results for both his family and the state. When the Titan Prometheus tried to raise humankind above its appointed place in the universe, both Prometheus and humankind suffered. Yet Aeschylus did not naïvely believe in a universe ruled by an irrational, implacable justice that mechanically crushed the errant, whether innocent (as in the case of Oedipus) or not. Aeschylus' greatness lay in his ability to transform the old myths with their harsh morality. He was able to provide a new interpretation that made them more palatable—if not easier to live with—to the people of his generation.

Aeschylus did this in two ways. First, he identified the essential law of suffering, which dictates that it is only by enduring what fate inflicts that humans can rise to the highest levels of knowledge. Thus the chorus in his play *Prometheus Bound* proclaims that it has learned by watching the suffering of the protagonist and contemplating his fate. Aeschylus is saying that even if humans cannot fully comprehend the sufferings of the individual, they should still have faith that justice is being maintained. Despite appearances, the divine order prevails. One should not be misled by the fate of any individual, including that of Prometheus, because even here Zeus is somehow maintaining order, and if we could understand the larger view of things, his action would be seen to be justified.

At another level Aeschylus offered a solution to one of the grimmest of the old tales, the story of Orestes. His trilogy on the subject, the *Oresteia,* was performed in 458 B.C., just three years after the democratic reforms of the court system by Ephialtes, and is usually thought to reflect his approval of the changes. It can also be seen as an example of how a story that enshrined the values of the past, in this case the tradition of the vendetta, could be updated and in the process secularized by being placed in the context of the evolving democracy of contemporary Athens.

In the traditional account, Orestes is presented as trapped in the archaic pattern of crime followed by punishment that is passed on from generation to generation. At the point where Aeschylus begins the story, Agamemnon has sacrificed his daughter to ensure the successful departure of the Greek fleet for Troy, and on his

Urged on by his sister Electra, Orestes dispatches his mother's lover, Aegisthus, while Clytemnestra gestures in futility.

return home he is slain in revenge by his wife, Clytemnestra. Orestes in turn is directed by Apollo to murder her and is then pursued by the Furies, elemental spirits of the old world order, for having shed kin blood. Athena intervenes to resolve the contradictions of the archaic form of justice and persuades the Furies to accept the verdict of acquittal rendered to Orestes by the homicide court of Athens, the Areopagus. Thus Aeschylus was able to transform the old concept of justice by showing how the city-state, with the assistance of the gods, was capable of administering justice. Henceforth the Furies become the Kindly Ones, maintaining order in the new spirit of humanitarian justice that is reflected in the new court system at Athens. Thus the *Oresteia* offers a good example of the blending of the old and the new and of how the developing democracy was able to direct the old mythology into new channels.

THE CLASSICAL AGE, PART I (450–430 B.C.)

Power, Eloquence, and Democracy

From early times, power in Athens rested in the hands of kings, tyrants, and aristocrats whose decisions were arrived at within the privacy of their palaces or assembly chambers. By the mid–fifth century B.C., however, power was clearly established in the Assembly of the people and the popular law courts. In the past private council-

The massive Basilica at Paestum. Working slightly later, the architects of the Parthenon at Athens were able to lighten the inherent heaviness of the plain Doric temple structure.

lors and senior aristocrats had made their opinions known to their masters or to one another, respectively, but it was now necessary to conduct debate in the open, before large numbers of people. Legislative, judicial, and administrative matters were entirely public affairs. Decisions had to be reached in the clear light of day.

The new decision-making process called for a great elaboration of an ancient skill, eloquence. Greeks had always loved to converse, and oratory was known long before the existence of the Athenian democracy, but it was the fifth-century B.C. development of Athens that gave it its greatest impetus. There is nothing mysterious about this. The essence of oratory is persuasion. Although the terms *rhetoric* and *oratory* are often taken as synonyms for *manipulation* and *deceit,* they do not necessarily deserve these associations. The truth is that any assembly of people that has to make a decision, whether in policy making, law, or judicial sentencing, needs speakers who can clearly present and if necessary reconcile opposing viewpoints. Order, especially in large assemblies, prevents presiding magistrates from taking leading roles in questioning witnesses and guiding debates. If Athenian magistrates had been able to act in this fashion in the past, the developed democracy, with its assemblies and sometimes courts of thousands, made such action impossible. In judicial cases litigants had to argue their own briefs, and in the legislative gatherings a speaker who could clarify, analyze, and sum up matters was an essential element of the decision-making process. Vital issues such as taxes, war, and peace, as well as the day-to-day aspects of administration, were decided by the Assembly and the courts; before such decisions could be reached, they had to be discussed at length. There were no newspapers, reporters, columnists, or editorial writers to digest, synthesize, and sift. As a result, set speeches in which the orators presented the ramifications of the issues and tried to make the best presentation of the views they wished to convey were unavoidable. Different speakers presented different interpretations and swayed their listeners accordingly. In time Athenians became connoisseurs of good speeches and appreciated the techniques of the master orators.

New Ladders to the Top

For generations Athenian aristocrats had taken for granted their leadership positions within the state. In the past their special military capacity and valor—their *arete,* as it was called—had made them the most useful members of society. With the rise of the hoplites and the growth of the cities, however, new qualities of leadership that placed greater emphasis on civilian skills were demanded. The old combativeness of the aristocrats, so essential in the past, now needed to be restrained. It was becoming less and less acceptable to regard excellence as the special prerogative of wealth and social position, and one of the greatest achievements of the fifth century B.C. was to establish behavior itself as a measure of nobility, and justice, self-control, and the other moral virtues in themselves as qualities that the gods might regard with favor.

Contributing to the transformation of the old values was the revolution in the ways and means of leadership. When an education in excellence could be acquired only by being born into the right family, and when wealth and tradition were an age-old inheritance, the very means of becoming a leader was denied the ordinary citizen or even the citizen of wealth who lacked the necessary background. However, when the practical working of the democracy redefined the meaning of excellence and made it equivalent to political know-how, and gave primary emphasis to oral expression, the way to leadership was open to anyone with talent who could acquire the requisite skills. By making leadership a matter of talent and technique, this in turn created a demand for educators who could supply the necessary skills.

Success: The Sophists' Approach

The demand for a new educational system directly geared to preparing students for a political life was met by professional educators known as the Sophists. It was not that the Athenian democracy gave birth to the Sophist movement as such but that, as in so many other areas, the Sophists found their greatest opportunity at Athens. They came from all over the Greek-speaking world, claiming to be able to teach the art of politics for a set fee. This fee could be quite high, but it covered several years of education. Still, it was not the charging of fees that was the significant aspect of the Sophist movement but rather its revolutionary claim of being able to teach political competence, which common opinion until then had believed was rooted in family and wealth. The Sophists proved by the success of their pupils that this skill was now detachable from such factors and could be taught like any other and that there was nothing mystical about it. Their aim, whatever their methods, was simply to prepare a man for a successful political career. They taught a man to reason dialectically, to argue back and forth all sides of a case, to discover the most effective arguments for whichever side he needed to present, and then to convert this into a persuasive speech.

The kind of truth pursued by the Sophists was relative truth, appropriate only to the case at hand. In the context of the democracy, this made eminently good sense. What was needed in the day-to-day running of the city was an ability to argue the reasonableness or expediency of this or that course of action, the relative "truth" of whether particular wars should be fought, alliances joined, and honors conferred—the kinds of decisions we call *political* and whose ultimate truth is often unascertainable both at the moment the decision has to be made and even years later by historians. Similarly, in the courts defendants and prosecutors alike had to make the truth of their cases seem the closest approximations of reality. Sophistic techniques could be used on either side, and a considerable development of the understanding of what constituted guilt and innocence, and crime and appropriate punishment, resulted from the process.

The Logical Consequence: "Man, the Measure of All Things"

Given the implications of the Sophist approach, it is understandable why a great debate raged around the subjects of the foundations of morality and a citizen's obligations to the state. Other factors also made the issues topical. As a result of travel and migration overseas, Greeks had for generations been in contact with foreign cultures, and the writings of the geographer Hecataeus and the historian Herodotus had made at least some of them aware of the extraordinarily wide divergences of lifestyles everywhere. The question thus arose: is morality merely convention (*nomos*), or is there a higher sanction to be found in something else, say, in nature (*physis*)? Quickly the terms *convention* (*nomos*) and *nature* (*physis*) became the poles of a great debate that went on for centuries.

Within the terms of the discussion, *nomos* could be taken for the whole collection of laws and customs inherited by a city, a set of rules drawn up in rational fashion for the regulation of the state, or an arbitrary system established by a group of people in their own self-interest. It was the second definition of *nomos*—the establishment of the rule of law against the arbitrary actions of despots or oligarchs or even the irrelevant customs of the past—that the Greeks regarded as the great discovery of the sixth and fifth centuries B.C. With the growth of freedom, however, these laws themselves began to assume some of the irrational and tyrannical aspects previously attributed to tyrants and aristocrats. Hippias of Elis, for example, called *nomos* a "tyrant that forced men to do many things contrary to nature." Set in opposition to convention was nature, which could stand for the unwritten but unconditionally valid natural law, as contrasted with the particularities of local custom, or for the rights of the individual against the arbitrary rule of the state.

The figures of the first round of this debate are not nearly as well known as those of the later period, when Socrates, Plato, and Aristotle entered the discussion and pushed it to its limits. Nevertheless, as pioneers they have a special place in the history of this great topic.

It was the Sophist Protagoras who was responsible for the famous statement that man is the measure of all things, which is supposed to summarize the entirety of the classical view. What he meant was not that everything is to be regarded from the subjective view of the individual but that all human laws and practices are simply a matter of convention. It is the city-state, its constitution, and its laws that decide morality. Consequently, there are as many moralities as there are cities or nations.

The practical conclusion that Protagoras and his fellow Sophists drew from this was that what counted was not so much the constitution or the laws but the people of the city. If they could be educated—or better, for the Sophists were not interested in the masses, if their leaders could be educated—the laws they made would be automatically good. Other Sophists reached somewhat more radical conclusions.

Phaleas of Chalcedon, for example, made a logical inference about convention when he observed that the maldistribution of wealth was the cause of all strife in the cities of Greece. He then presented a plan for reducing economic inequality among citizens. Democritus of Abdera, a countryman of Protagoras, spoke of the importance of a sense of friendliness among citizens and of the rich helping the less fortunate, an unusual thought for any ancient thinker. Going beyond the bounds of the usual city-state orthodoxy, he declared, "To the wise man the whole world is open; the good person has the entire world for his country,"[1] a declaration that would be taken up in the next century and would become an article of faith of all cosmopolitan creeds until the end of the Roman Empire.

The Heroic Vision of Sophocles

In the midst of the rapidly changing world of the fifth century B.C., the great tragic playwright Sophocles represents a transitional figure between the old and the new. Characterized by E. R. Dodds as the "last great exponent of the archaic world-view,"[2] he stands between the closed world of the old city-state, with its wholesale demands on the individual, and the newly evolving order, with its expectation that individuals would reason things out for themselves. Sophocles was a dedicated Athenian and deeply involved in the affairs of the state. A friend of the statesman Cimon and a colleague on different occasions in the generalship with both Pericles and Nicias, he was also a member of a special board of councillors appointed to deal with the crisis created by the Sicilian disaster.

Like his friend Herodotus, he did not attempt to justify the ways of the gods. He accepted the traditional view that if the proper order were violated, retribution would follow. What was of concern to him—and here his humanism makes contact

[1] Fragment 247.
[2] E. R. Dodds, *The Greeks and the Irrational* (Berkeley: University of California Press, 1951), p. 49.

with that of the Sophists—was the individual and his or her relationship to his or her destiny. Even if fate is unalterable, a person is still free in responding to it. One's reactions should not be dictated by the group or society but by the individual. Thus, in Sophocles' play, Oedipus has no control over the destiny that led him to kill his father and marry his mother, but he is free in choosing his response to this tragic situation. He does not allow himself to be crushed by his experiences but learns to rise above them, buoyed by his own strength of character. Similarly, the confrontation of individuals with their destinies forms the center of interest of Sophocles' other plays. Antigone, faced with the choice between burying her brother in accordance with the traditional laws and violating the decree of Creon, ruler of the city, who forbade the burial, chooses the former course of action and faces her doom with heroic nobility and self-possession. In justifying her actions she appeals to the priority of the "unwritten and unchanging laws of heaven" over those of men and reproaches her sister Ismene for not helping her in her deed. In self-defense Ismene argues that even if Antigone is right, they are not physically strong enough to resist the state. Antigone's retort to this is simple: "This world approves your caution—the gods my courage."[3] In defense of his decision to prohibit the burial of Antigone's brother, Creon argues that obedience of the laws is vital to the survival of the state. He accuses Antigone of stubbornness and insolence. As the heroine is led off to execution, she reflects on her fate and wonders why the gods have not come to her aid but quickly reasserts her confidence in her original decision. Finally, Creon, through the death of his son and wife, comes to recognize his own stubbornness and pride, and the play ends with the chorus counseling wisdom and fear of the gods as the only way to happiness.

In this one play are to be found all the great issues of the age (the play was first performed shortly before 440 B.C.). The reasonableness of the laws and the importance of maintaining their authority are expressed convincingly by Creon, but the chorus points out that although the city is the greatest achievement of human civilization, humans are still capable of blundering, and it is of course Creon's tyrannical and ill-judged application of the laws that brings on disaster. Here Sophocles reflects the Sophist view of the relativity of laws that are human creations. Antigone's stand on the unchanging laws of the gods, however, puts the issue in another light, suggesting that beyond convention there really does exist a firm basis for morality. At the same time, her challenge to the laws of the state creates a crisis for her, and she is driven back on herself. She is alone in her decision and must seek strength in her own character because the gods do not come to her assistance. The individual who chooses to reason things out for himself or herself according to his or her own inner vision, who will not simply be dictated to by custom or popular opinions, must hold fast to the original decision and the act of faith implicit in it. It is here that Sophocles complements Aeschylus, whose great contribution was his insistence on the necessity of faith in the ultimate working of divine justice. Sophocles shows how

[3]Sophocles, *Antigone,* in L. R. Lind, *Ten Greek Plays in Contemporary Translations* (Boston: Houghton Mifflin, 1957), pp. 92, 94.

this can actually be achieved in practice and how the individual who has this faith in the justice of the gods can find the inner strength to survive the ordeals of life. The calm assurance of Sophocles' characters in the face of their fate has been justly compared to that seen on the Parthenon sculptures, which were being created at the time *Antigone* was being produced (447–431 B.C.).

The Invention of History: Herodotus Organizes the Past

Herodotus, the "father of history," also dealt with a heroic theme: the great clash between the Greeks and the Persians. In many respects Herodotus was broader in scope than his successor, Thucydides, and the later Greek historians who narrowly focused on Greek affairs and had little interest in the culture of non-Greeks. Herodotus provides a sympathetic understanding of both the Greeks and their enemies. A native of Halicarnassus in Asia Minor, Herodotus inherited the Ionic tradition of inquiry (*historie*) into the phenomena of the physical world, and by applying the technique to human society and asking why the Greeks and the Persians came into conflict, he created the discipline of history. His answer is not a dispassionate analysis of the causes of the war but rather a colorful tale that combines cool rationalization, vivid narrative, and traditional religious viewpoints. His idea of causation is the traditional one of injury followed by retribution, so that his account of the clash between the two peoples is a long description of the chain of grievances on both sides going back to mythical days. Herodotus believed that the gods intervened in history to put down the ambitious and the proud, and he made no attempt to explain why the innocent should also be crushed in this process. Like Sophocles, he was not interested in accounting for the workings of Providence. His achievement was the creation of a new way of looking at the past and a method of organizing information about it. He distinguished between the legendary past and the historic present and attempted to maintain a balance in his treatment of different peoples. He was not content to deal with colorful personalities but sought to get behind them to the institutions that produced them and to the factors in the natural environment that limited their actions.

Classical Art: The Ideal of Civic Harmony

Between 450 and 430 B.C., under the patronage of the Athenian state, some of the greatest masterpieces of architecture and sculpture of all time were created. These were the days of the sculptor Phidias, the painter Polygnotus, and the architects Ictinus, Callicrates, and Mnesicles, whose work on the Acropolis and elsewhere in the city (in the case of Polygnotus) made Athens the embodiment of classical Greece.

The architectural forms and artistic themes were essentially the same as were seen before. There were no daring innovations in temple design or sculptural decoration. Greeks still struggled with Centaurs, Amazons, and Trojans, and the gods contended with the giants, as in so many traditional sculptural and pictorial scenes. What was new was the spirit that transformed these forms and themes and the ac-

"THE MAJORITY FAVORED SURRENDER": HERODOTUS' JUDGMENT OF THE GREEKS

Although Herodotus is often regarded as a mere storyteller, his historical judgments were acute and fair, if at times unpalatable. Here Herodotus speaks of Greek behavior in the wars against the Persians.

The expedition of the Persians, though it was supposedly directed against the Athenians, in reality threatened all of Greece. Of this the Greeks were well aware ahead of time, but they did not all take the same attitude to the approach of the Persians. Some had already gone over to them and were confident that they would not suffer during the passage of the barbarians. Others, who had refused compliance, were thrown into a state of panic. This was in part because they thought that there were too few ships in Greece to oppose the Persians successfully, but also because it was clear that the majority of the Greeks were unwilling to fight and instead favored going over to the enemy.

At this point I have to state an opinion at which I know most people will take offense, even though I believe it is true. Had the Athenians, for fear of the approaching danger, abandoned their country [and gone overseas], or submitted to the power of Xerxes, there would have been no attempt to resist the Persians by sea [in which case the Persian army could not have been held back and the war would have been lost]. Therefore, if someone were to say at this time that the Athenians were the saviors of Greece, he would not be far wrong. For the truth is they held the scales; and whichever side they chose must have carried the day. They it was who, when they determined to maintain the freedom of Greece, roused up that portion of the Greek world which had not gone over to the Medes; and so, next to the gods, they repulsed the invaders. Even the terrible oracles which reached them from Delphi and struck fear in their hearts, did not persuade them to abandon Greece. They had the courage to remain faithful to their land and await the coming of the foe.

—Herodotus, *The Histories* 138–139. Based on the tr. of George Rawlinson (London, 1860).

companying sophistication of artistic technique. The gods became more human while still retaining an essential aloofness, whereas men and women seemed to share in the divine character of the gods. The opposition between celestial and terrestrial realms was resolved in a miraculous sense of balance in which contending forces were present but controlled. There is nothing static or coldly formal about the great classical creations. Human emotions and divine power and energy were not eliminated or suspended but integrated. Perhaps we can see in these poised works the balance of the Athenian state, which had just achieved an equilibrium of forces. For a brief moment, Athens was able to unify all the traditionally conflicting elements in the state: the rich and the poor, the aristocrats and middle classes, male and female, the educated and uneducated, foreigners and citizens.

The logic and solidity of the Greek temples of the early classical period have already been noted, and to the casual eye the Parthenon seems but a modification of the same basic design. Nevertheless, there are important differences that work in

The Parthenon, the greatest architectural achievement of classical Athens.

a number of subtle ways to make it like nothing else in the history of Greek temple building.

The principle of mathematical proportionality that had been used in the construction of the earlier temples was also used in the building of the Parthenon. Thus the same proportion is to be found in the ratio of the height of the temple to its width, the width of the cella (where the cult statue was housed) to its length, and the number of pillars in the sides and ends of the surrounding colonnade. To knowledgeable Greeks the proportionality of the temple would have had intrinsic appeal on a number of levels. One was the generally satisfying knowledge that the proportions had a rational, mathematical basis. The other, deriving from the Pythagorean belief that numbers and mathematical harmonies underlay and explained the beauty and order of the universe, would have appealed to a desire for a deeper explanation of the beauty of the building.

Had the Parthenon been constructed according to purely mathematical proportions, it would in all likelihood have been rigid and lifeless, and if the ancient architect Vitruvius is right, it would also have suffered from optical distortions. Perhaps for these reasons the architects made certain adjustments or compensations in the structure. The stylobate, or base, was made to curve more than 4 inches higher in the center than at the sides and over 2 inches higher in the center than at the ends. This curvature was carried up into the roof structure by the columns, which were made to curve inward by almost 2½ inches. To counteract and balance this curvature, some of the elements at the top of the entablature incline outward. In other words, the temple was carved like a piece of sculpture to achieve satisfying human dimensions, pleasing to both the eye and the mind, blending the real and the ideal, so that whether viewed by philosopher or layperson it immediately conveyed the same sense of grace, lightness, and beauty instead of the heaviness that might otherwise have been perceived in such a large, geometrically shaped building.

Although the Parthenon is architecturally famous in its own right, it is graced by a series of sculptural decorations that also have achieved fame. These are the sculptures of the metopes that surround the temple on the outside, the pediments at each end, and the frieze of the cella that housed the cult statue.

The metopes depict four traditional scenes in which the forces of uncontrolled emotion, disorder, and pride are pitted against the disciplined rationality and moderation of the Greeks and their gods. Greeks fight Centaurs, Amazons, and Trojans, and the gods struggle with the giants. What the viewer is presented with—or was presented with when these carvings were intact—is a generalization into which one can read one's own impressions, seeing the stories either in their original and familiar sense or as allegories depicting the ordering of the Athenian state, the subjection of its citizens to law, and the state's victories over foreigners, especially Asians. The pediments represent themes peculiar to Athena. In the east is her birth from the head of Zeus and in the west her competition with Poseidon for the guardianship of Athens—which Athena won, though Poseidon continued to receive special honors. Apparently accompanying Athena and Zeus in the former was Hephaestus, the god of the technical arts, who shared a major temple with Athena in the city below. The viewer here is led to understand that from its beginning the city was the recipient of the blessings of the gods, which included the gifts of wisdom and power (symbolized by Zeus and Athena) as well as the more prosaic arts of human livelihood (Hephaestus).

The frieze around the cella represents in great detail the Panathenaic procession, the central part of Athens's greatest festival. This most important celebration recalled the early origins of Athens, when the scattered villages of Attica were brought together in the common worship of Athena. The whole population was involved in this procession—even the *metics,* or resident foreigners, were given some functions to perform. In the artistic representation of this community celebration, we have perhaps the best example of the classical spirit of idealization and exaltation of humans to the company of the gods. However, the figures are not Greeks in general, nor is the procession some universal Hellenic ceremony; it is something peculiarly Athenian. Not only are the individuals in the sculpture idealized, but the frieze as a whole is an idealization of the Athenian state. All its members are represented—the old and the young, men and women, citizens and metics—all harmoniously bound together in the public worship of Athena. Here the classical spirit is most finely attuned to the inner balance and dynamism of the Athenian state itself.

The perfect balance of the
classical style: Lapith and
Centaur struggle with
each other in one of the
metopes of the Parthenon.

The godlike youth of Athens ride majestically in the Panathenaic procession frieze from the Parthenon.

THE LATER CLASSICAL PERIOD (430–338 B.C.)

The last 30 years of the fifth century B.C., during which Athens fought its bitter war with Sparta, have always been considered as dominated by the forceful but negative views of Euripides, Thucydides, and Aristophanes, the great intellectual masters of the age. This period is seen, as a consequence, as one of disintegration and moral and social revolution, with the full impact of Sophist ideas and the disasters of the war causing a split between the intellectuals and the community as well as between oligarchs and democrats. Indications of declining religiosity and the excesses of the democracy, as exemplified in such acts as the execution of the generals after the battle of Arginusae and the massacres at Scione and Melos, become examples of moral decline.

Although there is a great deal of truth to this interpretation, the nature of the evidence also has to be taken into account. Philosophers and intellectuals pursued a life of their own that may or may not have had anything to do with the conditions of the times, whereas humorists such as Aristophanes deliberately parodied and distorted what they saw for the sake of comic impact. All our interpreters were to some extent alienated from their community. Euripides lived as a recluse and eventually fled Athens altogether, and Thucydides was an exile for 20 years. Their pronouncements therefore need not be taken as evidence of a massive moral breakdown but rather as the expressions of gifted souls grappling with the problems raised by the continuing growth of the democracy, particularly by its conduct during the long and brutal war with Sparta.

Power and the People

During the last years of the fifth century B.C., the Peloponnesian War imposed excruciatingly difficult decisions on the Athenian democracy and made greater demands than ever before on the citizenry. These demands further stimulated the secularizing tendencies already present in the democratic processes themselves, as has been noted in connection with the drama of Aeschylus and the role of oratory in decision making. After 430 B.C., in part because of the war, the process advanced a stage further, as is particularly noticeable in the unmasking and secularizing of the sources of power within the state.

Despite spectacular advances in other areas, for citizens of modern democracies the nature and exercise of political power remain shrouded in mystery. Perhaps surprisingly, in fifth-century B.C. Athens, thousands of citizens were familiar with the uses of political power and were accustomed to acting as free agents in assemblies and courts that exercised full power. They were responsible only to themselves and their laws. There were no tyrants or aristocrats making decisions in private and then casting about for means of communicating them to the uninformed masses, and no secrecy surrounded the decision-making processes of the developed democracy. There was no need to pretend to a higher knowledge, and no establishment whose first loyalty was to maintaining itself at whatever cost. All the usual governmental pomp was set aside in favor of a common routine of daily business conducted, for the most part, under the guidance of very ordinary mortals. Subjects from the drainage of the agora to war and peace were debated publicly in all their hard reality. The hundreds of wrong decisions on major and minor issues were immediately laid on the shoulders of the mass of the people, who, despite efforts at excusing themselves (claiming, for example, to have been absent from the Assembly on crucial days), were still ultimately responsible for all that they did. Unlike modern citizen bodies, Athenians found it extremely difficult to find scapegoats for their blunders. There was no government to blame, no independent bureaucracies, no secret policies arrived at in private. They could vent their anger on their leaders—which they did frequently—but this was a minor matter considering how vulnerable they were and what little institutional power they exercised in any case.

Thucydides: Power, War, and Society

Thucydides served Athens as one of the ten generals elected in 424 B.C., but having failed against the Spartans in the north of Greece, he was exiled and returned to Athens only after the Peloponnesian War. His account of the war is considered one of the greatest histories ever written and one of the finest pieces of intellectual analysis of all time, but it is not a history in the modern sense of the term.

Thucydides' object was not just to achieve historical truth in the sense of presenting the facts accurately. He also sought to penetrate the surface of individual events to discover the universal and permanent laws concealed in them and to reveal causes that lead predictably to the same results. For example, he pointed out that although Athens might be universally hated because it wielded almost total power throughout Greece, this was not due to anything peculiar to the nature of Athens or the Athenian people but to the nature of power itself, which has its own laws and generates the same kind of reaction no matter who possesses it. War and justice, he concluded, cannot coexist; the powerful oppress the weak, and all states act in their own self-interest. He sought to lay bare the underlying but hidden structures of the state and the various constraints these imposed on its citizens in the conduct of interstate relations.

Thucydides regarded war itself as a problem to be solved by proper analysis. Events for him were not right or wrong, good or evil. He did not view them in ethical or moral terms but rather as questions of fact: What are the causes of conflict? What courses do social revolutions take once they begin? That people or states act from expedience or use whatever power they have at their disposal is not weighed for its good or evil consequences; Thucydides merely determined whether it was a fact. People and states must act according to their natures, and Thucydides' practical aim was to unravel the nature of both and leave the answer as a guide ("as an eternal possession," was his expression) to future generations. The Athenian people were no more exempt from these laws than any other. That they failed was a melancholy confirmation of Thucydides' bleak view of human nature.

"WAR IS A HARSH TEACHER": THE JUDGMENT OF THUCYDIDES

Thucydides judged the Greeks against a broader background than did Herodotus. During the bloody civil wars that sprang up in Greece during the Peloponnesian War, beginning with Corcyra 427 B.C., he found that human nature itself was at fault.

> So bloody was the progress of revolution, and the impression which it made was the greater as it was the first to occur. Later on, of course, the whole Hellenic world was convulsed, struggles being everywhere made by the popular chiefs to bring in the Athenians, and by the oligarchs to introduce the Spartans. In peace there would have been neither the pretext nor the wish to extend such invitations; but because in war an alliance [is] always available for either faction to attack their adversaries, and advance their own interests, opportunities for bringing in the foreigner were never lacking to the revolutionary parties. The sufferings which revolution caused the cities were many and terrible, such as have occurred and will always occur as long as human nature remains the same, though in a severer or milder form, and varying in their symptoms, according to the variety of the particular cases. In peace and prosperity states and individuals have better inclinations, because they do not find themselves confronted with overwhelming necessities; but war takes away the easy supply of daily wants, and so proves a harsh teacher that brings most men's characters to a level with their fortunes.

—Thucydides, *History of the Peloponnesian War 3.82.* Based on the tr. of R. Crawley (London, 1874).

Aristophanes: Another View of Power and the People

Aristophanes, the great comic playwright of the late fifth century B.C., had a keen eye for the pompous and the absurd, and took delight in skewering politicians, philosophers, poets, scientists, and musicians. He took on the gods, the people, the old, the young, men, and women.

Though critical of the democracy, he was not in sympathy with the reactionaries of the oligarchic coup of 411 B.C. or the Thirty Tyrants at the end of the Peloponnesian War. There were limits to his barbs. Although he often made the gods look ridiculous on the stage, he never made fun of the Mysteries of Eleusis. He made no jokes about menstruation or lesbianism, although his plays are otherwise full of coarse jokes about sex and excretion. If his plays taught social or moral lessons, they were never entirely without some complication. In *The Clouds,* for example, Strepsiades, a cunning but gullible farmer, finds himself in debt and thinks that by enrolling his son in "Socrates'" school he will be able to use his son to fend off his creditors in court. The son is coerced into attending the school, but later, when father and son quarrel, the son, relying on his "education," beats his father in violation of an important taboo in Greek society. The father now regrets his dishonest effort to cheat his creditors, and sets fire to "Socrates'" school and attacks his students. It says something of the tolerance of the Athenians that Aristophanes survived two oligarchic

ARISTOPHANES DEMOLISHES "SOCRATES"

In *The Clouds* a cunning old farmer named Strepsiades tries to escape from his creditors by taking lessons from "Socrates." Here is a sample of what he got:

STREPSIADES (*puzzled*): But look—Zeus, up on Olympos, don't you count *him* a god?

SOCRATES (*incredulous, scornful*): *Zeus?* What rubbish! There's no Zeus!

STREPSIADES (*awestruck*): What? Well! (*Recovering countenance a bit*) Who makes the rain? You just tell me that, for a start!

SOCRATES (*gesture towards the chorus of the comedy, who represent Clouds*): *They* do, of course. I'll explain. The evidence is overwhelming. Have you ever seen rain without clouds? *But,* on *your* theory it ought to rain out of a clear sky, with no clouds in sight.

STREPSIADES (*impressed*): Well, by God, that certainly fits with what you were saying. Do you know, honestly, I always thought it was Zeus pissing through a sieve! (*Cackles, then worried again*) But tell me—who does the thundering? That's what gives me the willies!

SOCRATES: *They* thunder—(*portentously*) in *random motion.*

STREPSIADES: Well, you *do* have some ideas! But how do you mean?

SOCRATES (*adopting lecturing manner*): When they are charged with fluid, and the laws of physics set them in movement, they hang low, laden with rain—through the laws of physics—and then, laden, they collide with each other and split—crash!

STREPSIADES: But who makes all those laws to get them moving? Isn't it Zeus?

SOCRATES: Oooooh no! It is *Atmospheric Rotation.*

STREPSIADES: Well, I never realised Zeus wasn't there any longer, but it was Rotation in charge. (*Suspiciously*) But—you still haven't explained to me about the noise, the thunder.

SOCRATES: Didn't I tell you that when the clouds are filled with water they collide with each other and produce a noise by virtue of their density?

STREPSIADES (*a little pugnaciously*): Well, what's the reason for thinking *that*?

SOCRATES (*patiently*): I'll explain with reference to your own experience. Have you ever filled yourself up with stew at a festival and then felt a bit funny in your guts, when a rumbling and bubbling runs all through them?

STREPSIADES: By God I have, and they give me terrible trouble when they're upset, and that bit of stew starts thundering—it's a terrible noise. Quiet-like at first—ppp! ppp! Then it steps it up—pppPP! And when I go and shit, it's *thunder*—ppppPPPPP!!!—just like the clouds!

SOCRATES: Well, just think what a fart you can produce from that puny belly of yours; and doesn't it stand to reason that the air above us (*points solemnly*)—infinite—can do a great crash of thunder? That, incidentally, is why the words "crash" and "crap" resemble each other.

— Kenneth Dover, trans., *The Greeks* (Austin: University of Texas, 1980), pp. 104–105. Used by permission.

coups and two democratic restorations. Even in wartime he could tweak the people and their leaders.

Euripides: Pondering the Injustice of the Gods

Since the democratic reform of the courts in 462 B.C., Athenians had become considerably more sophisticated and knowledgeable in their approach to questions of justice. The large citizen juries that replaced the old courts required a new kind of presentation by defendants and prosecutors alike. At the same time, new assumptions about what constituted guilt and how sanctions should be applied began to replace the deeply entrenched views of the past. It began to be assumed, for example, that every defendant had the right to make the best possible case for himself no matter how bad the circumstances might appear. Justice was no longer to be a function of social status. A case was to be resolved on the basis of the facts involved, not on the wealth and family connections of the individual concerned or on his alleged services to the state—though the latter often was the basis for a plea for special treatment by the jurors.

This new understanding of the nature of justice, with its underlying assumption of personal responsibility, clashed with the old view of guilt as somehow unrelated to the subject's internal state, something objective that he contracted whether innocent (as in the case of Oedipus) or not. This left the old mythology in a vulnerable position because it now appeared that the ways of the gods were less just than those of humans. What Aeschylus and Sophocles had consigned to the realms of faith and mystery could now, with the new techniques, be resolved in favor of a more earthly explanation. By Euripides' day the crudeness of the divine order of justice contrasted sharply (at least in the eyes of the more observant) with the one evolving in Athens, where there was a growing tendency to avoid blaming an evil cosmic system and instead to seek more ordinary explanations in human behavior and character. People, not gods, were to be held responsible. In addition, the solutions of Aeschylus' and Sophocles' earlier plays, which demanded a certain greatness on the part of the protagonists, clashed with the less-than-heroic middle-class values now predominating in democratic Athens.

Euripides (ca. 458–406 B.C.) faced this problem head-on and pursued the logic of the new understanding to the point where the old myths and legends often became practically unrecognizable. His characters complain bitterly about the injustice of the gods and humanity's fate. "You should be wiser than men, being gods," says the old man to the goddess Aphrodite in *Hippolytus*. Orestes and Electra, instead of being activated by respect for religion, as they are in Aeschylus' play, act for purely personal reasons and blame the gods for their deeds. Orestes knows that his father would not expect him to avenge his death by murder, yet Apollo commands the deed. "Where Apollo is stupid who is wise?" complains Electra in Euripides' play by that name. Do men know better than the gods who command such frightful deeds? Apparently they do, or should, Euripides suggests. Hercules, driven mad by the jealousy of Hera, kills his wife and children. Later, when he has regained his sanity at the end of the play, he reflects,

> I cannot believe that the gods commit unlawful acts . . . or that one god is master of another; for God, if he is truly God, needs nothing. These are the wretched imaginings of the minstrels.[4]

Whereas Aeschylus and Sophocles were able to ascribe a positive role to human suffering to justify it as a means to higher knowledge, Euripides observed that suffering just as easily degrades as elevates. Neither Hecuba in *The Trojan Women* nor Medea in the play by that name was able to rise above her suffering. Instead both were brought down to the levels of their tormentors and became maddened, vengeful murderers themselves.

It is no surprise that domestic violence makes its appearance with Euripides and that traditionally taboo issues such as the relations between husband and wife and between parent and children are aired with an unpleasant degree of realism. In *Medea* Jason, the hero of the Argonaut saga, becomes a pathetic middle-class figure, preoccupied with his station in society, ready to betray his much more heroic wife with the sophistic logic that although she saved his life and gave up her homeland for him, she had been more than compensated:

> From my deliverance you have gained more than you gave as I will show. You have had the opportunity to live among Greeks instead of barbarians and to learn what justice is and what it is like to live by law [*nomos*] rather than by the arbitrary compulsion of the strong.[5]

Jason at this point has violated the most fundamental of all laws and is about to contract a new marriage, in defense of which the best he can say is this:

> What I most desired was that we should live well and not be in need; for well I know that a poor man has no friends. Also I hoped to raise my children as befitted my house.[6]

Euripides' pursuit of the troubled state of human emotions led him to become, in one scholar's phrase, the world's first psychologist. His characters, confronted with the contradictions of the old myths, are left alone to struggle with their emotions. In the archaic world the passions of the mind and madness were thought to be things that came upon a person from the outside; now, with the gods confounded, these elements had to be accepted as part of human nature itself and not something existing in a demonic world over which people had no control. Now unmasked and confronted, they were still utterly terrifying and mysterious. If the problem of evil could no longer be shuffled off on an unseen world, it was still—or perhaps for that very reason more than ever—frighteningly real. The moment Euripides freed his charac-

---

[4]Euripides, *Madness of Hercules,* 1340.
[5]Euripides, *Medea,* 534–538.
[6]Ibid., 559–562.

ters from mythological beliefs, he was forced to show that they were still the slaves of overwhelming forces. Agamemnon, though convinced of the moral rightness of freeing Hecuba, the former queen of Troy, refused to do so because of his fear of the reaction of the army. Reflecting on this weakness of the king, Hecuba says, "No man is free; he is the slave of money . . . or fate, or else of the mob which rules the state."[7]

Socrates and the Sophists: The Quest for Certainty

The democracy of Athens demanded that its citizens think about weighty matters and take positions on a variety of legal, administrative, and policy issues. The Sophists prepared the people to enter public life and equipped them with the latest techniques of persuasion and dialectical analysis. In the courts, theater, the Assembly, and the agora, new ideas were relentlessly discussed and argued by some of the most provocative minds in history. Fifth-century B.C. Athenians had no comfortable insulation from the intellectual life of the city, nor had their philosophers as yet built ivory towers to which to flee. The great debate over the sources and validity of moral and political obligations that was now coming into public prominence was therefore significant not only to the intelligentsia but to the whole Athenian community.

For some the realization that laws were man-made conventions was a liberating experience. They were freed from what seemed to be the meaningless rules and irritating obligations of tradition. For others, who hoped to see the democracy founder, the new theories provided sophistic camouflage for treasonous theories. In Plato's *Gorgias* the speaker Callicles sees law as a conspiracy of the weak to restrain the strong, their natural masters. The same idea is repeated in *The Republic* by the Sophist Thrasymachus, who uses analogies from nature, where, he claims, the larger and stronger animals devour the weaker and the quick-witted outmaneuver the slow and stupid. He concludes with the aphorism that the "justice of men is in fact the expediency of the strongest" and that all states are rigged to suit the convenience of their rulers, whether they be the one or the many or the few. The immorality of Alcibiades and the brutality of the oligarchs in 411 and 404 B.C. chillingly demonstrated that these were more than the philosophic or neurotic musings of alienated intellectuals.

Another way in which the new theories could be seen to have practical, if less malevolent, consequences for the city was in the impulse of some thinkers to withdraw from public life. Aristippus of Cyrene, a student of Socrates, said that officeholding was a time-consuming and laborious form of slavery that the sensible person would avoid. Antisthenes, the precursor of Cynicism, tossed out the whole city-state concept and said that people should live not according to the laws of the city but according to the laws of virtue.

On the opposite side, two of the most vigorous minds in history, Socrates and Plato, came to the defense of the beleaguered city-state, and tried to find a new and irrefutable moral basis for it.

[7]Euripides, *Hecuba,* 864.

Socrates—insofar as it is possible to reconstruct his thought, for he left no written material—rejected the relativism of the Sophists and the belief that it is impossible to arrive at any secure basis for right and wrong. He agreed that customs differ from city to city and made a distinction between *right usage,* which might vary, and *abstract right,* which is eternal and universal. The animal world, he argued, was not suitable for comparison with human beings. For the basis of morality one had to pass to the suprahuman realm of Universal Right. The essential difficulty with human beings was their ignorance and lack of insight into the nature of good and evil. Politicians especially lacked this knowledge, and the political expertise of the Sophists, which Socrates classified as mere know-how or technique, was inadequate. Socrates was executed in 399 B.C. by the Athenians on charges of introducing strange gods and corrupting the youth.

Plato's Solution

Socrates' disciple Plato (ca. 429–347 B.C.) was a member of the Athenian upper classes and a relative of Critias and Charmides, two prominent members of the Thirty Tyrants who had ruled Athens after the fall of the democracy. Born shortly after the beginning of the Peloponnesian War, he was a witness to the catastrophic events of the last years of the fifth century B.C. The excesses of the Thirty, coupled with the execution of Socrates some years later, so disgusted him with public life that he withdrew from Athens for a time and visited Sicily and southern Italy, where his encounter with the Pythagorean sects had a profound effect on his life. He returned to Athens and around 387 B.C. opened a school beside the Academy gymnasium.

For Plato all existing constitutions were bad and all laws inadequate because they were incapable of meeting the innumerable new situations created by the complex and constantly changing events of daily life. What was needed was a ruler or rulers who possessed true knowledge of what was good for the state. This knowledge did not come from practical politics but was rather a transcendent understanding of the state and its nature. If people of such godlike insight could be found or trained, there would be no need for laws or constitutions, and the stability of the state would be permanently guaranteed. Like Socrates, Plato held that the possession of knowledge and wisdom, not of technical or practical ability, was the first and only true prerequisite for the statesman.

The ideal state, as described in Plato's masterwork, *The Republic,* should be divided into three approximately hereditary groups, the Guardians, the Auxiliaries, and the rest of society—that is, the handful of gurulike rulers, their military assistants, and the rest of society. These were not economic or social classifications. The rulers were forbidden to marry, have families, or possess property, as these interests could distract them from their essential purpose of guiding the state. Eugenics was to be used to produce the best candidates for the top groups, and there was to be no discrimination on the basis of sex. Women would be free, if they possessed the talents, to become either Guardians or Auxiliaries. Strict control of beliefs was to be exercised throughout the state, and there was to be no economic imbalance between the rich and the poor. A comprehensive education was to be provided for all, but the higher levels would be reserved for those who showed particular aptitude.

Between writing *The Republic* (ca. 375 B.C.) and the great work of his later years, *The Laws,* Plato made two trips to Sicily (367 and 361 B.C.) in a vain attempt to influence the tyrant of Syracuse, Dionysius II. When he returned to the task of establishing the constitution of the ideal state, which he continued until his death in 347 B.C., his confidence in the ability of people to be guided directly by reason was gone, and he was prepared to settle for what he called a second-best type of state. In this state people would be ruled by laws created by experts. Because these laws were to be framed following fixed and external models, all citizens were to be rigidly bound by them. Henceforth, God, not human beings, was to be the measure of all things. Driven by a mixture of high personal idealism and despair over the capacities of people to reach these ideals, Plato produced a caricature of the city-state in which conditioning, not consent, was to be the essential means of holding it together. Although the Athenian democracy continued to function ably in the welter of Greek interstate politics, Plato refused to consider the possibility that the mass of citizens could do anything to save themselves and looked for hope beyond his own turbulent times to the serene and unchanging world of the divine.

Aristotle and Isocrates: The Pragmatic Approach

Aristotle (ca. 385–322 B.C.), who also treated the question of how people should best live in the ideal state, was much less severe in his judgment of the abilities of the masses and a good deal more pragmatic than his mentor, Plato. Following a different theory of knowledge, which looked for truth in the workings of things rather than in ideal forms in a transcendent world, he analyzed over 150 constitutions to discover the laws that either kept them in existence or led to their destruction. Like Plato, he did not move beyond the city-state and assumed that the good life could be found only in this form of human organization. From his studies Aristotle seems to have concluded that what counted was not the precise type of constitution so much as its internal balance between two opposites, narrow oligarchy and extreme democracy. He emphasized the importance of office-holders and the kinds of office they held, and in general seems to have preferred citizens who were neither too rich nor too poor—the middle classes, in other words—believing that among these could be found most readily the two essentials of a stable constitution: justice and friendship. When these were absent, there was likely to be discontent, which would soon lead to revolution. The essential stabilizing element was proportional equality, which protected the poor from oppression, shielded the rich from expropriation, and rewarded the able.

Whereas Plato and Aristotle attempted to shore up the city-state by making more demands on its citizens and seeking a new basis for it in certain knowledge or workable laws, the rhetorician-educator Isocrates looked for help elsewhere. He deplored the anarchy of Greek politics, which set state against state and gave solace only to Greece's enemies, the Persians. He had no radical political solutions but made eloquent appeals to prominent fourth-century B.C. figures, such as Dionysius I of Syracuse and Philip of Macedonia, to lead a united Greece against its enemies. In opposition to Plato, he defended the study of rhetoric as a legitimate means of education, arguing that moral consciousness could be developed from a study of speech:

> I believe . . . that men become better and worthier if they are determined to speak well and if they have the desire to be able to persuade their listeners.[8]

For Isocrates the essentials of rhetorical education—analysis, composition, and the like—were valuable in themselves. Knowledge of the probable was attained by rhetoric, and topics analyzed by the rhetorical method attained a deeper significance. It was not, therefore, as Plato had claimed in his earlier writings, a discipline without content, dedicated to deception and distortion. These high ideals were much easier to proclaim than to live up to, and in the subsequent history of Greek oratory, Plato's judgment on the subject was unfortunately borne out more often than not.

ATHENIAN SOCIETY

The experiences of everyday life in a modern Western state are often not much help in enabling us to understand how the societies of the ancient world functioned. For instance, we usually take for granted the fact that despite the presence of disenfranchised groups in a modern state, the vast majority of the population will still be citizens. We would have difficulty in coming to grips with the reverse situation, where the number of noncitizens far exceeded the number of citizens (as in Sparta) or came close to 50 percent (as in Athens). When we talk about Athenians, what do we mean? Do we mean Athenians in the sense of Athenian citizens? In that case, however, what about Athenian women, whose legal status was equivalent to that of children? Are we to include *metics*—foreigners whose ancestors might have come to Athens generations earlier and who had no intention of returning "home"? Where do slaves and freedmen (ex-slaves) fit in? In terms of physical appearances, it was impossible to tell slave from free, *metic* from citizen. The cynical writer known as the Old Oligarch, while commenting on the privileged positions of slaves and aliens in Athens, explains why a slave would not step aside for a citizen on the street:

> Slaves and foreign residents (*metics*) have a great deal of license in Athens. You cannot strike them, and they will not step aside for you. There is a reason for this: if it were legal for you as a free born person to strike a slave, foreign resident or freedperson, you might often end up hitting an Athenian by mistake because ordinary Athenians do not dress any better than slaves and *metics,* nor are they superior in appearance.[9]

[8]Isocrates, *Antidosis,* 275.
[9]Pseudo-Xenophon, *The Old Oligarch,* 1.10, 2.7–8.

He is exaggerating, of course, for as soon as a person spoke it must have been possible to tell by the accent from where that person had come. Xenophon, one of Socrates' students, says that there were Lydians, Phrygians, Syrians, and people ("barbarians" is the term he uses) from every country among the resident alien population of Athens. We know also of Egyptians, Phoenicians, Carians, and Thracians. Athens, and especially its port town, Piraeus, must have had a tremendous mix of languages, dialects, physical appearances, and ways of life. Nevertheless, despite all appearances of heterogeneity and openness, Athenian society was no melting pot. Instead it adhered to the model of the closed, *polis*-type society, where the main basis for social stratification between the inhabitants of any region was that of citizen and noncitizen.

Citizenship: The Inside Track

Only Athenian citizens could own land, exercise all the rights of membership in the community, and share fully in its benefits. The franchise was exclusive and extended only rarely to outsiders. Lysias the orator, whose father had been persuaded by Pericles to migrate from Syracuse, lost his fortune during the regime of the Thirty Tyrants and solidly backed the democracy through all its tribulations, yet never received citizenship. Until 450 B.C. it was sufficient grounds for citizenship that one's father was an Athenian; after that date both parents had to be citizens. Residence in a *deme* (local district) was essential to establishing full citizenship, and the *deme* assembly was responsible for the first examination and enrollment of candidates for the citizenship on the *deme* rolls. In his eighteenth year a potential citizen presented his application to the *demarch* (the chief magistrate of the *deme*), and the whole *deme* assembly voted to accept or reject it. If the candidate failed here, he could appeal to a court in Athens, but if rejected by the court, he could be sold into slavery. Successful candidates next needed the endorsement of the Council, and then two years later their names were written on the list of those eligible to attend the main Assembly of Athens. So concerned were the Athenians with maintaining a strict watch on the citizenship rolls that periodic checks were made to see that no one had surreptitiously entered his name on the list or that no underage candidates had been admitted. In a formal legal and political sense, women belonged to a *deme* only through their relationship with a husband, father, or guardian.

For a long time the ownership of land was a prerequisite for membership in the assembly, and the landless were relegated to a position of half-citizenship. Under the tyrants, land allotments were made to many of the poorer citizens, who were thus enabled to become full members of society, and by the end of the sixth century B.C. the possession of land ceased to be a requirement of full citizenship.

Since Solon's time (ca. 600–550 B.C.) Athenians had been divided into various categories by census classifications, which were never abolished by law. Even under the full democracy, when access to office was practically guaranteed to everyone, a few positions, such as treasurer of the goddess Athena, were reserved for the very rich only. And at least in the eyes of the law, the lowest group, the *thetes,* were automatically excluded from office-holding. In practice, however, according to Aristotle, no candidate for office would ever admit belonging to this class.

Rich and Poor and the Athenian Economy

Despite ease of access to office and popular control of the Assembly and the courts, the distinction between aristocrat and commoner, rich and poor, was very much alive at Athens. Down to the end of the fifth century B.C. it was considered chic to proclaim one's family name, marry within the caste, and keep up family traditions and fortunes. Young aristocrats wore their hair long and competed fiercely against one another in sports, music, dancing, and horse racing. The aristocratic Alcibiades boasted to the Spartans that when Athens seemed to be at the end of its resources during one of the many crises of the Peloponnesian War, he was able to enter seven chariots in the Olympic Games and win first, second, and fourth prizes. "It is not idiocy," he said, "when a man at his own expense benefits not only himself but also his city."[10] In the eyes of middle-class Athenians, however, the aristocratic lifestyle included more questionable practices, such as rowdy drinking parties and pederasty. An anonymous critic commented that the life of young aristocrats at Athens consisted mostly of hangovers, idleness, and bathing. They knew nothing, the source claimed, beyond "drinking, bad singing, gourmet cooking and outlandish luxuries."[11] This, of course, has to be set against the aristocratic view of the "people" as "ungrateful, fickle, vicious, jealous, uncultured."[12]

In the fifth century B.C. rich and poor together benefited from the empire of Athens. The rich received jobs and official positions in large numbers, as well as opportunities to buy large, profitable estates around the Aegean. The common people got land in the form of colonial allotments overseas as well as many new jobs generated by the demands of maintaining the fleet. Revenue from the empire made it possible for the state to provide pay for juries and for councillors to attend the Council and for the masses to attend the festivals. More importantly, imperial revenue paid for the fleet. In the fourth century B.C., when the rich had to pick up the tab for the fleet, their enthusiasm for empire (and the democracy) rapidly waned.

Distinctions of wealth were not eliminated by the democracy, however. The general Nicias, whose blundering led to the defeat of the Sicilian expedition, had 1,000 slaves in the silver mines of Laurium, which brought him an income of 60,000 drachmas a year at a time when 130 drachmas was considered a subsistence income, and Demosthenes' father left an estate worth 84,000 drachmas. However, such estates were not large. The gift of about 40 acres to the grandson of the famous Aristides seemed a significant amount to Demosthenes, and the largest estate known was about 740 acres, which must have been exceptional. The vast majority of Atheni-

---

[10]Thucydides, *History of the Peloponnesian War,* 6.16.

[11]Aristophanes, *Daitales,* fragment 216.

[12]Pseudo-Plato, *Axiochus,* 369b.

ans—over 80 percent according to one calculation—were landowners to some degree, but most of these were small farmers whose holdings did not exceed 25 acres. The soil of Attica was notoriously poor, and encouraged thrift and hard work. Living within one's income came easily to such people. The small farmers were independent and conservative—as Aristophanes put it, "Marathon men, close-grained and stubborn, made of oak and maple."[13]

In the fifth and fourth centuries B.C. Piraeus was the foremost port in the Mediterranean, and Athens itself was a great commercial center. The majority of workers in the nonagricultural sector of the economy were small-scale craftsmen and artisans who owned their own workshops. There they created their products, which they then carried to the agora to sell. Large-scale production was on the whole exceptional, and the largest known workshop was in the armaments field and employed 120 slaves. The ceramics industry, one of Athens's largest, was also at the level of small-scale production. The majority of potteries consisted of the master potter, who might also be the painter, and a number of slaves who assisted him with the preparation of the clay, supervised the firing, and so forth. There were no middlemen, and the potteries themselves served as shops for their goods. Nevertheless, these little industrial concerns provided sufficient income to permit their owners to devote themselves full time to public careers. In the late fifth century B.C. the aristocratic leadership gradually passed into the hands of the well-to-do middle classes such as the tannery owners Cleon, Anytus, and Timarchus, the lamp manufacturer Hyperbolus, and the knife and furniture producer Demosthenes (the father of the orator).

Metics, Foreigners, and Slaves

An important segment of the Athenian community consisted of the resident noncitizens, or *metics.* These may have been recent arrivals, or they may have lived in Athens for generations without having been assimilated into the citizen body. They could not own land (without a special grant) or property, or even lend money on land as security. They could not marry Athenian citizens, nor could they participate in the public life of the city. They were subject to special taxes and the duties of the liturgies (acts of public generosity) as well as service in the army or navy in times of crisis. Still, they had a privileged position compared to other foreigners. They were properly registered in the *deme* rolls, and at least down to the beginning of the fourth century B.C., when the custom fell into disuse, they had patrons who represented them in court. They could attend the public festivals, and live and worship as they pleased. If wealthy, they could be influential behind the scenes.

They came from all over the Mediterranean and the Greek-speaking world, and brought their labor and talents to many different occupations. They were barbers, bakers, dyers, and painters as well as skilled craftsmen in the fields of textiles, leather, ceramics, and metalwork. Two of the biggest workshops in Athens, both shield factories, were owned by *metics.* In the final stages of the construction of the

[13]Aristophanes, *Acharnians,* 223.

Erechtheum on the Acropolis, out of 86 workmen whose status is known, 24 were citizens, 42 *metics,* and the remaining 20 slaves. Contracts for construction were awarded to *metics* as well as to citizens. The merchant who sold the gold leaf for the decoration of the Parthenon, for example, had a Phoenician name.

Metics as well as foreigners who did not belong strictly to this class developed other careers in Athens besides those in trade and industry. This was especially true in the skilled professions, and artists, doctors, philosophers, and educators who wished to escape from the narrow confines of their own home states or were forced into exile for political reasons poured into Athens. The philosopher Anaxagoras, a friend of Pericles, was from Asia Minor; the Sophists Protagoras, Gorgias, Hippias, and Prodicus were from Thrace, Sicily, the Peloponnese, and the Cyclades, respectively. Aristotle was from the north of Greece; Diogenes the Cynic from Sinope in the Black Sea area; Zeno, the founder of Stoicism, from Cyprus. The famous Hippocrates of Cos practiced medicine in Athens, and Hippodamus of Miletus planned the city of Piraeus.

Slaves were present in large numbers in Athens during classical times. Some idea of the numbers is suggested by the proposal of a fourth-century B.C. orator, Hyperides, to free 150,000 slaves in the mines and elsewhere in the country at a time of crisis. There were no large estates in Attica requiring cultivation by chain gangs, but the mines devoured vast numbers of slaves. Most businesses that required regularly employed labor, as contrasted with those needing only occasional help, made use of slaves. The mines were operated by slaves working for citizen contractors who took out leases from the state. Other slaves were employed in the metal and arms workshops and by individual potters, building contractors, and the like. Generally, the freeborn were employed independently, the only exception to this being in the public works, where slave, *metic,* and freeborn worked side by side for the same wages. Although slaves were common, not everyone could afford them. The poor, as Aristotle commented, used their wives and children as slaves.

An important aspect of slavery in Athens was the degree of freedom possessed by some of those in bondage. Many slaves were hired out by their masters, and might go from job to job as needed or be put in charge of little workshops, where they could labor in much the same fashion as free craftsmen. Many of those who worked in this way were allowed to keep part of their income from their labor and could in time buy their freedom and continue their businesses as before. One of these freedmen, Pasion, had 120,000 drachmas invested in land, a shield factory that brought in 6,000 drachmas yearly, a bank that brought in 10,000 drachmas, and loans totaling 234,000 drachmas. For his services to the state—he provided 1,000 shields and 5 triremes—he was made a citizen.

Men, Women, and Families

From the viewpoint of the community as a whole, the first duty of Athenian men and women was to the state. The needs of the city circumscribed and defined the roles of both men and women and restricted the freedom of both. Self-fulfillment and self-expression were restricted to a few well-developed, community-approved lifestyles. Men were defenders of the city and of their households and active participants in the city's political life. Their households were considered essential to the survival of the city itself. Athenian males, no less than Athenian females, had little choice of whom and when they should marry or even whether they should marry. When they became household heads themselves, they had little choice over whether they should support their parents, give dowries to their daughters and needy relatives, or even marry a female relative and divorce their wives if they were the only surviving next of kin. All these matters were determined by social custom and enforced by community opinion, which ruled everyone's lives in the face-to-face society of Athens.

Husbands and wives alike were responsible for maintaining the honor, reputation, and economic standing of their households. To fail to do so was to invite criticism and public shame. Economic neglect, failure to maintain religious traditions, inappropriate sexual activity by any member of the household, or inadequate participation in local and national affairs could destroy the reputation of the household and with it its effectiveness as an indispensable unit of the community.

In economic terms husbands and wives collaborated to maintain the joint property that constituted their household and without which they could not raise their children or function socially or politically. Much more than in modern life, the household provided men and women with a ready identity recognized and honored by society at large. The economic worth of the household—its capital, so to speak—enabled parents to raise their children, provide the economic foundation of the next generation, and guarantee some security in old age. Work was shared by all members of the household—husband, wife, and children—along with relatives who might be living with them, and slaves if they had them. All collaborated at harvest times and other moments of intense cultivation during the year. Apart from agricultural work, which was the principal occupation of almost all Athenians, women also worked as vendors, nurses, midwives, bakers, and innkeepers.

Athenian society upheld an ideal of seclusion of women in the home, yet women had distinct spheres of economic and social activities of their own that legitimately and necessarily took them out of their homes. They went out to make purchases and exchange and borrow goods from their neighbors. Clothes were washed at the fountain and regular trips to the well had to be made to keep the household supplied with water. Farms had to be worked, especially at times when the men were away on military campaigns, as they were a good portion of the year. "How," remarks Aristotle, "is it possible to keep the wives of the poor from going out of doors?" Women were brought to court by their husbands or fathers to arouse the sympathy of the jurors. They were central to the religious activities of the city and were paraded at festival times. Upper-class women who could afford slaves to do the work that most other women had to do for themselves tended to appear less in public, and conformed more to the ideal of seclusion. When they appeared in public their ghostly pale skin advertised their status and distinguished them from the tanned and wrinkled women of the poorer classes.

The heads of families were responsible for the maintenance of the religious traditions and special rituals of the family, and the care of the ancestral graves.

Husbands and wives spent a great deal of their time in religious celebrations associated with the birth and marriage of their children and the children of their kin and neighbors. It was these rituals, along with funerals and neighborhood (*deme*) sacrifices and festivals, that brought kin and neighbors together communally and helped shape their identities as Athenians.

The primary object of marriage was the perpetuation of the household rather than companionship. Age differences between spouses and different forms of education and interests are often thought to have constituted major barriers to the development of spousal affection. It is also claimed that men could find companionship with other men, concubines, prostitutes, and slaves. Many of these kinds of associations and liaisons were frowned upon, however, and it is hard to believe that in a majority of cases these kinds of relationships could have substituted for the affection of husbands and wives. The spousal relationship constituted the only intimate sexual relationship a male Athenian could have with an Athenian female and should not be dismissed out of hand despite the frequent cynical and misogynistic comments of the literary sources. The joint effort of running a household, raising and educating children, and seeing them through the various stages of their lives must have led, despite age differences and other obstacles, to mutual respect and friendship. Aristotle, at least, assumes the existence of friendship between spouses and makes the point that the real damage done by adultery was to the *philia*, the affection, of the husband and wife.

Enforcement of Morals

In the highly competitive, face-to-face society of Athens, the maintenance of the family's honor, broadly defined in economic, social, and political terms, was the joint responsibility of husband and wife. Either could destroy the social standing of their *oikos* by their inappropriate behavior. In economic terms, failure to maintain the family's resources or to increase them so that they could be passed on to the next generation was regarded as shameful. Adultery on the part of the wife effectively destroyed a household. Although the offending wife was not subject to criminal prosecution, her husband was compelled by law to divorce her, presumably to avoid suspicion that he colluded in her adultery, and she was excluded from participation in public religious life. This was a major impairment of her social life, given the degree to which religion penetrated every aspect of Athenian life. If caught in the act of intercourse the husband could kill the male adulterer on the spot or haul him off to court for summary execution if he admitted his guilt. Adultery, although occurring within the private sphere of the household, was regarded as a dangerous violation of public order because it could lead to personal vendettas between individuals and families.

Athenian society was deeply ambivalent about erotic relations between male citizens. In general, submission to sexual intercourse was regarded as shameful and incompatible with the independence of a citizen. It was seen as slavish to submit to another male sexually, and this activity could lead to dishonor as well as social and legal censure. However, no statute prohibited intercourse between consenting adult males, and the law did not directly infringe on the private realm except where the kind of sexual activities engaged in could lead to the removal of a man from the ranks of full citizenship or disrupt the order of society.

The law specifically prohibited male prostitution and the procuring of boys. It partially disenfranchised anyone who engaged in homosexual intercourse for gain, whether as a juvenile or an adult. Boys were protected against their relatives—fathers, uncles, guardians—who might hire them out. There were extremely strict laws protecting adolescent boys while they were outside their homes from the erotic attentions of older males such as teachers, gym instructors, chorus trainers, or the men who frequented the wrestling ground. In fact, boys were protected by law as strictly as were young women, with the difference that because boys were in training to be active citizens and soldiers they had to interact on a regular basis with older men. Finally, homosexual intercourse between a boy and an older man was prosecutable under the law of *hubris* (violence), even if the boy was alleged to have consented. The family could prosecute on the grounds of infringement of the boy's or the family's honor.

The penalties for violation of the law were severe because the dangers involved were great, not just to the individual boy or his family, but to the city itself, because a dishonored family might seek revenge, and feuds between families could disrupt the city. Pederastic activities could also remove potential citizens from service to the *polis* by disenfranchisement. Thus, the state necessarily acted to protect its households and itself against disruptions of this kind.

At the same time, Athenian society recognized the existence of the practice of pederasty and under certain circumstances, though very limited ones, the practice was sanctioned by custom. Competition in politics, public life, athletics, and the display of wealth, especially among the upper classes, spilled over into competition for the favors of women and boys. Men married late in life and women early, so romantic courtship of the kind we are familiar with today could not take place. Much energy of this type was shifted to the courting of young boys. Needless to say, the practice placed boys in a very difficult position because to be thought to have yielded was to ruin one's reputation and role as a citizen forever. When their beards were grown boys were no longer appropriate objects of pursuit. The masses over the years came to regard pederasty as an upper-class practice and orators were able to use the accusation of pederasty as a way of arousing prejudice in the jury against the person they were attacking.

Daily Life in Classical Athens

There were two cities of Athens: the Athens where the gods had their gleaming marble temples, and the Athens where most Athenians lived in shabby, crowded conditions. A third-century B.C. visitor to the city could comment in surprise, "A stranger coming on Athens unaware would find it hard to believe at first sight that this was the famous city of Athens." However, this was the remark of someone seeing the city after the time of Alexander the Great, when the Greeks were building well-planned cities all over the Middle East and when a place like Athens seemed quaint and old-fashioned.

The city of Athens below the magnificent Acropolis was a jungle of winding, narrow, unlit, unpaved streets, muddy in the winter and dusty in the summer. The open gutters that ran down the middle of the streets began to give way to proper drains and sewers only in the fourth century B.C. Most of the houses shared common walls of bricks or stones mortared together with mud. Thieves found it easier to break in through walls than through windows or doors. One famous thief was nicknamed "Brazen" because of his burrowing abilities. Windows were unglazed holes in the walls or roof. Mostly one story high, the houses of Athens had flat roofs reached by an outside staircase. In the hot weather of summer, everyone slept on the roofs.

The furniture of the typical Athenian house was minimal: tables, chairs or stools, and chests for storing clothes and other goods. Beds were made of wooden frames crisscrossed with webbing. Blankets and pillows were used, but sheets were unknown. Getting ready for bed at night was a simple process of dropping one's outergarments and crawling under the blankets.

Peoples of various crafts and trades tended to group themselves in specific parts of the city. Potters, leatherworkers, butchers, carpenters, and smiths of all kinds each had their own districts where they lived and practiced their trades. These neighborhoods were noisy, smelly, and crowded, but no one was likely to be without companionship for long. The great need was for privacy, not intimacy. The well-off tried to segregate themselves from the poor and often lived in comfortable houses, usually built around open courtyards onto which all the rooms opened. Even the rich, however, did not live ostentatiously. In the fourth century B.C. the orator Demosthenes could complain that whereas the houses of such famous men of the past as Aristides and Miltiades were no different from those of their neighbors, the rich of his day lived in houses as large as temples or other public buildings. This was an exaggeration, but it demonstrates that anyone who wanted to play an active role in city politics had to keep a low profile or suffer the consequences of envious, carping criticism.

The simplicity of Athenian lifestyles carried over during the classical period into meals and food. The staple diet was barley or wheat bread supplemented by vegetables, especially beans and lentils. Cheese, garlic, onions, and olives were also eaten in large quantities. Meat was a rarity for the ordinary people except at festival times. Fish was more common and probably, along with bread, was the principal food of the average Athenian. Sardines, anchovies, squid, octopus, and shellfish of all kinds as well as large fish such as tuna were popular. For dessert there was dried or fresh fruit, nuts, and honey cakes. In the countryside a popular food was a thin porridge made of barley meal flavored with such herbs as thyme and mint, which gave its consumers strong-smelling breaths that helped identify them as countryfolk when they visited the city. Wine, watered and sometimes flavored with aromatic herbs such as cinnamon or sweetened with honey, was the standard beverage.

Although daily living had its stresses and strains, they were very different from those that modern people experience. Life was not dominated by the clock or the never-failing, never-tiring machinery of the factory. Work was done seasonally or on demand; it was not regarded as an end in itself. Money was important, but making money was not one of the great driving forces of society. Family farms and businesses were passed on from one generation to the next, reducing some of the tension associated with the choice of careers and jobs. However, family feuds and neighborhood disputes could be ferocious and long-lasting. Insults were never taken lightly, and jealousies tended to cut down to size anyone who seemed to be getting too self-important.

Domestic life was, in many respects, undemanding. Expectations of comfort, hygiene, and cuisine were uniformly low. The preparation of most meals was a matter of putting bread (bought in the neighborhood bakery), olives, fruit, and vegetables on the table with water and wine. Fish or meat might be bought cooked or brought home and barbecued on a simple charcoal grill. Of course, there was no refrigeration. Clothes were made at home, but they were mostly simple rectangles of cloth that were draped over the body and held in place by clasps and belts. No one wore underclothes. The same clothes were worn day after day and lasted a lifetime, sometimes being handed down to the next generation. There was no need to worry about being out of fashion due to changing styles.

Men spent a great deal of time hanging around the workshops of the artisans, the food stalls, the barber shops, and the marketplace, gossiping and snacking. Women took the opportunity of trips to get water at the public fountain to keep up with what was happening in the neighborhood and the city. A great deal of informal education, especially for lower-class women and children, took place in the streets of Athens. Long before issues of major or minor importance were taken up by the Assembly or the Council, they were likely to have been thoroughly hashed over in the streets, workshops, and houses of the city. Indeed, the most stimulating aspects of daily life for all Athenians were undoubtedly the workings of the democracy itself and the religious life of the city. The festivals and the meetings of the Council, Assembly, commissions, and courts all took place near the people's homes. They were not distant, obscure rituals conducted by professional bureaucrats and politicians and only occasionally involving the mass of the people. From *deme* level on upward, Athenians were involved in the day-to-day affairs of the state as normal parts of their lives. Although the women of Athens were formally excluded from direct participation in the political and judicial processes, it is hard to believe that they, especially the older women—the grandmothers, mothers, elder sisters, cousins, and aunts— did not have some say, significant at times, about what happened in the public realm.

Day-to-Day Democracy: The People and Their Government

Like all governments, that of Athens was a system of sorts, some of it planned, much of it accidental. It had several characteristic principles of operation. All power was concentrated in the hands of the people, but because the people could not perform all the tasks necessary in such a large state, they had to delegate this power to various magistrates and boards. Deliberately, there were no clear-cut distinctions between the branches of government. The same body of people could be at one time a legislative assembly and at another a supreme court. Roughly, however, the main divisions corresponded to the traditional components of government: the Assembly (the legislature), the various magistracies and boards of the commissioners (the executive), and the court system (the judiciary). However, underlying the government of the city itself was the administrative and political system of the *demes*.

The Demes   The Athenian democracy had its secure foundations in the local *deme*, or precinct organization. Attica, the geographic region in which Athens was located, had over 139 of these local units, each with its own assembly and elected officers, its religious ceremonies and festivals. *Demes* owned property, levied taxes, and organized local cults. The *deme* assembly met regularly and took care of all neighborhood business. The *deme* was, in effect, a *polis* in miniature.

The *demes* formed the political and administrative infrastructure of Athens. Their role in the government goes a long way toward explaining the success of Athens's experiment in radical democracy. In the *demes'* assemblies and committees, the local small farmers, tradespeople, and aristocrats met and hashed out their differences. It was here that they learned the essential process of give-and-take and gained the experience that they needed when they were called to serve in the city's administrative and political system. Beyond practical experience in day-to-day politics, the *demes* provided the actual mechanism by which appointments were made to the Council and the commissions of Athens.

The Assembly   The Assembly (*ecclesia*) of the Athenian people, when properly called into being, was the sovereign power of the state. It met four times in every 36-day period (*prytany*) of the civil year, or 40 times a year. These meetings followed a regular agenda, which included (though not all at the same time) such items as votes of confidence in the current magistrates, defense needs and food supplies, accusations of treason, petitions from individuals to approach the Assembly on public or private concerns, foreign affairs, and religious matters. Almost all these issues were handled through a prepared schedule of motions that originated in the Council (*boule*) and was published before the meeting. In addition, there were special meetings that required no particular program beyond the matter at hand. Pay was budgeted only for the regular meetings, which required five days' notice together with the publication of the agenda. Emergency sessions were called by trumpeter and signal fires.

The Assembly was open to all Athenian males 20 years old and above who were not otherwise barred from attending. Normally, however, someone would begin attending only after the completion of the required two years of military service. Those who attended were given tokens that entitled them to collect the equivalent of a day's wages (1 to $1\frac{1}{2}$ drachmas).

Originally, meetings were held in the agora, but in classical Athens (except in cases of ostracism) they took place on the Pnyx hill, which had been carved into the shape of an outdoor auditorium with a sloping, fan-shaped floor reaching out from the speaker's platform. In the fifth century B.C. the Pnyx had a capacity of about 6,000. This figure doubled in the next century. Average attendance in the fifth century B.C. seems to have been around 6,000, which may seem low considering the 25,000–30,000 eligible citizens, but is actually high, given the number of meetings held (a minimum of three per month), not counting special meetings.

The Assembly had full legislative, judicial, and executive control of the state. There was no scattering of power among the different branches, and when the Assembly reached a decision, it was final. There was no need for further consultation or referral to another agency, senate, or supreme court. The people in the Assembly could declare war; make peace; elect its most important officers (the generals); condemn individuals to death, exile, or fines; audit accounts; confer honors; and perform many other tasks. The Assembly controlled the diplomatic life of the city, received ambassadors, designated and instructed its own envoys, formed alliances, and debated foreign policy. In military matters it determined the number of ships in the fleet, the size and objectives of the expeditions, and the generals. It supervised the conduct of war and disciplined commanders; Thucydides the historian, who failed in a campaign against the Spartans, was one of those who suffered.

Apart from its general supervision of state affairs, the main function of the Assembly was the formulation of policy. Although many items were routine and could be handled quickly, major decisions could be hammered out only after long debate. Issues such as the decisions to use the income from the newly discovered silver veins at Laurium for war ships, to fight rather than submit to the Persians, and to resist Sparta and Macedonia were argued fiercely in the Assembly and could be settled only there. Policies regarding the allies, cases of secession, and the hundreds of decisions in the day-to-day handling of wars were other common issues.

The Executive Branch: The Council and the Commissions   It is clear that large assemblies, numbering in the thousands, could not cope with the details of routine administration. Dozens of temples and public buildings had to be maintained; ships had to be equipped and replaced, dockyards kept up, equipment procured; streets needed to be cleaned; taxes had to be collected; poets and choruses had to be assigned for the festivals. Over such matters and a majority of court cases, the people did not maintain direct control but instead delegated the responsibility to dozens of boards of commissioners and less often to individual magistrates. Once the Assembly reached a decision, it was usually up to some other agency to see that it was carried out.

The general administrative principle of the democracy was to create boards of 10 to 50 commissioners (at times as many as 500) to handle specific functions on behalf of the Assembly. These officers were appointed by two methods, lot and election. The majority of commissioners (over 1,800) were appointed by lot, whereas a little over 50 were elected. The coordination and supervision of the majority of the boards of commissioners was the responsibility of the Council, the chief executive and administrative agency of the Athenian people. In the late fifth and fourth centuries permanent laws (*nomoi*) were decided on by commissions of up to 1,000 members (*nomothetai*) drawn from the 6,000 jurors. These committees of *nomothetai* met for a single day only, listened to the arguments for and against the proposed law and then voted by a show of hands.

The council consisted of 500 members, but because this was still too large a number for the handling of routine affairs, a standing committee of the council was created, made up of one-tenth of the full membership. The members of this committee were called the *prytanes,* or presidents. All 50 came from one of the ten tribes into which the Athenians were divided, but the order of service of the ten groups was determined by lot, so that, except toward the end of the year, it was impossible even to guess which 50 would be assigned for any of the ten periods of the year. During their term in office the *prytanes* lived and ate in the Tholos, the circular building on the edge of the agora, close to the meeting place of the Council, the Bouleuterium. In addition to their regular council pay of five obols a day, they drew a supplemental allowance of one obol. Altogether this was the equivalent of a laborer's daily wage in Athens in the fifth century B.C. and somewhat less in the fourth century.

The presiding officer of the standing subcommittee was selected daily by lot and served for 24 hours. In the fifth century B.C. he was also chairman of the ten officers of the Council who presided at meetings of the Assembly, should one occur on the day he happened to be president. He was not eligible for a second presidency.

The whole Council was supposed to meet every day except holidays and days of ill omen—in all, about 300 times during the year. Its agenda (the *programma*) was prepared by the *prytanes* and followed a standard order of procedure, beginning with religious matters and the reception of ambassadors from other states. The secret ballot was used on occasion, but more often decisions were made by a show of hands, as in the Assembly. It was in the Council that almost all the essential business for the Assembly was worked out ahead of time in the form of motions. Easily accessible from the teeming agora, the councillors were very much in contact with what was going on in the city. We can imagine how, during the anxious debates on the fate of the generals after the battle of Arginusae, Socrates, who was among the presiding officers for the scheduled Assembly meeting, must have been lobbied by partisans of both sides, or how, when news of Philip of Macedon's rapid advance into Greece in 338 B.C. was received by the Council, its members, who were eating their dinner in the Tholos, got up, cleared the agora, notified the generals of the situation, and prepared to debate the matter before advising the Assembly.

The Functions of the Council   The Council had a number of major areas of responsibility, its first being the preparation of motions to present to the Assembly. As a general rule, nothing could come before the Assembly without prior examination and preparation by the Council, which therefore acted as a screening committee for the whole Assembly. It could make recommendations in the form of motions for or against a particular issue, or it could simply present the matter without offering any opinion at all. The Assembly, in turn, was free to approve, reject, or amend the proposed motions or substitute new ones.

Any individual, foreigner as well as citizen, could petition for a hearing by the Council, but it was up to this body to decide whether to quash the matter or present it to the Assembly. The Council could thus deny, or at least hinder, access to the people of Athens. However, there was a specified time in one of the regularly scheduled *prytany* meetings (the four that occurred every 36 days) that allowed an individual to approach the Assembly directly.

Besides preparing the Assembly's agenda, the Council also supervised a large number of boards of commissioners and had judicial functions. In the area of finances, the Council was the Assembly's chief administrative agency. When the city had an empire, the Council supervised the assessment, collection, and payment of the tribute.

The Council also had primary responsibility for the maintenance of the fleet, Athens's principal military arm. This involved the supervision of those responsible for the shipyards and arsenals as well as of new ship construction. Because the number of ships might reach 300—though only a small percentage of these might be in active service—this was a major responsibility. Despite the fact that the operation of Athens's largest and most expensive public enterprise was spread among so many boards and individuals, it operated efficiently. To cite one example, despite the loss of 170 ships in Sicily in 413 B.C., Athens had 100 ships in Samos two years later and 180 at the last battle at Aegospotami in 405 B.C. Starting once more from scratch after the Peloponnesian War, Athens had over 100 ships by 376 B.C.; by the middle of the century, 300 were available. The military training of the 18-year-olds (*ephebes*) and the cavalry came under Council purview, along with many religious functions, the checking of the list of orphans and the handicapped who were eligible for state support, and the examination of incoming archons and councillors-elect for the coming year.

The Judiciary

GENERAL PRINCIPLES   As in all other realms, the first principle in the administration of Athenian justice was the preservation of the sovereignty of the people. Nothing was allowed to intervene between the people and those bringing suit or being sued. Athens tolerated no legal profession and had no full-time judges or attorneys, no system of criminal detection and apprehension, no public prosecutors. In the Athenian view such specialists would take power from the people and concentrate it in their own hands. In the past the Athenians had seen how much power control of the judiciary had given to tyrants and aristocrats. In actual practice this principle translated itself into the conferral of minimal amounts of power on individual magistrates, the retention of ultimate control by large juries of the people, and other devices such as the right to bring suit against a presiding judge thought not to have acted impartially.

With no professional police to detect crime and no public prosecutor's office to lodge complaints in the name of the state, it was up to the individual injured to bring suit. This could happen in two ways. The first was where the injured party had been beaten, robbed, or otherwise directly mistreated by the accused, in which case the suit was considered private. In the second instance, if the crime could be construed to have somehow done damage to the community at large, any male Athenian in good standing with the law could bring suit, on the grounds that he, as a member of society, had suffered the injury along with everyone else. These suits were classified as public, and it was to this category that the charges against Alcibiades and Socrates belong.

Faced with the practical problem of maintaining control over the judiciary and at the same time administering justice to the (then) most litigious people in the world, the Athenians had recourse to the same principle that had worked so well for them in the administrative branch of government: the division of responsibility among a large number of magistrates or commissioners so that none would have much power or too complicated a task; in this way the average citizen would not be overwhelmed if he were to be selected for service. What emerged, therefore, was a system of justice that divided cases into many different but specific categories (homicide, family matters, orphans' cases, religion, etc.). Single magistrates (and occasionally groups) were responsible for each category. Their primary role was to screen cases and decide whether they were serious enough to be taken further. If they were, the next step in most private cases was to send it to an arbitrator. If this proved unsatisfactory to either party, the case went to one of the large citizen juries, with the original magistrate presiding.

THE COURTS   The principal court of Athens was the Assembly of the Athenians themselves. Its main concern was with matters of such serious nature that all of society was thought to be threatened and thus needed to be consulted on what action should be taken. An individual who claimed to have evidence of such a crime (an oligarchic plot against the state, for example) could approach the Council at any time and have the item placed on the agenda (i.e., once in every 36-day period). If he followed this course, the case would probably be referred to the Council or to one of the standing courts for further action. Only in the most urgent cases did the people as a whole sit in judgment. The majority of other cases had to be presented to the appropriate magistrate or board for prior examination. Thus the Forty (consisting of 40 jurors) functioned as a small-claims court that pronounced judgments on matters involving less than 10 drachmas. If the amount was greater than this, the case was referred to arbitrators. If they failed to provide satisfaction, it went to a court presided over by a member of the Forty. The most important officials were the nine archons, each of whom had his own special area of jurisdiction. In general, the bulk of the private cases came to the Forty; the six junior archons (or *thesmothetae*) handled the majority of public cases.

The courts of the people (*dicasteries*) must be distinguished from the individual magistrates and boards of commissioners to whom cases generally came for a preliminary examination. These courts were large, their size depending on the importance of the case, from 201 members for private cases to 501 or larger for public cases. Pericles was tried and fined by a court of 1,500 in 430 B.C., and a court of 6,000 considered the case of sacrilege involving Alcibiades before the Sicilian expedition.

Jurors for the individual courts were drawn from a pool of 6,000 chosen annually (the process is not known) from among the ten tribes. Jurors had to be 30 years of age or older and in good standing with the law. Originally a juror was automatically assigned to a particular court for the entire year, but late in the fifth century B.C., due to citizen losses in the Peloponnesian War and the spectacular bribery of one entire panel by Anytus (later one of Socrates' accusers), the process of assignment was reorganized according to an elaborate system of lot taking. First the requisite number of jurors were selected and then assigned to the courts in such a way that no one would know which jurors would be assigned to which cases until the day of the trial itself. The new system also guaranteed two other things: first, that whoever presented himself for jury duty would have an equal chance of being selected, and, second, that all the ten tribes would be fairly represented in the drawing process.

PROCEDURE   In both public and private cases the basic judicial procedure was as follows: accompanied by one or two witnesses, the plaintiff had first to summon the defendants to appear before a certain magistrate on a given day, stating the nature of the accusation and naming the day of the appearance. At the actual meeting before the appropriate magistrate, the plaintiff made his allegation (which after the middle of the fourth century B.C. had to be in writing). If the magistrate accepted the case, court fees had to be paid then and there. Generally, in private cases both parties made a deposit, and if the plaintiff did not pay immediately, there was no further action. At the conclusion of the case, the losing party had to reimburse the other for his costs. The fee schedule varied, depending on the importance of the case. In actions involving less than 1,000 drachmas, the fee was 3 drachmas; for cases involving under 100 drachmas, there was no fee. In public cases the accuser alone paid the fee, the amount of which is unknown. When all these preliminaries were completed, the magistrate established a day for the preliminary hearing (the *anakrisis*). In the meantime the accuser's charge was published in the agora.

At the preliminary hearing, oaths were taken on both sides; evidence was presented in the form of depositions of witnesses, contracts, laws, and the like; and objections were made. The principal responsibility of the presiding magistrate was to determine whether the plaintiff really had a case, whether he was the right magistrate to handle it, and whether the proper procedure had been followed. It was generally not his job to decide the case; he merely decided whether to go on to the next step. When he was satisfied on these matters, he then assigned the case either to arbitration, as was common in private cases coming before the Forty, or immediately to a court. If arbitration failed to satisfy both parties, the next step was to ask the *thesmothetae* to fix a day for a trial and to assign the appropriate number of jurors.

Failure of the defendant to appear at the preliminary hearing meant that the plaintiff was granted the judgment automatically (and vice versa). Private cases could be withdrawn at this preliminary stage, but someone who had brought a public

Fragment of a *cleroterion,* a mechanical device created by the Athenians to help avoid stacked juries. Each juror had a ticket that was selected at random and inserted in one of the slots. Colored balls, again selected at random, were then slid down the tube, part of which can be seen at the left. Depending on the color, each row of jurors was either selected or rejected.

charge was fined 1,000 drachmas if he failed to carry it through after the *anakrisis.* He was fined a similar amount if he failed to obtain one-fifth of the jurors' votes, the object in this and the previous instance being to reduce frivolous accusations with no substantiating evidence. Fines in public cases usually went to the state.

Religion, Drama, and the Festivals

Athenians were famous for the care they lavished on their public festivals, which visitors came from all over Greece to witness. Pericles, with classical restraint, said, "We provide plenty of means for the mind to refresh itself from business. We celebrate games and sacrifices all the year round."[14] The Old Oligarch put it more bluntly when he said that the Athenians had twice as many festivals as anyone else, with the result that public business suffered. In fact, the year offered Athenian citizens an opportunity to participate in as many as 50 festivals, one of which lasted up to nine days, and this does not include the innumerable *deme* festivals and private celebrations in honor of individual deities and family cults.

As in every other aspect of public life, the democracy had an impact here, generally by expanding the number of participants at every level. Boards of officials were selected to organize and supervise many of the festivals. One of the principal responsibilities of the chief archon was to select wealthy individuals (the *choregi*) for the honor of producing the choruses and plays for the City Dionysia festival, the most important dramatic festival of the year. Beyond official participation, however, hundreds and at times thousands were involved in the numerous athletic competitions,

[14]Thucydides, *History of the Peloponnesian War,* 2.38.1.

processions, dances, choruses, plays, and sacrifices that made up the festivals as well as in the preparations—sometimes taking as much as a year—that went into them. With the exception of the most secret aspects of the Eleusinian and other mysteries, there was little restriction on who could witness them. At some, *metics* paraded in glorious robes alongside citizens. These were truly community feasts that were essential to the proper functioning of the state. Through them the gods were properly honored, and each new generation of Athenians duly initiated into the religious and moral values of the city. All citizens were expected to attend, and the festivals were considered so vital that for at least two, and possibly more, the state funded both the participants' expenses and the cost of their theater tickets.

From July (when the Athenian year began) onward, festival succeeded festival. In December came a cycle of celebrations in honor of Dionysus. These are of particular interest because of the dramatic presentations that occurred during some of them. The first of these were the rural Dionysia, organized by the individual *demes*, which generally consisted of processions in which a large artificial penis was displayed to ensure the fertility of the crops sown in the previous months. In many of the *demes*, however, dramatic festivals were also part of the celebrations. Plays that had been performed on previous occasions at the major Dionysiac celebrations in Athens were staged.

The City Dionysia—or Greater Dionysia—in March was one of the festivals for which all citizens received money from the state. It began with a torchlight procession and the reenactment of the coming of Dionysus to Athens from Eleutherae, a village in the northwest of Attica. Then came several days of dramatic and musical contests whose exact order is unknown to us. There were competitions between 20 dithyrambic choruses from the ten tribes, ten each of boys and men, with 50 members in each. The producer for each chorus was a wealthy man nominated by his tribe and designated by the archon. This man chose both the poet and the musical instrumentalists. Prizes, such as bulls, tripods, caldrons of bronze, and amphorae of wine, were distributed. These songs and dances were short, to allow all 20 teams to compete, but could involve complicated steps and meters. At the end of each day there was another torchlight procession in honor of Dionysus.

On the following four days came the plays, three days devoted to tragedy and one to comedy. The dramas began with a sacrifice to purify the theater, which was regarded as sacred, and libations were offered. Next the tribute of the allies and the surplus money of the state were carried across the orchestra for all to behold. Then the sons of men who had fallen in battle, who had been brought up at state expense, were paraded in full armor. They listened to a short exhortation before taking the special seats allotted to them. Prisoners were released in honor of Dionysus, and the festival was also used as an occasion to confer honors on the friends of the democracy.

The last action before the plays began was the final selection of the judges of the plays. A number of these had already been chosen from the tribes and their names placed in sealed urns. These were now opened, and ten judges selected. At the end of the contest, each wrote his preferences, in order, on a tablet and placed the tablet in an urn from which five tablets were drawn at random. The judgments were read from these. Prizes for composers, composition, production, and acting were awarded.

The order of performance had already been settled, and now the plays were ready to begin. A trumpet sounded, and the 14,000 to 17,000 people in the audience settled down for four days of entertainment, during which nine tragedies, three satyr plays (semicomic pieces), and five comedies would be performed.

The Theater   Music and dramatic festivals were originally held in the Agora, but at the time of Pericles they were shifted to the newly built Odeon and theater of Dionysus on the slopes of the Acropolis, near the temple of Dionysus.

The new theater consisted of a round, level dancing space (the orchestra) on which the chorus performed its dances. Above the orchestra ranged the ramp of the theater, and on either side were access passages that allowed the chorus to come and go. The seats in the theater were made of wood and were not replaced with stone until much later. Behind the orchestra was the stage, a large wooden frame about 100 feet long. In front of the stage there may have been a low platform (this fact is disputed) connected to the orchestra by stairs, from which the actors could proclaim their pieces.

In the earliest plays there was only one actor and the chorus. Aeschylus increased the number of actors to two and Sophocles to three, and thereafter this remained the standard number. In the middle of the fifth century B.C. a prize for actors was introduced, and in time the stars of the theater came to command astronomical fees. The actors wore masks, but in classical times at least these had none of the exaggerated features—the staring eyes and high-piled hair—of later times. The masks were a necessity because the size of the theater made it difficult to see the faces of the actors, and because they also permitted the actors to switch roles quickly. Costumes in brilliant colors matched the masks. Actors needed strong, clear voices to reach the upper rows of the theater, and they were also expected to be able to chant and sing in recitative.

The chorus usually had 15 members, all carefully drilled to speak, sing, and dance as one. They were generally present during the whole play and helped to give it dramatic unity. In the days of the single actor the play consisted essentially of a dialogue between the actor and the chorus. The chorus sang its lines, but what actions accompanied this and what it did during the dialogue of the actors are difficult to say. It is likely that it interpreted the action of the play by appropriate rhythmic movements. Some choruses were much admired as masterpieces of craftsmanship in their own right.

Athenian audiences were made up of people from all segments of the community: *metics*, foreigners, men, women, and at times even slaves were included. Plato's comment in the *Laws* in regard to different persons' criteria of pleasure is revealing. He remarks that little boys enjoy the conjurors; older boys, the comic poets; and young men, educated men and women, and the public in general, tragedy. Such audiences were highly appreciative and critical. They were easily moved, "weeping, glaring wildly . . . marvelling at what they heard."[15] They clapped, hissed, and booed to indicate their approval or disapproval, singling out for special attention the technical skills (or blunders) of chorus, actors, and playwrights. Individual lines were attacked, and one line of Euripides' almost caused a riot on one occasion, forcing him to stand up and provide an explanation on the spot.

The audience sat from dawn to dusk listening to the performances, which went on without break. To fortify themselves, they brought refreshments, such as wine and dried fruits (the latter also substituted as missiles to be flung at actors they disliked). Physical violence was a capital offense, but occasionally rival *choregi* (wealthy men who financed the plays) came to blows. Once, when Alcibiades had put on a play, he was able to browbeat the judges into giving him the prize, even though the crowd favored his rival *choregus*. Politicians tried to get publicity out of the staging of the plays, and Nicias, who lacked eloquence, compensated for this deficiency by lavish productions that regularly won first prize.

In the theater, the agora, the courts, and the Assembly, the Athenian people were exposed to a stimulating and demanding social, political, and intellectual environment. Whatever its drawbacks, and they were many, no one could say that the life of the average Athenian citizen, male or female, was boring or that it revolved around unimportant things. Directly or indirectly, they participated in all the major decisions that affected their existence. They were liberally exposed to the current ideas. Few nations can boast a roster of names comparable to those of Athens in the period between the Persian wars and the opening of the age of Alexander. Even fewer can claim a society and system of government that brought these figures and their ideas into the everyday lives of the people.

[15]Plato, *Ion,* 535e.

Chapter 7

Philip, Alexander, and the Hellenistic World

BACKWARD MACEDONIA CHALLENGES GREECE

For two centuries a handful of cities dominated the history of Greece, as Athens, Sparta, Thebes, Corinth, and Argos were the focal points of all the major wars and of most of the social and intellectual development from at least the sixth century B.C. Then, quite suddenly, in the middle of the fourth century B.C., they were eclipsed by other states, none of which had had a significant role in the past.

For a decade after 356 B.C. the center of events in mainland Greece was the Sacred War waged by the minor state of Phocis against Boeotia, Locris, Thessaly, and Macedonia. During the same decade the Carian kingdom of King Mausolus in Asia Minor rose to importance and had a hand in the breakup of Athens's second empire. Somewhat earlier, Jason of Pherae had successfully united the immense potential of Thessaly behind him, but after his death the normal pattern of disunity established itself again. To the north the kingdom of Macedonia possessed the same potential as Thessaly, and it was Macedonia that finally emerged as the major power of the fourth century B.C. and put an end to the classical age of the Greek city-states.

Macedonia was unlike the rest of Greece in many respects. It consisted of two regions: the plain around the Thermaic Gulf of Macedonia proper and the highland region in the hinterland, over which the Macedonian kings exercised only a feeble sovereignty. It had a continental climate, and unlike the rest of Greece, it was not dotted with city-states. Its tribal system was still intact, and government above the tribal level consisted of an elected, though hereditary, monarchy. The kings, like many of their counterparts in similarly undeveloped societies, were at the same time priests, judges, generals, and treasurers. The nobles of the different tribes were bound to them by personal bonds of loyalty, and were considered the kinsmen and friends of the king. The upper classes, or at least the king and his court, spoke Greek and made a point of cultivating Greek culture. Artists and poets were invited regularly to Pella, the capital, and among those who stayed there were Euripides and the painter Zeuxis. The kings were recognized as Greeks by the officials of the Olympic Games, but Macedonia was not considered part of the traditional Hellenic world by the rest of the Greeks.

The potential of Macedonia was great. Its people were hardy, and there was plenty of rich land and great reserves of timber and metal. It had difficulty realizing its potential, however, because, more than any other state in Greece, it was exposed to outside pressures. Illyrians pressed in from the west, Paeonians from the north, and Thracians from the east. For generations the Greeks had maintained cities along the coast, and in the mid–fourth century B.C. the Chalcidian League could field an army almost as large as that of Macedonia itself. On the other side of the Chalcidice, Athens had an ongoing interest in the Thracian coastal regions, and Amphipholis was always a particular concern. So preoccupied were the Macedonians with their defense problems and with holding its upland and lowland regions together that it was generally safe for the Greeks to disregard them as a threat.

THE GENIUS OF PHILIP

When Perdiccas III of Macedonia fell in battle against the Illyrians in 359 B.C., his brother Philip was made regent and eventually became King Philip II. He had spent three years at Thebes during the time of Epaminondas and Pelopidas, where he had observed the tactical innovations and reorganization of the phalanx that enabled Thebes to overcome the Spartan hoplites at Leuctra and Mantinea. He certainly appreciated the military revolution occurring throughout Greece. Nevertheless, Philip's policies and strategies were peculiarly his own. He combined an extraordinary sense of timing with a Machiavellian ability to manipulate other states so that his enemies were able only slowly to divine his intentions and usually acted too late to thwart him. Although his military abilities were first-rate, Philip knew when to use force and when other tactics would be equally successful.

Heavily armed cavalry had been the traditional strength of the Macedonian army. Its nucleus was the Companion Cavalry, drawn from the nobles of the different tribes and attached to the king by personal loyalty. Philip strengthened the existing hoplite forces and modified the traditional phalanx form by giving the infantrymen much longer spears or pikes and spacing them farther apart, thus giving them more mobility. Philip also made use of light cavalry and light infantry. More important than the reforms themselves, however, was Philip's ability to infuse the army with a spirit of energy and enthusiasm that enabled its members to transcend their tribal backgrounds and become a single striking force. By dint of constant and successful campaigning, he was able to make the Macedonian army into a force without an equal in Greece or anywhere else.

Philip's first mission was to free Macedonia from the threat of the foreigners. First the Paeonians were subdued, then the Illyrians (358 B.C.). In gratitude for relief from Illyrian pressure, the king of Epirus offered his daughter Olympias to Philip in marriage. In the summer of 356 B.C. they had a son, whom they named Alexander.

While Athens was involved in the Social War, Philip took the important city of Amphipolis (357 B.C.). From there he moved to establish the fortress of Philippi, which guaranteed him access to the rich gold mines of Mount Pangaeus. Producing 1,000 talents a year, these mines made Macedonia economically independent and provided Philip with the essential resources for financing his ambitions. His next move was to eliminate the remaining Athenian possessions in the region, and in preparation for doing so he first secured the alliance of the Chalcidian League. Athens, still involved in the Social War, could only stir up the Illyrians and Thracians. It was unable to prevent the fall of Potidaea in 356 B.C. Two years later Methone, Athens's last possession, fell to Philip.

THE ORATOR AND THE KING: DEMOSTHENES AND PHILIP

Despite its humiliation, Athens seemed willing to accept its losses. In part this was because its main interests were in the Hellespont and the Bosporus, which were not directly threatened by Philip, and in part because of internal developments. Since 358 B.C. Athens's *theoric,* or festival fund, had become an independent agency, and Eubulus, its chief administrator after 354 B.C., had a rule passed that all surplus revenue should go to this fund. This meant that a premium was placed on maintaining peace because the fund was used to finance the attendance of the poor at the festivals. In times of war, the money would have to go into the war fund. Athens's naval power was not neglected, however, and with over 300 ships available it was still the most important naval power in the Aegean. It was at this time that Demosthenes, the greatest orator of the fourth century B.C., rose to prominence. He has been denounced as a blind chauvinist fighting the tide of the times and hailed as a heroic patriot defending Athens's liberty against tyranny. Neither description fits the orator, who was a practical politician striving to survive in the slippery political world of democratic Athens. From at least 351 B.C., when he delivered his first Philippic (speech against Philip), Demosthenes more than any other Athenian recognized the significance of the growth of Macedonian power. Aware that any single state that developed overwhelming superiority in Greece would automatically be a threat to Athens, Demosthenes consistently inveighed against Philip and tried to convince the Athenians of the potential dangers. Understandably, the Athenians, with no prior appreciation of the resources of a unified Macedonia and no other precedents, were slow to act.

Having deterred the foreigners and eliminated Athenian footholds in Macedonia, Philip moved against the Chalcidian League and eliminated it in a surprise

A statue of Demosthenes, of which this is a copy, was erected around 280 B.C. in the Agora of Athens.

winter campaign in 348 B.C. Philip was at last free to achieve another ambition: a place for Macedonia in the Delphic amphictyony, or Holy League, which included such important states as Athens and Thebes. This he did by ending the 10-year-long Sacred War and displacing Phocis from its seat in the league. The final step came when Philip, after securing all his other fronts, attacked Thrace and brought it under his control (342–341 B.C.). As a result, Macedonia was now in a position to close in on the essential grain route through the Bosporus and the Hellespont. Immediately, Athens proposed alliances with two key cities in these areas: Byzantium and Perinthus. When Philip attacked, Athens's support foiled his efforts to take them. Left with no alternative but war to remove the last obstacle to his plans to control Greece, Philip prepared for a land invasion of Attica.

The pretext of supporting the Delphic amphictyony against an offending city allowed Philip to march a large army into central Greece in the spring of 338 B.C. In desperation, Athens diverted the *theoric* funds to the military account and appealed to its old foe, Thebes. Athens's ancient rival was itself concerned with the rising power of Macedonia, and its reluctance to break its alliance with Philip was further weakened by an Athenian offer to pay two-thirds of the costs of the war. An alliance was made, and at Chaeronea in the summer of 338 B.C. the forces of Macedonia and Greece met in one of the most decisive battles of history. Philip strengthened his left wing, where he placed the Macedonian phalanx and the cavalry commanded by Alexander, while deliberately leaving his right wing weak. In the ensuing battle the

---

THE RISE OF MACEDONIA

Accession of Philip II	359 B.C.
Philip frees Macedonia of foreign pressures	358–356 B.C.
Thrace comes under Macedonian control	342–341 B.C.
Battle of Chaeronea ends Greek independence	338 B.C.
Assassination of Philip II	336 B.C.

Thebans were annihilated by the Macedonian cavalry and infantry, and the Athenians advancing on the left were enveloped or scattered and fled from the battlefield. Imposing lenient terms on Athens, Philip made peace and went on to Corinth, where he convened the Greek states and compelled them to form a league to which all but Sparta adhered. The Macedonian king was to be the chief executive and military commander of the league. A council was to represent the individual members, each of which was to remain autonomous. No state was to wage war against another because all the Greeks were henceforth to be bound to a common peace. Theoretically, at least, this much of Isocrates' ideal had been realized. There was no tribute, but the members of the league were expected to make contributions to the federal army and to join with the Macedonians in a war of revenge against Persia for the invasion of Xerxes. In anticipation of this, Philip sent an advance guard into Asia Minor in the spring of 336 B.C., but before he could follow it up, he was assassinated at the wedding of his daughter. Alexander, with the support of Philip's senior commanders, succeeded him.

ALEXANDER THE GREAT

At the age of 20 Alexander inherited all the glories and resources of the Macedonian kingship so carefully nurtured by his father. The army was in superb condition, and Greece appeared to be firmly under Macedonian control. But Alexander also inherited the problems of the Macedonian monarchs. These were first of all dynastic, although Alexander's elimination of three rivals to the throne quickly resolved that problem. His mother, Olympias, who had been divorced by Philip not long before his death, took private revenge by murdering the infant son of Cleopatra, the woman who supplanted her, and then forcing Cleopatra to commit suicide. Alexander handled the other problems with equal ruthlessness and speed. Those perpetual enemies of the Macedonians, the Thracians and Illyrians, were subdued in lightning campaigns (335 B.C.). When false rumors of Alexander's death encouraged the Greeks to revolt, he marched south and captured Thebes, razing all of it except for the temples and the house of Pindar the poet. The population was slaughtered or sold into slavery. Shaken by the destruction of one of their legendary cities, the Greeks quickly came back to their allegiance and hurriedly voted to comply with

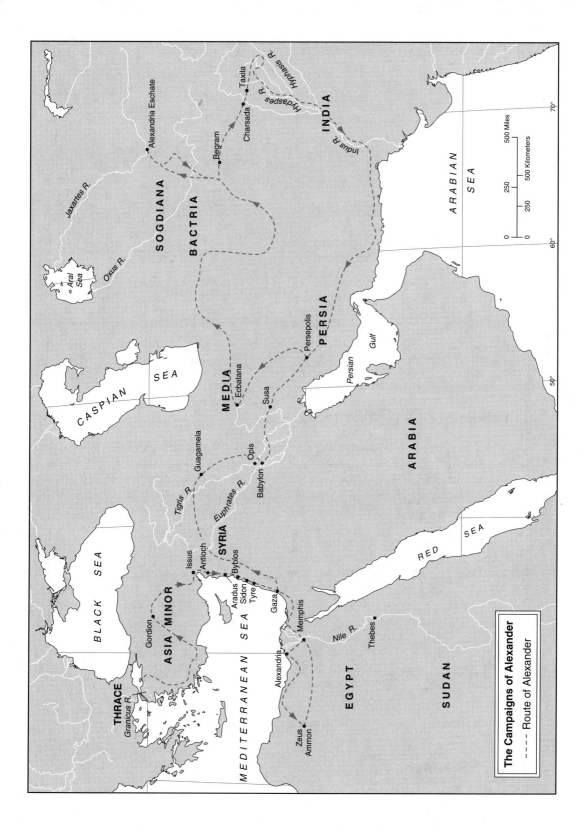

The Campaigns of Alexander
----- Route of Alexander

THE CONQUESTS OF ALEXANDER

Invasion of Asia Minor	334 B.C.
Battle of the Granicus	334 B.C.
Battle of Issus	333 B.C.
Fall of Tyre	332 B.C.
Occupation of Egypt and founding of Alexandria	332 B.C.
Invasion of Mesopotamia	331 B.C.
Battle of Gaugamela	331 B.C.
Campaigns in India	327–325 B.C.
Death of Alexander	323 B.C.

Alexander's requests for contributions for the invasion of Persia that Philip had planned.

In 334 B.C. Alexander and an army of 30,000 hoplites and 5,000 cavalry crossed into Asia Minor. At Troy he sacrificed to King Priam and placed wreaths on the tomb of his ancestor and model, Achilles. A shield said to have been from the Trojan wars was taken from the temple of Athena and was always carried thereafter by his bodyguard.

Conquest of the Persian Empire

Alexander's main objective in the first portion of his campaign (334–331 B.C.) was the destruction of Persian armed forces in the west. Because his fleet was mostly Greek and therefore untrustworthy, he chose a novel method of achieving this aim: a land campaign that would have the double effect of crippling Persian land forces while eliminating the naval bases of the Persian fleet.

The first clash with the Persians took place at the River Granicus, not far from the Hellespont. Here Alexander found a large collection of Persian cavalry and Greek mercenaries waiting for him on the opposite bank. As in all his battles, he was given the initiative by the Persian commanders, whose tactics lagged far behind recent military developments in Greece. Crashing across the river, Alexander scattered the opposing cavalry and then practically annihilated the defenseless infantry, justifying his ruthlessness by an appeal for the support of the League of Corinth for his Persian crusade, which technically made the mercenaries traitors to the Greek cause. He announced his victory by sending 300 suits of Persian armor to Athens as a dedication to Athena with the inscription, "From Alexander, the son of Philip, and the Greeks, except the Spartans." From the Granicus Alexander proceeded to liberate the Greek cities of Asia Minor that had been "freed" so many times before by different conquerors. An attempt by the Persian fleet to raise a revolt in Greece behind him failed, and in the autumn of 333 B.C. Alexander advanced to Issus, where the Persians under Darius III had gathered another large force of Greek mercenaries and Persian troops. The engagement was one of Alexander's three greatest battles, and he won it, like the others, by quickly seizing the initiative on the battlefield and making the enemy respond to his movements. Attacking, as was his custom, with the heavy Companion Cavalry, he dispersed his opponents and then swept around to envelop the other units from the rear. Darius fled, leaving behind his mother, his wife, and his children, whom Alexander treated with courtesy, winning an important propaganda victory by doing so. Darius had abandoned his family, to whom Alexander now extended his protection; by implication, Alexander asserted his right to succeed Darius as the Great King.

Instead of following Darius, Alexander swung south along the Phoenician coast in pursuit of his policy of eliminating both the land power and the seapower of the Persians. Sidon, Byblos, and Aradus quickly came over, but Tyre resisted, and for seven months a bitter siege was conducted before the city fell. Farther down the coast Alexander was again held up, this time for two months by the city of Gaza, which was finally taken after being defended to the last man. Alexander was then able to enter Egypt unopposed (late 332 B.C.). At Memphis he pleased the powerful Egyptian priesthood by sacrificing to the bull Apis, the living incarnation of Ptah, chief god of Memphis. The priests in turn crowned Alexander pharaoh of Egypt. He next sailed down the Nile to the Canopic mouth, where he founded Alexandria as a great business and commercial center. From Alexandria he traveled across the desert to the oasis of Siwa, to worship at the shrine of Zeus Ammon. There he was greeted by the priests as the son of Ammon. The Greeks equated Ammon with Zeus and assumed that henceforth Alexander regarded himself as the son of Zeus. This claim opened a rift with his senior Macedonian commanders, who found it hard to accept the implied slight to his father Philip, the king they rightly believed had made Macedonia great.

Leaving Egypt in the summer of 331 B.C., Alexander advanced northward and marched through Syria to the Tigris. Blocking his route to Babylon was a huge army that Darius had gathered from all over the empire. It was weak in heavy infantry because after Issus, Darius no longer had access to the sources of Greek mercenaries in the Aegean. However, he had compensated for this by increasing the amount of cavalry and by adding scythed chariots, which were supposed to cut down the Macedonian infantry. Although Darius chose the battlefield, Alexander, with his usual flair, was able to take rapid control of the tactical situation. His aim was to draw the enormously long Persian line out of position and then charge into any resulting gaps. To do this he advanced obliquely to the right, forcing the enemy to move with him. When a gap finally appeared between the center and the left wing, Alexander charged with his heavy cavalry and split the Persian line in two. As at Issus, Darius fled before the battle was over and was followed by large numbers of his troops. From Gaugamela, Alexander marched to Babylon, where he sacrificed to the gods and ordered the restoration of the temple of Marduk, which had been destroyed by the Persians. In midwinter he forced his way through the mountains into Persia proper and seized the treasures that had been accumulating at Persepolis for over two centuries. The palace of Xerxes was burned down during a drunken revel, although later apologists for Alexander claimed that it was a deliberate act intended to symbolize the end of Achaemenian rule and the wreaking of vengeance for Persian outrages in Greece. From Persepolis the army went on to Ecbatana, the Median capital, where Darius was supposed to have assembled another large army. There Alexander found that Darius had fled again, and the pursuit began once more. Covering almost 40 miles a day with his men, Alexander caught up with his quarry in July 330 B.C. On Alexander's approach, Darius was stabbed by his own guard, who then fled. When Alexander arrived, the king was dead.

CAMPAIGNS IN CENTRAL ASIA (330–323 B.C.)

With the death of Darius, Alexander's campaigns against Persia could have been regarded as closed. Alexander was now the Great King, and his troops might have assumed that he could return to move civilized regions to consolidate his conquests. However, Alexander had different plans. As Great King he inherited the responsibilities of the Achaemenids, chief of which was the retention of the heartland of the Persian Empire, Mesopotamia. To ensure this required control of the Iranian plateau and to hold it required in turn that the territory farther north and east be occupied to prevent the entry of the marauding nomads of central Asia. Another reason was that Alexander was determined to push his conquests to the edge of the known world, which he wrongly assumed did not extend much beyond the Indus. It was precisely at this point that he first encountered opposition from his own Macedonians. After Darius' death, Alexander had taken to wearing Persian dress on certain occasions involving Persian ceremonials and had begun to appoint Persians to positions of importance. Inevitably, the introduction of what to the Macedonians looked like outsiders into the very personal, inner circle of command excited jealousies. Later in the year of Darius' death, Philotas, son of Parmenio, the commander of the Companion Cavalry, was found guilty of treason and executed. Although innocent, his father was also put to death, being in too powerful a position to be allowed to live. Two years later Alexander got into a quarrel during a drinking bout with his old friend Cleitus, who taunted him with being the son of Ammon, not Philip, and declared that he owed his victories to Philip's generals and the Macedonians, not to his own skills. In a rage Alexander grabbed a guard's spear and stabbed Cleitus to death. Overcome by remorse, he spent the next three days without food or water in his tent until his companions persuaded him to return to his duties. A year later there was another conspiracy, and Callisthenes, Aristotle's nephew, was implicated and later executed. About this time Alexander married Roxane, the daughter of a Sogdian king; inevitably, more tensions were introduced. Further changes were brought about when Alexander ordered the training of Persians in the Macedonian style of warfare and brought Persian cavalry into his own ranks.

Despite these problems, Alexander was still in complete command of the army, and the years between 330 and 327 B.C. were spent in difficult campaigns in the wild northeastern districts of the Persian Empire. With these completed, Alexander prepared to embark on his last major campaign, the conquest of India. Imagining that what is now Pakistan and the Punjab constituted all of India, he did not see this as an unreasonable plan, and it would have given him the Indus as his eastern frontier. However, opposition within the region was formidable, and the last of Alexander's major battles was against Porus, one of the local kings, in the battle of the Hydaspes (326 B.C.). Moving through monsoon rains to what he thought was the edge of his new dominions, he reached the Hyphasis (Beas) River and discovered that there was even more land to the east and another great river. At this point his troops refused to go any farther, and Alexander was forced to retreat. Yet instead of retracing his footsteps and returning to Mesopotamia by the northern route, Alexander chose to march down the Indus to the Indian Ocean and then head west along the barren coast of southern Pakistan. After desperate suffering and tremendous losses, the army, or what was left of it, finally got through to safety.

The Aims of Alexander

When Alexander arrived back in Persia, he found that many of his satraps, both Greek and Persian, had behaved badly in his absence. He immediately set about re-asserting his control. Fearing Alexander's vengeance, his old friend, the treasurer Harpalus, fled with a large sum of money and tried to find sanctuary at Athens. There some of the gold found its way into Demosthenes' pockets, who was impeached, convicted, and driven into exile. Alexander's principal aim at this point, however, was to establish some kind of a joint Macedonian-Persian aristocracy. He had already established large numbers of colonies in Asia and had associated Persians with him in high government office. Now, in a mass wedding, he and 80 of the Companion Cavalry took wives from among the Persian nobility, and over 10,000 Macedonians had their relationships with Asiatic women recognized. All these efforts at fusing the two groups did not prevent a mutiny breaking out at Opis in 324 B.C., when Alexander discharged the veterans and prepared to send them home. The army tended to take the view that it had won Alexander's wars and now, in the moment of triumph, was being dismissed and replaced by the very people it had conquered. Alexander responded by discharging the whole army and retiring to his tent until his forlorn troops begged his foregiveness. With magnanimity and showmanship he welcomed them back, and a great feast was celebrated at which Macedonians and Persians sat down together and drank from the same cup while Alexander prayed for concord (*homonoia*) and a partnership in the empire between Macedonians and Persians. In the winter Alexander's closest friend, Hephaistion, died, leaving Alexander grief-stricken. The following year, while preparing for a great exploratory expedition to circumnavigate and conquer Arabia, Alexander contracted a fever. After lying ill for 10 days, he died on June 13, 323 B.C. He was 32 years old.

Alexander's brilliance as a general and leader of men dazzled his contemporaries and inspired countless imitators throughout history. There is no doubting his capacity to sweep others into his own heroic vision, and even today the accounts of his exploits have a magical quality that not even the most cynical can denigrate. Alexander was the living embodiment of the Homeric ideal of the speaker of words and the doer of deeds, and the mixture of courage, love of his fellow soldiers, flamboyance, generosity, ferocity, and ruthlessness were entirely appropriate in this worthy descendant of Achilles. His principal achievement, the destruction of the armed might of Persia, opened the way for the spread of Greek influence, but Alexander himself was no empire builder. What unity and legitimacy his kingdom possessed depended entirely on his own personality and promptly disappeared after his death. His successors are often portrayed unfavorably as hard-headed pragmatists who lacked Alexander's vision of fusing east and west, Greek and foreigner, but it is a poor comparison. Alexander, unfortunately, had no capacity to hold his far-flung empire together beyond his own flamboyant personality.

ALEXANDER'S SUCCESSORS

It is said that, as Alexander lay dying, his commanders asked to whom he left his kingdom and that Alexander replied, "To the strongest." Though probably apocryphal, the tale is a good commentary on what actually happened in the years after his death. His generals at first squabbled but eventually patched up a compromise. Philip III Arrhidaeus, Alexander's feeble-minded half-brother, and his son by Roxane, Alexander IV, were set up as figureheads. However, it was an impossible solution. Young Alexander was part barbarian and therefore unacceptable to the rank and file of the army. Because neither he nor Philip III could rule without regents, inevitably the struggle for power became a battle among Alexander's generals and lieutenants.

The senior commanders were soon eliminated. The cavalry general Perdiccas and the infantry chief Craterus were both killed in 321 B.C., the former by mutinous troops and the latter in battle. Antipater, the other senior commander, survived until 319 B.C. (Unlike most of the other potential successors, he died a natural death of old age.) The blood relatives also soon disappeared. Philip Arrhidaeus was murdered in 317 B.C. by the brutal Olympias, who in turn was put to death, and Roxane and Alexander IV were done away with around 310 B.C. by Cassander, the son of Antipater.

A second line of contenders consisted of Antigonus the One-Eyed, one of Alexander's governors in Asia Minor, and his son Demetrius. Two others were Ptolemy and Seleucus, members of the Companion Cavalry. Of these, Ptolemy was ultimately the most successful. In 321 B.C. he seized Egypt and consolidated his hold by hijacking the body of Alexander as it was being brought back to Macedonia for burial and giving it a magnificent tomb in his capital, Alexandria. He immediately set out to reorganize and exploit the riches of the Egyptian economy, and quickly built up a position of power for himself and his successors. This position remained intact for practically the next 300 years. Antigonus the One-Eyed came closest to reunifying the empire of Alexander, but he was defeated and killed in battle at Ipsus in Phrygia in 301 B.C. by a coalition that included Seleucus and Lysimachus, the governor of Thrace. Demetrius, after a spectacular career, drank himself to death, but his son, Antigonus II Gonatas, was an able ruler and established himself firmly as king of Macedonia and Greece. His descendants maintained themselves there until the appearance of the Romans in the second century B.C. Seleucus carved out a realm for himself that consisted of the eastern satrapies, to the extent that it was possible to control them, and some parts of Asia Minor. His son by his Persian wife Apama, Antiochus I, became head of the third major Hellenistic kingdom, and his descendants ruled there until the first century B.C. Thus in the generation after Alexander a pattern gradually emerged that was to dominate the Greek world to the time of the Romans. The Ptolemies held Egypt, Cyprus, Palestine, and Phoenicia (until the second century B.C.), together with some toeholds in the Aegean area; the Antigonids retained Macedonia and much of Greece with the exception of the areas under the control of the Achaean and Aetolian leagues, and the Seleucids held Syria, Mesopotamia (until the second century B.C.), much of Iran (until the mid–third century B.C.), and some of Asia Minor. In the third century B.C. the kingdom of Pergamum in western Asia Minor emerged as a distant fourth among the Hellenistic monarchies, and Rhodes remained a powerful independent state until weakened by Rome in the second century B.C. In mainland Greece the classical cities such as Athens, Thebes, and Sparta played no significant roles.

After a generation of war the once unified Persian Empire lay in pieces. In its place was a collection of warlike states that constantly feuded with each other while at the same time trying to keep down their indigenous populations. Whether Macedonians and Greeks were any better as colonial administrators than their imperial predecessors is hard to tell. It is even more difficult to estimate whether the peoples of the region would have been better off without any kind of imperial overlordship.

THE STATE AND SOCIETY IN THE HELLENISTIC WORLD

The Greek of the classical period was typically a citizen of a small city-state, used to moving in a world of small communities in which states such as Athens and Sparta seemed like giants, though still of essentially the same recognizable political type as his or her own native *polis*. By contrast, in the Hellenistic world there was no such constitutional catholicity but instead a multiplicity of political forms. The most prevalent type of government was monarchy, but even here there was a major difference between the huge kingdoms of the Ptolemies and Seleucids, with their heavily Eastern trappings, and the more conservative monarchy of the Macedonians. In between stood the smaller kingdom of Pergamum. In mainland Greece the old city-states still longed—and occasionally fought—for independence, although they generally remained firmly under the control of the Macedonian monarchy. Federal leagues were a new development. These combinations of city-states and rural cantons in the remoter districts of Greece had begun in the fourth century B.C. but emerged as significant powers in the third, able to fend off all the attempts of the kings to bring them under control. From the viewpoint of the old *polis* constitution, these were its lineal and most successful descendants. Although large in comparison to the classical ideal, they preserved the essential *polis* quality of autonomy. Unlike the monarchies, which lived on uneasy terms with the Greek cities in their midst, the leagues were true fusions of cities and the only genuinely progressive political innovation of the period.

Monarchies, leagues, and city-states do not exhaust the list of constitutional possibilities that the Hellenistic world embraced. There were large temple-states in Asia Minor and Syria run by powerful, dynastic priesthoods. These states maintained a considerable measure of independence down to the Roman period. The Judean temple-state in Palestine became completely independent in the mid–second century B.C. and remained so until the appearance of the Romans 100 years later. Little feudal principalities under their native aristocracies dotted the Seleucid regions, and everywhere newly founded capitals, military colonies, and cities multiplied the political forms under which the inhabitant of the Hellenistic world might live.

The Monarchs

The predominant political institution of the Hellenistic world was the altogether un-Greek absolute monarchy. However, this form of government was natural to the Macedonians and to the world Alexander had conquered, and the Greeks had no choice but to accommodate themselves to it. This happened with surprising quickness despite their longstanding antipathy to a strong executive and their tendency to characterize the subjects of kings as slaves. For example, Athenians could chant to Demetrius of Macedon,

> The other gods are either far away or cannot hear or do not exist or do not care for us. You we can see, not in wood or stone, but face to face . . . to you we pray.[1]

The Athenians even gave Demetrius the Parthenon as his residence. This unexpected servility is not exactly what it seems, however. Athenians by the end of the fourth century B.C., along with many other Greeks, were more inclined to worship manifestations or epiphanies of divine power than the more personal gods of the past. The kings of the Hellenistic world were particularly likely to be the focal point of divine emanations and were honored as benefactors and saviors who could be depended on to protect their people from their enemies. Thus Athens was "saved" from Cassander by Demetrius, Rhodes from Demetrius by Ptolemy, and the Asiatic Greeks from invading Celts by Antiochus. In addition, there was widespread belief in the philosopher Euhemerus' theory that the gods had originally been powerful kings who were later deified. All of this prepared the way for the divinization of the monarchs, and their official cults were extended everywhere throughout their kingdoms. An important component of these cults distinguished them from the strictly Eastern version of king worship: the element of personal achievement by the rulers (in the form of great victories, heroic deeds, or benefits conferred on humanity) which in Greek eyes justified their claim to a share in the godhead.

[1]Athenaeus, *Deipnosophists* ("Connoisseurs in Dining"), 6.63.253.

The kings were surrounded by a court aristocracy of which the two highest levels were known as the Kinsmen and the Friends, but the rule of the kings was absolute and unrestrained by any constitutional conventions. Officials could be removed without formality, and the king's will in the form of edicts and decrees had the force of law. He and his court were the state, and the kingdom he ruled was in no sense a community of people—a republic, commonwealth, or city-state—where individuals had the rights of citizens. The people were simply the subjects of the king, and life and death lay in his hands. In practice, however, his absolutism was tempered by a number of factors. He could not administer his huge realms without a bureaucracy, and weak or lazy kings were automatically its prisoners. Nor could he rule without the support of the Greeks dwelling in the country, in either the cities, colonies, or rural districts. Apart from the mercenary army and the bureaucracy, these were the king's main support, although they could not be trusted to provide troops or administrative services. For these the king preferred to collect taxes directly to pay his mercenaries and his officials.

Maintaining Greek Identity

With the exception of Egypt, the essential means of preserving the self-identity of the Greek ruling class was the city and to a smaller extent the military colony. In Egypt, where outside Alexandria and two other lesser cities there was no urbanization, the Greeks were scattered throughout the countryside in corporations (*politeumata*) that found their focal points in the local gymnasiums.

The *polis* was selected by Alexander as the main means of maintaining control over the vast regions of the newly conquered Persian Empire. Traditionally he is credited with founding 70 cities, and in this work he was followed by his successors. Seleucus I, for example, founded 16 Antiochs, 9 Seleuceias, 6 Laodiceas, 3 Apameas, and 1 Stratoniceia, named after his father, himself, his mother, and his wives, respectively. Military colonies often became cities but retained the distinctions of not owning their territory outright and being subject to military levies.

Generally, the cities had democratic constitutions. They had their assemblies, councils, and elected officials, and the principles of collegial or group magistracies and rotation in office were maintained. With few exceptions, there was no attempt to limit the franchise to a narrow oligarchy, although citizenship continued to be confined to Greeks who could prove Greek descent on both sides. In practice many non-Greeks were able to acquire the franchise through grants or marriage arrangements as well as by more surreptitious means.

Economically, the cities did not produce great wealth, although they did supply necessary services that are more difficult to categorize. Their food supply was almost always derived from their own territory, and industry was limited to the production of essential goods for local consumption. Imports consisted of luxury goods for the well-to-do, food in times of scarcity, and raw materials such as metal, stone, and timber. Wealth was mostly a matter of landholding, although fortunes were also made in trade and in some of the professions, where rhetoricians, doctors, athletes, and architects often did well. The nonproductive character of the cities should not be exaggerated, however, because there is no way of estimating how much their contributions in the fields of education, health, entertainment, and overall civility were also factors in maintaining the level of productivity in their regions. One of the most striking aspects of Hellenistic civilization is the extraordinary generosity of the well-off classes, who competed with each other in their benefactions. Again there is no way of calculating how much the wealthy contributed to their communities in this fashion, though at a guess it must compare favorably with what modern governments manage to squeeze out of the wealthy by means of taxation. If the cities by their very existence encouraged the wealthy to spend lavishly on such community functions as festivals, public buildings, and the food and water supply, then by this very fact they probably justified their existence. The alternative, which occurred in the late Roman Empire, was for the rich to withdraw to their country villas, where their wealth was spent on essentially private functions, and the masses were reduced to a form of serfdom.

In Greece itself, intercity relations changed considerably, although internally the cities themselves remained much as they had always been. Arbitration became a common means of settling local conflicts. The right of asylum was jealously guarded as one of the last vestiges of city-state independence, and the kings tried to win popularity by conferring this right on particular cities and shrines. Some cities agreed to liberate one another's citizens if the citizens were purchased as slaves. The exchange of citizenship between cities such as was effected by Athens and Priene and Athens and Rhodes became common throughout the Aegean area. As in the past, festivals were a means of bridging the gulf between cities, and many new ones were created in the Hellenistic period. The settling of internal disputes by means of judicial commissions from other cities was common. These judges first attempted to solve disputes themselves, and only if they failed did the local juries take over. The process eventually led to the development of a body of common law and legal practice that effectively transcended the narrow boundaries of the individual city-states.

The Greeks Try Representative Government: The Leagues

One of the most remarkable developments of the age was the emergence in Greece proper of federal leagues with true representative government. The ground for these leagues had been prepared long before they finally emerged as significant powers in the third century B.C. One of their predecessors was the religious association known as the *amphictyony*, which consisted of a number of states joined in a league for the purposes of worship at a common shrine. Among the best known were the amphictyonies of Delphi and Delos. The object of these leagues, which included all the major powers of Greece, was the maintenance of the cults and temples and to some extent the inculcation of certain rules among its members. During the festivals there was to be a truce, and the shrine itself was to be regarded as an asylum.

Although these associations brought the separate states together in religious worship, they had no ability to break down the independence of the states and offer a basis for intercity citizenship. Similarly, such organizations as the imperial leagues of Sparta and Athens created no more than a superficial unity, and each state jealously guarded its own citizenship. It was thus not in the more advanced parts of Greece that true federal leagues with universal citizenship first came into existence but in the more remote regions where the tribal and cantonal structure of society still existed and the city-state was not the predominating constitutional form.

The Aetolian federal state in western central Greece evolved in the fourth century B.C. from a loose tribal organization. It consisted of a council made up by proportionate representation of delegates from the constituent villages and cities and a primary assembly open to all citizens, which met twice a year. The Achaean League in the north of the Peloponnese also emerged as a significant power in the fourth century B.C., and at one time contained no fewer than 60 cities and villages. As in the Aetolian League, there was a primary assembly that met irregularly to deal with specific major issues such as war, peace, and alliances. Voting was by cities, which probably had their number of votes determined by their population. There was also a council whose role and composition are not clearly understood. In general, the leagues recognized the right of citizens to exercise their political rights throughout the federal territory, to move at will, to own property, and to marry whomever they chose. Internal affairs were left to the individual states, but foreign relations and military matters were the concern of the federal government by way of either the full assembly or the council. Military service was regarded as duty to the individual cities. Taxes were paid to both the federal government and the home states.

HELLENISTIC SOCIETY

The social structures of the Hellenistic age reflect two main characteristics. The first was the gap between those who professed Greek culture, whether ethnic Greeks or not, and those who held fast to their own native cultures. The second characteristic was the separation of society and state, so unlike the situation in the classical period of the *polis,* when the two had been practically identical.

The Peoples of the Hellenistic World

The peoples of the Hellenistic world were as diverse as their political forms. The homogeneous population of the Aegean region during the classical period was replaced by the incredibly fragmented and much larger populations of the old Persian Empire, each with its own individual history and inner complexities. Even the traditional Greek homeland was far from being a fully homogeneous region, for there were still major differences between areas that had urbanized in the Archaic period and places where the *polis* had only recently arrived.

Egypt was predominantly a land of peasants—some 6 million of them—among whom were scattered an unknown number of Greek and Macedonian colonists and settlers. The center of Greek power was Alexandria, a city at its height of perhaps a million people, both native and Greek. In the Seleucid Empire the diversity was infinitely greater. Iranian nomads wandered freely throughout the desertlike regions east of the old Persian capital of Persepolis, and Babylonia and Syria comprised some of the most advanced and sophisticated societies of the ancient world. Egypt's population has been estimated at 30 million, over which presided another unknown number of Greeks and Macedonians in cities scattered thousands of miles apart. Alexandria Eschate—"Farthest Alexandria"—on the Jaxartes River was closer to modern Calcutta on the lower Ganges than it was to its own capital, Antioch, 2,200 miles to the east.

The main problem faced by the Ptolemies and Seleucids was how to maintain themselves as a tiny minority in the midst of such alien cultures and large populations. In Egypt strikes and revolts forced the Ptolemies to make concessions and take more and more Egyptians into the government and the army, and in the Seleucid Empire the Parthians and the East Greeks of Bactria quickly won and maintained their independence at the expense of the central state. More so than the Ptolemies, the Seleucid rulers had to contend with a naturally difficult geographic region, enormous distances, numerous independent-minded Greek cities, native aristocracies, and temple-states. Egypt, by contrast, benefited from its traditional isolation and its long history of internal unification under a powerful monarchy. Even here, however, the Ptolemies faced enemies among some of the native priesthoods and stubborn peasant masses, who never ceased to regard them as alien conquerors. Even Alexandria, the capital, with its unruly heterogeneous population, presented great difficulties to the rulers. Divine monarchs thus faced intractable human problems.

It is difficult to generalize about the degree of influence Greeks had on indigenous peoples, and vice versa, throughout the Hellenistic period. What might be true for Egypt, about which more is known, may be invalid for Syria, Mesopotamia, or Iran. Greeks in general showed little interest in learning the languages or understanding the culture of the conquered peoples. This should not cause surprise. Like other imperial peoples, they were content to learn how to get along with those they had subjugated. In Egypt, Greek and Egyptian cultures simply coexisted. The Ptolemies, it is true, successfully blended Greek and Egyptian ideas of kingship and learned to work with the Egyptian priesthoods, but except for select groups of upper-class Egyptians who had to work with their Greek rulers, there seems to have been little cultural interchange. Greeks wrote in Greek, Egyptians in Egyptian. Greek artists and architects had almost no influence on their Egyptian counterparts. Two legal systems, one Greek, the other Egyptian, existed side by side. Elsewhere, especially in Syria and Palestine, Hellenic culture penetrated more deeply, and the encounter between cosmopolitan Judaism and Hellenism in Egypt and elsewhere represents one of the few genuine cultural exchanges in history.

Hellenistic Social Structures: The Old System Changes

In terms of social structures, the most characteristic feature of the Hellenistic age was the separation of state and society, the reverse of the situation in the classical age. In classical times there had been practically no government—no permanent legislative and judicial organs, no permanent bureaucracies or executives—as distinguished from the people. In the new world, however, the government, with its kings, courts, and administrative hierarchies, was emphatically not identical with the people but instead something apart from them; the state went out of its way to emphasize its different and independent sovereignty.

This is not to say that the *polis* vanished or ceased to function in the way it always had. However, citizenship now meant something different. Being a citizen of a *polis* still guaranteed a basic, well-defined place in the Greek universe. The social functions of the *polis* remained unimpaired. Greek life still revolved around the temple, the gymnasium, the agora, and the theater. The *polis* still had control of local affairs. It still interacted with other cities. Its larger political life, however, was overshadowed by the more powerful courts of the kings. To be an Athenian, a Spartan, or a Corinthian had literally once meant everything—a share in the state's power, the loot of its wars, and the profits of its empire. Now, that sense of political independence was lost and with it the basis of the culture of the classical age.

Paradoxically, the breaking of the narrow citizenship-power connection provided new possibilities, especially in the realm of culture. Despite its wars, the Greek world had always been a community of cities and peoples. As long as the old formula of the classical *polis* prevailed, however, strict control of the franchise tended also to restrict the culture on which it was based. In the Hellenistic period this changed, and even in Greece proper we see exchanges of franchise between cities, the use of mediation, and the extension of asylum to refugees. Intellectually it had long been recognized that being a Greek was more a matter of culture than race, and that many "barbarians" were in fact closer to being true Greeks than were a good number of the Greeks themselves. Practically speaking, though, until the kings took political power into their own hands, there were great restrictions on the opportunities open to Greeks and non-Greeks alike.

In classical Athens the government and to a lesser extent the armed services were so designed that, with some significant exceptions, nearly anyone could become anything. Outside the elective offices, talent was not particularly rewarded or sought out, and amaterurism was the general rule. By contrast, in the new states the professional was supreme, and it mattered little where he came from as long as he was Greek or at least claimed to be one. At the festivals professional actors, musicians, and athletes replaced the amateurs of the past and made their rounds from city to city. Physicians, technicians, engineers, generals, and scholars were in great demand and moved as the opportunities presented themselves. For instance, the mathematician Apollonius of Perga was able to do most of his pioneering work on conics at Alexandria under the patronage of the Ptolemies and then transfer to Pergamum, where he dedicated a revised edition of his masterwork to his new sponsor, King Attalus. Above all, the new kingdoms needed bureaucrats—accountants, managers, and scribes—to organize and operate their administrative systems, and mercenaries to supply the backbone of their fighting forces. In such a world the old restrictive idea of citizenship, where participation in government, religion, and the army depended on the possessions of the franchise, was simply obsolete.

Seated on an elaborate chair, a languid lady of the Hellenistic upper classes attends to her toilette. Isolated from any meaningful role in public life, the Hellenistic well-to-do lavished their attention on their private affairs.

With the clear division between state and society and the reduced importance of the citizenship, it now became more important than ever to be well-to-do. The distinction between rich and poor had always been the main dividing line between the classes of the old *polis*, but even outside Athens the existence of assemblies had guaranteed some power to the lower classes. Now, although all the new cities were formally democracies and possessed assemblies, the upper classes were firmly in control. The bourgeoisie constituted the new elite, and in a sense it became the only new citizenry of the supposedly cosmopolitan Hellenistic world. The lower classes were progressively disenfranchised and sank in importance.

Gender Roles and Everyday Life

One important consequence of the weakening of the tie between society and the state was the effect it had on gender roles. Like almost every other aspect of life in the Hellenistic world, the roles of men and women and the intimate structures of the family itself were affected by the new circumstances under which all Greeks now found themselves.

In classical times the influence of the head of the household, the *kyrios,* depended in large measure on the very real power he possessed in the community at large. His despotism at home reflected the enhanced position males enjoyed in the day-to-day life of the classical *polis*. In Hellenistic times, however, and especially outside the confines of Greece proper, mercenaries began taking over military responsibilities from ordinary male citizens, and the kings usurped their political control. In the classical *polis* citizenship had bolstered the power of the heads of families. Prestige gained in the service of the city translated into a strong sense of self-esteem. Now, along with the decline of citizens' responsibilities came a decline in their power.

Some men, perhaps a majority, came to terms with the new realities. Those with enough money discovered the pleasures of the private realm. The quality of housing, clothing, and furniture all improved. Perhaps they came to appreciate the fact that the threat to life and limb declined. Mercenaries were not inclined to fight to the finish. When one side or the other seemed to be on the point of winning, the battle often ended. Then there was the great safety valve of overseas emigration for the ambitious, the dissatisfied, and the misfits. Both men and women availed themselves of the opportunity. In the past the absence of a dowry might have condemned a woman to spinsterhood for life in the house of some relative, where she was often treated as a semislave. Now the dowryless young woman, along with the footloose young man, could escape overseas, facing unknown dangers but at least free of the mean constraints of their native city or village.

The stimulus to social change also came from another, unexpected source. From the time of Philip II and probably long before, the women of the Macedonian royal family played highly visible roles in the political and even military life of the nation. It has often been remarked that the Macedonians in general were more like the Greeks of the Homeric age than their own times, and the strong women of the *Odyssey* such as Penelope and Arete would have seemed much more real to the Macedonians than to the sexually polarized Greeks of the south. Macedonian queens were not only active in the political and military spheres; they originated and sponsored religious festivals, patronized literature and the arts, and contributed to the needs of the community from their own private resources. Queen Arsinoe II, wife first of Lysimachus and then of Ptolemy II, founded the festival of the Arsinoeia honoring Aphrodite and constructed the largest building of the then known world at Samothrace for the mystery cult of the Cabiri.

With such striking and colorful leaders to show the way, it is not surprising that a few women in the Hellenistic period began to enter the professions, to write poetry, to paint, to engage in philosophic speculation, and to publish scholarly works. Much more sympathetic interpretations of women's viewpoints were attempted by male writers, presumably in response to the existence of a reading public among women. In earlier versions of the story of the voyage of the Argonauts, the bloodthirsty Medea slew and dismembered her brother. In the new version of Apollonius of Rhodes, it is her consort, Jason, who does the gory deed. It is no accident that the Hellenistic age was a period when love poetry and the novel flourished and the emphasis on the heroic shrank. It is ironic that much of this development occurred under the sponsorship, intentional or otherwise, of the Macedonians, who by normal Greek estimation were hopelessly behind the times.

In cities such as classical Athens, where citizenship meant a great deal economically and socially, sexuality was not a private matter. The Athenians, perhaps, went to extremes to ensure the perpetuation of citizen families and to repress female sexuality in particular, but these were not exclusively Athenian concerns. Combined with a lack of economic resources, these factors made the restriction of the numbers of children raised practically mandatory throughout the whole of the old Greek world. Too many daughters in any Greek family usually meant a proportionate reduction in the family's net worth. From an economic viewpoint, each dowry paid out meant a loss to the family's wealth. Especially in bad economic times, there was a general tendency to expose female rather than male infants, to feed them less, and to disregard their education and physical development.

Much of this changed in the more affluent, less restricted environment of the Hellenistic east. There was more money in circulation and less social repression. In the first two centuries after Alexander, Greeks in vast numbers headed east to fill the armies and bureaucracies of the Hellenistic kingdoms. Greek women were in short supply, and because it was the policy of the Hellenistic kings to maintain the Greek population, women were in a position to pick and choose their mates. Dowries ceased to be so overwhelmingly important, and, if we can generalize from the experience of Ptolemaic Egypt, there was less necessity to expose unwanted children, although the practice did continue. Family and kin interfered less in marriages; they were usually too far away to have much influence. Marriage contracts from Egypt spelled out the obligations of husbands and made it clear that the family was to be the main focus of their attention; they were not to fritter away money on prostitutes or boyfriends or to sell any property held in common by the spouses. A Greek wife in Egypt could at least demand a lot more from her husband in terms of marital fidelity than could her counterparts in Greece proper, where concubinage and other liaisons were taken for granted. The idea of returning a dowry because a husband kept a mistress, as some Greek contracts in Egypt stipulated, would have been unthinkable in earlier times.

Greek women in Egypt had other advantages. In areas where Greeks had settled in large numbers, the old traditions of patriarchy undoubtedly survived, but in areas less intensely settled by Greeks, women came into contact with the liberal customs of Egypt and had a choice between using Greek or Egyptian law codes. Greek women became aware of the more active economic and social role of Egyptian women. In divorce proceedings they could opt for the Egyptian legal practice of allowing wives to initiate their own proceedings without the intervention of a legal guardian. In economic matters Greek women in Egypt had a more significant role than anywhere else in the Greek world. They bought, sold, and leased land, farmed it themselves, or rented it out.

Of course, there was also a much seamier side to Hellenistic social life. Prostitution was widespread. Freed from the constraints of the traditional system, men and women were more vulnerable to the uncertainties of life. We hear of children being kidnapped and sold into prostitution and slavery. One can imagine that being the wife of a nomadic mercenary soldier, who was serving now one commander, now another, could not have been much fun—exciting, perhaps, but hardly secure. Women often had to fend for themselves. If a husband was killed or died, a woman might not have had any other relatives to fall back on, none of the old, dependable, fail-safe devices that the traditional Greek *polis* offered to respectable women and their children. In the unregulated free-for-all of the Hellenistic world, the ambitious, the independent-minded, and the unscrupulous probably did well, but for others the lack of traditional supports and restraints must have meant great hardship.

A HELLENISTIC MARRIAGE CONTRACT

Hellenistic marriage contracts spelled out the obligations of husbands toward their wives and families, and attempted to compensate for the lack of traditional, *polis*-style safeguards. Here, in a marriage contract of 311 B.C., a man called Herakleides agrees to certain conditions in taking Demetria as his wife:

> It shall not be lawful for Herakleides to bring home another wife in insult against Demetria, nor to have children by another woman nor to do evil against Demetria on any pretext. If Herakleides is discovered doing any of these things and Demetria proves it before three men whom they both accept, Herakleides shall give back to Demetria the dowry of 1000 drachmas which she brought and moreover forfeit 1000 drachmas of the silver coinage of Alexander.

Source: Roger S. Bagnall and Peter Derow, *Greek Historical Documents: The Hellenistic Period* (Chico, Calif.: Scholars Press, 1981), p. 199.

CULTURE AND RELIGION IN THE HELLENISTIC WORLD

From a cultural viewpoint the Hellenistic period witnessed the permanent uniting—to the extent it was possible—of Greek and Near Eastern cultures. For centuries these cultures had influenced each other, mostly at a distance. The alphabet, religious and mythological themes, artistic motifs, and possibly ideas about the *polis* and hoplite-style fighting had been transmitted from the Near East to Greece during the Archaic Age or even earlier in some instances. With the conquests of Alexander the two worlds became closely intermeshed; Greeks and Greek cities were scattered from one end of the Near East to the other, from India to the Aegean.

Indigenous peoples reacted to the arrival of the Greeks in various ways. Where they could, they threw off Greek military control as quickly as possible; more often they passively accepted their fate. At the command of their Macedonian overlord, the inhabitants of Babylon deserted their ancient city for a new city built nearby. The sullen resentment of the Egyptians was expressed in sporadic revolts and apocalyptic literature that described the coming defeat of their oppressors and the restoration of the glories of Egypt.

The culture that responded most vigorously to the Greek challenge was Judaism. At one level Jews firmly and completely rejected Hellenic culture, but at other levels—especially, though not exclusively, outside Palestine—they attempted to come to terms with it. That prepared the way for an offshoot of Judaism to come to terms successfully with Greek philosophical and intellectual culture. In the work of the Christian Platonists of Alexandria during Roman times, the integration of eastern and western cultures was to be as successfully complete as it ever would be.

Old Gods and New Gods

The gods of the old homeland of Greece found it hard to move when the Greeks spread eastward in the footsteps of Alexander. From ancient times they had been identified with particular cities and places—Athena with Athens, Apollo with Delphi, Aphrodite with Corinth. People had grown accustomed to regarding individual Olympians as their special protecting deities and to having this right recognized by others. Athena, though worshiped elsewhere, was closely identified with the city that bore her name. She had done special things for Athens, and hers alone was the Parthenon and the festivals that honored her in the Athenian religious year. She had been present with the Athenians at the foundation of their city and was with them through all their trials and victories. There was no way in which this kind of association could be transplanted. If emigrant Athenians wished to worship her, they could of course do so, but there were no temples established in her honor and no recurring festivals in the cycle of the year to remind people of her. Besides, the new cities of the east were packed with emigrants from all over the Hellenic world, each with its own deity. There was no homogeneous population that believed, as Athenians had always believed, that Zeus and Apollo were their divine ancestors and Athena their protective goddess. They could only worship her until such time as temples were built to her—assuming that they were to be built to her and not to some other god or goddess—in private cult associations. Such associations or corporations were entirely voluntary and personal. By contrast, in Athens the cult of the goddess Athena was an essential part of civic life, to which everyone was bound. In the new cities such worship was a matter of private devotion, and the associations organized to conduct this worship become one of the standard features of the Hellenistic world and one of its most radical transformations.

In the new world the Greeks were scattered over an enormously wide landscape, altogether unlike the closely defined territories of their past. In Egypt, where the Ptolemies did not permit the building of cities outside the three major ones, the Greeks were scattered in settlements throughout the countryside and by necessity came into close contact with the natives. Although the Seleucids encouraged city building in their realms and thereby enabled the emigrants to congregate, the new establishments were often located close to or actually on the sites of earlier eastern villages or cities. Seleuceia-on-Tigris was founded at Opis, a native village, and its founder, Seleucus I, transferred to it a good part of the population of old Babylon. Antioch itself was established on an old native site. There was thus a close intermingling of the two populations, and like it or not, the Greeks had to pay attention to the gods where they now dwelt.

There were a number of ways in which the Greeks could discharge their obligations to their host deities. They could honor them through the officially established priesthoods, for example, by paying for sacrifices and prayers to be offered in their honor. They could also identify the eastern gods with their own, as they had been doing for centuries, and worship them appropriately. By syncretism the Egyptian Thoth became Hermes; the Syrian Atargatis, Aphrodite; and a whole host of

The amalgamation of east and west: Hygeia, a classically modeled goddess representing Health, stands beside a thoroughly alien-looking Asclepius, the Greek god of healing. Over his head is an inscription in Greek lettering. Significantly, however, it is in a Semitic language.

storm and sky gods, Zeus. Sometimes a bridge between the Greek and eastern worlds was built when the priests learned Greek and attempted to communicate with their conquerors. In Babylon the priest Berossus and in Egypt the priest Manetho translated or paraphrased the sacred Babylonian and Egyptian texts into Greek. Jewish apologists attempted to explain and defend Jewish beliefs to the Greeks and later to the Romans.

Nevertheless, there was still something missing. The eastern gods remained eastern, served by alien priesthoods. What was needed was a transformation that would take away the Greeks' sense of strangeness while allowing them to believe they were honoring the gods of their new lands. Although many transformations were made—Cybele, Atargatis, Adonis, and Attis were among the most popular—none was more successful than Serapis, Isis, and Horus.

Serapis and Isis: A Case of Successful Manipulation

Serapis was the conscious fusion of the Egyptian god Osiris, a mortuary and fertility deity, with the divine bull calf Apis. This amalgamation was brought about by the first Ptolemy with the assistance of the Egyptian priest Manetho and the Greek Timotheus, an official interpreter of the Eleusinian mysteries. As associates Serapis had his wife, Isis; their son, Horus; and Anubis, the god who conducted souls to the next world. This combination failed to appeal to Egyptians, who remained attached to the old forms of their gods, but it was a great success among the Greeks and eventually spread everywhere in the Greco-Roman world. Serapis was regarded as a kind and gentle god who did not punish his devotees. His image in the temple (the Serapeum), which is known through copies and literary accounts, was heavily bearded and dark, decorated with silver, gold, and precious stones such as emeralds and sapphires. On his head was a basket for measuring grain, the symbol of his lordship of the earth. Mysterious and majestic, he exercised a special fascination for both Greeks and Romans.

The new cult operated on two levels. For the majority of followers Serapis was an attractive, universal god who could be worshiped and prayed to everywhere through cult associations and private shrines. But for a very special group—those with a certain desire or need for religious involvement—there were the mysteries of Isis, the consort of Serapis. The ceremonies and rituals of initiation connected with these mysteries were probably also devised by the same Greek-Egyptian-Macedonian trio who had successfully launched the worship of Serapis. The Greeks were already familiar with mystery religions, such as the beloved religion of Eleusis, which conferred the hope of immortality on its initiates. Eleusis and its mysteries, however, were confined to one particular place in Greece, whereas the mysteries of Isis, like Isis herself, were universal. The new ceremonies were quite different from the old Egyptian rituals of Isis, which had publicly dramatized her mourning and search for the dead Osiris. In fact, there were no initiates in the Egyptian form of Isis worship. The kind of salvation offered by the mysteries of Isis (and other mysteries for that matter) was not freedom from sin and assimilation to God as his children, but escape from fate or destiny and a share in the god's potency or power. Fate loomed large in the minds of people of the period after Alexander. Escape from its inevitability through the power of a god such as Isis, who was able to overcome it, was avidly sought.

Fate, Astrology, and the Uprooted

If the interstate politics of the old Greek world had been chaotic, there were always, at least, the permanent anchors of the cities themselves. Battles and wars might be won or lost, but the cities went on forever. They had existed from the beginning—from mythological times—and their exclusivity had perpetuated their sense of identity. Athenians were Athenians and Corinthians Corinthians, and there was no mistaking the identity of each.

This was not the case in the cities of the new Hellenistic world, where Greeks from everywhere jostled with the natives and where the characteristic language was not Attic or Dorian or Ionic but a new kind of Greek—*koine*, or the "common tongue"—which blotted out the distinctive regional variations. Without roots, the Greeks after Alexander felt particularly vulnerable to the constant wars and changing alliances among the major powers, as well as to the normal experiences of life. Individuals rose and fell with dizzying rapidity. Fortunes were made and lost overnight. The old codes and conventions based on community practices had little

The compassionate Serapis responded to the need of people in the Hellenistic age for a god who could help lighten their burdens in a fast-changing world.

influence on the behavior of the newly liberated emigrants and the flamboyant successors of Alexander. The gods who had ruled in the past—justly or unjustly—were now as nothing compared to Fortune (Tyche), who played with people like children, loving to turn things upside down unexpectedly. Fortune was as deceitful as she was unpredictable, and people swept along by the torrent of events without the sustenance of the old customs and institutions of the city-state could only pray for deliverance. Understandably, they prayed to Fortune herself and made her the protective deity of a dozen new cities in the east.

Another revolution affected people almost as much as the opening up of the new world: the new astronomy and the world view that went with it, which began to make its appearance in the fourth century B.C. and achieved its final form in the Hellenistic period. In the old view of things, which had held throughout most of classical times, the earth was regarded as a disk or saucer surrounded by water, with the sky superimposed above like a bowl. Underneath was Hades, the shadowy abode of the dead. In the heavens were the clouds, planets, and stars. The gods moved freely throughout this limited, rather cozy universe and were always close at hand. Then two of Plato's students, Eudoxus and Heracleides, revolutionized this vision. Eudoxus demonstrated that the planets obeyed regular laws and moved in circular fashion within a number of spheres. Heracleides speculated that the earth, a sphere, revolved on its own axis daily and that Mercury and Venus revolved around the sun (also a planet), although all three, along with the remaining planets, revolved around the earth. These astronomical theories were quickly translated into cosmological and anthropological theories that placed the earth at the lowest level of a hierarchy of planetary bodies of progressive refinement and regarded the human soul as a spark of divine fire locked in the material body. After Alexander, the east made two contributions that completed the picture of the new universe: the accurate Babylonian observations of the positions of the heavenly bodies and the belief in their influence on human lives. Out of this fusion came the pseudoscience of astrology, which was to dominate both the intellectual and the popular view of the universe and God for the rest of antiquity and even later.

In its strictest form, astrology is atheistic because it views the universe as a self-running mechanism that operates according to totally predictable laws without any outside intervention. Its most basic assumption is that if true knowledge of the operation of one part of the cosmos (in this instance the movements of the heavenly bodies) is known, information about the operation of the other parts—human destiny, for example—can be inferred. Hence, if the movements of the stars and planets can be brought into coordination with important events in the life of an individual—such as birth—it will be possible to predict that person's fate. In this mechanistic world there is no room for divine intervention or free will, and the individual's fate is as fixed as the movements of the heavens themselves. A less strict view was that the heavenly bodies were themselves gods who might be appeased by appropriate religious action, and it was this view that was most popularly accepted. In both views, the underlying assumptions about the nature of the universe as enshrined in astrology were considered incontestable and had a profound effect on the age's religions and philosophic outlook.

Monotheism and Mysticism

Plato's profound dissatisfaction with what he regarded as the imperfections and instability of governments and laws led him to abandon the material world and seek permanence in the realm of the divine, which alone was real and unchanging. It was not just the ever-changing world of city-state politics that Plato dismissed as unreal but everything in the sensible world. According to his definition, things apprehended by the senses are mutable and finite and therefore unknowable by the mind; only the essences of things are unchanging and therefore the proper objects of knowledge. Even essences shared only partially in the highest three categories of Being: the One, the Good, and the Beautiful. The most elevated and humanly satisfying task that anyone could engage in was therefore the pursuit of these categories and beyond them their highest embodiment, the Unknown and Undefinable God. This essentially private concern with the divine that was characteristic of the new age was light-years removed from the external religiosity of the old *polis*, whose gods were satisfied with lip service and the performance of sacrifices, games, and processions in their honor.

Plato's contribution was particularly significant in the area of the new astronomy. The calculations of his students Eudoxus and Heracleides had shown that the planetary bodies moved majestically according to predictable and regular laws. From this Plato inferred the existence of an unseen intelligence—a World Soul—behind the visible universe, marvelously regulating all its parts. He further reasoned that the World Soul found its counterpart in the human soul, which struggled to bring order to the chaotic material world of the body and bring it into harmony with the universe. Wisdom, therefore, was the ordering of people in accordance with the divine system of the universe. Thus in one leap Plato succeeded in reconciling religion and the new astronomy and in setting up an ethics of personal salvation in place of the collectivist model of the past. For a significant intellectual minority the contemplation of the universe and its harmonious working was from this time forward a source of inner security and consolation.

Ethics and the Popular Philosophies

In the classical *polis* the civic religions' lack of ethical content had not been a problem until quite late in their development. The practically creedless cult of the gods was complemented by a powerful system of conventional usage and practice that governed day-to-day life. Custom was the basis of morality and governed every aspect of the individual's life. The trouble with this arrangement was that one depended on and shored up the other, and citizens who left their community were on their own, without the customs or the religious practices of the city-state to sustain them. The potential for moral chaos and psychological disruption in such a situation was extremely high.

The situation was not as bad as it might appear, however. The citizens of states where convention was most highly developed, such as Sparta, were susceptible to moral vertigo when they stepped outside the community, but those of other states, such as Athens, had long traditions of personal autonomy and individuality. Since the late fifth century B.C. there had been much speculation about alternative ethical systems, totally private types of morality that were independent of the conventions of the state and at times directly opposed to them. Hence the appeal of the new philosophies Cynicism, Epicureanism, and Stoicism. Their aim was to give people adrift in an unstable world a sense of permanence and independence. The new thinking was supposed to make people self-sufficient and, if possible, invulnerable to the whims of Fortune—free of the powers of the planets as manifested in the unpredictable events of daily life. Cynicism got its start at Athens with Diogenes of Sinope (ca. 400–325 B.C.). Athens was also home to the founders of Epicureanism and Stoicism: Epicurus of Samos (370–340 B.C.) and Zeno of Citium (335–263 B.C.).

Cynicism and Epicureanism   The Cynics taught that the principal source of trouble in life was excessive attachment to society, its conventions, and its material trappings. Such possessions or attachments as a husband, a wife, children, native country, or material goods of any kind made a person extremely vulnerable to the whims of Fortune. Therefore, to be truly free, a person should be liberated from these things. Teles argued that the obligations of citizenship were a form of slavery and—contrary

---

A CYNIC'S VIEW OF RICHES

Give to the poor feeding from a common bowl the money wasted on vanities. Is the eye of Justice blind, the law thwarted? How can men accept as gods those who neither hear nor see such evils? . . . Who can find Justice when Zeus, our parent, treats some men as their father, but others as their stepfather?

—Cercidas of Megalopolis, ca. 250 B.C.

---

to commonly held opinion—suggested that exile from one's homeland constituted no great loss. Many people, such as women and slaves, he observed, are excluded from political life as a matter of course, yet this does not prevent them from being content with what they have. He claimed that it was not the poor who were burdened down with responsibilities but the rich, who had to worry about their properties and possessions. The most famous Cynic of all, Diogenes, trained himself to suffer the hardship of the elements by rolling in the snow in winter and exposing himself to the sun in summer. Regarded as a saint by his followers (and as mad by Plato), he was the subject of many apocryphal tales. On one occasion he was supposed to have been hauled before Philip of Macedonia and accused of being a spy, to which he replied by saying that he had indeed come to spy, but only on the king's insatiable greed. When asked by Alexander what service he could do for the philosopher, Diogenes replied, "Stand out of my sun."

Common among Cynics was the image of the individual as an actor on the stage performing according to the direction of Fortune. Fortune, said Teles, is like a playwright who designs a number of parts: the shipwrecked man, the exile, the beggar, the king. What a good man has to do is simply play well any part assigned to him. Fortune may indeed destroy a person like a storm sinking a ship at sea, but at least the individual will go down like a man.

The Epicureans also aimed to make people free, but they looked beyond the conventions of social life that were the main targets of the Cynics. They believed that a person who could avoid disturbances would be free, and because the principal sources of upset in a person's life are fear and desire, these are the main things to be eliminated. Neither the fear of death, the gods, or pain nor the desire for unnecessary things should concern us. As one of the Epicurean epitaphs put it,

> There is nothing to fear in God nor anything to feel in death. Evil can be endured, good achieved.

The object of life accordingly was pleasure, but pleasure for the Epicureans was more the avoidance of pain than hedonistic self-indulgence. The reason for this is simple: pleasure, when excessive, can be as disturbing as pain and should therefore be taken only in moderation. Only pleasures that are simple and attainable regularly without elaborate measures deserve pursuit. Too much effort in any direction is likely to bring disequilibrium. Thus a person should avoid the noise and bustle of political life along with its honors and responsibilities. "Live out of the public eye," was the advice of Epicurus. Choose the plainest food. If you regularly eat only dry bread, a piece of cheese will give extraordinary satisfaction. "Thank blessed nature that she had made essential things easy to come by and things attained with difficulty unnecessary," was another of his sayings. Above all we should restrain desire: "If you wish to make [a man] rich do not add to his money but subtract from his desires." And "a person who has the least need of riches enjoys them most."[2]

The antidote to fear is knowledge, said the Epicureans, but not the pursuit of knowledge for its own sake, which is nothing but vanity. We need to know only as much as will secure us from being afraid of any natural phenomenon or the divine beings who rule the universe. Nothing exists except atoms and the void through which they fall. The cosmos and everything in it are material. Natural phenomena such as thunder and lightning have a physical explanation and should not be ascribed to the anger of the gods. The gods do indeed exist, but they have no concern or interest in human beings or in the world, which operates on purely mechanical principles without outside intervention.

Epicurus stressed friendship as well as good memories as an important aspect of the happy life, and his garden at Athens was a tranquil oasis for a contented band of his followers, both men and women.

Stoicism   Like Plato, the Stoics accepted the new astronomy, which noted and explained the regular movements of the heavens by natural causes. Because the universe was orderly, they concluded that it must be the product of a wise design. They argued that despite appearances to the contrary, Providence, Fate, or Destiny leads all things to their appointed ends. If we had a wider vision of things than our usually purely personal one, we would see that this was so.

Stoics saw the human soul as a divine spark that strives to bring order to the body and bring it into harmony with the universe. It is therefore of the essence of wisdom to conform to the order of the cosmos as it is apprehended by reason and, as the Stoics said, to "live according to nature." By extension they concluded that there were not numerous ways of life for an individual to follow but only one. As Zeno, the founder of Stoicism, put it,

> All men should regard themselves as members of one city and people, having one life and order as a herd feeding together on a common pasture.[3]

Stoics believed that most things in the universe follow the divine order, either by instinct, as in the case of the lesser creatures, or by necessity, as in the case of the stars, which are of the same substance as God himself and therefore cannot resist his will. Humans, however, have free will and are capable of rejecting or accepting God's

[2]Seneca, *Letters,* 21.7, 14.17.
[3]Plutarch, *The Virtue of Alexander,* 1.6.

A STOIC HYMN

Lead me O God and thou my Destiny
To that one place which you will have me fill.
I follow gladly. Should I strive with Thee,—
A recreant, I needs must follow still.

—Cleanthes, ca. 300 B.C.

Source: Cleanthes, "God Leads the Way," in C. C. Martindale, trans., *The Goddess of Ghosts*, 2nd ed. (London: Burns, Dates & Washbourne Ltd, 1925), p. 25. Reprinted with permission.

---

plan for them—or at least they have the illusion of freedom because failure to follow the divine blueprint can lead only to profound personal unhappiness and the rejection of one's own true nature. A person should therefore cheerfully and willingly embrace God's plan as manifested by reason, and not resist or struggle against it.

This is not a version of Christian ethics, though at times Stoicism and Christianity seem close to each other. The Stoics believed that each individual had a fixed place in the universe, and that one's duty lay in performing whatever functions were attached to it and not in striving for change. The good Stoic was to accept everything that happened without rebellion or complaint, thus preserving one's inner calm and tranquillity. Virtue was to be practiced for its own sake, no matter what the outcome. The individual was to leave self behind and be content with doing right, whether or not one actually achieved one's goals. The result of this pursuit of virtue was to make a person like God, free and independent and above the fluctuations of earthly life.

Although the Stoics rejected the narrow confines of the city-state and believed in the universal brotherhood of humanity, this did not mean that they thought these ideals could be realized in practice. According to Chrysippus, people were like seats in a theater; some were simply better than others, and nothing could be done about it. Equality was to be achieved in human souls because other conditions, such as wealth or poverty, health or sickness, were of no importance. A slave, they said unconvincingly, could be as free in his or her soul as the freeborn.

The Greek Challenge to Judaism

Since the Jews' return to Jerusalem from the Babylonian Exile after 538 B.C., great emphasis had been placed by Jewish leaders on the role of Mosaic law in the regulation of ethical behavior and cultic practices. Theoretically, answers to all of the problems of daily life could be found in the law, but in practice certain challenges could not be easily answered by reference to the Torah, the first five books of the Hebrew scriptures. The author of the Book of Job, for instance, was not satisfied with current answers to the problem of evil and why God permitted the good to suffer and the evil to flourish. In the form of a brilliant dialogue he shows the inadequacies of traditional responses such as the claim that God tests people by suffering or that he always punishes the wicked and blesses the righteous. In the last analysis Job settles for the position that God's dealing with human beings is too mysterious to fathom and that one's own individual sufferings cannot outweigh the very evident goodness of God and of the world he created.

The author of the Book of Ecclesiastes, Koheleth, goes even further, saying that the rich and the poor, the wise and the foolish, the ethical and the unethical, are all alike swallowed up in death. The same fate overtakes everyone. God's ways are incomprehensible, and there is no way, at least rationally, to reconcile the justice of God with the events of daily life. Death is the fixed destiny of all creatures. Everything has been laid down by a God who is as distant and unapproachable as the Unknown God of Plato. All that one can do is resign oneself to one's position and enjoy whatever good things life happens to bring. In a manner similar to the *Epic of Gilgamesh,* Koheleth says, "So, I commend mirth; for there is nothing good for man under the sun except to eat, drink and be merry" (Eccles. 8:15). Ethics for him is a matter of expediency because no one knows what really constitutes the good life. One should be neither overly righteous nor overly wise, and should keep a careful watch on one's thoughts and utterances. Although rooted in the same scriptural tradition of wisdom literature as Job, Koheleth was heavily influenced by Hellenistic Greek thought, and his cool rationalism and distinctive personality were novelties in the scriptures.

Intellectual challenges of this type provoked considerable reflection among Jewish intellectuals about the nature of Judaism and its relationship to other cultures. However, there were more serious challenges to the very existence of Judaism as a national religion. Under Seleucus IV (187–175 B.C.), the Macedonian king of Syria, attempts were made to seize the revenues of the Temple at Jerusalem. These attempts failed, but under Seleucus' successor, Antiochus IV (175–163 B.C.), the conflict between Hellenism and traditional Judaism came to a head. The Jewish high priest of the time, Jason, was a strong advocate of Hellenic culture and proposed to Antiochus that he be allowed to "set up a gymnasium and a training place for the youth in Jerusalem, and to enroll the people of that city as citizens of Antioch [i.e., Jerusalem would become a Greek city with the name of Antioch]" (2 Macc. 4:9). The horror of a gymnasium where Greek athletic activities would be performed by nude young Jews and of instruction in Greek culture taking place in Jerusalem provoked outrage in conservative Jewish circles. Guerrilla actions were first tried, then full-scale warfare. Led by Mattathias of the Hasmonean priestly family and after his death by his son Judas Maccabeus, the revolt was at first successful. The Temple, which had been polluted by the sacrifice of a pig, was recovered and purified. The war dragged on, however, and in 160 B.C. Judas was killed. His brothers Jonathan and Simon took his place, and eventually Simon captured the Macedonian citadel in Jerusalem, and the Syrian monarch Demetrius II was forced to recognize the independence of Judaea. In the eyes of many Jews, however, the Hasmoneans were corrupted by their own success, and the revolutionary party split into two factions, the Sadducees, who continued to support the ruling family and were not averse to the pleasures of Hellenistic lifestyles, and the law-abiding Pharisees. Many other splinter groups also formed. Although a majority of Jews still clung to the hope of a restored Temple and state and the military overthrow of their enemies, a minority came to believe that the savior (the Messiah), when he came, would not be a worldly king.

The Jews of the dispersion (the Diaspora), as opposed to the Jews of Palestine, had a somewhat different set of problems to confront. They had to contend with the culture of both the Greeks and their other non-Jewish neighbors throughout the Near East. Obviously, the law could not be as easily or exactly observed in a non-Jewish environment as in Palestine, and its demands had to be adjusted accordingly. Three precepts of the law—circumcision, the observance of the Sabbath, and the avoidance of pork—became the most obvious distinguishing characteristics of Jews outside Palestine. Beyond these identifying marks, it was the monotheism of the Jews and their high standards of morality that impressed their neighbors as distinguishing features. Yet where no obvious conflicts were involved, Jews were able to borrow ethical concepts from their Hellenic compatriots and use the traditional Greek moral language of the virtues to present their own ethical teaching. There was even some borrowing in theology, as Greek-speaking Jews took over Stoic arguments against polytheism and idolatry and Stoic demonstrations of the existence of God.

One of the principal centers of Jewish culture outside Judaea was Alexandria. There, beginning around 250 B.C., the Hebrew scriptures were translated into Greek, and a great deal of other literature was composed, most of it with the object of keeping the Jews of Alexandria loyal to their faith amid the temptations—moral, religious, and intellectual—of Ptolemaic Alexandria. Another purpose was to refute pagan criticisms of Judaism and to present it as an ancient and reasonable faith.

The most significant work of reconciling Judaic and Hellenistic cultures was performed by the great philosopher-mystic Philo, who lived in Alexandria at the end

---

DEATH, IMMORALITY, AND SIN

Individual immortality and ethical behavior as a condition for eternal life are among the themes found in *The Wisdom of Solomon,* composed during the Hellenistic period:

God did not make death
    and he does not enjoy the destruction of the living.
He created all things that they might have being;
    the creatures of the world are wholesome. . . .
For God formed humankind for immortality,
    and made humans the image of his own nature.
But through the envy of the devil death entered the
    world, and those who belong to him experience it.
But the souls of the upright are in the hand of God.

—*The Wisdom of Solomon,* 1.13–14, 2.23–3.1

of the first century B.C. Philo's object was to show that scriptural beliefs contained in revealed and perfected form the philosophy and ethics of the best of non-Jewish thought. The method he used to achieve this end was the allegorical technique used by the scholars of the Museum, the Ptolemies' research institute at Alexandria in Egypt, to account for the crudities of Greek mythology, which were at odds with more recent ideas of proper moral behavior. Allegorical interpretation seeks a deeper moral or philosophical meaning beneath the more obvious surface events. For instance, the life of Abraham is seen as symbolic of the human soul's pilgrimage out of a world of materialism and decadence and into a purer and more refined environment. Philo saw Yahweh, the energetic and emotional Jewish Lord of History, in Platonic terms as a distant, austere, infinitely perfect God who communicates with the world through a series of mediators. Over these mediators presides the Logos, which in Stoic thought is a kind of indwelling principle of coherence in the material world that guides all things (including humans) to their own proper ends. As will be seen, the idea of the Logos crops up again in early Christianity.

GREEK HIGH CULTURE ADAPTS TO A NEW ENVIRONMENT

The conditions of the age after Alexander encouraged the spread of literature and art and the participation of the most distant areas of the Greek world in its production. Bion of Borysthenes in Ukraine developed the famous Cynic diatribe (a kind of moral sermon), and Menippus of Gadara, a city just south of Lake Galilee on the east bank of the Jordan, invented a much admired form of satire that found imitators in Varro and Seneca among the Romans and Lucian among the Greeks. Also from Gadara were the fine epigrammatists Meleager and Philodemus. From Sidon and Askelon on the Phoenician and Palestinian coasts came a whole line of poets, philosophers, and historians: Antipater, Boethus, Antiochus, Apollonius, Artemidorus, and many more. Others came from Armenia, Persia, Babylonia, and even farther east. Poetry was still a vital medium of communicating, understanding, and passing on traditional culture. It responded to the needs of the new age in unusual ways.

New Uses for Poetry

Alexandrian poetry is often learned and allusive. It loves to show a knowledge of obscure mythologies and has a special interest in etiology—the process, for example, by which the Scythians or the Galatians are accounted for by being made the descendants of Heracles' son Scythes or of the nymph Galataea, respectively. Two of the great Alexandrians, Apollonius and Callimachus, are hard to read because so much of their poetry consists of far-ranging and obscure mythological and etiological discussions. What must be considered is the strong sense of isolation from Greek history, culture, and tradition that the inhabitants of the new world felt and their

---

LOVE EPIGRAMS

Meleager, from Gadara in Palestine, was famous for his short love poems or epigrams. The following extracts are from his collection, *The Garland:*

Thou sleepest, Zenophila, tender flower. Would I were Sleep, though wingless, to creep under thy lashes, so that not even he who lulls the eyes of Zeus might visit thee, but I might have thee all to myself.

O briny wave of Love, and sleepless gales of Jealousy, and wintry sea of song and wine, whither am I borne? This way and that shifts the abandoned rudder of my judgment. Shall we ever set eyes again on tender Scylla?

Source: Based on W. R. Paton, trans., *The Greek Anthology* (Cambridge, Mass.: Harvard University Press, 1916), pp. 174, 190.

---

strong need to relate their new foundations to the old world. It was to fill this need that the poets of the Hellenistic age composed their seemingly unappealing poems. By creating a web of stories, they integrated the new cities with the old and provided them with a legitimate sense of belonging far beyond the city's foundation charter from the king. Famous poets such as Apollonius of Rhodes were invited to write foundation poems for the new cities, but local poets and antiquarians could fill the bill as well. More curious from the modern standpoint was the acceptance of these tales as historical. It was considered legitimate to take a place name and work it into a tale involving some like-sounding hero or god. What mattered was the process—the method of making contact with the legitimate legend—not the credibility of the final account, which apparently did not matter to the Greeks at all. The final result of all this mythologizing was that all the peoples of the Mediterranean world and even of the lands beyond were brought together in a great pseudohistory that was the historical equivalent of the newly expanded geographic understanding of the known world. It remained intact until Christian times, when the classical version of prehistory was replaced by the Hebrew account of the origin of the nations in Genesis.

The New History: Greeks and Non-Greeks

Some historians responded to the new tastes of the reading public by borrowing dramatic techniques from the theater to make their subject more lively and readable. Duris of Samos wrote a history of the period from the battle of Leuctra to about 280 B.C., and Phylarchus of Athens picked up there and continued down to 220 B.C. Duris' portrayal of Demetrius Poliorcetes as a hero destroyed by self-indulgence and pride and Phylarchus' descriptions of the attempted reforms of the Spartan king Cleomenes III are among the most vivid in ancient history. More traditional histories were also composed. Ptolemy I wrote an account of Alexander's conquests from official documents, and two other officers of Alexander, Nearchus and Aristobulus, also contributed sober accounts. All three versions are reflected in the surviving history of Alexander written by Arrian in the Roman Empire period. Another fine historian was Hieronymus of Cardia, whose writings on the wars of the successors of Alexander survive in fragmentary quotations in the works of others, including Plutarch. The majority of Hellenistic history writing, of which there was a great deal, tended to follow the lines of Duris or had propagandist aims. Most of it has perished.

Polybius in the second century B.C. (ca. 198–ca. 118 B.C.) was the only other great historian of the Hellenistic period. Although written in a dry and uninteresting fashion and with distinct biases against Macedonia and Aetolia, his history of the rise of Rome to dominance in the Mediterranean between 220 B.C. and 167 B.C. is a great one. He attempts to bring all of history into focus by concentrating on this crucial event of his times. He had a full understanding of both sides, having been first a member of the ruling party of the Achaean League and then a close friend of the Roman general Scipio Aemilianus. He had a passionate desire to uncover the truth and made a point of familiarizing himself with Mediterranean geography. Unfortunately, in practice his prejudices against democracy, his admiration for oligarchy, and his belief that Fortune gave Rome a special role in history tended to vitiate his own principles.

An interesting response to the spread of Hellenism was the attempt by some of the indigenous peoples to assert their own histories and cultural values. In the third century B.C. two priests, Berossus in Babylon and Manetho in Egypt, wrote histories of their respective lands in Greek. Later in the same century Fabius Pictor was the first Roman to write an account of his city's history for Greek consumption. A string of Jewish historians and apologists from Demetrius (ca. 220 B.C.) to Josephus (first century A.D.) strove to make their culture and past palatable to Greek and Roman tastes, only to be ignored and instead see crude anti-Semitic fables embraced by the reading and nonreading public alike. To be fair to the Greeks, their attitudes toward the historical records of other indigenous peoples (including the Romans) were equally cavalier. To them the accounts of Romans, Assyrians, Egyptians, Persians, and Jews seemed fabulous and unbelievable. The Greeks were convinced that they alone possessed the true account of prehistory, and unless other accounts could make reference to it, they were automatically dismissed or altered to suit the accepted version. Greek ancestors could be found, if necessary, for any nations they encountered, who in this way could be worked into the Greek scheme of early history. Although the Romans accepted the Greek notion that they were the descendants of the Trojan refugee Aeneas, they rejected other tales that would have made Odysseus, Heracles, or Evander the Arcadian their ancestors. It was not until Christianity that the Near East had its revenge, and then the Greek version of national origins was overwhelmed in favor of the Hebrew account in the book of Genesis.

Utopian Literature: Greek Society's Unfulfilled Hopes

The imagination of the Greeks was greatly stimulated by the enormous expansion of their world after Alexander. Romances and novels in which travel and distant places were involved circulated widely. The Alexander Romance, from a combination of Greek and Near Eastern sources, began circulating in the Hellenistic period and eventually spread all over Europe and Asia in innumerable versions.

Accounts of utopias were also popular. Euhemerus, a client of the Macedonian king Cassander, wrote a story about a utopia that popularized his theory that the gods were originally earthly rulers who were later deified. Euhemerus' utopia was located, he claimed, a few days' voyage off the coast of Arabia. Its inhabitants all possessed the franchise; there was no slavery and practically no private property. Everyone received sustenance according to their needs, but those with higher responsibilities received more than the others. Cassander allowed his eccentric brother Alexarchos to found a city called Uranopolis—"the Heavenly City"—on the Mount Athos peninsula in the north of Greece, but unfortunately we know next to nothing of it except for a few coins and scattered literary references.

Iambulus, another utopianist writing in the mid-third century B.C., described an island in the Indian Ocean that he claimed to have visited. It was one of seven called the Islands of the Sun, and its inhabitants called themselves the children of the sun. Borrowing from Euhemerus, Iambulus depicts these children of the sun as living in a blissful community without war or inner strife. There was no slavery or private property, and wives and children were held in common. Crops grew without attention throughout the year. There was no disease, and population was controlled by voluntary euthanasia. Everyone took turns performing the essential work of the community, and leisure time was given to mutual enjoyment and the worship of the divinity. Onesicritus, who was in Alexander's entourage, circulated the tale that the inhabitants of one area of the Indus Valley lived to the age of 130 years (Iambulus' children of the sun committed suicide at 150), ate together communally, used no money, and admitted lawsuits for only two crimes, homicide and battery. Medicine alone was studied among the sciences, the rest being considered dangerous.

Theater: Leaving the *Polis* Behind

The people who sat in the theaters and *odea* (roofed performance halls) to hear the plays and musical productions of the classical period were an altogether different kind of audience from their Hellenistic successors. The former belonged to independent, tightly knit communities where art, poetry, and the theater were integral parts of the religious and civic life of the cities. The community, not the individual, was the patron of the arts, setting the standards and making the contracts for architectural and theatrical productions. In the Hellenistic age all this was reversed. The connection between power and citizenship was broken, and now only the kings exercised genuine political power. They were also the principal patrons of the fine arts.

There was still a tremendous demand for plays. Festivals old and new were performed all over the Greek world. Tragedy continued to be written, and both old and new compositions made their appearance from one end of the Mediterranean to the other. The names of 70 tragic playwrights are known, although the tendency to emphasize the classical tragedies of the fifth century B.C. at the expense of these later writers means that we know little about them. Fortunately, a sufficient amount of Hellenistic comedy survives, so that we can form some idea of what the audiences of that period thought was amusing.

The comic playwrights of fifth-century B.C. Athens made fun of the decisions, politics, and politicians of their day and devoted little attention to plot development or the characters involved. By contrast, the comedy of the century after Alexander (known as New Comedy) was almost devoid of political satire. Instead, it concentrated on social manners, particularly in family situations, and on moral questions such as greed and poverty, love and guilt, servility and pride. Of the many known plays in this field, only those of Menander survive in sufficient quantity for us to make a fair estimate of this kind of theater.

Menander (ca. 342–ca. 292 B.C.) was a contemporary of Epicurus, with whom he served as an ephebe (military cadet), and a student of Theophrastus, Aristotle's successor in the Lyceum. His plays, like almost all those of New Comedy, follow a standard plot. A young man loves a girl whom he cannot marry for one reason or another—she may be a noncitizen or too poor or a slave for whom the owner demands an impossible price. Somehow the difficulties are overcome, either because it is discovered that the girl is really the daughter of a well-to-do citizen who had exposed her at birth or because the necessary money is forthcoming (through the machinations of a clever slave, perhaps), and the play ends happily. Menander's plays have a comfortable sense of optimism about them. The evil characters are not overwhelmingly evil—nor are the good saints. The largest obstacles in life seem to be things such as family disapproval or shortage of money. Gone are the heroic characters of Sophocles and the tortured figures of Euripides, struggling with giant problems of fate, suffering, and human responsibility. In their place are ordinary and realistic human relationships: men preoccupied with the pursuit of money, soldiers who think that human relations can be bought or created to order, greedy prostitutes, and self-indulgent, superficial young men. Balanced, just relationships are Menander's ideals; his sins are passion, anger, and the pursuit of unnecessary things such as too much money or a reputation. Moderation in all things will produce a sense of equanimity and balance. His best characters (there are no heroes) show a capacity for self-examination but not great deeds.

The failings of the bourgeoisie and its interpersonal relations are the subject of New Comedy. No attempt is made to focus on the real villains of the age: the tyrannical sovereigns, brutal generals and soldiers, arrogant rich, and indifferent middle classes. What Menander and his fellow comic poets did was take the advice of the philosophers and withdraw to a world of small, ethical problems while ignoring (except for passing remarks) the larger issues of society that had escaped their control and now rested in the hands of the kings, their courts, bureaucracies, and mercenary armies. The break with the past is complete. In place of a community struggling with its problems and seeing them reflected on the stage in philosophical plays are individuals on a very restricted and limited scale trying to cope with their own private, psychological problems and interpersonal relations.

Popular tastes were not neglected. If anything, the contrary was true—the theater was taken over, certainly by the Roman period, by popularizing tendencies. For one thing, the physical arrangement of the theater had changed, and costuming and a high stage pushed the action back into a separate world, making the Hellenistic and Roman theaters much more like ours than like their classical predecessors. The actor came to dominate the plays, and the Romans gave greater emphasis to music, so that during the Roman Empire music-hall variety-type shows and the operetta had practically usurped the stage from the traditional plays. A major factor contributing to this development was the rise in popularity of the mime or playlet in the Hellenistic period. Either sung or spoken, mimes were written to appeal to the masses. Their stock themes were adultery and seduction, and they often burlesqued the traditional tales of the tragic and comic theaters. Amusing and fast-moving, they had enormous appeal. Originally staged as sideshows to the main performance, they eventually replaced the traditional plays altogether.

The Golden Age of Greek Science

The golden age of Greek science came in the centuries that followed the conquests of Alexander the Great. Long years of philosophical and mathematical research culminated in the work of Aristotle, who established the principle that conclusions should be drawn only from a mass of material gathered by empirical methods. Aristotle applied this basic principle of research to biology, where he did his finest scientific work; some of his observations were not surpassed until modern times. Using the same technique of empirical examination, he analyzed the plots of hundreds of plays to establish a theory of tragedy and gathered over 150 constitutions to try to determine what elements in them contributed to the preservation or destruction of the city-state type of society. Although Plato had emphasized mathematics and made it an essential part of his curriculum, his quest for ideal forms underlying the physical universe had a bad influence on scientific development by encouraging researchers to look for metaphysical forms rather than following Aristotle's principle of scientific induction from field observations. Nevertheless, for about two centuries after Alexander, there was an outpouring of scientific studies unexcelled until the modern scientific renaissance.

One of the reasons for this development was the Hellenistic kings' cultural involvement in higher education. The Ptolemies established a major research center at Alexandria, the Musuem and libraries were founded at Alexandria, Pergamum, Antioch, Rhodes, Smyrna, and probably elsewhere. Athens, eclipsed by Alexandria in the sciences and in literature, remained the world's center of philosophical and rhetorical studies.

The Museum at Alexandria was the center of the scientific movement and attracted researchers from all over the Greek-speaking world. Sponsored and financed by the Ptolemies, the Museum was not, as the term signifies in our usage, an institution dedicated to collecting items from the past. Rather, it was a place where creative

HELLENISTIC TECHNOLOGY AND SCIENCE

The most spectacular demonstration of Hellenistic technology and science is found in the complicated instrument known as the *Antikythera mechanism*. It was discovered in the remains of a first-century B.C. shipwreck found near the island of Antikythera located between Crete and the Peloponnese. The device is a calendrical sun and moon computer that coordinates lunar and solar months with the positions of the planets, the zodiacal path of the sun, and the rising and setting of the most noticeable stars. It is equipped with a number of tables and concentric dials, the latter being operated by a series of gears that include a sophisticated differential assembly (at *E*). An outside crank (at *A*) provides the power necessary to activate the device. Scholars speculate that the mechanism might have been held in the hand of a statue and used as a kind of exhibition piece.

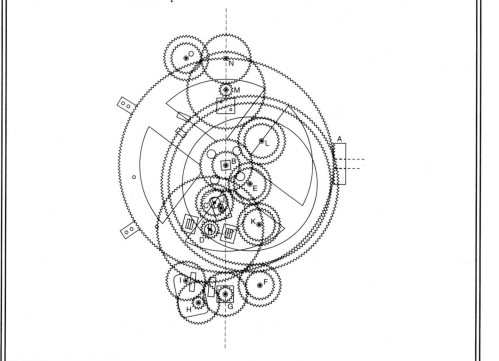

investigation in a number of important fields in the sciences and literature was conducted.

Astronomy and Mathematics   Reflecting the metaphysical and theoretical predisposition of its researchers, the most spectacular achievements of the Museum were in astronomy and mathematics, but there were also significant advances in medicine and mechanics. The predominantly laboratory sciences, physics and chemistry, however, developed hardly at all at the Museum.

Since the discoveries of Plato's student Eudoxus in the fourth century B.C., the predominant view of the universe was that Mercury and Venus revolved around the sun and that the sun, moon, and other planets revolved around the earth in concentric spheres. Aristarchos of Samos (ca. 310–230 B.C.), one of the most brilliant scholars of the Museum, went further and advanced the hypothesis that all the planets revolved around the sun, which was fixed, and that the stars, which were also fixed, were at enormous distances from the earth. Aristarchos also endorsed the theory of Heracleides of Pontus that the earth revolved daily on its axis. Unfortunately, there was no way of making the observed phenomena of the movement of the planets and stars—especially stellar parallax and the apparent increase and decrease in the size of the stars as the earth moved toward or away from them—agree with this system. Although the supposition of the immensity of the universe would account for the absence of explanations for these phenomena, no one was willing to accept such a hypothesis. Besides, there were workable alternatives that "saved the phenomena"—the apparent movement of the planets—so Aristarchos' heliocentric theory never caught on.

Hipparchus of Nicaea (ca. 190–126 B.C.), another Alexandrian scholar, calculated that the length of a mean lunar month was 29 days, 12 hours, 44 minutes, and 3⅓ seconds, which is less than 1 second off from modern findings. He also discovered the precession of the equinoxes.

The greatest advances of the Hellenistic sciences were in mathematics, particularly geometry, which had a special appeal to the metaphysically minded scholar-scientists of the period. The first of the great mathematicians was Euclid (ca. 300 B.C.), whose book on the fundamentals of geometry became a standard text for the next 2,000 years, and it was not until the nineteenth century that mathematicians managed to create what has come to be known as non-Euclidean geometry. Archimedes (ca. 287–212 B.C.), famous for his protracted defense of Syracuse against the Romans and his discovery of the principle of specific gravity while taking a bath, also calculated the value of π and invented integral calculus. His practical inventions included the compound pulley and the endless screw, which was used to drain mines in Spain and irrigate fields in Egypt. Apollonius of Perga, a somewhat younger contemporary of Archimedes, is the third of the great mathematicians. His treatise on conic sections was an exhaustive monograph on the subject and influenced mathematicians down to Newton.

A number of figures besides Archimedes dabbled in practical mechanics. Ctesibius (ca. 260 B.C.) dealt with ballistic formulas and invented a catapult that worked on compressed air. Hero of Alexandria (first century B.C.) discovered the principle of virtual work as a result of his experimentation with levers and pulleys. He also invented an early form of the theodolite, the dioptra, a portable water level for use in surveying, and a simple steam engine.

Medicine: Scientific, Clinical, and Folk   Medicine made great strides in the Hellenistic period that were not excelled until the time of Harvey. Alexandria was the setting for most of these developments, and this is where the two greatest researchers,

Herophilus of Chalcedon and Erasistratus of Ceos, did their work. The former was an anatomist whose discoveries included the sensory nerves and their connection with the spinal cord, the duodenum, and the distinction between the cerebrum and the cerebellum. He believed that the brain was the center of the nervous system as well as the seat of intelligence and that the arteries carried blood. On the basis of dissection, which included vivisection, Herophilus gave the first accurate description of female anatomy. He discovered the ovaries and possibly also the fallopian tubes. Unlike his predecessors, Herophilus did not regard women as a special class or as exceptions to the normal rules that governed health. Erasistratus recognized that the heart was a motor that supplied the blood to the various parts of the body; unfortunately, he fell back on the theory that the arteries carried air. His most important discovery was the distinction between the sensory and motor nerves, which Herophilus had missed. He was more interested in physiology than anatomy, and discussed the role of diet and the process of nourishment in the body's tissues.

Theoretical medical research made little advance after Herophilus and Erasistratus, and clinical studies came to dominate under Philinus, Herophilus' successor at the Museum. Proven therapeutic practice rather than theoretical anatomy or physiology dominated his school, whose best-known member, Heracleides of Tarentum, concentrated on pharmacology and toxicology as well as dietetics and medical history. Asclepiades of Prusa, who took an almost diametrically opposite approach to that of Heracleides, cured diseases by a regimen of diet, exercise, massage, and cold baths. He placed no reliance on drugs and argued that health could be recovered by the "restoration of the symmetry of the atoms" of which the body was composed. In the early Roman Empire the encyclopedist Celsus composed a treatise summarizing the advances made in medicine since the time of Hippocrates.

Art and Society

The patrons of art in the Hellenistic world were as varied as Hellenistic society itself. The kings as founders of cities—especially capital cities—were the principal patrons, but individuals among the upper and middle classes, as well as the cities themselves, were also important purchasers of art. Corresponding to the extraordinary variety and taste of its patrons, Hellenistic art ranged from the monumental 400-foot frieze at Pergamum to tiny, exquisite gems that were the special feature of Hellenistic jewelers. Everything from the most flamboyant and vulgar baroque to the elegantly restrained classical was available—for a price. Copies of archaic and classical statues in every grade, quality, size, and material could be obtained through art dealers in all the major cities. Thus the *polis* selecting art and commissioning buildings for its own community needs was replaced by the individual shopping to fill his or her needs. Kings used art of all kinds (and quality) for propaganda purposes, but private persons also made purchases, either for their own homes or collections or in their capacities as benefactors of their cities. A class of amateur art connoisseurs arose, and in art as well as literature there developed a split between the *cognoscenti* and the masses, for whom it was assumed that only the obvious and gross were appropriate.

Among the artists themselves the times also brought changes. The hugely expanded demand for copies and decorations of all kinds added the dimension of trade to high art. The widely dispersed character of the Hellenistic cities made it necessary for artists to travel a great deal and mix with other artists from all over the world in large, joint projects. Indicative of the broadening character of the new society is the fact that we know of several professional female artists, one of whom, Helena, painted a scene of Alexander's battle with the Persians at Issus. Her picture may have served as the original for the well-known Alexander Mosaic at Pompeii, which shows Alexander and Darius confronting each other in the midst of battle.

The New Cities   The cities, especially the capitals, were the showplaces of the Hellenistic kings. Although fortresses of the rulers, they were far more than mere armed camps. They were the visible and permanent symbols of all that the kings and the ruling elite stood for, and it was as founders of cities that the Hellenistic kings made their most original contributions to history.

The first step in the construction of a new city was the hiring of a competent architect who could create a plan to suit the site and at the same time satisfy the military, administrative, and cultural aims of the founder. As in so many other things, the path for achieving this had long been prepared by a tradition of city planning going back to at least the sixth century B.C. Hippodamus, the founder of the art of town planning, was active in the fifth century B.C., and some superb examples of his method can be found in two cities laid out in the following century, Priene and Miletus in Asia Minor. Careful planning organically related all the essential parts of the city—the agoras, temples, gymnasiums, theaters, residential quarters, docks, and so forth—to its site. In the case of Priene, the location was a difficult hillside, whereas for Miletus the site was a promontory jutting into the sea with accommodations for several harbors. Pergamum, the capital of the Attalids, presented formidable problems to the planners. It had a superb but difficult location on a steep hillside, and the eventual solution was to divide the city into a number of levels. Although the capitals were the most spectacular examples of Hippodamian planning, cities of similar types were built from one end of the Hellenistic world to the other. As late as the second century B.C. the work was still going on, even in far-flung Afghanistan and Pakistan, where the well-designed grids of Begram, Charsada, and Taxila testify to the persistence of the Hellenic ideal.

Once the initial stages of layout and construction had been accomplished, the next step was to decorate the city fittingly. For this task the workshops of Rhodes, Athens, Alexandria, and elsewhere could be called upon, artists and craftsmen (now distinct groups) could be imported to do the work on the spot, or some combination of these two could be arranged. Because so many of the new cities were the creations of the kings, it is understandable that their presence should have been strongly felt. The cities bore their names, and their coinage circulated their likenesses, but there was also royal sculpture to remind the citizens of their masters.

Sculpture, Propaganda, and Daily Life   In the fourth century B.C. there had been a steady movement toward realistic portraiture in sculpture. In literature, this ten-

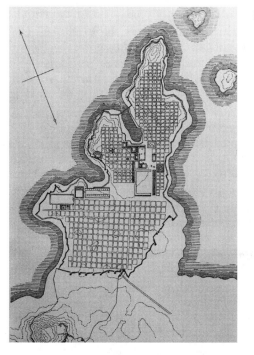

Plan of Miletus in Asia Minor (ca. 100 B.C.).

dency found its counterpart in biography. The historian Xenophon wrote the life stories of the Spartan Agesilaus and the Persian Cyrus, and in the Hellenistic period biography emerged as a fully developed literary genre in its own right. In the same period portraiture became a distinct field in sculpture, and both biography and portraiture found ideal subjects in the flamboyant lives of the Hellenistic kings, queens, and generals. The best sculptures were able to balance realism and psychological insight and convey a sense of the king's superhuman burden as well as their special share in the divine potency.

The kings communicated with their subjects by less obvious means also. In Alexandria the cult of Serapis—the deity who cared for his worshipers—could hardly fail to suggest the rule of the Ptolemies, who also aspired to the same image of benevolent concern. The kings of Pergamum consciously intended the Altar of Zeus on the hill at the summit of the city to be another Parthenon. Its approach was designed to resemble Mnesicles' Propylaea at Athens, which concealed the view of the Parthenon until the moment when the visitor emerged from between the last pillars and suddenly beheld the Parthenon above in three-quarters view. Like the Parthenon, the Altar of Zeus had a frieze, but its didactic purpose was much more evident. Instead of having to strain to see through the column shafts, as at Athens, the viewer of the Pergamum frieze could look at the sculptures almost at eye level. If there was doubt as to their meaning, the viewer could consult the inscription that accompanied each figure. The frieze, consisting of almost 400 feet of contorted, muscular giants and gods locked in fierce combat, conveyed the same message as that of the Parthenon: the victory of the gods over the forces of chaos and of the Greeks over the barbarians. Thus the Attalids, by their victories over the invading Celts, claimed to play the same role as the defenders of Greek civilization against barbarism that Athens claimed for itself in the wars against the Persians. It was a stunning piece of sculpture, vigorous and energetic, but utterly unlike the calm, restrained works of Phidias at Athens. Yet it was a true reflection of the power, turmoil, and freedom of the age.

Hellenistic writers largely gave up the heroic and bloodthirsty themes of early literature for more intimate and personal topics such as love and the ordinary events of everyday life. The same is true of art, where love in every facet, from the tender and ingenuous to the explicit and vulgar, was explored in detail. Every physical and psychological human aspect was investigated, and individuals of all walks and stages of life, not just the youthful gods and godlike aristocracy, were considered fit subjects. Slaves and peasants, old men and women, the deformed and crippled, children at play and asleep, drunken gods and men, were depicted in an incredible variety of poses and materials. For the first time smiling statues made their appearance, but the virtuoso artists of the period could represent any mood they or their patrons wished to convey. Sagging skin and protruding veins were shown as readily as smooth

The great range of Hellenistic sculpture is suggested by these two extremes: the complicated, contorted figures of Laocoon and his sons and the simple statuette of a contented, overweight old woman.

The eternal appeal of the classical style. Compare these harmoniously arranged struggling figures from the tomb of Mausolus with the similarly balanced Lapith and Centaur in the Parthenon metope on page 154.

flesh and muscles. Another popular fashion was veristic portraiture, which depicted with illusionistic exactitude vignettes of real life. Rural scenes with nymphs, peasants, and satyrs dancing in Arcadian simplicity were the counterpart of the bucolic poems of literature.

During the classical age there was no real distinction between the educated or intellectual class and the rest of society. Everyone attended the plays, recitations, and choruses of the poets and dramatists. During the Hellenistic age, however, a new phenomenon made its appearance: the person who read in private, possessed a library, and tended to associate with like-minded people. At the professional level there were the scholars of Alexandria and the other centers of learning and the philosophers and rhetoricians who wandered the world making their services available to those seeking an education. To this class symbolic and classicizing art appealed greatly. Lysippus produced a statue called *Opportunity* whose face was covered with hair to represent the difficulty of recognizing opportunity and whose head was bald to symbolize the difficulty of grasping it. The statue had wings on its feet and a razor in its hand to illustrate the speed and abruptness with which opportunity presents itself and must be seized. The friezes of Pergamum were an encyclopedia of learned mythology as well as symbolism. Classicism, the reproduction of forms canonized in the fifth century B.C., made its appearance before the Hellenistic age in the tomb of Mausolus in Caria, and ever after conscious appeals were made to this definitive period in Greek art. Over 800 years later, in the last years of the empire, we find Roman aristocrats using classical forms in the ivory plaques they exchanged among themselves.

The homes of the newly affluent middle classes as well as the new cities themselves created a great demand for copies of the ancient masters and for other forms of decoration such as paintings, mosaics, moldings, and the like. Copies of all kinds were mass-produced. Unfortunately, almost no paintings of the Hellenistic period survive, although some idea can be formed from those on the walls and in the floor mosaics of the towns and villas around the Bay of Naples destroyed in A.D. 79. So much of classical and Hellenistic art survives only in copies that it is difficult to estimate how good the originals actually were. Not a single original piece by the masters, such as Phidias, Praxiteles, Polyclitus, or Lysippus, has been identified with certainty.

BECOMING GREEK: EDUCATION IN THE NEW WORLD

The new world created fresh demands in the fields of communication and education. In old Greece the cities were still able to fulfill their educational functions without much change from the past. Conservative tradition was enshrined in the community's way of life and provided the essential moral framework for both old and young. The city, with its festivals, courts, assemblies, and general method of doing public business, inculcated each new generation with the ways of the past. Except in higher education, the city had no need of any artificial educational system independent of the community itself. Reading, writing, and calculation were taught as purely mechanical skills in private schools for a few, but there was no education beyond that unless an *ephebeia,* a military youth-training program, had been established in the city. Moral education, of course, took place in the larger environment of home and city.

In the new lands none of these assumptions about education held true. Greek cities in the east were little islands in an alien sea. Their inhabitants were themselves natives of a dozen different Greek cities or regions. It was therefore necessary to create a wholly new educational system to provide for the perpetuation of Greek culture. The primary component of this new institution was the gymnasium, and its director, the gymnasiarch, became one of the most important persons in the new cities. Becauses the object of the gymnasium was to inculcate Greek values, the languages and cultures of indigenous peoples were not part of its curriculum.

The Gymnasium Goes Academic

The early gymnasiums had been informal affairs, located in the suburbs where the necessary space was easily obtainable. A good water supply for the baths was considered important, and trees for shade were also desirable. Athens's three oldest gymnasiums were combinations of religious shrines, parks, athletic fields, and lecture halls. Later, more were built, one even in the agora itself. In the Hellenistic period this tendency to bring the gymnasiums within the walls of the city was given reinforcement as their importance as educational centers grew. In Egypt, where Greek settlements were scattered throughout the countryside and cities were few, the gymnasium became the real center of Greek political, social, and cultural life. Similarly, when native peoples such as the upper-class Jews of Jerusalem wished to acquire Greek culture, they imported the institution of the gymnasium. As a result of this formal development, the gymnasium came to be quite an elaborate affair, carefully planned and laid out as an integrated architectural unit. The essential elements consisted of a running track, an area for discus and javelin throwing, a wrestling place (the *palaestra*), and buildings with space for baths, changing rooms, lecture halls, libraries, and supplies. Depending on the space available, these could be arranged at will. In Delphi and Pergamum, which were built on the sides of hills, the various buildings and tracks were distributed on different terraces, but the more ordinary arrangement was to surround a large area with a wall or colonnade and place the various rooms and halls along the sides. Statues were common decorations, and the walls were often covered with paintings, lists of pupils and athletic victors—and graffiti.

The traditional object of Greek education had always been the maintenance of a balance between intellectual and physical education, although there was a general tendency to move more heavily in one direction than the other. Thus the gymnasiums of the classical period had emphasized sports, whereas in the Hellenistic period and later in the Roman period athletics gave way to scholastics. The change was due to a number of factors, foremost of which was the aristocratic aspect of the physical education program in the early period, which emphasized competition. The subsequent rise of professional sports tended to lessen the importance of amateur athletics, but the most significant factor in the shift toward academics was the new role the gymnasiums played in the Hellenistic city as they became the centers where Greek ideas and ideals were kept alive. With the loss of independence, the city's agora and its other meeting places declined in importance, and the new focus of social and cultural life became the gymnasium. Education became a detached and independent process, no more an integral part of the life of the city. Its standards, too, had to derive from elsewhere; the city itself was no longer the norm and measure of things. These sources included the general Greek environment, such as the common festivals that united Greeks from all over the world. Even in only partially Hellenized areas they had an important function. In Palestine the five-year games held at Tyre brought both true Greeks and Hellenized natives together from all over the region. On one occasion the contingent from Jerusalem brought 330 drachmas with it, but remaining true to their beliefs, they dedicated the money to shipbuilding in Tyre rather than to the sacrifices of the city god, Melkart-Heracles.

The Curriculum

More important than the festivals in setting the new educational standards, however, was the study of the classics, the great literary works thought to enshrine the most characteristically Greek views and attitudes. Preeminent among these were the works of Homer and the three tragedians Aeschylus, Sophocles, and Euripides, with the greatest emphasis being given to Euripides. Hesiod, Pindar, Alcman, Alcaeus, and Sappho were also studied, and of the more recent works Menander's comedies, Apollodorus' *Argonautica,* and the epigrammatists' poems were popular. Prose was less studied. Of the historians, Herodotus, Xenophon, and especially Thucydides were standard fare, and among the orators Demosthenes was considered supreme. In secondary schools, for youths from 14 to 18 years of age, these texts were studied minutely by the most mechanical means. Painstaking lists of unusual words were prepared and supplemented by endless recitations and memorizations. Students learned to recognize the identifying marks of classical literature and tried to model their own writing on it. There was no interest whatsoever in original or creative writing. The object was to reproduce as closely as possible the style, syntax, and diction of the models. Beyond that the purpose of studying the classics was the inculcation of moral values and the discovery of the wisdom contained in them. Needless to say, this produced all sorts of problems, especially where the shocking practices of the models were at odds with the middle-class values of the Hellenistic and Roman periods. The result was allegorical interpretations of the questionable actions of the heroes and gods, just as biblical commentators were forced into similar positions by the peculiar deeds of some of the patriarchs in Genesis. The main problem in the study of both classical and scriptural texts was the total absence among Hellenistic readers of a sense of the atmosphere in which the works were composed and their assumption of or desire to find an unchanging set of values in the texts. Some did appreciate the historical relativity of the compositions, but the majority of the commentators found easier solutions in imaginative explanations, such as Plutarch's claim that Homer's description of the adulterers Paris and Helen retiring to bed at the end of Book III of the *Iliad* was really intended to cast discredit on evildoers.

An Unexpected Side Effect

The same classical texts were studied in the same kind of institutions everywhere in the Hellenistic world, which had the effect of providing broad cultural unity wherever a gymnasium was established. It was here that the models evolved in Athens of a detachable educational system came into their own and provided the Greeks with a solution to the perplexing problem of maintaining their identity amid alien and powerful cultures. But the more important effect of this system of education was that it broke down the old exclusivity of the Greek cities, which had made the assimilation of outsiders so difficult. Now all that a person needed to become a Greek was a knowledge of the language and a gymnasium education. For the lower classes, who could not afford the latter, this meant little, but for those who had the resources and wanted this kind of an education, either for themselves or for their children, the door was at least ajar. This last proviso is included because theoretically the gymnasium was open only to native Greeks, though in practice non-Greeks were able to slip onto the gymnasium lists and merge with the Greek upper classes.

Higher Education and the Job Market

Not many Greeks possessed an education beyond what the local gymnasium offered, and those who wished to pursue higher studies generally had to travel to one of the larger cities that had chairs of rhetoric and philosophy, the mainstay of the university curriculum in the ancient world. Of these two subjects, rhetoric tended to predominate for largely practical reasons.

Despite the curtailing of the Greek city's autonomy, its affairs were conducted much as they had been in the past. After Alexander the generally democratic type of constitution prevailed everywhere almost until the beginning of the Roman period, and with it came the same kinds of public-speaking requirements as in the past. Councils, assemblies, courts, and judicial commissions all demanded formal presentations by people appearing before them. The same was true of external relations between the cities, and we have numerous accounts of delegations being sent by groups among the contending city factions to argue their cases before the kings and later the emperors. But even in more provincial settings than the courts of kings, the rhetoricians had their part to play. For example, in the New Testament tale of Paul's arrest for inciting a riot in Jerusalem, we read of his accusers coming down to Caesarea and bringing with them the rhetorician Tertullus to conduct the prosecution before the Roman magistrate (Acts 24:1). Although the great deliberative oratory of the past declined along with the freedom of the cities, it remained true that the person with oratorical ability could contribute most to the welfare of his city. He could do this at home through his ability to persuade his own people of the wisdom of certain courses of action and abroad in his capacity to negotiate successfully with the other cities and powers in the Hellenistic political world.

The result of this practical necessity for rhetorical ability, coupled with its traditional importance in Greek education, was that the study of the subject became the crown and object of almost all higher education, though with gestures to the study of philosophy. It was claimed, as Isocrates had argued in his debate against Plato, that the effort spent in learning how to speak properly had the corresponding moral effect of teaching the learner how to think and live properly. It was eloquence that distinguished the educated from the uneducated and the Greek from the non-Greek.

THE HELLENISTIC AGE: ACHIEVEMENTS AND LIMITATIONS

The Hellenistic age is difficult to evaluate. Naturally, much depends on whose viewpoint is being considered and whether contemporary sensibilities are to be regarded as appropriate yardsticks. Did the conquered peoples of western Asia and Egypt fare better or worse under their Macedonian and Greek overlords than they had under their previous rulers? Would they have been better off under their own elites? If unity is to be taken as a criterion of success, then the experiment of the Macedonian kings, including Alexander, must be viewed as a failure. Unlike the Persians and before them the Assyrians, they were unable to sustain the union of the diverse peoples of the Near East in anything like a coherent state. Political fragmentation and instability led to endless, often pointless wars among the successor states of the Persian Empire. On the other hand, the ferocious techniques of control used by the Assyrians, Babylonians, and Persians to keep their heterogeneous world in order were abandoned by their successors. Nor did Greeks and Macedonians have things entirely their own way. Celtic invasions of Greece, Macedonia, and Asia Minor were a serious cause of alarm in the third century B.C. Macedonian control of Iran was soon broken, and vigorous resistance movements existed in Egypt and Palestine.

It is often said that the Greeks and Macedonians paid little attention to the cultures of the peoples they conquered, but again we must ask what kind of yardstick is being used. Did their predecessors show any greater sensitivities toward their subjects, or is it to be expected that imperial regimens will show a certain amount of sympathy (that is, something beyond mere curiosity) for the cultures of the conquered? If anything, the cultural world of the Hellenistic age was considerably more open to contributions from indigenous peoples than the previous dominant cultures had been. For example, the Ptolemies of Egypt passed themselves off as pharaohs and patronized Egyptian temples, thus helping to sustain Egyptian culture. The atmosphere of the Hellenistic age was also highly successful in breaking down the narrow, self-defeating particularisms of the Greeks themselves. In one area, religion and religious literature, the Hellenistic period was characterized by a highly productive interchange between dominant and native cultures, and indeed a cultural fusion of East and West was achieved in the emergence of classical Christianity in A.D. 200–400. Ultimately, perhaps, we should see the Romans, a non-Greek people, as the main legatees of the Hellenistic age. Heavily influenced at various times but not overwhelmed by Greek culture, they in turn extended Greek culture widely. In their promotion of Christianity in the late Empire period, the Romans were, in effect, advancing an amalgam of Greek and Near Eastern religious influences. Broadly construed, the Hellenistic age may be regarded as the principal mediator between the cultures of the Near East and those that ultimately became the dominant cultures of the West.

Chapter 8

Early Rome

THE WESTERN MEDITERRANEAN AND EARLY ITALY

In ancient and modern times the western Mediterranean has been the focal point of the countries surrounding it. High mountain ranges and plateaus cut off the coastal areas from the interior and prevent easy communication with the land masses behind them. Long, narrow coastal plains in Africa and Spain lead up to high, arid mountains and plateaus. In Africa, the Atlas range and beyond it the vast waste of the Sahara constitute even today the southern boundary of the Mediterranean region and a major barrier to communication between this area and equatorial Africa. The rich agricultural plains of Italy—Tuscany, Lazio, and Campania—face the sea and are backed by the steeply rising peaks of the Apennines. The Cévennes and the Alps direct the inhabitants of the south of France away from continental Europe and toward the sea. Great rivers—the Ebro in Spain, the Rhône in France, and the Tiber in Italy—flow into the Mediterranean, drawing the peoples of the uplands toward the coasts, where the great cities, almost all of them founded in ancient times, are located. Conveniently situated islands—the Balearics, Sardinia, Corsica, and Sicily—aid communication and in antiquity served as handy stopping places for the maritime traffic coast-hugging. Distances are short in this world. In one of the more dramatic scenes from the Roman Republic, Cato the Elder (second century B.C.), who was arguing in the Senate for the destruction of Carthage in Tunisia, opened the folds of his toga and let fall a bunch of ripe figs that had been picked outside Carthage just three days before, lending emphasis to his point that a vigorous neighbor such as Carthage, even though in Africa, was much too close for comfort.

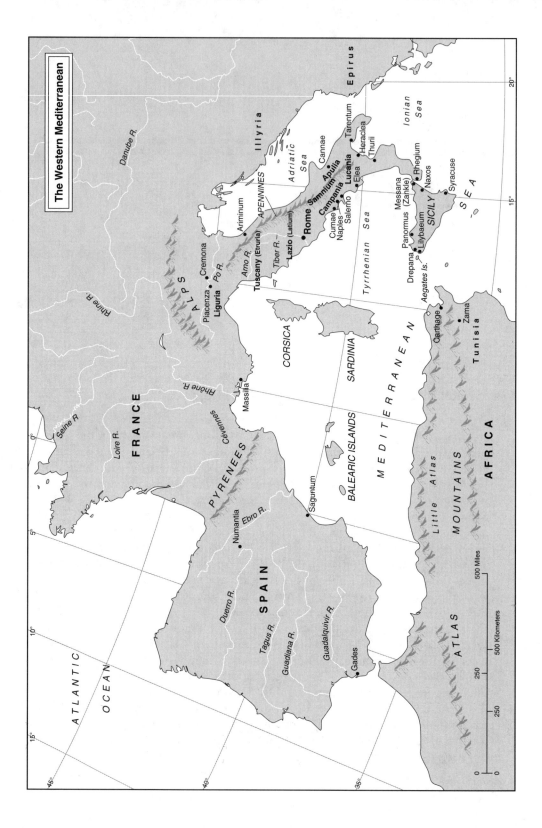

The Western Mediterranean

Greeks, Phoenicians, and Celts

The western Mediterranean was one of the richest mineral and agricultural areas in the ancient world. In Roman times, southeastern Spain, the Ebro valley, southern France, Italy from the Arno River to Salerno, and the hinterland of Carthage were covered with vineyards and olive groves. The export trade was brisk. Even today the grid pattern of the Roman field system can be seen stretching for mile after mile in the countryside of modern Tunisia. Grain from Sicily, Africa, and Sardinia fed Rome for centuries and allowed Italian farmers to concentrate on wine and oil production as well as on other cash crops.

It was the metals of the west, however, that first attracted the attention of the eastern civilizations. The Phoenicians were the first to stumble across the mineral wealth of Spain. In time its great potential was realized, and it became the Mediterranean world's principal source of silver, copper, and tin. Somewhat later the iron resources of Etruria began to be tapped. Then, from the middle of the eighth century (ca. 750 B.C.), a flood of Greeks began moving across the northern rim of the western Mediterranean, paralleling the path of Phoenician traders who were moving primarily along the coast of Africa toward the Atlantic.

From at least the sixth century B.C., the area north of the Mediterranean, stretching from Spain through France, southern Germany and Austria, was occupied by warlike Celtic-speaking peoples. Much longer than the Greeks and Romans, they resisted the Mediterranean impulse to form states or build cities, and generally remained content with less complex forms of society such as the chiefdom. Their presence and presence of others like them—the Germanic peoples, for instance—forever made the development of the state and of urban culture in the west a much slower and more precarious process than it had been among the Greeks. The state in a permanent form did not come to northern Europe until the ninth century A.D., and Celtic peoples, left to their own devices in fringe areas of Europe such as Scotland and Ireland, resisted state formation down to the eve of modern times.

Italy: Geography and History

Italy is divided into a number of clearly identifiable geographic regions by the switching back and forth of the Apennines, its great central mountain range. These mountains begin at the point where the Alps reach the Mediterranean coast at the Riviera, then cut all the way across Italy to the Adriatic Sea at a point below Ariminum (modern Rimini). There they begin to turn southeast and recross the peninsula until they touch the Tyrrhenian coast in Lucania. From there they continue on south through the toe of Italy, reappearing in Sicily, and again in Africa as the Atlas chain.

This zigzagging of the Apennines creates three great natural lowland regions. The first two, the Po valley in the north and Apulia in the south, open onto the Adriatic. In the west, the third, which contains the districts of Etruria (Tuscany), Latium (Lazio), and Campania, opens onto the Mediterranean proper. Between Apulia and

Unaffected by classical Greek ideas of form, this small bronze statuette from Sardinia breathes the independent and alien spirit of the west.

Campania the mountains flatten out to form a large plateau, known to the Romans as Samnium, which dominates the plains on either side.

In ancient times the richest agricultural land and almost all the mineral wealth of Italy were to be found in the western lowland region. In addition, the natural lines of communication lay in this area rather than in the mountainous central highlands or on the narrow Adriatic coastal plain. Rome, with its central location astride these routes, could prevent movement north or south or from the Mediterranean into the interior. Long before there were any roads leading to Rome, all the lines of communication converged on the site where a number of hills overlooked a ford on the lower reaches of the Tiber.

Its position in the middle of Italy meant that Rome was vulnerable to attack from many sides. However, Rome had an advantage in its central lines of communication. As long as it could keep its enemies from coordinating their attacks—or hold one enemy off while coping with the others—Rome could use its communication lines to deploy its forces quickly from one frontier to another. Diplomacy, therefore, was an important element in Rome's dealings with its neighbors, and the principle of divide and conquer was a matter of survival for the early Romans.

The Peoples of Italy

The Italy of Rome's early years was a complicated mosaic of peoples, cultures, and languages. Celts began to infiltrate across the Alps in the early fifth century B.C. and then came in massive numbers around 400 B.C., settling first in the Po valley and then extending themselves southward along the Adriatic coast. The Greeks had been in Italy and Sicily since the eighth century B.C. Their main concentrations were in the south along the instep of the boot, in the area known as Magna Graecia, but they also had important settlements on the Adriatic and the Tyrrhenian coasts. The Phoenicians were influential in Etruria, where they found allies to support them against common enemies: the Greeks of Italy, Sicily, and Marseille. With the exception of the late-arriving Celts, however, these peoples never ventured deep into the hinterland, and the interior of Italy remained in the hands of two groups of earlier arrivals. The first was made up of Indo-European–speaking peoples, of whom the most important were the Venetians of the Po valley, the Oscans and Umbrians of the central highlands and east coast, and the Latins of the west. The second group, which did not speak Indo-European languages, included one of the most important of the peoples of Italy, the Etruscans. Others of lesser note were the Messapians of Apulia and the Ligurians of the northwest. Thus Italy of the early Roman phase was a babel of languages, dialects, and cultures in various stages of development, from the primitive to the most sophisticated.

Of all these peoples, the Oscans were most widespread and the Celts probably the most dangerous. The Latins were confined to the small area between the Tiber and Campania, hemmed in by enemies on all sides. The Oscans and Celts, however, were pre-state, tribal peoples who only slowly made the transition to an urban form of life, and then only partially. Organizationally they were backward compared to the Etruscans, Greeks, and Latins, but because of their numbers, military aptitude, and raiding habits, they gave the urban-based peoples of Italy some difficult moments before they were finally overcome.

The Etruscans

Among the peoples of Italy it was the Etruscans (and with their help, the Romans) who made the most remarkable responses to the new influences coming out of the east.[1] Around 700 B.C. the inhabitants of the rich area between the Arno and the Tiber created a flourishing city-state civilization that was recognized throughout the Mediterranean for its opulence and at times for its peculiar customs. To the Greeks

---

[1]Like so many other ancient peoples, the Etruscans had the misfortune of having their history written for them by their conquerors, and although the Romans admitted their admiration of the Etruscans in a number of areas, they suppressed or ignored much evidence of their accomplishments. Only after centuries of archaeological research has any independent witness been established at all.

they were *Tyrsenoi* (from which comes "Tyrrhenian Sea") and to the Romans *Etrusci* or *Tusci* (hence Etruscan or Tuscan).

The Etruscan cities formed a loose federation that met annually to discuss joint action and to celebrate religious festivals in the Greek fashion. Traditionally the number of cities in the federation was 12, but from the archaeological remains we know of the existence of others, many of whose ancient names are still unknown. While occasionally cooperating, the cities of Etruria also fought bitterly among themselves. Down to the fifth century B.C. they were ruled by kings in whom were combined the functions of priest, general, judge, and political leader. After that date an annually elected official (the *zilath*, or in Latin, *praetor*) presided, assisted by a college of magistrates. There were no senates and no assemblies of the people. Society was divided between aristocrats and a large, servile lower class that was further separated into a number of grades, but there was no free middle class. Aristocratic women enjoyed what seemed to the Greeks to be an astonishing amount of freedom. They accounted for it by accusing the Etruscans of materialism and loose morals.

Economically, the wealth of Etruria lay in its great deposits of iron, copper, tin, and zinc and in its fertile agricultural areas. Etruscan decorative bronzes and jewelry were unsurpassed in the ancient world, and Etruscan farmers achieved high levels of excellence, inventing, among other things, the *cuniculus,* or tunnel method of draining river valley bottoms. By eliminating meandering streams and marshes, this technique reduces erosion and expands cultivable land.

Although in the Roman period the Etruscans were confined within the geographic boundaries of Etruria, at an earlier date they had an empire that included Campania and some of the Po valley. This empire, together with Etruria's own resources, allowed Etruscan aristocrats to enjoy unprecedented prosperity—and to supply, via their graves, the museums of the modern world with some of the greatest art of antiquity.

Etruria was at its height between 650 and 450 B.C., but repeated collisions with Greeks, Latins, Oscans, and Celts shattered its military power, and the Etruscans, like their allies, the Carthaginians, entered into a period of eclipse.

Etruscan Culture's Legacy to Rome

Literature was not a well-developed aspect of Etruscan culture. Chronicles or simple histories of the individual cities did exist, and there is mention of an author of tragedies, but no poetry, either epic or lyric, is known. However, there was a body of seers and diviners, the *haruspices* (singular, *haruspex*), who, in the early period at least, passed on their learning by word of mouth. Etruscan religion, like the religions of the Near East (but unlike those of Greece and Rome), was believed to have been revealed by the gods and had a strong element of the ecstatic that both attracted and repelled the Romans. Officially, the haruspices were held at a distance by the Romans and consulted only in times of extreme emergency. The Romans preferred the consultation of their own state-controlled prophetic books, the Sibylline oracles.

The examination of the entrails of sacrificed animals, particularly the liver, was one of the principal branches of the *disciplina Etrusca,* the Etruscan art of divination.

It was thought that the liver reflected the state of the world at the moment the sacrifice was made and thus could reveal the will of the gods as well as the future to those who could read the signs. In the ancient Near East the art of examining livers had been reduced to a standardized technique, and model terra-cotta livers were created to assist in the process of interpretation. In northern Italy, near Piacenza, a similar model liver in bronze was found in 1877. It is divided into 16 compartments with 24 inner divisions to which the names of various gods have been assigned. According to Cicero, the divisions on the left side of a sacrificial liver were unfavorable and those on the right favorable. Markings and unusual shapes and colorations could then be given a positive or negative interpretation by the priest and the results passed on to the inquirer.

For the interpretation of lightning or thunder the heavens were similarly divided by the haruspex, who took a position facing south, divided the heavens into 16 portions, favorable and unfavorable, and then watched to see where lightning flashes began and ended or from what direction thunder was heard. All aspects of life were governed in this fashion, and the pronouncements of the haruspices provided rules for the establishment of an orderly society. The founders of cities, for example, and the builders of temples, public buildings, and private homes were guided by specific aspects of the discipline. In these cases the land, which was first pointed out by some sign from the gods (such as the vultures seen by Romulus and Remus at the founding of Rome), was laid out according to a cosmic model. The purpose of this was to create a sacred space clearly distinguishable from the surrounding undifferentiated profane space, which was peopled by demons. A magic circle was inscribed about cities by means of a plough. This circle, such as the *pomerium* around Rome, designated the enclosed area as holy and protected against evil influences by its resident deities. Contact with this space ensured the inhabitants a continuous source of power deriving from its sacred character.

From the Etruscans the Romans borrowed this technique for discovering the will of heaven but not the personnel that went with it, the haruspices. Instead, the taking of the auspices (signs), as it was called in Rome, was reserved for the elected magistrates, assisted if necessary by the college of augurs, which consisted of distinguished political figures, usually former magistrates, not professional priests. Julius Caesar, for example, was both an augur and a *pontifex,* or priest. The auspices had to be taken before any major decision was made, and there was a special spot on the Capitoline Hill, the *auguraculum,* reserved for this purpose. All this was taken so seriously that in the first century B.C., when a Roman noble built a house that blocked the view of the magistrate looking for signs in the sky from the *auguraculum,* the house had to be torn down.

Town Planning and Architecture   From the Etruscans the Romans also learned the technique of establishing boundaries (*limitatio*), which they used in setting up their colonies and dividing the territory of the surrounding countryside, acts that were both practical and religious. The results of these land divisions can still be seen in many areas of the Mediterranean world, especially in North Africa and the north of

The Temple of Venus Genetrix dominates the Forum of Caesar in Rome (dedicated in 46 B.C.). The practice of placing temples at the end of long enclosures was borrowed from the Etruscans by the Romans and eventually became a standard architectural feature of cities throughout the Empire.

Italy, where thousands of square miles are broken up into neat, rectilinear grids that pass over natural obstacles without interruption.

Architecturally, the Etruscan temple differed from the Greek, which was free-standing, and could be walked around. Instead, the Etruscans placed their temple on a high platform at the rear of a sacred enclosure. It had long, overhanging eaves and a high gable, and the worshipers' attention was immediately focused on the temple when they entered the sacred place. This principle of placing a temple axially at the far end of an enclosure became a standard Roman architectural device that is found throughout the Roman world. In this arrangement the individual is subordinated to the order and symmetry of the buildings and to the gods of the state who inhabit them. Unlike the classical Greek arrangement of temples and buildings, where the human being is the accepted measure of things, the Romans early came to place the person in an orderly arrangement, symbolizing their belief that all people had preordained places in the scheme of life, places fixed by the gods and interpreted by the state.

Unlike the Greeks, the Etruscans did not use stone in building, except for the construction of tombs and tomb decorations, until the Hellenistic period. Their temples were of wood, surmounted by terra-cotta decorations, some of which have survived and are true masterpieces. Elaborately carved sarcophagi, the lid of which portrayed the deceased either lying prone or raised on an elbow, were popular. Whole cities of the dead were laid out in grid fashion after the style for cities of the living, and tombs were elaborately cut in the rock or piled over with mounds of earth. The tombs themselves are engineering achievements and have preserved their treasures in the damp earth of Italy almost as well as the tombs of Egypt guarded theirs.

Another medium in which the Etruscans excelled was decorative bronze work, which the Greeks admired greatly and imported in quantities. Surviving cups, lamp stands, candlesticks, tripods, incense burners, mirrors, and toilet boxes are among the finest examples of Etruscan art. Etruscan jewelry was superb, and in their miniature techniques, their use of granulation and filigree, and their art of engraving, the Etruscans were unsurpassed.

Etruscan Origins   One of the great unresolved mysteries of the classical period is the origin of the Etruscans, and neither modern debate nor archaeology seems any closer to resolving the problem.

The culture that immediately preceded that of the Etruscans is known as Villanovan, an Italian version of the great Urnfield culture found north of the Alps that lasted from about the twelfth to the seventh century B.C. Urnfield culture, so called from its practice of burying the cremated remains of the dead in urns placed side by side by the hundreds, consisted of settled agricultural communities of some size that produced cereals and used the traction plough in place of the hoe or digging stick. Initially using bronze, Urnfield culture gradually switched to iron, the time of the change varying from place to place. Archaeologically, Villanovan sites show a well-developed society based on agriculture, and the surprise is that in Etruria in the seventh century B.C. it developed quickly and without interruption into the full-fledged, much admired Etruscan culture known to history. Every known Etruscan city is preceded by a Villanovan settlement, a fact that has led to the debate about whether the Etruscans were transformed Villanovans or whether the new culture should be explained by the arrival of immigrants from somewhere else, usually the east.

In antiquity a historian of early Rome, Dionysius of Halicarnassus, advocated the first position, whereas Herodotus maintained that the Etruscans were transplanted Lydians from Asia Minor. There are undeniable affinities between Etruscan arts and practices and those of the east. *Tholos* tombs similar to those found at Mycenae and on Crete have been found in Etruria, and the practice of divination by means of the entrails of animals has parallels in Mesopotamia. Many artistic motifs are also found in both areas. There is even an inscription in what appears to be Etruscan on the Aegean island of Lemnos, which could, logically, have been the site of one of the stages of Etruscan western migration. Nevertheless, the possibility of the unbroken, peaceful evolution of Villanovan into Etruscan sites cannot be ignored, and the particularly rich development of the Etruscan cities after the seventh century B.C. can probably be best explained in terms of the exploitation by the natives of Etruria of the great metal deposits that happened to be in that part of the Villanovan world. Etruscan culture cannot have been transplanted as a whole from one part of the Mediterranean to another.

Neither the invasionist hypothesis nor the nativist hypothesis is fully convincing, and what needs emphasis is the fact that Etruscan civilization developed in Italy and in its fullness appears nowhere else. Whatever foreign elements made their contributions to the original Villanovans, the resulting culture was the response of a local community to local social and economic conditions, thereby effecting the transformation of both the natives and the external elements—whatever they may have been—at the same time.

THE LATINS AND EARLY ROME

In the prehistoric site that would become known as Rome there was nothing that can be identified specifically as Roman. The city that was to dominate Italy was no more than one of a number of villages occupying the many hills of Latium and struggling to maintain themselves against their aggressive neighbors, who periodically descended on them to raid or make temporary or permanent settlements. The Romans later recalled the arrival of the hillsmen from the Sabine country, the Etruscans from across the Tiber, and the many other wandering groups from within Latium itself who settled down to form a composite city on the hills overlooking the Tiber.

These hills were much steeper then than they are now, offering a refuge from raiding bands, floods, and wild animals. The archaeological picture from the tenth to the seventh century B.C. shows little villages crowding the tops of the hills, with their cemeteries on the hillsides or at the valley bottoms. In this loose, almost anarchic setting it is easy to imagine migrating clans, individual drifters, and families cast loose from other cities and regions settling on unoccupied lands and working out communal relations with similar groups of earlier settlers. In later times it was recalled that eight of the hills constituted a religious federation (deceptively called the Septimontium) and that their boundaries were marked by three bridges, which could be opened or closed at will, across the Forum stream. The god Janus was the protector of these bridges. When he finally received a dwelling place in Rome, the opening of the gates of his temple signified that the bridges were up and the stream could not be crossed (war). Likewise, the closing of the gates meant peace—the bridges were down and the stream could be crossed.

The Founders of Rome

The Romans, unlike the Greeks, had no recollections of Mycenaean greatness regarding their origins and no Homer to transform their folk tales into poetic legends and myths. The Romans often chose to emphasize the simplicity and heterogeneity of their beginnings.

Although the Romans were literate from the sixth century B.C., it was a long time before they felt a need to organize the chaotic mass of legends, folk tales, archaic rituals and calendars, treaties, law codes, and family histories that constituted the source of their early history. So late were they in setting about this task that no generally acceptable date for Rome's founding was available until the first century B.C., 400 years after the founding of the Republic and almost 600 years after the founding of the city. The result is that the early history of Rome is, even to the present, a quagmire of scholarly dispute.

The Romans' impulse to give a coherent explanation of their origins came in several stages. As their power expanded, they found themselves compelled to give some kind of intelligible account of themselves to their new neighbors and subjects, so by about the mid–third century B.C. an established version of their beginnings began to emerge.

The problem was how to fit the strictly local Latin and Roman traditions into the wider, Greek view of things. For centuries the Greeks had plied the Mediterranean from one end to the other and had already worked out synchronous chronologies for the prehistories of most of the peoples they came in contact with, linking them with their own prehistory and such helpful but vague wanderers as Heracles, Jason, Odysseus, and Evander. The local peoples, who knew no more than their

---

EVENTS OF EARLY ROMAN HISTORY

Founding of Rome (traditional date)	753 B.C.
The monarchy	ca. 750–500 B.C.
Etruscan domination	ca. 625–500 B.C.
Founding of the Republic (traditional date)	509 B.C.
Oscan threat to Rome and the Latins	ca. 500–400 B.C.
Conflict of the Orders	ca. 470–287 B.C.
The Twelve Tables	ca. 450 B.C.
Licinian-Sextian laws	ca. 367 B.C.
Hortensian law	287 B.C.

---

own traditions (and even these not very well), were in no position to make such complicated connections, for they lacked the information and even the interest. The Greeks, however, had a passionate need to make sense and order out of the anarchic stories of the Mediterranean peoples.

A number of possible founders of Rome, including Odysseus, had already been put forward by the Greeks. However, because the Romans were not eager to acknowledge a Greek founder, they settled on another possibility, the Trojan hero Aeneas, and laboriously worked him into the chronology of Romulus, who may have been part of the native legend. Six additional kings were given schematic reigns to fill in the gap between Romulus and the traditional date of the founding of the Republic (509 B.C.): Numa Pompilius, Tullus Hostilius, Ancus Marcius, Tarquinius Priscus, Servius Tullius, and Tarquinius Superbus. The historical reality behind these kings is impossible to recover at this point. All we can say is that they probably represent early leaders of the developing community, of whom some were Sabine (Numa and Ancus), some Latin (Romulus and Tullus), and some Etruscan (the two Tarquins and possibly Servius Tullius, despite his Latin-sounding name).

Combining the archaeological evidence with the traditions of the literary sources, we have the following four-stage process of development at Rome. Stage 1, lasting from approximately 900 to 800 B.C., finds echoes in the mythology of the arrival of the Trojan hero Aeneas. Stage 2 covers the period of the foundation of the city, approximately 800–750 B.C., which corresponds to the legendary story of Romulus. At this time the Palatine and Forum areas of Rome show signs of habitation. The third stage (ca. 750–600 B.C.) includes the expansion of the Palatine and Forum areas and the development of the other hills—the city of the legendary kings Ancus Marcius and Tarquinius Priscus. Finally, in Stage 4, during the last decades of the seventh century B.C. and the early part of the sixth (ca. 625–575 B.C.), we have the archaic city under Etruscan influence. At this time all the villages had coalesced to form a single entity, the city of Servius Tullius and Tarquinius Superbus.

As the power of the kings increased, they attempted to check the strength of the heads of the great families (the patricians) by the addition of new senators. A

A coin issued by Julius Caesar around 47 or 46 B.C. showing Aeneas escaping from Troy carrying his father and a statue of Athena (the Palladium). Founding legends were taken very seriously by all ancient peoples, and Caesar was able to put to good use the claim that his family, the gens Julia, was descended from Aeneas and the goddess Venus.

great building program was undertaken to consolidate popular support for the regime, and the largest temple in Italy was erected to Jupiter on the Capitoline Hill. A rampart was built around the city, and the Forum (market) area was drained and paved. According to tradition it was Servius Tullius who abolished the old system of having the clan heads draft their followers, and instead made property qualification

---

ORIGINS AND IDEOLOGY: THE ROMAN MELTING POT

The Roman historical tradition accepted—and sometimes glorified—the belief that the founding of Rome was a joint venture in which a number of peoples of different ethnic origins participated. At the time of Augustus, the historian Livy (59 B.C.–A.D. 17) summarized this view in his description of the thoughts that ran through the mind of Tanaquil, the ambitious wife of Tarquinius Priscus, who became Rome's fifth king. She argued with herself that her husband was getting nowhere in their native Tarquinii in Etruria, where the people despised him because his father had been a foreigner, a Greek. If he would only go to Rome, she believed, things would be different:

> Rome was a most attractive place. Here was a new people among whom things happened quickly and where individuals rose because of merit. Surely there would be opportunities there for a courageous and energetic person. After all, Tatius, a Sabine who ruled jointly with Romulus for a short time, had been king in Rome; Numa had been summoned from foreign parts, from Cures, to rule there; King Ancus had a Sabine mother, and only Numa was of noble ancestery in his lineage.

Although obviously anachronistic and never of more than the most limited application, there was still a lot of truth in this view of Rome, and with varying degrees of openness from century to century the city adhered to it as a principle of statecraft.

—Livy 1.34

the sole criterion for service in the army. Greek pottery flowed into Rome, and the city's population expanded rapidly as it came to participate in the general prosperity of the Mediterranean world. For the first time, the Romans, or at least some of them, became literate and came into contact with the more developed world of the Greek and Near Eastern populations, with all that this implied for the ordering of the city and the revamping of its religious, political, and military institutions.

THE REPUBLIC

The Patrician State

By the late Republic (133–30 B.C.), it was an established Roman convention to portray its kings as a series of progressively deteriorating monarchs, of whom the last, the Etruscan Tarquin the Proud (Tarquinius Superbus), was the worst.

In the Roman tradition, Tarquin is the stock tyrant of Greek moralistic writing: arrogant, brutal, and corrupt. He and his sister-in-law (his wife-to-be) conspire to kill first their respective spouses and then the ruling king—his lover's father. The reign, thus begun with the shedding of so much blood, progresses from one outrage to another until finally a Roman nobleman by the name of Brutus (The Stupid) had the courage to organize a revolt and drive out the oppressors. With surprising smoothness and perfect unanimity two consuls were chosen to replace the deposed king,

A coin of M. Junius Brutus issued around 54 B.C. proclaims "Liberty" on one side and "Brutus" on the other. Just as Julius Caesar made much of his family connections with Aeneas, Brutus propagandized the fact that his supposed ancestor had been responsible for winning Rome's freedom from the tyranny of the Tarquins.

and so without bloodshed Roman freedom was won, an event that all classes celebrated joyfully. The historian Livy makes the point, however, that this was a conditioned freedom. The anarchic Romans needed the discipline of the kings, and were saved from the catastrophe of pure democracy and complete freedom by the reliable hand of the Senate and the annual election of dependable nobles. Understandably, the theme of the expulsion of the Tarquins and the liberation of the Roman people became one of the heroic sagas of Roman history, providing endless material for dramatists, propagandists, and moralists.

Unfortunately, the Romans had no historian to deflate this edifying interpretation of the fall of the tyrants, as did Thucydides with a similar tale enjoyed by the Athenians, and were it not for the chance survival of some fragmentary outside sources we would have no account of the founding of the Republic but the self-serving version of the Roman aristocrats. These sources enable us to see the expulsion of the kings against the wider background of a shifting series of alliances and leagues among Etruscan and Latin cities. It becomes clear that the Tarquins were expelled not by an internal uprising but in an encounter involving the Etruscan city of Clusium (under its king, Lars Porsenna) on one hand and Rome (under the Tarquins), the Latins, and the Greek city of Cumae on the other. It was under the protectorate of Porsenna, who expelled Tarquin from Rome, that the Republic came into existence. All the talk of liberty and deliverance from oppression was a later elaboration, just as the Athenian version of the liberators Harmodius and Aristogeiton sought to conceal the fact that it was a Spartan army, not Athenian patriots, that liberated Athens. The exaggerated account of the reign of Tarquin and the emphasis on the smooth transition from the kings to the Republic were intended to play down the revolutionary implications of the dethronement of a legitimate king by force of arms. Aristocrats of the late Republic looked back and wondered whether the early history of the city might not encourage other potential revolutionaries bent on proclaiming liberty for themselves against alleged oppressors. It was a tradition that could not be suppressed, however, and the term *libertas* (liberty) has an interesting history of its own in the propaganda of the warring political factions of the late Republic. Still, although the traditions of later periods may have distorted the account of the founding of the Republic, the event itself was a turning point in Roman history.

The new state embodied a fundamental opposition to the old that it expressed in the term *Republic* (*res publica,* or the public realm), which was set in opposition to the kingdom (*res privata,* or the private realm) of the Etruscan kings, who were depicted as regarding the state as their own private possession. The source of power was the people properly assembled (*iure sociati*), and the magistrates of the Republic were never above the state but part of it.

Magistrates and Assemblies

In the confusing days after the departure of the Tarquins, the only force in Rome that could be depended on for stability was the army, controlled by the aristocracy. More and more it became the ruling body of the city. Set up as a deliberative assembly, it carried on the legislative, judicial, and elective responsibilities of government. From the *centuries,* or units, of which it was composed, the assembly came to be known as the Centuriate Assembly (*comitia centuriata*). Eventually there were 193 of these units. The Senate, a much smaller body, constituted the second branch of government. Originally it was a council of the most important clan heads that had advised the kings. Although it had no formal or constitutional power, it had a great deal of informal influence. When the ruling king died, the auspices were said to return to the Senate, which meant that it had the job of finding someone acceptable—to both the gods and the Senate—to replace him. Another ancient source of authority, summed up in the phrase, "authority of the fathers" (*auctoritas patrum*), was the Senate's claim to have the power to ratify resolutions of the Centuriate Assembly before they were enacted. Under the Republic, the Senate, consisting of about 300 ex-magistrates, continued its advisory role, and its influence increased as the power of the state grew. In practice if not by law, consuls and other magistrates were obliged to seek its advice on all major internal and external policies.

The first officers of the new state seem to have been a group of magistrates called praetors, ruling in collegial Etruscan fashion and presided over by a *praetor maximus.* Later two of the group were given preeminence as *praetores majores,* who exercised power jointly. In this fashion what was later known as the Consulate was gradually elaborated. It is unlikely that the Romans, as was once thought, invented on the spot the consulship as it existed in later times: a collegial body of two magistrates, elected annually, with equal powers. Instead, the stress of events, particularly the demands of warfare, probably dictated the selection of two individuals from among the magistrates to provide leadership. During the following half-century the constitutional aspects of the complicated working of two individuals, each holding supreme power but working closely together, were worked out. To carry on the religious duties of the kings, the Romans created the King of Sacrifices (*rex sacrorum*), who, like the kings, was solemnly inaugurated for life. Unlike them, however, he had no political, military, or judicial roles. He was the head of the priestly hierarchy, but that was the limit of his career.

The New City: Architecture and Religion

The emergence of the new Roman state was further signaled by the creation of a civic center in the Forum, which had been a shapeless, indeterminate marketplace. First the king's house (Regia) was transferred there from the Palatine Hill and became the place where the King of Sacrifices performed his functions. It was now no longer the inaccessible private dwelling of a king but the public residence of a magistrate, located in a public place. It was established in calculated relationship to the Temple of Vesta, goddess of the hearth, and the house of her ministers, the Vestal Virgins, also now transferred to the Forum, where the hearth of the new community was to be found. The king and the Vestals were conceived as continuing the offices and cults without which the state could not continue, but in a setting adjusted to the needs of the new community. In the old order the king embodied the priestly, military, judicial, and political powers of the state, and these functions were viewed as inseparable and vital to its functioning. The new Republic preserved the functions but redistributed them in such a fashion as to bring about a thorough reorganization of the state without departing from its underlying religious concepts.

At the other end of the Forum from the Regia and the Temple of Vesta, the Comitium, or meeting place of the people, was created. Now the Forum had two poles, the one political and secular, the other religious, giving visible evidence of the existence of a new state based on a new set of presuppositions, the most fundamental of which was that the business of the community was no longer the private affair of an individual but belonged to all the people; Rome was to be a Republic, not a monarchy.

The expulsion of the kings is one of the great turning points in Roman history. Although often neglected, it is comparable in its significance to the religious revival and realignment of the Republic in the time of Augustus and to the adoption of Christianity by Constantine. The new state found expression in the beginnings of a new constitution, not fully elaborated but clearly different from the one that preceded it, and in religious reform. Both were materially expressed in the new Forum, which was to survive as an influential reminder of the change down to the end of the Roman Empire almost 1,000 years later.

The Plebeian Revolution

Despite the achievement attained by selective borrowings from the past, the new Roman state lacked cohesiveness. By definition the revolution was a victory for the patricians, who took over when the Tarquins were unseated; it was not necessarily a victory for the rest of Roman society. The patricians, through their clients and their special relations with one another, dominated the Senate and the army and through them the state. The remainder of society was excluded from political power.

One of the principal problems the dominant patricians faced was the tendency for powerful clans among them to try to carve out private realms for themselves at the expense of the community as a whole. In the struggle the remainder of society suffered from the aristocracy's greed, arbitrariness, and abuse of power. Debt bondage and other forms of dependency on the aristocracy increased, as they had in Greek cities during similar stages of development. Dangers also threatened from outside Rome. We read of bad harvests, famine, and pestilence. Since the end of the sixth century B.C. the Oscans had been pushing down from their crowded highland homes into the plains of Latium, and this time there was no organized Etruscan power to hold them back. In 474 B.C. the naval might of Etruria had been destroyed by the Greeks of Sicily. Before the end of the century the Etruscans were to be driven out of Campania, their richest province. All of Etruria as well as Rome suffered the consequences. After a promising beginning in the early years of the fifth century B.C. the Roman building program came to an end. Imports from Greece soon stopped, and Rome was faced with economic stagnation, increasing indebtedness among the lower classes, and general social unrest.

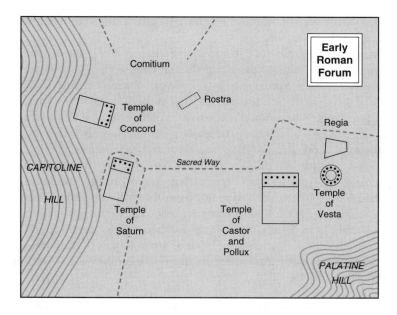

At some point in the fifth century B.C., social relations in Rome had so deteriorated that in a desperate effort to protect themselves from the misgovernance of the patricians, the plebeians resorted to a cultural device traditional among Italian peoples: the creation of a Sacred Band. The plebeians withdrew from the city and swore an oath to be loyal to each other and to sacrifice their lives for the common cause. As a Sacred Band, the plebeians held their own meetings as an alternative to the meetings of the patrician-dominated Centuriate Assembly. They established their own temple to the goddess Ceres as a counter to the Temple of Jupiter on the Capitoline Hill, the religious center of the patrician state. Custodians called aediles were appointed to care for it. They elected their own leaders, the tribunes of the plebs, and swore loyalty to them. Initially two in number to oppose the two patrician consuls, the tribunes eventually grew to constitute a college of ten. Tribunes and aediles were protected by a sacred law (*lex sacer*) that declared that anyone who injured them would be held "sacred" (*sacer*), that is, would be handed over to the gods for vengeance. Practically speaking, this meant that anyone could kill violators of the sacredness (*sacrosanctitas*) of the plebeian representatives without fear of retribution, divine or human.

The tribunes claimed the right to offer protection (*auxilium*) and if necessary to intervene with their veto (*intercessio*) on behalf of plebeians threatened by the misconduct of patrician magistrates or the institutions they controlled. Protected only by the sacred oath, tribunes stepped in between victim and persecutor. According to the Roman historian Livy, patrician magistrates were brought to trial and were even condemned to death before the assembled plebeians. The reality behind this memory was probably the out-of-hand lynching of patricians who had violated the sacred character of the tribunes.

By invoking the protection of the gods and acting as a religious community, the plebeians were able to legitimate their activity, but they were also able to wring important concessions from the patricians by refusing or threatening to refuse military service at critical moments when the city was threatened by outside invasion. In the early stages of the struggle between patricians and plebeians (the Conflict of the Orders, as it is known), the objectives of the plebeians were largely defensive and protective, and their method of procedure was informal. Gradually, however, the plebeians developed a sense of political identity and began to see themselves as constituting a quasi-independent political community within the Roman state. From this consciousness derived the second major assembly of Rome, the Council of the Plebs (*concilium plebis*), a parallel and alternative assembly to the patrician-controlled Centuriate Assembly.[2] Originally there were 4 urban tribes, corresponding to the four regions of Rome, and 16 rural tribes, because the majority of Romans, plebeians and patricians alike, were rural farmers. In the third century B.C. the number of tribes was finally fixed at 35.

The Twelve Tables   Another achievement of the plebeians was the publication of Rome's first law code, the so-called Twelve Tables. It was considered by the Romans to be the source of all law, private and public, governing such matters as the rights and duties of families, forms of marriage, inheritance, the definition of some crimes and their punishments, and the right of appeal. It was learned by heart by generations of children and played a role analogous to the Magna Charta or the Bill of Rights. The laws themselves were not favorable to the plebeians, and for a long time the administration of the law itself remained under the control of the patricians. Nevertheless, the fact that some aspects of the law had been made public was an achievement, and the general principle of establishing a single code that applied to all members of society by a uniform, universally known process was a step of major importance. It represented a continuation of the conscious molding of institutions to serve the needs of the people rather than the tacit assumption that the law was divine and outside human control, requiring a sacred priesthood to administer it. This came to be reflected in the use of language, where *ius,* the term for the secular concept of law, came to be applied to one body of law, and *fas,* which was reserved for sacred law, was applied to another.

In other respects the Twelve Tables show attempts to bridge the gap between the conflicting elements of the state. For example, the ostentatious display of luxury at funerals, a practice the patricians shared with the Etruscan nobles, was restricted. Various crimes were mentioned and assigned specific penalties—another step toward curbing the arbitrary actions of aristocratic judges.

---

[2]At a later stage of constitutional evolution, the use of the *concilium plebis* for elections and legislation became common. When convened by a consul or praetor rather than a tribune, the Council was known as the Tribal Assembly (*comitia tributa*).

A CONSERVATIVE'S VIEW OF THE TRIBUNATE

In the first century B.C. the conservative senator Cicero wrote a work bearing the same name as Plato's famous dialogue *The Laws*. In his dialogue Cicero says the following about the tribunate. Cicero is speaking in response to his brother Quintus.

Quintus, you see the deficiencies of the tribunate very clearly, but it is unfair when criticizing an institution to omit its advantages and pick only on its weaknesses. By this method the consulship could be condemned if we were to just emphasize the bad deeds of some people who held that office. I recognize that there is potential for mischief in the power of the tribunate, but we could not have the good that was sought when the office was established, without the evil also. "The power of the tribunes of the people is too great," you say. True, but the power of the people themselves is much more cruel—and more violent. Yet this power is made milder when there is a leader to control it. Think what it would be like if there were no leader at all! For a leader is conscious of his own danger, whereas the people have no sense of danger whatsoever. "But" you will say, "the tribunes sometimes stir up the people." Yes, but they often calm them too.

—Cicero, *De Legibus* 3.23

The Patrician-Plebeian State

The beginnings of patrician-plebeian concord in the fifth century B.C. were savagely interrupted by the sack of Rome by the Celts, or Gauls, as they were known to the Romans, in 390 B.C. The resulting misery and economic dislocation unsettled the community, and the patrician-plebeian struggle began all over again at a new level of intensity.

The main problems were those of land distribution, debt, and access to political office—a trio of problems that plagued all ancient societies. There was rarely anything unique about the problems themselves, and the only variable factor was the different ways in which they were handled from one society to another. Sparta and Athens, for example, took a radical approach, whereas Rome followed a much slower and more conservative course. As an expanding state, Rome was able to avoid facing these issues for some time. It was not until the Licinian-Sextian laws of about 367 B.C. that the right of plebeian access to public land (i.e., land won by the state in war) was established. These laws also attempted to cover the problem of debt by decreeing that interest already paid should be deducted from the principal and the whole paid off in three years. Various attempts were made to cope with high interest rates and debt in the following years, but it was not until 326 (or 313) B.C. that the *lex Poetelia*, described by Livy as a new beginning for liberty, prohibited imprisonment for debt.

A vital issue settled in 367 B.C. was that of the admission of nonpatricians to the consulship. The problem here was not a law against the admission of these people, because no such law existed and plebeians had in fact been elected to the consulship in the first half of the fifth century B.C. What was involved was the breaking of what had become a de facto custom, which required a law for its reversal. Gradually, non-patricians began to make their way into the highest offices, and a new elite, the patrician-plebeian nobility, emerged. Among the old families who were willing to cooperate with the rising plebeians were the Fabii, Aemilii, Sulpicii, and Servilii, who found compatible partners in the Licinii, Sextii, and Plautii—names that were to appear regularly in the lists of Republican magistrates for the next three and a half centuries.

Plebeian access to other magistracies followed. The same year that the Licinian-Sexton laws were passed (ca. 367 B.C.), the number of commissioners who regulated various religious functions was increased from two to ten, of whom five were to be plebeians (*decemviri sacris faciundis*). The patrician *curule aedileship,* which was set up in 367 B.C. to share the administration of the city with the plebeian aediles, was soon open to plebeians also, and the important new office of praetor (established in 366 B.C.), which took over the consul's civil jurisdiction over the city, was opened to them in 336 B.C. Other offices to which the plebeians gained admission were the dictatorship (a temporary emergency appointment) in 356 B.C. and the censorship in 351 B.C. However, it was not until 300 B.C. that they achieved access to the important priesthoods of the pontiffs and augurs by the *lex Ogulnia*. In that year the number of pontiffs was raised from five to nine, and the number of augurs from four to nine, the additions in both cases being plebeians. Also in 300 B.C., at the end of lengthy development and elaboration, the right of appeal to the people in capital cases and in cases involving scourging was established by the *lex Valeria.*

Additional steps toward breaking down the exclusivity of the patricians came in 304 B.C. with the publication, by the aedile Cn. Flavius, of a handbook of legal phrases and procedures (*legis actiones*) and the posting in the Forum of a calendar that showed days on which public business could be transacted. These measures complemented and continued the reforms introduced by the Twelve Tables, because it was not only the law that was made public but also many of the secrets by which it was manipulated.

Part of the curtailment of the patricians and the increase in importance of the plebeians is reflected in the activity of the first great Roman statesman we can actually identify by name, Appius Claudius. As censor in 312 B.C. he allowed freedmen to enroll in the tribe of their choice and admitted sons of freedmen to the Senate. The first measure was probably directed toward resolving a problem occurring in newly incorporated territory that continued to be inhabited by its native population, some of whom would have been slaves. It was logical to allow these individuals, upon their manumission and acquisition of Roman citizenship, to enroll in their own local tribes instead of compelling them to register in the four urban tribes, where their influence was greatly curtailed. This measure, which would have gone a long way toward breaking the control of local landlords, was reversed in 304 B.C. but revived several times thereafter in succeeding centuries. What to do with former slaves was an issue not easily resolved by the Republic.

The final step in the long history of the patrician-plebeian state came in 287 B.C., when the Tribal Assembly became the principal law-making body of the state and its decrees—or plebiscites, as they were called—acquired the force of law without needing the endorsement of the Senate. This law, the *lex Hortensia,* came as a result of over a century and a half of struggle. After 287 B.C. the decisions of the Tribal Assembly and the Centuriate Assembly had equal force and bound all citizens, whether rich or poor, freeborn or freedmen. Henceforth the Tribal Assembly rather than the Centuriate Assembly became the principal legislative body of the state. At approximately the same time it acquired the right to ratify treaties with foreign powers and became a court of appeal for those who had been fined.

THE SOCIAL AND POLITICAL ACHIEVEMENT OF EARLY ROME: CONSENSUS

The remarkable social, political, and military achievement of Rome's early centuries must be emphasized. It was in these obscure, distant, almost mythical times that the Romans came up with their own, wholly original version of the *polis.*

In many respects the emergence of the city of Rome was unremarkable. Cities were springing up all around the Mediterranean—in Syria, Phoenicia, Greece, North Africa, and southern Spain. In Italy there were plenty of models for the Romans to imitate: Greek in the south, Etruscan in the north. However, the Romans took only the most general blueprint of the city from others. The idea that the people (however actually defined) were sovereign and that the magistrates were not

---

A WORD WITH A LONG HISTORY

con•sen•sus \kən-'sen(t)-səs\ *n, often attrib* [L, fr. *consensus,* pp. of *consentire*] (1861) **1:** group solidarity in sentiment and belief **2a:** general agreement: UNANIMITY (the ~ of their opinion, based on reports that had drifted back from the border—John Hersey) **b:** the judgment arrived at by most of those concerned (the ~ was to abandon the project)

usage The phrase *consensus of opinion,* which is not actually redundant (see sense 2a; the sense that takes the phrase is slightly older), has been so often claimed as a redundancy that it has become relatively rare in edited prose. Sense 2a has not become extinct but sense 2b has far outstripped it in frequency of use. Sense 2b is also growing in attributive use esp. in the phrase *consensus politics.*

¹con•sent \kən-'sent\ *vi* [ME *consenten,* fr. L *consentire,* fr. com- + *sentire* to feel—more at SENSE] (13c) **1:** to give assent or approval: AGREE **2** *archaic:* to be in concord in opinion or sentiment **syn** see ASSENT—**con•sent•ing•ly** \ –iŋ-lē\ *adv*

Source: By permission. From *Webster's Ninth New Collegiate Dictionary* © 1988 by Merriam-Webster Inc., publisher of the Merriam-Webster ® dictionaries.

above the law was standard. The assumption that the hoplite (heavy infantry) phalanx was synonymous with the people was also taken for granted, but what emerged from the Roman experience was something very different from anything that had evolved in Greece or elsewhere. Rome was a unified society, yet it was made up of two separately defined groups, patricians and plebeians, each with its own institutional means of doing public business. Although the formula seems like one designed for stalemate and inactivity, it somehow provided Rome with the strength not just to fend off all invaders—a triumph in itself, given Rome's vulnerable position—but to engage in a round of conquests that no Etruscan, Greek, or Phoenician *polis* came anywhere close to equaling. Clearly, what this dual system did for Rome was to provide patricians and plebeians, rich and poor, with a satisfactory means of working together, a method of achieving consensus within a diverse citizen body. Apparently it worked well enough to bring out the best in most citizens. For centuries Rome's citizens were able to persuade themselves, as well as millions of non-Romans, that it was worthwhile to belong to this unusual state.

Chapter 9

The Building of an Empire

THE GROWTH OF ROME IN ITALY

At the same time that the Greeks were fighting epic battles against the Persians in the east, the Romans and their allies, the Latins, were having difficulty with the elementary but chronic problem of warlike hillspeople migrating into the rich plains of Latium.

Rome had a challenging geographic location. Situated in central Italy at an important crossing point on the Tiber, it tended to become the focal point of all travel and migration up and down the peninsula. Its survival depended on its ability to control this crossing. Once this had been accomplished, Rome would have the advantage of internal lines of communication that would in turn help it dominate the rest of Italy. Nevertheless, in these early years just being able to fend off warlike local enemies on all sides was an achievement in itself. Early in the fifth century B.C. the Oscan-speaking Volsci had pushed all the way to the Tyrrhenian Sea coast and as far north into Latium as Velitrae, only 20 miles from Rome. For most of the century, therefore, Rome's main foreign policy concerns were the movements of peoples and the management of its sometimes difficult relations with other members of the Latin federation to which it belonged.

Rome and the Latins

The ties that bound the villages and towns of Latium together—their common cult centers, language, and belief in a common origin—were much more strongly felt

---

WARS OF THE ROMAN REPUBLIC, I

Wars with the Oscans	ca. 500–400 B.C.
Capture of Veii	396 B.C.
Sack of Rome by the Celts	390 B.C.
Latin revolt	340–338 B.C.
Samnite Wars	326–304; 298–290 B.C.
Battle of Sentinum	295 B.C.
War with Pyrrhus	280–275 B.C.
First Punic War	264–241 B.C.
Second Punic War	218–201 B.C.
Battle of Cannae	216 B.C.
Battle of Zama	202 B.C.

---

than were similar ties among the Greeks. The cities of the latter had generally grown up in something close to isolation from one another in the small plains, landlocked harbors, and islands of Greece, whereas the Latins were forced to live side by side in the wide-open plain of Latium. Their neighbors on all sides were threatening foreigners with alien cultures and languages, and their ability to defend themselves lay in common effort rather than individual strength or the possession of inaccessible strongholds.

As members of the ancient, loosely organized Latin League, the cities of Latium had for centuries shared the reciprocal rights (*iura*) of marriage, commerce, and probably also migration. Citizens of Latin cities could make contracts with Roman citizens and depend on Roman courts for their enforcement, and the rights of Roman citizens would be protected by courts in Latin cities. These rights were particularly important in the matter of marriage because citizenship was closely associated with parentage, and the transmission of property depended on the recognition of citizenship. In Athens after Pericles, for example, both parents had to be Athenian to guarantee their children citizenship. In Latium, by contrast, citizens of different states could freely intermarry with full testamentary and paternity rights. It is also generally assumed that Latins could migrate and settle in one another's cities, acquiring in the process the citizenship of the new state without forfeiting the right to return to their places of origin. This early conditioning in openness was fundamental to Rome's ability to expand outward, progressively incorporating first its Latin neighbors, then the peoples of the rest of Italy, and eventually the whole Mediterranean world. The early stages of these developments are worth examining in some detail because it was then that Rome stumbled onto some of the most fundamental techniques of the unique form of imperialism it was to use time and again in later phases of its Mediterranean expansion.

Early Roman historians, determined to make Rome great from its earliest days, depicted it as having been the supreme power in the Latin League from the time of the kings. However, even with Etruscan hegemony of the city and control of the land

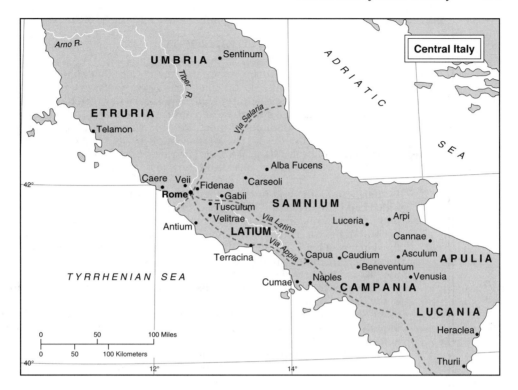

route between Etruria and Etruscan holdings in Campania, there is no need to assume that Rome dominated all the Latin cities. Rome remained in the league even when the city was under the Etruscans, and it was only after their expulsion, with the help of the town of Clusium, and Rome's subsequent battles with the league after the founding of the Republic, that Rome found itself at odds with its old allies. As it turned out, the Latin cities were in no position to impose special conditions on Rome's return to the league, as they needed Rome's support against the most recent and significant descent of hillspeople into Latium, in which all the territory from the interior mountains to the sea at Terracina and Antium fell under the control of the Volsci. The Romans in turn needed the shield of the Latin cities to the south in order to concentrate on the Etruscans in the north, so both sides were bound by mutual interest to keep the other as strong as possible. Accordingly, the Latins and Romans renegotiated the terms of their relationship in what is known as the Cassian Treaty (*foedus Cassianum*) in 493 B.C. Later the Romans were to attempt to claim that the treaty explicitly conceded them supremacy in the league.

The wars of the Latins and Romans against the Oscans are described with much embellishment by Livy and feature such legendary figures as the traitor Coriolanus, who led the Volsci to the gates of Rome (491 B.C.), and the hero Cincinnatus, who

CELTIC FEROCITY

Neither Greeks nor Romans had any reason to love the Celts. Both had suffered humiliating defeats at their hands, but the main reason why Celts were regarded with such fear and disdain was their culture. Unlike most societies around the Mediterranean, Celtic society was oral, nonurban, and unsettled. Celts drank distilled alcohol and ate butter and large amounts of meat. To Mediterranean people they were huge—if slow-witted. Celts were not backward technologically, but they seemed to belong to a primitive political and social world. Their fighting techniques, in particular, were regarded by Greeks and Romans as irrational and uncivilized.

In their wanderings and in battle the Celts use chariots drawn by two horses which carry the driver and the warrior. When they meet with cavalry in battle they first throw their javelins at the enemy, and then step down from their chariots and fight with their swords. Some of them so despise death that they enter the dangers of battle naked, wearing only a sword-belt. They bring to war with them their freedmen attendants, choosing them from among the poor. They use them in battle as chariot drivers and shield-bearers.

They have the custom when they have lined up for combat to step in front of the battle-line and challenge the bravest of their enemies to single combat, brandishing their weapons in the challenge to single combat, they sing a song in praise of the great deeds of their ancestors, and of their own achievements, mocking and belittling at the same time their opponent, trying by such techniques to destroy his spirit before the fight. When their opponents fall they cut off their heads and tie them around their horses' necks. They hand over to their attendants the blood-covered arms of their enemies, and carry them off as booty, singing songs of victory.

Spoils of war they fasten with nails to their houses, just as hunters do of the heads of wild animals they have killed. Them embalm the heads of the most distinguished opponents in cedar oil, and carefully guard them in chests. They show these heads to visitors, claiming that they, or their father or some ancestor had refused large sums of money for this or that head. Some of them, it is said, boast that they have not accepted an equal weight of gold for the head they show, demonstrating a kind of barbarous nobility. Not to sell a thing that constitutes the proof of one's bravery is a noble, well-bred kind of thing, but on the other hand to continue to ill-treat the remains of a fellow human being after he is dead is bestial.

—Diodorus Siculus, *The Library of History*, 5.29

was called from his plough to defeat another Oscan tribe, the Aequi, at Mount Algidus in 458 B.C. But even Livy cannot conceal the mundane character of these conflicts. By the end of the century the threat had come to an end, and Rome was able to divert its attention to its old feud with the nearby Etruscan city of Veii. At issue was control of the salt pans at the Tiber mouth and of the route by which the salt was conveyed inland, the Via Salaria. Initially the Romans wrestled with Veii for possession of Fidenae, the only other crossing of the Tiber in its lower reaches, and then they attacked Veii itself. After a long siege the city fell to M. Furius Camillus in 396 B.C.

According to legend, when Camillus saw the great quantity of loot from the captured city, he prayed that Rome's good luck would not provoke the envy of men or the gods, but he stumbled inauspiciously as he was pronouncing the words, and only six years later Rome fell to a band of marauding Celtic warriors.

The Sack of Rome

By 600 B.C. Celtic culture had spread throughout most of central Europe and France (the so-called Hallstatt phase, ca. 700–500 B.C.). Another major period of Celtic expansion (the La Tène phase) began about the middle of the fifth century B.C., and around 400 B.C. bands of armed Celts poured across the Alps into the Po valley and routed the Etruscans living there. At the same time, the Greek city of Syracuse, under its energetic leader Dionysius, was pressing from the south and was at war with the Etruscan city of Caere, which was friendly to Rome. In the midst of these events, the appearance of the Celts at the rear of the Etruscans gave an unexpected boost to the Greeks. According to one version, the Celts even sought them out to propose joint action. In this context the rout of the Romans by the Gauls (Celts) at the battle of the Allia in 390 B.C. and the subsequent sack of Rome may not be as haphazard as they appear from the Roman sources, which ignore events elsewhere in Italy and make Rome the focus of the Celtic invasion.

Psychologically, the effect of the sack of Rome by the Celts must have been devastating. Undoubtedly, at this time the Romans reflected on the relentless pressures of the Oscan highlanders during the preceding century and on the often demonstrated undependability of the Latin League, and resolved to free themselves from these dangers in the future. Prompted by these motives, they reformed the army, added some new magistrates, and launched a period of expansion that ultimately provided them with safe frontiers, far from Rome and even far from Italy itself.

The New Army

The old legionary Roman army had been modeled on the massed phalanx characteristic of Greek armies of the first part of the fifth century B.C. The reformed Roman army was much less rigid. It consisted of 30 maniples, each made up of two centuries commanded by centurions. Each maniple had 120 to 160 men armed with a short cut-and-thrust sword. They had throwing javelins in place of the old thrusting spears. The legion depended henceforth on a very flexible tactical style of fighting that required a much higher degree of coordination and experience than in the past.

Cohesion and professionalism were provided largely by the centurions. These men were drawn from the ranks, not from the elite classes, who provided the higher officers, military tribunes, quaestors (financial officers), and consuls. Centurions were thus not officers in the traditional sense of being outsiders from a different class who represented a potentially different set of interests from those of the enlisted men. They were instead rankers promoted on the basis of competence and trust.

Unlike the officers who belonged to the legion as a whole, centurions were attached directly to the individual maniples, the tactical units of the legion. Another reform that accompanied these changes and made them workable was the introduction of pay. A complete break with the past was thus achieved. The new legionary army was not the equivalent of the hoplite phalanx of a Greek city, which consisted only of those who could afford the necessary equipment for warfare. Instead, the legion more accurately reflected the integrated patrician-plebeian state of Rome, where the upper classes maintained control of the higher commands while the other classes supplied the bulk of the troops and some of its most critical subofficers, the centurions. Nevertheless, the Roman army was still a militia, an army of amateur citizen-soldiers. It was recruited and dissolved annually.

The End of the Latin League

The immediate effect of the sack of Rome on the city's external relations was its loss of control of the Latin League, which went its own independent way until 358 B.C., when the Cassian Treaty was once more enforced. During this time Rome found allies elsewhere—in Etruria, among the cities of Campania, and with the Samnites of central Italy—among peoples who viewed Roman imperialism as a lesser threat than the marauding bands of Gauls. The Etruscans, in particular, were losing ground throughout Italy. Their naval power was destroyed by the Sicilian Greeks off Cumae in 474 B.C., and by 400 B.C. they had lost Campania, their richest possession, to invading Oscans. By mid-century they were driven out of the Po valley by the Gauls, who remained a constant threat on their northern and northeastern frontiers. By contrast, the Samnites were just entering the period of their greatest power.

The alliance with the Samnites in 354 B.C. came at an opportune moment for Rome. For years the Latins had anxiously watched Rome grow beyond what seemed to them its proper place in a league of equal city-states, and in an attempt to alter the changing relationship before it was too late the Latins, joined by the cities of Campania, revolted in 340 B.C. Both were quickly overwhelmed by the Romans with the assistance of their new allies, the Samnites, and in 338 B.C. the war came to an end. What ensued is one of the epoch-making events in Roman history, for instead of the confiscations and expropriations to which defeated enemies were usually subjected, the Romans treated their old allies in quite a different manner. To appreciate the importance of this change it is necessary to review the stages by which Rome arrived at what was to become, after 338 B.C., a standard feature of Roman statecraft throughout its subsequent history.

Municipia   Since the sixth century B.C. the nearby Latin city of Gabii enjoyed an unusual relationship with Rome, ratified by a treaty that, according to first-century B.C. antiquarian Dionysius of Halicarnassus, could still be seen in his time in the Temple of Dius Fidius in Rome. Under the terms of the treaty, citizens of Rome were full citizens of Gabii, and, more importantly, those of Gabii were full citizens of Rome, to the extent that as early as 422 B.C. a citizen of Gabii named Antistius may have been elected a tribune of the plebeians at Rome. Local government was left intact at Gabii.

Before 340 B.C. another Latin town, Tusculum, was incorporated into Rome in a similar fashion, and L. Fulvius Curvus, the Roman consul of 322 B.C., was the first of a long series of citizens from that town to appear in the Roman list of magistrates. Finally, Caere, a neighboring Etruscan city that had extended asylum to Roman exiles and to the Vestal Virgins (who had carried with them Rome's sacred objects for safekeeping) during the Gallic invasion, was granted the right of public hospitality. This right guaranteed Caeritans in Rome all the rights of Roman citizens without any of the obligations such as taxes or military or public service. All these were apparently ad hoc arrangements, which the Romans, because of their special knowledge of the internal situation of the cities concerned, could assume in advance would work. In the case of the Latin cities (Gabii and Tusculum), the barriers were less significant, and the Romans could extend full citizenship rights; with the Etruscans of Caere there was a more guarded conferral of rights. Caeritans did not have to serve in the army, but they could not run for office either.

These precedents provided Rome with practical alternatives when it was casting about after the war for substitutes to the Latin League, which by now had outlived its usefulness. The first step was to dissolve the league. Then four of its former members were selected for complete incorporation in the Roman state, with grants of full citizenship (*civitas optimo iure*) but without the abolition of local government or laws. Henceforth, the inhabitants of these cities, like the inhabitants of Gabii, enjoyed dual citizenship and were subject to both taxes and military service while exercising the privilege of full participation in the Roman political process. Next the precedent of Caere was extended to a string of Oscan towns in Latium and Campania. These were partially incorporated into the Roman commonwealth, and their inhabitants were granted Roman citizenship, but they did not have the power to vote in the assemblies (*civitas sine suffragio,* citizenship without the vote). Technically, these newly incorporated cities were known as *municipia.*

Colonies Two other governing techniques came into use at this time and became, with the two just outlined, standard Roman methods of coping with the problem of newly acquired territory with non-Roman or non-Latin populations. First, nine Latin cities were left as independent states, thus forming a ring of border fortresses around the newly extended Roman territories. Citizens of these states kept their Latin citizenship and had reciprocal relations of commerce and marriage (*commercium* and *conubium*) with Rome, but not with one another. In addition, the Romans continued a practice long in use by the Latin League: the founding of colonies in newly acquired inland areas that required fairly large numbers of settlers for security. The league had regularly done this in the past as a joint action whereby on recently conquered land a completely new city-state was established, made up of citizens from all the members of the league, including Rome. This practice was continued and extended by Rome so that colonies were eventually placed in key locations throughout

Italy to become the foundation of Roman power in the peninsula. People were attracted to move to the Latin colonies by large grants of land, although at least for Romans such a move had a drawback: their citizenship was changed (or reduced) from Roman to Latin, and they could no longer serve in the legions or participate in political life in Rome. They could regain their citizenship, however, by leaving the colony and settling permanently once more in Roman territory. It seems that membership in Latin colonies was not restricted to those who were already Roman or Latin citizens; any Italian ally could sign up for enrollment. Therefore, one of the results of the planting of Latin colonies was to bring at least some other Italians directly into the Roman political system at a status close to that of Roman citizens.

The second governing technique was a modification of the first. This consisted in establishing small groups of Roman citizens (usually about 300 families) in coastal areas that needed a resident garrison. These small settlements, which were known as Roman colonies to distinguish them from the larger Latin colonies, were ultimately established at many points on both the Adriatic and Tyrrhenian coasts and became models for Roman colonies overseas. Citizens who joined these colonies did not lose their Roman franchise and were freed from service in the legions, although this was no great concession because they were on permanent garrison duty anyway. The grants of land they received were small and local government was elementary, again in contrast to the fully organized city life of the Latin colonies. Inhabitants remained subject to the control of the magistrates in Rome.

These techniques by which towns were granted full Roman citizenship (*civitas optimo iure*) or partial citizenship (*civitas sine suffragio*), or by which Romans and Latins were established in colonies in new territories, were consciously used as a means of resolving the Latins' complaints that they were being treated unequally while at the same time preserving the city-state structure of both the Romans and the Latins. The colonies were also useful safety valves for surplus population in the home states. The system was an achievement in federal organization that allowed for a maximum degree of flexibility and adjustment to local differences without endangering the solidity of the state as a whole. The direction of military and foreign affairs was the responsibility of the federal government at Rome and was open in varying degrees to those desiring to share in it from outside the city. By contrast, local government, except for the functions mentioned, was left intact and was exclusively in the hands of the elected magistrates of the individual city-states.

From Rome's viewpoint the solution of 338 B.C. was enormously advantageous. Directly or indirectly, by whole or partial grants of citizenship, Rome added over 200,000 new citizens to its population (a 42 percent increase) and over 300 square kilometers to its territory (a 37 percent increase). All of Latium and Campania, two of the richest and most developed areas of Italy, now constituted the basis of Roman political and economic power. With these resources Rome was able to control the ever-present threat of the central highlanders, who had never previously been handled by anyone, and eventually to fight Carthage to a standstill for control of the western Mediterranean.

The Samnite Wars

The most powerful single state in the Italian peninsula in the second half of the fourth century B.C. was the Samnite federation. Strategically located on a saddle of mountain land overlooking two of the major plains of Italy, Campania and Apulia, Samnium was in a position to dominate all of central and southern Italy. By the mid–fourth century B.C. it was well on the way to doing so. Previous Oscan incursions from the highlands had swept the Greeks and Etruscans out of Campania (with the exception of Naples), but when Rome incorporated the Campanians into its commonwealth in 338 B.C., the Samnites were confronted for the first time by an organized block of people reaching from south of Naples to Etruria. In addition, Rome had interests in Apulia, into which the Samnites were infiltrating, where the cities of Arpi and Luceria had requested Roman help. The great conflict was thus a struggle between the urbanized, agricultural populations of the plains and the pastoral highland peoples. For almost a generation the wars dragged on—bloody, confused, unending.

The main struggle took place in two phases: between 326 and 304 B.C. and between 298 and 290 B.C. Strategically, Rome's problem was how to avoid being caught between the Samnites to the south and its other enemies, the Gauls and Etruscans, to the north. Very conscious of the possibility of having to fight on two fronts, Rome went to great lengths to secure peace on its northern frontier while contending with the Samnites on the south. Almost to the end Rome was successful in this task, and when the Gauls and Etruscans finally did join in the fighting, it was too late to make any difference.

The initial phase of the war saw Rome attempting direct assaults on the Samnite mountain stronghold from Campania and failing miserably. The battle of the Caudine Forks in 321 B.C., which resulted in a whole Roman army being forced to surrender, was in the opinion of the Romans their worst defeat in history. Subsequently, Rome's links with Campania, the Via Latina and the Via Appia, were cut, and several of its colonial outposts overwhelmed. With the failure of this strategy, Rome turned to another, and this time found a way to take Samnium from the rear.

The new approach involved a series of diplomatic and military moves across the peninsula to the Adriatic so that Roman armies could march down the coast into Apulia to the rear of the Samnites, where the Romans had established a colony at Luceria in 315 B.C. Other Roman colonies (Alba Fucens and Carseoli) were planted as fortresses on the other side of Samnium, and so instead of Rome being enveloped, it was the enemy that was surrounded. The last major battle was fought in Sentinum in 295 B.C., when the Romans confronted and defeated a coalition of Samnites, Gauls, and Etruscans; five years later peace was made among all the contending parties.

Rome immediately set about consolidating its hold on central Italy by founding new colonies and extending the road system. The solid band of Roman territory across the peninsula now provided internal lines of communication and allowed

ROMAN FEROCITY: THE BATTLE OF SENTINUM

Although the Romans regarded themselves as the champions of the more urbanized and presumably more civilized areas of Italy, they were not far removed from the barbarous customs of their enemies. In the desperate battle of Sentinum in 295 B.C. against a combined army of Gauls (Celts) and Samnites, one of the consuls, Decius Mus, "devoted," himself *and* his enemies to the gods to win victory. Decius' father had similarly "devoted" himself to the gods.

Twice the Romans compelled the Gallic cavalry to give way. At the second charge, when they advanced farther, and were briskly engaged in the middle of the enemy's squadrons, they were thrown into confusion by a method of fighting new to them. A number of the enemy, mounted on chariots and wagons, made towards them with such frightening noise from the trampling of the cattle and the thunder of the wheels that the Roman horses were terrified. The victorious cavalry were scattered in panic; in blind flight men and horses fell to the ground. The disorder spread to the legions and many of the first ranks were trampled underfoot by the horses and wagons which swept through their ranks. As soon as the Gallic infantry saw their enemy in confusion they pursued their advantage and did not allow them time to recover themselves.

Decius shouted to his men, asking where they were fleeing to or what hope there was in running away. He tried to stop them as they turned their backs, but finding that he could not persuade them to keep their posts because they were so panicked, he called on his [deceased] father, Publius Decius. "Why do I postpone any longer the fate of our family?" he cried. "It is destined for us to serve as sacrificial victims to avert dangers to our country. I will now offer the legions of the enemy, together with myself, to be immolated to Earth and the Gods of the Underworld."

Having said this he ordered Marcus Livius, a priest whom he had ordered not to leave his side when they went into battle, to dictate the form of the ritual in which he was to devote himself and the legions of the enemy on behalf of the army of the Roman people. He was accordingly devoted with the same prayers and in the same dress in which his father, Publius Decius, had ordered himself to be devoted at the battle of Vestris during the Latin War. Immediately after the solemn ritual prayers he added the following: "I drive away dread and defeat, slaughter and bloodshed, and the wrath of the gods, celestial and infernal; with the contagious influence of the Furies, the Ministers of Death, I will infect the standards, the weapons and armor of the enemy. The place of my destruction will be that of the Gauls and Samnites also." After uttering these curses on himself and his foes he spurred forward his horse where he saw the line of the Gauls was thickest, and rushing on them met his death.

From then on the battle seemed to be fought with a degree of force that seemed scarcely human. The Romans . . . stopped their flight. . . . Livius the priest, to whom Decius had transferred his lictors [attendants] with orders to act as propraetor, cried out aloud that the Romans were victorious, having been saved by the death of the consul, and that the Gauls and the Samnites were now the victims of mother Earth and the Gods of the Underworld; that Decius was summoning and dragging to himself the army devoted along with him.

—Livy, 10.28–29

troops to be moved quickly from one front to another. Rome was now the dominant power in Italy. It could isolate potential enemies in the north and south, and concentrate its forces against one while holding off the others. Apart from these military, strategic, and diplomatic advantages, Rome was seen throughout most of the Samnite Wars as the defender of the urban-agricultural populations against the infiltrating mountaineers. It was this threat, in fact, that had first involved Rome with the Campanians, and the process was shortly to be repeated with the Greek cities in the south.

Tarentum and Pyrrhus

Rome's appearance in Apulia put it into competition with the Greeks of Tarentum and the protectorate they attempted to maintain over the other Greek cities of the south. Given the usual feuding both within Greek cities between upper and lower classes and among Greek cities themselves, it was inevitable that some internal party would supply the impetus or at least the pretext for Rome to intervene directly and displace Tarentum's protectorate with its own.

In 282 B.C. the aristocrats of Thurii appealed not to Tarentum but to Rome for help against the Oscans of Lucania, and Rome responded by supplying a garrison of Roman troops. About the same time four other Greek cities were similarly garrisoned. Tarentum retaliated by sinking part of a Roman flotilla that had entered its waters and then appealing for help to one of the great military adventurers of the post-Alexander world, Pyrrhus of Epirus. Hopeful of duplicating Alexander's eastern conquests in the west, Pyrrhus arrived with an expeditionary force in 280 B.C. and announced, by way of justification, that as a descendant of Achilles he was waging a second Trojan War on behalf of the Greeks against the (Trojan) Romans. In two battles in 280 and 279 B.C. at Heraclea and Asculum, he defeated Roman armies, but not without serious losses to his own troops. Attempts at negotiation failed, and the Romans, encouraged by their allies, the Carthaginians, rejected proposals for a confederacy of southern Italy of which Tarentum would be the head. Never one to remain for long at any task, Pyrrhus left to help the Sicilians clear their island of Carthaginians. When this expedition failed, he returned to Italy, where in his third battle with the Romans, near Beneventum in 275 B.C., he was defeated and forced to withdraw from Italy. Three years later Pyrrhus removed his garrison from Tarentum, and the city fell to the Romans.

With the fall of Tarentum, Rome's conquest of the peninsula, except for the Celtic north, was complete. There was no power left to challenge Rome, and its general defense of the urban populations against the traditional enemies of the Greeks of Italy—the Oscans and the Gauls—won Rome esteem in the eyes of Greeks throughout the world. Pyrrhus was one of the most colorful characters of the period, and his military abilities were not taken lightly by either the Greeks or the Macedonians. Roman success against his elephants, cavalry, and infantry was evaluated accordingly. A delegation from the Macedonian king of Egypt, Ptolemy Philadelphus, arrived in Rome in 273 B.C. bearing gifts, and Greek historians such as Duris and

Timaeus took note of the new power rising in the west. Timaeus picked Rome as the defender of Greek liberties against the other traditional enemy of the Greeks, Carthage, and made a synchronism between Rome's and Carthage's founding dates to lend dramatic emphasis to his point.

THE PUNIC WARS

Carthage, like Rome, had grown considerably since the two cities had made their first treaty in 509 B.C. By the time of their clash in the third century B.C., Carthage had come to dominate all the Phoenician cities in Africa and possessed a maritime empire reaching from Ptolemaic Egypt to the Atlantic. It was renowned for its wealth and the stability of its constitution, which Aristotle so admired that he included it as the only non-Greek example in his collection of constitutions.

Carthage's wealth depended not only on its mercantile activities but also on its rich agricultural hinterland, from which food supplies were exported to the urbanized Greek east. The city was ruled by a wealthy oligarchy; the masses of the people, exempt from military service and cared for by rich patrons, lacked the political consciousness of the Greeks and Romans and were known for their submissiveness. Military and civilian powers were separated not for any theoretical reasons but because commerce was the predominant way of life at Carthage. Generals were elected and held office for as long as was necessary for them to accomplish their missions. Failure was treated with great harshness, and unsuccessful commanders were often crucified.

Among the legacies the Etruscans left Rome was their alliance with Carthage, based on a lack of competing interests and shared enemies. Initially the differences between the cities were marked. Rome's wealth, such as it was, lay in agriculture. Its military power consisted of heavy infantry, and its immediate concerns were with Italy. Carthage's interests were maritime and commercial, and its military power lay in its navy. Eventually, the situation changed, and the success of each power in enlarging its respective sphere of influence inevitably brought them into confrontation. With the advantage of hindsight, Livy was to comment that Rome's involvement with Campania led to the war with Pyrrhus, which in turn led to the wars with Carthage. It was not a calculated collision; both powers edged their way into the conflict, and there was no careful weighing of national interests and realizable war aims.

The First Punic War (264–241 B.C.)

The occasion for the conflict arose, as might be expected, in southern Italy and Sicily, where Roman and Carthaginian interests were beginning to overlap. In the past an internal squabble in a Sicilian city might have meant little to Rome, but with its growing involvement in southern Italy, its sensitivity to such events expanded proportionately.

Campanian mercenaries in the service of Syracuse had revolted and seized the Sicilian city of Messana. In 264 B.C. they were hard-pressed by Hiero of Syracuse, and different factions within Messana appealed to the Romans and Carthaginians for help. The Carthaginians were closest and got there first, putting a garrison in the citadel.

At Rome the request for aid caused a major debate. Some saw the Carthaginian seizure of Messana as a prelude to an attempt to end the old balance of power between the Greeks and Carthaginians in Sicily by a complete victory for the Carthaginians. The fact that Messana was only a few miles from Italy and lay deep in traditional Greek territory, coupled with the fact that the Carthaginians already occupied Corsica and Sardinia, meant that such a move would convert the entire Tyrrhenian Sea into a Carthaginian lake. Other Romans had a personal interest in the Campanian mercenaries who were in control of Messana and in southern Italy in general. Campania had been part of the Roman commonwealth for three-quarters of a century, and Campanian senators (the Atilii and Ogulnii, for example) were powerful in Rome at this time. It might also have been argued that the Romans had more in common with the Greeks of Sicily than with the Carthaginians, their erstwhile allies. In the impasse, the decision was passed to the Roman people, who, according to biased aristocratic sources, were swayed by greed in favor of war against Carthage.

The Romans entered this conflict with a number of unresolved problems, the first of which was the question of realistic war aims. Should they restore the balance of power in Sicily? This would be a minimum achievement. Should they drive the Carthaginians out of Sicily altogether or even attempt an assault on Carthage itself? Because there had never been a need to debate these matters, there was no clear thought on how the war should be waged, and events themselves dominated the early years of the conflict. After initial land victories in Sicily, the Romans, following in the footsteps of Pyrrhus, began to push the Carthaginians back into the west of the island, only to discover that this could never be more than temporarily successful as long as the Carthaginians held their main ports, Lilybaeum, Drepana, and Panormus (Palermo). It was then that the need for a Roman navy became apparent, although at this stage the implications of such a commitment had not been thought through. With a surprising lack of hesitation, the Romans formed a fleet in 260 B.C. and circumvented the superior seamanship of the Carthaginians by transforming sea battles into land battles by the invention of a device called the *corvus,* a gangplank that also acted as a grappling iron locking two ships together, thus allowing Roman marines to make quick work of their opponents. With the creation of the fleet and the achievement of tactical superiority over the Carthaginians, the slow process of siege and blockade began. Ultimately this approach was to bring victory, but not before the Romans had attempted some shortcuts that threatened the whole concept of naval power.

In 256 B.C. Rome sent an expedition against Carthage in the hope of concluding the war quickly. It failed, and Roman naval power was decimated by storms and mishandling, so that by 249 B.C. Rome was back where it started. For the following

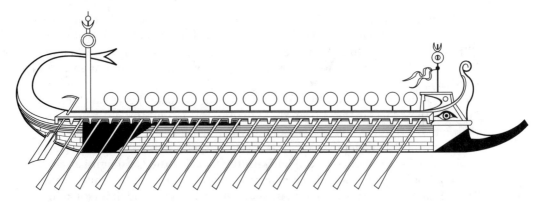

A reconstruction of a Carthaginian war ship of the time of the First Punic War found, along with the remains of a sister ship, off the coast of Sicily in 1971–1973. The hold of the one illustrated contained a cache of *cannabis sativa*. The discoverers of the ships speculate that it was used to help the rowers endure the stress of their long hours at the oars.

eight years the war languished until by one supreme effort a new fleet was created and the Sicilian blockade resumed. The Romans won a naval battle off the Aegates Islands, and Carthage, exhausted and unable to supply its forces in Sicily, including those of its most successful commander, Hamilcar Barca, agreed to negotiate (241 B.C.). The settlement resulted in the loss of Sicily, the payment of an indemnity, and various other clauses, which the Romans used as a pretext shortly afterward to seize Corsica and Sardinia.

Rome's first war with Carthage, called the First Punic War, revealed the strengths and weaknesses of both sides. Rome suffered from incredibly inept generalship because of its system of annual rotation in office and the resulting lack of consistent strategy. However, Rome's tenacity, manpower reserves, and willingness to seek victory contrasted with Carthage's half-measures and its dependence on mercenaries. Roman luck made a difference too, and its ally, Hiero of Syracuse, more than once helped out in bad times.

Between the two rounds of wars (264–241 B.C. and 218–202 B.C.) the Romans and the Carthaginians became deeply involved in their own affairs. In the Adriatic, Rome put down the pirates of Illyria, who were terrorizing the Greek coastlands, and replaced Macedonia, supreme since Philip and Alexander, as the power to be reckoned with in this area. Shortly afterward, the Gauls, who had been quiet all during the war with the Carthaginians, began a major advance on Rome. Terrified, the Romans resorted to human sacrifice and the consultation of the prophetic Sibylline books but finally defeated the Gauls at Telamon in 225 B.C. This victory gave the Romans the opportunity to finish off the Gallic threat, and a series of campaigns was launched against the Gauls' homeland in the Po valley. Roman colonies were established at Cremona and Placentia (Piacenza), but before the task was completed, the second war with Carthage broke out. Twenty years elapsed before the Romans renewed their efforts in the north.

The Carthaginians were also engaged in expansion, and under the energetic Hamilcar Barca began the resubjugation of Spain and the exploitation of its physical and human resources. Hamilcar, his son-in-law Hasdrubal, and his son Hannibal established close relations with the Spanish natives, and the last two, following Carthaginian custom, intermarried with Spanish royal houses. The Barcid dynasty in Spain grew in power, and the attention of the Romans was often drawn there by Rome's ally Massilia (Marseille).

The War with Hannibal (218–201 B.C.)

The pretext for the outbreak of the Second Punic War was found in Hannibal's attack on Saguntum, over which the Romans claimed some kind of protectorate, although the city lay well within the Carthaginian sphere of influence. An ultimatum was rejected by Carthage, and as soon as Hannibal heard the news, he marched his army out of Spain, through France, and across the Alps into Italy.

The strategies each side used in the Second Punic War were dictated largely by the results of the first. The Carthaginians, recognizing that Rome could be defeated only on land, conceded control of the sea to Rome; the Romans, for their part, planned to continue where they had left off in 241 B.C., using Sicily as a base to invade Africa while blockading a Carthaginian invasion from Spain. Hannibal upset this plan by slipping past the Roman forces into Italy, thereby forcing the cancellation of the war in Africa. His strategy was based on the assumption of Hellenistic warfare that a thoroughly professional general leading professional troops could defeat an amateur citizen levy and on the presumption that as a result of defeats in the field, the Roman confederation, like all other leagues, would disintegrate. In the first instance Hannibal proved to be correct, although his own genius was a factor that outweighed the others and made textbook cases out of his battles, confronting the Romans with a threat they had never before faced.

From 218 B.C. onward Hannibal remained unbeaten, and one great Roman defeat followed another, of which Cannae in 216 B.C. was the greatest. So great were the Roman losses that adolescents and slaves had to be drafted into the army. The annual rites in honor of the goddess Ceres, which could be celebrated only by women, had to be canceled because too many women were in mourning and mourners could not participate in the rituals. But then the weight of history began to tell as Hannibal came up against the Roman conquests of the past century that had divided Italy into two halves, giving the Romans internal lines of communication and preserving intact the heartland of Roman influence. Hannibal was kept in the south, the Gauls were fended off in the north, and although individual cities might revolt against Rome, as did Capua and Tarentum, Hannibal could not prevent their recapture. Nor could he capture Rome itself. His army was not large enough, and it lacked siege equipment. Roman colonies continued to perform their assigned function as self-sustaining fortresses in enemy country, and Roman roads allowed the legions to be shifted quickly from front to front. With its fleet, Rome could bring in supplies and deny them to Hannibal. Still, even with these advantages Rome would not have beaten Carthage had it not been for its victory in other theaters of the war and the emergence of a Roman military genius, P. Cornelius Scipio.

Scipio's first successes came in Spain, where he drove out the Carthaginians (210–205 B.C.) and established his reputation as a charismatic leader and a general of the caliber of Hannibal. Given the opportunity to invade Africa, he forced Hannibal's withdrawal from Italy and then defeated him in a pitched battle at Zama in 202 B.C., when for the first time the Romans achieved cavalry superiority in the field. Carthage surrendered all overseas possessions and all but 10 war ships, and agreed to pay a huge indemnity and not to wage war in Africa without Rome's consent. Rome won because it was able to compel Carthage to fight on Roman terms, even though the genius of Hannibal had averted defeat for years. Rome's control of the seas forced Hannibal to march overland to Italy, prevented Philip V of Macedonia, an ally of Hannibal's from 215 B.C. onward, from effectively aiding him, and allowed Rome to make its final assault on Africa from Sicily. The Romans could bring supplies into Italy from all over the Mediterranean while denying the Carthaginians the same facility. In Scipio they finally found a leader who raised their citizen-soldiers to new levels of technical ability, introduced new weapons and sophisticated new tactics, experimented with mobile tactical units (cohorts), and passed on a legacy of brilliant generalship.

ROMAN TERRITORIAL EXPANSION AFTER THE HANNIBALIC WAR

Italy and Spain

The most obvious result of the Punic Wars lay in the extension of Rome's commitments overseas and in Italy. Before this time Rome's principal concern was for its immediate possessions in central Italy. With the defeat of Hannibal, however, the Romans found themselves deeply involved in northern and southern Italy, Spain, southern Gaul, Illyria (in the Balkans), and North Africa, and through these areas with the eastern Mediterranean.

Much of northern and southern Italy had gone over to Hannibal during the wars, and as punishment Rome confiscated huge areas of land from its former allies, more than doubling its own landholdings in the process and producing an entirely new political map of Italy. Pieces of Roman territory, designated as public land, stretched from one end of Italy to the other, still occupied in many instances by their original owners. The connecting of these scattered parcels (usually the best land possessed by the original owners) by roads and their settlement, occupation, and development by Romans were to be among the greatest projects undertaken by Rome in the second century B.C., offering fantastic opportunities for self-enrichment to many, especially to the upper classes. Although the south required little pacification after the departure of Hannibal, the Ligurian and Celtic tribes of the north were conquered only after a series of lengthy campaigns lasting from 200 to 180 B.C. Even then the job was not complete, as the tribes of the Alps remained unsubdued until the time of Augustus. Romanization took place concurrently with pacification, and large colonies and major connecting roads were created.

Spain fell to Rome as part of the spoils of the Punic Wars. For strategic and economic reasons Spain had to be brought fully under Roman control, for it was from Spain, with its human and mineral resources, that Carthage had launched its nearly fatal attack on Rome in 218 B.C., and Rome was determined that nothing like that should happen again. Accordingly, in 197 B.C. Spain was divided into two Roman provinces, and the slow process of bringing this gigantic land mass under control began. Spain was inhabited mostly by nonurbanized peoples, and the Romans used the same techniques of diplomacy and war they used so successfully against similar peoples in Italy. As in all Roman undertakings abroad at this time, the object was not the direct annexation of territory but the elimination of groups that might pose a threat to Rome's interests in the area and the establishment of relations on a client-patron basis. Because these interests were never clearly defined and because the client-patron relationship was moral rather than legal, misunderstandings and ambiguities inevitably resulted.

Between 197 and 133 B.C. Rome conducted a series of campaigns resulting in the subjection and eventual Romanization of much of the Iberian Peninsula.

Later in the century Rome acquired the province of Transalpine Gaul, guaranteeing direct access to Spain from Italy. The campaigns for the conquest of Spain were characterized not by the significance of the battles or the numbers involved but by the consistency with which the legions were beaten by the skillful guerrilla tactics of the Spanish and by the broken treaties, lax military discipline, atrocities, and ruined reputations on the Roman side. Not until 133 B.C., when the Celtic-Iberian town of Numantia was destroyed by Scipio Aemilianus, who earlier had reduced Carthage to rubble, could Rome's hold on Spain be called secure. As late as the time of Augustus, recalcitrant tribes in northwestern Spain were still disturbing the *pax Romana,* the Roman peace. It is no coincidence that some of the dates Roman historians assigned to the decline of the Republic coincide with Rome's disastrous experiences in the Iberian Peninsula.

Macedonia and the East

Before the war with Hannibal, Roman suppression of piracy in the Adriatic had brought it into immediate contact with Macedonia, and the usual process of making friends and allies, by which Rome established its influence, began.

Following Philip's stab in the back after the battle of Cannae, when the Macedonians allied themselves with Hannibal, Rome became more involved in the area east of the Adriatic, establishing its first formal alliance with a Greek state, the Aetolian League. With its hands freed after the defeat of Hannibal, Rome now gave its

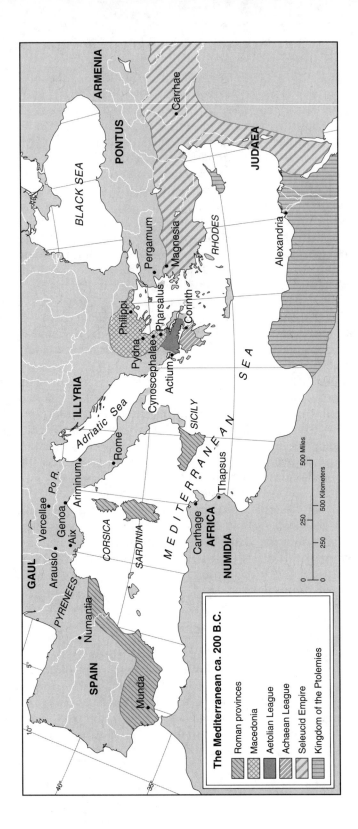

The Mediterranean ca. 200 B.C.

Roman provinces
Macedonia
Aetolian League
Achaean League
Seleucid Empire
Kingdom of the Ptolemies

GAUL
SPAIN
PYRENEES
Numantia
Munda
Arausio
Vercellae
Genoa
Aix
Ariminum
Rome
Po R.
CORSICA
SARDINIA
Carthage
AFRICA
NUMIDIA
Thapsus
SICILY
ILLYRIA
Adriatic Sea
Philippi
Pydna
Cynoscephalae
Actium
Pharsalus
Corinth
Pergamum
Magnesia
RHODES
Alexandria
JUDAEA
Carrhae
ARMENIA
PONTUS
BLACK SEA
MEDITERRANEAN SEA

500 Miles
500 Kilometers
0   250   250
0   250   500

5°
10°
40°
35°

WARS OF THE ROMAN REPUBLIC, II

Sporadic wars in the Iberian Peninsula	197–133 B.C.
Second Macedonian War	200–196 B.C.
Battle of Cynoscephalae	197 B.C.
War with Antiochus	192–189 B.C.
Battle of Magnesia	190 B.C.
Third Macedonian War	172–167 B.C.
Battle of Pydna	168 B.C.
Achaean War: Sack of Corinth	146 B.C.
Third Punic War: Sack of Carthage	149–146 B.C.

attention to the Greek sphere, as it was doing simultaneously to its other legacies of the Punic Wars in northern Italy and Iberia. Encouraged by new allies in Greece and by Rhodes and Pergamum across the Aegean, Rome challenged Philip to withdraw from Greece. When he refused, Rome launched a war against him. At Cynoscephalae in 197 B.C. the famed Macedonian phalanx met the Roman legions in battle for the first time and went down in defeat. Rome's object, as in Spain and elsewhere, was not the direct acquisition of territory or the complete destruction of Macedonia as a center of power but only its weakening and curtailment within suitable limits. This was achieved by balancing Macedonia against Aetolia and winning over the Greek states by granting them their freedom. Unfortunately, the Greeks had difficulty in coming to terms with the limitations placed on their freedom by the Romans, and it was to take more wars and the breaking up of Macedonia before the ambiguities of their relationship were finally resolved.

Typically, the first of these wars was provoked by Rome's first Greek ally, the Aetolian League. This militarily powerful but culturally backward league had hoped in typical Greek fashion to fill the power vacuum left by Macedonia, but was disappointed not only in this but even in its territorial ambitions with regard to the annexation of a few adjoining Thessalian towns. The war also involved Rome with the king of Syria, the Seleucid Antiochus III, with whose possessions in Asia Minor Rome now came into contact. The evacuation of Greece in 196 B.C. had won Rome much good will, so that when Antiochus, in response to the urging of the Aetolians, landed in Greece in 192 B.C. to "liberate the Greeks," he received a cool reception. In due course he was bundled out of Greece by the Romans, who quickly returned. He was completely defeated at Magnesia in Asia Minor in 190 B.C. The Romans imposed an armament reduction and an enormous indemnity, which eventually led to the destruction of Seleucid power in the east. Rome's staunch allies in Asia, Rhodes and Pergamum, were generously rewarded, and a new balance of power was established in the eastern Mediterranean with the Peace of Apamea in 188 B.C. Egypt, weak at this time, had no intention of challenging Rome, especially after seeing its two old rivals, Macedonia and Syria, go down to defeat so easily.

Decoding Rome's Intentions

Rome's handling of Greece through a combination of cynical manipulation and reliance on its traditional client-patron approach continued to lead to more misunderstandings and blunders on the part of its allies and enemies alike. In taking on alliances with Greek states and cities, Rome inevitably became involved in the complicated political and social entanglements that had frustrated every effort of philosophers, statesmen, and generals for the preceding 500 years. Rome was constantly besieged by Greek individuals, factions, and governments attempting to manipulate it in their own self-interest against other Greeks. At one time the Senate was confronted by no less than four sets of Spartan envoys, each of whom claimed to speak as a legitimate spokesman for his country. Such a situation put the Greeks at the mercy of the Romans, but it also dragged the Romans into the demoralizing world of Greek diplomacy, where they quickly learned (or perfected) the arts of casuistry, equivocation, and mischief-making.

A complaint by an ally, or perhaps a suspicious move by one of the powers being watched by Rome, led, time and again, to increase suspicions and investigations by commissions that in turn often provoked confrontations. Such a combination of circumstances led, after Philip's death, to a final confrontation in Macedonia between his son Perseus and the Romans. The consolidation of Macedonia's economic and human resources and a marriage alliance with the Seleucids, together with the personally urged allegations of Eumenes, king of Pergamum, led to another war and the final overthrow of the Macedonian kingdom at the battle of Pydna in 168 B.C. In the aftermath Macedonia was divided into four impotent, autonomous republics. With the loss of its kings, one of the world's great nations passed into oblivion. At the same time the Romans dissolved the Greek Boeotian League (whose democratic organization found little sympathy at Rome, where democracy was identified with instability). Rome also weakened Rhodes, its former ally, who had mistakenly offered to mediate between Rome and Perseus when Rome seemed to be having difficulty bringing the Macedonians to a decisive confrontation on the battlefield. Pergamum was also involved in mediation attempts and likewise suffered eclipse as Rome's foremost ally in Asia Minor. Once again Rome refused to take on the responsibility of formal supervision of the conquered areas, although it did assume a direct financial interest by continuing to collect, at a reduced rate, the taxes the Macedonian kings had levied in the past. After clearing out the unreliable anti-Roman elements throughout the Greek cities, the Roman legions returned once more to Italy, laden with immense booty.

The Low Point of Roman Imperialism

This was not Rome's last involvement in the tangle of Greek politics. Rome did in Greece what it had done in Italy and the western Mediterranean: it eliminated one power block after another and slowly inculcated the rules under which politics were to be exercised. Allies were often slower to learn the rules than enemies, as the examples of Aetolia, Rhodes, and Pergamum had already demonstrated. Now the Achaean League, another old ally of Rome, miscalculated just how much freedom it was allowed to settle affairs in its own area, the Peloponnese, where it maintained a permanent dispute with Sparta. This time the issue was resolved by the dissolution of the league and the barbaric sack and destruction of the ancient city of Corinth as an object lesson to the rest of Greece (146 B.C.). Greece as a whole now came under the general supervision of the Roman governor of Macedonia, which had been made into a province two years earlier after yet another revolt. The same year (146 B.C.) saw the sack and destruction of another great city, Carthage, Rome's old rival for power in the west, after a three-year siege. The same combination of Roman suspicions and the complaints of allies that had so often brought on confrontations in Greece had the same effect in Africa, where the basic economic strength of Carthage and the constant stream of complaints from the Numidians finally brought Rome to a decision it had avoided in the past: the destruction of the city. Yet another province, Africa, was added and came under the direct surveillance of a Roman governor.

In pulling together the loose ends after the Punic Wars, Rome emerged in 146 B.C. as the dominant power not just in the west but in the whole Mediterranean. Under formal supervision were the overseas provinces of Sicily, Sardinia-Corsica, Macedonia, Africa, the two Spains, and shortly afterward Asia Minor and southern Gaul. Cowed and enmeshed in the Roman system of client-patron relations were the important states of Syria, Egypt, Pergamum, and Rhodes as well as dozens of petty states and cities. The social structure that had served so well within Rome and had enabled it to build unobtrusive power in Italy was now extended to the whole Mediterranean and was to be the basis for the unification of the whole region in the Roman Empire. At precisely this moment, however, the new policeman of the world fell victim to internal disorder, corruption, and revolution, brought on, paradoxically, by its efforts to bring the Mediterranean into line with its own sociopolitical goals and assumptions.

SOCIETY AND THE STATE IN THE ROMAN REPUBLIC

Modern democracies pride themselves on the fact that, legally at least, citizenship in their states is a very simple matter. An individual either is or is not a full citizen. There are no intermediary or secondary classifications. In principle, a full citizen, except in certain instances (e.g., if a person has been convicted of a particular crime), has all the rights and privileges enjoyed by all other citizens, and can claim equal treatment under the law. In Roman society, by contrast, the inequality of everyday life— economic, social, cultural, and even gender-related—was built into the formal structure of society. Romans made explicit the divisions of wealth, education, and social standing. The higher one's status, the more votes one had. Votes, the Romans said, should be weighed, not counted.

In the Republic, members of the Roman state could be either full citizens, citizens without the right to vote, or Latins with a variety of privileges coming close to,

---

STERN ROMAN FATHERS AND MOTHERS

The second-century statesman and historian Polybius, like many other Greeks, looked with amazement and a bit of horror at the power Roman fathers had over their children:

> Some fathers, while still magistrates, executed their own sons, a thing contrary to every custom or law. They placed a higher value on their country's interests over natural family ties (65.4.5).

The matriarchal Cornelia, daughter of Scipio Africanus and the mother of two revolutionary sons, Tiberius and Gaius Gracchus (among the twelve children she bore) takes Gaius to task in the following letter. The document may be genuine, although most of the literature of the period is heavily influenced by pro- and anti-Gracchan propaganda.

> I would not hesitate to take a solemn oath that no enemy, except for those who murdered [your brother] Tiberius, has caused me such trouble and distress as you have by your actions, you who ought, as the only survivor of all those children I bore, to have made sure I had the least anxiety possible in my old age. You should have taken into consideration how little of my life is left and acted to please me, and consider it unfilial to act against my advice. . . . But if you are determined on your course of action, seek the tribunate when I am dead. In fact, do what you like when I am no longer aware of it. . . . If you continue as you are I fear that through your own actions you will bring such trouble on yourself that you will never be happy.

—Cornelius Nepos, *Fragment 1*

---

but still falling short of, those of full Roman citizens. One could be freeborn, a slave, or a freedman or freedwoman—each a separate legal category. Even full Roman citizens were unequal among themselves in certain ways. Some citizens were the hereditary clients of other citizens and owed them obligations as their patrons (and vice versa, for patrons had responsibilities toward clients). Whereas some citizens were legally independent (*sui iuris*) and could own and sell property, marry, or divorce as they willed, others, even in adulthood, were still under the legal control of their fathers or guardians. Age and gender were also special categories with individually assigned rights and responsibilities.

In a society structured on these lines, one's economic location in the system was not necessarily of the first importance, but rather whether one was a foreigner or a citizen, free or slave, client or patron, Latin or ally, male or female, married or unmarried. These were more crucial to an individual's status than the possession of wealth, education, or ability. In fact, there were many able, educated, wealthy slaves and freedmen who were at least formally, and in the eyes of the law, less favored than freeborn citizens who lacked these advantages.

The Roman Family, *Patria Potestas,* and Gender Roles

Besides these classifications, a full citizen might come under other categories, such as being legally independent (*sui iuris*) or still under the control (*potestas*) of someone else. In the case of either a man or a woman this other person could be one's father. However, if a woman had been married under the strict *manus* (in the hand, or under the power) form of marriage, she came under the *potestas* of her husband, not of her father.

The power of the father (*patria potestas*) in a Roman family was unique, unlike that in any other Mediterranean land. The head of the household, who was the oldest living male (*paterfamilias*), literally had the power of life or death over his children, although in practice custom placed restrictions on its exercise. This power extended beyond the usual decision as to whether newborns should live or be exposed. In certain circumstances (for example, in the case of sexual offenses, including adultery) the *paterfamilias* could execute his own *adult* children; in fact, it was his responsibility, not that of the state, to do so. Even married daughters who had committed serious offenses but whose marriages were of the non-*manus* type were handed over to him for judgment. The *paterfamilias* could decide who his children should marry and, more interestingly, whether they should stay married or get divorced. He owned all the family property, so even his grown sons and grandsons could not, technically, own anything until he died. However, he had no control over the public life of his sons, who might hold higher offices than he had ever attained. His responsibilities were heavy, for he ruled the household and owned its property not so much for his own private gratification as for the benefit of the family, which was regarded as a separate entity with its own traditions, history, religious rituals, and protective deities. The *paterfamilias* was the religious head of the household as well as the property owner and ruler. He was responsible for the continuity of the family, its name, its burial places, and the cult of its ancestral spirits.

A woman, even more than a man, came under the strict control of her family. If she married according to the *manus* form of matrimony, she ceased to be part of her own immediate family and passed over completely into her husband's. She worshiped the guardian spirits of his family, and his ancestors became hers. Whatever property she brought with her became his, and if he died, she came under the guardianship of one of his male relatives. If the other, non-*manus* form of marriage was followed, the wife remained legally within her own family and under the power of her own *paterfamilias*. In this instance any property she brought with her by way of dowry was hers, and in the case of a divorce or the death of her husband, the property remained hers and reverted to her family. The guardian in this instance would be one of her own kin. Women, unlike men, never escaped guardianship and at least theoretically could never control or dispose of property without the guardian's approval.

In practice matters were often quite different. For example, a *paterfamilias* was bound by custom to consult his family council before taking action on any important issue. This council was made up of the important adult members of the family.

To go against its recommendation was considered a breach of custom. A *paterfamilias* had to be around to exercise his power, and whether many survived long enough to attempt to control their grown sons, let alone their grandsons, is an open question. Given the late age at which men married, the length of time Roman heads of household spent away from home on campaigns or in the forum, and the high numbers lost in battle, the real influence of wives and mothers (*materna auctoritas*) may have been much greater than the strict letter of the law recognized. Many women who were supposed to be under the control of a guardian must have de facto been free to do what they wanted. Technically it was always possible to escape *patria potestas* by a roundabout process called emancipation (*emancipatio*), but this could be done only with parental cooperation, obviously limiting its usefulness.

The kind of marriage chosen also contributed to the degree of a wife's independence. In the second century B.C. the non-*manus* form became more common. This meant that wives remained in control of their own property, which could be quite substantial, especially after they received their share of their paternal inheritance. Husbands would have to think twice before engaging in any action that might bring down on their heads an irate father-in-law or an energetic, well-connected brother-in-law. This legal situation may not have been regarded as an intolerable intrusion in a man's private affairs. Marriage was regarded primarily as the source of legitimate children, and once this function had been served, a husband in an unhappy marriage had plenty of socially tolerated alternatives for his sexual energies. Concubinage was not considered wrong or sinful; slave women and women of lower social status were always available, and liaisons with them were not regarded as threats to the marriage. Naturally, this was the husband's viewpoint; it was quite another matter for the wife. Dalliance with male slaves or lower-class males would not be tolerated because it raised the possibility of spurious children and serious challenges to the family name, property, and most important of all for the upper classes, reputation. The only solution for a wife who found her husband's neglect or philandering intolerable was divorce, which was easy enough. A wife's ability to remedy a problem through the influence of her own family should not be underestimated, however.

Roman Families and Their Slaves

The Roman family often included not just parents and their unmarried children but also their slaves, their freedmen, and the offspring of both. The Romans were liberal in their manumission policies, so in many households slaves had a good chance of winning their freedom (or at times of purchasing it) and becoming Roman citizens. However, even after manumission, family ties persisted. In the eyes of the law, a slave had no father, and on manumission the freedman took the name of the former owner. For example, when Tiro, the slave of the famous orator M. Tullius Cicero, was freed, he became Marcus Tullius Tiro. Sometimes the only surviving member of a particular Roman family was a freedman and on him devolved the responsibility for maintaining the family graves and the cult of the ancestral spirits.

Often the family burial plot contained the remains of the original family and their freed slaves, all bearing the same family name.

All of this made for great confusion in familial relations. Marriage relations between husband and wife were complicated by the presence of male and female slaves. Slave marriages existed but were not recognized as legal; they had their own complications, which only added to the muddle. There was always the danger that the owner of a slave couple would sell one of the members of the slave marriage or one of their children, thus creating emotional havoc for the slaves (and possibly also for the master himself or his wife and children). The status of the offspring of such slave relationships was also highly complicated because during the marriage one of the partners might be manumitted; then what was the status of the children born after that point? What of those born earlier? Or a freedman in a household might begin to consort with a slave woman in a stable relationship and have children by her, leading to yet more legal tangles. The complexities do not end here. Slaves could purchase other slaves. When a male purchased a female slave as a wife, she actually had the status of being a personal slave to her husband, though strictly speaking she belonged to *his* master because everything a slave owned belonged to the slave's owner. In practice this tactic could have the effect of reducing the likelihood of the slave wife being sold off into another household.

These examples suggest only some of the legal, emotional, and social headaches in Roman families that possessed slaves—a fairly large segment of the population because not only the rich but even the middle classes owned slaves. Also, to balance this fairly benign picture of domestic slavery, it should be added that slavery in rural areas, especially on large estates or in the mines, could take a much harsher form. In the countryside, where slaves worked in chain gangs, there must have been little chance of manumission. There slaves were exploited to the maximum and were often treated with great cruelty, from which there was no escape except flight, death, or, very rarely, revolt.

Clients, Patrons, and *Fides*

Given the importance the Romans attached to the family and the power of the head of the household, it is not surprising that paternalism prevailed throughout the state and greatly influenced political and social relations.

From ancient times certain families and individuals considered themselves the clients (*clientes*) of other families and regarded the heads of these houses as their patrons (*patroni*), with whom they had special ties of a nonlegal, fiduciary kind. Freedmen automatically became the clients of those who had manumitted them, and in a less precise way great noble households acquired patronship relations with non-Roman communities, cities, and even states, such as those the Sempronii possessed with Spain or the Fabii possessed with the south of France. A complicated network of mutual duties and obligations expressed by the Latin term *fides,* or "faith," bound clients and patrons together and, though not expressed in the terms of formal law, possessed great moral weight.

A late–first-century B.C. statue of a Roman aristocrat displaying the portrait busts of his ancestors. Roman nobles interested in a political career exploited to the fullest the conservative public's respect for the deeds of the heroes of the past.

Patrons had comprehensive obligations toward their clients and were expected to supply such things as legal advice, representation, and, when necessary, political protection. Clients responded appropriately, aiding their patrons in whatever way they could, usually and most conspicuously by their political support and their votes. Neither patron nor client could give evidence against the other in court.

Of all qualities that Romans liked to think were most characteristically Roman, *fides,* which translates as "faith" but had broader connotations of credibility and dependability, was the most favored. It had wider applicability than merely to the relationship of client and patron and permeated all Roman social relations. It existed between a man and his friends (*amici*), between upper and lower classes, even between Rome itself and its various allies and friends. The very word was connected with the term for treaty, *foedus,* from which our own word *federal* comes, and with belief. *Fides* was one of the abstract deities, like Concord and Piety, that the Romans so liked to venerate and had a temple in the city going back to the most ancient times. It was not a legal but a moral and social concept. It could not be enforced in the courts, and like so much else in the Republic, it depended on custom and the opinion of the community for its enforcement. Understandably, *fides* was an essential aspect of any noble's dealings with his clients or his equals, and Roman self-identity, both individual and national, was closely connected with this concept. Foreign nations or their leaders were criticized for their lack of it, and to impugn a person's *fides* at Rome was very serious business. The strength of the Republic was seen as flowing from the commitment of the different groups of society to this ideal rather than from any formal, legal, or constitutional structure. Obligations and duties (*officia*) were not spelled out in elaborate, ironclad contracts but rather were left to the interpretive moral sensibilities of the parties involved and depended on the changing conditions of day-to-day life.

Dignity, Honor, and Order

Beyond these legal and moral classifications that distinguished full citizens from half-citizens, free from slave, and client from patron, another series of categories based on the concept of honor further classified Romans and divided them from one another.

In modern industrial societies, power is spread throughout a variety of economic, political, cultural, and religious institutions, and much of the leadership also derives from these sources. Nevertheless, specialization is such that service in one type of institution tends to disqualify a person from at least simultaneous service in another. It is difficult to envision a society where the reverse might be the case—where, for example, a business or labor leader would at the same time be a general, judge, practical politician, and priest.

There were no powerful autonomous institutions such as corporations, unions, churches, or universities in ancient Rome, and leadership in almost all aspects of public life was in the hands of the same small, wealthy group of individuals. These men, great landowners for the most part, were also Rome's priests, judges, generals, and statesmen. Julius Caesar, one of the city's best-known politicians and generals and a man of questionable morals, was also head of the state religion (*pontifex maximus*), as was Scipio Nasica, the political opponent and assassin of Tiberius Gracchus, one of the tribunes of the people in 133 B.C. The holding of the various priesthoods was considered an important adjunct to a successful career in politics.

Distinctions in Roman society were based not on an individual's professional skills or even wealth but rather on the capacity for public service in a broad sense. The Romans arranged their society and its politics to this end. Talents and skills that we regard highly, such as those of scientists, doctors, and artists, were relegated to the private realm and were never considered qualifications for service to the state. Instead the Romans looked for individuals who in war would be able to lead their armies and in peace would be looked up to as sources of wise legislation, jurisdiction, and religious guidance.

With such an emphasis it is easy to see why honor (*honor*) and dignity (*dignitas*) were the two most important, interrelated values in Roman life and why community esteem rather than popularity was so important. This might be viewed as demonstrating that Rome was a backward, primitive society, still in the process of emerging from its heroic age. However, the way Rome set about bestowing honor on individuals was not a simple method of handing out awards to the bravest or the most

---

IDEALS OF THE NOBLES

The grave inscriptions put up in the third and second centuries to honor the Scipio family are an important source of information on what motivated the politically active segment of the Roman elite. The following is the epitaph of Gnaeus Cornelius Scipio Hispanus, active around 150 B.C.

> Cn. Cornelius Scipio Hispanus, son of Gnaeus, praetor, curule aedile, quaestor, twice military tribune, member of the Board of Ten for Judging Lawsuits; member of the Board of Ten for Offering Sacrifices.
>
> By observing our ancestral customs I increased the distinction of my family. I raised children. I imitated the deeds of my father. I upheld the honor of my ancestors, so much so that they are glad I was born of their line. The magistracies I held ennobled my family.

—H. Dessau, *Inscriptiones Latinae Selectae* (Berlin, 1892), 9.1.2.15

---

nobly born but an intricate, orderly procedure that had the effect of tying the social and political realms closely together, something few societies have been able to accomplish or to maintain for very long.

A key concept in this process was order (*ordo,* a word that has passed directly into the most modern Western languages), which for the Romans constituted the foundation of public life. It was a concept that survived the fall of both the Roman Republic and the Roman Empire.

The Orders   *Orders* were groupings of individuals in society according to estimated worth. Each order possessed a certain rank or dignity, which gave a person belonging to it precedence and privileges over someone of a lower order. By the late Republic the word *order* was applied to all sorts of groupings, such as skilled craftsmen, freedmen, and scribes, but it is only the rights and privileges of the two most important orders, the equestrian and senatorial, that properly reflect the meaning of the term. The reason is that the lower orders, such as scribes and carpenters, had little to distinguish them formally from one another, whereas the privileges of the senators and knights (*equites,* hence, *equestrian)* clearly did differentiate those who held these titles from the rest of society. The distinctions were more than nominal. They were juridical, political, and financial, for members of these orders had privileges and rights—such as the capacity to serve as jurors, bid for state contracts, and stand for higher office—that were denied the rest of society. Yet it must be stressed that neither of these orders constituted a kind of hereditary feudal aristocracy.

The Equestrian Order

Entry into the highest order, the Senate, was by membership in the equestrian order, which in a sense contained the Senate. Senators voted in the equestrian centuries of the Centuriate Assembly, but eventually the juridical position of each order became clearly defined. By the end of the second century B.C. the two were quite distinct in terms of their rights and special privileges. A senator could not bid for a state contract, for example, whereas a knight could. Socially, however, the two were always very closely related and enjoyed constant interchange.

Admission to the equestrian order was not based on wealth, although a fixed base net worth of 400,000 sesterces was required. A more important prerequisite was recognition by the censor, whose role in classifying people in Roman society was moral as well as financial. In principle the censor was to look for the kinds of accomplishments that would qualify a person for inclusion in the first level of the aristocracy and even potentially in the Senate itself. For example, a man had to be virtuous in the Roman sense: he had to have proved himself dependable on the battlefield, in the courts, as a legislator, and as a patron who cared for his clients. Negatively, certain statuses, such as being a former slave or having known moral failings, automatically removed a person from consideration. In the calculation of a man's worth, the skills of private enterprise and success in making money had to be related to the larger community in positive, public ways by means of benefits (*beneficia*) conferred on it. The mere possession of wealth (or culture for that matter), regardless of the amount, would not automatically qualify a man for entry into the equestrian or senatorial order as long as he remained committed to a private way of life. Once in an order, it was a different matter, and in time these criteria were applied less rigidly. Nevertheless, public service was at all times considered a prerequisite for entry into the aristocracy.

Practically, commendation or recommendation by a member of the aristocracy, preferably by a powerful senator, was essential in the process of advancement, and this in turn depended on the needs of particular individuals and families for new talent, which often could be supplied only by reaching down to the lower ranks. The process is not terribly well known because "new men," as they were called, were reluctant to document their rise in a society where old family names meant so much. Although the military tribuneship, which was of equestrian rank, was an elective office, it is not known whether nonequestrians were elected to it and so automatically acquired this rank, or whether the Romans preferred to elect individuals who were equestrian to begin with. The latter is probably the case, considering the conservative character of the voters and the aristocracy's tight control over the electoral processes.

The Senate

From early times, Romans in positions of authority, public or private, were expected to consult competent advisers before undertaking any important activity. The *paterfamilias*, for instance, was supposed to consult a council (*consilium*) of family members and friends on weighty matters and to follow majority advice. If we view the state as the Roman family writ large, with the magistrates acting as *patresfamilias*, the Senate was their council.

The authority of the Senate in the Roman constitutional system is difficult to define because it had no official function beyond that of advising the elected magistrates. The formal powers of legislation, declaring war, and making peace rested with the people in the assemblies. Over time, especially during the Punic Wars, the informal power of the Senate, known as its authority (*auctoritas*), grew spectacularly. For all practical purposes the Senate took control of the state. In particular, foreign policy and the conduct of war were considered the Senate's special prerogatives, but there was no change in its statutory position, and legally there was nothing to stop consuls, praetors, or tribunes from calling the assemblies of the people to enact legislation, pass judgment, or vote independently of the Senate. Nevertheless, the power of the Senate was enormous. At its root lay the fact that in the Republic, social and political structures coincided. In the Rome of that period, political, military, social, moral, and economic eminence were all interrelated, and although there were wealthy, cultured people outside the Senate, they had little power, and their social position was proportionately low. The power of the Senate was such that all commands in war and all provincial governorships went to its members, and even when the people agitated for a role in deciding who received such positions—as they sometimes did—the choice still lay between senators, not between senators and nonsenators.

The Senate was recruited de facto from among the equestrian order, for membership in it was not something hereditary that could be passed on from father to son. However, sons of senators were automatically members of the equestrian order, and it was not uncommon for senatorial fathers to have sons who chose to remain equestrians (as was the case of the grandfather of Augustus, according to the biographer Suetonius), or the reverse, for an equestrian father to have a senatorial son. The two orders were closely related, then, with some family members—brothers, cousins, uncles, nephews, grandsons—being senators and others knights. It was possible for generations to slip by without a particular family branch producing a senator. A family might drop out of the senatorial order to recoup its finances or simply because of lack of interest and ambition among its members in a particular generation. A special inner group among the senators was the nobles (*nobiles*), whose ancestors had held the consulship.

The Cursus Honorum   Entry into the senatorial order was in some respects similar to entry into the equestrian order. It required action by the censors, one of whose main jobs was filling vacancies in the Senate and removing unworthy senators. Censors could not just pick their candidates at random: they had to come from a list of ex-magistrates. In a sense, therefore, it can be said that the people elected the Senate, though only indirectly because of the censors' role in the process. The result, in any case, was that the Senate consisted of already-proven officials, all of whom had military as well as civilian experience. The quaestorship, the lowest of the regular magistracies, was held between the ages of 27 and 30. The praetorship was to be held not before 40, and the consulship not before 42.

From early times the tradition developed that in the senatorial career ladder (*cursus honorum*) certain offices were prerequisites for election to the next higher one. The lowest of the regular magistracies in the *cursus* was the quaestorship. This position was either military or civilian, depending on whether the successful candidate was attached to a military unit as an officer on a general's staff or went off to a province as a governor's aide. Those who held this office had usually previously held other elective offices, such as the military tribunate or some judicial post. Entry into the Senate came automatically with the quaestorship by the first century B.C., although earlier having held the patrician or curule aedileship had been a prerequisite. Someone at this level would have had very little influence and would remain a "backbencher" unless elected to higher office.

The next required office in the senatorial *cursus* was the praetorship, which was essential for candidacy for the consulship. However, the intermediary step of tribune of the plebs or aedile was advisable to continue the slow buildup of an individual's reputation with the various segments of the voting population. Visibility was an essential factor in advancement, as were the ties of faith (*fides*), clientship (*clientela*), and friendship (*amicitia*), the components of the informal political system that underlay the formal system and made it work.

The aedileship was another administrative office to which minor jurisdiction was attached. Aediles were responsible for the care and maintenance of the public buildings, streets, and water and grain supply, and the supervision of the marketplaces, traffic, and religious celebrations. There were only four aediles, so a fair amount of business must have come their way, along with numerous opportunities for making contacts and doing favors (*beneficia*) for individuals or for the clients of individuals from whom they hoped to receive support when running for the next office. In the late Republic their responsibility for the games at religious festivals gave the aediles a special opportunity to curry favor with the public by making their own private contributions to spectacular celebrations that the allotted funds would not support. As aedile, Caesar went heavily into debt to put on a series of magnificent games. They won him wide popularity but eventually forced him to look for a good province to rule as governor so that he could pay off his creditors.

Tribunes also had good opportunities for making contacts with the people on a day-to-day basis and winning the kind of recognition that might serve them in good stead later. At least in the classical period of the Republic, until the mid–second century B.C., this did not mean currying popularity but performing useful functions for those who counted in Roman society through actions such as vetoing measures obnoxious to various members of the nobility or proposing and supporting laws these people wanted. All this demanded a fair amount of political sensitivity to the consequences of one's actions, and tribunes always had to keep in mind who they might offend or please by a particular action. Such a system obviously did not encourage the swift passage of run-of-the-mill legislation, let alone innovative proposals.

The successful candidate for praetor, one rung from the top, could end up as one of Rome's two chief judicial officers or as a governor of a province with military and civilian jurisdiction. In the first capacity the praetor's principal role was that of deciding how the laws should be administered in particular cases. He did not require technical knowledge of the law, which was available from unofficial specialists, the *jurisconsults.* What he did need, however, was the ability to take cases and decide whether they deserved a hearing. Then, in consultation with the parties involved, he selected the judge and the conditions under which the case would be tried. This role of the praetor and of the jurisconsults, together with the publication of the rules under which an individual praetor would adjudicate during his year in office, provided the foundation for the great edifice of Roman law, which was to be systematized in the imperial period (first century A.D. onward).

After the praetorship came the consulship, the highest position in the Republic. Although the consuls were primarily military men, they were also the chief civil officers of the state with the right and the duty to call the Senate or the assemblies of the people together to legislate, elect, or pass judgment. Like all Roman offices, the consulship was collegial, which meant that each consul had to take into account the veto power of his partner. There was also the built-in restriction that a consul's *imperium,* or power, ended precisely on December 31 (or, before 153 B.C., on March 14), when he once more became a private citizen. The process of prorogation, or extending the office as a promagistracy, was the only standard way of avoiding a quick return to civilian life.

The Cursus Honorum *and the Army*

The **Cursus Honorum** *and the Army*   Unlike most modern societies, where civilian and military hierarchies are rigidly separated, the professionalism of military officers prized, and civilian control of the military regarded as essential for freedom, Rome preferred a close intermingling of military and civilian careers. The consuls were at one and the same time generals and civilian heads of state. The Senate itself was made up of ex–military officers who had been elected to political office and who might at any moment be called to serve in a campaign. Senators were not technocrats, lawyers, or political careerists but rather aristocrats, citizens, soldiers, and politicians.

In Rome there was no such thing as a purely nonmilitary political career. Indeed, a successful military career was essential to political advancement, as the unmilitary-minded orator Cicero knew only too well. Voters respected victorious commanders and promoted them to higher office or reelected them in times of crisis. In a triumphal parade a Roman general celebrated the victory of the Roman people over their enemies, and at the same time received the maximum amount of glory and honor that the people could bestow on an individual. A kind of symmetry existed between the career goals of the triumphing general and the needs of the state. Religion, politics, war, and ethical values were fused to form a seamless whole. In this way, all classes and all citizens were bound to each other in a great national project: warfare.

The Senate and the Provinces

Before the third century B.C. the scope of a senatorial commander's opportunities was limited by the small scale of Rome's military involvements and the restricted responsibilities that this implied. All the wars were fought in Italy, and the campaigning seasons were short, even if the wars themselves were long. The Senate consequently had little difficulty monitoring what was going on. In peacetime, a commander's opportunities were even more limited. With the Punic Wars, however, came longer campaigns, more distant theaters of war, and greater responsibilities. Even when the wars were over, there were still major opportunities, for now there were permanent overseas provinces to be ruled. First there was just Sicily and Sardinia, but then in the second century B.C. Spain, Africa, Macedonia, Asia, and southern Gaul were added, and in the first century B.C. came Gaul proper and a whole series of eastern provinces. It was as though Rome was put on a permanent wartime footing as far as career opportunities were concerned.

The governing of permanent provinces was something new in Roman history. In the past the Senate had been responsible for the city of Rome itself and such territory in Italy that did not belong to the self-governing municipalities and colonies or to the allies. Broad areas of responsibility known as *provinces* had been regularly assigned in the past to military commanders, and the term was even used to describe the responsibilities of the praetors. One praetor, for example, had the *provincia urbana* and the other the *provincia peregrina*—that is, one was in charge of the administration of law for Roman citizens and the other was in charge of its administration for foreigners. Now the term was applied to whole countries for whose administration Rome had decided to take on permanent responsibility. Because Rome had no experience in this kind of administration and did not believe in professional civil servants, even for its own government, it was forced to rely on the only other kind of experience it had in foreign affairs: military campaigns. Governors, either consuls or praetors, were therefore sent out every year to govern the provinces with *imperium* (supreme power), just as Rome's military commanders, who were also consuls and praetors, were given *imperium* to conduct war on behalf of Rome.

The first task facing a newly appointed governor was to collect his staff, which, considering the responsibilities, was extremely small. His adjutant was a quaestor, 25 to 30 years old, assigned by lot from the group selected for that year. The quaestor's job was chiefly financial, but he could be delegated to do almost anything by his superior, from holding court to commanding troops. The governor could also take a number of legates or aides with him—three if he was a consul—who were also generally senators, some of high rank. Cicero took his brother Quintus, who was of praetorian rank, with him when he was assigned to Cilicia. In a more warlike situation Lucius Scipio had his brother Publius, the victor over Hannibal, on his staff as a legate when he was assigned the province of Greece in 190 B.C. with permission to carry the war against the Seleucid king Antiochus III into Asia. In addition, a number of friends and relatives might be invited to come along for the experience. Tiberius Gracchus, the revolutionary tribune of 133 B.C., had earlier been the companion of his brother-in-law Scipio Aemilianus, the commander of the Roman army then besieging Carthage. The governor's professional staff was minute. It consisted of his private secretary (*accensus*), a few scribes (who were Rome's only professional civil servants), a doctor, a haruspex, and some others such as his lictors, who carried the rods and axes (*fasces*) that were the symbols of his office.

Administrative Responsibilities   The administration of the provinces placed great demands on the officials Rome selected in this haphazard fashion, and not just on their integrity. Although the governor had absolute power over his subjects, the problems he had to face were huge. Conditions varied widely from region to region. Sicily had 65 cities, and Asia was probably richer than Italy itself, but the west was still backward and tribal, and had no urban life worth talking about. Governors had little guidance. They came and went in rapid succession, taking with them their staffs, so that there was no opportunity to build up a permanent local administration that would help an incoming governor adjust to local conditions. His starting point was the provincial charter (*lex provinciae*), which was drawn up at the time the province was founded and constituted the basic law of the province. For example, it established such things as the statuses of the various cities and of their inhabitants, always a thorny problem, but it left much to the discretion of the governor. Information might be picked up from previous governors, but politics could easily interfere with the communication. And there were always plenty of people in Rome who had special, personal interests in the provinces and who were not slow in letting a new governor know how they felt he should act where their affairs might be involved.

The system put great strains on governors in other ways. As noted, the Roman political process had an important military aspect, and its highest office was a generalship. Names were obviously made more easily on the battlefield than in the law courts. There was therefore a temptation to use provincial wars as stepping stones to the next office or the next command. Governors could expand wars, or if it looked like their replacements might be in a position to steal their laurels, they could rush to finish the fighting before the replacements arrived. For example, Julius Caesar's designated province was Cisalpine and Transalpine Gaul, but by the end of his proconsulship he had added all of Gaul proper and had made separate assaults on Germany and Britain. In the west, especially, where the population was largely tribal and unsettled, governors faced a standing temptation to seek a quick victory in the short time allowed by their term of office.

Civil administration posed another set of problems to the governors and often strained their morality to the breaking point. They received some expense money but no salary, and if a governor was scrupulously honest, the holding of such an office could be expensive. Verres, the corrupt governor of Sicily whom Cicero prosecuted, cynically remarked that a governor had to acquire three fortunes when in the provinces: one to pay off the debts incurred in running for public office in the first place, one to bribe the jurors if he was unlucky enough to be brought to trial, and one to live on for the rest of his days.

Provincial administration was complicated by a number of factors. It was important to get along well with the local oligarchies, who were Rome's principal supporters in the provinces and who might have powerful friends in Rome, but this could easily compromise the evenhanded administration of justice. The most difficult problems were in the richer provinces, where the Romans inherited a complicated system of taxation from their predecessors, the Hellenistic kings, who had hordes of bureaucrats to handle their fiscal problems. Because the Romans chose to

Roman soldiers and administrators engaged in some undetermined task, possibly taking a census, laying out a colony, or drafting troops. This scene from the Altar of Domitius Ahenobarbus (ca. 100 B.C.) is one of the few depictions of soldiers of the Republican period.

remain above such matters but not to forgo the income, they had to resort to private enterprise, as they so often did in matters lying beyond the interest or competence of the Senate. Private—actually only semiprivate—companies (*societates*) were allowed to bid for the job of collecting taxes in the provinces. The company that won would then send out its agents (*publicani*) to make the collections, which had to cover expenses as well as provide a worthwhile profit. These companies were systematically organized, and drew their directors (*magistri*) and shareholders (*socii*) from among the equestrian class. They were enormously influential both in Rome and in the provinces. A governor with ambitions to advance had to be cautious how he acted on complaints brought against their representatives in the provinces. It took a great deal of courage and integrity to fight the system. One who did was the consul Rutilius Rufus, who took on the companies while governor in Asia in the first century B.C., and on his return to Rome was tried, condemned, and forced into exile by the equestrian-controlled courts. This was a notorious case, however, and the average governor would probably have been content if he succeeded in avoiding serious problems during his tenure in office.

Corruption and Efforts at Reform There is no guarantee that a permanent administrative service created by the Senate would have done a spectacularly better job of running the provinces, because it presumably would still have been reporting to the Senate. Any reform would have had to begin with the Senate itself and with the whole political process in Rome. Even under the Empire, when abuses of the kind common in the Republic were supposed to have been brought under control, we still hear of extortion and other crimes in the provinces. However, there were some means of redress during the Republic, combining formal and informal features in typical Roman fashion. Some senatorial families, such as the Gracchi in Spain and the Fabii in southern France, had special interests in particular provinces, and appeal could be made to them. Of course, much depended on the political battles that were taking place in Rome at the time the complaint was made and who was on whose side. The formal method was to bring an accusation (the commonest one being extortion) and introduce an action for its remedy (*res repetundae*). After 149 B.C. there was a permanent court to handle these accusations, but it was difficult to get a judgment. If the senators were the jurors, as they were down to 123 B.C. and then again after 83 B.C., they would be slow to condemn a fellow club member, and equestrians who manned the court at other times were often only concerned with the attitude of the accused toward the tax companies that they ran or in which they held stock. There was no public prosecutor's office, so the action had to be initiated by the wronged provincials themselves and might be hindered by the current governor, who could intimidate witnesses and otherwise harass the parties involved. Then at Rome a senator had to be found who would introduce the case. If the provincials were lucky enough to win the case, they acquired Roman citizenship (if they wanted it) and double the amount they had lost. The defendant was generally expelled from the Senate and exiled.

Although the full effects of Rome's method of governing its provinces did not become apparent until well into the first century B.C.—and then the concern was mainly for the damage being done to Rome itself—certain defects were present in the system from the beginning.

Collegiality, which was of the essence of the political process at Rome, was not in force in the provinces. The governor alone was responsible for what went on there, restrained only by his term of office, his estimate of the local political situation, and the few informal sanctions that might be brought to bear on him. He might do little or nothing except in the most routine fashion, or, depending on his inclination and the type of province he ruled, he might be benevolent or cruel, just or unjust. He could keep his hands clean, as Cicero did during his term of office in Cilicia, attempt reform, as Rutilius did in Asia, or regard the province as so much real estate to be exploited, as Verres did in Sicily. Rome's heavy reliance on custom to govern social relations was misplaced in the provinces. At home a magistrate was restrained by centuries of experience and hundreds of unwritten practices that did not exist in the provinces. It was to take a political revolution to create a system that could control the governors, and even then the complaints continued.

The Roman Army and Society

More than most ancient states, the Roman state was a tightly integrated nation of warriors. Romans were first and foremost soldier-citizens. Being a citizen automatically involved service in the legions. Military service was not a special privilege or duty of any particular group; eligible citizens of all classes, except the poorest (*pro-letarii*), were subject to the draft from their seventeenth to their sixtieth year. In practice, however, 16–20 campaigns was usually considered the maximum that one needed to serve. Because the voters were the same people who made up the legions, there was no large gap between what the army wanted and what the state wanted, at least not until the late Republic (after 133 B.C.), when the state began to disintegrate. The burden of military service did not fall on the poor, as it so often does in modern states, but on the middle and upper classes, who were rewarded with proportionately larger amounts of political power. Military and civilian careers coincided and complemented each other. The highest awards and honors were reserved for military success, not for high performance in such spheres as the arts, trade, finance, and industry. These occupations had their place in the Roman scheme of things, but at a distinctly lower level than in the Forum and the battlefield. The high degree of integration of army and society enabled Rome to project an amazingly great degree of power relative to its population.

A final element that contributed significantly to Rome's military success was its ability to integrate its allies in its war aims and battle plans. Every Roman army was made up of a core unit of legions, but brigaded alongside the legions, under Roman command, was an approximately equal (and sometimes greater) number of allied contingents. The allies, apart from supplying much needed additional manpower, also provided support in areas where Rome was traditionally weak, such as in cavalry.

Ultimately Roman military strength is to be traced not to the superior fighting qualities of the legions, although they were high, but to the nature of Roman society itself. Put simply, Rome was able to get more out of its own citizens and its allies than any other ancient society. Its true genius was displayed not in its army but in its political and social system.

AN ESTIMATE OF ROMAN SOCIETY

What can be said in favor of a system that blatantly favored the rich over the poor, the well-born over the lowly? Can anything be said to justify such elitist principles?

One kind of defense—and the easiest—is to point out the inconsistencies and weaknesses of modern societies, where despite egalitarian sentiments the rich and powerful still exercise special influence in the elective, legislative, and judicial processes. The Romans would claim that this kind of system leads to concealment, cynicism, and irresponsibility and that at least in Rome it was perfectly clear who was powerful and, more important, who was responsible. In a crisis the Roman people could simply exercise their prerogative by making their own choice, either of a general, a piece of legislation, or a judicial condemnation. Outside crisis situations, it was easy for the public to keep track of what was going on. The Senate consisted of only about 300 members, of whom 20 to 30 were key figures, all of them well known. The elective system exposed the individual to some degree of public scrutiny, and the seniority system was so slow that there was always a choice between trying a well-known older man or reaching down to the lower ranks to pick someone with talent, although of course this happened only in desperate situations, when enough of the old guard had been killed or shown, as they often were, to be inept.

Romans could claim that they achieved a fine blend of formal ranking by wealth as well as by public esteem—a blend of economic muscle and aristocratic excellence. Entry into the Senate or the equestrian order was not automatic and demanded some proof of public confidence in a candidate's ability and character. Theoretically, wealth was not an end in itself but a means of providing services to the community. Public offices had no salaries, and legal services were required by law to be free. Romans could point to the inability of most modern democracies to integrate the wealthy classes into the state as a particularly grievous failing. They could justly claim that modern individual philanthropy by the rich is too haphazard and arbitrary to compensate for their overall lack of involvement in the formal public life of the community. Socialist and communist states would be considered to have failed also. The mere elimination of a class, Romans would argue, does not eliminate human craving for distinction but merely drives it underground, where it is more difficult to control.

Needless to say, this kind of a debate could not have taken place at all in the context of the Republic. Language and the presuppositions underlying our use of words would have made it impossible. The concepts of the inherent rights of the individual, merit, and egalitarianism are too distinctively modern and alien to the Roman mentality to have permitted a meaningful discussion, and even if properly understood they would have been rejected as self-contradictory and unrealizable. It would take yet another revolution, the advent of Christianity, to dethrone the old classical assumptions and replace them with a new set of values.

Chapter 10

The Transformation of the Roman Republic

THE OLD ORDER FADES

In 200 B.C., despite the great increase in territory and power that had come with their victory over Carthage, a majority of Romans still lived in the same narrow stretch of land in central Italy that had constituted the Roman heartland before the Punic Wars. Except for a few scattered colonies, the rest of Italy was, as in the past, in the hands of a variety of non-Roman cultural, linguistic, and ethnic groups. Overseas, Sicily, Sardinia, and Corsica were provinces, but Roman presence there was minimal.

Shortcomings of the System

The Romans' unwillingness to expand and their geographic confinement to central Italy were in turn reflections of their psychological assumptions about the nature of the state and how society should be structured. Old ideas about city-state life, which reached back to Rome's beginnings, assumed that citizens should live within a day's walking distance of the capital. When Roman citizens were settled by state action in colonies outside Roman territory, they were, at least before the second century B.C., automatically reduced to the second-rate status of Latin citizens. Even within Roman territory, individualistic farmsteading was not encouraged; normally, Romans were expected to settle in organized groups complete with preexisting charter, laws, and political structure. In the eyes of the ruling oligarchy, if not of the masses, the city-state had definite territorial limits beyond which it could not expand without ceasing to be a state in which public office was exchanged among a small number of families in a free give-and-take process. After 241 B.C. the number of tribal units, which until then had been increasing as more territory was added, was fixed at 35, and in the future individual tribes were simply expanded to cope with new additions of territory. Only by keeping expansion under strict control was it possible for the old system to function.

Paradoxically, Hannibal's invasion had left the old system not only intact but stronger and narrower than ever at precisely the time when new conditions were crying out for an entirely new system. The war with Hannibal made a gift of governmental control to the Senate, which still was not a constitutionally established organ of government but nevertheless exercised even tighter control than in the past. Success, by confirming the Romans in their old ways, was the wrong formula for new times. A small coterie of some 20 families passed the highest office of state from hand to hand among themselves. By the mid–second century B.C., only four new families had been admitted to the consulship.

There was no change in the belief that land, farmed by aristocrat and peasant alike, was the basis of the Roman economic system. Commercial, financial, and industrial interests were accommodated only reluctantly. Taxes were raised for current needs, and surpluses, when they occurred, were returned to the people. Budget planning was unthinkable, as were paid professional administrators (except at the lowest levels), politicians, and lawyers. The nobility gave their services freely to the state in these capacities, being forbidden by law as well as ancient custom to receive pay for such efforts. All state contracts were let out to private companies, and in general an absolute minimum of resources was earmarked for formal government. To manage the Roman Empire in 200 B.C. there were 10 senior and 18 junior magistrates, all elected annually (every five years in the case of the censors), of whom exactly half were concerned entirely with affairs within the city of Rome itself.

The army was similarly unprofessional and consisted of annual levies of amateur, peasant soldiers who were expected to supply their own weapons, food, and clothing, commanded by amateur officers who served a year and then returned to private life. Only reluctantly did the state begin to supply its soldiers with arms, food, and clothing, and even then made deductions for their cost from the soldiers' meager allowance. Service in the army was seen as a duty and privilege of full citizens only, and those lacking the requisite amount of property, which constituted their "stock" in the corporate state, were excluded from this privilege.

Rome's cultural life in 200 B.C. was as simple as its economic and administrative arrangements. Coarse native mime and farce, family histories, translations of Greek plays, and a few attempts at epic poetry in Latin by non-Romans satisfied the minimum demands of Romans for literature and drama. Unlike in the more developed Greek east, the Roman reading public was minute. Architecturally, Rome did not compare with even provincial Greek cities, let alone such metropolises as Athens or Alexandria, and visiting Macedonians from the court of King Philip V poked fun at the capital city of the Western world. In social terms Rome was still archaic by

Greek standards; family and kin ties prevailed over the more individualized pattern of ethics and legal relationships characteristic of societies in the Hellenistic east.

The Transformation   Within little more than a century, all of this was to change. The whole of Italy south of the Po was to possess the franchise, and Romans were to be found everywhere throughout the Mediterranean. By the end of the second century B.C. new provinces in Spain, Macedonia, Africa, Asia, and part of Gaul were added, and Roman power was everywhere supreme. Vast amounts of money in the form of loot, tribute, and indemnities flowed into Rome. Although most of this money stayed at the top, some trickled down to the masses in various forms, such as improved services and communications, a share in war booty for soldiers, and most important, the elimination in 167 B.C. of the *tributum,* the principal tax to which Romans were subject.

With little impulse on the part of the Romans to build up capital, the money poured into public building programs and items of conspicuous consumption. Throughout Italy in the second century B.C. a great network of trunk roads was constructed, linking one end of the country with the other and tying colonies directly to Rome. In the north the Po valley was dissected by the Via Aemilia and the Via Postumia, which linked Genoa on the west to Aquileia and Ariminum on the Adriatic. Another consular road, the Via Aurelia-Aemilia, ran along the coast from Rome to Genoa. Other major roads were constructed in the mountainous regions of central Italy, and two great highways, the Via Appia and the Via Annia, gave access to the

If Greeks and Macedonians saw little of cultural note in the Rome of the second century B.C., a major transformation was already under way as the Roman upper classes were acquiring a taste for Greek art and commissioning a whole range of subjects, including these fine gems. The fact that so few portraits of individual Romans survive from this period makes these tiny images particularly valuable.

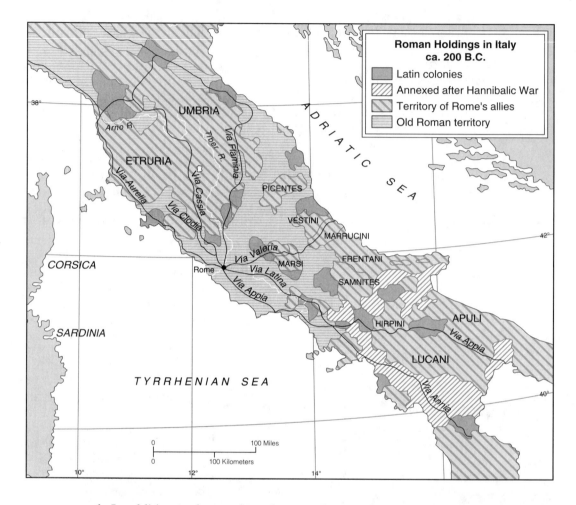

Roman Holdings in Italy
ca. 200 B.C.
- Latin colonies
- Annexed after Hannibalic War
- Territory of Rome's allies
- Old Roman territory

south. In addition to the trunk roads, secondary roads sprang up to serve local needs and connect bypassed towns with the main routes. New colonies were established in strategic locations, and on occasion individual grants (*viritim*) of public land were made to attract migrant peasants from the overcrowded parts of central Italy. The slow process of clearing the forests and draining the swamps of the Po valley was begun, making this immensely fertile region available for cultivation.

Under these influences, the character of Italian agriculture began to change. The peasant subsistence farmer, the backbone of the army, began to give way to the long-term volunteer, whose loyalty was more likely to be to his commander—or to the person who could pay his wages—than to the state. New types of cash crop farming were introduced, taking different forms in different parts of Italy. In the south giant ranches (*latifundia*) were devoted to the raising of huge herds of cattle and sheep, watched over by slave herders. Although road construction was not undertaken with economic objectives in view, it had the effect of opening up previously inaccessible and unprofitable Roman landholdings to Roman farmers, large and small. Archaeological surveys show that land use intensified during the second century B.C. in many parts of Italy, as the primeval forest was cut down and land came under cultivation for the first time. Northeast of Rome was a large area in which specialized farms produced vegetables, poultry, fish, and all sorts of luxury items (snails, boars, stags, and thrushes, for example) for the Roman market. Served by three great trunk roads, the Via Flaminia, the Via Cassia, and the Via Clodia, this was a natural area for intensive farming. Similar "truck farming" regions were probably associated with cities throughout the peninsula. Elsewhere in Italy, great groves of olive trees and vineyards were planted to supply the needs of an affluent population and to provide exports for growing markets overseas, especially in the west. In the provinces, too, roads were constructed, such as the Via Egnatia, which traversed Macedonia, and the Via Herculea in Spain.

The impact of the wealth of the Mediterranean was soon seen in other ways. Rome went on a building spree that continued, on and off, for 500 years, leaving the huge monuments of brick and concrete so much admired by visitors to Rome over the centuries. Two new aqueducts, the Aqua Marcia and the Aqua Tepula, were constructed and the older aqueducts repaired, with the result that the water supply of Rome was more than doubled. The censors of 184 B.C., Cato and Flaccus, spent huge sums improving the drainage and sewage systems of the city. Over the years additional sums were poured into new bridges (the Mulvian and Aemilian), basilicas (Sempronian, Aemilian, and Opimian), a dozen or more temples, and half a dozen shrines, in addition to warehouses, porticoes, granaries, sidewalks, shopping areas, arches, and statues. The first marble buildings were constructed in the second century B.C., and a gilded ceiling was seen for the first time in Rome in the Capitolium. Elsewhere in Italy, similar building projects embellished towns with baths, forums, basilicas, and temples, some funded by the central treasury in Rome, others by local notables or municipal councils. L. Mummius, who sacked Corinth, adorned the towns and provinces of Italy with booty, as his surviving inscriptions proclaim. Huge private fortunes were accumulated, and villas and town houses, in the past marked by simplicity of style and construction, were now built with all the luxurious embellishments that eastern architects and artists could devise. Eventually these villas evolved into the landscape-type mansions of the first century B.C., with their grounds laid out in imitation of natural scenery. Towers, bridges, pavilions, statues, trees, and artificial islands and streams adorned the grounds, and there were aviaries, fish ponds, baths, and every known amenity.

Cultural Changes: Rome and Greece

In the second century B.C., in addition to the other problems brought on by its military successes, Rome had to face and cope with the allurements of Greek culture. It would not be an exaggeration to say that Romans were culturally illiterate in the fields of poetry, drama, and history before the second century B.C., although some efforts were being made in the direction of the first two at this time, chiefly by outsiders. However, Latin was still too rough for prose writing, and was only slowly being made

"HE WANTED TO APPEAR TO BE CULTURED"

When it became fashionable among the Roman elite to display knowledge of Greek culture, practical Romans did not bother to purchase educated Greek slaves to act as tutors (they might have had difficulty in doing so, as this story suggests). Instead, they had their own slaves trained in Greek literature just as they had them trained to be cooks, hairdressers, accountants, or farm managers. The following story suggests how slaves might have acquired their skills.

A very rich man called Calvisius Sabinus inherited the estate of a freedman (and, it should be added, the mentality of a freedman as well). Never was it so outrageous that such a man should have such wealth. His memory was so poor that he would on occasion forget the name of Odysseus, or Achilles or Priam—individuals we all know as well as we know our teachers. No *nomenclator* [the slave whose job it was to remind his master of the name of the person he was talking to], no matter how old, made as many mistakes in imposing names on clients rather than getting them right in the first place, as Sabinus did when he referred to Trojans and Greeks. Yet he wanted to appear to be cultured. He hit on the following solution. At great expense he bought slaves. One of them had the job of memorizing the whole of Homer by heart; another had to memorize Hesiod, and so on for the nine lyric poets. It is no surprise that he had to fork out an enormous price for them: he could find none already trained for sale. He had to contract them out to be trained.

Then, when he had acquired his gang of slaves he would pester his dinner guests. He kept his slaves by his couch and would continually ask them for lines to quote, even though he would often forget what they had said in the middle of a sentence.

—Seneca, *Letters*, 27

suitable for poetry and drama. Yet it was at precisely this time that Rome had the greatest need to communicate with the rest of the world and explain its institutions and politics to the educated classes of the Mediterranean. Public opinion was important in the Greek-speaking world, and it was essential for the Romans to respond to questions being raised throughout the Mediterranean about where Rome had sprung from; what enabled it to conquer Pyrrhus, the Gauls, and the Carthaginians (the last two ancient enemies of the Greeks); and what justification, if any, it had for possessing an empire.

The first answers to such questions were supplied by Greeks writing about Rome from a distance, such as Timaeus of Tauromenium in Sicily, who lived in Athens in the early third century B.C. Not until the end of the Punic Wars were Romans able to give an account of their institutions and history. Writing in Greek, Fabius Pictor wrote a history of Rome that emphasized its strength, moderation, tenaciousness, and good faith as well as the wisdom of its Senate and its strict moral code. With Cato the Elder, in the first half of the second century B.C., Latin history writing first came into existence, representing a new level of self-confidence on the part of the Romans, who now rose to the challenge of Greek letters by composing their own literature in their own language. This was an achievement matched by no other people with whom the Greeks came into contact. For Cato, in fact, the Greeks no longer counted; the Romans and the Italians had nothing of which to be ashamed. On the contrary, he believed they had incorporated the best of the Greek world with the best of their own rich heritage—a pardonable exaggeration with which many Greeks in the second century B.C. must have agreed. From this time on, numerous accounts in Latin by members of the senatorial class provided the growing reading public of Rome and Italy with suitably patriotic, moralizing histories, often laced with polemic tracts from the internal political battles of the century. There were few qualms about adapting history to the political needs of the Roman upper classes, and history was seen as a means of glorifying one's achievements and the achievements of one's family as well as propagandizing for further advancement.

In Cato's younger days Roman poetry and drama were rudimentary, with Livius Andronicus and Naevius providing translations of Greek poems and plays, but the first half of the second century B.C. saw the full flowering of Latin in the works of Ennius, Pacuvius, Plautus, Terence, and others. Epic poems glorifying Rome's past and its destiny were produced, and Ennius' aphorisms, which reflected the nobles' vision of Rome, became commonplaces quoted throughout subsequent Roman history. Plays celebrating Roman historical events were written but never became popular. Comedies, especially those of Plautus, were always popular, although the settings and the stock figures were Greek for fear of offending conservative Roman tastes. There was no place for Aristophanic humor in Rome, where the aristocracy took its role as a governing class seriously and unquestioningly. Mime and farce, which were native to Italy, were the popular fare of the lower classes and eventually displaced the plays of Roman comedy altogether.

Although Greek grammarians were present in Rome in 167 B.C., they were expelled six years later. When three famous Greek philosophers—Carneades, the head of the Academy; the Stoic Diogenes; and Critolaus the Peripatetic—came to Rome to plead a case on behalf of Athens, they electrified the youth of the city with their lectures. Nothing like Carneades' lecture on justice and its application to the problem of empire, delivered on two successive days—on the second of which the speaker refuted all the theories he had put up on the previous day—had been heard before. Cato urged that the philosophers be given a quick answer to their plea so that they could return to their schools in Athens as soon as possible, while the "youth of Rome could listen, as in the past, to their laws and magistrates."[1] Even Scipio Aemilianus, the Roman patron and friend of the Greek historian Polybius, attacked the corrupting influence of Greek ideas, especially the disastrous effect of wealth on the Roman ruling class. Scipio Nasica prevented the building of a permanent theater in Rome in 154 B.C. because he feared it would lead to the speedy corruption of the citizens, and such a theater was not built for a century. A permanent amphitheater for games,

---

[1]Plutarch, *Life of Marcus Cato*, 22:5.

which were becoming increasingly popular, was not built in Rome until the end of the first century B.C., presumably on the grounds that one of the best ways of controlling this form of amusement was to keep the audience from becoming too comfortable.

Religion   Roman religion showed the effects of the upheavals brought about by the acquisition of an empire. Traditionally, Roman religion had been an integral part of state affairs. Of course, there was a private religion or devotion practiced within families and by individuals, but the state was involved with religion as part of its proper function. Political figures held religious offices as a matter of course, and the maintenance of the peace of the gods (*pax deorum*) was as much a part of the functioning of the state as fighting wars or hearing legal cases—the other two primary duties of Roman magistrates, who had inherited the triple roles of priest, general, and judge from the Etruscan kings. However, after the expansion of Rome, the old system was clearly inadequate, and the very localized character of the religion made it impossible to export. Religious functions were to be performed in Rome, and various figures who were priests as well as consuls or praetors were hindered in the performance of their duties and in some instances could not leave Italy at all. As Rome grew and the bonds of clientship (*clientela*) dissolved, the confinement of religion to the higher officials of state and to state functions created a vacuum. Eastern religions moved in to fill the void. The worship of the Great Mother (*Magna Mater, Mater Deorum,* or Cybele) was introduced officially in 205 B.C., and unofficially the worship of Dionysus crept into Italy and was savagely repressed as being dangerous to Rome both politically and morally. However, the two religions remained as the forerunners of many others, including the one that was ultimately to triumph: Christianity.

New Classes Emerge

Not all the wealth that flowed to Rome was in the form of cash or movable property. Huge numbers of slaves accompanied the returning conquerors and were put to work in various segments of the economy—in agriculture, industry, the mines, and the home. No one knows the numbers, but the impact was sufficient to jolt the entire economic structure of Italy out of its traditional ways and to introduce a completely new factor into Roman society. Because Roman masters had a propensity for manumission and slaves, when manumitted by Romans, acquired the franchise (unlike their Greek counterparts), the existence of a large servile population guaranteed Rome large numbers of new Roman citizens from the second century B.C. onward. The freedman class was generally made up of former domestic or urban slaves engaged in skilled and professional activities; in comparison to the average freeborn Roman, these people were well-to-do. They therefore tended to enter the middle rather than the lower classes.

An even more significant development of the second century B.C. was the increased importance of the equestrian class, the *equites*. This general term was applied to individuals outside the Senate who possessed a high census rating because of their wealth as well as other qualifications. Because senators were barred from contract-

New directions: A Roman general portrayed in Hellenistic style in the first century B.C. The Roman ancestors would not have approved.

ing, banking, and trade and because manufacturing was looked down on by the elite, the equestrian class was able to exercise a near-monopoly in these increasingly important areas. One group of equestrians (called *publicani,* or publicans, because they served the public sector) was organized into small companies that contracted with the state for the lease of mines, the construction of roads and public buildings, the manufacture of arms, the supply of food and clothing for the armies, and so on. Because the second century B.C. was a particularly lucrative period for building contracts and arms supply, the influence of the publicans increased proportionately, although it was some time before they attempted to translate this new-found power into direct political influence in opposition to that of the Senate. Another group, also from the equestrian order, was engaged in trade, banking, and manufacturing. Because so much capital had recently come to Rome, loans were readily available, and Rome soon became the financial capital of the Mediterranean. Although senators could not engage directly in such activities, their surplus capital was let out on loans, and both senators and equestrians invested heavily in land in many parts of Italy, especially in the south. The differences between senators and equestrians should not be exaggerated, as they both belonged to the same ruling class and shared common financial and economic interests. Nevertheless, the more actively involved groups of equestrians, along with the large new servile and freedman classes, had no traditionally established place in Roman society. Much of the turmoil and unrest of the second and first centuries B.C. involved the slow process by which these new groups carved out niches for themselves in the conservative Roman social structure. The changes did not come about easily.

The lower classes, which with the traditional patrician class had formed the basis for the society of the old Roman Republic, changed enormously during the second century B.C. In the past members of these classes were almost exclusively rural and fit into the social fabric of the state quite readily as clients of the nobility. As clients they could be either tenants on the great estates of the nobles or free, independent proprietor farmers. Either way, the social structure was geared to a very stable economy and the unchanging though complex relationship of client to patron. In addition to the clients there were others among the lower classes who from time immemorial had remained outside the clientage system but had never, at least in the country districts, constituted an important political force.

Despite their properly Roman dress and pose, the couple of the late first century B.C. are ex-slaves, as the accompanying inscription (not shown) indicates.

All this began to change rapidly under the new conditions of the second century B.C. First there were the enormous losses of the Punic Wars and subsequent wars of conquest in Spain, Greece, and North Africa. Peasants who in the early Republic could readily take time from their work to repel raiders or engage in summer campaigns in Italy now often found themselves assigned to quasipermanent armies in the provinces overseas. It could be years before they returned home, and their farms inevitably suffered. Throughout the first half of the second century B.C. a considerable body of men, estimated at close to 50,000, was annually in arms. But this was not the only force that transformed the peasant subsistence farmer of Italy.

With growing markets in Italy and the introduction of new cash crop farming techniques, peasants found themselves with yet another alternative to their previous economic modes of existence. With the capital acquired in the form of war booty, they could transform their holdings into a profitable enterprise based on slave labor, granted the right conditions of access to transportation and a good market. Probably not many peasants achieved this transformation, and intensively exploited farms were more likely to represent the investments of overcapitalized senators and members of the equestrian class. With much new land coming into production in various parts of Italy, especially in the north, there were new possibilities and new incentives to move, further weakening the old social system, which had been based on the long-term occupation of the same farmstead and the hereditary client-patron relationship. Withdrawal from this relationship, either by emigration or by its transformation, had not occurred on such a scale before. In addition, uprooted peasants and veterans flowed to Rome and to the towns of Italy, where they found partial employment in the great houses of the nobles and the huge (and growing) building programs and service industries, thus creating a true urban proletariat for the first time in Roman history.

THE GRACCHAN REVOLUTION: SOCIAL AND POLITICAL CONTEXT

Even before the major outbreak of violence in Rome in 133 B.C., there were numerous manifestations of unrest. Recruitment for wars in both Greece and Spain was a constant cause of discontent. There was a mutiny in the army in Greece in 198 B.C. and insubordination there eight years later; in 189 B.C. Manlius Vulso was forced to relax discipline and to bribe his troops to get them to fight. Aemilius Paullus, the victor over the Macedonians at Pydna, had great difficulty initially with his undisciplined troops, and they later complained loudly of the small amount of loot they received and even attempted to prevent his triumph. The Spanish war particularly caused major outbursts. Recruitment was difficult from the beginning, and discontent was chronic. Draft riots broke out in 151 and 138 B.C., and the tribunes, upon being appealed to by prospective recruits, imprisoned the consuls who were conducting the enlistment. Raw recruits were often sent out when veterans refused to serve.

SLAVE WOMEN

The following text from Cato the Censor's manual on cash crop farming suggests how a landowner, interested in making a profit, should make use of his slaves. It is interesting because it gives some insight into what rural slave women (and, no doubt, freeborn women also) might be expected to do. The advice is directed to the slave manager, the *vilicus*.

Slave housekeepers should attend to the following duties. If such a house-keeper has been given to you by your master as your wife, confine your attentions to her alone. Make her respect you. Restrain her extravagance. She should not visit her neighbors or other women often, either in the house or in her quarters. She is not to go out to eat or wander around the neighborhood. She is not to initiate religious worship herself or have others do it for her without the say-so of the master or mistress. . . . She must be clean and keep the farm-house clean and neat. Every night before she goes to bed she must clean the hearth. On the Kalends, Ides, and Nones of every month and on every holiday she is to hang a garland over the hearth and pray to the household gods (the *lares*) for abundance of food. She must keep food on hand for you and the slaves. She should keep a large flock of chickens and many eggs. She should have supplies of dried pears, sorb-apples, figs, and raisins; also, sorb-apples, pears, grapes and sparrow-apples preserved in *dolia* [large ceramic pots buried in the floor]. Grapes in grapeskins and fresh Praenestine nuts are to be kept in pitchers, likewise buried in the floor. Scantian apples are to be kept in *dolia* and other fruits that are usually preserved, as well as wild fruit. All these she should store carefully every year. She should also know how to make good flour and how to grind spelt [a grain] finely.

—Cato, *De Agricultura* 143

Attempts were made to cope with these indications of dissatisfaction, and new laws, the *leges Porciae,* so improved conditions of military service and guaranteed the personal rights of Roman citizens that by 150 B.C. the death penalty for citizens had fallen into general disuse. Secret ballots were introduced after mid-century for elections, trials, and legislation, indicating concessions to popular demands. The latent power of the tribunate was slowly awakened, and in an increasing number of instances tribunes were willing to use their awesome power on behalf of groups or individuals who felt that the state was not rendering them justice. Some nobles were not above appealing directly to the people and using tribunes on their own behalf. Scipio Aemilianus, the destroyer of Carthage, was twice elected consul and assigned provinces with the assistance of the people in flagrant defiance of custom and law. His close friend G. Laelius proposed an agrarian law that excited fierce opposition in the Senate and had to be withdrawn. Laws against corrupt electioneering practices (*leges de ambitu*) were enacted in 181 B.C. and 159 B.C., and by the end of the century there was a standing court responsible for the examination of such cases.

This again indicates the rising power of independent voters, free of the patron-client system. Attempts were made by conflicting interests to control the power of the tribunes by manipulating the state religion (*leges Aelia et Fufia*) and, at about the same time, to break the hold of the nobles on the priesthoods by the introduction of a law that would require the vacancies in the priestly colleges to be filled by popular election rather than by the traditional, careful process of co-option, which allowed the nobles to control these important offices closely.

All this points to the gradual breakdown of the old, predictable social bonds that had united the nobles in a common front and bound the masses to the upper classes by ties of patronage. With Rome's lower classes expanding as dispossessed small farmers and veterans migrated to the city and mixed with increasingly heterogeneous classes of slaves and freedmen, the social relations of the past based on kinship and personal relations gave way to new relationships based on common economic or political interests or mere propinquity. Votes, which in the past had belonged to a patron by ancient customs, began to be thought of as free and could be sought by anyone caring to solicit them. Laws against corrupt electioneering did not work, and sponsoring expensive spectacles or attaining significant military achievements became alternative ways to high office, although it was not until the next century that the most flagrant abuses were found in this area. The upper classes, the senators and the equestrians, gradually gave up their rigorous ideals of public service, and found substitutes in the increasingly attractive private realm, which offered the comforts of luxurious villas, expensive clothes and foods, and the satisfaction of their intellectual, aesthetic, and sensual appetites, which they had neither been permitted nor could afford to indulge previously. Taxes introduced by Cato on slaves with special skills or talents, ornaments, women's clothes, and other items failed to check incipient luxury, and similar taxes on statues and other *objets d'art* had no success.

The railings of Cato and other moralists against erecting public statues (including statues to women) and their general allegations of moral corruption point to a major reordering of values in the second century B.C. There was a fine dividing line between the acquisition of glory (*gloria*) in the service of the state and outright self-inflation. The values that had made Rome great in war and adversity led in peace to monstrous examples of egomania and self-indulgence.

Tiberius Gracchus: The Emergence of Popular Politics

The enormous social, cultural, and economic changes of the second century B.C. were channeled into an old constitutional framework designed for a city and territory a fraction of the size of the empire at that time. The political machinery of the Republic was called upon to perform tasks for which it had not been designed. In 133 B.C., when it was presented with major legislation that flew in the face of over half a century of development, it failed completely. The result was a division in the ruling class following roughly the lines of division that had begun to appear in Roman society at large.

EVENTS OF THE LATE REPUBLIC

Tribunate of Tiberius Gracchus	133 B.C.
Tribunate of Gaius Gracchus	123–122 B.C.
Jugurthine War: Marius in Africa	111–104 B.C.
War with the Cimbri and Teutons	105–101 B.C.
Social War	90–88 B.C.
Revolt of Mithridates VI	88 B.C.
Dictatorship of Sulla	82–79 B.C.
Slave revolt of Spartacus	73–71 B.C.
Pompey's campaign against the pirates	67 B.C.
Pompey's conquest of the east	66–62 B.C.
Conspiracy of Catiline	63 B.C.
Conquest of Gaul by Caesar	58–52 B.C.
Civil wars	
Battle of Pharsalus	48 B.C.
Assassination of Caesar	44 B.C.
Battle of Philippi	42 B.C.
Battle of Actium	31 B.C.

The agents of this change were not outsiders to the ruling elite who had emerged directly from the new forces at work in Roman society, as one might expect, but descendants of two of the most prominent families in the aristocracy, the Cornelii and Sempronii. On their mother's side Tiberius and Gaius Gracchus were the descendants of Scipio Africanus, and by marriage they were connected with the most distinguished families in Rome. Their brother-in-law was Scipio Aemilianus, who in 133 B.C. was commanding the Roman forces besieging Numantia in Spain. Tiberius was married to a daughter of Appius Claudius, who had been both consul and censor and now enjoyed the title of *princeps senatus,* the foremost man in the Senate; Gaius's father-in-law, Licinius Crassus, was soon to be *pontifex maximus* (chief priest) and consul. Conveniently, Crassus' own brother was consul in 133 B.C., the very year that the elder Gracchan brother, Tiberius, entered into the office of tribune of the plebs with a radical plan to transform the foundation of the Roman state.

In the view of Gracchus and his supporters, many of Rome's problems were caused by the steady disappearance of the peasant farmer, who was being pushed off the land by the rich landowners. This in turn was making it difficult to obtain adequate numbers of the right kind of recruits for the legions. Though partly correct, this analysis failed to do justice to the exceedingly complex problems of the second century B.C. or even to the reasons for the inadequate number of troops. By mid-century there was indeed a decline in the number of peasant farmers available for legionary service. There was also increasing reluctance on the part of many to serve in the new kinds of wars being fought, wars not so much for the defense of Rome as for the protection or acquisition of an overseas empire. Besides, there were new economic opportunities in Italy that made soldiering a less than attractive alternative.

Whatever the explanation for the decline in numbers on the draft rolls, the conclusion was still the same: there were too few recruits for the army. It was to solve this problem as well as to build up their faction's power that the Gracchans proposed their solution. The idea was to tap the huge resources of public land over which the state had sovereignty and put it to use by granting inalienable plots to individual farmers who, with their descendants, would be forever liable to legionary service while also politically obligated to the Gracchans for the original land grant. There would thus be much less opportunity for these new farm owners to escape the draft, by either administrative malfunction or deliberate avoidance. So, at a stroke, the regular supply of troops would be guaranteed or at least augmented. It was estimated, presumably, that the bait of land would outweigh the general reluctance of the peasantry to serve in the legions at all.

There were two difficulties with this program. The first was that the public land under discussion had already been parceled out in inextricable confusion between legal renters and leaseholders, who considered themselves de facto owners, and illegal squatters, both Roman and non-Roman, including in some instances the original possessors, who had never vacated their confiscated land. Tiberius and his supporters first had to clear these people off the land and somehow equitably settle a large number of complicated suits before initiating their own settlement program. Because many of the leaseholders as well as the squatters with doubtful title were well-to-do, this proposal was calculated to stir up a storm of protest, which in fact it did and continued to do long after Tiberius' death. The second problem, unanticipated at least in its size, was the large number of rural dwellers at the other end of the scale who were suddenly offered either outright grants of land, which meant an increase in their property holdings, or the confirmation of title to perhaps some of the land on which they were already squatting. Naturally, there were more of these than of the first group of well-to-do possessors, and when the law came up for the vote, Rome witnessed the extraordinary sight of masses of country people pouring into the city to support the measure. With excellent markets now available for farm products, the ownership of land or the extension of one's possessions was an irresistible attraction, which for the moment overcame the problems of time and distance normally deterring rural voters from traveling to Rome. The Gracchans now found themselves at the head of an unplanned democratic movement. When other members of the aristocratic coalition backed off, Tiberius went ahead with the law, which first required the unprecedented and ticklish removal from office of an opposing tribune.

With the passage of the law and the election of a commission (consisting of Tiberius, his brother, and his father-in-law!) to administer it, the rural mob withdrew from Rome, and political life began to return to normal. However, there arose the inevitable threat of the prosecution of Tiberius for illegality when his term of office was up on December 9, 133 B.C. To forestall this, Tiberius attempted to have himself reelected to the tribunate. Not having the rural voters at his command as he had earlier in the year, he turned to other groups that the upheavals of the second century B.C. had also brought to the surface. To the equestrian and better-off nonsenatorial classes he offered the bait of favorable legislation of various kinds, later developed by his brother Gaius. But these new supporters were either unable or perhaps not as willing as the rural crowds might have been to defend him against a determined assault by his opponents, who physically broke up the assembly on the day of the election and in the confusion killed him and many of his followers.

Gaius Gracchus

Ten years after Tiberius' death his brother Gaius, who in the intervening years had performed his required military service and acted as commissioner for the discharge of his brother's agrarian law, entered the same office of tribune of the plebeians as Tiberius had held in 133 B.C., but with a new strategy and a new plan of action. This time an appeal was made immediately to several of the newly emerging groups, though not to the rural crowds who had proved so difficult to handle in 133 B.C. The publicans were offered the contracts for collecting the taxes of Asia, which dwarfed all others in size, as well as large contracts for constructing roads, granaries, and public buildings. In addition, the equestrian class, to which the publicans belonged, was to be given control of the extortion court (*quaestio de repetundis*), which tried cases of senatorial misconduct in provincial administration and until then had been in the hands of the senators themselves. This new arrangement would ensure the publicans a high degree of political freedom from senatorial interference as they collected the taxes of Asia. Promises of large amounts of land in Africa for well-to-do groups in Italy, grain at a fixed price for the urban crowds, some laws governing military service and personal rights, Roman citizenship for the Latins, and Latin citizenship for the Italian allies were the baits offered to the final elements of the Gracchan coalition. This extraordinary combination of interests enabled Gaius to wield power for two consecutive years and enact most of the promised legislation, but in time the inevitable negative forces with which the Roman constitution abounded, in particular the tribunician veto, gradually dissolved the alliance. In 121 B.C. Gaius found himself out of office and without power. During an attempt by his opponents to abrogate one of his laws, he was killed along with many of his supporters, including the ex-consul Fulvius Flaccus, and his body was thrown into the Tiber.

The end of Gaius was another illustration of the Senate's inability to rule and of the power of the new forces within the Republic. Gaius' coalition of equestrians, well-to-do groups, and the urban crowds had enabled him to control the Tribal Assembly for a period, but it did not constitute the basis for a permanent government. At the same time, the very existence of this coalition of forces showed the paralysis of the old senatorial oligarchy and the ineffectiveness of its ruling techniques. Granted that in the end the Gracchan coalition disintegrated and the old system reasserted itself, it was nevertheless only a matter of time before new leaders would experiment with the emerging forces. The Gracchans also demonstrated the power of these new groups in Roman society, especially the rural voters, the equestrian class, and the urban crowds, and they also pointed out the discontent of the Italian allies.

By emphasizing the power of the equestrian class, they suggested that there was a basis of power other than landed wealth, and by inviting the rural voters, the Italians, and the urban crowds to involve themselves in the legal and political processes, they helped stimulate the political consciousness of these groups and encouraged them to hope for more than they had ever received. It was to these groups that politicians were to turn more and more. Eventually the revolution, culminating in the rise of Augustus, was to guarantee them a place in Roman society that the old aristocracy was unable to concede to them voluntarily. In a crisis the elite could generally depend on the loyalty of their mobs of retainers, clients, and like-minded friends to crush movements such as that of Tiberius Gracchus, but in the years after 133 B.C. the popular leaders (*populares*) learned how to counteract this power with mobs of their own. When this happened there was no alternative but to bring in the army, thus violating the most basic constitutional principle that soldiers should not cross the *pomerium,* the sacred boundary of the city.

FROM THE GRACCHI TO AUGUSTUS: THE ROMAN REVOLUTION

The century after the Gracchi was one of slow adjustment to the great issues they had raised. One by one, without following any particular program or plan, each issue was resolved in turn. The problem of recruitment for the legions was settled by Marius in 107 B.C., when he eliminated property qualifications for service. Conscription was henceforth reserved for emergency situations. The Italian allies fought for and won citizenship in a bloody war between 91 and 89 B.C. The Senate was expanded to twice its original size by Sulla, and most of the new members were drawn from the equestrians, thus hastening the unification of the senatorial and equestrian orders in the government of Augustus.

The most intractable problem was determining who was to rule and by what means. The old understanding about this had been undergoing change for years, but no new agreement had yet been worked out: Maintaining public order in times of political crisis remained insoluble until Augustus introduced a permanent militarized police force, the Praetorian and Urban Cohorts.

At issue was the question of the composition of the ruling oligarchy. In the past, by tacit agreement a handful of families had passed the chief offices of state among themselves, and the Senate, by exercising discipline over its own membership, had been able to maintain control of the political power of the state. Toward the end of the second century B.C., however, this discipline weakened, and political power began to fragment. Although the old coterie of nobles was still regularly able to place its candidates in high office, it was unable to dominate the Senate and the political process as it had in the past. When a new ruling oligarchy emerged almost a century later, most of the old families were gone, and their replacements came from a much wider social and geographic background. Numerically, too, the ruling class was larger than in the past. Nevertheless, the social viewpoints of the newcomers did not essentially differ from those of their predecessors. What had changed was the locus of political power and the source of senatorial discipline, both of which now lay outside the Senate in the hands of the new political head of the state, the emperor.

The Rise of Marius

The external enemies that Rome faced in the generation after the Gracchi were not major powers on the order of Carthage or the Hellenistic states of an earlier period. Rather, they were prestate peoples, and the wars of this time followed the pattern of the guerrilla campaigns that Rome had fought in Spain. They were long, protracted, and unconventional, the kind that easily brought out the ineptness and weakness of the senatorial system of command.

In 116 B.C. Rome became involved in the disputed succession to the throne of the African client-kingdom of Numidia. By 111 B.C. Roman troops were fully engaged, and for a number of years the war dragged on dismally, with Roman commanders unfavorably contrasting with their wily opponent, the Numidian king Jugurtha. Exasperated by repeated failure and the slow pace of the war, the people turned to Gaius Marius, a "new man" of equestrian background, who promised them a quick end. With great popular acclaim he was elected to the consulship for 107 B.C.

The problem Marius faced in the African war was a basic one of guerrilla warfare: he had to have considerably more troops than the enemy, but with another war in progress elsewhere and permanent manpower shortages, it seemed unlikely that he would be any more successful than his predecessors. However, by the simple but bold expedient of enrolling the propertyless in the legions, Marius resolved the manpower shortage. By 105 B.C. the war was over, just in time to allow him to return to Italy to bring another war, this time against the German tribes, to a successful conclusion.

Toward the end of the second century B.C. two large German tribes, the Cimbri and the Teutons, were driven from their homeland in Denmark by the flooding of the sea, and they began a slow march southward. Repulsed in the Danube area, they moved toward Italy and made their first contact with the Romans in 113 B.C. Thereafter they continued their wanderings, colliding with other Roman armies, which they easily overcame. A major defeat for the Romans at Arausio (Orange) in southern France in 105 B.C. brought on the possibility of an invasion of Italy. Once more the people turned to Marius and elected him consul for the next five years, flatly disregarding the law that prohibited such successive tenures of office. Immediately Marius set about a thoroughgoing reorganization and retraining of the legions, grouping the original 30 maniples in units of 10 each, called *cohorts,* each with about 500 men. The cohorts were further subdivided into 6 centuries. The corporate identity and continuity of the legions were fostered by giving each one its own "eagle," or standard.

Meanwhile the German tribes had once more postponed their invasion of Italy. When they did return, Marius defeated them separately, the Cimbri at Aix in southern France in 102 B.C. and the Teutons the following year near Vercellae in northern Italy.

Marius, Saturninus, and Veterans

After the German menace had been removed, the old system of senatorial rule began to reassert itself and Marius' power declined, but not before he engaged in yet another experiment.

Under the old draft system it was assumed that discharged soldiers would return to their farms and resume life where they had left off, but what was to be done with Marius' propertyless veterans, who were now an officially acknowledged part of the army? Somehow they had to be cared for, and the easiest solution seemed to be to make them land assignments. For this purpose Marius aligned himself with the ambitious tribune L. Appuleius Saturninus and pushed for the enactment of a land law. Passage did not come easily, however, and in the impasse Marius brought his veterans into the legislative assembly and secured passage by force, thus writing yet another chapter in Roman history (100 B.C.). Although Tiberius Gracchus had used the rural voters and the city mob to pass his measures, and his brother had tried to forge an alliance of the equestrians and the city people, it was not until Marius that the final step of combining tribunes, military commanders, and veterans was taken. It was too effective a combination to be ignored in the future. However, Marius was no revolutionary, and a little later, when Saturninus resorted to violence in furthering his own ambitions, Marius abandoned him, and Saturninus was killed in a riot.

The Social War

The issue of citizenship for the Italian allies appears to have gone underground in the years after Gaius Gracchus, but in 91 B.C. it resurfaced violently. In the intervening years there had been no letup in the exploitation by Romans of public land all over Italy, and in general the Italians felt that they were getting less than their share of the spoils of conquest. They served in the army and fought Rome's wars but were losing out in the changed conditions of the second and first centuries B.C. When the issue of the bestowal of citizenship was raised by the tribune M. Livius Drusus in 91 B.C. but defeated by Roman shortsightedness, the Italians rose in revolt and set up an independent state, which they called Italia, with its capital at Corfinium in central Italy.

The so-called Social War was bitterly contested and not fully ended until as late as 80 B.C., but the main issues were resolved by grants of citizenship in 90 B.C. and 89 B.C. to cities that had not revolted and to individuals who gave up the revolt and surrendered. At last, all of Italy south of the Po was united under a single constitution and a single political system. Even then, however, the oligarchy at Rome tried

Social War propaganda of the allies: A soldier, with a bull representing Italy beside him, tramples a Roman standard. On other coin issues of the allies the bull is shown goring the Roman wolf.

to avoid the political implications of the extension of citizenship by preventing the distribution of the new citizens throughout the tribes for a number of years.

Sulla

War continued to offer opportunities to the able and ambitious among the nobility, and the dominant figures of the next half-century—Sulla, Pompey, Crassus, and Caesar—all rose to prominence through their generalship and their ability to convert success on the battlefield into political power in Rome.

L. Cornelius Sulla had served under Marius in the war against Jugurtha and had recently distinguished himself again in the Social War. He was elected consul for 88 B.C. Now another opportunity presented itself. In the east the kingdom of Pontus had expanded under a series of energetic rulers and had come into conflict with Roman client-kings in the area. This escalated into a major conflict when the king of Pontus, Mithridates VI, invaded the Roman province of Asia in 88 B.C. and massacred, it is said, 80,000 resident Romans and Italians.

The command of the war against Mithridates went to Sulla but was challenged by Marius, who, in collusion with the tribune P. Sulpicius Rufus, had himself designated commander. Just as Marius had once gone to the then revolutionary extent of using his veterans to force the passage of a land law, Sulla now simply marched his troops on Rome, drove out Marius, killed Sulpicius, and invalidated his laws. After enacting some new provisions, he left for the east.

Advancing from Asia, Mithridates' forces crossed into Greece but were driven out by Sulla after a series of battles. By 85 B.C. Mithridates was ready to negotiate, and terms were worked out whereby he agreed to vacate the province of Asia and pay an indemnity. Two years later Sulla was back in Italy, ready to reestablish his political power, which had collapsed in the interim. With his veteran army and the assistance of a number of young nobles who rallied to him, including M. Licinius Crassus and Cn. Pompeius (Pompey), Sulla routed his opponents and initiated a reign of terror, showing himself once again an apt pupil of the violent politicians who had preceded him. To raise money and eliminate his political opponents, he hit upon a novel method of murder, the proscription list, which gave the names of his enemies together with the prices he was willing to pay for their deaths. About 200 senators and over 1,600 equestrians perished in these proscriptions, and from the proceeds of their estates Sulla was able to pay his troops and then settle down without fear of opposition to the task of reforming the constitution.

As dictator from 82 B.C. to 79 B.C., Sulla pushed through a series of reforms intended to introduce a measure of order to the chaos of recent political life at Rome. He curtailed the power of the tribunate, increased the number of quaestors and praetors, and established a rigid schedule according to which the different magistracies were to be held. He attempted to control provincial governors, whose power, like that of the tribunes in Rome, had grown and was increasingly attractive to ambitious individuals, by ruling that they should not start wars on their own or march their troops across the boundaries of their provinces.

His most important and lasting change was his reform of the Senate, whose numbers had been halved by his own massacres and the battles with the supporters of Marius. To the surviving 150 or so members he added about 400, mostly from the equestrian order. Henceforth, the composition of the Senate was radically altered. As a class it was now considerably broadened, and if the old families still continued to dominate the high offices, it was not in the coherent fashion of the past, and new men began to make their appearance in the lower magistracies. It is against the background of this much enlarged Senate that the events from Sulla to Caesar must be viewed. The details of the wars that fill this period are not nearly as important as the rapid development of events in the Roman political system.

Pompey

After Sulla's death in 78 B.C., wars continued to offer new opportunities to ambitious generals, and the Senate demonstrated again and again its inability to control them. It was now too unwieldy and its membership too diffuse to exercise the kind of tight, coherent action necessary to restrain the power of the newly emerging dynasts Pompey, Crassus, and Caesar.

Pompey, one of Sulla's generals, was the first to demonstrate this weakness. When confronted with a series of revolts in Italy and Spain, he maneuvered the Senate into giving him a series of special high commands (propraetorian and proconsular), even though he was still not a member of that body. Crassus, another of Sulla's generals, enhanced his reputation by ending the great slave revolt of Spartacus in 71 B.C., and together with Pompey he was able to procure his election to the consulship for 70 B.C. Promptly both men saw to the restoration of the tribunate and set about removing what was left of Sulla's reforms.

Three years later a law was proposed to give Pompey a special command with unlimited power (*imperium infinitum*) against the pirates whose depredations had grown ever since Rome had curtailed the independent maritime power of Rhodes. The command was so large and so unusual that it provoked a storm of protest in the Senate, where only Julius Caesar, who had been elected to the quaestorship just two years earlier, spoke on its behalf. The bill (*lex Gabinia*) was finally passed in scenes of great disorder by the popular assembly, and Pompey entered his command. By means of excellent organization of his resources, he cleared up the pirate menace in three months and was soon peacefully settling the remnants of their forces on vacant land in Cilicia.

In 66 B.C. another opportunity presented itself. The war with Mithridates had been revived, but after initial successes under L. Licinius Lucullus, it was not going well. It was now proposed that Pompey finish it off. Under the terms of the Manilian law, supported again by Caesar and by the "new man," Cicero, Pompey was given command of the provinces of Cilicia, Bithynia, and Pontus and of the war against Mithridates. Between 66 and 62 B.C. Pompey swept through the east, first defeating Mithridates and driving him to flight, then continuing into Armenia and from there back to Syria and into Palestine, where he settled a dispute over the throne of Judaea. Single-handedly, he redrew the map of the eastern Mediterranean, founding cities and making provinces and treaties with client-kings. In the process, he increased Rome's annual income by 70 percent.

Pompey, Crassus, and Caesar

In Italy, meanwhile, Cicero reached the pinnacle of his career when, as consul in 63 B.C., he suppressed a revolt of a group of disgruntled nobles led by L. Sergius Catilina. In anticipation of Pompey's return, Crassus continued to build up his political strength and sponsored the promising career of Julius Caesar. Others also claimed Crassus' support, such as P. Clodius, whose alleged affair with Caesar's wife led to her divorce and Caesar's famous comment about the necessity of his wife's being above suspicion.

The return of Pompey gave new impetus to Caesar's advance. Rebuffed by the Senate in his attempt to have his eastern settlements approved and land appropriated for his veterans, Pompey turned first to a tribune for help and, failing there, to Caesar, one of the consular candidates for 59 B.C. Crassus also backed Caesar, and with the combined support of Crassus and Pompey, Caesar was elected consul and immediately saw to the passage of the measures desired by his allies. This alliance is sometimes, though inaccurately, called the First Triumvirate. The following year

Caesar went off to his province, Gaul, where he remained for the next seven years. By the end of this period he had annexed for the empire a gigantic new stretch of territory, reaching from the Pyrenees and the Atlantic coast to the Rhine. The resources of this territory, both in manpower and in money, constituted the foundation of what amounted to an independent kingdom.

Although Caesar's command was the most prolonged and the most spectacular, the other members of the alliance also had their military commands during this period. Crassus and Pompey were consuls again in 55 B.C. and were granted the provinces of Syria and Spain, respectively, for five years. The three men thus had control over most of the military resources of the empire.

At the end of 55 B.C. Crassus went off to Syria in an attempt to refurbish his military reputation, but two years later he was killed by the Parthians at the disastrous battle of Carrhae. This event, coupled with the death in 54 B.C. of Pompey's wife, Caesar's daughter Julia, led to the disintegration of the alliance. Rome was left with two dominant figures, one of whom was putting the ruthless finishing touches to one of Rome's most successful and profitable imperialistic ventures. Over a two-year period communication between the two men gradually broke down, until finally Caesar's enemies maneuvered the Senate into declaring him a public enemy and prevailing upon Pompey to "save the Republic."

Clodius and His Gangs

Another destabilizing influence worked within the city of Rome itself. A shaky consensus among the elite allowed it to put down the Gracchan movements and the sedition of Saturninus, but in each case the elite lost some of its authority and prestige. After every manifestation of popular unrest was crushed with violence, its ability to intimidate declined. The self-interested consensus of the elite did not lead to, or reflect, a consensus in the community at large. This was especially true of the city of Rome, with its increasingly large mixed population of freeborn, freedmen, slaves, and immigrants from all over Italy and the Mediterranean. The densely packed urban population of Rome, reaching nearly a million by the late Republic, was no longer governed by the old social rules. These rules had traditionally depended on discipline created by regular military service, the responsibilities of farm ownership, and the acknowledgment of the authority (*auctoritas*) of the magistrates and the upper classes in general. Now recruitment for the legions took place largely in rural areas; farms had been lost and the ties of clientage were weakened. Other forms of association, primitive trade unions, fraternal associations, and burial societies (*collegia*) began to assume more and more significance for the urban population. The *collegia*, which had ancient roots, also taught the ordinary people of Rome the usefulness of informal, low-level organizational techniques. These associations dovetailed with the long-established local neighborhood associations of the city, the *vici*. The existence of a dependable subsidized grain supply from the time of Gaius Gracchus also contributed to the growing independence of the *plebs urbana,* the urban people, or the *plebs sordida,* as the upper classes called them. The proletariat (*proletarii,* the lowest census category) should not be confusesd with the *plebs urbana* of which it was a part. The *plebs urbana* contained a much wider spectrum of people.

Nevertheless, it took the extraordinary leadership of the aristocratic Publius Clodius to turn the *collegia, operae* (gangs), *tabernarii* (shopkeepers), and *opifices* (artisans) of Rome into an effective political force. What his goals were beyond his desire for revenge against Cicero, with whom he had a vendetta and whom he succeeded in having exiled, are still unclear, and may well have been unclear to Clodius himself. His gangs could shut down the normal functions of government and intimidate the magistrates. Even the great dynasts Pompey and Caesar had to learn to take Clodius into account. Clodius first opposed Pompey, but then reversed himself and worked with the dynasts to bring about the joint consulship of Pompey and Crassus in 55 B.C. Gridlock later in the decade between Pompey and Caesar played into Clodius' hands and led to further chaos in the streets.

Even after Clodius' death in a confrontation with a gang organized by the oligarchs, the now politicized *plebs urbana* continued to act independently under new leaders. In a final confession of weakness, and in violation of the strongest constitutional traditions of the free state, armed troops were brought into the city to put down the *plebs* and maintain order. The problem of an independent minded, violent-prone urban population was a problem left to be solved by Augustus and his successors.

The Civil Wars

The civil war that followed the breakdown of relations betwen Caesar, Pompey, and the Senate lased from 49 B.C. to 45 B.C. Pompey was defeated at Pharsalus in Greece in 48 B.C. and was murdered shortly afterward while seeking refuge in Egypt. There were two other major engagements, at Thapsus in Africa and Munda in Spain, and in 45 B.C. Caesar returned triumphantly to Rome. There were no proscriptions, and Caesar assiduously extended clemency to his defeated foes.

Like Sulla, Caesar added new members to the again depleted Senate, expanding its numbers from 600 to 900. At the same time, he made it clear that the traditions of rule of the Republic were at an end. Early in 44 B.C. he had himself declared Perpetual Dictator and commented that Sulla had committed a major political blunder when he resigned the dictatorship in 79 B.C. The Ides of March soon followed.

Between 47 B.C. and 44 B.C. Caesar had initiated a huge number of programs, many of which were incomplete at the time of his death. He tackled and solved, at least temporarily, the problem of debt, reformed the calendar, established colonies for his veterans, and initiated an enormous building program at Rome. There were also many legal and constitutional enactments. On the Ides of March in 44 B.C., while making preparations for the war against Parthia to revenge Carrhae and the death of Crassus, Caesar was struck down by a group of senatorial assassins led by M. Junius Brutus and C. Cassius Longinus. Almost immediately, a whole new round of civil wars broke out.

Perhaps Caesar's most important legacy was his selection of his sister Julia's grandson, Gaius Octavius, as his heir. Octavius was adopted into Caesar's family with the name of G. Julius Caesar Octavianus—Octavian for short. At the time it looked like a bad choice. Octavian was only 18 and sickly, yet he quickly created a place for himself beside Caesar's more experienced officers. In an involved series of actions, Caesar's generals Antony and Lepidus, together with Octavian, established themselves as a ruling triumvirate. After purging their enemies in a bloody proscription that included Cicero, they divided the Roman world among them. Brutus and Cassius were eliminated in battle at Philippi in 42 B.C., and thereafter the triumvirs ruled in an uneasy alliance. Lepidus was dropped in 36 B.C., and the two remaining partners inevitably began to drift apart.

While Octavian consolidated his hold on Italy and the west, Antony, now managing Roman affairs in the east, conducted an unsuccessful campaign against the Parthians. On his return he began to depend more and more on the resources of Egypt as well as on its capable ruler, Cleopatra. Using Antony's relations with Cleopatra as a weapon, Octavian launched a successful campaign to turn popular opinion against him, the most damaging accusation being that Antony wanted to transfer the capital of the empire to Alexandria. Matters finally came to a head in 31 B.C., when Octavian formally declared war against Cleopatra; officially this was not to be another civil war but a war against a foreign enemy. At Actium in Greece, Antony and Cleopatra were decisively beaten and subsequently committed suicide. The civil wars were over, and Octavian, or Augustus, as he is better known to us, was left alone on stage.

THE FALL OF THE ROMAN REPUBLIC

The fall of the Roman Republic is as vast and complicated a subject as the fall of the Roman Empire, although not nearly as well known. In many respects it is also a more absorbing story because the gradual transition from the free institutions of the Republic to those of the autocracy has many more contemporary parallels than the invasion of the Empire by the northern barbarians.

The collapse of the Republic resulted from the complicated interaction of a large number of factors, some acting in an immediate and direct way, others in a less obvious fashion. It is easy enough to list the suspected causes but much more difficult to explain how they are related or to weigh their individual importance.

There can be no doubt that the changes in the wealth, sophistication, education, and values of the upper classes had an important bearing on the transition from Republic to Empire. So did the revolutions in agriculture, finance, and commerce that accompanied Rome's rise to world power. But there were other factors. The citizenship expanded enormously, and the Senate was first doubled by Sulla, then increased again by Caesar. There were problems with debt, the courts, and relations between the classes, as well as with raising troops and maintaining order in Rome

---

CICERO'S VIEW OF THE ROMAN ELITE

Our leading men think they have transcended the summit of human ambition when the bearded mullets in their fish ponds eat out of their hands—while they meanwhile let everything else go to pieces.

—*Letters to Atticus*, 2.1

---

and the Italian countryside. Lack of discipline and irresponsibility were increasing in all segments of society.

The ancients inclined toward moral explanations for the collapse, believing that the decadence, greed, and ambition at all levels of Roman society were responsible, whereas modern investigators tend to regard these factors as superficial manifestations of deeper ills and look for the causes in political, social, and economic factors.

The main outline of events is clear enough. From the mid–second century B.C. there was an increasing tendency toward political fragmentation in the ruling classes and consequent dissipation of power. The Senate gradually lost political control of the state and never regained it. Although the fall of the Republic had important social underpinnings, it was essentially a political, not a social, revolution.

Rome's Military Commitment and Its Effects

Rome's rise to power in the Mediterranean did not involve it in a great deal of direct administration and economic exploitation, although there was some of both. What it did commit Rome to in a major way, however, was an unending military defense of its acquisitions. Rome never gave up its conquests or forgot its legacies, even though at times it may have been slow to exploit them, as in the case of Cyrene, which was not organized as a province until 20 years after it had been bequeathed to Rome by its ruler.

Rome's commitment to maintaining peace in the Mediterranean created a major problem because it demanded standing armies, and these in turn required either large numbers of draftees who could be quickly rotated in and out of the legions or long-term enlisted men. Because Rome was committed to fulfilling its manpower needs from the lists of the property owners, the second alternative was ruled out. Whether because of a decline in the number of property owners or because of increasing resistance to military service, fulfilling the needs of the standing armies— let alone supplying emergency levies—by the old method was becoming more and more difficult.

In retrospect this can be seen to have had some advantages. The reluctance (or unavailability) of draftees to fight long wars at great distances from Rome put some limitations on glory-seeking generals and even on the ambitions of the Senate and the people of Rome. After Marius, however, there was no such restriction: the draft still operated but no longer restrained commanders, and the more charismatic could always attract the numbers of soldiers they needed. The Senate, which had controlled the draft in the past, thus lost control of the state's manpower reserves, and power shifted to legions where volunteers made up a majority of the troops. Not that these soldiers were conscious revolutionaries. There was no rebellion of the proletariat in the legions against the state. Rather, the landless and the poor now had a role and an option. They could choose to fight or not to fight, and they could select the leader for whom they would fight. The rest lay with the commanders.

Had the Mediterranean of the late Republic been a naturally peaceful area, there probably would have been no fall at all or at the most a gradual transformation. However, the constant wars from the time of Marius, coupled with the weakened condition of the Senate, gave repeated opportunities to ambitious and able commanders, and as long as the wars went on, there was no one to restrain them. In peacetime the situation was somewhat different, but then the more successful could combine their resources—as Pompey, Crassus, and Caesar did in 60–59 B.C.—at which point their will was irresistible. The power of commanders tended to increase, not decrease. Successive years as consul or proconsul meant years of continuous patronage. Marius was consul five times in a row from 104 to 100 B.C., Sulla held the *imperium* from 88 to 79 B.C., and Caesar had nine straight years in Gaul. With these commands came the power to select and appoint officers, dispense the funds assigned to the war, and divide the booty. Nor was there any need for these generals to share their glory or power with anyone other than those with whom they chose to share it. The age of Marius, Sulla, Pompey, and Caesar was an age of individualists who were restricted only by their vision of what and how much they wanted. In a sense this was the way it had to be. The old restraints had been swept away by Rome's commitment to maintaining order in the Mediterranean, and if the old system had been found wanting, how else was a new one to be found except by experimentation?

The New Roman Society

So far emphasis has been placed on the immediate effects of Rome's military commitment, but at the same time other major developments presented yet another series of opportunities to Rome's new leaders.

The Social War ended an old problem by eliminating de jure discrimination against the Italian allies, and the way was now open for Rome and Italy to merge. The problem was how to fit the Italians, especially the upper classes, into the existing Roman system. If Rome had been more open-handed earlier or if the infusion of the Italians had occurred at a less chaotic time, the Senate might have been able to cope with the influx, but it needed time, and now there was no time left. The old aristocracy, slowly failing over the years, was not able to deal with the large number of newcomers, and its general attitude of social superiority must have been as grating to the Italians as it had been to rising new men at any time in Rome's past. It was therefore left to the individual Roman noble to make what use he chose of the results of the Social War and the reforms of Sulla. Caesar, who began his career later than the other dynasts, had the good fortune and the political astuteness to develop the Italian connection to the fullest.

The problem of the equestrians had largely been solved by Sulla's changes and the events that followed his death. After 70 B.C., for example, no more was heard of the composition of the courts, which had been a standing battle since the time of Gaius Gracchus. Even the economic distinction between the equestrians and the Senate began to disappear as it became increasingly acceptable for senators to participate as silent partners in the public contracts of the state. These changes removed the edge from the struggle between the two orders, and by the end of the Republic a new equestrian-senatorial government was in the making. Still, the oligarchs were as incapable of coping with the flood of new men from the equestrian order as they were with the Italians. It took someone like Caesar, who surrounded himself with equestrians, or his adopted son and heir, Octavian, who was of equestrian stock on his father's side, to appreciate the opportunities here. Thus, of all the dynasts, only Caesar had the luck and the ability to put together a powerful coalition of the new forces of the Italian municipalities, the equestrian class, the new senatorial houses, the people, and the common soldiers. This coalition constituted the foundation for the new state created by Octavian.

Literature and Society

Paralleling and complementing the evolution of a new political order was a cultural revolution of equally significant proportions. In the chaotic years between the Gracchi and Augustus, Rome was transformed from a provincial city-state into the sophisticated cosmopolitan capital of a world empire. Italy and Rome overflowed with Greek works of art, and philosophers, literary figures, doctors, architects, and rhetoricians from the east catered to the growing educational needs and luxurious tastes of the new ruling classes.

Yet while Rome was rising to new levels of cultural sophistication, its social cohesiveness was disintegrating. In the past Romans had been tied to one another by legally weak but morally powerful bonds of kinship, patronage, friendship, and duty, but the newly emerging society was fragmented. Remnants of the old patriciate clung to their old privileges, whereas elements of a new imperial nobility that included such diverse groups as freedmen, equestrians, and military men strove to establish their places in society. Others sought only to avoid political entanglements and enjoy their riches in peace and quiet. Women made independent by the decline of the rigid patriarchal system acquired riches and education and moved with freedom at the highest levels of society. As each of these social groupings evolved and developed its own codes of behavior, the simple consensus of the past dissolved, and the easy

LIBERATED WOMEN OF THE LATE REPUBLIC

In the last centuries of the Republic upper-class Roman women gained a considerable amount of independence, both personally and over their property. Lower-class women also achieved a certain measure of independence and found careers as actresses, dancers, and musicians, and in less reputable occupations. After the murder of Caesar, his avengers needed money to pursue their campaign against the assassins, Brutus and Cassius. First the Triumvirs proscribed the property of their enemies, but when they found they were still short, they decided on a different tactic. Note the important role played by the people.

The Triumvirs addressed the people on this subject and published an edict requiring 1400 of the richest women to make a valuation of their property, and to furnish for the service of the war an amount the triumvirs would see fit. . . .

The women decided to approach the women-folk of the Triumvirs. They got a hearing from the sister of Octavian [the future Augustus] and the mother of Antony, but they were repulsed from the doors of Fulvia, the wife of Antony, whose rudeness they could scarcely endure. They then forced their way to the tribunal of the Triumvirs in the Forum, the people and the guards dividing to let them pass. There, through Hortensia, whom they had delegated as their representative, they spoke as follows:

"As befitted women of our rank addressing a petition to you, we had recourse first to the women of your households. But having been treated with discourtesy by Fulvia, we have been driven to come to you in person publicly. You have already deprived us of our fathers, our sons, our husbands, and our brothers, whom you accused of having wronged you. If you take away our property also you reduce us to a condition unbecoming our status, our manners and our gender. If we have done you wrong, as you say our husbands have, proscribe us as you do them. But if we women have not voted any of you public enemies, have not torn down your houses, destroyed your army, or led one against you; if we have not hindered you in obtaining offices and honors—why do we share the penalty when we did not share the guilt?

"Why should we pay taxes when we have no part in the honors, the commands, the politics, for which you fight against others with such dreadful results? 'Because this is a time of war,' do you say? When have there not been wars, and when have taxes ever been imposed on women, who are exempted by their gender among all humankind? . . ."

While Hortensia was giving her speech the Triumvirs were angry that women should dare to speak publicly while the men were silent, and that they should demand reasons for their acts from the magistrates. . . . They ordered the lictors to drive them away from the tribunal, which they proceeded to do until cries were raised by the people outside. Then the lictors stopped and the Triumvirs said they would postpone consideration of the matter until the next day.

On the following day they reduced the number of women who were to present a valuation of their property from 1400 to 400, and decreed that all individuals who possessed more than 100,000 drachmae, both citizens and strangers, freedmen and priests, men of all nationalities without a single exception . . . should lend them at interest a fiftieth part of their property and contribute one year's income to the war expenses.

—Appian, *Civil Wars*, 4.32–34. Based on the translation of Horace White (London, 1893).

These sensitively carved portrait gems show the familiarity of the Romans of the first century B.C. with the wide range of Greek portrait styles. From the left: Cicero (probably), Caesar, and the young Octavian.

identification of society and the state, which had been characteristic of the Republic, vanished.

It was in the context of this rapidly changing society that Roman literature came of age. In part this was due to the emergence of the kind of un-Roman, apolitical leisurely class just mentioned, but the traditional devotion of the Roman upper classes to a life of public service, despite its weakening, also had a hand in the final shaping of Latin literature.

As the ruling class of the Republic fragmented, the Senate gradually ceased to be the place where the most important decisions were made. Increasingly, public issues were aired and settled in army camps, the courts, the assemblies, and even the campaign trail. In such an environment the ability to communicate and persuade was paramount, and it was in the practice of public oratory that Latin prose was molded. New men such as Cicero rose on the strength of their rhetorical ability, and descendants of the old nobility quickly learned that the mastery of words could speed their advance through the *cursus honorum*. The ability to write also began to be recognized as a significant political weapon. Although in the second century B.C. Cato had shown what could be done with the publication of speeches, it was not until the time of the Gracchi and the years that followed that the full potential of the written word was realized. Speeches as well as propagandizing autobiographies and biographies were published by major figures to justify and further their careers. An enlarged reading public encouraged popularizers to churn out undependable though readable histories of Rome from the time of its founding down to their own time. Simultaneously, the quality of the theater, which had been high in the previous century, declined catastrophically, as low-grade farce and mime drove out tragedy and comedy. Purely personal poetry, epigrams, love elegies, and lyrics evolved to reach extraordinary heights in the emotionally charged poems of Catullus. Under Augustus this tendency to Hellenistic-style private literature was challenged momentarily, and in Virgil, Horace, and Livy the public and private realms were as perfectly blended as they were ever to be in the Rome of the late Republic.

Cicero   Cicero, whose career coincided with the decline of the Republic, is the best known but by no means the only example of a public figure whose great literary talents were combined with a vigorous career of public service. A man from the new Italian municipal aristocracy, he lacked most of the normally essential prerequisites for advancement in Rome, such as family connections and military ability. His awesome oratorical and literary talents compensated for these deficiencies and enabled him to play an important political role throughout most of the declining years of the Republic. Initially his talents were fostered in the courts and on the campaign trail and then before assemblies and in the Senate. It was his ear for the music of Latin and his sense of its rhythms that gave the language a form and fitted it as a vehicle of thought and expression for all time. Like those of so many of the public figures of his age, his writings cover an extraordinary range of subjects and literary genres, from poetry to antiquarian topics and from chatty letters to dignified orations. More than any other body of literature, his writings bring to life the concerns, personalities, and emotional conflicts of the late Republic. For 40 years he produced an unfailing flow of speeches, philosophical works, letters, and technical tracts. No other figure of the ancient world revealed so much of his personality as Cicero. We know of his affection for his family and his unceasing concern for the Republic, but also of his vindictiveness, duplicity, and extraordinary conceit. Of course, he was not the only master of oratory or prose. Caesar, for example, practiced a very effective but much plainer variety of oratory, and his terse written reports to the Senate from Gaul, the *Commentaries,* are masterpieces of both Latin literature and political astuteness. It is with Cicero, however, that one gets the full flavor of the age.

History and Propaganda   The higher value placed on public over private careers had the effect of bending Roman literary production to fit the political needs of factions and would-be leaders. The example of Cato has already been mentioned, but it was left to G. Fannius, the one-time friend of Gaius Gracchus, to show how effectively history could be put to the uses of a clique. His account of the events of the Gracchan revolution, written from the viewpoint of the ruling oligarchy and exculpating the murderers of the Gracchi, was so effective in swamping his opponents' version that it became the accepted view of those turbulent times. Contemporary history of this kind merged with autobiography and pure propaganda in the early part of the first century B.C., when a host of public figures wrote accounts of their careers. Rutilius Rufus, an embittered ex-governor who had been exiled after a notoriously unjust trial, wrote an apologia defending his actions. Marius and Sulla produced self-congratulatory accounts of their careers and were imitated by others, including Julius Caesar and Augustus. Sulla's biased memoirs were incorporated into the equally biased work of Cornelius Sisenna, who wrote of the Social War (90–88 B.C.)

and the civil wars that followed. Sallust, a supporter of Caesar, picked up where Sisenna left off. Except for fragments, both works have perished, but two of Sallust's monographs, on the Jugurthine War and the conspiracy of Catiline, have survived. His venomous portrait of the times, combined with Cicero's and the poet Catullus' images of public and private corruption, have left an indelible, if distorted, impression of the age.

Although the active politicians concentrated their literary efforts on contemporary history and propaganda tracts, the work of writing histories in the traditional annalistic or year-by-year style passed into the hands of popularizers and romanticizers such as Claudius Quadrigarius and Valerius Antias. With an eye primarily on the demands of a public more interested in entertainment than strict truth, these writers unscrupulously twisted facts and copiously invented material wherever their sources failed them. Fortunately, there was another, more serious side to the writing of history. The past had always been grist for the propaganda mills of Rome, and in an age of increasing historical awareness more people became conscious of the obscurity and archaic character of many Roman customs, religious rituals, place names, and the like. Learned antiquarians turned their attention to these matters, and produced crabbed commentaries on such questions as how Rome acquired its name and the significance of the various place names and ancient festivals. The great master of this field in the first century B.C. was M. Terentius Varro, whom Caesar appointed to head Rome's first public library. From his pen came a ceaseless flow of books on Roman antiquities and such related topics as linguistics and law, although he also wrote on estate management, philosophy, and even mathematics and astronomy. Dozens of other antiquarians and encyclopedists struggled to make sense of what had once been accepted without query and to sum up their findings in publications. Even the busy Cicero was stimulated to write a history of oratory, and Caesar wrote on astronomy and grammar.

In the next generation Roman historical writing reached maturity in the great account of the rise of Rome by Livy. Unlike its predecessors, which for the most part exist only as fragments cited by other writers, considerable segments of the work of Livy have survived.

Coming at the end of a long period of development, Livy had the advantage of being able to make use of the works of the earlier historians as well as the research of the antiquarians. Candidly moralistic, Livy invited the reader

> to examine closely the lives, the customs, the kinds of men and the means they used in politics and war to first win and then retain our empire; next to see how, with discipline gradually weakening, morals at first became as it were discordant; then how they began to disintegrate rapidly and finally collapse in ruin until we come to our own times when we can neither endure our vices nor accept the remedies needed to cure them. The study of history is a healthy and worthwhile activity. It presents to the reader a huge variety of models to be followed or avoided, and it does so with complete clarity. It works equally well for the individual and for the state.[2]

[2]Livy, "Preface," *Book 1*, 396.

Understandably, his history is full of edifying examples of virtue and vice, and despite his great narrative ability, his characters tend to become idealized and somewhat wooden. Nevertheless, Livy's scope and his capacity for sustained narrative far outdistanced the literary talents of his predecessors, and his work soon replaced theirs.

Poetry and the Ideals of Public Service   The poets of the late Republic were much influenced by Alexandrian assumptions about what could and could not be attempted in poetry. Long epics on mythical or historical subjects were considered impossible, whereas short, highly polished poems, full of learned allusions, were much in vogue. Epigrams, pastoral idylls, mythical sketches, and short, artificial epics were characteristic of this kind of literature. Typically, C. Helvidius Cinna, one of the most important proponents of these views at Rome, worked for nine years on the production of his masterpiece, the *Zmyrna,* of which, ironically, only three lines survive. On the other hand, Catullus raised lyric poetry to heights of unaffected passion in his addresses to Lesbia. Having fallen in love with the sophisticated wife of a Roman aristocrat, he soon discovered she had no interest in the kind of complicated love he entertained for her. Spurned, he was forced to come to terms with his own contradictory feelings:

> I hate I love—don't ask why;
> I do not know. I only feel it and I'm tormented.[3]

Like Sappho 500 years earlier, he turned to the gods for help:

> O gods if you have any pity or help anyone at death,
> Look at me: if I have lived a decent life
> Snatch this awful curse from me.
> It creeps from limb to limb, numbing them,
> Driving out all joy from my soul.
> I do not ask that my beloved return to me
> Nor what cannot be, that she be chaste,
> But only to be well again, cured of this hideous disease.
> O gods, do this for my love of you.[4]

Unlike the Greeks, who wrote of the effects of love in women, Catullus described his own feelings, and where the literary language failed him he was bold enough to introduce slang and colloquial idioms. A similarly personal attitude, though in a completely different context, was brought by Lucretius to an unlikely subject, the materialistic philosophy of Epicurus. Filled with a missionary zeal to free men from the fear of the gods and death, Lucretius set out in magnificent verse form his own interpretation of Epicurus' views. Where Catullus was fashionable, witty, sensuous, and ultimately successful only in short verse, Lucretius was serious and dignified, and his life's work was devoted to the production of one long poem. In the next generation

[3]Catullus, *Poems,* no. 85.
[4]Ibid., no. 76.

Tibullus and Propertius carried on the now highly fashionable tradition of concern with affairs of the heart rather than those of the state. Tibullus could proclaim, in un-Roman fashion, that although he hated war, he was a "good general and soldier in the service of love," and Propertius could say that "the conquest of people is worth nothing in comparison to love." All these figures reflect an age in which the horizons of the ruling classes were broadening culturally while contracting politically. Shifting from a preoccupation with the competitive aspects of political life, they discovered the joys of leisure, wealth, and social prominence. As the ferocity of the political arena intensified, the attractions of the private life of luxury grew more enticing.

Virgil and Horace   The old traditions were not entirely moribund, however, and in Virgil's great epic, the *Aeneid*, Rome found the finest expression of its ideals of public service, though transmuted by the new environment. The *Aeneid* is set in mythological times and focuses on the wanderings of the Trojan hero Aeneas and his final settlement in Italy. Yet despite the mythological setting, Virgil made no attempt to reproduce the zest and spontaneity of Homer's heroes. He was too modern, and the age too psychologically self-conscious, to permit this. Aeneas, accordingly, is no naïve, barbaric Achilles but a man of great complexity, not always sure of what he is doing, struggling to find out from obscure signs what destiny intends for him. In an age that saw the disintegration of Rome's old moral consensus, Virgil was able to show how the dependable virtues of the past could be adjusted to work in the present. His hero rejects the temptation to slip into a life of voluptuous ease when he abandons Dido and her rich Carthaginian kingdom and resumes his apparently endless journey. He refuses to yield to weakness or to seek solutions through violence and resists both his own angry passions and those of his friends and foes. Midway through the tale the dimensions of his quest are revealed to him in a journey through the underworld. Here Aeneas is told of his descendants, who will make Rome great and extend its "authority [*imperium*] to the ends of the earth and its spirit to the height of Olympus."[5] He is warned of the horrors of civil war, and the section closes with a declaration of Rome's imperial responsibility:

> Your charge o Romans is to rule the nations by your authority [*imperium*]; this is to be your special craft: to establish the tradition of peace; be merciful to the conquered; and to put down the haughty.[6]

For sustained dignity, seriousness, and nobility of theme, Virgil's epic is unsurpassed. However, it reflects the passing of an era. In the poem's concentration on the single figure of Aeneas, its scornful attitude toward the mob, and its preoccupation with order and obedience, we miss the vigorous, competitive spirit of the Republic. More than any of the other literary figures of the times, Virgil captured in his work the change in values that was taking place as Augustus assumed the burdens and responsibility of rule that in the Republic had been spread throughout an entire class.

[5]Virgil, *Aeneid,* 6.782.
[6]Ibid., 6.851–853.

Although Horace says nothing of Roman public life, he talks a great deal about moral conduct and the traditional values that were assumed to have made Rome great. Virtue is praised over wealth, moderation over excess, and the simple, frugal life over the luxurious:

> The man who wants only what he needs
> is not deterred by the turbulent seas
> nor the furious storm winds
> when Arcturus is setting or Haedus is rising. . . .

> If Phrygian marble or purple garments
> brighter than the stars, or wine from Falernum,
> or the perfumes of the east
> cannot comfort the troubled man,
> why should I build a palace in the latest style
> with pillars that generate envy?
> Why would I trade my Sabine glen
> for the burdens of wealth?[7]

His poems, skilled and carefully worked, demonstrate the kind of harmonious balance he would have liked to find in society itself. Far more than in the elevated verses of Virgil, we can see in Horace the manners, customs, and figures of the times. Here is the flesh and blood of the new age, the rich, the poor, the middle classes, the city and country folk. In the following vignette we can catch a glimpse of the Rome of Horace's age as well as sense some of the poet's frustrations with its limitations:

> A confident poet will often be put in a panic
> And fright when the cheapseats, so stupid, so stolid, so superior
> In numbers, inferior in taste and good sense, and quite ready
> To fight if the knights demur, call out for a bear
> Or a prize fight in the middle of the play. Those roly-prolies!
> They came here to SEE something! But so does everyone else
> Who goes to the *theatre* today, including the knights.
> Pleasure has switched her allegiance from the ear to the eye.
> It gets more and more spectacular: the curtain stays up
> Four or five hours, while the troops dash by, the cavalry,
> Then the infantry (obscene, those mob scenes). Kings are dragged in,
> Their hands bound behind them. . . .
> Chariots, carts, wagons, and boats go whooshing
> Across the stage, closely followed by captured statues,
> Ivory or Corinthian bronze. Democritus *laughed?*
> Were he still in earth, he'd have enough reason for mirth
> Just watching the people gape at their favorite new monster,
> A giraffe or a nice white elephant; he'd look at the audience
> Rather than the play, as a much more interesting spectacle.[8]

---

[7]Horace, *Odes,* 3.1.

[8]Horace, *The Satires and Epistles of Horace,* trans. Smith Palmer Bovie (Chicago: University of Chicago Press, 1959), pp. 255–256. Copyright by The University of Chicago Press.

Chapter 11

The Roman World
from Augustus
to the Third-Century Crisis

THE REFORMS OF AUGUSTUS

The problem facing Octavian when he returned to Italy after defeating Antony was how to find a political and constitutional formula that would embrace the whole state—the people, Senate, equestrian order, and army alike—in a new and lasting relationship. In addition, the system of imperial government, so haphazard and irresponsible in the past, badly needed to be overhauled and made responsive to the needs of the provincials. The formula would have to contain elements of the old and the new, but no one, not even Octavian—or Augustus, as he was called after 27 B.C.—knew the correct proportions. Some of the components were already to be found in the faction of Caesar, but the task confronting Octavian was that of making faction and state coincide.

The Army, the Senate, and the People

The most pressing problem was that of the army. Between 31 B.C. and 13 B.C. Augustus reduced it from 60 to 28 legions, in the process settling over 100,000 veterans in colonies in Italy, Africa, Asia, and Syria. Under Sulla resettlement had been financed by a bloody proscription; fortunately, the means for accomplishing Augustus' enormous resettlement were supplied by the treasures of Egypt, which Augustus seized after the defeat of Antony.

The matter of imperial defense was resolutely faced by making the permanent legionary forces in the provinces large enough to cope with the problems of the frontiers without having to raise emergency armies and by regularizing length of service, pay scales, and discharge benefits. Regular pay came out of the old Republican treasury, and in A.D. 6 a special military treasury, funded by a sales tax and death duties, was set up to pay retirement bonuses to the 9,000 or so veterans who were discharged annually.

The political problem of the army was not so easily solved. Somehow Augustus had to discover a legally acceptable means of keeping control of the legions, or Rome would once more be plunged into the horrors of civil war.

Having held the consulship continuously from 31 B.C., Augustus suddenly renounced his powers in 27 B.C. and declared the reestablishment of the Republic. Pressed by the Senate, he retained the consulship and also proconsular control of the legions. Although this solution had at least constitutional form, it was not completely satisfactory. For example, it halved the number of consular positions available to the nobility and saddled Augustus with many routine duties. After a serious illness and an attempted coup, he resigned the consulship in 23 B.C. but was compensated by being given special proconsular power (*maius imperium*), greater than that possessed by any other proconsul, which allowed him to intervene in the provinces wherever he thought it necessary. This proved to be a generally satisfactory solution to the problem of how to control the legions and became one of the pillars of the new constitution.

These constitutional formalities, however, did not much concern the average soldier or the people, and it was here that the dynastic principle that was to have a major role in Roman history came into prominence. As the adopted son of Caesar, Augustus had inherited the devotion of Caesar's troops, and this phenomenon of loyalty to the son of the previous ruler became another of the foundations of the Empire. After Augustus, every emperor had to be either the adopted son or the real son of the previous emperor if he was to gain the support of the army and the people.

Relations between Augustus and the upper classes were considerably eased by his concern for constitutional formalities, but he exploited other, less formal approaches with great ingenuity and apparent genuineness. For example, whereas Caesar had little patience with the Senate and offended it unnecessarily, Augustus went out of his way to be deferential. He did not flaunt his power, and maintained a simple and modest standard of living. He wore homespun togas and lived in a dwelling that any of the nobles might have possessed. In the matter of titles, which were so important at Rome, his preference was for informal *princeps,* or "elder statesman." In the Republic this term had been applied to ex-consuls whose prestige and authority were such that they were able to dominate the Senate and the government, though not in any formal or legal sense. Augustus' use of the title implied that he ruled in a similar traditional way, by his authority and not by virtue of any alteration in the constitution. Although no one could overlook the fact that Augustus' influence went far beyond his *auctoritas,* after 50 years of bloodshed the upper classes were willing to close their eyes to the reality of his power as long as they did not also have to face the external trappings of an autocracy.

In other respects, Augustus managed relations with the Senate with tact and dignity. Its numbers were gradually reduced from 1,000 to 600, and membership was made hereditary, although Augustus retained the right to nominate new members. The census qualification was put at 1 million sesterces, but special emphasis was placed on integrity and capacity for public office.

The powers and jurisdiction of the Senate and of Augustus tended to overlap in a number of areas, and the lines of demarcation were left deliberately vague. Both made appointments to the provinces, but the Senate sent governors to the peaceful, senatorial provinces, whereas Augustus sent his governors to the remainder, the imperial provinces where the legions were stationed. Governors were now paid regular salaries, and their terms were extended from one year to three to five years. The temptation to exploit their positions was thus reduced, and their lengthened tenure allowed them sufficient time to acquire expertise in the exercise of their duties. By these means and by the judicious reform of the tax-collecting system, Augustus was able to establish the provinces on a sound administrative basis.

In the course of seeking suitable legal forms for his extraordinary powers, Augustus selected one constitutional form from the old patrician state and one from the plebeian. The first was proconsular *imperium,* which gave him control of the army, and the second was tribunician power, which was voted to him in 23 B.C. Together they were to be the real foundation of the new state. The choice of tribunician power was particularly popular with the people. For centuries they had turned to their tribunes for the redress of all kinds of grievances, and now they could turn to their tribune-emperor. It was also a good choice from a purely practical, constitutional viewpoint. As tribune, Augustus could veto or enact legislation, intervene on behalf of individuals, hold court, or call the Senate into session, yet the office had none of the tyrannical connotations of the kingship or even, from the people's view, of the consulship. By the same willing oversight by which the Senate and the upper classes came to accept Augustus' perpetual proconsular power as the price of peace, the people were willing to acquiesce in their loss of power by accepting Augustus as their permanent tribune.

Religious and Social Reform

Augustus attempted to stem the rising tide of moral change that had developed in the late Republic by enacting a comprehensive program of social, religious, and moral reform. Because many men and women of the upper classes preferred to remain celibate and regarded the raising and education of children as too much trouble, Augustus enacted penalties for childless couples while creating special benefits for those with children, although later he was compelled to reduce or even remove the penalties and increase the benefits. To cope with adultery, which was widely condoned, and to extend the power of the state over the family, Augustus made the act a public crime to which severe penalties were attached. Sumptuary laws were enacted to control luxury, and attempts were made to control the haphazard manumission of slaves and the number of the poor eligible for free grain.

THE AUGUSTAN SETTLEMENT

With biting irony the historian Tacitus (died ca. A.D. 120) describes how Augustus brought to completion the transformation of the Republic. However, Tacitus gives scant credit to the overwhelming nature of the problems facing Augustus after a century of upheaval, let alone his adroitness and general success in solving them:

> When after the destruction of Brutus and Cassius there was no longer any army of the Repbulic . . . and when with Lepidus pushed aside and Antony slain . . . then dropping the title of Triumvir, and proclaiming that he was a consul, and that he was satisfied with a tribune's authority for the protection of the people, Augustus won over the soldiers with gifts, the populace with cheap grain, and all men with the attractions of peace. So he grew greater by degrees while he concentrated in himself the functions of the Senate, the magistrates, and the laws. He was wholly unopposed, for the boldest spirits had fallen in battle, or in the proscription, while the remaining nobles, the readier they were to be slaves, were raised the higher by wealth and promotion, so that, aggrandized by revolution, they preferred the safety of the present to the dangers of the past. Nor did the provinces dislike that condition of affairs, for they distrusted the government of the Senate and the People, because of the rivalries between the leading men and the rapacity of the officials, while the protection of the laws was unavailing, as they were continually upset by violence, intrigue, and finally by corruption.

Source: Based on Tacitus, *The Annals of Tacitus,* tr. A. J. Church and W. J. Brodribb (London: Macmillan, 1906), pp. 2–4.

The *princeps* placed special emphasis on the traditional religion and morality of Rome. His very title, *Augustus,* had religious connotations and could be taken to mean that his rule had been inaugurated with all due concern for the augural requirements of Roman religion, or it might have drawn attention to his authority, the word for which was derived from the same Latin root.

The idea that prosperity and peace in the state depended on the pious fulfillment of religious duties to the gods was an ancient one in Rome, and in the Republic the magistrates had taken particular responsibility for maintaining the *pax deorum,* the peace between gods and men. Augustus made a point of stressing his concern for this traditional belief by restoring temples—82 by his own account—and becoming a member of the sacred colleges of pontiffs and augurs. He revived many cults and ancient practices, and in 12 B.C., when Lepidus died, he became *pontifex maximus.* From this date he was not only the secular but also the religious head of the state.

The peace and tranquility that Augustus' rule introduced were deeply felt by all of Italian society, not least by its literary figures and artists. Augustus had the good fortune of finding in Virgil, Horace, and Livy spokesmen for the regime who were in genuine accord with its goals.

Mother Earth, the personification of the fertile land of Italy, from the Altar of Peace. The Augustan message emphasized the return of peace and the restoration of the old order.

Both Virgil and Livy were inspired by the epic rise of Rome, its sufferings, its piety, its great destiny. In the hero Aeneas, Virgil discovered the ideal figure of the Augustan Age: sober, tenacious, pious, a slave to duty. Livy, as has been noted, traced the history of Rome from its meager beginnings to his own day, filling it with patriotic and moral examples, and Horace elegantly expounded in his *Odes* the virtues of the Romans, their frugality, hardiness, and simplicity. However, Ovid failed to adjust himself to the new current of morality and was banished, for instead of writing elevating moral tales, he produced the *Art of Love,* a humorous sexual handbook that was not taken well by the sober Augustus.

More directly Augustus used the coinage of the Empire to herald his achievement in bringing peace to the world. The plastic arts, too, were made to reflect this theme. One of the best-preserved monuments of the age is the Altar of Peace, a simple structure surrounded by walls decorated with friezes whose serenity and order are immediately striking, and which to this day convey a profound sense of the Augustan peace.

Just as the newly established Republic had found expression in the development of the Forum, Augustus' refounding of Rome was also expressed in a building program in the same area. The Forum was now, at last, given definitive shape by the construction of the Temple of Caesar at one end and the rebuilding of the other three sides—the Basilicas Julia and Aemilia and the Rostra (the platform from which the speakers addressed the people). Caesar's own forum, just behind the Senate House, and a new one, the Forum Augusti (centered on the great Temple of Mars the Avenger), were built at right angles to it, somewhat farther to the northeast. In addition to the Forum and the Altar of Peace, Augustus' other projects included the Theater of Marcellus, the Temple of Apollo on the Palatine, his own mausoleum, and innumerable restorations of older buildings. An entirely new monumental center was constructed in the Campus Martius by Agrippa, Augustus' son-in-law. This included a basilica, baths, a temple, gardens, porticoes, an artificial lake and canal, and a huge hall, the Saepta, intended for voting purposes. Elsewhere in the city a great variety of new buildings were erected, including theaters, libraries, temples, arches, and warehouses. The drainage system was enlarged and overhauled, and the water supply was practically doubled. When the people complained on one occasion of the high price of wine, Augustus told them to drink the water that he had so liberally provided them.

The styles of the building programs reflected Augustus' own complicated aims. They ranged from the startlingly Hellenistic Altar of Peace to the somberly conservative Italian-style basilicas, theaters, and forums. Even the building materials represented both innovation and conservatism. Concrete, which had been used sparingly for some time, now passed into common use. Marble was introduced for the first time on a large scale, and one of Augustus' boasts, according to the biographer Suetonius, was that he had found Rome brick but left it marble.

The reign of Augustus also brought other, more tangible benefits to the Roman people. For the first time in its history the city of Rome was provided with a proper urban administration. In addition to Augustus' personal bodyguard, the Praetorian Cohorts, a police force of 3,000 men (*Cohortes Urbanae*) was created, as well as a firefighting force of 7,000 (*Vigiles*). New aqueducts were built, and the sewage system was thoroughly overhauled. A permanent board of commissioners (*Curatores Aquarum*) was appointed to maintain the supply of water. Similar commissions were created to look after flood control (*Curatores Riparum Tiberis*) and the food supply (*Cura Annonae*). Entertainment was not neglected, and the first permanent amphitheater in Rome's history was erected. Only a century later the satirist Juvenal was to use the bitter epithet "bread and the circus" to describe the imperial people of Rome.

The Succession

Augustus rose to power as the adopted son of Caesar and maintained himself as *princeps* by his careful management of the constitution and his sensitivity to the residue of republican feelings among his subjects. These were the essentials of his rule: his personal and dynastic popularity with the people and the army, and his acceptance by the Senate as the "best man" in the state. The appearance of a monarchy was avoided, and technically all the emperor's powers were conferred on him by the Senate and people, and would cease to exist when he died. Therein lay the problem. How could power be passed on in an orderly way, without civil strife, after his death?

The problem nagged at Augustus, and at some point he made up his mind that the stability of the state could be maintained only if power were to be transmitted to an heir who bore his name. Unfortunately, Augustus had no sons, and his daughter Julia's sons, Gaius and Lucius, died young. That left Tiberius, his wife's son from a previous marriage, and it was this man, already in middle age, whom Augustus finally adopted and associated with himself in the ruling of the Empire in A.D. 4. In turn, Tiberius was forced to adopt as his heir his brother's son, Germanicus, whose mother had been a daughter of Antony and Augustus' sister Octavia. Thus, when Augustus died in A.D. 14, Tiberius succeeded as the son of Caesar to the loyalty of the people and the army, having already been constitutionally invested with most of the powers of the *princeps*.

ROUNDING OUT THE EMPIRE

The Julio-Claudians

Under Augustus the fragmented conquests of the Republic were rounded out and consolidated. With the conquest of Galicia in the northwest the subjection of Spain was at last completed. The interior of Gaul, though conquered by Caesar, had not yet been properly organized; it was now divided into three new provinces. Under the impression that Asia was not enormously more distant from the Rhine than the Rhine was from Spain, Augustus planned to add Germany, and probably everything else east of the Rhine, to the Empire. In A.D. 6 a massive pincer movement from the upper Rhine and the Danube, involving 12 legions, was organized to incorporate Germany up to the Elbe, but just as the offensive was about to get under way, Illyriia (formally Yugoslavia) to the south revolted. By A.D. 9 Tiberius had finally suppressed this revolt, but the same year three legions in Germany under P. Quinctilius Varus were wiped out in a surprise attack. This brought to an end Roman plans for the conquest of Germany, and the lands to the east of the Rhine were evacuated.

In the south the Romans had greater success. By 15 B.C. the alpine regions were subdued and organized into two provinces. After the suppression of the great Illyrian revolt of A.D. 6, the lands to the south of the Danube were consolidated into two provinces, Dalmatia and Pannonia, and a large command farther east known as Moesia, which reached the Black Sea. In the east there were no new conquests. Augustus did not try to avenge the defeat inflicted on Rome in 53 B.C. by Parthia but instead negotiated a settlement under which Armenia was to be a buffer state ruled by a king who acknowledged—or was supposed to acknowledge—Roman suzerainty. Other

PEER REVIEW: AUGUSTUS' CONTEMPORARIES JUDGE HIM

On the death of Augustus, Tacitus reports various opinions about his accomplishments:

> Intelligent people . . . spoke variously of his life with praise and blame. Some said that dutiful feeling towards a father [the duty to avenge his adoptive father, Julius Caesar], and the necessities of the state in which laws had then no place, drove him into civil war, which can neither be planned nor conducted on any right principles. . . . The only remedy for his distracted country was the rule of a single man. Yet Augustus had reorganized the state neither as a monarchy nor a dictatorship but as a Principate [the rule of the first man in the state, the *princeps*]. The ocean and remote rivers were the boundaries of the Empire; the legions, provinces, fleets—all things were linked together; there was law for the citizens; there was respect shown for the allies. The capital had been beautified on a grand scale; only in a few instances had he resorted to force, simply to secure general tranquility.
>
> It was said, on the other hand, that filial duty and state necessity were merely assumed as a mask. His real motive was lust for power. Driven by that he had mobilized the veterans by bribery, and when a young man with no official position, had raised an army, tampered with a consul's legions, and pretended attachment to the faction of Sextus Pompey. Then, when by a decree of the Senate he had usurped the high functions and authority of praetor . . . he at once wrested the consulate from reluctant Senate, and turned against the Republic the arms with which he had been entrusted against Antony. Citizens were proscribed and lands divided. . . . Even granting that the deaths of Cassius and Brutus were sacrifices to a hereditary enmity (though duty requires us to ignore private feuds for the sake of the public welfare), still Sextus Pompey had been deluded by the phantom of peace, and Lepidus by the mask of friendship. Subsequently, Antony had been lured on by the treaties of Tarentum and Brundisium, and by his marriage with the sister of Augustus, and paid by his death the penalty of a treacherous alliance. No doubt, there was peace after all this, but it was a peace stained with blood.

Source: Based on Tacitus, *The Annals of Tacitus,* trans. A. J. Church and W. J. Brodribb (London: Macmillan, 1906), pp. 2–4, 9, 10.

client kingdoms, such as Judaea and Cappadocia, served similar purposes as buffer states for the empire in the east.

During the Julio-Claudian period (27 B.C.–A.D. 68) the Roman frontier with the outside world was a fairly fluid affair. There were no fixed borders with clearly laid-out defenses, as in later times. The legions slept in tents or in winter quarters made of wood, and camps were not much more complicated than the quickly constructed marching camps normally used on campaigns. Between widely separated legionary bases there was often no active defense at all. Instead, the legions were maintained as mobile striking forces deployed to make forays into enemy territory, to

---

THE JULIO-CLAUDIAN EMPERORS

Augustus	27 B.C.–A.D. 14
Tiberius	A.D. 14–37
Gaius (Caligula)	37–41
Claudius	41–54
Nero	54–68

---

crush revolts in the provinces behind them, or to intercept major incursions from across the borders. The client-states provided another source of protection. They could absorb much of the weight of a first attack while providing for their own internal security.

Roman security depended most of all on the maintenance of the already well established reputation of the legions. Under Tiberius, Roman prestige on the Rhine frontier, which had been severely damaged by the loss of Varus' legions, was gradually restored, but no major wars of conquest were fought. A good administrator, Tiberius was able to cut in half the unpopular sales tax, which had been 1 percent, and he left a large surplus in the treasury when he died.

Tiberius' problems of succession were even more complicated than those of his predecessor. The heir apparent, Germanicus, died in A.D. 19, and Tiberius' next choice, his own son Drusus, was poisoned by the sinister Praetorian Prefect Sejanus, although the emperor was not to learn of this until much later. This left his grandson Tiberius Gemellus and a somewhat older grandnephew, Gaius. They were made joint heirs in A.D. 36. When Tiberius died the next year, Gaius, with the support of the new Praetorian Prefect, Macro, was proclaimed emperor. It was a disastrous choice because Gaius, or Caligula (Little Boot), as he was nicknamed, proved to be mentally unbalanced. He soon murdered Gemellus and initiated treason trials for the purpose of appropriating the fortunes of rich senators whose wealth he needed to pay for his wild extravagances. When it was rumored that he intended to make his horse a consul and that after training maneuvers for an invasion of Britain he had marched the legions to the English Channel only to order them to pick seashells, the Praetorians took matters into their own hands and murdered him. In his place they put his uncle, the aging Claudius.

The bookish Claudius, who had studied under Livy and had written histories of the Etruscans and of the Punic Wars, was generally considered unfit for Roman public life; he had not even been adopted into the Julian family (the family of Julius Caesar) and was practically unknown outside the palace. To gain military prestige and consolidate his support with the army, he decided to annex Britain using two new legions raised by Caligula. Not a military man himself, he made good selections in his commanders and delegated Aulus Plautius, with four legions, to lead the invasion. Among Plautius' legionary commanders was the future emperor Vespasian, who owed his position to the influence of Narcissus, one of Claudius' freedmen. Initially the invasion went well, and Roman control of the south was quickly established (A.D. 43–47). The conquest of Wales and the north of Britain was a different story, and it was to be another 30 years before the rest of Britain was secure.

Claudius proved to have unexpected administrative abilities and organized permanent departments of finance (*a rationibus*), correspondence (*ab epistulis*), and petitions (*a libellis*) headed by freedmen who ran them efficiently but whose great power won many enemies for their master.

The emperor's fourth wife, Agrippina, schemed to have her son by a previous marriage, Nero, placed on the throne, and to speed the succession she poisoned Claudius in A.D. 54. Under the tutorship of Seneca and the Praetorian Prefect Burrus, Nero's reign opened favorably, but soon a savage battle for power began in the palace in which Seneca and Agrippina eventually perished. Nero emerged as an irresponsible, amoral dilettante whose principal concerns were music and literature, and as the reign advanced his eccentricity increased, provoking conspiracies that further contributed to the downward spiral.

Major wars were fought in the east during Nero's reign by some of the best generals Rome had produced in many years. In a series of campaigns against the Parthians, Cn. Domitius Corbulo brought Armenia within the Roman sphere of influence, and gave Nero an opportunity to stage and preside at an elaborate coronation of its king in Pompey's theater in Rome, which was gilded for the occasion.

In Judaea, mishandling of provincial affairs by successive Roman procurators provoked a major revolt in A.D. 66 and required the dispatch of a full-scale expedition to put it down. The commander selected was T. Flavius Vespasianus (Vespasian), whose career, after successful service in Britain under Claudius, had suffered a setback because of his unfortunate habit of falling asleep at Nero's recitals. Perhaps more important was the fact that his patron, Narcissus, had opposed the marriage of Claudius and Agrippina, so for both men passage into political oblivion followed inevitably upon Nero's accession to power. Vespasian pressed the war in Judaea efficiently and had practically ended it when civil war broke out over Nero's successor.

Most of Nero's irresponsibilities had had little effect on the provinces or the armies, but in A.D. 67 he came to suspect his generals of treason, and ordered Corbulo and the commanders of the Rhine legions to commit suicide. The governor of Spain, Galba, avoided a similar fate by choosing instead to revolt, and Nero precipitously committed suicide. In A.D. 69, the Year of the Four Emperors, a bloody round of civil wars was fought in which first Galba was slain by the Praetorian Guards and then his successor, Otho, was killed in battle against the Rhine legions who invaded Italy in support of their candidate, Vitellius. The Danube and Syrian legions next announced for Vespasian and marched on Rome, the former getting there first, having crushed the forces of Vitellius on the way. The following summer Vespasian arrived in Rome, leaving his son Titus to finish the siege of Jerusalem; in 70 the city was captured, and the temple destroyed.

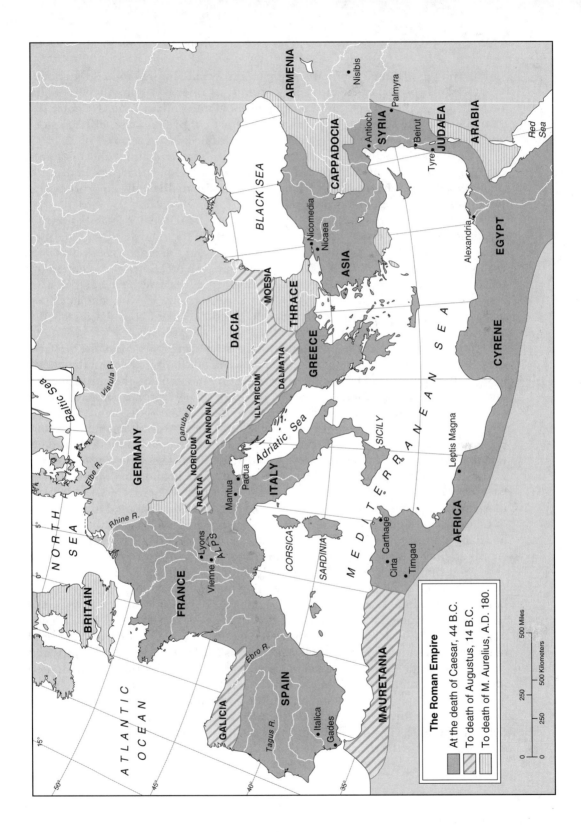

The Roman Empire

At the death of Caesar, 44 B.C.
To death of Augustus, 14 B.C.
To death of M. Aurelius, A.D. 180.

500 Miles

500 Kilometers

ATLANTIC OCEAN

NORTH SEA

Baltic Sea

BRITAIN

GERMANY

FRANCE

SPAIN

GALICIA

MAURETANIA

ITALY

CORSICA

SARDINIA

SICILY

AFRICA

CYRENE

EGYPT

MEDITERRANEAN SEA

Adriatic Sea

ILLYRICUM

DALMATIA

PANNONIA

NORICUM

RAETIA

DACIA

MOESIA

THRACE

GREECE

ASIA

CAPPADOCIA

ARMENIA

SYRIA

JUDAEA

ARABIA

Red Sea

BLACK SEA

ALPS

Rhine R.

Danube R.

Elbe R.

Vistula R.

Tagus R.

Ebro R.

Lyons
Vienne

Mantua
Padua

Carthage
Cirta
Timgad

Leptis Magna

Italica
Gades

Alexandria

Tyre
Beirut
Antioch
Palmyra
Nisibis

Nicomedia
Nicaea

THE FLAVIANS AND THE FIVE "GOOD EMPERORS"

Vespasian	A.D. 69–79
Titus	79–81
Domitian	81–96
Nerva	96–98
Trajan	98–117
Hadrian	117–138
Antoninus Pius	138–161
Marcus Aurelius	161–180

The Flavians and the Five "Good Emperors"

The Flavian dynasty that Vespasian established was based in the rural bourgeoisie of Italy and thus was in marked contrast to the aristocratic and eccentric Julio-Claudians who had ruled to the time of Nero. The tone of the new regime was one of modesty, simplicity, and strict adherence to the old ways. However, the weakness of the Senate and the power of the armies that had set up Galba, Otho, Vitellius, and Vespasian in turn had been demonstrated for everyone to see and was a lesson not easily forgotten.

Vespasian struggled to restore financial stability, which had been upset by the extravagances of Nero and the destruction caused by the recent civil wars. New senators were added, especially men from the equestrian order and from the provinces. Since Claudius the permanent departments in Rome, such as finance and correspondence, had been in the hands of freedmen, but were now transferred to equestrians—the first step in the creation of a civil service outside the traditional framework of the Senate.

Vespasian was less successful in his dynastic policies. From the beginning he had made it clear that he intended that his sons Titus and Domitian would succeed him. Although the former died before any clear judgment could be reached about him, Domitian ruled long enough (A.D. 81–96) to earn the hatred of the Senate, and he was murdered in a palace conspiracy that included his own wife Domitia (the daughter of Corbulo, Nero's great general). Domitian was an able administrator and made excellent official appointments, but his growing paranoia converted the later years of his rule into a reign of terror. Tacitus the historian and Pliny the Younger looked back on these years as a time of humiliation and terror.

Domitian's successor was the elderly senator M. Cocceius Nerva, who had ingratiated himself with the legions by adopting Trajan, the popular commander of the Rhine army. Trajan's family hailed from Italica (near Seville) in Spain, and he was thus the first emperor of provincial origin. After a two-year reign Nerva died, and Trajan, his energetic successor, began a series of campaigns to round out the Roman frontier. Dacia (modern Romania) was added between 101 and 106 to secure the

Danube frontier, and in A.D.114 Trajan began an invasion of Armenia and Mesopotamia. After initial successes, a major revolt in his rear forced him to retreat, and he died in Cilicia in 117. It was announced that on his deathbed he had adopted his nephew by marriage, P. Aelius Hadrianus, or Hadrian (reigned A.D. 117–138).

Hadrian promptly abandoned Trajan's eastern conquests and spent most of his reign (12 out of 21 years) traveling all over the Empire visiting the provinces, overseeing the administration, and checking the discipline of the army. He was a brilliant administrator who concerned himself with all aspects of government and the administration of justice. He established cities in Egypt, Asia Minor, and the Balkans, and he initiated the construction of the great wall in the north of England that bears his name. He was a deeply cultured man who surrounded himself with orators and artists. He had strong ideas about architecture, and one of his greatest creations, the Pantheon, stands intact to the present day. He was less tolerant when it came to non-Greek cultures, and his rebuilding of Jerusalem and the erection of a temple to Jupiter on the site of the old Temple provoked a major revolt (the Bar Kochba Rebellion of A.D. 132–135) that was brutally put down.

Hadrian's first chosen successor, his close friend L. Ceionius Commodus, died in A.D. 138, and he next turned to an elderly senator, T. Aurelius Antoninus (better known as Antoninus Pius, reigned A.D. 138–161), whose family came from Nemausus (Nîmes) in the south of France. Antoninus was in turn instructed to adopt as his successor his nephew M. Annius Verus (Marcus Aurelius, reigned A.D. 161–180) and Lucius Verus, the son of Commodus. Unlike the restless Hadrian, Antoninus lived quietly in Rome, never stirring from the city during his reign, and for 23 years the Empire stagnated.

A descendant of a Spanish family, the prim Marcus Aurelius ruled for eight years in association with Lucius Verus, a man whom he regarded as worthless. When Verus died in A.D. 169, he was not replaced. A confirmed Stoic, Marcus Aurelius had plenty of opportunities to test his commitment to this philosophy, for wars and other disasters dominated his reign. In the east a series of campaigns was waged between A.D. 162 and 166 under the nominal command of Verus, whose troops brought back with them a virulent plague that ravaged the Empire.

Under the Flavians and their successors, the Roman frontier gradually lost its fluid outlines and came to possess clearly identifiable boundaries marked by walls, palisades, fences, towers, roads, and well-built, permanent legionary fortresses. The old client-states were absorbed, and the new defensive aim was to provide security against small-scale infiltration as well as much larger incursions. The advantage of this policy was that it allowed even the border provinces to develop cities and agriculture along Mediterranean lines, and places such as the Danube valley, once remote and undeveloped, now began to flourish. Under Marcus Aurelius this policy was put to the test. As a result of the eastern wars, the Rhine and Danube frontiers were weakened, and in A.D. 167 several large tribal confederations, among them the Marcomanni and the Quadi, broke through the defenses and advanced into Italy and Greece before being stopped. Aurelius spent the best part of the next 13 years in fierce campaigns against the Germans and was poised for another advance when he died in A.D. 180.

THE SEVERAN EMPERORS

The luck the Empire had been having with its rulers came to an end on the accession in A.D. 180 of Commodus, the son of Marcus Aurelius. From the time he was 15 he had been joint ruler of the Empire with his father, and immediately on Marcus' death he asserted his authority by making peace with the Germans, against whom the Romans had been fighting continuously since 167. To the dismay of the Senate, he returned to Rome and promptly began spending enormous sums on extravagant spectacles in the circus while leaving the running of the government to his cronies. Dressed as the hero Hercules, he performed feats of archery in the arena, which delighted the mob. In 182 an unsuccessful assassination attempt launched him on the course that Nero and Domitian had followed, but he managed to survive for another 10 years before finally succumbing to a plot engineered by his mistress and the Praetorian Prefect.

His replacement, the elderly senator Pertinax, gives a good indication of the changing conditions of the second century. Although a distinguished senator and at the time of his elevation the holder of the Prefecture of the City—the highest post that a senator could have—Pertinax was the son of a freedman from northern Italy and had served in the equestrian service before becoming a member of the Senate. A rigid disciplinarian, he was soon murdered by the Praetorian Guard, who then proceeded to the degrading auction of the Empire to whomever would pay the largest bribe. The highest bidder was senator M. Didius Julianus.

On the news of this event, the frontier legions took matters into their own hands, and a four-year civil war ensued. The troops in Syria proclaimed C. Pescennius Niger emperor; those in Britain, D. Clodius Albinus; and the Danube legions, their commander, L. Septimius Severus. Located closer to Rome than the others, the Danube legions got there first and disposed of Julianus. Severus then disbanded the Praetorian Guard and replaced it with veterans from his own ranks. Proclaiming

---

THE SEVERAN EMPERORS

Septimius Severus	A.D. 193–211
Caracalla	211–217
Elagabalus	218–222
Severus Alexander	222–235

Albinus his heir in the west, in order to secure his rear, he set off for the east, where he defeated Niger in A.D. 194. Antioch, which supported Niger, was sacked and lost its position as the capital of Syria. Byzantium, which had also resisted him, was razed. Turning west, he then took on Albinus and after a struggle defeated him. Lyon then suffered the fate of Antioch and Byzantium, and because a number of senators had supported Albinus, Severus turned on the Senate, executing many of its members and confiscating their estates. At the same time he announced his adoption as the son of Marcus Aurelius. His sons Caracalla and Geta were declared his heirs.

Under the Antonine emperors—Antoninus Pius, Marcus Aurelius, and Commodus—many North Africans had found their way into high positions in the army and the imperial administration. Among these was Severus, a native of the ancient Phoenician city of Leptis Magna in Libya. An old slander that seems to have circulated widely claimed he spoke Latin with an accent; he was, in fact, the first truly provincial Roman emperor. Septimius' wife, Julia Domna, was also a provincial, a Syrian aristocrat whose family held the hereditary priesthood at Emesa.

From A.D. 197–202 Septimius campaigned in the east against the Parthians and extended the Roman frontier to include Mesopotamia. Six years later he set out for Britain with the intention of finally incorporating Scotland in the Empire. The task proved more difficult than he anticipated, and in 210 he arranged a peace and withdrew the legions behind Hadrian's Wall. He died the following year.

On his deathbed Septimius was supposed to have urged his sons "to live in peace with each other, to enrich the soldiers and despise the rest of the world." The advice was only partially heeded. Geta was soon murdered by his brother Caracalla, who then went on to calm the restless troops by increasing their pay. He campaigned successfully in Germany against the Alamanni and afterward in the east against the Parthians. Revenue was raised to sustain these undertakings by extending the Roman franchise in A.D. 212 to all free inhabitants of the Empire and then doubling the inheritance tax to which only citizens were liable. Although this act, known as the Antonine Constitution, has its cynical side, its symbolic value was high. It gave a sense of unity to the peoples of the Empire and fulfilled some philsophers' dreams of creating a single world community of citizens. Henceforward Rome was to be the common home of all the scattered inhabitants of the Empire.

In A.D. 217 Caracalla was murdered by the Praetorian Prefect Macrinus, another North African, who became the first equestrian to ascend the throne. However, Macrinus had not calculated on the wiles of Julia Maesa, the sister-in-law of Septimius Severus, who announced to the troops that her grandson, Varius Avitus, priest of the sun god Elagabal, was the son of Caracalla. Loyal to the Severan dynasty, the legionaries killed Macrinus and declared Avitus, or Elagabalus, emperor in his place. The new emperor proved to be an eccentric who squandered vast amounts of state funds, and, after being persuaded to adopt his cousin, Severus Alexander, as his heir, he was disposed of by the Praetorian Guard at his own grandmother's suggestion. Severus Alexander was only 14 when he ascended the throne and throughout his reign was firmly under the thumb of his mother, Julia Mammaea. The jurist Ulpian and a number of senators in the emperor's council were good influences on the

SOME IMPERIAL WOMEN

The early emperors of Rome ruled through a small group of family members, kin, friends, freedmen, and slaves much as the great nobles of the Republic had run their personal estates. Most of imperial decision making occurred within a very small circle of intimates, meeting within the palace. Understandably, the women of the imperial family were often among the most influential insiders.

Throughout his life Augustus depended on the advice of his intelligent, strong-minded wife, Livia, who also served as a model of old-fashioned Republican propriety. Her fidelity was never challenged, although enemies of Augustus saw her as a ruthless intriguer who manipulated Augustus in favor of her son Tiberius. Certainly Tiberius thought she was overbearing. He is supposed to have left Rome in A.D. 26 to live in Capri mainly to avoid her, although he had plenty of other reasons for wanting to get out of Rome.

Plotina, Trajan's wife, took an active role in promoting his kinsman Hadrian's career. At her urging Trajan gave his grandniece Sabina to Hadrian in marriage. When Trajan died suddenly on his return from campaigning in Mesopotamia without having designated an heir, Plotina had a hand in seeing that the throne passed safely to Hadrian. One story has it that she concealed her husband's death and had an actor impersonate him, announcing in a tired voice that he had adopted Hadrian as his son.

Marcia, the lover of Commodus, the unbalanced son of Marcus Aurelius, eventually turned against him and conspired to have him killed. When poison failed, she and her fellow conspirators persuaded his personal trainer to strangle him.

Perhaps of all the imperial women, Julia Domna, wife of the emperor Septimius Severus, and her daughter, Julia Mamaea, mother of the emperor Alexander Severus, were the most influential. Septimius, a native of Leptis Magna in Libya, cast around for a suitable wife before becoming emperor, and supposedly led by a horoscope, proposed to Julia Domna, a member of a powerful Syrian family. The marriage was a strategic success for Septimius. In the struggle for the throne following the death of Commodus, her family connections helped solidify his control of Syria. She accompanied her husband on his campaigns in the east and was honored with the title *mater castrorum,* "Mother of the Camp." Temporarily forced out of political life by the Praetorian Prefect Plautianus, another native of Leptis Magna, she devoted herself to literature and philosophy, gathering a distinguished group of scholars, jurists, doctors, and writers around her. Plautianus soon overreached himself and Julia had the satisfaction of seeing the great Syrian jurist Papinian, a relative of hers by marriage, appointed in his place.

Her sons, unfortunately, did not measure up to either her or her husband's expectations. Septimius left Geta and Caracalla as joint heirs on his death, but the arrangement did not last long. Geta was stabbed on his brother's orders and died in Julia's arms. Julia seems to have exercised some restraint on the unstable Caracalla and after a short reign he was assassinated. Julia herself died soon afterward of breast cancer.

Julia Domna's sister, Julia Maesa, engineered the fall of Macrinus, Caracalla's successor, and regained the throne for the Severan family by persuading the legions that her grandson Elagabalus was the illegitimate son of Caracalla. The male line of the Severi was no match for the female and Elagabalus proved as unsuitable an emperor as Caracalla. Anticipating trouble the resourceful Syrian family forced Elagabalus to adopt his cousin Alexander Severus, the son of Julia Maesa's other daughter, Julia

continues

Mamaea, as his successor. This was a better choice, and Alexander proved to be highly popular. Feeling threatened, Elagabalus and his mother attempted to have Alexander killed but found the tables turned on them by Julia Maesa and Julia Mamaea. Both Elagabalus and his mother were assassinated by the Praetorian Guard and Alexander was selected to rule in his place. His grandmother soon died, and his mother, Julia Mamaea, took her place as the power behind the throne. Alexander ruled from 222 to 235 A.D. Unfortunately, his reign coincided with a deterioration in the overall military situation and Alexander proved to be a weak leader. On campaign in Germany the troops turned on him and murdered him and his mother, initiating a 50-year period of great instability in the imperial succession.

young man. However, on campaign in Germany in A.D. 235 he attempted to negotiate with the enemy and was killed by his own troops, who saw his diplomacy as an attempt to bribe, rather than fight, the enemy. They apparently would have preferred to fight the Germans and keep the money for themselves. What followed was the half-century of political, economic, and military chaos known by modern historians as the Crisis of the Third Century.

Under the Severan dynasty the Empire entered a new phase. Its founder, Septimius Severus, pushed the frontier forward in Syria, Arabia, and North Africa. Recognizing the inability of troops spread out along an extended frontier to deal with any real threat, Severus created a mobile central field army of over 30,000 men made up of legionary detachments (*vexillationes*) and large contingents of cavalry from Africa and Syria. The army became more professional and even democratic to the extent that the old, well-established connection between the upper classes and the officer corps was weakened, as large numbers of able provincials and men of the lower classes were able to enter its ranks. A somewhat similar form of democratization took place in the administration. It too expanded as greater emphasis was placed on the role of the equestrian class over that of the senatorial. Three newly recruited legions were given equestrian commanders, as were all the provinces in the east. The Severi also reached out more to provincials. By one count, 60 percent of the financial administrators (procurators) were from either Africa or the east. A succession of brilliant lawyers held the position of Praetorian Prefect and began the systematic organization of Roman law. These reforms ultimately provided a foundation on which the emperors of the later third century were able to reconstruct the apparently doomed empire and save it from the crisis that had all but engulfed it.

Chapter 12

The Roman Peace

CHALLENGE AND RESPONSE

A Tendency to Anarchy

The size and complexity of the Roman Empire made it extraordinarily difficult to govern. It had neither geographic nor cultural unity. There had never been a time when the regions of the Empire were politically united, and after the passing of Roman rule, they were never to be united again. Beyond a little trade, what could possibly have tied Britain to Egypt or Belgium to Syria? They were too far apart, even as they are today, and too culturally dissimilar to have had a natural community of interests.

The government and society that Rome managed to impose on this area were flimsy and artificial, always under challenge by local forces, which tended to reassert themselves in moments of Roman weakness and tear apart the connections that had been laboriously built up.

The Cement of Empire

The cement that held the Empire together for as long as it did was social, cultural, and military. It consisted first of Rome's ability to involve the different classes of the Empire in the processes of government and society and so integrate them with one another that none were permanently alienated. The Romans had no systematic ideology of empire and instead substituted the slow, pragmatic application of what they did know well: their own social system with its hierarchical organization of society on the basis of wealth and public service. Patronage established connections across class lines, and careers in the army and civil service allowed the able and ambitious to rise to high office. Based on this uniform social system, a homogeneous culture derived from the study of a handful of classical texts in Greek and Latin allowed Syrians to communicate with Africans and Spaniards with Britons in a way that had never before been possible and has not recurred since.

Ultimately everything depended on the ability of the army to maintain the peace within and without the Empire. This in turn depended on the willingness of the Empire to foot the bill for the army. It was a complicated equation in which costs could not be allowed to outweigh the benefits for a long period, and when they did, as happened in the west after the fourth century, the Empire collapsed. In the east the equation of costs and benefits was better maintained, and the Roman Empire survived a full 1,000 years after its disappearance in the west.

Distance and Time: The Secret Enemies of the Roman Peace

If we include the Mediterranean Sea, the geographic extent of the Roman Empire at its height was only slightly less than that of the continental United States. It stretched from the lowlands of Scotland to the Sudan and from the Ukraine to Morocco. Great villas, towns, and fortresses lined the 1,000 miles of Rhine and Danube frontier. Far into the interior of North Africa the town of Timgad was laid out in grid fashion by the veterans of the distinguished army legion, Legio III Augusta, and was graced with an amphitheater, baths, libraries, and portico-lined squares.

Travel had always been easy in the coastal areas of the Empire, and three weeks of good sailing could bring a traveler from one end of the Mediterranean to the other. Centuries of Roman effort built up a great network of roads that linked the inland regions with this central thoroughfare. Nevertheless, land transportation was always slow and expensive, and the cost of hauling bulk goods prohibitive. In the late Empire a 1,200-pound wagonload of wheat doubled its price over a journey of 300 miles. It was cheaper to transport grain by ship from one end of the Mediterranean to the other than to send it 75 miles overland.

Rivers such as the Rhine, Danube, Rhône, Nile, and Euphrates were vital means of communication with the interior regions. The government maintained a constant concern for the upkeep of the roads, the state-operated land transportation system (*cursus publicus*), and the guilds of maritime shippers (*navicularii*). The transportation system was divided into light and heavy divisions, the former providing official travelers with horses and carriages, and the latter being responsible for the movement of heavy goods such as food, clothing, arms, and building materials. On the light *cursus* travelers could average about 90 miles per day. The guilds of shippers were originally independent contractors but were gradually incorporated into the state transportation system and rewarded with special exemptions from the taxes and other burdensome municipal responsibilities that the middle classes in the Empire had to bear. Eventually all sorts of regulations governed the transportation system. Regulations for the number of horses, carriages, and carts that might pass a given point in a single day, together with the maximum loads, were set down—and ignored. Inspectors supervised the system, looking out for unauthorized users and out-of-date or forged passes.

Roman administrators and troops were thinly spread over the gigantic regions of the Empire, and the task of visiting and supervising them was close to overwhelming. In emergencies, such as the breaching of the frontiers by invaders, the ability of the Empire to respond was directly related to the speed with which it could gather accurate information about the size of the horde, its composition, direction, speed of movement, and the like, and then summon troops of appropriate armament and number from other theaters to cope with the invaders, drive them out, and repair the damage to the frontier fortifications. Throughout its history, distance and time were the secret enemies of the Roman peace. Despite the high quality of its 50,000 miles of roads, the transportation network remained that of an underdeveloped country. Burdened with a similarly weak economy and low technology, the Empire quickly depleted its reserves when pressures built up beyond a certain level. Under the Roman social formula only so much could be squeezed out of the system, and to achieve anything more would have required a radical reordering of society that not even utopianists dreamed of.

SOCIETY AND THE STATE IN THE EMPIRE

Cultural Pluralism and Cultural Unity

The Empire was no empty land mass waiting to be filled by conquering Romans who themselves constituted a homogeneous community. The provinces won by the wars of the Republic were filled with peoples whose histories were as long and diverse as those of the Romans themselves.

Although knowledge of Latin and Greek would take a traveler comfortably from one end of the Empire to the other, the bulk of the native populations retained their native languages until almost the end of the Empire. Celtic, Germanic, Semitic, Hamitic, and Berber languages along with the cultures they sustained were deeply rooted in the various regions of the Empire. An artificial boundary following roughly the lines of the Rhine and the Danube marked the official point at which prestate and urban world, Old Europe and Mediterranean, confronted each other. It would be a mistake, however, to attach too much importance to frontiers. In reality, a kind of permanent moral and cultural frontier existed within the Roman world itself between those who accepted the urbanized form of Greco-Roman high culture and those who, passively for the most part, resisted it. Polyglot, multiethnic, and multicultural, the Roman Empire was one of the great melting pots of all time.

The depth of civilization varied from area to area, being deepest in the eastern Mediterranean and thinnest in the west, generally in inverse ratio to the distance from the Mediterranean seacoast. Iron Age Celts and Germans in the west, who had only recently been introduced to written laws and literature, were united under Rome with Syrians, Mesopotamians, Jews, and Egyptians, whose literacy and literature went back for thousands of years. Half of the Empire was underdeveloped, and the other half was overdeveloped.

Opposing this tendency to cultural anarchy, which was the natural state of the Empire, was Greco-Roman civilization and its supporting educational system. Outside the older, developed cultures of the east it had no competitors, and by the end of the second century A.D. it provided a uniform, high culture for the upper classes everywhere, which informally even percolated down to the masses.

The provincialization of Greco-Roman civilization is one of the most remarkable features of the period. Roman satirist Juvenal complained of the number of eastern intellectual and literary figures at Rome, and in fact some of the greatest masters of Greek and Latin in this time were provincials. Lucian, the brilliant satirist, was Syrian; historians Arrian and Dio Cassius were from Bithynia, as was moralist-rhetorician Dio Chrysostom; Apuleius and Tertullian were African. Although the upper classes shared the common heritage of Greek and Latin and could travel comfortably in the knowledge of being able to find their own type everywhere, a great educational (though not social) gap existed between them and the masses. The acquisition of an education was a long, expensive, (and often boring) process that only the upper classes could afford.

The purpose of the Roman educational system was not merely to teach how to read and write but how to read and write *well.* There was a huge difference between the practical literacy of a soldier, merchant, or ordinary town councillor and the highly literate and bookish education of the upper classes. Like wealth and titles, culture was regarded as a mark of distinction and almost as eagerly sought.

The languages studied were limited to two, Greek and Latin, and at that not the languages of current use but the Greek and Latin of the classical authors. Other languages and their literature were regarded as barbaric and thus ignored. In Latin, Virgil, Terence, Sallust, and Cicero were the favorite authors; Homer, Thucydides, the Attic tragedians, and Demosthenes were read in Greek. These masters were accepted as authorities, and students were expected to mold their styles after them. Imagination and originality were discouraged, and form and style were considered more important than content. The classical texts were dissected line by line, the rules of grammar and syntax learned by memory. Technical proficiency was prized above all, and generations of students went through untold suffering to master the nuances of a classical style. As an old man, Saint Augustine, the great bishop of Carthage, could still recall the horrors of his early days in school and rhetorically claimed that death was preferable to what was suffered in childhood studies.

The ultimate goal of the educational system was the mastery of the spoken word. There was a close connection between civic life and the art of public speaking, and because the educated regarded a public career as their normal lifetime occupation, an oratorical ability of some level was indispensable. Business that today is handled in writing or informal telephone conversations was then conducted for-

The two extremes of the Roman world: elegant aristocrat (left) and rough peasant (right).

mally and in person. The average middle- or upper-class person could expect to have to speak at one time or another in public before magistrates seated on tribunals, before their fellow city councillors, to the people, before jurors and judges, or to soldiers, and the effective speaker was one formally trained in rhetoric, the art of persuasion.

The municipalities of the Empire took a keen interest in the higher levels of education, and any city that thought anything of itself provided chairs of grammar and rhetoric. The emperors, as patrons of the arts, privately endowed chairs at Rome and Athens, but there was no philosophy of education as a tool for socialization in the modern sense. Education was narrowly conceived as the prerogative of a small elite that had the time and the money to spend on it. Extending this kind of education broadly would have seemed absurd and probably impossible.

The middle classes strove for culture and advanced as far as their resources would permit them. Textbooks and summaries of all kinds existed, and great collections of miscellaneous information on every conceivable subject were produced in quantity. Summaries of history, philosophy, science, and geography could be picked up from any bookseller. Even the so-called well-educated people tended to accumulate odd bits of information—mythological, antiquarian, and historical—and their knowledge of philosophy, the sciences, and mathematics was minimal, even by ancient standards.

Culture, the Masses, and Daily Life   Although the culture of the educated had a bookish, academic quality, Greco-Roman civilization reached out to the masses of the people, especially the city-dwellers, in a number of informal ways.

The mere fact of living together in a city had the effect of extending to other classes the high culture of the upper classes. There was a much greater degree of physical proximity between the classes than there is in modern society. To begin with, the cities were designed principally for use by pedestrians, not vehicles, and it was assumed that there would be large population densities in the downtown, forum areas, where most public business was transacted. Here trials were conducted, elections held, and public announcements made. The people met again in the theaters, amphitheaters, gymnasia, and baths and at the formal religious celebrations held periodically throughout the year. Roman imperial officials, town councillors, and magistrates could be easily identified and approached. Merchants and shopkeepers went about their daily business, and life was carried on in a very personal, intimate manner. Gossip and rumor, functioning as the media of ancient town-life, carried tales all over the city, sparing no one.

The cultured and well-to-do classes of the cities of the Empire were not segregated elites who had little contact with the rest of society. The very ideals of urban life demanded an interchange between the classes, and the summit of a man's career was to have himself honored by his fellow citizens as patron and benefactor of his city. The rich were expected to make tangible contributions to the public life of the city by serving, unremunerated, as magistrates, giving festivals, maintaining the food and water supply, erecting public buildings, and generally contributing to the essentials of a civilized life. These services were known as liturgies. The purely private enjoyment of wealth and the gratification of intellectual curiosity or aesthetic tastes were considered aberrations. Although the rich had their country villas, their primary residences were their town houses.

In an even more informal way the culture of the upper classes was passed on through the medium of classical art. New cities were arranged in grid patterns, and markets, temples, basilicas, and theaters were designed according to carefully conceived plans. They conveyed a sense of order and dignity to the town-dwellers and to visitors from the countryside, and some cities, such as Timgad in the wilderness of the Algerian Atlas Mountains, were deliberately created as showplaces to impress the barbarians. Hundreds of cities existed in areas where today there are few. Africa had 500, for example, and there were about 300 in Asia Minor (modern Turkey). A great deal of cultural diffusion must have occurred even without any formal government plan. The Romans, for the most part, were concerned with the cities as administrative, not cultural, centers.

Urban Life and Romanization

A peculiarity of the Romans (at least to our way of thinking) was their careful gradation of cities in ascending order of importance. In reality, no better way could have been devised to display in very graphic fashion the hierarchical arrangement of Roman society itself and Rome's dominating position in it. Native peoples throughout the Empire could not miss the overt distinctions of rank among cities and the advantages of those near the top of the pyramid.

At the head of the ranks of Roman cities came those that enjoyed the title of Roman colony and at the same time possessed what was called the Italian Right (*jus Italicum*). The latter privilege, in practice not very common, granted immunity from taxation and from the authority of the local Roman governor. All other cities and territories, of whatever status, paid the standard land and poll taxes, the *tributum soli* and *tributum capitis*, respectively. Italy, as the homeland of the Romans, was immune in this period from these taxes.

Below these specially favored colonies came the other Roman colonies, and below them the cities (*municipia*) of Roman and Latin citizenship. Latin municipalities were of two kinds, those whose elected magistrates received Roman citizenship automatically on election (*Latium minus,* or the Lesser Latin Right) and those whose local senators (decurions) automatically received Roman citizenship, regardless of whether they were elected (*Latium maius,* or the Greater Latin Right). Everyone else in these cities was, of course, a Latin citizen and as such barred from the imperial civil service and the Roman magistracies. Practically speaking, this was not a major disadvantage, and Roman law was administered in both Latin and Roman municipalities. Alongside Roman and Latin foundations were the native cities (*civitates*), villages (*vici*), and districts (*pagi*), in which the majority of the non-Roman population continued to live under its own laws and customs.

During the Empire the Romans encouraged their subjects to build and settle in cities, thereby giving up their old rural haunts and inaccessible fortresses on strategic sites. These new foundations were rapidly advanced to first the Latin status and then the Roman, and in this way whole areas of the west were Romanized. The ultimate achievement was the winning of the title of Roman colony, to which great prestige was attached. Leptis Magna, the birthplace of emperor Septimius Severus, was originally an ordinary non-Roman *civitas*, ruled by Punic magistrates. By the end of the first century A.D. it was a *municipium,* probably with Latin status, and then under Trajan it became a full Roman colony. Finally, under Septimius Severus, its native son, it received the Italian Right. By the end of the second century A.D. cities with un–Roman-sounding names such as Nisibis in Syria were made titular colonies, and Lebanese Tyre and Heliopolis were given the coveted Italian Right.

In the eastern half of the Empire, where there were few Romans and citizenship was not widely extended to the native population, the pre-Roman system of local and regional government continued to operate. In the Greek areas a great network of cities existed, each with its own carefully defined and often disputed territory, ruled from within by an oligarchic elite according to its own laws, which might date to its foundation. Elsewhere non-Greek cities existed alongside later Greek foundations, as in Palestine, Lebanon, and Syria, or there were Greek cities with large numbers of non-Greeks in their populations.

This complexity was guaranteed to test the flexibility of Roman governors and administrators, who in their careers might at one stage be in contentious Alexandria, which was always ready to erupt into riots between Greeks and Jews, or in peaceful

Sicily, where nothing ever happened, or in tribal Britain or Africa. Each region had its own particular set of problems—military, cultural, and social. It was a fine training ground for tolerance or, perhaps more usually, benign neglect.

The Uses of Amusement: Games and Gladiators

At the time of Augustus, the Roman calendar had 77 days of public games honoring the gods; within two centuries the number had risen to 176. The gods had reason to be pleased with the Romans. Good portions of some months were practically given over to such games. April, for instance, had the *Ludi Megalenses* (honoring the Great Mother), April 4–10; the *Ludi Cereales* (for the goddess of cereal grains), April 12–19; and the *Ludi Florales* (for a fertility goddess), April 28—May 3. Another good month was September, with the *Ludi Romani* from the fifth to the nineteenth. At these games people in Rome had a chance to see chariot races in the Circus Maximus or, if they could get tickets, theatrical performances at one of the many theaters that from the first century B.C. sprang up around the city.

The circus races pitted four professional teams, the Red, White, Blue, and Green factions (*factiones*), as they were called, against each other in 4-horse races, although teams of up to 8 or 10 horses were also known. According to the poet Ovid,

Although repetitious in appearance, Roman cities offered the amenities of urban life to people from one end of the Empire to the other. Left, enduring brick and concrete buildings line a street in Ostia, the port of Rome; right, Pompeii from the walls.

the circus was also a good place to meet women because the seating was not segregated the way it was in the theaters and amphitheaters. Nevertheless, the main attraction was the races themselves, especially the spectacular crashes that often occurred as the flimsy chariots careened around the circus, pulled by galloping teams of horses.

More people could cram themselves into the great race track of Rome, the Circus Maximus (capacity 250,000), than into all the other theaters in the city combined, but more days of the games were devoted to the theater than to racing. Theatrical performances in the Empire were gaudy spectacles of music, song, and dance aimed at entertaining mass audiences of up to 10,000 people. Occasionally plays of the classical period of the Republic were revived or individual scenes from tragedies performed, but the most popular entertainment was a kind of raunchy vaudeville in which mythological scenes were acted out, often grotesquely, on the stage. Sex and violence were staple elements. Understandably, actors in these performances had bad reputations and were regularly banished from the city by emperors trying to exert some kind of control over unruly audiences.

Gladiators   Gladiatorial shows had a different origin than did the *Ludi,* the state festivals honoring the gods. Originally they were staged as funeral games honoring the dead, and as ways of drawing attention to the virtue of the deceased. They were not financed by the state but by the individual who felt he had an obligation (a *munus; munera,* pl.) to the dead person. By the first century, although still ostensibly motivated by religion, the *munera* had become an important part of the method by which politicians drew favorable attention to themselves and won votes. In a successful bid for the office of aedile, for example, Julius Caesar presented 320 pairs of gladiators in honor of his father—who had died 20 years earlier! Both Pompey and Caesar put on extravagant wild beast hunts. Pompey's games saw the slaughter of 20 elephants, 600 lions, 410 leopards, and the first rhinoceros ever seen in Rome. Not to be outdone by his rival, Caesar also had masses of animals slaughtered at his games including, for the first time, a giraffe.

Given the political potential of such displays it is understandable why Augustus made a point of monopolizing the spectacles and giving magnificent games himself. From his time onward the gladiatorial *munera* were combined on the same day with wild beast hunts in the morning, the execution of low-status criminals around midday, and gladiatorial shows in the late afternoon. It would be an oversimplification of a complex ritualistic event to argue that all that motivated Augustus and his successors was the desire to retain control of the people through bloody but fascinating entertainment. "Bread and the circuses," Juvenal's famous aphorism, applied to the theater and the chariot races of the *Ludi,* not the *munera.* The motivation was more involved.

As the great benefactor (*euergtes*) of the Roman people the emperor was expected to display his munificence independently of the formal religious festivals of the whole community (the *Ludi*). The tradition of grand display was already well established in the Republic, and it suited the emperors to continue it because by

---

MURDEROUS GAMES

On three occasions I gave gladiatorial shows on my own behalf and fifteen times for my sons and grandsons. About 10,000 men fought in these games. . . . On twenty-six occasions I put on wild beast hunts for the people in the circus, forum or amphitheater in which about 3,500 animals were killed.

—Augustus, *Res Gestae* 22

[In celebration of his victories] Trajan gave shows that lasted 123 days during which 11,000 wild and tame animals were killed, and 10,000 gladiators fought.

—Dio, *History of Rome* 68.15.1

---

putting on great shows, they could demonstrate both their own power and the power of the Roman people. Through animal hunts the people could see in an impressively visual way how their power extended throughout what seemed to be the whole world. Through their emperor the people of Rome could order distant nations to provide them with their most exotic animals: lions from Libya; hippopotamuses and crocodiles from Egypt; leopards and giraffes from Africa; tigers and elephants from India; and bears, lynx, and elk from Europe. The wild beast hunts were gaudy celebrations of the immense power and wealth of Rome. Who else but the people of Rome could afford the complete waste of such valuable assets? The slaughter of animals also had symbolic value. In Roman times nature was not as distant as it now seems, nor as well understood. The wilderness was much closer at hand and far from tamed. Wild beasts were seen as cruel and dangerous, not as endangered species, and their slaughter represented the assertion of order over the chaos of wild nature. Even urban populations needed to be reassured that nature was under control, and the arena represented an excellent place to make this point.

The gladiatorial fights were seen in a different light. Gladiators were drawn from the ranks of criminals, slaves, and prisoners of war. They were trained to fight skillfully in stylized forms of combat: the practically naked net-and-trident man was pitted against the man in armor, the "Thracian" against the "Gaul," cavalry against cavalry, charioteers against charioteers. The crowd looked for skill and bravery. They especially looked to see how the gladiators faced death. Sometimes in recognition of a particularly brave performance the crowd declared in favor of a gladiator who had lost, and let the *editor,* the giver of the games (usually the emperor), know how they felt. Drawn from the *perditi homines,* the lost and ruined men of the Empire, gladiators were given a chance to redeem themselves by the display of the most important of all Roman virtues, bravery. By this means they found a way of reintegrating themselves in the society from which they had been ejected by crime, loss in war, or just bad luck.

One final important point about the games must be made. Even though the people of Rome were ruled in the Empire period by emperors, they had not forgotten they were once sovereign. They expected the rulers to pay attention to them and listen to their grievances and demands. If they lacked free speech as individuals they had no qualms about speaking their mind as a group, and the arena provided an excellent venue for the expression of public opinion. Tiberius, who took a statue for his own enjoyment from a public place, was forced to return it after the people complained. Over the years the emperors were forced to hear demands for reduction of taxes and lower grain prices; there complaints about officials. Both Julius Caesar and Marcus Aurelius, who wrote letters and talked to clients and officials during the games, were reminded by the crowd to pay attention. Tiberius, who hated the games and did not attend them, developed a very bad reputation with the people. On the other hand, Claudius and Commodus, whom the elite despised, were much appreciated by the people because they were attentive watchers, or in the case of Commodus, actual participants. The *munera* played an important role in the Romanization of the Empire. In imitation of what went on in Rome, provincial elites spent vast sums of money putting up amphitheaters. Some 272 are known to have existed. Many survive to the present, including the largest of all, the Colosseum.

Religions of the Empire

The great cultural diversity of the Empire was reflected in the chaotic variety of religions, cults, philosophies, and theosophies that offered themselves to the inhabitants of the Roman world. They ranged from the austere, ascetic monotheism of Judaism and Christianity and some of the philosophies to the flamboyant and bloody rituals of Cybele. There were officially sanctioned and supported state cults that functioned openly and splendidly, and small, private groups that met and worshiped in secret. Every taste and class was accommodated. The emperors, although tolerant, tried to maintain some kind of order by putting down practices that did not fit in with their idea of an orderly society or seemed to represent some kind of political threat. Human sacrifice was stopped in Gaul and North Africa, Druidism was stamped out in Celtic lands, and even astrology and magic captured the emperor's attention at times. Simultaneously, the emperors tried to boost the civil religions of the Empire.

Emperor Worship   The emperor was the high priest and head of the Roman state religion, and as such was responsible for maintaining right relations between the gods and humankind. While alive he was a semidivine intermediary between human beings and the gods, and when dead he was a god himself.

In the east, rulers had long been worshiped as being more clearly sources of divine power than the remote deities of traditional belief, although they too were worshiped. It made good sense politically to honor a man-god, for this conveniently combined cult and homage in a single act. In the Republican period the Greeks had identified the goddess Roma as the source of Rome's power and worshiped her, sometimes along with an individual Roman general. Thus the cult of Roma and the general T. Quinctius Flamininus, who "liberated" Greece from Macedonian domination in 197 B.C., was established at Chalcis, where it survived for more than 300 years. During the Principate the cult of Rome and Augustus, replete with temples, altars, and priests, spread throughout the eastern provinces and eventually, following prodding by the emperors, to the west as well. In Italy and Rome homage was paid to the *genius*, or "spirit," of the emperors following the tradition of the cult of the *genius* of the *paterfamilias* (the head of the Roman household) within his own family. Logically, other members of the imperial family were incorporated in the cult of the reigning emperor. Thus, all the peoples of the empire could be viewed as being members of a single family, with the emperor as their kindly but firm *paterfamilias*.

Civil Religions and Cults

The imperial cult was not intended to replace the traditional civil religions or cults that flourished in profusion all over the empire. Most of the cults of the Hellenistic period continued into Roman times. Under the *pax Romana* the worship of Isis spread to the west, where she won thousands of new adherents. An Iranian religion, Mithraism, was popular in the army and offered an attractive combination of doctrine, ritual, and ethical practice. Its adherents believed that the cosmos was in constant tension between the forces of good and evil, light and darkness, life and death. The soul, although immortal, is contaminated by association with the body and must be liberated by an ascetic struggle in which Mithras, who has already conquered death and ascended into heaven, assists. A high level of ethical behavior was expected, but psychological support was supplied by the regular meetings of the Mithraic community, which took place in small, cavelike chapels and included a sacred meal. However, the appeal of Mithraism was limited because it excluded women.

Syncretism and fusion, as in Hellenistic times, was common. In North Africa, Saturn was associated with Jupiter; in Gaul, Mercury was identified with the native Celtic deity Lug and Jupiter with Taranis. At Bath in Britain, Minerva was identified with the local spring goddess, Sulis. Everywhere the ancient festivals and sacrifices continued to require, as always, the financial support of the cities and the upper classes for their suitable enactment. Thousands of people sat or stood in theaters, amphitheaters, town squares, or temple doorways to witness religious spectacles of one kind of another. The shrine of the healing god Asclepius at Epidaurus in Greece had a theater that could accommodate 15,000, and in other parts of the Empire theaters were specially built adjacent to temples to accommodate worshipers at festival times. The celebrations included sacrifices, banquets, dancing, music, games, and processions. At times there were theatrical reenactments of religious or mythological events. Many of the mystery cults, such as those of Eleusis, also staged large-scale, dramatic affairs attracting thousands. Religious festivals were widely publicized outside individual cities in the hope of attracting worshipers (or just tourists, because both would pay). The more magnificent the celebration, the larger the crowds. Pilgrims and tourists alike carried the word of these religious celebrations far and wide.

The Health of Paganism   The strength but also the weakness of the cults and civil religions of the Empire lay in their close ties with the communities in which they were embedded. When their fortunes rose, so did those of the cults: the temples were maintained or embellished, the festivals were splendidly celebrated. The reverse was also true. When cities and communities declined, so did their ability to maintain the cults, which, unsustained by public support, faded. Gods not worshiped ceased to be gods at all or degenerated to the level of local superstitions. Nevertheless, there is little evidence that in the early Empire the traditional cults did not satisfy the religious needs of the people. At least in the cities, if the local cults did not appeal or were not conducted according to one's tastes, there were always other choices. The unity and relative peacefulness of the empire promoted the spread of religions and made exotic alternatives available everywhere. Among those that benefited from these conditions and found a secure niche throughout the Empire were the ancient national religion of Judaism, an approved cult, and its recent, heretical offshoot Christianity, which took centuries before it, too, was approved.

Judaism and Christianity   Judaism and Christianity were both exclusive in their membership and both placed emphasis on the close adhesion to strict ethical practices and dogmatic beliefs. Judaism, in addition to the attractiveness of its high moral standards and its lofty monotheism, was one of the most ancient religions of the Empire. It possessed an important collection of religious books, which propounded in organized fashion its history, laws, and philosophy. It offered a coherent account of the origin of human beings and their history from the earliest times. Its liturgy had the advantages of both the philosophers' lecture hall and the sense of community and brotherhood of the mystery cults.

Christianity borrowed these traits from Judaism but dropped the more extreme demands of the law such as circumcision and the laws of purification. To the Jewish belief that God was the Lord of History, Christians added the assertion that history had found its culmination in the lowly person of Jesus of Nazareth, who was executed by the imperial prefect Pontius Pilate during the reign of the emperor Tiberius.

The message and mission of Jesus emerge out of the world of late Jewish eschatology. Like many of his contemporaries, Jesus believed that the world was enthralled to demonic influences and that liberation would come through the intervention of God, who would overwhelm the forces of evil and set up his own kingdom over which sin and death would have no power. In the past, God had acted in a preliminary way to deliver his people from bondage in such events as the call of Abraham, the Exodus from Egypt, and the end of the Babylonian captivity; now, however, he was preparing to act in a final, decisive manner.

Jesus did not proclaim a new ethical or moral system. He was not primarily a teacher, and his message was not startlingly original; much of it was to be found in traditional Jewish or even pagan ethics. He viewed his mission, rather, as the proclamation of the coming of a new period of history, the Kingdom of Heaven. This he believed was to be brought about not by human means, such as the violent overthrow of governments, or by the observation of laws or ethical rules, but by the active intervention of God in human affairs. Moreover, Jesus' ministry was intended, somehow, to inaugurate the new age. Reaching back to the prophet Isaiah, he identified himself with the servant figure, whose sufferings would atone for the sins of Israel, a scapegoat whose death would usher in the Day of the Lord. Again drawing on the symbolism of Israel's past, Jesus described his death during the Last Supper discourse in terms of the symbols of the Passover. Just as the Exodus was a mighty act by which God had freed the Israelites from Egypt and made them his people, so Jesus' death, his "passover," or passage to the next world, would be the means by which a New Exodus leading to a New Covenant would be brought about. By means of this New Covenant (or Testament), the reign of God was to be initiated, freeing humankind from sin, death, and the power of the demonic world.

For the earliest Christians the kingdom was inaugurated not only by Jesus' death but also by his miraculous resurrection from the dead and his ascension to heaven. New members were brought into the community by the ritual of baptism, which identified them symbolically or sacramentally with the key events of Jesus' life, his death and resurrection. Christian life itself revolved around common worship, preaching, and exhortation. Collections of the sayings and deeds of Jesus were made and told and retold. The common meal shared by early Christians took on the overtones of Jesus' Last Supper with his apostles and became the setting for discussions, readings, and interpretations of Jesus' life and actions. Among the major issues settled in the early years of the Christian community was the question of whether Jesus' message was to be limited to Jews or could be extended to gentiles as well. One of the principal figures in this momentous debate was a Hellenized Jew, Paul of Tarsus. The decision in favor of a wider audience had vital implications for the future of Christianity, the Greco-Roman world in which it came to maturity, and even the world outside the frontiers that was ultimately to achieve a triumph of sorts over Rome.

Rabbinic Judaism   During the first century A.D. there were many competing—though interacting—forms of Judaism in Judaea and among Jews outside Palestine (the Diaspora). In Palestine, two schools, the Sadducees and the Pharisees, differed over doctrinal issues such as the immortality of the soul and punishment after death. In interpreting scripture and the law Sadducees took a literal approach, insisting that only the written scriptures were acceptable sources of revelation, whereas Pharisees were more flexible. The latter claimed that the *Torah* (the law) came in two forms, the one written and the other oral, each necessary and complementary to the other, each God given. Besides these two main schools (further divided into subsects), there were numerous other groups of Jewish ascetics, revolutionaries, mystics, and believers in apocalyptic restoration. Of these the most important were the Essenes and the Qumran, or Dead Sea community (whose library was discovered in caves above the Dead Sea in 1947). The communities of the Diaspora possessed yet another variant of Judaism.

The destruction of the Temple in Jerusalem by the Romans in A.D. 70 and further devastation following the Bar Kochba Rebellion of A.D. 132–135 resulted in a spiritual upheaval in Judaism comparable to the one that followed the destruction of the Temple of Solomon (the First Temple) by the Babylonians in 587–586 B.C., and led directly to the flowering of Rabbinic Judaism. With the elimination of the Second Temple the influence of the Sadducees faded, the Qumran and Essene sects were destroyed or scattered, and the apocalyptic movements discredited. Now, in the absence of the Temple, the synagogue became the vital focus of Jewish religious life. The rabbi as interpreter and wise man replaced the priest, and prayer became a surrogate for animal sacrifice. Of the many traditions of Judaism, Pharisaism proved to be the most vital and capable of responding to the needs of postrevolt Judaism, and it was from this root in particular, though not exclusively, that Rabbinic Judaism developed. In time the oral tradition of the Pharisees was written down and edited. It received definitive form around A.D. 200 in the work known as the *Mishnah,* the basic document of Rabbinic Judaism, which contains statements of the law and the original commentaries of the rabbis. Although it contains some material going back to the third century B.C., the bulk of the Mishnah derives from the first two centuries A.D. From about A.D. 200 to 500, loosely organized groups of scholars in Palestine and Babylonia commented on the Mishnah in a process that ultimately led to the production of two other fundamental documents, the Palestinian and Babylonian Talmuds.

Philosophy, Religion, and Magic   By the time of the Roman peace, philosophy had long since given up its metaphysical search for knowledge and instead devoted itself to the humbler, more practical questions of human conduct. It did not even concern itself with theories of morality but instead sought to give concrete answers to pressing questions of daily life. What is virtue? How should wealth and power be used? How should people cope with change and loss? How involved should a citizen be in civic life? What is human happiness?

All the great schools of philosophy of the past were ransacked to provide answers to these questions. Philosophy was converted into religion and made to reply to questions that the old philosophies and religions had not even raised. It was as though it had been decided that what was needed was not new knowledge but practical answers to pressing moral issues. It was not theoretical information about the nature of human life that was sought but rather instructions on how to conduct one's everyday life: art not science, salvation rather than wisdom, revealed truths in the place of reasoning and speculation. The ability of reason to give secure answers was questioned, and more definitive sources of authority were sought. Syncretism was in the air, and the boundaries between philosophy, science, magic, and religion became blurred to the point where all of these terms became interchangeable. Even Christianity could claim to be a philosophy, meaning a way of life or a way of ascending to God.

For the middle and upper classes, Seneca, Musonius, Epictetus, Plutarch, and others provided examples, sermons, and exhortations to virtue. Seneca turned Stoicism into a religion and criticized abuses of wealth and pleasure, including cultural pursuits, arguing that the true objective of philosophy was to live well. He urged people on, somewhat cheerlessly, in the struggle against evil and developed such a high concept of God that some Christians later concluded that he must have been a convert.

Musonius, who was exiled by Nero, preached gentleness to wrongdoers and forgiveness of injuries, and argued against the double standard for men and women. Apollonius of Tyana taught brotherly helpfulness, courage, and temperance. He spoke against the luxury of the baths at Antioch and the frivolity of the Athenians. He criticized Nero as an effeminate tyrant and encouraged rebellion. Demonax successfully argued the Athenians out of staging gladiatorial contests by saying that they would first have to give up the Altar of Pity in the city before they could introduce such contests. Dio Chrysostom denounced both the sensuality of the rich and the selfishness of the mob. For him the true community was one from which greed, intemperance, and violence were banished and in which everyone lived under law. He glorified the simple life of the peasants and preached moderation to the emperor Trajan. Plutarch's vast knowledge was used in a lifetime devoted to the moral education of his contemporaries. Unlike so many of his gloomy, moralist friends, who viewed life with a deep pessimism, Plutarch cheerfully emphasized the power of positive thinking. People, he said, should think of the good things they have and look for the hidden hand of God in the disasters that befall them. Most of the bitterness of calamities comes from their own doing, he argued, not from events outside themselves.

The masses sought answers to the same kinds of questions that plagued the educated and received answers from hosts of prophets, preachers, oracle mongers, and magicians. The higher speculations of the moral theologians were put into handbook form or popularized by street preachers. Unwashed and rude Cynic philosophers disdained convention and harangued the passers-by, preaching renunciation of all social ties and responsibilities. Proteus Peregrinus, one of the more flamboyant of the Cynics, criticized the emperor Antoninus Pius at Rome and the powerful Herodes Atticus at Athens. Herodes, he said, merely gratified his vanity by his huge benefactions in Greece and elsewhere. Proteus committed ritual suicide in 165 and was hailed as a holy man throughout Greece. Apollonius of Tyana lived as an ascetic, performed miracles, and so impressed his contemporaries that after his death, his cult spread widely.

Others were not so reputable. Alexander of Abonoteichos deliberately set out to mine the potential of the superstitious age. Selecting an out-of-the-way town with a gullible population, he planted a newly hatched snake in a goose egg and then substituted a fully grown snake with a false head. Thus established, he proceeded to hand out answers to sealed questions, which he claimed he never opened. The fraud was attacked by Lucian of Samosata, one of the few disbelievers in an age of credulity.

Roman Society

Citizenship and Status   The complexities of ethnicity, language, culture, and religion were further confused by a bewildering variety of constitutional and legal systems. Almost all the old legal classifications of the Republic continued during the

Empire. First there was the complication of citizenship, because one could have Roman, Latin, or simply native (*peregrine*) status. Of course, Roman citizens were potentially capable of a full political life at Rome, but in addition they had certain rights in criminal law not possessed by anyone else. In cases in which the charge was capital they could appeal from a local court to Rome, and often the mere status of an individual as a Roman would deter local authorities from dispensing summary justice. It was not that Roman citizens were exempt from obeying the local laws of provinces but that as members of the ruling power, their political standing was something a local magistrate needed to take into account. Saint Paul, who had Roman citizenship, made good use of this during his travels in the Roman world, where he often came into conflict with local ruling bodies. Even within the citizenship there were gradations, as some Romans belonged to immune cities and so escaped the standard forms of taxation, or were Romans with freedman (ex-slave) status and so had other built-in restrictions, such as the inability to serve in the legions or hold public office. Then there were persons of the Latin Right, which entitled them to practically the same legal but not the same political privileges as Romans. Being married or single, old or young, independent (*sui iuris*) or under guardianship, male or female, also had important legal consequences. Finally there were slaves, whose only rights were vaguely defined in the Law of Nations (*jus gentium*) and in some specific enactments handed down by the emperors.

Most of the problems arising from citizenship were resolved in A.D. 212 when the emperor Caracalla extended Roman citizenship to almost everyone in the Empire by the Antonine Constitution. This brought the vast majority of the population fully within the scope of Roman constitutional and civil law, so a uniform code could be applied everywhere. Although an egalitarian tendency can be detected in Caracalla's extension of citizenship, there was no concession to democracy. To the extent that the privileges of citizenship were thought to have been watered down by the increase in numbers, there developed another system of classification that counteracted this and ensured the preservation of the traditional system based on wealth and public esteem. This was the distinction between high-status individuals (*honestiores*) and low-status individuals (*humiliores*).

High and Low Status: Honestiores *and* Humiliores

By the second century A.D. the distinction between high- and low-caste inhabitants of the Empire, regardless of their citizenship, was an established fact of law. *Honestiores* could claim special treatment under the law and were subject to much less stringent criminal punishments than *humiliores*. For example, a provincial governor could not execute persons of high status and could exile them only after consultation with the emperor, whereas *humiliores* received summary judicial treatment and punishment. This distinction cut across citizenship bounds, so that ultimately it was more advantageous to be a member, especially a powerful member, of the upper classes with high status than to be a poor citizen with low status.

Those who belonged to the *honestiores* included first of all senators and equestrians, then decurions (local senators), soldiers, veterans, and some professionals. The scramble for citizenship became a scramble for inclusion in one of the higher classifications. Such inclusion was one of the ways the Romans could ensure their continuing interest in local administration and the army because service in either brought membership in the higher caste. This was not quite as discriminatory as it seems because those who scrambled hardest also needed the higher status the most. These were the property owners of moderate holdings whose material goods made them targets for exploitation by the tax collectors, soldiers, and imperial administrators. The lower classes, as always, had little to protect them beyond public opinion, their membership in some organization patronized by the powerful, such as burial societies, or direct dependence on some powerful individual. Toward the end of this period even this system of privilege failed to protect the middle-class property owners from the exactions of the tax collectors, and there was a great deal of pressure either to move up to such a high status, either equestrian or senatorial, as to be out of reach, or to stop such attempts altogether and become the client of someone powerful enough to offer adequate protection.

The Family   It is difficult to make generalizations about the family in the Empire because all the family types discussed to this point—Middle Eastern, traditional Greek, Hellenistic Greek, Jewish, and Roman, as well as some new forms—were represented among its diverse peoples. Just because the Romans brought a rather superficial unity to the various regions of the Empire did not mean that its inhabitants abandoned their own cultures and social traditions. Probably the more relaxed customs of the Hellenistic world continued to make inroads among the inhabitants of older Greek cities, but social customs, especially concerning marriage, children, and the transmission of property, are notoriously slow to change. Where Romans settled in large numbers they brought and maintained their family traditions, but even in the Republic the Romans themselves were far from culturally or socially homogeneous.

For the first time we catch glimpses of northern European family styles among the Celtic and Germanic populations living in the Empire. More than anything else it was the greater freedom enjoyed by women among these peoples that caught the disapproving attention of the conservative, patriarchal Greeks and Romans. The ultimate condemnation was reserved for such warrior-queens as the British tribal leader Boudicca, who led her troops into action against the Romans. Horror tales were also told of German women who slit the throats of prisoners (non-Romans in this case) over huge bronze cauldrons as sacrifices to the gods for victory in battle.

With the emergence of Christianity the kind of family and marriage relations that had been common among Jews began to spread among diverse elements of the Empire's population. Ultimately this family type had a very important influence on social relations, but not in the first centuries of the Empire. In its earliest form Christianity had the potential to alter familial relations profoundly. It challenged the old concepts of patriarchal dominance by suggesting that all members of the Christian community were equal and that the family of Christians had replaced the family of the secular world. These radical implications were never pursued to their logical conclusion, however, and ultimately traditional patriarchal powers prevailed.

WOMEN, CHRISTIANITY, AND SOCIAL CONFLICT

In the following selection noted theologian Elisabeth Schüssler Fiorenza points out the radical differences between early Christian and Roman assumptions about the role of women and the family. The same would be true to only a slightly lesser extent of traditional Greek assumptions about the position of women:

> The Christian missionary movement conflicted with the existing order of the patriarchal household because it converted *individuals* independently of their social status and function in the patriarchal household. Christian mission caused social unrest because it admitted wives and slaves as well as daughters and sons into the house-church, even when the *paterfamilias* was still pagan and had not converted to Christianity. . . .
>
> The social implications of religious conversion were realized in the house-church as the discipleship community of equals. Independently of their fathers and husbands, women held membership and gained leadership positions in the Christian missionary movement. Even in the beginning of the second century female and male slaves still expected their freedom to be purchased by the Christian community. . . .
>
> According to Mark's Gospel, the discipleship of equals is the community of brothers and sisters who do not have a "father." It is the "new family" that has replaced all the natural, social kinship ties of the patriarchal family. It does not consist of rulers and subjects, of relationships of superordination and subordination. According to Paul it is the *ekklesia,* the "assembly of the saints" who have equal access to God in the Spirit and are therefore coequal members in the body of Christ.

These radical assumptions about the early Christian community did not survive much later than the second century A.D.

Source: Elisabeth Schüssler Fiorenza, *Bread, Not Stone: The Challenge of Feminist Biblical Interpretation* (Boston: Beacon Press, 1984), pp. 74–75.

Among traditional Romans, children still technically came under the control of the *paterfamilias,* but his influence continued to wane. More and more women controlled their own property and as a result presumably had greater freedom in their marriages. However, because most army recruiting now took place among provincials, fewer Roman husbands would have been on campaign for long periods, so it is hard to estimate the degree of freedom Roman women had in this period compared to the Republic. The ideology of female inferiority remained unchanged.

Apex of the Social Pyramid: The Senate   Under the Republic, senators not only provided Rome with its generals, political leaders, judges, and high administrators but also controlled the city's political life. When the emperors took over the latter role from the Senate, they still needed capable personnel, but because of Roman prejudice against a professional military or civil service, such people came from only the senatorial and equestrian classes. The dilemma of the emperors was therefore how to use the Senate's great ability to produce, screen, and test personnel without conceding it too much political power. So conservative was the Roman tradition that it was to take over two centuries before an independent recruitment system replaced the old method.

The great strength of the Senate lay in its tradition of public service. By custom the Roman upper classes found their fulfillment in holding state offices and not in private business ventures or artistic or philosophical dilettantism. Even though the Senate lost its political power as a corporate, governing body, it never lost its social position. Throughout the whole period of the Empire it remained the focus of the ambitious among the upper classes everywhere and even expanded its influence as more and more provincials entered it. Even when the Senate lost contact with the political, administrative, and military branches in the third-century crisis and its members ceased to be employed in high commands or as governors, its social standing and privileges continued and ultimately outlasted even the western Empire itself.

In a status-conscious society, membership in the senatorial order represented the ultimate achievement of a man's life. It was an exclusive club where the wealthiest and most illustrious inhabitants of the Roman world were to be found along with its current and future rulers. In a practical sense, too, membership in the Senate was of enormous advantage. Specific privileges included access to the highest offices, commands of armies, governorships of provinces and cities, and all the attendant opportunities for accumulating or increasing wealth and power. Down to the third century all the emperors were drawn from the ranks of the senators. Whatever the dangers involved—and they were great when suspicious emperors occupied the throne—it was a most attractive class to belong to. In an age when public recognition meant everything, the broad purple stripe of the senatorial toga was the symbol of the highest achievement and received due recognition from the citizenry.

REQUIREMENTS AND COMPOSITION   The requirements for membership in the Senate were still largely those of the Republic: wealth and the holding of public office. However, sons of senators now belonged automatically to the senatorial order, though not necessarily to the Senate. As before, there were presenatorial posts, such as the military tribunate, which senatorials were expected to fill, thus maintaining the upper classes' important contact with the army. Then followed the offices of quaestor, aedile or tribune of the plebs, praetor, and finally consulate. Posts in Rome were unpaid and required the expenditure of considerable amounts of money. The satirist Martial, for example, tells the story of a woman who promptly divorced her husband when she found out he was standing for the praetorship.

The Senate was neither a closed hereditary system nor a meritocracy. Senatorial families tended to die out, and the most prominent were often targets for hostile emperors. Constant infusion of new members from the upper ranks of the equestrian class was therefore a necessity, and this class in turn drew on the one beneath it, the curial or decurion class, which made up the aristocracy of the provincial cities.

In this way a healthy upward movement was maintained, and over the years the composition of the Senate gradually changed. From being exclusively Roman in the early Republic, the Senate was dominated by Italians in the late Republic and under the Julio-Claudians. Then came a steady influx from the western provinces. Seneca, who acted as tutor and adviser to Nero, was from Spain, as was his brother Gallio, who was governor in Achaea when Saint Paul was accused of stirring up trouble in Corinth. The emperor Vespasian was from the rural districts of Italy, and his successors Trajan, Hadrian, Antonius Pius, and Marcus Aurelius were descendants of Italian settlers in Spain and southern Gaul. Africans began to enter the Senate around A.D. 100. Lusius Quietus, who helped put down the revolt in Judaea under Hadrian, was a Moor, and in 193 another African, Septimius Severus from Leptis Magna in modern Libya, ascended the imperial throne. The eastern provinces began to make their contributions at about the same time, and in the second century new senators came from the Danube provinces and Dalmatia (in the former Yugoslavia). By the third century A.D., more than half the Senate was from the provinces, mostly Africa or the Greek east.

CULTURAL TRADITIONS   In addition to serving the Empire in a practical way, senators had the leisure time to devote to literature and the opportunity to acquire a good education.

Tacitus, who was the son-in-law of Agricola, one of the great governors of Britain, and a governor himself in Asia, composed a brilliant, bitter history of the first-century emperors. A friend of his, the younger Pliny, wrote a series of stylish letters that constitutes one of the principal sources for the social history of the Empire. Suetonius' *Lives of the Caesars,* which is full of biographical information and scandalous anecdotes, was favorite reading among the middle classes. Many senators dabbled in poetry, and all practiced rhetoric, both in the law courts and privately. Pliny tried out his *Panegyric* to Trajan on his friends in a recital lasting three days and suffered equally at their hands. His writings were so popular that senators at the end of the Empire in the west were still studying him and producing similar pieces of vapid rhetoric. In the second century a flourishing movement known as the Second Sophistic (after the Sophists of the fifth and fourth centuries B.C., who had invented formal rhetoric) revived the style and vocabulary of earlier Greek oratory and brought to the fore a number of highly talented individuals such as Aelius Aristides and Dio Chrysostom, who delivered lectures all over the Empire and cultivated the favor of the emperors and the Roman aristocracy.

The Second Tier: The Equestrians   In the Republic the equestrian class had formed the second level of the aristocracy. Like the Senate, it consisted of two groups, those actually involved in state and public affairs and those who were content to live their lives on their estates with only minimum participation in civic life. Between the senatorial and equestrian classes there was no essential social or economic distinction. Both belonged to the leisure classes, had their capital invested in land, and shared the same conservative viewpoints.

In the Empire the same generally held true, but with some important exceptions. Although there were still few senators, 600 if we count only those who were actually in the Senate, the equestrian class had expanded enormously. For example, Gades in Spain and Padua in Italy each had 500 equestrians on their citizen rosters. All over the Empire the propertied classes vied for membership in this class and the privileges it conferred. Outwardly these consisted of the narrow purple stripe on the toga and the right to sit in the first rows of the theater and circus, minor perquisites perhaps but, in view of the high degree of status consciousness in the Empire, important enough to be sought. More significant was the special privilege of exemption from municipal burdens that equestrians shared with senators and their right of access to the highest level of the aristocracy, the Senate.

Although many among the propertied classes were content to enjoy the privileges of membership in the equestrian order, it had another, more formal aspect that attracted the more ambitious.

THE EQUESTRIAN CIVIL SERVICE   Obviously, the Senate could not supply all the officers and administrators needed by the Empire, even allowing for Roman reluctance to create a bureaucracy. There was also the problem that many offices were not of sufficient dignity to permit a senator to hold them but nevertheless required a certain amount of ambition, education, responsibility, and initiative. Thousands of men were needed to command the non-Roman units of the army, the auxiliaries; to supervise and manage the emperor's private properties and estates; to act as jurors; to run the departments of the central government; and to perform other important tasks. Unwilling to set up a true civil service system and dispense with the basic idea of dignity, public service, and patronage as the prime criteria for officeholding, the emperors from Vespasian on simply expanded the equestrian order and drew upon it for their manpower needs. Gradually a junior administrative service parallel to that of the Senate grew up and began to attract those interested in such a career from all over the Empire.

In principle, at least, military service was a prerequisite for an equestrian career. Members of the local municipal aristocracy who chose this kind of a career could enter the equestrian branch of the army directly and perform their three tours of duty (*tres militiae*) as prefect of an auxiliary unit, legionary tribune, and prefect of the auxiliary cavalry, or they could enter as centurions and follow that career, sometimes preferred because it offered permanent service after the *tres militiae*. In either case, having had considerable experience, they would then enter the equestrian civil service as procurators. In this capacity they could serve in a vast number of governing and administrative posts.

At the lower levels equestrians supervised the numerous estates, mines, and possessions of the emperor. They were his tax collectors and his overseers of the mint and the public transportation system (*cursus publicus*). At higher levels they were governors of minor provinces, especially the more recently conquered, such as Austria (Raetia) or Judaea. In Rome they were in charge of the food supply (*annona*), the fire department (*vigiles*), and the Praetorian Guard, the latter commanders (the Praetorian Prefects) being second only to the emperor in power.

Alongside the military equestrian career there developed a purely civilian one that drew upon literary figures, academicians, and lawyers. The first two tended to end up in areas involving diplomacy, correspondence, and foreign languages; the legal specialists provided their services directly to emperors, governors, and procurators. As the administrative branch grew, law became more important, and lawyers began to play a proportionately greater role. The legal powers of the Praetorian Prefects expanded, and when the two great jurists Papinian and Ulpian were prefects under the Severi, they set about a thoroughgoing reorganization of the administration.

In general, the equestrian class made available to the emperor a broader and more dependable pool of talent than the Senate, but mostly from the same kind of desirable social background. From the viewpoint of the propertied classes of the Empire and even for the ambitious among the lower classes, the equestrian order and an equestrian career offered the incentives of social advancement, good pay and security, and the privileges of a higher legal status.

The Decurion or Curial Class: The Third Tier   The municipalities of the west and Roman colonies everywhere were microcosms of Rome itself. They had their senates (*curiae*) and their magistrates, which they elected annually on the Roman model, at least in theory, not at random but on the basis of character, public service, and wealth.

Generally, the local senates in the west consisted of 100 members, although in the east they were much larger. Each city had its own charter and laws, and took care of its own administration. The local magistrates saw to the collection of the imperial taxes and were responsible for the maintenance of peace in the city and the upkeep of its public services. This involved supervising the possessions of the city, its land, mines, and properties, and from this income seeing that its temples, walls, and public buildings were maintained, its water and food supplies were guaranteed, and its essential games and festivals to the gods were performed. Because the income generally fell short of these demands, the local ruling classes were expected to make up the difference out of their own pockets. In good times there was a great deal of competition among the rich to show their generosity and receive in return the shouted approval of the population in the streets and arenas and the erection of an honorary statue or inscription. Often such benefactors also ended up paying for the inscription or even the statute, being content, they claimed, that the population had voted the honor. Being a member of the local senate and a magistrate was thus an expensive business, but it was assumed that public accolades and recognition constituted adequate compensation for the cash outlay. When this assumption was challenged in bad times, the Empire had a serious crisis on its hands.

Like the senatorial and equestrian classes, the curial classes were themselves divided in ranks of dignity, and they jealously maintained their gradations of honor. A standard feature of municipal life that enshrined this principle was the wealthy's custom of setting up commemorative endowments that made provision for the distribution of money to the townspeople on certain days, such as festivals. These

Provincial elites: Syrian man (left) and woman (right) with inscriptions in Syriac (a dialect of Aramaic) and Greek. Although the poses are Roman, the style—the wide-open eyes and the simplified facial features, for example—represents a departure from the Greco-Roman tradition and anticipate the taste of the late Empire.

distributions were made on a strictly hierarchical basis, more going proportionately to the magistrates than to the members of the Senate and so on, down the list to the lowest levels, with the poorest receiving the least. The notion that the poor per se might be deserving was quite foreign to the mentality of the people of the Roman world.

There was a great craving for distinction of any kind, and each class imitated the one above it to the degree that its financial resources permitted. If senators and equestrians established foundations and endowed them with millions or hundreds of thousands of sesterces, the other levels of society created their endowments in the thousands, hundreds, or even, pathetically, tens of sesterces. It was this desire for public recognition that accounts for the vast numbers of inscriptions that are the main source of social history in the Empire.

Freedmen and Augustales: Status Among Former Slaves

A large segment of Roman society was held in slavery, but liberal traditions of manumission made for a large class of freedmen who either had been freed by their masters or had saved enough to secure their own manumission. Because a lot of the trade, shopkeeping, and manufacturing of the Empire lay in their hands, they were often extremely wealthy and ambitious. It was logical, therefore, for the Romans to extend to freedmen the same kind of social regimentation that existed among the freeborn, with the double purpose of securing the services of the ambitious and the talented and minimizing discontent.

The sensitivity of the Romans to dignity would not permit ex-slaves to participate fully in the political system, but their ingenuity created a way around this by the invention of the college of *Augustales*. This corporation, which was extended to the cities of the Empire and was responsible for the upkeep of the imperial cult, consisted of the wealthiest freedmen. Chosen by the local senates, this group came to constitute a kind of aristocracy among the ex-slaves. Although barred from office, they had the right to wear purple-bordered togas, which distinguished them from the masses, both freeborn and servile, and often were granted the insignia of public office, though not the office itself, a common sleight of hand by which the Romans got around impossible situations of social and political life. Like city magistrates, they paid a heavy fee upon entry into their society and were then expected to contribute lavishly to the expenses of city activities. The rewards were the same as for the freeborn magistrates: public applause and recognition at the festivals and games and the erection of honorary inscriptions and statues. Their names are associated with every known benefaction: sponsoring festivals, games, and banquets; erecting all kinds of public buildings, such as baths and arenas; and giving small donations such as wood and oil for the baths. Their vulgarity as *nouveaux riches* was a well-known literary theme, but nevertheless, side by side with the magistrates of the cities of the Empire, they enjoyed (or suffered) the publicity and reduction of their fortunes by the masses, who knew how to extract some return for the only thing they had to offer or withhold: their applause and recognition.

The Collegia: Status for Everyone   The compulsion to organize into groups and then develop further classifications within the groups extended even to the lowest levels of society.

From the first century A.D. burial societies (*collegia*) were permitted by the government and rapidly spread all over the Empire. The purpose of these societies was to bury the dead and honor their memory with inscriptions and with celebrations at banquets at which all the members gathered. Each society had its own charter and bylaws, elected its own officers, and had its own patron deity in whose honor it gathered. Members paid an entrance fee and gathered periodically to eat a banquet or celebrate a festival of the god. The societies could own property, and the wealthier ones owned shrines, meeting houses, and gardens where they held their events. It was considered one of the civic duties of the curial classes and of the *Augustales* to give gifts to or endow these burial societies. Such benefactors were then honored by being elected patrons of the society—the usual Roman social trade-off. There was a practical side to this custom. The Roman cult of the dead was deeply ingrained, and its perpetuation was of the utmost importance. If a family should die out, the burial society would indefinitely continue to honor the memory of its deceased, especially if they were benefactors.

Procession of *vici magistri:* The equivalent at Rome of the *Augustales* elsewhere, the *vici magistri* were responsible for protecting the cult spirits of their districts (*vici*) as well as the *genius* of the emperor. These well-to-do freedmen took their responsibilities seriously and proudly displayed their piety and their role in the public life of the city by erecting this expensive monument in the first century A.D.

The organization of these societies was modeled on that of society at large and imitated exactly the etiquette of the ruling classes. Strict precedence was observed at the gatherings, and donations from patrons were distributed to the membership in graded amounts, just as a distribution to the population at large was made in the cities. Because these societies were open to all members of society, servile or free, male or female, all classes could indulge their desire to have a title, achieve some distinction, and be above someone else. Even the lowliest might win the duly recognized title of tribune or quaestor of such a society and to that extent participate in the larger civic life.

There were other motivations for joining *collegia*. In the fluid society of the early Empire, the desire to form artificial communities, especially in the cities, was very strong. Here the uprooted and the alienated could gather for mutual support, protection, and pure conviviality. From top to bottom the Roman world was grouped and categorized, each level rated on a general scale of dignity and each group further internally subdivided. Movement from one level to another was possible but slow, often taking generations. In the meantime, a father might console himself, as we often see in the inscriptions, with his own achievements while hoping to see his sons rise higher. A common type of inscription is that in which parents with Greek names and freedmen status celebrate the election of a son with a different, Latin name, as aedile or quaestor of some local senate. This man's son might go on to a successful career in the equestrian civil service, perhaps emerging as a senator, governor, or even emperor.

UPWARD MOBILITY

In the late Republic and early Empire large numbers of slaves, especially urban slaves, were manumitted by their masters and mistresses. Because citizenship was conferred at the time of manumission, it was fairly easy for freedmen to blend with the freeborn population, and even easier for their children to do so. In this inscription clearly well-off parents, whose names indicate that they are ex-slaves, put up a memorial to their son, who had "made good" in the town of Capena near Rome. Unlike his parents, the son's name does not suggest servile status. He instead possesses the full titulature of a freeborn Roman citizen, a point made with pride by the parents, who (or at least the father) were at one time slaves of the imperial household of the Flavian dynasty (A.D. 69–96):

> T. Flavius Mythus, freedman of Augustus, and Flavia Diogis, parents, have set aside [this burial area] for their most devoted son, T. Flavius Flavianus, son of Flavius, of the Quirinal Tribe, aedile and quaestor-designate of the federate city of Capena. They do this also for themselves, their freedmen and their freed-women and their descendents. This property, consisting of about 4 jugera marked off from the Cutulenian farm, comes with a bath house and adjacent buildings on both sides of the road. An aqueduct supplies water from the Cu-tulenian farm.

Source: H. Dessau, *Inscriptiones Latinae Selectae* (Berlin, 1892), no. 5770.

THE GOVERNMENT, THE ARMY, AND SOCIETY

The Emperor and His Limitations

The emperor who presided over the sprawling regions of the Roman world was no autocrat whose well-developed machinery of government enabled him to rule despot-ically over his docile subjects. Power came to him not from heaven but from the Sen-ate and people of Rome, and as late as the sixth century A.D. Pope Gregory the Great could say that the difference between barbarian kings and Roman emperors was that the latter were the lords of free men. However, the emperor was extremely powerful. He was the head of the Roman religion, the commander-in-chief of the armies, the principal lawmaker, and the ultimate court of appeal. It was only by convention that this power had to be disguised, and over the years the disguise melted away. Even so, the limitations on the emperor's powers were very real, and none of the emperors had anything like the resources of the modern totalitarian ruler.

The emperor's responsibilities were overwhelming, the first being to defend the Empire against its outside enemies. For this the army had to be maintained in constant readiness over thousands of miles of frontier. New recruits, armaments, and supplies had to be shipped to the farthest corners of the world in a regular, dependable fashion. Suitable officers from generals to centurions had to be selected, trained, and appointed—no easy task in any army of 350,000 to 400,000 men spread over 45 provinces. The military responsibilities alone would have taken all the time of an emperor, as in fact they did in times of invasion or civil war. Military responsibilities, however, were only part of the emperor's problems. He had to maintain peace within the Empire as well as without.

Relations with the Senate were never easy and remained one of the great unresolved problems of the Empire. The Senate was the common meeting ground of the wealthiest and most influential figures in the Empire and the source of all its high administrators and military officers. Its members were the opinion makers of the Empire, with tentacles extending everywhere. Every emperor had to consider the possibility of treason in his midst, and Domitian used to complain that emperors led miserable lives because only their murders could convince people that conspiracies against them were real.

Before the rise of Rome, Greek cities had been racked by internal dissent and fought each other endlessly. Tribesmen had forever been at one another's throats, and only the introduction of Roman rule brought peace. Although it was the proud boast of the Empire that, in the words of Epictetus, "there are no longer any wars, no battles, no brigandage, no piracy," in reality the natural state of things tended constantly to reassert itself. The mobs of Alexandria and Antioch rioted regularly, and the cities, especially in the east, competed ferociously for first place in their provincial rankings. In civil wars they joined opposite sides, as Lyon and Vienne did in the war to see who would succeed Nero and as Nicomedia and Nicaea, Antioch and Laodicaea, Tyre and Beirut, did in the civil war following the death of Commodus. In addition, each province had its own particular set of problems. In Bithynia in Asia at one stage it was overbuilding; in Algeria and Morocco, the raids of desert tribesmen; in Judaea, religious unrest. The real task of the emperor was to find competent and trustworthy personnel to rule and guard such cities and regions.

Sometimes the solutions devised by the emperors were worse than the original problems. Bad governors, rioting soldiers, and unscrupulous officials were often a greater threat to peace than the unruly urban factions and rural tribesmen themselves. One governor cavalierly dispensed justice to his subjects on a sliding scale—more compensation for a high-ranking person than a low-ranking one—necessitated, he claimed, by the greater risk involved. Tiberius warned his governors to shear his sheep, not flay them, but the long list of trials of governors accused of misdeeds shows that this command was often ignored. Perhaps it was some consolation to the provincials that there were any trials at all. Of the 40 known cases that came to trial from the time of Augustus to that of Trajan (27 B.C.–A.D. 117), 28 ended in conviction.

Getting the Job Done: Imperial Administrators

At the beginning of the Principate, the main personnel resources of the emperor were a handful of senatorial governors, equestrian legates, and financial agents

---

SLAVES RUNNING THE EMPIRE

The early emperors ran the empire the way the great nobles of the Republic ran their great estates. They did this with the assistance of their family, friends, freedmen, and slaves. The following inscription suggests how important slaves could be in the running of the Empire and what influence they wielded, not to mention what kind of households they themselves had.

> To Musicus Scurranus, slave of Tiberius Caesar Augustus, manager of the Gallic treasury in the province of Lyons. This monument is put up by his slaves who were with him in Rome when he died. He was a worthy master.

Venustus, agent	Epaphra, butler	Facilis, footman
Decianus, accountant	Primus, valet	Anthus, butler
Dicaeus, secretary	Communis, steward	Hedylus, steward
Mutatus, secretary	Pothus, footman	Firmus, cook
Creticus, secretary	Tiasus, cook	Secunda ?
Agathopus, doctor		

Source: H. Dessau, *Inscriptions Latinae Selectae* (Berlin, 1892), 1514.

(procurators), members of his own family and close personal friends (his *consilium*, or council), and the freedmen and slaves of his household. To a surprising degree, the emperors ran the Empire the way a Roman *paterfamilias* ran his family. Government tended to be informal and personal, characterized by exchanges of letters (which the emperor himself read), recommendations by friends, and purely personal choices and decisions arrived at in consultation with the *consilium*. The real professionals were the freedmen and slaves of the emperor's household, and to a large extent, even with the development of the equestrian civil service, this remained true to the end of the Principate. By modern standards, or even the standards of the ancient Near East or China, the Empire was grossly underadministered. A few thousand individuals, most of them amateurs or part timers, ran an empire of over 50 million inhabitants. In terms of efficiency, this was an extraordinarily successful operation; conversely, Roman administrative aims were very limited and were governed largely by political considerations. Peace had to be maintained, the frontiers defended, taxes collected, and independent sources of power prevented from developing. Given these goals, a large bureaucracy was not only superfluous but undesirable. The principal work of administration at the local level, even the initial steps of collecting the taxes, was left to the individual city councils or senates of the Empire. Initially regarded as an honor, these responsibilities eventually became a tremendous burden and contributed to the failure of the Empire. Nevertheless, the overall result was to keep Roman presence in the provinces minimal, outside the frontier areas where the legions were stationed. In this respect the emperors continued the traditions of the Republic.

Governors   Governors of the frontier provinces had the double task of ruling the civilian population and commanding whatever armed forces happened to be there. These might consist of only a few auxiliary units, as in Austria, or two or three legions, as in Syria or the Rhine area. As chief administrator, judge, and general, the governor needed as much political ability as military.

In the peaceful provinces the prime responsibility of the governor was to maintain order. He had to do this without the assistance of the legions or even of a well-developed bureaucracy. His staff was minute. At most he was allowed three or four assistants, and beyond that he had to round up his own staff among his friends in Rome and the provinces and among his own servants. When Fronto, a close friend of Marcus Aurelius, was appointed governor of Asia in the mid–second century A.D., he asked friends from Cirta, his hometown in Africa, to come along, as well as some literary figures from Alexandria and a military expert from Morocco. Some other individuals from Cilicia were also invited.

The political position of the governor was crucial. With no military forces to speak of at his disposal, the peace of the province depended on his ability to maintain good relations with the ruling oligarchies of the cities. This could be complicated by collusion between these and other Roman officials already in the province, such as imperial procurators (financial agents), who reported directly to the emperor, or by personal contacts between the local aristocracy and powerful members of the Senate. Although theoretically the governor had the power of life and death over his subjects, he had to tread carefully and treat each case individually lest he stir up trouble for himself either in Rome or in the province itself.

The law of the province (*lex provinciae*), which was drafted when each province was initially set up, established the jurisdiction of the governor with regard to the various cities, towns, and districts of the province. Because these subdivisions could range from Roman colonies to simple rural districts, the governor had to be prepared to face all sorts of complicated questions involving boundary disputes, claims of change of status, privilege, and the like. All major crimes—such as murder, arson, rape, and adultery—and lawsuits involving large sums of money came to his court. Cases were heard directly by the governor, who sat surrounded by the friends he had brought with him from Rome as well as local Romans invited to join this group (the *consilium*). Complicating factors were whether the defendants were Roman and whether they were from the upper or lower classes (*honestiores* or *humiliores*). In addition to the legal difficulties, there was always the lurking political question of what effect his decision might have on the general peace of the province. There was no one to tell him what to do or exactly how far his jurisdiction extended. Should he refer the case to the emperor, as Pliny did when confronted with accusations against Christians, or should he settle the matter on his own? Should he dodge hot issues or turn a blind eye to the corrupt practices he found in the province? How should he cope with provincials who were exploiting their fellows? Should he take the risk of being told by the local oligarchs that he was no friend of Caesar if he defended the poor and lowly against their highly placed oppressors? Even the most conscientious governors must have been perplexed by issues such as these.

Bearing the Burden: Financing the Empire   A governor was not responsible for the finances of the province except in a very general sense. The actual maintenance of roads, city walls, aqueducts, temples, and other structures was the responsibility of the local senates, as were police surveillance and public entertainment. The city magistrates and senates were also responsible for the collection of the two main taxes, the poll tax (*tributum capitis*) and the land tax (*tributum soli*). The first was a tax of 1 percent of capital valuation that all provincials had to pay, and the second was a fixed tax on the produce of the land. To collect these taxes, which were then passed on to the Roman fiscal agents, the quaestors and procurators, a census of the inhabitants and the land in the province had to be maintained by the city councils. This census included the numbers of people, farms, acres devoted to pasturage and agriculture, vineyards, olive groves, and even trees.

Along with receiving the taxes from the cities and townships, the quaestors and procurators were responsible for collecting a number of other taxes. Of particular importance was the 5 percent inheritance tax, which went into the military treasury. There was also a 5 percent tax on what slaves paid their masters for manumissions and a 2 or 2.5 percent toll tax on goods in transit (*portorium*).

The Army and the Defense of the Empire

The Empire had over 6,000 miles of frontier to defend, from Hadrian's Wall in Britain to the North African and Arabian deserts. Some of the frontiers were rivers, such as the Rhine and the Danube, along which the army had constructed an elaborate chain of fortress towns, watchposts, palisades, ditches, walls, and military roads. In Syria another network of fortresses existed to defend the eastern half of the Empire against Parthia, the only major organized state with which Rome had to contend. In Africa constant vigilance was needed to keep the desert tribes from pillaging the settled areas. From year to year the army might be called on to cope with invasions of organized infantry divisions, mounted archers, heavily armored cavalry, or guerrilla infiltrators. Even assault by sea was not unthinkable.

Against these enemies Rome fielded an army of about 350,000 to 400,000 men, divided almost equally between citizen legionaries and noncitizen auxiliaries. The citizen soldiers were grouped in legions of some 5,500 men each, further divided into 10 cohorts and 60 centuries. Only 120 of these soldiers were cavalry. The auxiliary units were much more varied, consisting of cavalry units (*alae*) of 1,000 each and cohorts of 500 that could be either all infantry or part infantry and part cavalry. Serving among the auxiliaries were other, more barbarous units recruited outside the Empire called *numeri*. A Roman army could thus consist of a legion or a number of legions with whatever number of auxiliary units and borrowed legionary cohorts were deemed necessary for the campaign. Without changing the basic commitment to heavy infantry, the Roman army was able to find flexibility by employing the special skills of the auxiliary units, which were commanded by Roman officers but fought according to their own style.

The official view of the Roman legionary and his traditional enemy, the barbarian from beyond the frontiers, as depicted on a relief from the Forum of Trajan in Rome, second century A.D.

The Genius of the Roman Military   The cement that held this heterogeneous army together was the Roman officer corps. Legions were commanded by senatorial legates who had under them six tribunes, one of senatorial birth; the others were of the equestrian class. (An exception to this rule of command by senators was the legion in Egypt, which was under an equestrian officer.) There were also 60 centurions and, assuming an equal number of auxiliaries, 5 to 10 equestrian officers commanding the noncitizen forces.

The mixture of civilian and military experience that Roman officers of senatorial and equestrian rank possessed seems strange to modern eyes, which at least in peacetime regard the two careers as separate. However, from the viewpoint of Romans of the upper and middle classes there was a self-evident connection between civilian and military life. Depending on one's status or choice of career, a young man could begin either in the army or with civilian posts and then move on to other military and civilian positions.

Sons of senators went off at about the age of 18 to serve in the legions and in their mid-twenties might return as quaestors in the service of a provincial governor. Later, as legionary commanders or as governors themselves, they would once more be back in the provinces, having in the meantime held civilian posts in Rome such as the aedileship and praetorship.

Equestrian officers had even more varied careers. Usually they began as civilian magistrates in their hometowns and from there went on to become equestrian officers and serve their three tours of duty (*tres militiae*) of three or four years each, during which they were rotated through command of an auxiliary cohort, back to the legions as military tribune, and then on to the command of an auxiliary cavalry unit. For example, they might spend a few years commanding one of the Syrian auxiliary units in Pannonia (Hungary), then more years with the noted army division Legio III Augusta in Africa, and finally a few years with a cavalry unit in Britain. Technically they were still civilians and could at this point return to civilian life; if exceptionally able, they might proceed directly to the command of a legion, with senatorial rank. More commonly, they went on to a career in the equestrian (procuratorial) civil service.

Another line of advancement was through the ranks of the centurions. Simple soldiers, with luck and ability, could become centurions and advance through the complicated grades to the highest position, that of repeat senior centurion (*primus pilus bis*). From this position they could enter the equestrian civil service, as did the equestrian officers who went through the *tres militiae,* or they could remain in the army for the rest of their careers.

From the viewpoint of military cohesion, it was the influx of these educated civilians from the towns of Italy and the provinces that provided much of the talent necessary for the proper operation of the army. The army was concerned primarily with maintaining peace, and it performed a great number of civilian functions in addition to its military duties. It was the single greatest reserve of technically trained people in the Empire—engineers, surveyors, builders, and administrators of all kinds. It was principally from this source that the emperors drew their technical staffs, judges, governors, and legionary commanders. Far from being a peripheral element in the Empire, the army had a much more central role than most modern armies. The constant movement of officers and the promotion of ordinary soldiers guaranteed a unity to the scattered legions and auxiliary units. The civilian character of the equestrian officers was an unusual feature that opened the army to whole classes of people whose careers would otherwise have terminated with a minor office in a provincial town. Men of talent could transfer their expertise to the army and find a whole new world of imperial service opened to them. The close connection between military commands and civilian administration made the army an integral part of Roman life and guaranteed that it would not become overprofessionalized. This also had its weaknesses, but at least in peaceful times it proved a brilliant solution to the problem of integration of such a diverse region as the Empire. Although not intended as such, the Roman army was the prime agent of social unity and mobility in the Mediterranean world.

Recruitment and Conditions of Service   Legionaries were initially recruited in Italy and the western provinces, but by the second century A.D. the majority came from the provinces where the legions were located. Auxiliaries, although originally recruited in particular provinces, eventually came from wherever the individual units were stationed. The principle of obligatory military service was never dropped, and in fact when new legions were formed, they were made up of levies from Italy.

A SOLDIER'S CAREER: THE OVERACHIEVING VELIUS RUFUS

Gaius Velius Rufus, son of Salvius, primipilus [chief centurion] of Legio X Ful-minata, prefect of units from eight legions (I Adiutrix; II Adiutrix; II Augusta; VIII Augusta; IX Hispana; XIV Gemina; XX Victrix and XXI Rapax); tribune of Cohors XIII Urbana; leader of the army of Africa and Mauretania for suppressing the Mauretanian uprising; decorated by Emperors Vespasian and Titus in the Jewish War with the *corona vallaris* [first over the rampart], collars, discs, armbands, the *corona muralis* [first over the wall], two parade spears and two unit flags. In the Marcomannic, Quadi and Sarmatian Wars he conducted an expedition against them through the kingdom of Decebalus, king of the Dacians and won the *corona muralis,* two parade spears and two unit flags. He was procurator [financial administrator] of Emperor Caesar Augustus Germanicus in the provinces of Pannonia and Dalmatia [parts of Hungary and the former Yugoslavia]; procurator of Raetia [Austria] with the right of the sword. He was sent to Parthia to bring back Epiphanes and Callinicus, sons of King Antiochus [of Commagene, a client state in Syria-Mesopotamia] to Emperor Vespasian along with a mass of people subject to tribute. Marcus Alfius Olympiacus, son of Marcus, of the Fabian tribe, veteran *aquilifer* [eagle bearer] of the XV Apol-linaris dedicated this statue to him.

Source: H. Dessau, *Inscriptiones Latinae Selectae* (Berlin, 1892) 9200.

Throughout the Empire, providing recruits was one of the cities' most onerous burdens.

Legionaries served for 25 years and received 300 denarii a year in three installments; deductions were made for food and clothing. Another source of income was the cash donatives made by the emperors on major occasions, such as anniversaries of their accession to power. On discharge, the legionaries received either a plot of land or 3,000 denarii, together with the privilege of belonging to the higher legal category of *honestiores.*

Auxiliaries fared almost as well. Their basic pay was 200–300 denarii per year, and on discharge they received Roman citizenship for themselves and their children (though not for their wives). (By contrast, marriages of legionaries were not recognized until the end of the second century, a situation that caused all kinds of difficulties for their de facto wives and children.)

Pay and service conditions in the Roman army were considered good, and a soldier could hope to accumulate some savings, learn a trade perhaps, or even advance to high rank if he had particular ability. Non–Latin speakers could pick up Latin and make contacts with upper- and middle-class Roman officers that might prove useful later. Provincial Syrians, Africans, or Spaniards might start out uneducated and penniless in the auxiliaries and later emerge with a rough education, citizenship, some money, and new status. Discharged at the rate of 6,000 a year, the auxiliaries constituted an important addition to the Romanized population of the

Empire and a continuing source of recruits for the army because sons regularly followed their fathers into the old units.

Italians still enjoyed some advantages over the provincials. Recruitment for the Praetorian Guard took place in Italy, and with their knowledge of Latin, a length of service of only 16 years compared to 25 for the ordinary legionaries, higher pay, and location in Rome, Praetorian troopers had an edge over their legionary competitors in the scramble for advancement within the army. However, the bulk of legionary centurions always remained promoted legionaries, not Praetorians.

Chapter 13

The Empire from the Third-Century Crisis to Justinian

THE THIRD-CENTURY CRISIS

With the end of the Severan dynasty the Roman Empire entered a period of great peril, of almost perpetual political chaos and increasing economic dislocation. Simultaneously, invaders attacked in the east and across the Danube and penetrated far into the interior of the Empire, doing enormous damage. For over half a century the pressures continued until finally a series of great emperors succeeded in bringing Rome back from the brink of destruction and restoring peace in what amounted to a refounding of the Empire.

Imperial Security: A Fine Balance

The peace of the Roman world depended on achieving a balance between barbarian pressures and the ability of the legions to resist them and between the costs of war and the resources of the state. A key factor in this equation was the imperial succession, which in the third century practically collapsed. The result was chaos in key areas of the Empire as Roman armies, each supporting its own candidate for the throne, fought each other and abandoned the frontiers to the enemy without. At the same time, the probing of frontier defenses by groups of barbarians had changed in character. In the past this had been done for the most part by small, scattered raiding parties. In the second century A.D. larger confederations, such as the Germanic Quadi and Marcomanni and the Iranian Iazyges, managed to penetrate significant distances into the Empire—and this at a time when there was no problem with the imperial succession. In the third century similar confederations were able to cause far greater troubles for the Empire because of its own internal weaknesses. In A.D. 233 the Alamanni attacked across the upper Danube, and from then until the end of the century the pressures were unrelenting. The Goths, Sarmatians, and Iazyges concentrated in the lower Danube and Black Sea areas, while the Franks, Vandals, and Alamanni assaulted the Rhine and Danube frontiers.

These attacks were not planned by some coordinating council of Germanic chieftains. The confederations were not homogeneous, ethnic groups of long standing. They were warrior bands that came together under the leadership of successful, charismatic chiefs and could disappear as quickly as they had appeared or change sides at a moment's notice. Whole peoples seem to disappear as the result of some minor setback. Unfortunately, we have no directly relevant information from the varied groups of invaders themselves as to what was going on among them. Centuries of contact with the developed south had begun finally to undermine the ancient, anarchic, prestate traditions of northern Europe. The invasions of the third century are evidence of the slow accommodation of the peoples of northern Europe to the territorial state.

The northern frontiers were not the only source of difficulty for the Empire. Weakened by unsuccessful wars with Rome, the old Parthian dynasty fell in A.D. 226 and was replaced by a much more vigorous Persian regime, the Sassanids, who reorganized the state on a businesslike basis and in A.D. 231 invaded the eastern provinces of the Empire in an attempt to recover regions that had once belonged to Persia back in the time of Darius and Xerxes.

These years also saw a tremendous inflation in prices and the collapse of the Roman currency system. The silver content of the coinage dropped to 1 percent by the time of Claudius II (A.D. 268–270), and the price of grain went from 2 denarii per measure in A.D. 200 to 330 in A.D. 301. Surprisingly, it was the government that was hardest hit by inflation, because its taxes came as fixed money payments. However, because it had to feed and supply the legions, it eventually was forced to fall back on requisitions in kind. At the same time developments that were already under way in the second century were rapidly advanced by the pressures of the times. The role of the army in choosing emperors was reinforced at the expense of the Senate, and the emperors no longer made any pretense of being the first citizen, or *princeps*. They were military men and autocrats, and their court began to assume an increasingly important role. More and more key personnel came from the equestrian order until, under Gallienus (A.D. 253–268), senators were excluded from all military commands and most civilian positions. The number of Italians in the Senate declined, and provincials, especially from Africa and the east, increased in numbers and included many soldiers and equestrians. The state intervened more than ever in local affairs, and the burdens of municipal administration on the town senates of the Empire increased out of all proportion to the rewards of membership. By the same token, the relentlessness and continuity of the imperial administrative services during the anarchy of civil wars and invasions in the third century kept the Empire together.

The most important social changes of these years occurred in religion. For the first time Christianity began to find widespread acceptance among the middle classes of the Empire and to build up a respectable intellectual presentation of its tenets. At the same time its organization developed considerably, as the individual churches began to communicate more freely with one another and to meet in provincial councils to discuss their common needs and objectives.

POLITICAL ANARCHY

The outstanding defect of the political arrangement worked out by Augustus was its inability to guarantee the imperial succession. It was neither wholly dynastic nor wholly elective. The army and the people at large had longstanding traditions of loyalty to the individual emperors and their families, but there was always the possibility of an outsider supported by his own troops claiming the succession on one pretext or another and then actually taking the throne by force of arms. This had happened already in A.D. 69 and 193, and was to happen again and again after the last of the Severans, Severus Alexander, was murdered by his own troops in A.D. 235. Between his death and the accession of Diocletian in 284 there were 22 legitimate emperors and many more usurpers.

The successor of the Severans was a soldier's soldier, the huge Thracian Maximinus. He increased his popularity with the troops by granting them pay raises and conducting successful campaigns along the northern frontiers, but his financial demands provoked a rebellion in Africa, which was supported by a surprisingly active Senate at Rome. The African Gordian I and his son Gordian II were proclaimed emperors, and when they were slain in battle by troops loyal to Maximinus, two senators, M. Clodius Pupienus and D. Caelius Balbinus, were elevated as joint emperors and adopted Gordian's grandson as their heir. In attempting to recover Italy, Maximinus was murdered by his own troops after an unsuccessful siege of Aquileia, and Pupienus and Balbinus in turn were assassinated by the Praetorian Guard, who elevated Gordian III to the throne. On campaign in the east, Gordian was slain in a mutiny, and the Praetorian Prefect Philip took over in A.D. 244. It is indicative of the evolving character of the Empire that it was left to Philip, an Arab from Shahba, south of Damascus, to celebrate with great pomp the millennium of the founding of Rome in 247 A.D.

Philip's reign came to an end in 249, and he was succeeded by one of his generals, Decius. To pacify the angry gods, whom he felt must have been responsible for the disasters besetting Rome, the new emperor launched the first empirewide persecution of the Christians. Soon afterward he was killed in battle with the Goths in the lower Danube area. Decius was succeeded briefly by Trebonianus Gallus and his son Volusianus, and then by the Moor Aemilianus. The next emperor was Valerian, the commander of the Rhine legions. He had good relations with the Senate and at its suggestion appointed his son Gallienus as a second Augustus, or co-emperor, in 253. Responsibility for the Empire was now divided for the first time, and while Gal-

---

EMPERORS DURING THE THIRD-CENTURY CRISIS

Maxminus the Thracian	A.D. 235–238
Gordian I	238
Gordian II	238
Balbinus	238
Pupienus	238
Gordian III	238–244
Philip the Arab	244–249
Decius	249–251
Trebonianus Gallus	251–253
Volusianus (son of Trebonianus)	251–253
Aemilianus the Moor	253
Valerian	253–260
Gallienus (son of Valerian)	253–268
Claudius II (first of the Illyrian emperors)	268–270
Quintillus (brother of Claudius)	270
Aurelian	270–275
Tacitus	275–276
Florian (brother of Tacitus)	276
Probus	276–282
Carus	282–283
Carinus and Numerian (sons of Carus)	283–284

---

lienus remained in Gaul, Valerian went to the east to repel the Persians. In A.D. 257 he launched the second empirewide persecution of the Christians, which was called off by Gallienus in 260 upon the capture of his father by the Persians. In the same year the western half of the Empire, including Britain, Gaul, and Spain, was split off from the rest by the usurper Postumus, who was recognized by Gallienus and did an effective job in defending the Rhine frontier against invaders. In the east Palmyra, under its rulers Odenathus and then his widow, Zenobia, proclaimed its independence and was recognized as a client-kingdom.

Gallienus' rule was beset by the greatest disasters Rome had yet suffered. Gothic fleets ravaged the Aegean, sacking Ephesus and burning its great Temple of Diana in A.D. 262–263. Then, around 267 the Heruli, a German tribe, captured and sacked the cities of Byzantium, Athens, Corinth, Argos, and Sparta. Gallienus coped as best he could and initiated a series of military reforms that placed emphasis on cavalry units (*vexillationes*). He finally defeated the Goths in 268 at Naissus in the Balkans but was assassinated the same year by the Illyrian generals Claudius and Aurelian.

With the defeat of the Goths and the advent of the Illyrians, Rome's fortunes began to rise again slowly. Claudius II was succeeded by Aurelian in A.D. 270, and the step-by-step process of reuniting the Empire began. The Palmyrenes were overcome in 273, and in 274 Postumus' successor in the west, Tetricus, submitted. Aurelian could justly claim the title of *Restitutor Orbis,* the Restorer of the World. During his reign Rome abandoned Dacia (modern Romania) and the Agri Decumates, the region between the headwaters of the Rhine and the Danube, as undefendable, and great walls were built around the city of Rome. Aurelian also attempted currency reforms and proclaimed the sun god as the universal god of the Empire. In A.D. 275 he succumbed to a conspiracy and was succeeded briefly by the aged senator Tacitus (not the historian, although he claimed descent from him). After Tacitus' peaceful death (strange in these times), another Illyrian, Probus, succeeded to the throne. Uncomfortable with his rigid discipline, the troops rebelled and killed him in 282, and the Praetorian Prefect Carus became emperor. Soon the troops proclaimed the one-time Illyrian shepherd Diocles emperor (A.D. 284), and as Diocletian he began the work of the refounding of the Roman Empire.

DIOCLETIAN AND CONSTANTINE

Under Diocletian the Empire found peace again. His general Maximian cleared the invaders out of the west and was rewarded by being made "Augustus," or senior co-emperor, in 286. In A.D. 293 the imperial college was expanded to four as both Diocletian and Maximian adopted as "Caesars," or junior emperors and successors, the generals Gaius Galerius and Flavius Constantius, respectively. To cement the relationship, Constantius put away his common-law wife Helena (the mother of the future emperor Constantine) and married Theodora, Maximian's stepdaughter. The multiplication of emperors permitted a more effective defense of the Empire, and Roman armies were able to beat back their enemies on all the frontiers. The founding in 334 of Constantinople (modern Istanbul) as the second capital of the Empire on the site of the old Greek city of Byzantium contributed significantly to the security of the eastern half of the Empire.

The Reforms of Diocletian

A born administrator, Diocletian began a thorough reorganization of the Empire. He greatly expanded the size of the army and attempted to create a stable currency. His most successful reforms were the reorganization of the requisitions in kind (which had become the principal source of income for the state in the third century) into a regular system of levies (*indictiones*) and the creation of a true budget. The administration of the Empire was now expanded and professionalized to provide the necessary taxes, manpower, and supplies for the reconstituted state.

Down to the third century the government of the Empire depended in large measure on an informal system of aristocratic government over which the emperor, with direct control of the somewhat more fully organized equestrian civil service, presided. Upper-class provincials were held responsible for the bulk of imperial administration, including the collection of most of the taxes, and were in turn supervised by upper-class Romans. The concept of the administration as a permanent collection of career officials, whose loyalty was to the bureaucracy and the state and who were largely independent of the cities and the magistrates, generals, and emperors who came and went, was slow in developing. Even under Diocletian, when the administration had developed considerably, the local curial classes were still relied upon to collect the taxes, although the supervision of them was increased enormously.

To a large extent the tightening of the administration simply meant the expansion of the old system. There were approximately 50 provinces when Diocletian ascended the throne, but these were often inefficient administrative units. Asia, for example, had 250 cities but only one governor. Diocletian's solution was to divide the province into six smaller units, each headed by a governor with a staff of about 100. Similar adjustments were made wherever the emperor or his staff thought them necessary or useful, so that ultimately the number of provinces expanded to 100, grouped in 13 dioceses under vicars. This reorganization took place only at high levels in the administration, and there was much less proliferation at the lower echelons. It has been calculated that there were about 30,000 civil servants by the end of the fourth century, a small number considering that the Empire had a population of perhaps 50 million.

The staff that looked after the provinces was also expanded and professionalized, though it remained for Constantine, Diocletian's successor, to bring the process of evolution to completion. The development began at the top with the office of the emperor and the bureaucracy (*comitatus*) that went with it. In place of a single emperor vainly rushing from one end of the Empire to the other, there were to be two Augusti with their delegated successors, the Caesars. This arrangement is known as the Tetrarchy, or the Rule of Four. The attendant staff of each emperor was doubled. Under the Augusti were the Praetorian Prefects, who as the chief aides or ministers of the emperors were responsible for all civilian and military operations in the Empire. Constantine disbanded the Praetorian Guard and relieved the Prefects of their military responsibilities so that they could devote themselves full-time to their civilian duties, which now consisted of supplying the army with all its material and manpower needs, supervising the provincial governors, and heading the judicial system. This separation of military and civilian functions was systematically carried out throughout the system.

The administrative reforms of Diocletian went hand in hand with his reorganization of the army. The ease with which invaders broke through the frontier defenses demonstrated the need for strengthening the army. Under Diocletian its numbers, which had been slowly rising, became almost double what they had been at the beginning of the third century. It is hard to believe that Diocletian would have gone ahead with his enlargement of the army if he (or his predecessors) had not already come to the conclusion that the Empire could bear the strain of increased numbers of troops and the supplies they needed. Obviously, if the army was to be expanded, there would also have to be a corresponding increase in the administrative side of the government to supply the large number of new recruits required together with

The College of Four (the Tetrarchy): Diocletian Tackles the Succession Problem

West		East	
Maximian	A.D. 286–305	Diocletian	A.D. 284–305
Constantius Chlorus		Galerius	
Caesar	293–305	Caesar	293–305
Augustus	305–306	Augustus	305–311
Severus		Licinius	
Caesar	305	Augustus	308–324
Augustus	306–307	Maximinus Daia	
Maxentius		Caesar	305–308
Augustus	308–312	Augustus	308–313
Constantine			
Caesar	306–308		
Augustus	308–337		
	Constantine (sole emperor) 324–337		

the weapons, armor, uniforms, food, cavalry mounts, and pay they needed. For whatever reasons—lack of time and ability or the anarchy of the period—previous emperors in the third century had attempted to muddle through with the resources they had at hand. Diocletian's special talent, however, was administrative, and like a new Augustus, he set about a thorough reorganization of the Empire in every area—military, administrative, fiscal, and economic. Like his great predecessor, he was extremely successful, and in the east his work enabled the Empire to survive for another 1,000 years.

Constantine

Toward the end of his reign, Diocletian, urged by Galerius, initiated another great persecution of the Christians (A.D. 303). They were dismissed from the army and the civil service, churches were burned, and the scriptures were confiscated. Members of the clergy were prime targets for the persecutors, and many were imprisoned and put to death.

On the retirement of Diocletian and Maximian in 305, civil war broke out again. Constantius died the following year, and his son Constantine was proclaimed Caesar in his place. Another contender, Maxentius, the son of Maximian, entered the contest but was defeated by Constantine at the battle of the Milvian Bridge in A.D. 312. Before the battle Constantine dreamed that he would win if he painted on his soldiers' shields the monogram of Christ, which later evolved into the *labarum,* Constantine's personal standard, a *chi rho* (☧) mounted on a cross. Constantine's victory convinced him of the might of the Christian god, and in 313 he returned the confiscated properties of the Church and extended privileges to the clergy. At once he found himself involved in the theological and disciplinary disputes of the Church, and the split in the African Church between the heretical Donatists and the orthodox was drawn to his attention. After trying to settle the problem peacefully, he resorted to persecution (A.D. 317–320) but failed again. In the meantime, his relations with the co-ruler in the east, Licinius, deteriorated, and war broke out between the two men. In 324 Licinius was defeated, and Constantine became the sole ruler of the Empire. At this point he became aware of the great battle raging between the bishop of Alexandria and one of his priests, Arius, which had split the churches of the eastern half of the Empire. After trying personal persuasion, Constantine called a council of the whole Church to meet in 325 at Nicaea and personally directed it until a moderate formula was agreed on. The battle did not end there, however, and the controversy continued for years.

In addition to problems of imperial rule Constantine was plagued by domestic difficulties. His favorite son, Crispus, the offspring of his first marriage, was also favored by his mother, the pious Helena, whereas his wife Fausta promoted the fortunes and careers of her own sons by Constantine. In 326 she falsely accused Crispus of assaulting her, and the emperor, without proper investigation, had his son executed. Later he became aware of his error and put Fausta to death. This tragedy clouded the emperor's later years and filled him with remorse for his crime, which he attempted to expiate by lavish gifts to the Church. Fearing for his salvation, he waited until close to the moment of death to be baptized.

Last Emperors of the Western Empire and the First Byzantine (or Eastern) Roman Emperors

West		East	
Constantine II	A.D. 337–340	Constantius II	A.D. 337–361
Constantius II (sole emperor)	351–361		
Julian (sole emperor)	361–363		
Valentinian I	364–375	Valens	364–378
Gratian	375–383	Theodosius I	379–395
Valentinian II	383–392		
Theodosius I (sole emperor)	394–395		
Honorius	395–423	Arcadius	395–408
Valentinian III	425–455	Theodosius II	408–450
		Marcian	450–457
Majorian	457–461	Leo I	457–474
Anthemius	467–472	Zeno	474–491
Romulus Augustulus	475–476	Anastasius	491–518
		Justin	518–527
		Justinian	527–565
		(Other emperors to 1453)	

Constantine died in 337, leaving the Empire to his three sons and two nephews. Inevitably this arrangement generated a struggle for power among the heirs, and in 353 after a series of bloody purges and civil wars the aloof and suspicious Constantius II emerged as sole ruler. Two years later he was forced by increasing imperial needs to appoint Julian, Constantine's only surviving nephew, Caesar in Gaul. There Julian had some success against the Alamanni, and when Constantius demanded that Julian lend him his Gallic troops for war against the Persians in the east, they rebelled and proclaimed Julian Augustus. Fortunately, Constantius died before civil war could break out, and Julian became sole emperor (A.D. 361–363).

The impulsive and rather naïve Julian had for years been a secret pagan and enjoyed dabbling in magic. Now he publicly proclaimed his loyalty to the ancient religion and the ideals of Hellenic civilization. Seeking to reverse the inroads of Christianity, he attempted to put paganism on a similar organizational footing and demanded high moral standards of its ministers. Inevitably he became embroiled in the continuing struggles between the Arians and the orthodox in the eastern half of the Empire, and after first restoring the troublesome patriarch of Alexandria, the famous Athanasius, deposed him again. As religious turmoil increased, Julian turned his attention to the frontiers. Campaigning against the Persians in 363, he was mortally wounded in battle, and his successor, Jovian (A.D. 363–364), was forced to make peace. With the death of Julian the dynasty of Constantine the Great came to an end.

THE COLLAPSE OF THE WESTERN EMPIRE

After the brief reign of Jovian, the Empire was entrusted to Valentinian I (A.D. 364–375), who appointed his brother Valens as Augustus of the east. Although despised by the educated classes of the empire, Valentinian was an emperor in the soldierly tradition of Diocletian and Constantine. A stern disciplinarian and a conscientious administrator, he attempted to protect the poor from the ravages of the well-to-do and was impartial in the religious disputes that continued to rage in the Empire.

A year after Valentinian's death in 375, the Germanic Visigoths, fleeing before the Huns, petitioned to be admitted into the Empire. Valens allowed them to cross the Danube and settle in vacant land, but soon the exactions of the imperial officials drove them to revolt, and in 378, at the disastrous battle of Adrianople, they overwhelmed the emperor and his army. The situation was redeemed to some extent when Gratian, Valentinian's successor in the west, appointed the able Spanish general Theodosius to succeed Valens and make a settlement with the marauding Germans. By diplomacy and military force Theodosius brought peace to the Balkans and reorganized the eastern Roman army, incorporating in the process large numbers of the invaders and placing special emphasis on cavalry. Both Gratian and Theodosius took active parts in the battles between Christians and pagans and between the Arians and the orthodox. Under the influence of Ambrose, the powerful bishop of Milan, Gratian dropped the ancient title of *pontifex maximus* and withdrew the Altar of Victory from the Senate at Rome. In the east Theodosius legislated against the

Arians and in 381 convened the Second Ecumenical Council of Constantinople, which reaffirmed the traditional orthodox beliefs. Ten years later he forbade all pagan rites.

When Gratian was assassinated in A.D. 383, Theodosius defeated his usurper in battle and retained Gratian's half-brother, Valentinian II, as his colleague in the west. Later, when Valentinian was also murdered, Theodosius was forced to fight another bloody civil war from which he emerged in 394 as the last sole ruler of the united Roman world. Ironically, his reign in this capacity lasted only five months, and when he died in 395, he was succeeded by his young and ineffectual sons, Honorius and Arcadius, the former taking the west and the latter the east. Both fell under the control of advisers and generals who fought savage battles for power among themselves precisely when the Empire most needed strong central control. Under the leadership of Alaric, the restless Visigoths took advantage of the weakness of the Empire to ravage Greece, desisting only when encouraged to move westward by Arcadius' principal adviser, the wily eunuch Eutropius. Initially Stilicho, the able Vandal general who commanded the western armies, was able to control the Visigoths, but in 408 he was assassinated and no one was left to stop their depredations. They sacked Rome in A.D. 410, and its fall sent reverberations throughout the Empire. Eventually the Visigoths left Italy and settled in southwestern Gaul as supposed subjects of the Romans.

The Rise of the German Kingdoms

In the winter of A.D. 406, two years before Stilicho's murder, great numbers of Germans crossed the frozen Rhine and pushed their way through the imperial defenses and into central Gaul. From there they moved on to Spain and Africa, where the Vandals established an independent kingdom that Rome was forced to recognize. By 455 they were strong enough to raid Italy, and for a second time Rome was brutally sacked.

By mid-century most of the west was in the hands of Germanic tribes. Britain had been abandoned in 407. The Franks were established in the north and central areas of Gaul, the Burgundians had settled along the Rhône, and the Visigoths had moved into the south. Still, both Romans and Germans could appreciate a common threat, and in 451 they combined against the Huns of Attila and defeated them near Troyes. For 20 years thereafter a series of shadow emperors controlled by barbarian chiefs succeeded one another until in 476 the mercenary captain Odoacer deposed the puppet emperor Romulus Augustulus and returned the imperial insignia to Constantinople, agreeing to act as representative of the eastern emperor with the title Patrician. In this uneventful fashion the formal administration of the unified Empire came to an end. In A.D. 493 Odoacer was in turn deposed by Theodoric, king of the Ostrogoths, with the blessings of Emperor Zeno. Theodoric ostensibly ruled Italy as the representative of the eastern emperor, as had Odoacer, but in reality the arrival of Theodoric and the Ostrogoths meant that Italy was now simply the latest Germanic kingdom to be carved out of Roman territory. The political transformation of the western Empire from a unified state to a number of Germanic kingdoms was now essentially complete.

THE RISE OF THE BYZANTINE EMPIRE

The Romans of the eastern half of the Empire were better able to defend themselves against marauding bands of invaders than their counterparts in the west. Militarily, the east was much less vulnerable to invasion from the north; the strong defenses of Constantinople made it extremely difficult for invaders to reach the inner core of the eastern Empire's rich provinces. Eastern emperors could draw on more plentiful supplies of troops from within their own territory and were not as dependent on large contingents of German mercenaries as the emperors of the west. The east, being more urbanized, populous, and richer, had greater financial resources to meet the needs of imperial defense, and its peoples accepted imperial autocracy with greater docility than those of the more independent-minded west. The east too was lucky in having a string of strong, long-lived emperors who managed to maintain the army, build up the bureaucracy, and retain the support of the Church during the turbulent fifth and sixth centuries. Theodosius II (A.D. 408–450) was able to fend off both the Huns and the Persians, and Zeno (A.D. 474–491) was able to rid himself of the Ostrogoths by assigning Italy to them. During his long reign, Anastasius (A.D. 491–518) managed to keep peace among the competing factions within the Church and fend off invasions from both east and west.

Under his successors, Justin (A.D. 518–527) and the brilliant Justinian (A.D. 527–565), the eastern Empire reached heights of great power, and serious efforts were made to reunify the Empire. North Africa was freed of the Vandals, and Roman armies once more marched into Spain and southern France. However, the overthrow of the Ostrogothic kingdom in Italy turned out to be a major blunder. Endless and often pointless campaigns finally destroyed the economy of Italy and exhausted the resources of the eastern Empire.

Justinian was more successful in his attempt to restore Roman greatness in the arts and administration. The chaotic mass of Roman law was reduced to order in the *Code,* published in 529, followed by the *Digest,* a work that brought together extracts from the opinions of the foremost Roman judges of the past, and the *Institutes,* a textbook for the training of law students. For as long as the eastern Empire lasted, the *Code* provided the legal framework for the administration of law for Roman citizens. Although it went far toward making the emperor absolute, its very existence provided checks on his power to make new legislation. Byzantine emperors (as historians call the rulers of the eastern Empire) were not despots because their actions were judged legal only when they conformed to the *Code.*

Secular literature had a final imperial renaissance in the sixth century. The great age of Christian literature had ended in the fifth century, and in the following age theological literature held a subordinate position. The historian Procopius of Caesarea wrote of theological disputes with cynical detachment, and rhetoricians such as Choricius prided themselves on the Attic purity of their style. In Egypt poets composed elaborate epics on pagan, mythological themes. After a great fire destroyed much of the city of Constantinople, Justinian undertook a major building program. The construction of the Church of Holy Wisdom, Hagia Sophia, was a stunning architectural achievement. It still stands as a monument to the ambition, originality, and vitality of this last fragment of the Roman Empire.

Chapter 14

The Transformed Empire

HISTORY MOVES NORTHWARD

It is not possible to study the fourth century for very long without realizing that a shift in geography had taken place. Areas that previously had been central to Roman history, such as Italy, now became backwaters, and peripheral areas became central. Before the fourth century the focus of history was the Mediterranean itself and the lands bordering it. Now there was a pronounced shift of the axis of the Roman world northward and eastward, away from the Mediterranean and toward the Atlantic and Danube. Eventually, after the Arab invasions of the seventh century, there was a further shift eastward, this time toward the Euphrates and Mesopotamia. With this last event the Mediterranean lost forever both the unity that Roman rule and culture had imposed on it and its centrality in Western history.

The Threat of Invasion

Already in the second century pressures on the Danube frontier and in Syria had drawn the Romans northward and eastward. Marcus Aurelius' Marcomannic campaigns kept him on the northern frontier for 12 years, and his colleague Lucius Verus had earlier spent 4 years in campaigns against the Parthians. Septimius Severus was similarly drawn to the east, and throughout the third century the northern and eastern frontiers, particularly the lower Danube and Euphrates, were the constant preoccupations of the emperors. Rome itself was now considerably off the beaten path, rarely visited and of no use as a base to the emperors, whose problems lay 500 to 1,500 miles to the north or east. New centers closer to the danger spots were essential. In the west Milan and Aquileia in Italy and Trier on the Moselle were good locations; in the Danube area Sirmium, Serdica, Thessalonika, Byzantium, and Nicomedia were tried at one time or another. In the east Antioch was the most obvious center.

Along with the transfer of the administration to the northern and eastern frontiers came a shift of wealth to these regions. All along the Danube flourishing cities came into being, and new roads, bridges, dockyards, and villas were built. The treasury of Gaul was located at Trier, along with a mint and an armament factory. Emperors Constantius I and Constantine had their headquarters there, and a considerable amount of building activity resulted. Enormous baths and warehouses were constructed as well as a great basilica, which still survives. The gates were renovated, and new villas for the senior bureaucrats built in the countryside. Other emperors had their favorite sites also. Diocletian made his capital at Nicomedia in Asia Minor; Maximian erected his palace at his birthplace, Sirmium; and Galerius adorned Thessalonika with magnificent buildings. Antioch, though sacked by the Persians in the previous century, was another flourishing center, with its mints, baths, lighted streets, armament factories, and linen industry.

Constantinople: Focus for the New World

The logical step of establishing a major military and administrative center near both the Euphrates and Danube frontiers was taken by Constantine in 324. After considering Sirmium, Serdica, and possibly Thessalonika, he selected Byzantium on the Bosporus. It had a superb location at the strategic and easily defended bottleneck between Europe and Asia. Supplies could be brought in by land as well as by sea, and it straddled the vital east-west road that led from northern Italy down the Danube to the Bosporus, then over the Anatolian plateau by way of Nicomedia, Ancyra, and Caesarea to Antioch. It was also close to the great intellectual centers of Greece, Asia Minor, and the East.

The founding of Constantinople (the City of Constantine, as Byzantium was renamed) had profound historical repercussions. Whether Constantine intended it or not, the new city provided a focus for a kingdom quite unlike the one that was developing in the western half of the Roman Empire. The language and culture of the region were Greek. Its economic resources were superior to those of the west, and even its social structure offered more hope for permanence. Land was divided more evenly among the different classes, and the eastern senatorial aristocracy was not dominated, as it was in the west, by an old core of great landowning nobles. There was a different understanding, too, of the role of the emperor that promoted a more stable, unified kingdom. Culturally, the east was far more deeply Hellenized than the west, and even areas that had previously not been noted for their contributions, such as Cappadocia, rural Syria, and Egypt, now began to produce significant intellectual

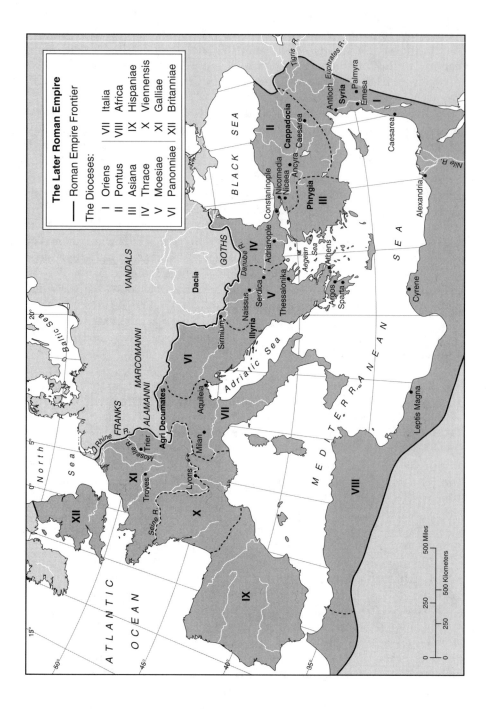

The Later Roman Empire

— Roman Empire Frontier

The Dioceses:

I	Oriens	VII	Italia
II	Pontus	VIII	Africa
III	Asiana	IX	Hispaniae
IV	Thrace	X	Viennensis
V	Moesiae	XI	Galliae
VI	Panonniae	XII	Britanniae

VANDALS

GOTHS

MARCOMANNI

ALAMANNI

FRANKS

Baltic Sea

BLACK SEA

Tigris R.

Euphrates R.

Nile R.

Antioch • Syria • Palmyra
Emesa • I

Cappadocia
Caesarea •
Nicomedia Ancyra •
Constantinople • Nicaea •
Phrygia III

Caesarea •

Alexandria •

MEDITERRANEAN SEA

Aegean Sea
Adrianople • Athens
Serdica • Argos • Sparta
Naissus • Thessalonika
Illyria
Sirmium •
Dacia
Danube R.

Cyrene •

Adriatic Sea

Leptis Magna •

Aquileia •
Agri Decumates
Trier • Milan •
Moselle R. Rhine R.
Lyons •
Troyes •
Seine R.

North Sea

ATLANTIC OCEAN

XII

XI

X

IX

VIII

VII

VI

V

IV

II

I

III

15° 50° 45° 40° 35°

20° 5° 0°

| 0 | 250 | 500 Miles |
| 0 | 250 | 500 Kilometers |

figures. In the great invasions of the fifth century, the east was able to fend for itself, whereas the more vulnerable and weaker western half of the Empire collapsed before the onslaught.

THE CULTURAL CENTER SHIFTS: THE TRANSFORMATION OF THE CLASSICAL WORLD

By the old standards the third century A.D. was an extremely impoverished period in Rome's history. There had been a great outpouring of encyclopedias and learned commentaries on the classical works of the past toward the end of the previous century and at the beginning of the third, but even this type of literature soon declined in both quantity and quality. The visual arts were equally affected. Even the copying of statues died out, and the great revival of sculpture in the next century confronted an almost complete lack of skilled craftsmen and artists trained in the classical tradition.

Despite cultural impoverishment, the time of the Empire's crisis was, from a different perspective, a period of intellectual and spiritual ferment. It is true that the old creativity had disappeared, but to compensate, new fields of inquiry and thought had opened. New classes of people emerged to investigate them and reconcile old and new traditions.

Opening Up the Classics

Although the old educational system continued to be as sterile and traditional as ever, it received a major boost in the third century when the government turned away from the senatorial classes to the lower-ranking equestrians for its top administrators while still insisting on high standards of education. The new officials were expected to conform to the ancient norms of classical behavior, which had belonged as a kind of birthright to the previous incumbents but had to be consciously acquired by the newcomers by diligent study of the great masterpieces of the past from Homer to Virgil. As a result, a whole new class of men with fresh minds became enthusiastic students of the classics and in the next century brought about a renaissance the like of which was not to be seen for another 700 years. In poetry there were Claudian, Ausonius, and Rutilius Namatianus, all of them pagans. Among the Christians were Paulinus, Ambrose, and Prudentius, the last the greatest Latin poet since the time of Augustus. For the first time in two and a half centuries the field of history produced a major figure, the Antiochene Ammianus Marcellinus, writing in Latin. He was the most important historian since Tacitus, whom he excelled in some respects. In Greek, Eusebius, bishop of Caesarea and friend of Constantine, broke important new ground in historical methodology.

A striking aspect of third- and fourth-century culture was its challenge to the old elitist suppositions about what constituted a genuine education and who could achieve it. There was a great deal of dilution and diffusion of classical learning as the rising classes of new men in the imperial civil service attempted to acquire the values and standards of the positions to which they aspired, which in the past had been the private possession of a snobbish, cultural elite. This kind of classical learning may not have been immediately relevant to the administrative job at hand, but the traditional association of high culture and public service could not easily be eradicated, and the Romans shied away from employing those they considered to be mere technicians for their higher civil service posts. Specialists were available, to be sure, but they served *under* the classically educated generalists. In the east this combination of scholar and bureaucrat proved a success and provided the emperors of that region with a stable administration for the next 1,000 years. In the west it was a different story, as the aristocrats withdrew from the cities to their villas in the countryside and the clergy retired to their monasteries, abandoning the army and the civil administration to their fates. By a quirk of history it was this movement into the countryside that finally extended Latin to the rural districts of the western Empire and led to the development of the Romance languages at the expense of the native tongues of Gaul and the Iberian peninsula.

Christianity and Classical Traditions

The most significant cultural challenge of the age was the task of coming to terms with Christianity. This took place at many levels of society and in many places, but from a purely intellectual viewpoint the most serious challenge was to present the new religion in a form acceptable—and intelligible—to the traditionally educated middle and upper classes of the Empire. Although people from these strata of society were attracted to many aspects of Christianity, the cultural context in which it evolved was alien and in some instances repugnant to classical sensibilities. The Hebrew theological concept of sacred history, of God as the Lord of History acting in such events as the Exodus or through the prophets and bringing about salvation through a new Exodus in the death and resurrection of Jesus, was simply outside the ken of people educated in the old fashion. Miracles and prophecies did not present much of a problem, nor did the belief that Jesus was the Son of God, but what of such themes as the suffering servant of Isaiah, the radical call to holiness, the hope of the Second Coming, and other peculiarities of late Judeo-Christian eschatology? It was impossible to accept Christianity without in some way coming to terms with its cultural origins. The scriptures, both the Hebrew scriptures and the New Testament, in all their bewildering (from a Greco-Roman viewpoint) complexity, had to be dealt with. It is a tribute to the integrity and vitality of Greco-Roman culture—supposedly in decline—that it accepted the challenge. Some of the best minds of the age devoted themselves to this task. Such people as Irenaeus of Lyons; Clement and Origen of Alexandria; the Cappadocians Basil, Gregory of Nazianze, and Gregory of Nyssa; Ambrose of Milan; Tertullian and Augustine from Africa; and many others would have made their mark in an earlier age in the secular world of politics, the army, and literature. Now they devoted themselves to understanding this alien religion, translating it into a language intelligible to Greeks and Latins, and, equally challenging, devising an organizational structure for the scattered Christian communities of the Empire. By any estimate it was a formidable undertaking.

THE NEW RELIGIOUS ENVIRONMENT

The Democratization of Excellence

At times the areas of agreement between pagan and Christian seem more significant than their differences. Christianity offered no radical challenges to commonly accepted Greek and Roman views of society, and there was no head-on collision over such fundamental questions as the ownership and use of property—including slaves—or the hierarchical arrangement of Roman society, which set one person above another and loaded privileges on some while denying them to others. Pagans and Christians often shared common views on such different ethical issues as abortion, the exposure of infants, astrology, prostitution, the immorality of the pagan gods, and the often frivolous and materialistic character of urban life. They even shared much the same views of the material world around them.

Since the fourth century B.C. it had been generally held that the cosmos consisted of a series of concentric spheres that revolved around one another in a fixed hierarchy, with the earth at the center. These spheres were composed of matter of differing grades of fineness. At the highest and purest level were the stars; then in descending order came the spheres of the sun, the planets, the moon, and finally, at the lowest and poorest level, the earth. Despite such an assumption that the earth was at the bottom of the cosmic hierarchy, the average Christian or pagan did not believe that the world of matter was wholly or intrinsically evil. For the Christian there was the irrefutable endorsement of matter in the belief in the resurrection of the body at the end of the world and in the assumption of human form by God's son in the mystery of the Incarnation, and pagans hardly needed to demonstrate their acceptance of the material world. Alongside this mainstream view, however, there lurked in both groups a suspicion of matter and the belief that the body was a weight that dragged down the soul, the purer element, whose natural tendency was to strive upward toward heavenly things. Thus the great pagan philosopher Plotinus could declare that he was ashamed to possess a body and wondered what deterioration had reduced man to his present state, and Saint Anthony, the Christian hermit, blushed when he had to perform any of the normal bodily functions. The body, it was imagined, needed to be subdued and brought under the control of the soul by ascetic practices, which ranged from the intellectual exercises of the Neoplatonists to the fantastic mortifications imposed on themselves by the Syrian and Egyptian ascetics, such as Saint Simeon the Stylite, who sat for 40 years on his pillar outside Antioch without descending.

Yet at the same time there was a growing feeling among many that it was possible for the individual to realize a new self and rise to previously impossible heights of moral excellence. In the past, it was thought that moral worth was the preserve of those who could, by reason of birth or wealth, achieve high military or civil office and that it was in the performance of the functions attached to these positions that an individual achieved true goodness and the fullest development of human potential. To a lesser extent the practice and study of rhetoric and philosophy could also be a source of this excellence, and in the third century the mystical philosophy of Plotinus held out yet a higher ideal of human achievement through intellectual union with God. On the other hand, the lower classes, engaged in time-consuming menial tasks, were automatically excluded by their occupations from the possession of moral goodness. However, with the advent of Christianity, even the ordinary man or woman could aspire to high levels of moral achievement without holding exalted civil or military rank or without the expense of a classical education. By a simple act of conversion or initiation, a person could begin to lead a new life of moral enlightenment. The knowledge that was acquired in this conversion or initiation was not mere information about God and the cosmos but a special kind of understand-

Visionaries and authorities of the new order: a saint on his pillar ignoring the temptations of the devil (represented by the serpent), while a ladder permits the devout to approach him for consultations; another saint, probably one of the Evangelists.

ing or insight that affected the whole person, transforming mind and emotions alike. It penetrated into the person's innermost being, converting and radically altering his or her life. Thus were the traditional concept of culture and the moral excellence it was assumed to entail transformed, democratized, and extended in religious form to the masses of the Empire.

A revolutionary aspect of third- and fourth-century religious development was the comprehensive attempt of Christians to reach as wide an audience as possible. By the time of Constantine, Christianity was on its way to becoming a mass religion, and its organizational structure was well equipped to handle its new role. It was no longer restricted to the small fervent cells of the past, and following Saint Paul's maxim, it tried to be all things to all people. To the intellectuals and educated classes it presented the learned apologies of its philosophers from Clement of Alexandria to Augustine, couched in the language and style of argument that these classes would recognize. To the masses it presented the same message in less abstruse fashion, and to all it extended the same hope of immortality, freedom from slavery to fate, the stars, the demons, and sin, as well as the possibility of overcoming human weakness and vice.

Religious Enthusiasts: A Problem for the Authorities

Of course, some people felt more deeply moved by these religious currents than others, and the third and fourth centuries abounded with religious enthusiasts of all kinds. Some felt that they were the intermediaries of the gods who had been selected to convey a special message to humankind.

Such emperors as Aurelian, who made the sun god the preeminent deity of the Empire; Constantine, who made Christianity the supreme religion; and Julian, who tried to turn the Empire back to paganism, felt the tug of religious conviction profoundly. Often the visionaries were regarded as heretics, and the establishment, whether Christian or pagan, tried to suppress them. In the second century the Phrygian Montanus proclaimed that a new Jerusalem would soon be revealed, and people poured out of the towns and villages to await with him the coming of Christ. A council of bishops promptly condemned him, but the movement lingered for centuries, and the problem of holy men, whether prophets, martyrs, or ascetics, was a difficult one for the authorities. The riotous monks of Egypt were a well-known menace to both the ecclesiastical and the civil establishments, and in Africa, Constantine attempted to suppress the rigorous Donatists, who had split the Church because of the orthodox clergy's alleged indulgence of those who had shown weakness during the Great Persecution of Diocletian.

For the average person, whose visionary capacities were limited, it was important to cling as closely as possible to favored beings who seemed to have been especially chosen by God to perform great spiritual deeds and whose charisma contrasted shatteringly with the ordinariness of the usual ministers of religion. Quite spontaneously, the practice of honoring the memory of the saints sprang up. Relics were treasured and circulated, and the churches and monuments built to enshrine their remains quickly became places of pilgrimage. Feasts were established in their honor and grew to occupy an increasingly important place in the annual cycle of religious celebrations. A new kind of literature, hagiography—the study of the lives of the saints—became one of the most common forms of popular reading for the next millennium and a half.

Self-Realization: Pagan and Christian Ways

Among educated pagans it was commonly accepted that the traditional gods were mediating spirits or demons but that God himself was infinitely removed from human beings, uncontaminated by matter and revealed only through his creations, which emanated from him in a descending series. According to Plotinus and the Neoplatonists, he could be reached by intellectual contemplation because the soul had a natural tendency toward union with God and sought completeness by identifying with him. This was not a matter of technique or ritual, and there were no special exercises or sacraments. Union could be achieved only by intellectual asceticism and contemplation, which required long years of training and education, especially of a literary kind. Understandably, this kind of rarefied Neoplatonism was accessible only to the few, but in watered-down forms it became the most popular type of religion practiced by the educated classes of the late Empire.

Christians agreed that the universe was peopled by invisible powers, the demons, and that God was indeed accessible to humankind, but whereas pagans feared the demons and struggled on their own to reach the Divine, Christians triumphantly declared that the demonic world had been overwhelmed by the intervention of God in the historical person of Jesus. All that remained was a mopping-up operation, part of which, unfortunately, involved the dismantling of demon-ridden pagan society and the building of a new community in its place. With many pagans, Christians shared the belief in the possibility of the individual realizing a new self through revealed knowledge and achieving liberation from the spirits and demons of the world. Although the mystery religions and the theosophies of the educated claimed to be able to transmit this knowledge, they lacked a coherent theology and an organization to do this effectively. For the Christian, access to the source of power over the unseen world was easy and secure, and did not depend on the maintenance of enthusiasm over long periods. A person was indeed converted to the new way of life, but that life was as regular and well organized as city life itself. The Christian could turn for help to the rituals and sacraments of the Church or to the clergy, the holy men, the angels, or the saints, as well as to the local church community itself. This support was comprehensive, for it was economic and social as well as spiritual. And it was worldwide. By the fourth century a Christian could move just about anywhere in the Empire and expect to find the same organization, ritual, and beliefs. Letters of introduction from the home church eased entry into the new community, where spiritual life could continue as before.

Faith and Reason

To the upper-class pagans who took the trouble to observe them, the early Christians seemed to be a supremely irrational group of fanatics. Marcus Aurelius and Galen the doctor were appalled at their uncritical assumptions, their lack of logic, and their stubbornness. The critic Celsus thought they were a dangerous sect, a people who considered themselves apart from the state and whose loyalties lay to another organization altogether. In the third century, however, the gap between educated Christians and pagans was narrowed by the development of a sophisticated Christian apologetic. By the time of Constantine a bridge of understanding, if not toleration, had been built between the two worlds by a succession of brilliant philosopher-theologians.

Clement of Alexandria (ca. A.D. 150–ca. 215) was the first to go beyond the early apologists and attempt a thoroughgoing reconciliation of faith and reason. Christians, he argued, had no reason to fear philosophy, for just as the Law was the tutor or guide of the Jews leading to Christ, so God had made philosophy the guide of the pagans. It, like reason, was a gift of God. Hence, he could argue, philosophizing was synonymous with being a Christian. Clement's brilliant disciple Origen also happened to be a pupil of Plotinus' master, Ammonius Saccas. For Origen the best in the pagan world had been nourished by God's providence before the

In art Christian and pagan often appealed to the same classical sources: a priestess of Bacchus making an offering (left), and Saint Michael the Archangel (right). These early images, each originally one of a pair of panels known as a diptych, were carved in ivory and constituted the outer leaves of formal announcements of events such as weddings.

appearance of Christianity, and a Christian could therefore not completely reject either Greek culture or the Roman Empire without refusing to accept part of God's providential plan for humankind. However, Christianity was the true education (*paideia*), and Christ the True Philosopher would lead human beings to the truth. The historical personality of Jesus was played down by these theologians, who instead emphasized Jesus as the Divine Logos, or Word, who was God's agent in creating and ruling the cosmos, a concept that would be familiar to the Neoplatonists, who believed in a whole series of beings mediating between God and humankind.

Both Christians and pagans placed great emphasis on prophecies and miracles, and in the eyes of Christians one of the most compelling arguments in favor of their beliefs was the fact that the coming of Christ had been foretold in the Hebrew scriptures. This line of argument was considered particularly cogent in antiquity because of the great reverence for the written word and the wisdom of the past. Miracles were used as arguments because Christians were not debating rationalists or nonbelievers but only believers of a different kind. The argument usually went along the lines that pagan miracles were worked by demons or that the miracles of Jesus were of a superior, moral kind. Origen borrowed the method of allegorical interpretation, which had been used by generations of scholars to avoid the obvious meanings of classical texts and to find new truths in them. In the absence of the tools of higher criticism it enabled both Christians and pagans to explain away the more awkward problems in their respective bodies of literature. Until the development of modern historical techniques in the nineteenth century, the cultural worlds of the Hebrew scriptures, late Judaism and early Christianity remained a lost, unintelligible world. Its place was taken by a set of doctrines and ethical prescriptions formulated in Greco-Roman terminology.

THE EMPIRE AND THE CHURCH COME TO TERMS

Explaining the Church

The emergence of the Church as a major institution and the attempt of the government to bring it within the framework of the state were the most important developments of the third and fourth centuries. By themselves, the administrative and military reforms of Diocletian and Constantine and the artistic and architectural revivals of the fourth century would have been an interesting epilogue to the end of the classical world, but it was the emergence of the institutional Church that provided the connecting link between this world and the later stages of the development of Western history.

The life of the Church revolved around a series of rituals, of which baptism and the Eucharist were the most important, and the day-to-day contact of the average Christian with the Church was through these events rather than through any more personal or formal contacts with the clergy. The message of Christianity was deeply embedded in ritual, and the incidental education that derived therefrom was probably a good deal more important than exhortations and explanations from the pulpit.

The Christian liturgy borrowed heavily from Judaism. The calendar of feasts followed by the Church was Jewish, with the principal feasts of the year, Easter and the Descent of the Holy Spirit, occurring at the same time as Passover and Pentecost, respectively. It was only after much bitter debate that the date for Easter was changed and given its present position in the calendar. Sunday soon displaced Saturday as the most important day for Christians, and each week they gathered to celebrate the resurrection of Jesus and wait for his Second Coming.

Baptism, a Jewish ceremony of washing, was required for initiation into Christianity. Although at the beginning all that was necessary was a profession of faith, the practice of giving instructions in the essentials of the religion soon became common. A succinct expression of these essentials was found in the Symbol or Creed of the Apostles. Hence, from an early date, in addition to a moral conversion and the performance of ritual acts, Christian converts were expected also to think correctly and to know the essential doctrinal beliefs in their religion.

The principal—and most original—act of the Christian community was the celebration of the Eucharist. This ritual consisted of two parts, the first borrowed from the synagogue service and consisting of prayers, readings, homilies, and hymns to which candidates for baptism were admitted. The second and most mysterious part, to which only the fully initiated were admitted, was a simple meal revolving around the blessing of an offering of bread and wine and then its ritual consumption by the participants. In origin it was a common Jewish domestic ritual to which Jesus had given special meaning at the Last Supper. It was seen by early Christians in a number of ways—as an anticipation of the Messianic banquet to be enjoyed with Jesus in the Heavenly Kingdom, a symbolic repetition of the sacrifice on Calvary, and as a mysterious reenactment of the Last Supper itself.

The liturgy had a dynamic of its own and made certain demands on the celebrant and congregation alike. Because its principal act, the Eucharist, consisted of a number of parts, of which the first was a series of readings and a homily, or sermon, the celebrant had to be literate and possess some degree of education to be able to comment on the readings and expound the essentials of Christian beliefs. The scriptures of the new religion were enshrined in its rituals, so that for the first time the masses were exposed to a literature not designed exclusively for an educated elite. The rituals themselves were powerful educational tools, so that even without any explicit inculcation by the clergy (or even in the face of it), certain points were emphasized again and again and thus sank imperceptibly into the consciousness of the congregations. Year after year the liturgy celebrated the birth, death, and resurrection of Jesus and other events of his life. A whole history and prehistory, beginning with Adam and passing through the events of the scriptures, was taken for granted, as were suppositions about the movement of current history toward a grand finale, the Second Coming of the Lord. Local barriers were dissolved in the celebration of the liturgy, and the Christian community was seen not as an isolated entity but as part of a larger body that extended everywhere in the world, embracing all peoples. Paradoxically, this development occurred just as the secular state was beginning to disintegrate and other forms of communication were disappearing.

It was in the liturgy that the wider, organizational Church and the local communities made contact because the rituals could be performed only by a properly appointed celebrant. The bishop (or his representative) had a powerful position in the community. One element of his strength lay in the fact that he represented the outside world to his particular church because his mandate came from there, not from the people. He was an accepted member of the community, however, and, whether popular or not, was viewed as the means through which the grace to live a spiritual life would come. He was present at all the main events in the lives of his people from birth to death, strengthening, consoling, educating. His power was not political or even religious in the old sense. It was something quite new, and around the person of the bishop a new community began to form that was unlike anything that had existed before.

The Visual Expression of the New Union

For both Greeks and Romans the temples were buildings whose primary purposes were to honor the gods and goddesses by providing suitable dwelling places for them as well as protection for their cult statues from the elements. The exterior was emphasized, and the interior, cramped and dimly lit, was much less important. The sharp corners and boxy lines of the Greek temple set it apart from the surrounding space and placed it solidly on the ground. It was intended to be looked at and walked around. By contrast the worship needs of the new faith created a demand for fresh architectural forms. Its churches were not principally the dwelling places of a god, and what Christians needed most was large interior spaces where the people could gather to celebrate their rituals, preferably with unblocked views of the altar and the celebrant. Conveniently, this kind of building was readily available in the secular basilica, whose shape, coincidentally, also happened to serve the needs of the new imperial autocrats.

The rectangular basilica was an old Italian architectural form designed to serve the community's social, commercial, and legal needs. Every Italian city had one or more basilicas, located in or near the forum, the town's business area. Their purpose was to provide shelter from inclement weather for large numbers of people, so special emphasis was given to the interior; the outer form was of secondary importance. Barrel and cross vaults provided the essential structural elements of the building, and light was supplied by clerestory windows high above the floor. The results were impressive, and in the hands of the new secular and religious authorities, all the potential of this ancient architectural form was realized. New visual and spatial dimensions were opened up. In the basilica, unlike the temple, space was itself important, and the classical Greek effort to limit it by sharp corners and right angles gave way to the curves of the vaults and ceilings, which conveyed the impression of distance and limitlessness. With illumination coming from high above, mysterious effects of

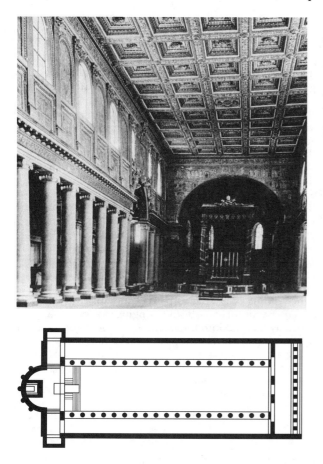

Despite considerable decorative changes over the centuries, the great Basilica of Saint Mary Major in Rome has remained structurally unaltered since its construction around A.D. 440. Flanked by two aisles, the majestically proportioned nave suggests the grandeur of the basilican style of architecture.

light and shade became possible. Another element was the colossal size of the basilicas of the Constantinian period. The central nave of Maxentius' basilica, for example, measured 260 by 80 feet, and the ceiling, supported by three soaring cross vaults, was 115 feet above the marble floor. A riot of colored pavements, mosaics, wall decorations, and coffered ceilings confronted the eye in all directions, yet all the elements were integrated and a focus was provided by the structure's axial lines, which drew the gaze immediately to the apses at either end.

In such a building the individual was dwarfed but at the same time swept up into the structure. Under the huge vaults, all people were drawn together as one. Whereas in the classical view the individual regarded the temple from his or her own particular vantage point, in the basilica the individual was submerged and overwhelmed by the mass of people gathered there, his or her special viewpoint lost in so large a setting. As part of the mass, however, the individual was included, not excluded, and together with his or her fellows was lifted up to the infinite, whether this was the godhead or the emperor.

THE POWER OF THE BASILICA

At Trier, Germany, the basilica built by Constantine survives intact. This fine description of it by a modern scholar gives an impression of all basilicas of the period:

> Originally [its] red brick was hidden under plaster, painted around the windows (in two tiers) with yellow vine tendrils and little cupids, all on a red background. Most of the walls were pierced by pipes, and there was space under the floor, too, for the circulation of hot air. Forehall and nave were paved with a honeycomb design in black and white, while geometric patterns of many-colored marble and gilt glass covered the walls up to the second tier of windows. . . . The apse, a throne platform in its midst, was sheathed in gold and mosaics; over all, a gilt-coffered ceiling. There were no columns in the 250-foot nave to detract from the impression of enormous size; no interruption to the floods of light that played over the surfaces of gold, ochre, green, red, black, and white; nothing but air, it seemed, to support a vault a hundred feet above the floor. One's gaze rose involuntarily into space, floated like a mote in the stillness, rebounded from the range of colors, but came to rest inevitably at the gathering of lines in the apse. There sat or stood the emperor on ceremonial occasions for the announcement of victories, the reading of new laws, the reception of embassies. The whole building had a point. Beautiful in itself, and bringing to a focus many brilliant arts and skills, its beauty merged into the purposes of the state. It declared the power of its creator, a being who, to the awe of barbarians and peasants, could enclose so vast a space *and heat it.*

Source: Ramsay MacMullen, *Constantine* (New York: Dial Press, 1969), p. 50. Copyright © 1969 by Ramsay MacMullen. Reprinted by permission of Dial Press.

The basilican plan was as perfectly adapted to the needs of the new religion as it was to those of the imperial government. In place of the emperor was the bishop celebrating the Eucharist for the assembled congregation or pronouncing his homily from the high pulpit. In this setting the individual Christian was absorbed into the mass of fellow worshipers and linked to the bishop, God's intermediary between Heaven and Earth. In the mystical action of the ritual a person was lifted out of time and into the heavenly realm of the Eternal Banquet with God. The basilica's removal of the limits of space served the needs of the new religion particularly well. The worshiper passed through the dull, outer portals and was suddenly swept up into a magnificent, heavenly world. Yet all was organized and serene. The individual had a place, but he or she was no longer, as in the Greek view, the measurer of things. The world, the Church, the congregation, and the bishop were arranged in a hierarchical ascending framework as clearly as the secular state. The congregation was below the bishop as the people were below the emperor, yet they were not cut off from these figures but somehow united with them. The functions of all were defined and established. In the world of the fourth century it was not so much that human vision was turned inward as it was turned elsewhere, away from the meanness and insignificance of the world to the infinite beyond. In such a setting the individual could discover a place only by relating to his or her fellow citizens and coreligionists in the established secular and ecclesiastical hierarchies.

Society and the Church

The Church of the fourth century was as highly structured as civil society and possessed almost as many gradations, distinctions, and honors. For the curial classes who moved in large numbers into the hierarchy of the Church, there was no loss of status, and they were able to continue in their old roles as public figures in a new and more attractive environment. As civil society gradually slipped into chaos and repression, however, the administrative organs of the Church looked more and more attractive to the old, service-oriented aristocracies of the Empire. In addition to public positions that had honors and privileges attached to them, the Church began to have increasingly large holdings of land, buildings, and funds that needed the same kind of management that in the past the curial classes had lavished on their beloved cities. More important, the Church provided these people with a sense of community and with congregations over which they could rule without the alienation that they had experienced as civil administrators. Instead of representing a savage and distant government in its most immediate and oppressive form, squeezing taxes out of an unwilling citizenry, the ecclesiastical administrator presided over a community whose adherence to him—as well as its financial contributions—was voluntary. Constantine's endorsement of the ecclesiastical organization and his showering upon it of judicial, social, and economic privileges made it even more attractive. Henceforth, a flood of talented people from all parts of the Empire, who in the past would have ended up as governors and generals or even emperors, began to appear as bishops and patriarchs of the Church. Ambrose, Athanasius, Basil, the two Gregories, John Chrysostom, and Augustine were among the most dynamic, talented, and ambitious figures of the age. They had one thing in common: all were bishops.

At the head of each duly established church was a monarchical bishop who possessed autocratic powers over those under him. He could ordain to the priesthood and the lower orders, admit new members to the community, and expel others. He was in complete control of the finances of the church, and his appointment was for life unless deposed by a council of other bishops; the people could not depose him. Beneath this powerful figure were ranged in descending order priests, deacons, subdeacons, readers, acolytes, singers, exorcists, porters, gravediggers, hospital attendants, and many others. Rome in the mid–third century had 154 clergy, not an exceptional number compared to Carthage two centuries later, which had over 500. Emperor Justinian tried to keep the numbers at Constantinople under 500. Beside the churches and their staffs there were charitable foundations, such as hospitals, orphanages, and homes for the aged, widows, and travelers, which also required supervision, staffing, and management. As early as the third century the Church in Rome was caring for 1,500 poor persons and widows.

In this sixth-century mosaic from Saint Vitale in Ravenna, Italy, Bishop Maximianus and his clergy surround the Emperor Justinian, practically crowding the soldiers out of the composition. Although the scene probably reflects the situation at the imperial court as Maximianus would have liked it to be, the bishops of the late Empire did in fact wield immense power. Note the *chi rho* on the soldier's shield at left.

The Role of Women in the New Order   Despite the important role played by women in early Christian communities, they were eventually excluded from the all-important functions of baptizing, exorcising demons, preaching, and administering the Eucharist; all of these activities were reserved for men. The language of religion as well as the imagery and symbolism of the churches were all predominantly male. Although there was a tradition in the Syrian church that the Holy Spirit, the third person of the Trinity, was feminine, this doctrine was rejected by the orthodox majority. So was the alternative church organization of Marcion, which allowed women to baptize, exorcise, and preach.

As the hierarchical structure of Church government developed and the role of the clergy in civil society grew, the influence of women declined proportionately. As long as Christians were limited to meeting in each other's homes for the celebration of their rituals, the role of women must have remained significant. However, once Christianity became an accepted religion in the Empire and was promoted to the status of its official religion, the effect was to accentuate enormously the role of the clergy. The rituals of the churches now became elaborate public ceremonies, and the clergy's role as guardians of behavior and belief was greatly strengthened. In all of these developments, the contribution or involvement of women was at best peripheral. Once again the public realm prevailed over the private. In the public expression of religion, women were relegated to the sidelines.

The Christian family reproduced many of the features characteristic of Jewish family structures. It was also influenced heavily by traditional Greco-Roman assumptions about the predominance of the male head of the household and the subordination of all other household members to him. The gradual elimination of slavery during the later Empire, the unacceptability of concubinage for observant Christians, and rules against easy divorce all contributed to the strengthening of the nuclear family and the tensions within it. Christian misogyny repeated most of the biblical and Greco-Roman stereotypes of women and probably resulted from the effort to put the demands of the new religion into practice at the family level.

This rather bleak picture of the role of women must be balanced by other perspectives. The Hellenic and biblical traditions of the natural inferiority of women had to be reconciled with Jewish and Christian beliefs in the equality of all human beings in the sight of God and the call of all, male and female alike, to the heights of holiness. Especially in the Syrian Christian world, great emphasis was placed on the role of Mary, the mother of Jesus. In the fifth century the cult of the Virgin spread widely throughout the rest of the Greco-Roman Christian world and found a permanent place in its tradition. Female martyrs had shown the same degree of fortitude as their male counterparts during the centuries of persecution, and their triumphs and glories were celebrated in the popular and widely read *Lives of the Saints*. Their relics were sought as eagerly as those of male martyrs, and their shrines became sites of pilgrimage. The Gospels gave prominence to the role of women in the life of Jesus, and it was clear from the writings of Paul that women had had a major role in the ministry of the early Church. And like men, women had the option of withdrawing from the world and forming their own religious communities where they could, in large measure, escape male dominance. Monasteries of women, like those of their male counterparts, tended to accumulate land and property and have considerable influence on nearby secular communities. Nevertheless, Christian women generally remained outside the mainstream of the organized Church and, like their Jewish sisters, found themselves confined to the private realm of the family and to passive roles in the religious life of their communities.

THE EMPEROR, THE ADMINISTRATION, AND THE ARMY

The Division of Power

As early as the time of Marcus Aurelius the difficulties a single emperor had in coping with the problems of imperial defense were being felt, and Avidius Cassius was delegated to handle the east while Aurelius himself faced the northern invasions. In the third century A.D. only radical regionalization enabled the Empire to survive the simultaneous attacks from the north and east. Gallienus allowed the usurper Postumus to cope with all the western provinces and permitted the upstart state of Palmyra under Odenathus to handle the eastern frontier while he fought the Goths on the Danube. By the time of the accession of Diocletian in 284 it was clearly impossible for any one emperor to rule unassisted an Empire that reached from Scotland to the Sudan, at least while it was under severe military pressure. The practical solution arrived at was to divide it into a number of parts. From 285, when Diocletian appointed Maximian as Caesar in the west, until 476, when the last western emperor was deposed, the united Empire was ruled by a single individual for only a few years.

Although this was the de facto solution to the problem of imperial administration, the way in which emperors and Caesars came to power was as chaotic as ever. As in the past, dynastic sentiment was strong in the army and among the people, and from Constantine onward sons or relatives, and at times even children and women, were elevated on the death of a ruling emperor. Usurpers, usually generals acclaimed by their own troops, had therefore to seek the recognition of the reigning emperor (as long as one remained) or challenge him in the field. An alternative for an aspiring claimant was to remain a power behind the throne, and this was increasingly common in the fifth century when German generals rose in the service of Rome. These officers preferred this role, for in addition to being unacceptable as emperors, they would probably also have lost contact with their own troops, on whose loyalty they depended above all else.

The instability of the imperial office from the third century onward was a major factor in the weakening of the Empire in the west. There the tradition of autocratic rule was less firmly established, and the senatorial class was extremely powerful. The west was also militarily more exposed than the east, with the result that the emperors there had a much more difficult job fulfilling their role as protectors of the state against both the barbarians without and the powerful within.

The Mystique of the Imperial Office

From the time of Augustus a religious aura surrounded the person of the emperor, and in the provinces at least he was worshiped as a god even during his lifetime. This all-too-natural veneration of power was given new prominence from the time of Septimius Severus, until by the end of the third century the emperors were ruling as the earthly representatives of Jupiter himself.

Under the Severi, images of the emperor and his family decorated the altars of towns and the chapels of the legions, and received the adoration (*adoratio*) of provincials and soldiers alike. Geta, one of Severus' sons, issued coins in his own image, showing him wearing the crown of the sun god and venerating his father, who was assimilated to the highest divinity. His mother, Julia Domna, appeared on coins as Cybele, the Mother of the Gods, or as the Mother of the Augusti, seated on the throne of Juno. The gods now became the assistants and companions of the emperor, and the heavenly court was modeled after the image of the imperial court on earth. New titles were added: the emperor was the Restorer of the World, the Inaugurator of the Golden Age; he was saluted as Undefeated, Eternal, Perpetual. It was more significant to swear by the imperial *genius* than to swear by the gods. With Aurelian, the official title of the emperor became *Deus et Dominus,* God and Lord. Under the same emperor the sun god was adopted as the supreme deity of the Empire and a new college of pontiffs, independent of the old pontifical college, was created to serve his needs, as was a new temple at Rome. Everything having to do with the emperor was sacred. His household was the *domus divina* (divine house), he dwelt in a sacred palace, his decrees and pronouncements were termed sacred, and those admitted to his presence were expected to kneel before him and venerate him as they did his images. Finally, after eight and a half centuries, the royal crown reappeared, and crown, scepter, orb, purple cloak, and triumphal regalia became the standard symbols of office.

Under Diocletian the evolution reached fulfillment, and the emperor and his Caesar took the names *Jovius* and *Herculius,* respectively, becoming the agents or vice-regents of Jupiter on earth (or, if their subjects preferred it, the very gods themselves—the theological niceties of the point were never precisely defined). Court ceremony was now firmly established in its most minute detail, and the emperor disappeared into the private recesses of the palace, to appear only on the rarest of occasions and then in full, unapproachable regalia. The cycle had come fully around. Roman history began with the regal period, passed through the Republic and Principate, and ended with an autocracy. Appropriately, because the emperor's power had become godlike, the allegiance of the people to him no longer had a secular, political basis but was now religious. Constantine could issue coins (ca. A.D. 330) that depicted a hand stretching forth from the heavens to extend to him a crown. When the Empire became Christian, there was no fundamental change. In the Republic the magistrates had been priests who were responsible for the maintenance of good relations between divine and earthly realms, or the peace of the gods (*pax deorum*). In the Empire this duty fell to the *princeps,* and when Constantine became a Christian, he still regarded it as his responsibility to maintain this relationship, although now it was the *pax Dei,* the peace of God. He also continued to hold the office of *pontifex maximus,* as did his successors down to the time of Gratian (ca. A.D. 375). Among the emperor's duties, therefore, was the care of the Church in order that God might be offered a pleasing sacrifice by human beings. If that involved suppressing incorrect belief, error, or indiscipline, so be it. The emperor was not simply entitled but *bound* to intervene in religious affairs.

Administration: Coping with the Crisis

In the third century the old class system of the Empire came under tremendous pressures. Until A.D. 260 the method of recruiting top administrators and army officers from the senatorial and equestrian classes continued, but with increasing numbers coming from among the latter group. Septimius Severus found it necessary to appoint equestrians to senatorial posts, giving them the title of acting governor (*procurator vice praesidis*), and the emperors after him increasingly tended in the same direction as the slow, conservative Senate, with its limited membership (still around 600), fierce jealousies, and self-centered aristocratic values, proved unable to provide the kind of leaders the Empire desperately needed in its time of crisis. With Gallienus, senators were finally excluded from all military commands and most of the governorships and administrative posts. Not that this was the end for the Senate by any means. Especially in the west, the old aristocracy continued to accumulate land, intermarry, and build up enormous fortunes. The Senate at Rome never lost its attractiveness as the oldest and most exclusive club in the Empire.

The New Administrators   With Diocletian, who ascended the throne in A.D. 284, a new era began. Under his rule the army expanded to almost twice its previous size, creating a demand for masses of new officers from the rank of general on down, all coming from the equestrian classes. Similarly, his doubling of the number of provinces from 50 to 100 created hundreds of new equestrian positions as well as 50 new provincial governors, now called *praesides*. The result was that the equestrian order expanded greatly, and the most natural candidates for the new positions were found among the local gentry of the Empire, the decurions. In the past their main function had been to attend to the administration of the cities, collecting taxes and so forth. Some, of course, had already been recruited into the imperial civil service, but now many more left their local councils to take equestrian positions in the army or civilian administration. This was an attractive move because apart from the opportunities offered by a new and wider career outside their own cities, the posts carried the higher status of the equestrian rank and freedom from the expensive burdens of city administration. There was even the possibility of returning to their native provinces with their new titles and positions as servants of the emperor.

Qualifications for the new careerists, whether in the military or in the civilian branches (although technically all were now military and wore military uniforms), were increasingly detached from the old bases of honor, wealth, and public service that had dominated in the old system. Now what counted was ability and education, however the latter was acquired, whether in the leisurely aristocratic way of the past or by more technical schooling under professional educators, now in great demand. The new army commanders were of a distinctly nonpatrician background, but of course this was nothing new in the third century. Diocletian was the son of a freedman from Dalmatia, and his colleague Galerius had once herded cattle in Hungary. Constantine's father was a rural magnate from Naissus in the former Yugoslavia. Although ability and education were important for active careerists, wealth did not lose its power, and successive administrations railed at the practice of well-to-do decurions buying codicils or titles to a particular office and rank without ever actually performing the duties attached to it.

The End of the Equestrian Order

Constantius II (A.D. 337–361) continued the policy of his predecessors and established a second Senate with 300 members at Constantinople. This grew rapidly, reaching almost 2,000 by the end of the century, with a similar increase at Rome. More and more offices were elevated from equestrian to senatorial rank, and equestrians were appointed to them. Understandably, the effects of the earlier expansion of the equestrian order now began to be felt in the Senate. Decurions struggled to be promoted to the rank of senator, instead of to the equestrian order, and the wealthy, whenever they could, bought the title. The attractions were the same as before—exemptions and privileges, especially the exemption from curial services. Senatorial rank also promised its holders added security from the harsh exactions of imperial governors and administrators. The exemption from curial responsibilities was early seen as a major problem, and by 436 it was restricted to those with the highest senatorial rankings. With the expansion of the senatorial order and the freer bestowal of the senatorial rank, the equestrian order gradually died out or was absorbed in the senatorial order. By the beginning of the fifth century it had ceased to exist, and in its place was the vastly expanded—and cheapened—senatorial class.

Social Character   The Senate of the second half of the fourth century was a very mixed body. In the west it contained a core of great landowners, some of whom claimed to be able to trace their ancestry back to the nobility of the Republic, but there were also Germans such as the Vandal Stilicho, who married the niece of the great emperor Theodosius, and Bauto the Frank, who was married to the daughter of another emperor, Arcadius. There were Armenians, Alans, Sarmatians, and even a few Persians. Sometimes peasants rose to high rank, as was the case of Justin (the uncle of the famous emperor Justinian), who became emperor of the eastern Empire in A.D. 518. The rhetorician Libanius sneeringly cites examples of senators who had risen from humble origins—they were sausagemakers and cloakroom attendants, he claims—repeating the same kind of comments that Roman senators had been making about newcomers into their ranks since the Republic.

An important feature of the western senatorial aristocracy was its local character. Most official appointments made by senators occurred in their own part of the world, and their influence was therefore as much their own as imperial. The thoroughness with which taxes were collected and shipped to the central administration depended on how cooperative these local magnates chose to be. When imperial judges sat in court, the local aristocrats sat beside them. More and more the peasantry was faced with a choice between the exactions of the emperor's tax collector and the protection offered by the local magnate—along with its price. People's horizons shrank, and their loyalties became focused on the lord of the manor, who now began to assume a more important role than the distant emperor as lawgiver, judge, and protector. In the east, where there were few great landowning families and the bulk of the new senators were from the aristocracies of the cities, the situation was different, and the Senate there constituted a true aristocracy of office and service. An important consequence of this was that in the east a large number of the new senators were Christian because Christianity was so much more advanced there than in the west.

The new Senate at Constantinople never gained the prestige of the old Senate in the west, and the power of the eastern emperor was proportionately greater. It was predominantly a Senate of service, and the ideal of the scholar-bureaucrat gave the eastern Empire a solidity sorely lacking in the west, where the two roles tended to be separated (to the considerable detriment of the state). Ultimately, then, the emperors succeeded in creating a true state bureaucracy and maintaining the allegiance of the educated and well-to-do classes in one half of the Empire but not in the other. In the west the emperors failed, and the upper classes went their own private way.

The Disappearance of the Middle Class

With the expansion of the army and the administration, the middle classes of the Empire came under extreme pressure. The attractions of service in the imperial administration were more than balanced by the improved efficiency of the tax-collecting system. As decurions moved upward into the equestrian and senatorial orders, fewer and fewer could be found to replace them, and the burdens increased on those who remained. The central administration continued to demand that essential city services be maintained and that the increased taxes be paid—all of this with reduced numbers and no increase in economic productivity. Laborers and artisans fled from the fields and workshops into the army or simply elsewhere—to other cities and towns where they thought better opportunities might await them. If there was great stability in the first two centuries of the Empire, the third and fourth saw great movements of people back and forth as the emperors on one hand encouraged them to move by creating new opportunities and on the other tried to restrict them in order to make the new tax system work. Under Constantine the clergy acquired exempt status from curial responsibilities, and a new exodus into the administration of the Church began, despite efforts by the government to restrict the number of decurions who were ordained. Periodic attempts were also made to expel those of curial origin from the Senate, but there was no way of reversing the process. Richer, luckier, perhaps more able decurions moved up into the exempt classes, and the poorer or unluckier were simply pushed down into the lower classes and numbered among the *humiliores*. Gradually the process of simplification reduced the classes of the Empire to two: one comprising the newly expanded senatorial order, the clergy, and the employees of the state, all privileged and, in varying degrees, well-off, and the other made up of the masses of the Empire, all unprivileged and extremely poor.

The division was most noticeable in the west, where for centuries the senatorial order had been building up its great landholdings. Mere handfuls of great families owned most of the land of Italy and Gaul. Under these circumstances the patronage of a powerful neighbor, whether bishop, senator, or military commander, was the only source to which the average citizen could turn for protection against the tax collectors or for help in bad economic times. This development was not exclusively western, however. Toward the end of the fourth century Syrian villagers were in the peculiar position of having to pay the local military commander a fee to use his soldiers·to protect them from the imperial tax collectors. More typically, though, the local patron was a great landowner whose fee for protection was some kind of claim or lien against the peasant's property. Over the years, either by this method or by crushing taxation, the free peasantry became tenants (*coloni*) of the landowners. The emperors tried to fight this kind of patronage because it interfered with the flow of tax money, although some were genuinely concerned with the plight of the commoners; Valentinian, for example, established the office of city defender (*defensor civitatis*), which was intended to protect the poor by offering them cheap and speedy justice.

The New Financial System: Rationalization and Resistance

The change in personnel was only one aspect of the transformation wrought by Diocletian and Constantine. The fiscal basis of the government was also radically altered at this time. In the past, Rome, like all ancient Mediterranean states before it, collected only enough taxes to pay current bills. There were no annual budgets and no fluctuating tax rates. For political reasons the government was extremely slow to change the rate of existing taxes or impose new ones. Expenses were paid directly out of current income. When a sudden crisis occurred, the only way money could be raised was by the sale of state possessions or the confiscation of the estates of the wealthy. The Severan emperors had tremendously increased the pay of the soldiers, and larger and larger quantities of debased coins began to come into circulation. The result was that prices rose and the real income of the state, the army, and the bureaucracy declined. To compensate, the collection of taxes in kind became the principal source of income for the state, and soldiers and bureaucrats now received, in addition to payments in cash, requisitions in kind, including free uniforms, rations, and weapons. With the abandonment of fixed taxes as the principal source of income, the government was finally in a position to come up with a true budget, for instead of trying to meet expenses out of a fixed income it could requisition its actual needs—so much grain, so many uniforms, and so on. Although requisitioning in kind was an accomplished fact by some point in the third century A.D., it was left to Diocletian to rationalize the process.

The first step was to determine the actual resources of the Empire, and this was accomplished in a series of censuses held over a number of years throughout the provinces. The results were then expressed in ideal fiscal units (called *iuga* and *capita*), which allowed a uniform system of measurement to be extended to the whole Empire and permitted the staff of the Praetorian Prefects to have a good idea of available resources. Conversion tables were worked out, establishing the ratio between actual land values, productivity, and rural population. For example, in one region,

20 Roman acres of first-class arable land, 5 acres of vineyards, or 60 acres of third-class land was calculated as one unit (*iugum*). Human beings and livestock were similarly calculated in terms of *capita,* and the two figures were added to give a total of the resources of the particular region. Next, the Praetorian Prefect estimated how many supplies he needed for the coming year, and, knowing how much each province was worth, he was able to set a rate, which at least theoretically fluctuated each year depending on the needs of the state.

The burden of Diocletian's taxes fell principally on agriculture, the largest segment of the economy, and on the rural population. The collection of taxes was still the responsibility of the unfortunate curial classes of the cities, who had to be prepared to make up arrears out of their own pockets. Senators escaped these duties but were subject to a modest surtax (the *gleba* or *follis*), and merchants had to pay a five-year levy in gold or silver, which proved to be extremely burdensome. Because the efficient operation of the budget depended on the permanence of the fiscal units, Diocletian decreed that all peasants and decurions were always to remain in the places in which they were registered in the census. In a similar vein, though completely without success, he enacted a decree that fixed prices for all goods, commodities, and wages.

The emperor's subjects understandably resisted the new tax system. Corruption was rampant, and maneuvers of all kinds were used to avoid payments. One emperor complained of how his bureaucrats used "minute calculations of impenetrable obscurity" to cover their embezzling and then demanded receipts for past years, which most people, assuming they owed nothing, had long ago thrown away.[1] Another trick the tax collectors used was to exploit the inefficiency of the bureaucracy by writing off the arrears, which often were allowed to accumulate, in order to clear up the books. Crafty tax collectors gave their victims credit at high interest rates and then waited until a general indulgence wiped out the due taxes altogether. Another administrative abuse was the failure to revise the censuses periodically, and because land use and population fluctuated, the census often did not reflect the true situation in a given region. The worst feature of the system was its generally unprogressive character, which applied the same tax rate to rich and poor. Although senators were subject to a surtax, their land was often undervalued, and they could postpone payments and fend off the tax collectors until inflation reduced the amount or an indulgence eliminated it.

Justice, Law, and the Social System

A major responsibility of the emperor was the administration of justice. During the third century the local courts had faded away, and governors had become automatically the court of the first instance. Because appeals went to the emperor, the result

---

[1]A.H.M. Jones, trans., *The Decline of the Ancient World* (London: Longmans, Green & Co., 1966), p. 175.

SHORTCOMINGS OF THE ROMAN LEGAL SYSTEM

Roman justice was slow, costly, and often corrupt. The Justinian Code aimed at preventing lawsuits from "becoming almost immortal and exceeding the term of human life" by establishing certain time limits for the passing of judgment and for decisions on appeals. Distance slowed communications, courts were clogged, and governors were busy at their numerous tasks. As with civilian administration and legionary commands, the Romans resisted professionalization. The administration of justice was regarded as merely one of the functions of a magistrate who had other duties to perform, both civilian and military, and he was allowed considerable latitude. He was expected to take into account all the aspects of a case—including its social and political dimensions—not merely its legalities. The result was that the system of justice faithfully reflected the social system, which explicitly recognized the inequality of people and accorded those higher in the system a more favorable treatment than those lower down. The case was classically put by a Greek who, after being made a prisoner of war, had elected to live among the Huns of Attila:

> The laws are not the same for all [in the Roman Empire]. If a rich man breaks the law he can avoid the penalty for his wrongdoing. But if it is a poor man who does not know how to pull strings, he suffers the penalty of the law—unless he departs this life before trial, while proceedings drag on interminably and vast expenses are incurred.

Source: A.H.M. Jones, trans., *The Decline of the Ancient World* (London: Longmans, Green & Co., 1966), p. 197.

was that with only 50 provincial governors, who had other duties besides their judicial functions, and only one emperor, the courts were clogged with cases. There was the further problem of the uncertainty of the law, which did not receive its definitive form until the publication of the uniform code of Justinian in the sixth century. In the meantime, attorneys could embarrass judges by quoting from authoritative sources unknown or even inaccessible to them. The situation got so bad that in A.D. 426 Valentinian III issued a decree giving foremost authority to the five great jurists of former years, Papinian, Paulus, Ulpian, Modestinus, and Gaius. Where they differed, a majority vote was to be taken, with Papinian as the tie breaker.

The emperor himself was the chief legislator, and his pronouncements were the principal source of law. These consisted of judgments (*decreta*) and answers to inquiries of judges (*relationes*) and of private citizens (*rescripta*). There were also imperial edicts and constitutions, which were general laws either for the whole Empire or particular provinces. The confusion created by this haphazard system was great and only slowly resolved, first by the publication of the Theodosian Code (A.D. 438) and finally by the monumental product of Justinian in 529.

THE ARMY, THE EMPIRE, AND THE BARBARIANS

The army during the Roman peace had been stretched along thousands of miles of frontier. There were no reserves, and expeditions could be mounted only by drawing units from the frontier garrisons. This was a self-defeating process because any weakness in the screening forces constituted an invitation to the barbarians to break through into the Empire and make off with what they could lay their hands on before reinforcements arrived.

Already in the third century efforts were being made to build up a mobile reserve, which would be able to cope with major incursions that the frontier forces could not handle. In these forces emphasis was placed on cavalry units (*vexillationes*), which were ranked with the legions.

The standard division of the old army had been the legion, to which were attached additional auxiliary units of 500 to 1,000 men each. Since Caracalla's edict extending the franchise to the Empire, the distinction between legionaries and auxiliaries on the grounds of citizenship disappeared, but the legions themselves as well as the *auxilia* remained. Now, however, the reserve armies (*comitatenses* or *palatini*) were formed by withdrawing units, usually of 1,000 men each, and adding them to the existing cavalry units. The original legions from which these units were taken continued to exist, but at lower manpower levels. The overall result was to create an army consisting of generally smaller, more manageable units, divided between the frontier forces (*limitanei*) and the central field armies. The majority of the troops (about 65 percent) remained on the frontiers, but their quality was not as high as the reserve forces. The result of this new policy was to permit the mobile field armies to respond quickly and effectively to major incursions. However, a by-product of the policy was the conversion of the frontier provinces into battlegrounds that were fought over again and again until their inhabitants did not care who ruled them as long as there was peace.

The composition of the army of the late Empire differed considerably from that of the Principate. Although the tendency toward hereditary recruitment from among the descendants of army veterans and the use of barbarians had already begun long before, there had never been the level of dependence on these two sources that there was after Diocletian and Constantine. Diocletian made the military career hereditary, requiring by law that the sons of soldiers enter the profession. He also revived the draft so that in addition to supplying pay and material, the cities of the Empire were now required to provide recruits as well. In the fourth century this was the main source of manpower, although resistance to this form of recruitment was high. The draftees had to be branded or even imprisoned at night to prevent them from escaping, and the government resorted to all sorts of threats and enticements to come up with the requisite numbers. Pay and service conditions were generally good, and there were special tax exemptions and other benefits. Still, the minimum height requirement had to be lowered from 5 feet 10 inches to 5 feet 7 inches in 367 to allow the government's net to be cast more widely.

Barbarians were recruited in two ways. The first method was to enroll them in regular army units as volunteers, and apparently large numbers did volunteer, being attracted by the promotional opportunities and the regular pay. The majority were Germans from various tribes, but volunteers came from as far away as Ireland and Persia. On entry into the legions they automatically received the citizenship. The essentials of Latin were quickly learned, and barbarians often rose to high rank. They gave dedicated service to Rome, and there is no evidence that those who served in the regular units in this fashion were any more untrustworthy than recruits from within the Empire.

The other method of recruiting barbarians was dangerous. This consisted of employing whole groups of the outsiders, whether in tribes or just as individuals, who put themselves under the leadership of some prominent warrior. These contingents fought alongside the regular Roman army units but were not subject to the same discipline and control. At first the numbers were small, but after the battle of Adrianople (A.D. 378), they were employed in increasingly large numbers. In part this was due to the heavy losses suffered by the regular forces in the civil wars of the late fourth century and in part to the great barbarian invasions of the same period. Large tribal units such as the Visigoths, Burgundians, and Alans forced their way into Roman territory and occupied or were assigned lands, in return for which they offered their military services. Finally, the Roman army in the west consisted of practically nothing but barbarian hordes under nominal allegiance to the Roman emperor. The Roman army slowly disintegrated, with the contingents in Britain, Spain, and Africa disappearing in the 450s and the last units in France in 486. Saint Severinus' biographer, Eugippius, described how the surviving regiments in Austria drew their last installments of pay in the 480s and were dismissed. He comments matter-of-factly:

> While the Roman empire still stood, soldiers were maintained with public pay in many of the towns for the defence of the frontier, but when that custom lapsed the military units were abolished together with the frontier.[2]

With such little fanfare did Roman rule on the Danube come to an end.

Romans and Germans

The nature of Germanic migration into the Empire is greatly disputed. Were the Germans who forced or petitioned their way in migrating peoples or warrior bands? The answer might be both, depending on the groups. In the case of the Visigoths, for example, the argument is strong that they were a warrior band that evolved into something more like a nation under the leadership of Alaric and his successors Wallia, Theoderic, and Euric. Originally formed from the amalgamation of three previously

[2]Ibid.

independent groups of Goths around the strong leadership of Alaric, the Visigoths were joined by other Germans as well as natives of the Empire. Like many other German groups, the Visigoths had been in contact with Rome for a long time, had served in its armies, and had been impressed by the majesty of its imperial façade. These experiences tended to erode the cultural barrier between the two sides.

The transition from Roman to Germanic rule was thus accomplished with less violence than might be expected. Life in much of the west continued as it always had; in some areas it may even have improved as a result of the disappearance of the grinding but largely ineffective fiscal administration of the Empire. In Italy and Gaul, German soldiers were billeted in cities, not the countryside, and were maintained on the basis of income granted them from state resources, not loot or confiscated property. Taxes that would normally have gone to the imperial treasury were directly assigned to individual soldiers so that the only real losers were the original imperial bureaucrats, who were now largely bypassed. The cities were administered locally by elected defenders (*defensores*). Legislation and legal practice remained as they were in the past, and the Theodosian Code was the principal reference work of the law. Roman judges and advisers now worked for the German courts rather than for the imperial civil service.

At least in these regions the picture of hordes of savage barbarians descending on the Empire with fire and sword and eventually settling down to a miserable existence in ruined villas and towns is false. The number of Germans was not great, and they were far from their homelands. They and their leaders had long been accustomed to Roman ways, and it made sense for them to work out a modus vivendi with the local Roman populations. Both Germans and Romans—especially the large Roman landholders—shared an interest in maintaining existing institutions. In time a new Roman-Germanic amalgam of landlords and rulers came into existence. In some parts of Spain and Africa, however, the transition was not so peaceful, and whole regions of the old northern provinces of the Empire lost any semblance of higher culture. The Germanic courts were anything but civil. The Visigoth Alaric's successor, Athaulf, was assassinated, and his children murdered. Theoderic's sons succeeded in similarly bloody fashion. Nor were all Romans willing to work with the Germans. Some, such as civic leader (and later bishop) Sidonius Apollinaris, would do so only when the chiefs were in allegiance with the Empire (or what was left of it). The poet Rutilius Namatianus mentions two magnates who abandoned estates in Gaul rather than cut a deal with the Goths.

The main barrier between Germans and Romans in the early years of the settlement of the west was, oddly, religion. Many Germans had earlier converted to an Arian form of Christianity, and so found themselves regarded not just as outsiders but as heretics by the native population. In time this barrier fell as the new settlers accepted the orthodox faith of the provincials among whom they lived. The conversion of the Franks from paganism to Christianity at the time of the baptism of their king, Clovis, around A.D. 500 represented another important step in the process of reconciling Roman and Germanic populations.

EPILOGUE

Of course the story does not end at this point. Roman rule in the east lasted for another 1,000 years until the fall of Constantinople to the Turks in 1453. In the west the story is more complicated. City life did not entirely vanish with the fall of the western Empire, but it no longer had anything like the importance it had had for the Romans. Roman law and administrative techniques were used by German kings alongside their own customary legal and administrative systems. Classical culture and many of its values survived, but in very different ways. A major Romanized and Hellenized institution, the Church, was a common meeting ground of Romans and Germans, and constituted a useful kind of cultural bridge between the two peoples.

Until the fifth century there had always been a well-defined, if fluid, boundary between the distinctively European north and the Mediterranean south, the one represented by Germanic and other indigenous European peoples who resisted urbanization and the formation of the state, and the other by peoples who were, in varying degrees of willingness, prepared to accept these forms of social and political organization. For centuries Rome had promoted state and urban culture. It had coerced Celtic, Germanic, and other native European peoples who lived within the borders of the Empire into abandoning their old forms of social and political organization and accepting that of the Roman state. Yet, paradoxically, once the frontier along the Rhine and Danube was removed, the Germanic peoples who settled within the old boundaries of the Empire, especially the Franks, *voluntarily* accepted a form of the state and began to extend it eastward into old "free" Germany. Northern Europe at this point began to abandon the chiefdom, which had characterized its political, social, and cultural life since the Bronze Age. This was a decisive break with the past. Only the Celtic fringe areas such as Ireland and Scotland continued to resist more developed state forms of government. In this sense the fifth century can stand for the final period in the elimination of barriers between north and south, east and west, European and Mediterranean, forms of culture.

Looking back, the whole of ancient history can be seen as a process of interchange between east and west. The city and the state were pioneered in the Near East. Subsequently, southern Europeans, the Greeks first, then the Etruscans, Latins, and others, succumbed to the allures of the more complex and rewarding kind of society and created the *polis* as their own special form of this community. It was within the context of the *polis* that all subsequent Mediterranean history took place, even during the Roman Empire, when the Romans came up with the unique idea of making all peoples in the Empire citizens of their city. But the east was to be heard from again, this time in the form of a powerful religious movement. In the remarkable centuries between A.D. 200 and 500 Greeks and Romans struggled to make this new phenomenon their own, much as their ancestors centuries before had wrestled with and domesticated the concept of the city and the state. If east and west could be said to have come to an understanding, it was during this last, dramatic process of adaptation. Like many cultural amalgams, however, the synthesis of biblical traditions with Greek and Roman culture was incomplete and ultimately failed to hold together. Since the dawning of the modern age, a new era of experimentation as radical as that of the early *polis* age (800–500 B.C.) or of the late Empire (A.D. 200–500) has been under way. Among the driving forces are many of the same ones that made those earlier periods so exciting, creative, and ultimately successful.

Suggested Readings

THE ANCIENT NEAR EAST

COHEN, RONALD, AND ELMAN R. SERVICE. *Origins of the State: The Anthropology of Political Evolution.* Philadelphia: Institute for the Study of Human Issues, 1978.

COOK, J. M. *The Persian Empire.* New York: Schocken, 1983.

DREWS, ROBERT. *The End of the Bronze Age.* Princeton, N.J.: Princeton University Press, 1993.

DRIVER, SAMUEL R. *Introduction to the Literature of the Old Testament.* New York: Meridian, 1956.

EDWARDS, I. E. S. *The Pyramids of Egypt* (rev. ed.). Harmondsworth, UK: Penguin, 1983.

GARDINER, ALAN. *Egypt of the Pharaohs: An Introduction.* Oxford, UK: Clarendon, 1961.

GURNEY, O. R. *The Hittites* (3rd ed.). Harmondsworth, UK: Penguin, 1991.

HALLO, WILLIAM W., AND WILLIAM KELLY SIMPSON. *The Ancient Near East: A History.* (2nd edition) Orlando, Fla.: Harcourt Brace Jovanovich, 1998.

HOFFMAN, MICHAEL A. *Egypt Before the Pharaohs.* New York: Knopf, 1979.

HORNUNG, E. *Conceptions of God in Ancient Egypt.* Ithaca, N.Y.: Cornell University Press, 1982.

———. *Ideas into Image.* New York: Timken, 1992.

KEMP, BARRY J. *Ancient Egypt: Anatomy of a Civilization.* London: Routledge, 1989.

KRAMER, SAMUEL NOAH. *The Sumerians: Their History, Culture, and Character.* Chicago: University of Chicago Press, 1963.

LICHTHEIM, MIRIAM. *Ancient Egyptian Literature,* 3 vols. Berkeley: University of California Press, 1973–1980.

LLOYD, SETON. *The Art of the Ancient Near East.* New York: Praeger, 1969.

MICHALOWSKI, KAZIMIERZ. *The Art of Ancient Egypt.* London: Abrams, 1969.

OPPENHEIM, A. LEO. *Ancient Mesopotamia: Portrait of a Dead Civilization.* Chicago: University of Chicago Press, 1964.

REDFORD, DONALD B. *Akhenaten: The Heretic Pharaoh.* Princeton, N.J.: Princeton University Press, 1984.

———. *Egypt, Canaan, and Israel in Ancient Times.* Princeton, N.J.: Princeton University Press, 1992.

REDMAN, CHARLES L. *The Rise of Civilization: From Early Farmers to Urban Society in the Ancient Near East.* New York: Freeman, 1978.

ROUX, GEORGES. *Ancient Iraq* (3rd ed.). Harmondsworth, UK: Penguin, 1992.

SAGGS, H. W. F. *The Greatness That Was Babylon.* New York: Hawthorn, 1962.

———. *Civilization Before Greece and Rome.* New Haven, Conn.: Yale University Press, 1988.

SHAFER, B. (ed.). *Religion in Ancient Egypt.* Ithaca, N.Y.: Cornell University Press, 1991.

SHERRATT, ANDREW (ed.). *The Cambridge Encyclopedia of Archaeology.* New York: Cambridge University Press, 1980.

TRIGGER, B. G., ET AL. (eds.). *Ancient Egypt: A Social History.* New York: Cambridge University Press, 1983.

UCKO, PETER J., ET AL. (eds.). *Man, Settlement, and Urbanism.* London: Duckworth, 1972.

WILSON, JOHN A. *The Culture of Ancient Egypt.* Chicago: University of Chicago Press, 1965.

THE GREEK WORLD

BLUNDELL, SUE. *Women in Ancient Greece.* Cambridge, Mass.: Harvard University Press, 1995.

BORZA, EUGENE N. *In the Shadow of Olympus: The Emergence of Macedon.* Princeton, N.J.: Princeton University Press, 1990.

BOSWORTH, A. B. *Conquest and Empire: The Reign of Alexander the Great.* New York: Cambridge University Press, 1988.

BURKERT, WALTER. *Greek Religion.* Cambridge, Mass.: Harvard University Press, 1985.

———. *The Orientalizing Revolution.* Cambridge, Mass.: Harvard University Press, 1992.

CHADWICK, JOHN. *The Mycenaean World.* Cambridge, UK: Cambridge University Press, 1976.

CHAMPION, TIMOTHY, ET AL. *Prehistoric Europe.* London: Academic Press, 1984.

COHEN, DAVID. *Law, Sexuality and Society: The Enforcement of Morals in Classical Athens.* New York: Cambridge University Press, 1991.

———. *Law, Violence, and Community in Classical Athens.* New York: Cambridge University Press, 1995.

DAVIES, J. K. *Democracy and Classical Greece.* Atlantic Highlands, N.J.: Humanities Press, 1978.

DODDS, ERIC R. *The Greeks and the Irrational* (2nd ed.). Berkeley: University of California Press, 1968.

DOVER, K. J. *Greek Popular Morality.* Indianapolis: Hackett, 1994.

EHRENBURG, VICTOR. *The Greek State* (2nd ed.). London: Methuen, 1969.

FINLEY, MOSES. *The World of Odysseus* (rev. ed.). New York: Viking, 1965.

FORREST, W. G. *The Emergence of Greek Democracy.* New York: McGraw-Hill, 1966.

GARLAN, YVON. *Slavery in Ancient Greece.* Ithaca, N.Y.: Cornell University Press, 1988.

GARNSEY, PETER. *Famine and Food Supply in the Greco-Roman World.* Cambridge, UK: Cambridge University Press, 1988.

GARNSEY, PETER, AND C. R. WHITTAKER, eds. *Imperialism in the Ancient World.* Cambridge, UK: Cambridge University Press, 1978.

GOLDEN, MARK. *Children and Childhood in Classical Athens.* Baltimore: Johns Hopkins University Press, 1990.

GREEN, PETER. *Alexander to Actium: The Historical Evolution of the Hellenistic Age.* Berkeley: University of California Press, 1990.

HALL, E. *Inventing the Barbarian.* Oxford, UK: Oxford University Press, 1989.

HORNBLOWER, SIMON. *The Greek World 479–323 B.C.* London: Methuen, 1983.

JAEGER, WERNER. *Paideia: The Ideals of Greek Culture.* 3 vols. New York: Oxford University Press, 1943–1945.

JONES, A. H. M. *Greek Democracy.* Oxford, UK: Blackwell, 1957.

KITTO, H. D. F. *The Greeks.* Harmondsworth: Penguin, 1951.

LACEY, W. K. *The Family in Classical Greece.* Ithaca, N.Y.: Cornell University Press, 1968.

LLOYD, G. E. R. *Early Greek Science: Thales to Alexander.* New York: Norton, 1970.

———. *Greek Science After Aristotle.* New York: Norton, 1973.

LORAUX, N. *The Children of Athena: Athenian Ideas About Citizenship and the Division Between the Sexes.* Princeton, N.J.: Princeton University Press, 1993.

MARROU, H. I. *A History of Education in Antiquity.* New York: New American Library, 1964.

MIKALSON, J. D. *Athenian Popular Religion.* Chapel Hill: University of North Carolina Press, 1983.

MURRAY, OSWYN. *Early Greece.* London: Fontana, 1980.

POLIAKOFF, MICHAEL. *Combat Sports in the Ancient World.* New Haven, Conn.: Yale University Press, 1987.

POMEROY, SARAH B. *Families in Classical and Hellenistic Greece.* Oxford, UK: Clarendon, 1997.

SNODGRASS, ANTHONY M. *Archaic Greece: The Age of Experiment.* Berkeley: University of California Press, 1980.

SNOWDEN, FRANK M. JR. *Blacks in Antiquity.* Cambridge, Mass.: Harvard University Press, 1970.

TCHERIKOVER, AVIGDOR. *Hellenistic Civilization and the Jews.* Philadelphia: Jewish Publication Society of America, 1970.

WALBANK, F. W. *The Hellenistic World.* Atlantic Highlands, N.J.: Humanities Press, 1981.

THE ROMAN WORLD

ALFOELDY, GEZA. *The Social History of Rome.* Baltimore: Johns Hopkins University Press, 1988.

BADIAN, ERNST. *Roman Imperialism in the Late Republic* (2nd ed.). Oxford, UK: Blackwell, 1968.

————. *Publicans and Sinners: Private Enterprise in the Service of the Roman Republic.* Ithaca, N.Y.: Cornell University Press, 1972.

BEARD, MARY, AND MICHAEL CRAWFORD. *Rome in the Late Republic.* Ithaca, N.Y.: Cornell University Press, 1985.

BRADLEY, KEITH. *Slavery and Society at Rome.* New York: Cambridge University Press, 1994.

BROWN, PETER. *Augustine of Hippo: A Biography.* Berkeley: University of California Press, 1967.

CLARK, GILLIAN. *Women in Late Antiquity: Pagan and Christian Lifestyles.* Oxford, UK: Clarendon, 1993.

CORNELL, T. J. *The Beginnings of Rome.* London: Routledge, 1995.

CROOK, JOHN A. *Law and Life of Rome: 90 B.C.–A.D. 212.* Ithaca, N.Y.: Cornell University Press, 1967.

DIXON, SUZANNE. *The Roman Family.* Baltimore: Johns Hopkins University Press, 1992.

EARL, DONALD C. *The Moral and Political Tradition of Rome*. Ithaca, N.Y.: Cornell University Press, 1967.

EVANS, JOHN K. *War, Women and Children in Ancient Rome*. London: Routledge, 1991.

GARNSEY, PETER, AND RICHARD SALLER. *The Roman Empire: Economy, Society, and Culture*. Berkeley: University of California Press, 1987.

GOFFART, WALTER. *Barbarians and Romans: Techniques of Accommodation*. Princeton, N.J.: Princeton University Press, 1980.

GRUEN, ERICH S. *The Last Generation of the Roman Republic*. Berkeley: University of California Press, 1974.

HEURGON, JACQUES. *The Rise of Rome*. Berkeley: University of California Press, 1973.

KEPPIE, LAWRENCE. *The Making of the Roman Army*. Totowa, N.J.: Barnes & Noble, 1984.

KRAEMER, ROSS SHEPARD. *Her Share of the Blessing: Women's Religion Among Pagans, Jews, and Christians in the Greco-Roman World*. Oxford, UK: Oxford University Press, 1992.

MACMULLEN, RAMSAY. *Enemies of the Roman Order: Treason, Unrest and Alienation in the Empire*. Cambridge, Mass.: Harvard University Press, 1966.

———. *Paganism in the Roman Empire*. New Haven, Conn.: Yale University Press, 1981.

———. *Corruption and Decline of Rome*. New Haven, Conn.: Yale University Press, 1988.

MEEKS, WAYNE, A. *The Moral World of the First Christians*. Philadelphia: Westminster Press, 1986.

MILLAR, FERGUS. *The Roman Near East: 31 B.C.–A.D. 337*. Cambridge, Mass.: Harvard University Press, 1993.

NIPPEL, WILFRIED. *Public Order in Ancient Rome*. Cambridge, UK: Cambridge University Press, 1995.

RICHARDSON, EMELINE. *The Etruscans: Their Art and Civilization*. Chicago: University of Chicago Press, 1964.

SALLER, RICHARD P. *Personal Patronage Under the Early Empire*. New York: Cambridge University Press, 1982.

———. *Patriarchy, Property and Death in the Roman Family*. Cambridge, Mass.: Cambridge University Press, 1994.

SANDERS, E. P. *Jewish and Christian Self-Definition*. Philadelphia: Fortress Press, 1980.

SCHUERER, EMIL. *History of the Jewish People in the Time of Jesus Christ* (rev. ed.). Edinburgh, UK: Clark, 1973.

TALBERT, RICHARD J. A. *The Senate of Imperial Rome*. Princeton, N.J.: Princeton University Press, 1984.

TAYLOR, LILY ROSS. *Party Politics in the Age of Caesar.* Berkeley: University of California Press, 1949.

TREGGIARI, SUSAN. *Roman Freedmen During the Late Republic.* Oxford, UK: Oxford University Press, 1969.

————. *Roman Marriage.* Oxford, UK: Clarendon, 1991.

WHITE, K. D. *Roman Farming.* Ithaca, N.Y.: Cornell University Press, 1970.

WIEDEMANN, THOMAS. *Emperors and Gladiators.* London: Routledge, 1992.

Illustrations

Maps and plans originally prepared by the author and revised by Alice Thiede for this edition.

Index